The Silent Majority

Politics and Society in
Twentieth-Century America

A list of titles in this series appears at the back of the book

The Silent Majority

SUBURBAN POLITICS IN THE SUNBELT SOUTH

Matthew D. Lassiter

PRINCETON UNIVERSITY PRESS

PRINCETON AND OXFORD

Published by Princeton University Press, 41 William Street, Princeton, New Jersey 08540

In the United Kingdom: Published by Princeton University Press, 3 Market Place, Woodstock, Oxfordshire OX20 1SY

Third printing, and first paperback printing, 2007
Paperback ISBN: 978-0-691-13389-8

The Library of Congress has cataloged the cloth edition of this book as follows

Lassiter, Matthew D., 1970–
The silent majority : suburban politics in the Sunbelt South / Matthew D. Lassiter.
p.   cm.—(Politics and society in twentieth-century America)
Includes bibliographical references and index.
ISBN-13: 978-0-691-09255-3 (alk. paper)
ISBN-10: 0-691-09255-9 (alk. paper)
1. Southern States—Politics and government—1951–   2. Sunbelt States—Politics and government.   3. Suburbs—Southern States.   4. Suburbs—Sunbelt States.
5. Metropolitan areas—Southern States.   6. Metropolitan areas—Sunbelt States.
I. Title.   II. Series.

F216.2.L37 2006

320.975'09173'3—dc22   2005040568

British Library Cataloging-in-Publication Data is available

This book has been composed in Caledonia

Printed on acid-free paper. ∞

press.princeton.edu

Printed in the United States of America

10   9   8   7   6   5

Contents

List of Illustrations   vii

List of Tables   ix

Acknowledgments   xi

Abbreviations   xv

Introduction   1

PART I   *The Triumph of Moderation*   21

CHAPTER 1
The Divided South   23

CHAPTER 2
HOPE in the New South   44

CHAPTER 3
The Open-Schools Movement   69

CHAPTER 4
The Strange Career of Atlanta Exceptionalism   94

PART II   *The Revolt of the Center*   119

CHAPTER 5
The "Charlotte Way"   121

CHAPTER 6
Suburban Populism   148

CHAPTER 7
Neighborhood Politics   175

CHAPTER 8
Class Fairness and Racial Stability   198

PART III   *Suburban Strategies*   223

CHAPTER 9
The Suburbanization of Southern Politics   225

Chapter 10
The Failure of the Southern Strategy   251

Chapter 11
Metropolitan Divergence   276

Chapter 12
Regional Convergence   301

Epilogue   324

Notes   331

Index   365

Illustrations

FIGURES

2.1 Three Leaders of Atlanta's Corporate-Political Alliance, 1961   49
2.2 "We *Want* Public Schools," 1959   61
2.3 Grand Opening of Atlanta's Lenox Square Mall, 1959   65
3.1 "NOW . . . Shall We Blind These Eyes To Knowledge?" 1959   73
3.2 HOPE Flyer, 1959   75
3.3 HOPE's President Testifies to the Sibley Commission, 1960   83
4.1 Press Conference to Announce School Desegregation in
    Atlanta, 1961   98
4.2 Aerial View of Downtown Atlanta and Stadium, Late 1960s   110
5.1 Aerial View of Downtown Charlotte, 1970   125
5.2 First Rally of the Concerned Parents Association, 1969   140
5.3 Black Citizens of Charlotte Demand Two-Way Busing, 1969   145
6.1 Concerned Parents Association, "Struggle for Freedom"
    Flyer, 1970   149
6.2 Suburban Parents at an Antibusing Protest, 1970   152
6.3 Beverly Woods Subdivision, "United We Stand" Flyer, 1970   155
6.4 "Integration, Yes! Busing, No!" 1970   164
7.1 Fairgrounds Rally to Boycott Busing in Charlotte, 1970   187
7.2 Black Students Protest Discrimination in Suburban
    Schools, 1971   190
8.1 Maggie Ray of the Citizens Advisory Group at Her Myers
    Park Home, 1974   201
8.2 District Judge James B. McMillan, Charlotte, North Carolina   207
9.1 Nixon Campaign Flyer, South Carolina, 1968   235
10.1 Memorandum on the Southern Strategy, 1969   263
10.2 Governor Linwood Holton Escorts His Daughter to
     School, 1970   264
10.3 Governor Jimmy Carter on the Cover of *Time*, 1971   271
12.1 White Support for a Federal Role in School Integration,
     South and Non-South, 1964–2000   309

MAPS

1.1 Distribution of the Black Population of the Eleven States of
    the South, 1960   27

2.1 Distribution of the Black Population of the City of Atlanta,
Fulton County, and DeKalb County, 1960   51
2.2 Distribution of the Black Population of Georgia, 1960   55
4.1 Distribution of the Black Population of Metropolitan
Atlanta, 2000   116
5.1 Distribution of the Black Population of the City of Charlotte
and Mecklenburg County, 1970   127
8.1 Distribution of the Black Population of the City of Charlotte
and Mecklenburg County, 2000   216
11.1 Distribution of the Black Population of the City of Richmond,
Henrico County, and Chesterfield County, 1970   282
11.2 Distribution of the Black Population of the City of Richmond,
Henrico County, and Chesterfield County, 2000   294

Tables

9.1 Percentage of the White Southern Vote Received by
Segregationist/States' Rights Candidates in Three
Presidential Elections, 1948–1968   229

11.1 Decline in White Enrollment, 1968–1986, and Percentage
of Black Students in Majority-White and Racially Isolated
Schools, 1986, Large City-Suburban Consolidated
(Countywide) School Districts in the South   278

11.2 Decline in White Enrollment, 1968–1986, and Percentage
of Black Students in Majority-White and Racially Isolated
Schools, 1986, Large Urban School Districts in the South
without Metropolitan Integration Plans   300

12.1 Decline in White Enrollment, 1968–1986, and Percentage
of Black Students in Majority-White and Racially Isolated
Schools, 1986, Large Urban School Districts outside
the South   317

Acknowledgments

I have made a lot of friends and accumulated a lot of debts in the process of writing this book, a journey that I began in Virginia and completed in Maine and Michigan, with many research trips to Atlanta and Charlotte and a few detours in the mountains of North Carolina along the way. The professors I met during my undergraduate years at Furman University helped set me on this path, with special thanks to Marian Strobel and Jim Edwards. Paul Gaston advised the dissertation at the University of Virginia, and I hope that the finished product lives up to the standard he established in his own book about the original version of the New South. Along with Mary Gaston, Paul helped make Charlottesville a wonderful place to live, and his fusion of scholarship and activism inspires me today more than ever. Ed Ayers provided generous support as well as a model through his own scholarship on the promises and perils of southern history. My time at the University of Virginia also benefited greatly from interaction with Brian Balogh, Nelson Lichtenstein, Michael Klarman, Alon Confino, Michael Holt, and Julian Bond.

Many of the ideas in this book began as conversations with my graduate school colleagues in the Southern History Seminar at UVA, including Juliette Landphair, Matthew Dunne, Josh Rothman, Gregg Michel, Anne Rubin, and Vince Clark. From basketball to dinner parties, my experience in Charlottesville would have been incomplete without Li Fang, Tara Smiley, Tom Flemma, Andy Morris, Pete Sheehy, and Andy Trees. A special thanks to four good friends whose comments and criticism have been invaluable: Bob Guffin, Phillip Troutman, Doug Smith, and Andrew Lewis. Doug and Andy read the entire manuscript more than once and provided insightful and trenchant feedback.

At Bowdoin College, I benefited enormously from time spent with the interdisciplinary politics and bowling crew: Marc Hetherington, Suzanne Globetti, Joe Bandy, Joe Lane, Pete Coviello, Eric Chown, and Jonathan Weiler. I also would like to thank colleagues at the University of Michigan, especially Michele Mitchell, John Carson, Scott Kurashige, Matthew Countryman, Fred Cooper, Sonya Rose, Kathleen Canning, Charlie Bright, Maris Vinovskis, Kevin Gaines, Penny Von Eschen, Martha Jones, Damon Salesa, Terry McDonald, Kali Israel, Rebecca Scott, Jay Cook, Phil DeLoria, Maria Montoya, Tony Chen, Rob Mickey, Scott Campbell, Julius Scott, Paul Anderson, Tom Guglielmo, Stephen Ward, Jesse Hoffnung-Garskof, Dario Gaggio, Tom Green, Rick Hills, Jonathan Marwil, and David Cohen. Sue

Juster, Mills Thornton, and Greg Dowd read the manuscript as a work-in-progress and offered substantive advice on revisions. And my gratitude goes to Gina Morantz-Sanchez and Geoff Eley, because Ann Arbor would not have been the same without their counsel and hospitality.

A semester's worth of discussions with the graduate students in each version of my Urban Crisis/Suburban Nation seminar at the University of Michigan expanded my horizons in ways that they should recognize in these pages. I owe a special acknowledgment to Andrew Highsmith, who read the manuscript at a late date and provided sharp commentary, and to Matt Wittmann and Lily Geismer as well. Timely assistance in the final stages of the project came from three superb undergraduate research assistants, Katie Cramer, Jacob Strumwasser, and Liz Moselle. The staff at the University of Michigan Map Library helped me navigate census software I barely understood, and the maps in the book look the way they do because of the efforts of Ken Anderson. I also appreciate the feedback provided by participants in seminars at the University of Georgia, Duke University, Furman University, and the Urban Planning and School of Education programs at the University of Michigan.

Many other scholars were generous with their time and energy. Tom Sugrue, Bruce Schulman, and David Chappell provided encouragement and sound advice, and David Goldfield and Julian Zelizer also offered close readings. My research interests overlap substantially with those of Kevin Kruse and Robert Self, and our many conversations combined with the interpretations in their recent books have substantially improved my own. Jim Hershman supplied a stream of brilliant ideas, and my arguments about the relationship between class and caste reflect a debt to him. I also appreciate the assistance that this project has received, in various ways, from Gary Gerstle, Meg Jacobs, David Freund, Lizabeth Cohen, Stephen Smith, Nancy MacLean, Roslyn Arlin Mickelson, Arnold Hirsch, Maureen Flanagan, Kathy Nasstrom, Joe Crespino, Jack Dougherty, Brian Ward, Wendy Plotkin, Tim Tyson, Jeff Norrell, Tom Hanchett, Bryant Simon, Leslie Dunbar, and Steve Suitts. Thomas LeBien acquired the manuscript for Princeton University Press, and it is a much better and much shorter book thanks to his skills as an editor. I am also grateful to Brigitta van Rheinberg for shepherding the manuscript through the production process, along with the assistance of Alison Kalett, Dimitri Karetnikov, Dale Cotton, Cindy Crumrine, and the editors of the Politics and Society in Twentieth-Century America series.

A postdoctoral fellowship from the National Academy of Education and the Spencer Foundation allowed me to take a sabbatical year to revise the dissertation, and I also enjoyed fellowship support from the history departments of the University of Virginia and the University of Michigan. Many thanks to the staff at a number of archives and special collections departments, including Emory University, the Atlanta History Center, the Atlanta

University Center, Georgia State University, Clemson University, the University of North Carolina at Charlotte, the Southern History Collection at UNC-Chapel Hill, the Charlotte-Mecklenburg Public Library, the University of Virginia, Virginia Commonwealth University, and the Virginia Historical Society. Jonathan Wells of the Charlotte-Mecklenburg Planning Commission supplied statistics on annexation, and William Overhultz and Julian and Elsie Mason opened up their homes and personal records to a visiting scholar. The *Charlotte Observer* proved especially charitable with its photography archive, and Joyce Reimann at the Charlotte-Mecklenburg Public Library went well beyond the call of duty in helping me track down elusive negatives.

Friends and family often asked why it takes so long to write a history book, and so here's the answer. For keeping me grounded in Ann Arbor, many thanks to Jeb and Galen Sorom, Kurt Maier, Megan Gibb, Laura Hudson, Anne Lesemann, and Bridget Fahrland. Rob Sica, Dave Sica, Brian Erb, Mark Daniels, and Marty O'Sullivan distracted me with politics, philosophy, and more. My grandparents, Jim and Miriam Heiskell, taught me the value of education and always kept the door open in Atlanta. My parents, Ike and Sally Lassiter, have supported me throughout this endeavor and deserve more thanks than words can adequately convey. Even if many of us have moved a long way from Atlanta over the years, having lots of siblings and a large extended family means always being able to find a place to stay when on the road, not to mention plenty of conversations about the South and the nation.

Tracy Davis works on a daily rather than a decade-long deadline, as she has reminded me more than once during the past ten years. Her support, and her patience, have been an intrinsic part of this project from the beginning. I have learned a great deal during our time together over the years, and along our journey from North Carolina to Michigan, and neither this book nor my life would be nearly as good without her. Her love and friendship provide a constant reminder of what really matters, and this book is dedicated to her with my deepest gratitude and love in return.

Abbreviations

CAB	Citizens against Busing (Memphis)
CAB	Citizens against Busing (Richmond)
CAG	Citizens Advisory Group (Charlotte)
CEPS	Citizens for Excellent Public Schools (Richmond)
CORE	Congress of Racial Equality
CPA	Concerned Parents Association (Charlotte)
CRC	Charlotte-Mecklenburg Community Relations Committee
CUFF	Citizens United for Fairness (Charlotte)
DLC	Democratic Leadership Council
GACHR	Greater Atlanta Council on Human Relations
GOP	Republican Party
GUTS	Georgians Unwilling to Surrender
HEW	Department of Health, Education, and Welfare
HOPE	Help Our Public Education (Atlanta)
HUD	Department of Housing and Urban Development
ICA	Interested Citizens Association (Charlotte)
IMPACT	Involved Memphis Parents Assisting Children and Teachers
LCCR	Leadership Conference on Civil Rights
LDF	Legal Defense Fund (NAACP)
LWV	League of Women Voters
MARTA	Metropolitan Atlanta Rapid Transit Authority
NAACP	National Association for the Advancement of Colored People
NAG	National Action Group against Busing (Michigan)
OASIS	Organizations Assisting Schools in September (Atlanta)
QEC	Quality Education Committee (Charlotte)
SLP	Southern Leadership Project
SOS	Save Our Schools (New Orleans)
SRC	Southern Regional Council
UCCA	Unified Concerned Citizens of America
VCPS	Virginia Committee for Public Schools
WEC	Women's Emergency Committee to Open Our Schools (Little Rock)
WECPF	West End Concerned Parents and Friends (Richmond)

The Silent Majority

Introduction

"As a member of the silent majority," a white father from an affluent suburb of Charlotte, North Carolina, declared in 1970, "I have never asked what anyone in government or this country could do for me, but rather have kept my mouth shut, paid my taxes, and basically asked to be left alone." James McDavid, Jr., lived with his family in one of the new white-collar subdivisions developed outside Charlotte during the postwar growth boom that transformed the political culture and the physical landscape of the American South. Along with middle-class homeowners throughout the nation, the consumer lifestyle of the McDavids depended upon government programs that provided massive subsidies for suburban sprawl and efficient implementation of residential segregation. Federally funded highways crisscrossed the automobile-dependent metropolis, federally guaranteed low-interest mortgages and generous tax deductions made a racially exclusive version of the American Dream affordable for white suburban families, and federally bankrolled urban renewal policies systematically concentrated almost all of Charlotte's black residents in a compact ghetto located on the other side of downtown. Along with thousands of other parents from Charlotte's outer-ring suburbs, McDavid had written his congressman in outrage after a federal judge ordered a comprehensive busing plan to overcome the stark metropolitan patterns of state-sponsored housing segregation. From the perspective of his all-white subdivision, McDavid denounced busing as a form of reverse discrimination in violation of the color-blind philosophy of neighborhood schools and then issued a blunt threat to the politicians in Washington: "I think it is time the law abiding, tax paying white middle class started looking to the federal government for something besides oppression."[1]

During the civil rights showdowns of the late 1960s and early 1970s, white-collar families that claimed membership in the Silent Majority rallied around a "color-blind" discourse of suburban innocence that depicted residential segregation as the class-based outcome of meritocratic individualism rather than the unconstitutional product of structural racism. "I couldn't believe such a thing could happen in America," explained Don Roberson, a prosperous physician from the upper-middle-class suburbs who became a grassroots leader of the antibusing movement in Charlotte. "So many of us made the biggest investment of our lives—our homes—primarily on the basis of their location with regard to schools. It seemed like an absurdity that anyone could tell us where to send our children." "My first reaction was one of disbelief," remembered insurance executive Thomas Harris, another officer in the Concerned Parents Association, the local manifestation of the Silent Majority during the Charlotte busing crisis. "I did not believe there was any possibility whatsoever that the government was going to dictate where my kids were going to public school. It was crazy; it was not going to happen." From the other side of the metropolis, a black father who served as a plaintiff in the busing litigation acknowledged the potency of this class-driven interpretation of the city's protracted desegregation saga. "People thought we were destroying the whole American dream for them," James Polk observed. "To whites, that meant pull yourself up by your bootstraps, buy a nice home and two cars, live in a nice neighborhood and go to a nice church, send your kids to the appropriate school. . . . We understood that a lot of white people would raise holy hell."[2]

Through the populist revolt of the Silent Majority, millions of white homeowners who had achieved a residentially segregated and federally subsidized version of the American Dream forcefully rejected race-conscious liberalism as an unconstitutional exercise in social engineering and an unprecedented violation of free-market meritocracy. In 1968, the Kerner Report issued by the National Advisory Commission on Civil Disorders asked the middle-class residents of the segregated suburbs to reconsider the meritocratic ethos of color-blind individualism and ponder an unpopular interpretation of their own history: "What white Americans have never fully understood—but what the Negro can never forget—is that white society is deeply implicated in the ghetto. White institutions created it, white institutions maintain it, and white society condones it." The Kerner Commission also issued a dire warning: "To continue present policies is to make permanent the division of our country into two societies; one, largely Negro and poor, located in the central cities; the other, predominantly white and affluent, located in the suburbs and outlying areas." During the decade after the civil rights movement defeated the acknowledged "American Dilemma" of racial segregation mandated by law in the Jim Crow South, the bitter busing and housing battles that spread throughout the nation confronted a New American Dilemma—the fusion of class segregation and racial discrimination embodied in the urban-suburban divide. In response to the civil rights offensive against the structural forces of residential segregation, a grassroots suburban backlash rippled upward into national politics and established powerful and lasting constraints on the integrationist agenda of racial liberalism. The political culture of suburban exclusion and middle-class entitlement forged a resilient bipartisan consensus that ultimately exempted most affluent neighborhoods throughout the nation from any collective responsibility for the government programs that simultaneously developed the post-war metropolis and contained the inner-city ghettoes.[3]

The stories told in this book stand at the intersection of the metropolitan struggles for racial integration, the political mobilization of middle-class neighborhoods, and the spatial policies of suburban sprawl in the modern South. The regionwide scope of my project begins with the triumph of racial moderation over massive resistance during the southern accommodation to the *Brown v. Board of Education* decision of 1954 and then follows the trajectory of school integration and court-ordered busing in the Sunbelt metropolises of Atlanta and Charlotte. My account of the suburban strategies that reshaped southern politics investigates the postwar growth of the Republican party and the fabled Silent Majority of the Nixon years before culminating in the national retreat from integration remedies through key turning points stretching from Richmond to Detroit. Three fundamental transformations between the 1940s and the 1970s connect the local community studies in this book with broader regional and national trends. During the decades after World War II, the metropolitan Sunbelt replaced the rural Black Belt as the center of political power in the South, and a two-party system dominated by the interests of large corporations and the priorities of white-collar suburbs supplanted the traditional culture of white supremacy that governed the Jim Crow era. In a concurrent development, the considerable success of the civil rights movement in dismantling the legal caste system and discrediting overt racism, in combination with the rapid expansion of a suburban landscape organized around residential segregation and socioeconomic privilege, resulted in the evolution of a middle-class outlook expressed through the color-blind language of consumer rights and meritocratic individualism. And finally, the ascendance of the metropolitan Sunbelt played a crucial role in the fading of southern distinctiveness and the national collapse of the New Deal Order, a process of regional convergence marked by the parallel suburbanization of southern and American politics.

This book is about the grassroots politics produced by residential segregation and suburban sprawl and the interplay between the local and the national in the emergence of the center-right dynamic that has dominated American politics since the late 1960s. An investigation of the grassroots insurgency of the Silent Majority, and the broader story of middle-class political culture and suburban development across the postwar South, calls into question many of the conventional interpretations of electoral realignment in modern America. The widespread tendency to attribute the conservative shift in American politics to a top-down "Southern Strategy," launched by the Republican party in order to exploit white backlash against the civil rights movement, misses the longer-term convergence of southern and national politics around the suburban ethos of middle-class entitlement. And the enduring framework of southern racial exceptionalism, embodied in the artificial dichotomy between "de jure" and "de facto" segregation, has likewise distorted our understanding of the civil rights era by obscuring the ways in which state-financed suburbanization and state-sponsored residential segregation established a novel model of race relations, national in scope. During the postwar decades, the political economies of southern metropolises such as Atlanta and Charlotte and Richmond increasingly resembled their sprawling counterparts in the North and West, with pervasive structures of racial and class segregation imbedded in the built environment rather than enforced by Jim Crow legislation. The grassroots politics of suburban populism—from antibusing crusades and taxpayer revolts to homeowner movements in defense of racial and class exclusion—galvanized a bipartisan response marked by the persistent refusal of all three branches of the federal government to provide meaningful remedies for the historical legacies of metropolitan inequality and the contemporary processes of residential segregation.[4]

My exploration of the political culture of the metropolitan South attempts to accord equal weight to the analytical categories of class and race by examining their intersection in the grassroots contexts of suburban development and electoral realignment. I argue throughout the book that the overreliance on race-reductionist narratives to explain complex political transformations—such as the "rise of the Right" and "white backlash" and the "Southern Strategy" and the "Republican South"—downplays the centrality of class ideology in the outlook of suburban voters and ignores the consistent class divisions among white southerners evident throughout the civil rights era. The explanatory framework of color-blindness is not intended to accept at face value the claim that racial prejudice simply disappeared from middle-class attitudes, or to disregard the many ways that its proponents benefited from the "possessive investment in whiteness," but instead to capture a coherent way of thinking about and speaking about neighborhood boundaries and political citizenship that had become a paramount feature of suburban discourse by the second half of the 1960s. Racial inequality is a constant theme in American history, but the manifestations of racism are evolving and multifaceted, refracted through frameworks such as economics and geography. The ascendance of color-blind ideology in the metropolitan South, as in the rest of the nation, depended upon the establishment of structural mechanisms of exclusion that did not require individual racism by suburban beneficiaries in order to sustain white class privilege and maintain barriers of disadvantage facing urban minority communities. The suburban politics of middle-class warfare charted a middle course between the open racism of the extreme right and the egalitarian agenda of the civil rights movement, based in an ethos of color-blind individualism that accepted the principle of equal opportunity under the law but refused to countenance affirmative action policies designed to overcome metropolitan structures of inequality.[5]

Richard Nixon called suburban families the Forgotten Americans, and then the Silent Majority, and finally the New American Majority. As populist appeals to Middle America, these labels represented a suburban strategy designed to conceal class divisions among white voters while taking advantage of the convergence of southern and national politics. In a typical articulation of the color-blind platform, Nixon informed "the great silent majority of Americans" that "there is no reason to feel guilty about wanting to enjoy what you get and get what you earn, about wanting your children in good schools close to home, or about wanting to be judged fairly on your ability." The president explained that liberals "believe that the only way to achieve what they consider social justice is to place power in the hands of a strong central government which will do what they think has to be done, no matter what the majority thinks." The Republican party instead understood that the United States represented "the land of opportunity, not the land of quotas and restrictions." Nixon conceded that "some people oppose income redistribution and busing for the wrong reasons, but they are by no means the majority of Americans, who oppose them for the right reasons." He assured members of the Silent Majority that it was not selfish to want to see less of their hard-earned money "taken away by government taxation," and it was not racist to object to having their children "taken away from a neighborhood school and transported miles away." Nixon also consistently proclaimed, as he told a gathering of Republican activists in Atlanta, that the "so-called southern issues . . . are the same here as they are in America"—opposition to forced busing, desire for lower taxes, support for military strength abroad, demand for law and order at home, and color-blind justice for all citizens. Echoing from the grassroots to the White House, these narratives of white victimization and suburban heroism transformed the landscapes of southern and national politics and repudiated the history of metropolitan inequality highlighted in the Kerner Report.[6]

THE SPATIAL TURN IN POLITICAL HISTORY

The "Southern Strategy" explanation of the political transformation of the modern South is wrong. Following the lead of Kevin Phillips's 1969 book *The Emerging Republican Majority*, many scholars and pundits have embraced a top-down thesis of electoral realignment that credits the regional base of the Republican party to a race-driven Southern Strategy allegedly perfected by Richard Nixon between 1968 and 1972. In this version of the origins of the New Right, presidential candidates Barry Goldwater and George Wallace emerge as the two most influential losers in American political history, the progenitors of a racialized conservatism that shaped the GOP's coded appeals and united working-class and middle-class white voters in an alliance of reactionary populism. When required to explain the national disintegration of New Deal liberalism, and the setbacks for the civil rights movement on metropolitan landscapes across the United States, the Southern Strategy school offers a corollary called the "Southernization of American politics." In its most schematic formulation, this top-down narrative of conservative backlash wipes clean the slate of northern history before the mid-1960s and connects the dots between a wide-ranging series of episodes: Barry Goldwater's success in the Deep South, George Wallace's forays in the urban North, Richard Nixon's "law-and-order" and antibusing platforms, Ronald Reagan's "states' rights" speech in rural Mississippi, George Bush's "Willie Horton" television advertisements, and Newt Gingrich's invective against "welfare mothers." My emphasis on the suburbs and the Sunbelt challenges this refusal to abandon the trope of southern exceptionalism, which misses the broader story of the grassroots mobilization of the Silent Majority that reframed racial discourse and subsumed regional differences beneath a national politics of middle-class entitlement.[7]

In too many accounts of southern political realignment during the postwar era, the Deep South is the tail that wags the dog. I argue instead that the suburban strategies developed in the Sunbelt South, not a Southern Strategy inspired by the Deep South and orchestrated from the White House, provided the blueprint for the transformation of regional politics and the parallel reconfiguration of national politics. My perspective provides an alternative narrative, building on the demographic studies of political scientists and the new literature on the American West, that revolves around the class-stratified politics, economic conservatism, and color-blind racial ideology produced by the postwar suburbanization of southern society and the population shift to the metropolitan Sunbelt. At the grassroots level, the Southern Strategy conspicuously backfired in each of its four genuine incarnations: the Dixiecrat revolt of 1948, the Goldwater debacle in 1964, the third-party Wallace movement in 1968, and the Nixon administration's disastrous experiment with race-baiting politics in the pivotal 1970 midterm elections. Instead of accomplishing the mission of reassembling the Solid South through the manipulation of white backlash, all of these campaigns failed to carry the high-growth states of the Upper and Outer South and instead achieved pyrrhic victories in the Deep South strongholds that backed the losing candidate in all but one presidential election between 1948 and 1968. During the same period, the suburban residents of the metropolitan regions and the white-collar migrants to the Sunbelt South increasingly diverged from the racial politics of the Black Belt and converged with the class-based voting patterns in the rest of the nation. The South's central contribution to national political realignment came primarily from the suburban ethos of Sunbelt metropolises such as Atlanta and Charlotte, not the exportation of the political culture of the Deep South and the Black Belt.[8]

The disciplinary framework of American political history has been reinvigorated by an ongoing spatial turn that highlights the centrality of the grassroots in struggles over representative democracy and connects the structural insights of urban studies to the racial and class ideologies of white voters during the modern era. Pathbreaking community studies of the urban North have explored the racial contradiction at the heart of postwar liberalism, as the promise of equal opportunity for black citizens clashed with a white working-class backlash that defined segregated housing in secure neighborhoods as an essential feature of the New Deal social contract. In the blue-collar neighborhoods of the North and Midwest, as Thomas Sugrue and Arnold Hirsch have convincingly demonstrated, the counterattack against racial liberalism began with the Great Migration and not the Great Society, overlapping with the rise of massive resistance to the civil rights movement in the South. In the extension of this narrative, the backlash ethos of reactionary populism exploded in white working-class precincts during the racial conflicts of the 1960s and 1970s, resulting in the defection of the Reagan Democrats that destroyed Great Society liberalism and empowered Republican conservatism. These urban community studies provide a persuasive refutation of the "Southernization of America" thesis, alongside a compelling argument that the forces of racial backlash imbedded in the policies of postwar growth liberalism predated the showdowns of the sixties and the conservative mobilization of the New Right. At the same time, most of the new urban history has been written from an inside-out perspective, largely confined to episodes of direct racial friction within the city limits of the North and lacking a consciously suburban approach to the political landscape and the postwar metropolis. The next step for social and political historians is to establish a metropolitan framework that treats cities and suburbs as integral parts of the same narrative and extends the grassroots methodology to the South and the Sunbelt.[9]

A grassroots approach to political history reveals that the partisan affiliations of voters as Republicans or Democrats has often mattered less than the populist identifications of suburban residents as homeowners, taxpayers, and schoolparents. Scholars have only begun to examine the political culture of white-collar neighborhoods and the social movements of middle-class families in the sprawling suburbs of postwar America. Although most of the scholarship on modern conservatism remains wedded to a top-down viewpoint, recent books about the "suburban warriors" of the Sunbelt West have significantly expanded the grassroots narrative, from the Goldwater troops in the 1960s, to the tax revolts of the 1970s, to the evangelical mobilization of the 1980s and 1990s. But the linear emphasis of much of the Sunbelt literature on the roots of the New Right fails to incorporate the vast majority of suburban homeowners who were neither committed activists nor conservative ideologues. The political outlook of white families affiliated with the Silent Majority overlapped considerably with Republican conservatism but extended well beyond a right-wing base, reaching the national stage as a grassroots revolt of the center that demanded and received a bipartisan defense of suburban entitlement programs. Mike Davis's pioneering work on Los Angeles in *City of Quartz* provides the best model for interpreting the localist politics of property values and consumer rights practiced in the suburbs and the Sunbelt, resulting in an exclusionary brand of homeowner populism grounded in class privileges and racial barriers imbedded in the built environment. Postwar growth liberalism played as important a role as Sunbelt conservatism in establishing the three defining pillars of suburban ideology—homeowner, taxpayer, and schoolparent status. A deeper understanding of the political culture of middle-class entitlement and urban disinvestment requires analysis of the public policies and suburban strategies that simultaneously reshaped the metropolitan landscape and the electoral map.[10]

The populist revolt of the Silent Majority reveals the vitality and the volatility of the political center during an era of substantial turmoil. As Michael Kazin has demonstrated, the prevailing language of populism shifted substantially over the course of the twentieth century, from the traditional critique of big business to a gathering assault on big government, even as the localist defense of Middle America from enemies at the top and the bottom remained a consistent feature of mainstream political discourse. The broader trajectory of suburban decentralization and Sunbelt development destroyed the New Deal political order but ultimately produced an electoral climate in which neither the Democrats nor the Republicans could maintain a secure and ideological governing majority. The upward mobility subsidized by the entitlement programs of the federal government undermined the working-class base of New Deal liberalism and turned suburban swing voters into a crucial demographic that came to drive the electoral strategies of both parties. In the affluent white-collar neighborhoods that have commanded the attention of politicians and policymakers, the fusion of class-based individualism with color-blind innocence has effectively concealed the centrality of the state in forging metropolitan patterns of residential segregation. In popular culture, historical amnesia dominates the conventional wisdom of the suburbanization process, perhaps most notably in the frontier mythology advanced by conservative journalist David Brooks: "It's as if Zeus came down and started plopping vast towns in the middle of the farmland and the desert overnight. Boom! A master planned community! Boom! A big-box mall!" At the same time, the liberal tendency to explain southern political realignment through the narrow prism of civil rights legislation signed by Lyndon Johnson or rhetorical strategies adopted by Richard Nixon revolves around a fundamental misunderstanding of the long-term economic and demographic transformations produced by metropolitan development in the Sunbelt South.[11]

The interrelationship between suburban expansion and urban retrenchment represents the most important framework for investigating political realignment in postwar America, but the overemphasis on the metaphor of "white flight" reduces suburbanization to an appendage of urban history and provides an incomplete account of the development of metropolitan space. As a causal explanation, the white flight thesis obscures the constellation of government policies that drove postwar suburbanization, excising structural analysis in favor of a narrative that revolves around individual racism. In *Crabgrass Frontier*, the 1985 synthesis that legitimated the field of suburban history, Kenneth Jackson argued that "economic causes have been even more important than skin color in the suburbanization of the United States. . . . Because of public policies favoring the suburbs, only one possibility [for homeownership] was economically feasible. The result, if not the intent, of Washington programs has been to encourage decentralization." In the metropolitan Sunbelt, a typical resident of an outer-ring suburb constructed during the postwar boom never lived within the central city but instead had migrated from elsewhere, often from another state. In the urban South, the racial transition of particular neighborhoods generally reflected the foreseeable impact of official planning policies combined with the unscrupulous practices of the real estate industry. The civil rights agenda of court-ordered busing, which has received disproportionate blame for triggering white flight from urban schools and neighborhoods, actually produced an ambivalent legacy contingent upon the metropolitan scope of the integration remedy. Class-sensitive policies that included the suburbs resulted in relatively stable levels of school desegregation in a number of southern metropolises, while inequitable formulas that concentrated the burdens on working-class neighborhoods inflamed reactionary populism and accelerated white flight.[12]

An approach that connects metropolitan history to electoral realignment requires sustained attention to the interplay between race and class at the level of grassroots politics, including the populist ideology of homeowners and schoolparents, the unequal impact of public policies, and the inconsistent application of constitutional law. In his study of the urban crisis in postwar Detroit, Thomas Sugrue observes that "blackness and whiteness assumed a spatial definition," especially as the visibility of residential segregation reinforced prejudicial stereotypes about inner-city pathology and suburban meritocracy. My methodology builds on this theoretical insight with the argument that class identity also took on a powerful spatial orientation in the postwar metropolis. The physical location of homes and schools became the primary markers of a family's socioeconomic status—a synthesis of class indicators such as income, occupation, and education—resulting in a hierarchy of metropolitan power reflected in deep divisions among white neighborhoods ranging from voting behavior to integration exposure levels. In affluent suburbs marked by residential segregation and homeowner security, with whiteness not in jeopardy, color-blind ideology fused the naturalization of racial privilege with unapologetic enthusiasm for class exclusion. By the 1970s, the evolution of constitutional law enshrined class discrimination as a permissible outcome of public policy by redefining state-sponsored residential segregation as "de facto" socioeconomic segregation. In the intersection of electoral politics and metropolitan space, the protection of the class privileges of affluent suburbs consistently displaced the burdens of racial integration onto working-class white neighborhoods, a volatile process that severely undermined the moral authority of liberalism and simultaneously disproved the populist solidarity proclaimed by the champions of the Silent Majority.[13]

THE SUNBELT SYNTHESIS

The growth policies of New Deal liberalism and the emergence of the Cold War military-industrial complex shaped the spatial patterns of development in the postwar suburbs and transformed the South and the West into the Sunbelt, the booming region stretching from Virginia to California. The Federal Housing Administration and the GI Bill subsidized the American Dream of middle-class homeownership for millions of white families that left the countryside and the cities to move to the sprawling suburbs. By excluding racial minorities from new suburban housing and redlining non-white urban neighborhoods, federal mortgage policies during the initial postwar decades systematically enforced residential segregation and reinforced marketplace discrimination. The Interstate Highway Act of 1956 facilitated automobile-based commuting and corporate relocation to the metropolitan fringe and, in combination with federal urban renewal programs, enabled municipal governments to concentrate racial minorities within inner-city ghettoes. Cold War spending policies propelled a power shift to the southern and western states of the Sunbelt, where the population expanded between 1950 and 1975 at nearly twice the rate of Rust Belt counterparts in the Midwest and Northeast. White-collar migrants settled in suburban neighborhoods clustered around military bases, defense industries, and regional branch offices that reflected the explosive expansion of the technology-driven and service-oriented sectors of corporate capitalism. After the long recession of the seventies, the industrial centers of the Rust Belt increasingly emulated the Sunbelt model of high-tech innovation, business deregulation, flexible labor markets, and low-density sprawl. During the second half of the twentieth century, the single-family suburban neighborhood and the postindustrial Sunbelt economy emerged as the dominant methods of social organization, the primary focus of land-use planning, and the clear fulcrums of political power.[14]

In the dynamic metropolises of the postwar South, the corporate leaders who controlled municipal politics embraced a growth blueprint that could be called the Sunbelt Synthesis, a booster vision designed to transcend the burdens of the region's history through the twin pillars of rapid economic development and enforced racial harmony. By the 1940s, the pragmatic architects of the Sunbelt Synthesis recognized that the business agenda of industrial recruitment and regional modernization required a political culture of racial moderation. This conspicuous secession from the traditional values of the distinctive South found its most popular expression in the recurring celebrations of the arrival of a truly New South. In the region's fastest-growing cities, the futuristic New South ethos approached the status of a civic religion, a discourse of power that promised to synchronize the metropolitan landscape with the national standards of economic progress and suburban prosperity. In 1959, when metropolitan Atlanta surpassed the population landmark of one million residents, Mayor William Hartsfield proclaimed: "We roll out the red carpet for every damn Yankee who comes in here with two strong hands and some money." During the civil rights era, Atlanta's white leadership trumpeted a marketing slogan called the "City Too Busy to Hate," while corporate boosters in North Carolina's largest city championed an exceptionalist mythology known as the "Charlotte Way"— both of which embodied the mantra of a flourishing New South marked by moderate race relations in full alignment with national values. As in the nation at large, which operated under its own progressive mythology of racial harmony, the politics of moderation in the Sunbelt South attempted to move beyond the Jim Crow system of legal segregation through the spatial policies of suburban sprawl and urban containment.[15]

The practitioners of the Sunbelt Synthesis pursued a strategic commitment to racial peace through the planning policies of residential segregation. The corporate leaders of the New South, a group that has received excessive credit for guiding local communities into compliance with desegregation, also played the most significant role in constructing a metropolitan landscape of spatial apartheid that first reoriented and then outlasted the arrangements of Jim Crow. Between the 1940s and the mid-1970s, the local Chamber of Commerce served as a shadow government in almost every major city touted as part of the New South. Business interests dominated municipal politics through at-large voting systems that efficiently disfranchised working-class black and white neighborhoods. Levels of residential segregation in the metropolitan South increased substantially during the postwar decades, as municipal governments tapped federal funds to accelerate white-collar expansion on the suburban fringe and expand the central business district by relocating minority families to a disfavored sector of the city. The phenomenon generally condensed to the metaphor of white flight represented instead the intentional outcome of these city-building processes, as racial turnover inevitably followed in the section of the metropolis designated as the minority ghetto, usually among working-class white families who lacked the political power to alter growth policies. The corporate leaders of Sunbelt metropolises such as Atlanta and Charlotte perceived residential segregation as the progressive antidote to the interracial violence that tarnished the rural southern countryside as well as industrial cities from Birmingham to Detroit. This moderate version of managed race relations implemented at the level of the built environment embodied the ambitious New South project to achieve full reintegration into the nation.[16]

Municipal politics is a critical frame of reference for understanding the trajectory of the urban civil rights movement, as numerous community studies have demonstrated. In the cities of the New South, the particular arrangements of municipal politics shaped and constrained the strategies of local civil rights activists, especially middle-class black leaders who pursued racial advancement through a combination of backroom negotiations, electoral leverage, and eventually litigation. During the 1950s and 1960s, the staying power of corporate regimes depended upon unequal but resilient electoral coalitions between white families who lived in affluent neighborhoods and black voters who resided on the other side of town. The racial moderation at the center of the Sunbelt Synthesis simultaneously attempted to prevent segregationist violence at all costs and to defuse civil rights demonstrations through a philosophy of gradualism and negotiated progress that emphasized access to public accommodations. But the biracial alliances in these New South cities revolved around a devil's bargain for the integrationist agenda of the civil rights movement, because municipal politics also served as the conduit for the structural inequality produced by corporate capitalism in the contests over control of metropolitan space. Urban regimes in the metropolitan Sunbelt represented concrete moneyed interests—primarily the banking, homebuilding, construction, retail, and real estate industries—a power dynamic that blurred and in many cases eviscerated the line between public policy and private capital. Generally labeled the "power structure" or the "downtown establishment," these municipal coalitions stood at the nexus between the growth policies of the national state and the segregated development of metropolitan space, with principal leverage over the allocation of federal funds for transportation networks, urban renewal (castigated by opponents as "Negro removal"), and infrastructure for suburban subdivisions and shopping malls.[17]

The downtown leadership of New South cities adopted regional planning policies that segregated the metropolis by race and class while seeking to manage the centrifugal consequences of suburban sprawl set in motion by the public-private growth machine. Power and resources in the Sunbelt South flowed to a favored quadrant of the metropolis that I have designated the "island suburbs," a cluster of upper-middle-class and wealthy white neighborhoods located inside the city limits and protected by exclusionary zoning policies from racial integration and socioeconomic diversity. Archetypes of these island suburbs include the Buckhead section of northside Atlanta, the Myers Park area of southeast Charlotte, the graceful neighborhoods of Richmond's West End, the upscale subdivisions of east Memphis, and the prosperous enclaves of northwest Raleigh. Daily life in the island suburbs of the New South mirrored the consumer patterns and residential exclusivity of northern counterparts such as the Brookline section outside Boston or the Grosse Pointe neighborhoods adjacent to Detroit, with the crucial exception that city-friendly annexation laws in most southern states resulted in the incorporation of the Buckheads and Myers Parks inside the municipal boundaries. In the most critical element of the Sunbelt Synthesis, the downtown establishment championed the automatic annexation of new suburban developments and the consolidation of city and county school systems as the enlightened path of metropolitan cooperation that would ensure a healthy tax base and avoid the debilitating racial conflicts of the emerging urban crisis in the North. This Sunbelt version of regional planning aimed to minimize the impact of white out-migration from areas experiencing black residential expansion, and therefore maintain elite control of municipal politics, through steady annexation of middle-class voters who would enjoy the suburban lifestyle while remaining loyal to the New South synthesis of racial moderation in service of economic growth.[18]

At the grassroots level, white-collar families in the metropolitan South formulated their own variation of the politics of racial moderation, a neighborhood-based outlook that elevated the class priorities of quality education and national citizenship over the region's traditionalist campaigns in defense of white supremacy and states' rights. In the clashes over school desegregation during the decade after *Brown*, white moderation assumed a specific definition: open support for compliance with the law and preservation of public education rather than an absolutist defense of the racial caste line. After the Supreme Court invalidated the principle of "separate but equal," segregationist leaders from the rural South championed a caste-based policy of massive resistance that included the closing of public schools to prevent any degree of integration. White liberals and moderates from the island suburbs countered with a class-based desegregation compromise that revolved around "freedom of choice" and "neighborhood schools," explicitly marketed to metropolitan families as a "race-neutral" formula that would minimize integration through reliance upon residential segregation. This embryonic version of color-blind ideology accepted the one-way assimilation of meritocratic (meaning middle-class) black students into white schools, if often reluctantly, but also foreshadowed the fierce opposition to court-ordered busing of white children as an assault on the class achievements and consumer rights of upwardly mobile suburban families. In the 1970s, the antibusing movement based in the middle-class suburbs rallied around a color-blind defense anchored in the particular arrangements of the moderate-brokered accommodation to the *Brown* decision: that housing patterns in the metropolitan South corresponded to the (allegedly) de facto residential segregation of northern and western cities rather than historical forms of de jure segregation in violation of constitutional law.[19]

The Sunbelt Synthesis came under a multifaceted assault during the 1970s, as civil rights activists and urban working-class neighborhoods mobilized against the political monopoly exercised by the corporate leadership, and middle-class homeowners in outer-ring suburbs revolted against a broad range of metropolitan initiatives from annexation to busing. In a straightforward assessment of power and inequality across the New South, the *Raleigh News and Observer* acknowledged that "the present system is very responsive to the wishes of developers, businessmen, and similar groups but not to the average citizen, neighborhood associations and minorities." The municipal coalitions that had governed throughout the postwar era collapsed in some cities after demographic transition provided an opening for the formal exercise of black power, and they underwent substantial reconstitution in others after the busing litigation initiated by the NAACP sought metropolitan remedies for school segregation through the inclusion of the suburbs. The shifting currents at the grassroots level revealed that for all the populist rhetoric about a unified Silent Majority, racial conflicts consistently divided white communities along the neighborhood lines of class and geography. While the annexed island suburbs wielded their political influence to impose integration burdens on blue-collar neighborhoods, interracial working-class movements emerged to demand municipal reforms such as district elections and busing equalization. The Sunbelt metropolises of Atlanta and Charlotte appeared to offer the prototypes of the regional future, the peaceful and prosperous models of the New South. But the trajectories of the two cities also represent the divergent paths available to counterparts throughout the region—hypersegregated urban schools that illustrate the devastating failure of the *Brown* decision in the fragmented capital of Georgia, and a successfully integrated school system through a metropolitan busing plan that overcame a protracted revolt of the Silent Majority in the white-collar suburbs of North Carolina.[20]

Beyond Southern Exceptionalism

The era of southern exceptionalism is over. The historical linchpins of re-gional distinctiveness—a public culture of white supremacy rooted in legally mandated segregation, an underdeveloped economy dominated by the agri-cultural sector, and a single-party political system symbolized by the Solid South—dissolved as a result of the sustained pressure of the civil rights movement, the federal spending and corporate investment that stimulated the Sunbelt boom, and the postwar demographic migration to the cities and suburbs. In 1949, political scientist V. O. Key famously observed: "The fun-damental explanation of southern politics is that the black-belt whites suc-ceeded in imposing their will on their states and thereby presented a solid regional front in national politics on the race issue." The following decades decisively ruptured this phenomenon, as a steady stream of racial conflicts produced not regional unity but instead a divided white South, internally split along lines of class and geography. By the end of the 1970s, more than two-thirds of the electorate in the eleven southern states resided in metro-politan regions, where residential patterns of race and class mirrored the prevailing trends throughout the nation. Middle-class suburban voters be-came the driving force behind the steady postwar growth of the southern wing of the Republican party, including large numbers of white-collar mi-grants who relocated from the North and Midwest to work in the corporate economy. As the Sunbelt Synthesis of racial moderation and economic growth replaced the Black Belt politics of white supremacy, the regional dis-tinctiveness forged by the culture of Jim Crow gave way to the nationalizing trends of residential segregation and suburban exclusion. In 1974, in an ac-curate assessment of the disappearance of the exceptional South, journalist John Egerton observed that the region's "racial and economic and urban and political characteristics are very nearly the same as the dominant character-istics of the nation."[21]

The civil rights movement and the Sunbelt boom jointly destroyed the political mythology of the Solid South. During the decade after the U.S. Congress passed the Civil Rights Act (1964) and the Voting Rights Act (1965), federal enforcement and court-ordered busing transformed the re-gion's public schools into the most racially integrated in the nation, while the African-American electorate rapidly emerged as a powerful force in south-ern politics. The arrival of a competitive two-party system also depended upon the series of Supreme Court reapportionment decisions that began with *Baker v. Carr* (1962), which turned out to be as significant as *Brown* in reshaping the political culture of the South. The newly established principle of "one person, one vote" invalidated the rampant malapportionment that had long distorted the region's political climate, shifting power from the rural countryside to the metropolitan areas where a majority of people actually lived. With the cautionary note that any geographic model highlights general trends rather than exact science, my approach in the following chapters will adopt the formula advanced by Earl and Merle Black in *Politics and Society in the South*. The Black Belt describes counties that contained an African-American population of approximately one-third or greater, and the Deep South/Lower South labels include the five adjoining states with the highest percentage of black residents: Mississippi, Alabama, Louisiana, South Carolina, and Georgia. The Upper South/Outer South designations encompass the six-state subregion with large majorities of white citizens and high levels of metropolitan growth during the postwar era: Florida, Texas, Virginia, North Carolina, Tennessee, and Arkansas. My own emphasis on the Sunbelt/Black Belt divergence overlays this geographic formula, distinguishing metropolises such as Atlanta that are physically located in the Deep South but politically and demographically situated in the New South.[22]

The fiction of "de facto" segregation provided perhaps the most enduring, but also the most problematic, contrast between the exceptional South and the rest of the nation during the civil rights era. According to the prevailing regional distinction, enshrined in constitutional law and national discourse, racial inequality in the South represented segregation in law (de jure), while residential and educational patterns outside the region represented segregation in fact but not enforced by law (de facto). In the early 1960s, the NAACP initiated constitutional challenges against school segregation in several northern cities, but federal courts consistently ruled that the *Brown* mandate did not encompass the de facto landscape beyond the South. In the fall of 1963, when New York City faced mass boycotts by minority families that demanded busing to desegregate "racially imbalanced schools," the *New York Times* responded that the problem of "*de facto* segregation . . . is entirely different from that in the South. . . . The root is not in any systematic policy of racial exclusion fostered by law or administrative policy but in neighborhood population patterns." Congress reinforced this conventional wisdom in the Civil Rights Act of 1964, specifically excluding from the scope of desegregation policy any effort to "achieve a racial balance in any school by requiring the transportation of pupils or students from one school to another." That same year, white voters in the city of Detroit and the state of California approved referendums against open-housing legislation, grass-roots campaigns driven by property-rights defenses of residential segregation in a nascent display of the color-blind revolt against "forced integration." The powerful de facto mythology depended upon a fading regional contrast and a false narrative of national innocence, because public policies in the metropolitan South and North were still in the process of constructing a more intractable landscape of racial apartheid, an ultramodern version of de jure segregation.[23]

In the era of the Silent Majority, Richard Nixon announced that "we finally have in this country what the South has wanted and what the South deserves, a one-nation policy—not a southern strategy and not a northern strategy, but a one-nation strategy." The theme of regional convergence infused the president's appeals to the suburban voters whom he targeted in the 1968 election, the residents of the white-collar precincts that formed the Republican base in the Sunbelt South. During the next two years, the neighborhood schools movement in the suburban South fashioned the de facto mythology into a coherent color-blind platform that denounced court-ordered busing as a violation of the Civil Rights Act and defended the metropolitan landscape as identical to the large cities of the North. The Nixon administration promptly announced a new school integration policy that expanded the boundaries of de facto segregation to encompass the residential patterns of the metropolitan South. In concert with the color-blind demands of the Silent Majority, the White House recast public policies that sought "racial balance" and "economic integration" in suburban schools and neighborhoods as parallel forms of reverse discrimination, lacking constitutional authority to challenge the alleged class boundaries that defined de facto segregation. During the spring of 1970, Vice President Spiro Agnew reinforced this message during a trip to Georgia, where he appeared in front of the Confederate Memorial carved onto Stone Mountain, a longtime symbol of Old South resistance to racial equality. With Robert E. Lee and Stonewall Jackson riding by overhead, the vice president delivered a color-blind celebration of the Sunbelt Synthesis: "Just as the South cannot afford to discriminate against any of its own people, the rest of the nation cannot afford to discriminate against the South. . . . The New South embraces the future and presses forward with a robust economy fueled by industrial development. . . . The South that will make its greatest contribution to the American Dream is the New South."[24]

This book ends as a national story set in the suburbs, but it begins as a southern story set in the nation. Part I, "The Triumph of Moderation," starts by taking the reader on a tour of the varied geographic and political crossroads of the postwar South, revolving around the internal schisms that surfaced during the era of massive resistance to the *Brown* decision. The initial battles over school desegregation forced white southerners to take sides in a dramatic social and political showdown that pitted the survival of public education against an uncompromising defense of the racial caste system. At the center of this struggle stood a situationally silent majority of white moderates concentrated in the metropolitan regions, a group that sought to balance a general preference for the status quo with opposition to segregationist policies that preached defiance of the federal courts and abandonment of public schools. White liberals launched a comprehensive initiative to convince businessmen to lead their communities into compliance with

the law, but the turning point came from grassroots open-schools movements organized by ordinary middle-class parents from the island suburbs
of the major cities. Seeking to revitalize the collapsed middle ground, white
moderates in the metropolitan South devised a new class-based desegregation blueprint that discredited the reactionary politics of massive resistance
by evading the civil rights vision of good-faith integration. While part I
ranges broadly across the regional landscape, the bulk of this section ex-
plores the grassroots mobilization of the open-schools movement in Atlanta
and the long-term fate of the politics of racial moderation in the metropolis
acknowledged to be the headquarters of the New South. The saga of massive resistance marks a key turning point in the postwar narrative of southern transformation, the symbolic last stand for the caste politics of white supremacy and the collective debut for the suburban politics of color-blind
populism and middle-class consciousness.

Part II, "The Revolt of the Center," investigates the Silent Majority at the
grassroots level through a community study of the suburban uprising of
middle-class families during the five-year busing crisis in Charlotte. In 1969,
the metropolitan school district in Charlotte became the first place in the
United States to face a judicial mandate to overcome residential segregation
through two-way busing between the white neighborhoods on the suburban
fringe and the black schools of the urban core. Charlotte's antibusing movement rallied around a color-blind defense of neighborhood schools and
joined a national campaign to mobilize homeowners and schoolparents in
the middle-class suburbs, but events on the local landscape revealed that
the populist aura of the Silent Majority obscured substantial conflicts among
white families divided by class and geography. An interracial movement for
busing equalization eventually achieved a stable integration resolution in
Charlotte, in stark contrast to the fate of most other large cities throughout
the country, but not before the local revolt of the Silent Majority played a
crucial role in the reshaping of southern and national politics. The "Suburban Strategies" recounted in part III offer a regionwide perspective on
these developments, beginning with the postwar growth of the Republican
party in the metropolitan South and the subsequent reinvention of the New
Democrats as a moderate and interracial party of the center. The Nixon administration's short-lived experiment with an authentic Southern Strategy
backfired at the height of the busing controversy, but the alignment of federal desegregation policies with the grassroots demands of the Silent Majority established the spatial constraints on the scope of *Brown*. When the
Supreme Court rejected metropolitan integration remedies in pivotal cases
involving Richmond and Detroit, most suburban families throughout the
nation escaped accountability for the structural inequality highlighted in the
Kerner Report.

In the spring of 1970, after the NAACP secured a court-ordered busing plan for the city of Richmond, a white father named Benjamin Braswell announced: "I do not care what race my son's classmates are but it will not better my son's education to bus him anywhere. I will not stand for it. I was in the good old U.S. Navy during World War II to fight for the freedom of myself and my family and I stand ready, willing, and able to do it again in my own country if I have to." Tapping into the color-blind rhetoric of the Silent Majority, he explained that the "NAACP wanted the freedom of choice plan to begin with and I think that they were right. So what is right for them is also right for the Braswell family under the Federal Civil Rights Act." Two years later, the Reverend Robert Hall, Jr., sent an equally passionate letter to his Republican congressman, just before a federal appeals court invalidated a metropolitan integration formula that would have consolidated the predominantly white suburbs of Richmond and the majority-black schools inside the city. A white father of two children, Hall admitted that the prospect of busing originally "threw us into a near panic. . . . After much soul-searching, however, we decided along with many neighbors and friends to take positive steps to come to grips with the situation." He initially had not understood the rationale behind the integration mandate, but now he realized that "the objective is to completely dismantle a dual school system in order to make available the opportunity for a quality education to all children." Hall warned that the inclusion or exclusion of the affluent suburbs would determine whether racial integration succeeded or failed, because "the power base has been and still is white middle-class America." In conclusion, the pastor conceded that he did not "hold out much hope for imaginative leadership of the American people in sorting out this difficult and emotionally explosive issue." The experiences of white southerners as they sorted out this New American Dilemma, some enlisting in the Silent Majority and others transformed by the civil rights movement, is the story that follows.[25]

PART I

The Triumph of Moderation

CHAPTER 1

The Divided South

> Caught between the committed and dedicated partisans was a
> substantial and silent mass of plain citizens—confused and deeply
> disturbed. They were people who deplored desegregation and also
> deplored violence. . . . The failure of leadership in Washington
> which matched the default of Southern leadership made the
> ultimate showdown between state and federal force inevitable.
> —Harry Ashmore (1958), executive editor, *Arkansas Gazette*

ON JUNE 22, 1959, a liberal emissary named Benjamin Muse sat in the office of Governor Orval Faubus of Arkansas, an outspoken segregationist
leader of the South's political resistance to the *Brown* decision. Two years
earlier, Faubus had provoked a constitutional crisis by calling out the National Guard to prevent court-ordered school desegregation in Little Rock, a
maneuver that accompanied mob violence and prompted military intervention by the federal government. After a year of federally supervised desegregation, the governor closed all four of Little Rock's public high schools for
the duration of the 1958–59 academic year, under the authority of the state's
massive resistance program. When the Supreme Court rejected segregationist efforts to convert the city's white public schools into a taxpayer-
funded private system, Faubus proposed a constitutional amendment removing the state's obligation to provide free public education. Ben Muse, a
white liberal activist from the Southern Regional Council (SRC), had arrived as part of the group's regionwide mission to persuade recalcitrant
southern leaders that preserving public education represented a higher priority than maintaining the racial caste line without compromise. Founded
during World War II as an interracial organization dedicated to the promo-
tion of progressive public policy, the SRC's long-standing motto pledged "to
attain, through research and action, the ideals and practices of equal opportunity for all peoples in the South." Muse, the director of the Atlanta-based
organization's new Southern Leadership Project (SLP), told Faubus bluntly

A portion of chapter 1 was previously published in Matthew D. Lassiter, "A 'Fighting Moderate': Benjamin Muse's Search for the Submerged South," in *The Moderates' Dilemma: Massive Resistance to School Desegregation in Virginia*, ed. Matthew D. Lassiter and Andrew B.
Lewis (Charlottesville: Univ. Press of Virginia, 1998), 168–201. Reprinted with permission of
the University of Virginia Press.

that desegregation had become inevitable and that the time for defiance had passed. Even outside the media spotlight, the governor remained intransigent. "We haven't come to any such point," Faubus declared. "The whole South can keep on fighting. We can make the Supreme Court reverse its decision."[1]

In his search for the pragmatic South, Benjamin Muse found a more receptive audience among the civic elite of Little Rock. The Southern Leadership Project primarily targeted "moderate" members of the local "power structure," defined as prominent white businessmen whose distaste for the costs of defiance eclipsed their preference for Jim Crow. Corporate executives acknowledged the SLP message that televised chaos and shuttered schools had devastated their booster agenda to bring new industrial development and regional branch offices to Arkansas. A few months earlier, the Little Rock Chamber of Commerce had publicly endorsed a "controlled minimum" integration plan that would operate along the model popularized by business moderates in North Carolina—a pupil assignment scheme to comply with *Brown* by transferring a small number of black students to identifiably white schools after they passed a battery of aptitude screening tests. In combination with this corporate intervention, white moderates on the school board had issued a statement that Little Rock faced a choice between "open[ing] the schools with controlled integration, or . . . uncontrolled integration with all of its adverse effects, economic and social." Although many of Muse's contacts expressed personal opposition to racial integration, they praised the Chamber of Commerce for playing the decisive role in turning the tide of public opinion and paving the way for the anticipated reopening of public schools in the fall of 1959. Little Rock's civic leaders did not explain why the business community greeted the governor's demagoguery with two years of public silence before its belated involvement, but the president of the Chamber of Commerce did admit that his organization could not have overcome the forces of massive resistance without the assistance of the Women's Emergency Committee to Open Our Schools (WEC).[2]

The political mobilization of upper-middle-class white women from the island suburbs proved to be the turning point in Little Rock's massive resistance crisis. Female activists from some of the city's most exclusive neighborhoods started the WEC as an organization "dedicated to the principle of free public school education and to law and order. We stand neither for integration nor for segregation, but for education." The open-schools group boasted sixteen hundred members engaged in a multifaceted grassroots campaign of neighborhood gatherings, radio and television advertisements, and informational reports that emphasized the inadequacy of private schools and the economic consequences of the politics of defiance. Instead of confronting the ethical issues involved in compliance with the *Brown* decision, this rhetorical strategy redirected public discourse to the ways that massive resistance imposed severe penalties on white children and corporate interests. In the most critical episode of the Little Rock saga, the WEC organized a recall movement that replaced three segregationist members of the school board with corporate allies who supported minimal compliance with the law. The city peacefully implemented a "controlled integration" plan in the fall of 1959, representing a highly publicized triumph of racial moderation in the volatile South. In rejecting the absolute demands of the traditionalist caste ideology and defending the educational and economic values of a future-oriented alternative, the grassroots mobilization of urban and suburban families represented a rising power base in the postwar South, a political movement of middle-class consciousness that emerged as a collective force in response to the profound leadership crisis of the *Brown* era.[3]

During the era of massive resistance, the parallel default of political leadership at the national level and civic leadership at the municipal level facilitated the defiance of segregationist demagogues at the state level. At the height of the Little Rock crisis, the liberal Arkansas journalist Harry Ashmore charged that the "Southern leadership has no program and no policy except the negative one of delay at any price." But the roots of massive resistance, according to Ashmore, could be traced to the failure of national leaders to use "moral force . . . to persuade Southerners of the justice of the course the Supreme Court required of them," which had left the law-abiding white majority "confused and deeply disturbed." The contemporary and the historical searches for the "silent white moderates" of the civil rights era must be understood within the context of the decade-long policy of caution from two White House administrations, the fifteen-year career of the "all deliberate speed" *Brown II* mandate issued by the Supreme Court, and the persistent refusal of many prominent community leaders to speak out even in support of simple compliance with the law. The Southern Leadership Project—a direct response to the massive resistance dynamic of regressive state leadership, invisible local leadership, and timid national leadership—represented the most comprehensive liberal initiative to mobilize the region's "silent moderates" during the first decade after *Brown*. Despite lacking a mass membership, the Southern Regional Council embarked upon an ambitious operation to defeat massive resistance and guide the entire region into compliance with school desegregation through the political construction of a moderate South.[4]

White liberals in the South believed that grassroots civil rights activism and top-down federal intervention were necessary but insufficient forces in the struggle to eradicate the caste system and reshape the region's political culture. According to the SRC's mission statement, "Southerners themselves must ultimately work out democratic solutions to the South's problems." The arrival of open-schools protests against the implementation of massive resistance reinforced the SRC's long-standing faith in the existence of a moderate South—a silent majority—that historically had been submerged beneath the politics of white supremacy that empowered the region's conservative leadership through pervasive voting discrimination, systematic electoral malapportionment, and relentless intimidation of black activism and white dissent. During the late 1950s and early 1960s, the Southern Regional Council played a vigorous although largely clandestine role in the battle against massive resistance, through the comprehensive outreach to businessmen with the SLP and the covert provision of financial support and strategic advice to the open-schools groups forming in the major metropolitan centers. The liberal leaders of the SRC made a tactical decision to embrace the moderate open-schools movement as the political vehicle for their civil rights agenda, a practical response to the extreme threat of massive resistance that would have significant consequences for the long-term prospects of school integration and racial equality. The Southern Leadership Project failed almost completely in its attempt to convince the southern business community to speak out openly against segregationist rebellion and initiate a process of voluntary desegregation before the arrival of court orders and civic disorder. Instead the grassroots open-schools movement led by middle-class white parents from the cities and suburbs defeated the massive resistance program of the region's political leadership, but only by charting a middle path that discredited the politics of segregationist defiance by evading the ethical mandate of good-faith integration.[5]

The Origins of Massive Resistance

The battle lines in the South's massive resistance crisis can be traced to the profound regional transformations set in motion by the New Deal, World War II, and the advent of the Cold War. The midcentury restructuring of the regional economy shifted resources and influence to the urban businessmen and suburban families at the center of the new white-collar society. Corporate interests focused obsessively on the recruitment of outside industry and the economic development of the metropolis, a future-oriented outlook that combined an expansive growth agenda with conflict-averse racial moderation. Middle-class parents channeled their collective energy into localized projects such as the reform of their children's public schools, a consumerist ethos of individual meritocracy grounded in a spatial landscape of metropolitan residential segregation and postwar suburban prosperity. After the *Brown* decision, when the egalitarian challenge of the civil rights movement elicited the caste-driven response of massive resistance, the metropolitan priorities of business leaders and suburban families divided the white South along lines shaped by class ideology and racial geography. The initial

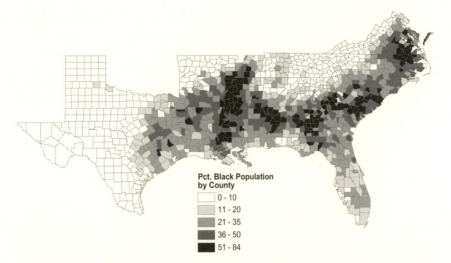

Map 1.1. Distribution of the Black Population of the Eleven States of the South, 1960, by County. The Black Belt region, consisting of counties where the African-American population exceeded one-third of the total, exercised disproportionate influence in regional politics during the massive resistance era despite decades of population depletion. Black Belt influence in southern politics faded rapidly after electoral reapportionment shifted power to the metropolitan centers. *Sources:* U.S. Census Bureau and Historical Census Browser, University of Virginia Library.

success of massive resistance depended upon a structural paradox of postwar southern development: the lingering concentration of political power in the rural Black Belt despite the emergence of the metropolitan Sunbelt as the region's economic and demographic engine (map 1.1). The eventual class-based resolution of the regional desegregation crisis represented a metropolitan rejection of Black Belt leadership that accelerated the shift of political power to the sprawling suburbs of the Sunbelt South.[6]

The primary explanation for the rise of massive resistance can be found in the failure of electoral reapportionment to keep pace with the metropolitan growth and middle-class expansion in the region's political economy. At the level of municipal politics, the Supreme Court's 1944 invalidation of the all-white primary empowered black voters in the major cities of the Sunbelt South, resulting in biracial alliances with affluent white neighborhoods that moderated the racial climate in the urban centers. At the level of presidential politics, election returns from the 1940s–1960s consistently demonstrated that the majority of white southerners identified with either the national wing of the Democratic party or the growing southern wing of the Republican party, a bipartisan dynamic that threatened Black Belt control of the so-called Solid South from two different directions. But at the state level, the rural politics of white supremacy flourished well into the 1960s, sustained not only by the blatant discrimination against African-American voters but also by the structural discrimination against all metropolitan residents resulting from systematic electoral malapportionment. The turn to massive resistance, especially in states of the Upper South where economic and demographic trends differed substantially from the Gulf Coast's segregationist strongholds, depended upon this effective disfranchisement of the cities and suburbs. Metropolitan voters did not gain proportionate influence in regional politics until the Supreme Court's decision in *Baker v. Carr* (1962) set in motion the reapportionment process nearly a decade after the strategy of defiance greeted the *Brown* mandate.[7]

The politics of moderation in the major cities and suburbs revealed the existence of a divided white South but also highlighted the ways in which the centrality of the "race issue" distorted ideological classifications along the regional spectrum. For many metropolitan voters whom historians have labeled the "white moderates" of the civil rights era, the middle-class belief in individual meritocracy was eclipsing the strict subscription to biological inferiority that underlay the political culture of white supremacy. But this moderate politics of class over caste also flourished because affluent, residentially segregated neighborhoods in the cities and suburbs faced little or no possibility of experiencing the specter of "massive integration" that animated the segregationist crusades based in the working-class precincts and the rural countryside. And by extension, the reactionary politics of racial caste generally trumped the reservoir of economic progressivism among working-class and rural white voters, which flared in moments such as the Populist movement and the New Deal (and could also be found in diluted form in the platforms of segregationist demagogues such as Governor George Wallace of Alabama). The race-dominated politics of the postwar South permitted urban corporate interests and suburban middle-class voters to occupy a position of relative moderation despite their essential fiscal conservatism and their consistent subordination of racial equality to the priority of economic growth. During the civil rights era, segregationist politicians based in the rural Black Belt and the Deep South states launched three regionwide efforts to resurrect the Solid South: the 1948 Dixiecrat revolt against the racial liberalism of the national Democrats, the turn to massive resistance during the *Brown* era, and Wallace's third-party presidential campaign in 1968. All three southern unity crusades foundered on the class-based divisions within the regional electorate, combined with the geographic divergence of the Deep South from the Outer South and the rural Black Belt from the metropolitan Sunbelt.[8]

The regional showdown over massive resistance initially empowered the caste-based forces of the Black Belt but ultimately propelled the South down the course charted by the class-based coalition in the metropolitan

Sunbelt. By the time of the *Brown* decision, the central players in the massive resistance drama had already staked out their respective positions. In 1950, key victories in the NAACP's deliberate assault on the "separate but equal" doctrine of *Plessy v. Ferguson* made it clear that the judicial invalidation of de jure school segregation loomed on the horizon. In 1951, the Southern Regional Council formally recognized that Jim Crow was incompatible with the principle of equal opportunity and for the first time proclaimed publicly that racial segregation was unethical and unconstitutional. By middecade, a majority of southern state governments had implemented a double-sided preemptive strike against court-ordered school integration: a transparent and incomplete effort to defend Jim Crow by equalizing funding between black and white schools, alongside legislation removing the constitutional guarantee of free public education in anticipation of a switch to a segregated private system. Metropolitan reformers, led by chapters of the League of Women Voters (LWV), worked for an alternative future-oriented objective: dramatically expanded support for public education as the cornerstone of middle-class values, industrial development, and regional modernization. Immediately after the *Brown* decision, the loudest voices came from segregationist organizations such as the Citizens' Councils, with a membership peak of approximately 250,000 and a power base in the smaller towns of the Black Belt. This grassroots uprising emboldened the region's conservative political leadership, symbolized by the 1956 Southern Manifesto in which 101 members of Congress pledged "to resist forced integration by any lawful means."[9]

The political architects of massive resistance devised an absolute defense of segregation in order to smooth over internal divisions among white southerners and unite the region behind a course of defiance to the Supreme Court. By the fall of 1958, when the governors of Virginia and Arkansas responded to court-ordered desegregation by closing public schools in four localities, massive resistance had become the dominant stance across the South. Many white citizens, including an eventual majority outside the Black Belt, did not support the segregationist policy of sacrificing public education and establishing a state-funded private school alternative. Massive resistance ultimately exposed the myopic vision of the rural leadership of the white South and transformed quotidian middle-class concerns about educational quality into a grassroots political mobilization against Black Belt recklessness. But out of intimidation or political impotence, distraction or disbelief, few white moderates organized in protest until after their own communities faced an immediate choice between legal compliance and public disorder, between maintaining total segregation and preserving public education. In the four Outer South states that rejected the strategy of massive resistance—North Carolina, Tennessee, Florida, and Texas—business interests and metropolitan voters exercised sufficient power in state politics to chart an alternative path of gradualism and tokenism. In the fall of 1957, three of North Carolina's largest cities "voluntarily" assigned a few carefully selected black students to previously all-white schools, representing the first significant breach in the southern wall of secondary school segregation and pioneering a suburban strategy of controlled desegregation circumscribed by aptitude screening and residential boundaries.[10]

In the beginning, massive resistance appeared to reflect a moral crisis of race relations, the ultimate test of the American Dilemma—would white southerners accept the principles of integration and equality contained in the *Brown* decision or would they choose the rebellious path of the Southern Manifesto and defend racial segregation to the bitter end? White liberals and moderates labored to redefine massive resistance as a pragmatic crisis of economic modernization and leadership resources—would local communities permit the destruction of public education for a new Lost Cause or would civic leaders resolve the desegregation debate in favor of the twin priorities of preserving public schools and maintaining economic prosperity? But in the broader trajectory of the postwar South, massive resistance ultimately crystallized as a political and spatial confrontation of class and geography—could the Black Belt leadership successfully impose a caste-driven resistance formula on the metropolitan areas of the Sunbelt South or would these extreme measures incite a revolt of the center by the region's fabled "silent moderates"?

The pragmatic liberal outreach and the grassroots moderate outlook converged in the project to redefine massive resistance from a defense of the "southern way of life" to a dangerous threat to white public schools and Sunbelt economic progress. Most suburban parents understood public education not as the appropriate place for a last stand in defense of white supremacy, but instead as the democratic institution at the center of a constellation of values shaped by racial privilege but grounded in middle-class consciousness: the upward mobility of their children in a meritocratic and modernizing society, the emblem of national citizenship and consumer freedom in a New South focused obsessively on the future. In response to the jeopardization of this suburban worldview, it would be in the crucible of massive resistance that a silent majority of white southern moderates first found a collective political voice, through a grassroots movement led by ordinary middle-class parents to protect their children's public schools. As the North Carolina model spread across the metropolitan South, this class-conscious triumph of racial moderation saved public education from the radical path of massive resistance, but only by replacing the civil rights agenda of social justice with an ostensibly race-neutral discourse of regional progress and individual meritocracy liberated from history itself, the latest and most resilient version of the New South mythology.[11]

VIRGINIA'S "FIGHTING MODERATES"

The triumphant metropolitan formula of gradual desegregation by individual black students, although ultimately embraced out of self-interest by a silent majority of white moderates, found its initial champions among white liberals who acted out of the best of intentions. In response to the extreme threat of massive resistance, southern liberals rallied around a pragmatic and cautious desegregation approach, a stance supported by many national liberals and most federal policymakers. "Undesirable or not," the progressive historian C. Vann Woodward wrote in 1957, "gradualism is an inescapable fact." After the *Brown* decision, Woodward later explained, "all over the South the lights of reason and tolerance and moderation began to go out under the resistance demand for conformity. . . . A 'moderate' became a man who dared open his mouth, an 'extremist' one who favored eventual compliance with the law, and 'compliance' took on the connotations of treason." This constricted public sphere represented a moral abdication of leadership by the moderate South, according to the famous assessment by Martin Luther King, Jr. In the "Letter from a Birmingham Jail," King warned: "We will have to repent in this generation not merely for the vitriolic words and actions of the bad people but for the appalling silence of the good people." In its comprehensive outreach to community leaders, the SRC recognized that the defeat of massive resistance required a compliance movement among white southerners that would begin in the critical realm of the public sphere, by replacing the volatile debate about race and segregation with a safer public discourse. Launched in 1959, the Southern Leadership Project proposed to galvanize moderate community leaders through practical appeals rather than moral suasion, emphasizing the educational and economic costs of defiance and the inevitability of compliance.[12]

The SLP's ambitious mission to steer the white South into compliance with the *Brown* decision reflected the pragmatic liberalism of Benjamin Muse, a journalist and former diplomat who served as director for the five-year duration of the project. Throughout the 1950s, Muse struggled to interpret his native region for a critical national audience through a weekly "Virginia Affairs" column in the *Washington Post* and regular essays in liberal periodicals. From a home base in the northern Virginia town of Manassas, he also participated directly in his state's massive resistance crisis as an enthusiastic booster of the grassroots open-schools movement. Muse's vocal opposition to racial discrimination placed him on a collision course with the Byrd Organization, the conservative faction that dominated Virginia politics from its base in the heavily black Southside region of the state. Even before the *Brown* decision, Muse routinely criticized the undemocratic nature of the state's political system, especially the Byrd Organization's reliance on the poll tax and its refusal to reapportion the legislature despite booming growth in the metropolitan centers and the northern Virginia suburbs. When the Organization embraced the Deep South brand of massive resistance, Muse explained in the *Nation* that the strategy of defiance represented the last gasp of the one-party system, because the vulnerable Byrd machine sought to manufacture racial unity in order to maintain rural dominance in the face of growing Republican strength in the metropolitan centers. As an antidote to reactionary state leadership, Muse predicted that a "compliance movement" would arise from urban and suburban Virginia, and he traveled throughout these communities imploring "silent moderates" to become "fighting moderates."[13]

As the majority of southern states adopted the path of massive resistance, Ben Muse advanced his own program of compliance with *Brown*, a comprehensive desegregation approach that revolved around an idiosyncratic vision of "good-faith gradualism." In 1956, in a lengthy essay in the *Washington Post*, he urged President Eisenhower to convene a gathering of southern leaders that would devise a systematic timetable in response to the Supreme Court's "all deliberate speed" formulation. To begin the process, Muse introduced a regionwide, county-by-county formula that ranged from immediate integration in Upper South localities with small percentages of black students to indefinite postponement in Black Belt strongholds of segregationist fervor. To critics who charged that his plan delayed constitutional rights, Muse argued that peaceful desegregation in the metropolitan and mountain counties would have a ripple effect, reducing tensions in more hostile areas. In the *New Republic*, he asserted that uncompromising integrationists and defiant segregationists were "equally obstructive to a solution of the South's great problem," and that gradualism based on genuine good faith could provide a rallying point for the "submerged moderates" of the South. In a public expression of the post-*Brown* identity crisis of southern liberalism, Muse concluded: "There is, of course, no middle ground. But I submit that moderation in this transition is the beginning of wisdom. All-out attack upon race discrimination brings sensations and explosions. It may bring the closing of some public schools. But genuine progress will not be made until the moderates on both sides rise up and make their influence felt. I say this because I would like to see race discrimination ended everywhere at the earliest possible date. Am I then a moderate?"[14]

Instead of Muse's vision of the slow but systematic implementation of integration in good faith, the executive and legislative branches of the federal government abandoned enforcement responsibility to private litigants and federal judges, and Virginia's elected officials filled the policymaking vacuum with the politics of defiance. In 1956, faced with clear evidence that suburban communities in northern Virginia planned to comply with court-ordered desegregation, the Byrd Organization jettisoned a local option formula approved by voter referendum and designed a massive resistance program to be implemented at the state level. Political malapportionment facilitated the turn to massive resistance, as the open-schools faction in the state legislature narrowly lost to a rural-based group of politicians who represented fewer than half of the state's residents. Two years later, when a clash between the federal judiciary and the state government appeared imminent, the organized opposition to massive resistance first emerged in one of the most affluent suburbs of northern Virginia. The Arlington Committee to Preserve Public Schools included members of religious, educational, and civic groups along with ordinary white parents who supported legal compliance and contended that state-subsidized private schools could never provide an adequate replacement for public education. In its mission statement, the Arlington Committee demanded local control of educational policy and insisted that the activists in the open-schools movement "are here concerned neither with perpetuating segregation nor in hastening integration."[15]

The open-schools movement in Virginia rapidly expanded into a formidable statewide revolt in the fall of 1958, after Governor Lindsay Almond closed public schools in three communities that faced immediate desegregation mandates. The enactment of the massive resistance program deprived thirteen thousand white students of public schooling in Norfolk, Charlottesville, and Front Royal. The save-the-schools movement rapidly mobilized in the port city of Norfolk, where white parents filed an equal-protection lawsuit to force the state government to reopen their children's schools. In Charlottesville, upper-middle-class white mothers opened temporary facilities to prevent local segregationists from converting to a permanent system of private education. Demands for open schools also came from a broad spectrum of PTA groups, religious organizations, and League of Women Voters chapters—a statewide surge championed by Ben Muse as the awakening of the "fighting moderates." Not until December, four months after the closing of schools, did corporate leaders express collective opposition to the program of massive resistance, but only in an off-the-record meeting between the governor and the Virginia Industrialization Group. By the time that business leaders in Virginia took a formal stand, the open-schools movement had already established a framework for compliance in the public sphere, and political sentiment in the state had shifted decisively. In Norfolk, for example, one hundred businessmen signed a petition explaining that "while we would strongly prefer to have segregated schools, . . . the abandonment of our public school system is . . . unthinkable." The manifesto appeared in late January, after months of grassroots activism by the parents in the open-schools movement and also days after the successful resolution of the litigation against massive resistance.[16]

Local open-schools movements soon joined forces in the Virginia Committee for Public Schools (VCPS), which ultimately included twenty-five thousand members in fifteen chapters based in the state's largest cities and suburbs. The organization decided to restrict membership to whites because of the "present climate of public opinion." The VCPS statement of principles declined to take a position on the issue of integration but warned that the sacrifice of public education would trigger corporate flight from the state, create a populace unqualified for representative government, and cause demoralization and delinquency among young people. VCPS literature observed that the organization "probably includes a majority who would prefer continued segregation of the schools," but all members were "brought together in the united belief that free public education must continue to be available to all who want it." The VCPS made endorsement of legal compliance a safe and respectable position through a highly effective public relations campaign that defended public education as an essential institution in a democratic society and emphasized the costs of defiance to the futures of white children. In the early months of 1959, federal and state courts invalidated the school-closing legislation, and black students peacefully broke the caste barrier in Virginia's secondary school system. That spring, with considerable assistance from a lobbying operation coordinated by the VCPS, moderate forces in the state legislature passed a local option plan over the fierce opposition of diehard massive resisters who sought to repeal the constitutional guarantee of free public education and subsidize an ersatz private system of segregation academies.[17]

The unprecedented political revolt by the open-schools movement revealed the fading clout of the Black Belt and foreshadowed the demise of the Byrd Organization, which would not survive the parallel empowerment of black voters and white suburbanites during the next decade. The decentralized policy of local option did allow rural segregationists in Prince Edward County to close their public schools for five years, but liberals such as Ben Muse rejoiced that "the state as a whole is no longer chained to the race problem of one small section." Yet with white moderates firmly in charge, the municipalities of urban and suburban Virginia proceeded to implement a bad-faith gradualist formula based on one-way individual desegregation limited by residential geography, avoiding the structural measures required to disestablish the dual school system. The triumphant consensus forged by the VCPS—that Virginians must choose either minimal compliance or no public schools—pushed any agenda of genuine racial equality to the margins of public discourse. Although Ben Muse consistently endorsed desegregation as a "matter of conscience and Christian ethics," and the massive resisters waved the banner of white supremacy, the grassroots open-schools movement refused to address the ethical or racial dimensions of the crisis at all. In the five tumultuous years since *Brown*, the extremism of massive resistance and the inherent limitations of the moderate philosophy forced white liberals to revise their strategic approach, postponing their vision of good-faith compliance and equal opportunity in favor of a defensive, class-driven appeal to save public schools for white students.[18]

THE SOUTHERN LEADERSHIP PROJECT

The Virginia experience quickly became the cautionary tale that the SRC projected for consumption by the defiant states of the Deep South, a warning of the need for white moderates at the local level to organize before rather than after the implementation of massive resistance. In its monthly *New South* publication, the SRC trumpeted the success of the Virginia Committee for Public Schools and explained that every state in the region faced a similar choice between "desegregation or no public education." The SRC also distributed a bleak forecast of the economic consequences that would have followed the permanent abandonment of public education in Virginia, including the departure of the state's industrial base and the absence of a skilled workforce adequate to the requirements of a modern society. White southern liberals drew two key lessons from the parallel showdowns in Arkansas and Virginia: that the refusal of open-schools groups to debate the moral issue of segregation versus integration represented the strategic breakthrough in moving the entire region from defiance to compliance and that pragmatic appeals to economic self-interest could convince business leaders in local communities to take a public stand for public education before court orders triggered massive resistance. The Southern Leadership Project represented the most comprehensive element of this compliance agenda, a five-year program to persuade local elites to adopt the tactics of the open-schools movements of the Upper South and comply with *Brown* before events spiraled out of control. "The politicians of the South have failed dismally to meet their responsibilities of leadership in this crisis," Benjamin Muse wrote in *Virginia's Massive Resistance*, a book designed to supplement the SLP's outreach efforts by offering a pragmatic path "out of the morass" for the silent moderates throughout the region.[19]

Between 1959 and 1964, SLP director Ben Muse visited more than five hundred contacts across the South, focusing on businessmen, newspaper editors, local politicians, and other prominent or potential white moderates. These intimate conversations, recorded in confidential memoranda sent to the SRC headquarters in Atlanta, provide a rare window into the local dynamics of leadership and citizenship that existed beyond the constricted arena of public discourse and the narrow glare of the media spotlight. As part of its broader task of interpreting regional mores for national leaders, the SRC forwarded the Muse memos to Thurgood Marshall of the NAACP and civil rights specialists Burke Marshall and Harris Wofford in the

Kennedy administration. The organization supplemented Muse's visits with a series of Leadership Reports, mailed to a list of several thousand regional leaders that included a heavy representation of corporate executives. Instead of appeals to "conscience and moral principle," the Leadership Reports emphasized economic arguments based on "common sense and self interest," portraying massive resistance as a futile last stand that would destroy the educational prospects of white children and devastate the industrialization agenda of the New South. Since desegregation was inevitable, the SLP argued, pragmatic southern leaders should manage the process of racial transition instead of allowing segregationist demagogues to create the conditions for civic chaos and mob violence. Through this combination of research and direct action, the SRC hoped to galvanize two types of southern leaders: the "cautious" liberals and "submerged moderates" who needed encouragement to take a public stand, and the more numerous "common sense" segregationists who presumably would be open to rational argument about the futility of resisting federal authority.[20]

The first year of the SLP revealed the strength of open-schools sentiment in the states of the Outer South and the popularity of North Carolina's minimalist desegregation model among leading white moderates. In his first mission as SLP director, Ben Muse traveled to Florida three times during 1959, as segregationists tried to replace the state's local option plan with massive resistance legislation. He advised Governor LeRoy Collins of Florida, a business moderate and champion of industrialization, to skirt the segregation/integration controversy through a New South emphasis on public education and economic progress. The SRC felt vindicated when Miami complied with court-ordered desegregation in the fall, although Muse quietly urged the Collins administration to increase the degree of integration instead of settling for tokenism. Several 1959 trips to Tennessee convinced Muse that cautious moderation also prevailed among newspaper editors, school board members, and business leaders in Knoxville, Nashville, and Chattanooga. All of his contacts promised that they would speak out against the closing of schools, although not until their communities faced a judicial mandate, and they generally advocated the class-based formula of limiting integration to a selective group of high-achieving black students. Additional journeys through North Carolina and Georgia assured Muse that the major urban newspapers in these states actively supported compliance and that many editors were quiet liberals who endorsed "good-faith gradualism." Although a vibrant open-schools movement called Help Our Public Education had arisen in Atlanta, editor Ralph McGill of the *Atlanta Constitution* reported that the city's business elite "have no guts" and would not act decisively against segregationist politicians. The SLP then arranged for two leaders of the Little Rock Chamber of Commerce to travel to Atlanta to warn their corporate counterparts against waiting too late before speaking publicly against massive resistance.[21]

"Business and industrial leaders are particularly wary of getting involved in the segregation furor," Muse concluded, but through the SLP they could be "inspired with a vision of a truly New South." In the winter of 1960, the arrival of the student sit-in movement announced that African-American protest, not pragmatic white leadership, would be the primary catalyst for social change in the region. As the Greensboro lunch counter demonstrations spread throughout the urban centers of the Outer South, the rapidity of events forced the SLP to shift from its initial emphasis on "voluntary compliance" to an ad hoc pattern of responding to racial showdowns as they occurred. Ben Muse moved away from the singular focus on schools in favor of a broader emphasis on equal access to public facilities, and in dozens of conferences he urged community leaders to resolve the sit-in controversy though biracial negotiations undertaken in good faith. In a balancing act that reflected the dilemma of pragmatic liberalism, Muse urged business leaders to desegregate lunch counters immediately while counseling black protesters to suspend demonstrations in favor of negotiated settlements. Although the eventual integration of public accommodations came only after renewed demonstrations and economic boycotts by the black community, white southern liberals who appreciated the catalyst of direct action still interpreted the breakthrough as a validation of their community-based agenda of interracial dialogue revolving around the local "power structure." Leslie Dunbar, the executive director of the SRC, acknowledged that while federal intervention and black protest had become the crucial triggers in the civil rights movement, "the white southerners who in scores of places assented to the student's demands laid the basis for a new hope—that the white South might at last be ready to take its destiny in its own hands and, without compulsion of the federal government and its courts, move to build a true community of persons."[22]

New Orleans became the next locale where the business establishment refused to heed the message of the SLP. Muse first visited New Orleans in late 1959, and Chamber of Commerce leaders told him bluntly that they would not repudiate massive resistance unless forced into action by a major crisis. In the spring of 1960, staff members of the SRC secretly began working with local activists in New Orleans to establish Save Our Schools (SOS) under the leadership of women reformers, ministers, and university professors. SOS mounted an advertising blitz that warned of the economic devastation caused by massive resistance and insisted that "the only realistic course was to support any reasonable plan, acceptable to the courts, which would keep public schools open." That fall, Louisiana Governor Jimmie Davis seized control of the New Orleans public school system to prevent compliance, and in response District Judge J. Skelly Wright invalidated the massive resistance laws passed by the state legislature. Behind the scenes, Muse labored in vain to convince business leaders to take a public stand during this descent into disorder. In November, four black first-grade girls finally entered two formerly all-white schools, accompanied by the most violent scenes of mob resistance since Little Rock. Thousands of people rioted in the streets, almost all white families boycotted the desegregated facilities, and the state legislature promised tuition grants for any students who transferred to private academies. Although SOS and other moderate groups lobbied continuously for peaceful compliance, the business community did not join the open-schools coalition until December, after four months of chaos. Additional desegregation in New Orleans proceeded far more smoothly the next fall, but the metropolitan brand of moderation that replaced the state program of massive resistance remained committed to policies of minimal desegregation rather than the SRC's vision of good-faith integration flowing from local control.[23]

Beginning in the fall of 1960, the SLP concentrated on the Deep South states where defiance flourished and support for gradual desegregation remained outside the boundaries of acceptable political discourse. A deep and uncharacteristic pessimism marked the reports from Muse's exploratory trip to the major cities of Alabama. Isolated white moderates and underground liberals expressed their fear to speak publicly for compliance and warned that only federal intervention could alter the dynamics of repression. Muse's memoranda concluded that southern moderates desperately needed the "moral force" of aggressive support for desegregation from the incoming Kennedy administration. He returned to Alabama in 1961, after the violent attacks on freedom riders dominated national headlines. Muse insisted that a hidden but moderate element existed in Alabama's cities, even though the newspapers and the civic leadership appeared to be "uncompromising segregationists." In January 1962, after Birmingham officials closed the city's parks and golf courses rather than accept court-ordered desegregation, local business leaders finally did take a public stand for compliance. Muse anticipated a "moderate upsurge" in Birmingham's future, but the SRC also recognized that its voluntary compliance agenda was not working in the Deep South, and that community after community appeared destined to repeat rather than learn from the failure of moderates in Virginia and Little Rock to mobilize in advance of disorder and defiance. The most tragic consequences of this profound collapse of the center remained on Birmingham's horizon, as the 1963 civil rights demonstrations and the city's brutal response revealed the simultaneous default of local officials and national politicians to enforce the rule of law.[24]

Between 1961 and 1964, the SLP sent Muse on five journeys to Mississippi, the state known by civil rights activists as the notorious "Closed

Society." Muse initially speculated that a majority of "educated Mississippi-ans are silently, or privately, moderate on the race issue," but the few white dissidents he could locate refused to speak out publicly and uniformly pre-dicted that a racial disaster was inevitable. He sharply criticized business-men involved with the Mississippi Economic Council who told him that while they opposed massive resistance, "the politicians are going crazy and we can't do much about it." The final SLP reports from Mississippi, written during the 1964 Freedom Summer, demonstrate the evolution in the south-ern liberal interpretation of the dynamics of desegregation and the setbacks to the SRC's philosophy that social transformation could originate from within the moderate white South. Muse advocated economic boycotts by the NAACP chapter in Jackson to pressure local business leaders and sent a report to the Johnson administration warning that only forceful federal ac-tion could prevent violence in the state. The SRC also shifted its resources from the cultivation of white moderates to the Voter Education Project, with the goal of transforming the South's political leadership through the empow-erment of the black electorate. In his final mission as SLP director, and in two additional books about the civil rights era, Benjamin Muse drove home the hard lessons of a decade of turmoil: the spectrum of southern leadership ranged from demagoguery to cowardice, the abdication of responsibility ex-tended to Congress and two consecutive presidential administrations, the mobilization of white moderates had been "very little and very late," and substantive change had come only through the combination of internal protest and external force. Good-faith gradualism had failed.[25]

"Hearts and Minds"

Massive resistance also failed. In the decade after *Brown*, the Black Belt agenda of preserving the caste system through a unified regional resistance backfired by forcing a divided white South to choose between the past and the future, framed as the competing priorities of absolute segregation versus open public schools. As the struggle over racial equality evolved into a pro-nounced crisis of educational preservation and economic modernization, the awakening of the "silent moderates" based in the metropolitan regions re-arranged the political fault lines of the Solid South. The rise of massive resis-tance as a political formula depended upon the peculiar dynamics of the one-party system, which bottled up the class and geographic divisions within the regional electorate. The actual implementation of school-closing policies became a crucible for the release of these ideological tensions, mobilizing ordinary middle-class citizens who lived in cities and suburbs against the consequences of rural control of southern politics. The grassroots open-schools movement previewed the rise of a class-conscious, consumer-oriented, and neighborhood-driven politics based in the suburban South, where the structures of the racial and spatial landscape increasingly reflected national rather than regionally distinctive patterns. In the future, the metropolitan priorities of rapid economic development and quality neighborhood schools and middle-class residential privilege, not the rural politics of white supremacy, would define the political center in the American South.

The denouement of massive resistance must be understood as a watershed moment in southern history, a political and ideological showdown that redefined and reinvigorated the middle ground, hastened the demise of the one-party system, and accelerated the power shift to the booming metropolitan regions where a majority of citizens actually resided. Some scholars of the civil rights era have argued that "the acceptance of token desegregation was a conservative reaction in defense of southern continuity and represented no real break with the past," an assessment that follows the tendency of contemporary analysts who reduced the divisions within the white South to a tactical disagreement between "smart segregationists" (white moderates) and "dumb segregationists" (massive resisters). But a sober recognition of the wide gulf between gradualism and equality should not obscure the ways in which the initial breach of the caste system shattered the psychological, political, and legal barriers of the Solid South. For caste-conscious segregationists, "token integration" represented a false promise by white moderates who had sacrificed the "southern way of life" on the altar of public education, and the only solution became Richmond editor James Kilpatrick's call for segregated private schools "from Southside Virginia to the Mississippi delta." For black southerners, the federal enforcement of court orders and the moderate consensus for legal compliance—although both were tardy and qualified—demonstrated that pressure tactics brought tangible results and that future progress would be negotiable and justiciable rather than beyond the pale. For white moderates, the arrival of desegregation destroyed the mythology of racial consensus, injected the philosophies of middle-class consciousness and color-blind meritocracy into the debate over racial privilege, and cleared the way for a genuine distribution of attitudes across the ideological spectrum.[26]

Although the SLP rarely convinced white communities to implement desegregation before crises occurred, and never persuaded business leaders to begin integration in good faith, the liberal strategy of changing the rhetorical terms of debate proved to be remarkably successful in defeating the political program of massive resistance. In the Sunbelt South, the emergent consensus for gradual desegregation and minimal compliance accompanied an unmistakable shift away from the public discourse of white supremacy in favor of a more complicated fusion of racial and class attitudes—a still inchoate ideology of individual rights, consumer liberties, and spatial privileges. Following the blueprint advanced by the open-schools movement, urban and suburban white parents maintained their firm commitment to public education as metropolitan school districts adopted policies of one-way desegregation limited by "freedom of choice" formulas and "neighborhood school" boundaries. During the decade after the collapse of massive resistance, the reapportionment wave launched by *Baker v. Carr* facilitated the ascendance of the Sunbelt metropolises over the Black Belt countryside, and the empowerment of black southerners through the Voting Rights Act of 1965 proved to be the coup de grace for the traditional politics of white supremacy. The primary demographic forces behind postwar political realignment in the New South became the sprawling middle-class suburbs and the expanding black electorate, not the defiant Dixiecrats and the defeated massive resisters.[27]

While civil rights activism and federal intervention proved to be necessary ingredients in the process of dismantling Jim Crow, the actions of white moderates were critical in undermining the defiant politics of white supremacy and constructing a grassroots alternative to the racial caste system. In chronicling this collapse of massive resistance, scholars often have credited the leadership of the business community for "engineering peaceful transitions to token desegregation" and initiating a process that "turned the tide and ushered in a new era in southern race relations." The five-year history of the Southern Leadership Project provides a systematic counterpoint to any emphasis on the centrality of public leadership by businessmen during the sustained crisis of school desegregation in the South. In the volatile climate of massive resistance, expressing open support for compliance became a stance of outright dissent and took on a political significance beyond the constricted range of moderate rhetoric. The profound default of traditional southern leaders created the vacuum in which ordinary suburban parents exercised the responsibilities of citizenship, standing up for the rule of law and the democratic ideals of public education. While business organizations maintained conspicuous silence, the leaders of the white southern opposition to massive resistance became the middle-class citizens, and especially the female reformers, of the Women's Emergency Committee in Arkansas, the Virginia Committee for Public Schools in the Old Dominion, Save Our Schools in Louisiana, and Help Our Public Education in Georgia. By 1963, recognition of this dynamic caused the SRC to redirect its efforts in the Deep South away from business leaders in favor of grassroots open-schools groups such as Alabamians behind Local Education and Mississippians for Public Education. When Jackson, Mississippi, implemented court-ordered desegregation without violence in the fall of 1964, the SRC claimed a major victory in its efforts to achieve compliance "peacefully and with good will."[28]

A year later, in the annual report of the Southern Regional Council, executive director Leslie Dunbar observed that "a seemingly invariable" lesson had emerged during the transition from massive resistance to desegregation in communities across the region: "No progress until the right of public discussion and dissent has been established." Since the most important battles of the massive resistance era took place in the public sphere, creating a consensus for legal compliance "has been the task and great achievement of save-our-schools groups." Six years after the SRC launched its comprehensive outreach to moderate businessmen, Dunbar acknowledged that "seldom has the 'power structure' led in gaining this right. Its weighty role comes later, after the windows have been opened." In an implicit repudiation of the pragmatic open-schools strategy, Dunbar also declared that "our society has been systematically oppressive, and the change from a discriminating to a non-discriminating social order cannot be a merely superficial alteration." Then the executive director of the SRC argued that the structural racism at the heart of the caste system had been understood most clearly by the extreme segregationists who opposed any desegregation compromise and the young black activists who gave new meaning to the promises of equality. In a series of essays published a year later, Dunbar went even further in crediting black southerners with showing white southerners— including white liberals—that segregation was simply a policy that could be changed by government intervention, instead of a deeply ingrained way of life that could only be dismantled with caution and through gradualism.[29]

Beyond the ebb and flow of massive resistance, urban businessmen and suburban families played critical roles in the interrelated processes that ultimately supplanted the caste-based legal order in the metropolitan South: the construction of the exclusionary residential landscape and the emergence of a new racial ideology of color-blind and class-based individualism. But the priorities of downtown business leaders and middle-class white parents, which converged during the era of massive resistance, also diverged in subtle but crucial ways that eventually would shatter the moderate consensus about the future of the New South. Approaching the politics of racial moderation through a metropolitan framework, urban businessmen pursued a growth agenda that emphasized the diversification of the economy, the annexation of the suburbs, the fortification of the downtown business district, and the systematic use of planning and development policies to segregate residential neighborhoods by race and income. Shaped by the configuration of this spatial landscape, middle-class suburbanites understood the growth consensus through a family-based, consumer-oriented, and fundamentally localist perspective, making quality education in secure neighborhood schools the foundation of their political and social worldview, not merely a function of industrial recruitment or regional prosperity. The inchoate middle-class consciousness that resolved the massive resistance crisis reflected an ascending suburban consensus that fused compliance with the law and full integration into the nation, a social ideology of meritocratic individualism rather than racial caste, an obsession with future success rather than past injustice, and the submergence of racial discourse beneath the color-blind politics of residential privilege.

In a series of 1955 speeches in the moderate suburbs of northern Virginia, Benjamin Muse told his audiences that racial segregation "has no justification in a democratic or a Christian society" and that "real integration can only come in the hearts and minds" of white southerners. This formulation consciously echoed the *Brown* decision's description of racial segregation as an injustice imposed upon the "hearts and minds" of African-American students. In the search for a pragmatic South, Benjamin Muse and the Southern Regional Council labored to change the minds of white southerners, believing that their hearts would follow. In retrospect, the limitations of the Southern Leadership Project are clearer: a desegregation consensus forged through the race-neutral rhetoric of white self-interest, rather than deeper examination of the meaning of equality in the context of the burdens of southern history, all too often represented not the first step of a good-faith process but instead reluctant acquiescence to the minimum requirements of the law. A full decade after *Brown*, the political failure of massive resistance had brought secondary school desegregation to every southern state, but the structural legacies of the dual educational system and the fundamental inadequacies in the moderate approach to race relations meant that almost 98 percent of black students remained in segregated institutions.[30]

The SRC's 1964 report endorsed the internal catalyst of the civil rights movement and the external catalyst of federal intervention in the South and proclaimed that "this nation is only still beginning the necessary work of making ours a republic of equal citizenship." The lessons of the previous decade seemed to contradict the organization's constant refrain that "each community in the South must find its own answers to social issues within the framework of law and conscience, . . . white and Negro, coming together in equal dignity to find the best ways to move ahead." But even as the Southern Regional Council praised protest from below and demanded intercession from outside, the resilient liberal faith in the necessity of transformation from within recognized an essential truth about the civil rights era. "The really key decisions will not be made by Presidents, Congress, or civil rights leaders," Leslie Dunbar told the SRC's annual convention in 1965. "They will be made individually by millions of homeowners, church-goers, parents of school children. . . . They will choose whether they want an . . . integrated society or one built on the principles of social exclusion and isolation."[31]

CHAPTER 2

HOPE in the New South

> We urban whites and blacks were locked in the same cage
> together. . . . We were going to have rampant racism and
> unfairness and corruption as long as we had the county unit system
> and malapportionment.
> —James Mackay (1986), former DeKalb
> County representative, General Assembly of Georgia

The Capital of the New South

All suburbs are not alike. Drive a few miles north from downtown Atlanta, on the older two-lane roads or the newer ten-lane highways, and the topography features rolling hills and wandering creeks, beautiful mansions with immense yards, acre-sized lots lined with pines and dogwoods, ranch-style brick homes surrounded by ivy and azaleas. Initially planned as "garden suburbs," the prosperous and exclusive residential areas of northside Atlanta have retained much of their original charm and character, even as the surrounding metropolis has become notorious for the excesses of suburban sprawl and the inequities of urban segregation. Neighborhoods such as Buckhead, West Paces Ferry, and Druid Hills now represent suburban islands within an urbanized landscape, insulated pockets of prestige and power with their own "edge city" dynamics, domestic sanctuaries demarcated by high-density commercial corridors and cluttered transportation networks. As historical boundaries of racial privilege have expanded into modern patterns of class prestige and consumer affluence, the prevailing ethos of northside Atlanta remains psychologically situated between and geographically isolated from the multiplying exurban subdivisions and the diminished urban core of the metropolitan region. A half-century ago, as the Georgia capital embraced the Sunbelt boom, the northside suburbs became the destination of choice for small-town white southerners entering the corporate economy, northern and midwestern professionals relocating to regional branch offices, and the adult offspring of Atlanta's intown elite. For the families that moved within this world of new money and polite company, "Atlanta seemed so small that everybody knew everybody else," according to Nan Pendergrast, a self-described "society lady" who grew up in Druid Hills, left Vassar College to marry a Georgia Tech graduate, settled down on a four-acre spread in West Paces Ferry, watched her daughter become a debutante, and helped launch a grassroots revolt that shook Georgia's political system to its foundations.[1]

Beginning in 1958, a determined group of white parents from the island suburbs of northside Atlanta constructed a powerful metropolitan rebellion against the massive resistance program of Georgia's rural leadership. Natives and newcomers joined together in an unprecedented social and political movement that took root in the churches, synagogues, PTA chapters, carpool lines, living rooms, and civic clubs of the newly developed suburban landscape. Upper-middle-class white women, describing themselves as "concerned housewives and mothers," dominated the public leadership of HOPE (Help Our Public Education), the ad hoc organization that coordinated Atlanta's open-schools campaign. As conscious representatives of the values of the New South, and enthusiastic citizen-boosters of the prevailing ethos of Atlanta Exceptionalism, these suburban activists fashioned a political style that combined the localist defense of their families and neighborhoods with a centrist ideology of educational reform and regional uplift. Tens of thousands of white Georgians actively supported the compromise desegregation path advanced by HOPE, a group that drew the open backing of Atlanta's news media and elected officials and the quiet assistance of the liberals in the Southern Regional Council.[2]

By 1961, when the city of Atlanta received national acclaim for the peaceful implementation of token desegregation at four public high schools, a clear and no-longer-silent majority of white Georgians had turned against the segregationist crusade to close public schools in defiance of the *Brown* decision. During this three-year struggle, the ordinary parent-activists in HOPE disproved the verdict that massive resistance had suppressed white moderation across a Solid South, and their victorious strategy cast into sharp relief the clash between the Black Belt and Sunbelt visions of the regional future. By decade's end, the middle-class discourse of protecting innocent children, strengthening public education, and pursuing economic prosperity would emanate from across the political spectrum. But the long-term fate of racial equality in metropolitan Atlanta also exposed the inherent liabilities in the strategic approach of white liberals and moderates, who insisted that the moral crisis of racial integration could be resolved only through an explicit focus on white self-interest and a conscious avoidance of ethical principles that grappled with the burdens of southern history.

The mobilization of Atlanta's island suburbs produced a new desegregation consensus that maintained the basic configuration of the dual school system but moved beyond caste barriers to accept the one-way integration of individual black students into white schools through a "freedom of choice" program. White moderates marketed freedom of choice as a "race-neutral" solution to the *Brown* dilemma, framed in the vocabulary of consumer rights and superimposed upon a racially structured educational system reimagined as "neighborhood schools." This class-driven formula anticipated the ideological currency of a color-blind ethos of individual meritocracy and socioeconomic privilege that naturalized a metropolitan landscape of pervasive racial discrimination and residential segregation. Expanding upon the open-schools movements in other southern cities, HOPE recast massive resistance as a showdown between the Black Belt retreat to the past and the Sunbelt embrace of the future, a potent strategy that successfully discredited the politics of white supremacy and effectively marginalized the egalitarian agenda of the civil rights movement. Through a race-neutral defense of public education, and a class-conscious vision of economic prosperity, the grass-roots activists in HOPE popularized an emerging suburban discourse that embodied the vitality but also the limits of the center.

The political defeat of massive resistance paved the way for the regional ascendancy of the Atlanta brand of racial moderation, elevating the future-oriented values of the New South over the traditionalist priorities of the Solid South. This ideological triumph of the Sunbelt Synthesis cemented the booster ethos of Atlanta Exceptionalism at the heart of the city's collective identity and symbolized the regional power shift to the dynamic metropolises of the postwar landscape. But despite liberal hopes that the demise of the one-party system would produce a progressive alliance of urban whites and blacks, the timing of this political transformation empowered the suburban South at the expense of both the countryside and the central cities. Atlanta's white moderates and liberals succeeded in saving the public school system from the immediate and severe threat of massive resistance, but only through defensive strategies ill-equipped to address the underlying forces of residential apartheid and metropolitan fragmentation that shadowed the future of the sprawling Sunbelt showcase.

Atlanta has always represented the epicenter of both the imagination and the ideology of the New South. While the original New South Creed of the late 1800s fused industrial growth and legal segregation into the managed mythology of regional modernization and racial harmony, the open embrace of white supremacy by the boosters of the post-Reconstruction era contradicted their insistence on the South's liberation from its own past. The Sunbelt Synthesis embodied in the trajectory of postwar Atlanta involved similar claims of immunity from the burdens of southern history, but this time pursued through an ultramodern formula that ultimately subsumed racial conflict beneath the overlapping frameworks of structural and spatial inequality, a frankly class-conscious and ostensibly color-blind philosophy of consumer-based individualism, unconstrained capitalist development, and intransigent suburban autonomy.[3]

The debunkers of the latest New South myths have emphasized the persistence of an "Atlanta Paradox"—"substantial racial segregation in a com-

munity with a reputation for good race relations, . . . a poor and economically declining city population in the face of dramatic economic growth."
But as in the nation at large, about which this verdict could just as easily be
written, contemporary Atlanta appears less as a paradox to be unraveled
than as an ideological and spatial landscape to be mapped. Although geographically situated within the Deep South, metropolitan Atlanta during the
postwar era most closely resembled a regional variation of the American
Dilemma and a postindustrial manifestation of the national urban crisis, albeit with the particular intensities of the Sunbelt economic blueprint. Deep
patterns of metropolitan inequality were not contradictory, but instead essential and intrinsic, to the twin slogans that infused the civic religion and
the futuristic ecology of Atlanta Exceptionalism—the "City Too Busy to
Hate" and "A City without Limits." For the New South architects of Atlanta's metropolitan landscape, residential segregation promised racial
peace through a city too fragmented to hate, and suburban sprawl represented Sunbelt prosperity synchronized with the growth ideology of American Exceptionalism. Atlanta's recent history, from the leading site of racial
moderation in the South's massive resistance showdown through the "post-
metropolitan" staging ground of the 1996 Olympics extravaganza, illustrates
the fusion of racial and class ideology into the politics of place and space embodied in the Sunbelt Synthesis.[4]

Biracial Politics

Atlanta represented the "bustling nerve center of the New South" during
the Sunbelt boom, as the national media and local boosters routinely reminded current residents, prospective investors, and corporate migrants. Although inextricably part of the relentless burnishing of the city's national
image, Atlanta's self-proclaimed designation as the de facto capital of the
Southeast also accurately captured postwar dynamics. Transcending its
modest origins as a railroad junction and its searing role in the Civil War, Atlanta efficiently capitalized on the resources and opportunities of Cold War
growth liberalism. Military bases and federal defense spending, most promi-
nently the Dobbins Air Force Base and the Lockheed Corporation in suburban Cobb County, spurred expansion on the metropolitan fringe. Almost
three thousand new corporations and regional branch offices arrived in
Atlanta between 1945 and 1960, drawn by an aggressive recruitment effort,
the availability of air conditioning, the low-wage and low-regulation economy, and the city's centrality in regional distribution networks as a highway
and airway crossroads. Atlanta's highly diversified economy revolved around
the white-collar sectors of finance, retail, and service; as early as 1950 manufacturing employed fewer than one-fifth of the metropolitan workforce, a

ratio that declined steadily to a level below one-tenth by century's end. The 1960 census revealed that the population of metropolitan Atlanta exceeded one million residents, a milestone celebrated with typical hyperbole and surpassed in the former Confederacy only by the southwestern metropolises of Houston and Dallas.[5]

The political culture of postwar Atlanta clearly reflected the priorities and the power of the downtown civic and political leadership, which enthusiastically championed the vision of a New South integrated into the nation through the reconciliatory agenda of the growth consensus, where racial dilemmas dissolved into the physical landscapes of Sunbelt prosperity. A year after the *Brown* decision, Mayor William B. Hartsfield devised his famous description of Atlanta as a "City Too Busy to Hate." This rhetorical flourish became Atlanta's semiofficial booster slogan during the civil rights era and shaped a hegemonic vocabulary of Atlanta Exceptionalism that framed the rhetoric of both the marketers and the critics of the city's mythology. ("Today's action indicates that Atlanta is a city too busy growing to hate," the leaders of the student sit-in movement announced in 1961 after business leaders finally agreed to their demands. "We are sure that this same attitude will prevail as Atlanta continues to progress.") A loyal national Democrat, Hartsfield became the political embodiment of the Sunbelt Synthesis, serving as mayor for all but two of the twenty-five years between 1937 and 1962. Racial moderation and economic growth formed the intertwined pillars of the Hartsfield administration, epitomized in the mayor's comment that he "always kept in mind that Atlanta was the headquarters of the Coca-Cola Company . . . and that anything that would reflect unfavorably on Atlanta would hurt the company." Atlantans understood that their mayor effectively spoke for the Chamber of Commerce and powerful elites such as Coca-Cola chairman Robert W. Woodruff (figure 2.1). While Hartsfield's invocation of the "City Too Busy to Hate" was fundamentally about the power of money, the slogan also provided a constant reminder that Atlanta Exceptionalism meant synchronization with national ideals and secession from Deep South mores.[6]

Atlanta's pioneering brand of racial moderation also represented the business community's pragmatic response to rising black influence in the sphere of municipal politics. Long considered an exemplar of middle-class black opportunity, the city boasted the prestigious black colleges of the Atlanta University Center and a downtown concentration of African-American financial power along Auburn Avenue. After the judicial invalidation of the white primary in 1944, massive voter registration drives turned the black electorate into a formidable force in local politics and made the endorsement of the Atlanta Negro Voters League critical to any candidate for citywide office. During the 1950s and 1960s, a crosstown alliance of upper-class white businessmen and their subordinate but privileged black counterparts

Figure 2.1. The three most powerful leaders of Atlanta's corporate-political alliance during the civil rights era. Robert Woodruff of the Coca-Cola Company, holding his trademark cigar, speaks to Mayor William Hartsfield (center) and Ivan Allen, Jr., the mayor-elect, at the Capital City Club in 1961. Courtesy of the William Berry Hartsfield Papers, Special Collections and Archives, Robert W. Woodruff Library, Emory University.

dominated city politics, based on the understanding that racial disputes would be resolved through quiet negotiation rather than public confrontation. Coalition dynamics in Atlanta closely resembled the "Progressive Mystique" that William Chafe has charted in Greensboro, where the dialectic of white moderation and black pragmatism produced a politics of civility that permitted modest reforms but reinforced systemic inequality. By making "good manners more important than substantial action," the biracial alliance remained under the control of paternalistic white elites who defended the status quo until forced to compromise by black protest or federal leverage, both of which triggered the overriding fear of negative national publicity. In practice, Atlanta's ruling consensus revolved around policies of class favoritism toward the more affluent members of both races; one journalist observed that the city's "political stability and leadership lay in a coalition of Negroes and 'nice' people, the respectable elements, including the conservative rich."[7]

As a discourse of power, Hartsfield's formulation of the "City Too Busy to Hate" captured the concrete ideological and institutional arrangements of the municipal governing coalition. Beginning in 1949, and continuing throughout the two-decade duration of the biracial alliance, a majority or near majority of the city's white electorate voted against the mayoral candidate of the downtown establishment, who drew consistent support from the crosstown coalition between black precincts and the affluent white neighborhoods of the northside. In return for the endorsement of the Atlanta Negro Voters League, Mayor Hartsfield openly consulted with African-American leaders, took symbolic steps such as the hiring of black policemen, oversaw the peaceful desegregation of municipal buses and golf courses, and routinely pledged that Atlanta would not tolerate the racial violence that inflamed many other southern cities. In the 1957 mayoral election, with the school desegregation crisis imminent, Hartsfield's victory over extreme segregationist Lester Maddox demonstrated the potency of racial moderation in Atlanta's temperate corner of the turbulent South. Accused by Maddox of being "a pawn of the NAACP" and the "Negro bloc vote," Hartsfield responded that Atlanta must avoid "the hatred and bitterness of Montgomery or Little Rock" and that his constituents "don't want Atlanta growth and prosperity to be stopped by racial controversy." This New South platform of open schools and legal compliance brought Hartsfield almost 97 percent of the black vote and 70 percent of the affluent white vote, while about two-thirds of the working-class and lower-middle-class white residents of Atlanta cast their ballots for Maddox and massive resistance.[8]

The politics of social class and the power lines of metropolitan space shaped Atlanta's voting arrangements, with the tacit understanding that economic development required moderate race relations, which in turn required residential segregation. The systematic housing segregation in the island suburbs of northside Atlanta reflected a fusion of public policy and private capital, including federal mortgage guidelines and local banking programs that mandated racial and class homogeneity, and the discriminatory impact of exclusionary municipal zoning and standard real estate practices. By 1960, eighteen contiguous census tracts located in the northern sections of Atlanta and Fulton County contained a population breakdown of 92,503 white and 1,355 black residents, with the majority of these racial minorities located in service-class neighborhoods or working as live-in servants (map 2.1). The overwhelmingly white neighborhoods of the northside included prewar garden suburbs originally governed by restrictive racial covenants and postwar subdivisions planned for the white-collar professionals in the corporate economy. On the other side of town, the Hartsfield administration expanded housing for minority families in exchange for the black elite's accommodation to urban renewal and expressway construction programs that employed "slum clearance" to fortify the downtown business district by displacing thousands of African-American residents. In an illustra-

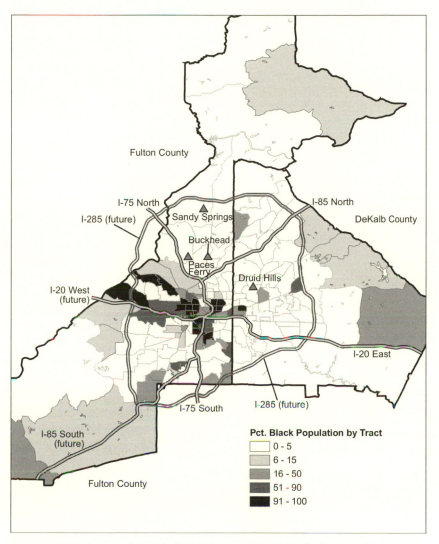

Map 2.1. Distribution of the Black Population of the City of Atlanta, Fulton County, and DeKalb County, 1960, by Census Tract. After the 1952 annexation of Buckhead, the city of Atlanta included most portions of Fulton County located within the future I-285 perimeter highway, as well as a small part of DeKalb. This map of the two most populous counties in metropolitan Atlanta reveals the concentration of the African-American population near downtown and the expansion trends as black families moved outward on the westside. The suburbs north of Atlanta experienced dramatic population growth during the 1950s and 1960s and remained overwhelmingly white and upper-middle class. Most of the open-schools activists in HOPE lived in the northside "island suburbs" of Buckhead, Paces Ferry, and Druid Hills. *Sources:* U.S. Census Bureau and the Atlanta Region Metropolitan Planning Commission.

tion of the Sunbelt South's preemptive version of managed race relations, the downtown establishment extended its imprimatur to ad hoc "mayor's committees" that negotiated the white-to-black conversion of specified neighborhoods, with the goal of preventing racial violence through a process of "peaceful transition." In a 1952 report, the Metropolitan Planning Commission proposed that "plans might be devised in connection with works programs such as expressway construction to make wholesale shifts of former white homes for colored occupancy at one time—with the consent and participation of all residents involved."[9]

The white leadership's pursuit of racial stability through spatial apartheid followed the national trend of public policy intervention in the housing market to ensure residential segregation but diverged from the pattern of many northern metropolises by acknowledging rather than ignoring the postwar housing shortage facing urban black communities. In addition to the intentional strategy of municipal leaders to trigger "white flight" from neighborhoods on the southside and westside that faced the pressures of black in-migration, the Metropolitan Planning Commission also selected undeveloped land for the construction of private single-family housing explicitly designated as "colored neighborhoods" in the suburbs. Atlanta's westside region, which already contained a 40 percent black population in the 1940s, became the primary focus of urban planning to provide both private and public housing exclusively for African-Americans. During the 1950s and 1960s, middle-class black families moved outward, especially along what would become the east/west I-20 corridor that bisects southside Atlanta, and remained allied with the business moderates who dominated coalition politics. Unable to effect a regime change with their votes, the white working-class and lower-middle-class residents of southwest and southeast Atlanta denounced the downtown establishment and occasionally fought back but usually fled. Protected from this centrifugal process by zoning policies and spatial buffers, the racial and class segregation institutionalized in the housing market, and negotiated consensus within the biracial alliance, the upscale island suburbs of northside Atlanta remained off limits, too secure to hate.[10]

The centerpiece of the corporate growth agenda involved the steady annexation of the northside suburbs, a regionalist vision designed to strengthen the biracial alliance and to guarantee a residentially segregated but functionally integrated metropolis. In 1952, the downtown establishment championed the Plan of Improvement, a proposal to triple the physical size of the city and incorporate about 100,000 primarily white residents of the booming suburbs north of Atlanta. The Chamber of Commerce and the League of Women Voters campaigned actively for the annexation plan, which under state law required approval by city residents and by a majority of the targeted population. Mayor Hartsfield warned that "if Atlanta's limits are fixed . . . then as a city it is finished." The Atlanta Negro Voters League delivered a crucial endorsement despite awareness that the Plan of Improvement would dilute its electoral power as the city's black population declined from 41 to 33 percent. Atlanta's white leadership clearly wanted to prevent the emergence of a majority-black city, but the incorporation of middle-class suburban neighborhoods also advanced the traditional good-government agenda of augmenting the tax base and facilitating metropolitan planning. In addition to enlarging the westside territory designated for African-American housing, the successful referendum on the Plan of Improvement laid the groundwork for the diffusion of the city's power base from downtown to Buckhead. The subsequent completion of the I-75 and I-85 expressways created commercial boundaries for the island suburbs within the city limits, with most of the annexed northside neighborhoods located inside the inner half of the inverted triangle formed by the north/south highways and the eventual I-285 perimeter.[11]

"We saved Atlanta with the Plan of Improvement," William Hartsfield later claimed. It was certainly true that the city's confrontation with Georgia's massive resistance program would have been markedly different without the formal inclusion of the white residents from Buckhead and the other island suburbs of northside Atlanta. The upper-middle-class parents of HOPE who organized Atlanta's open-schools movement, and the public schools of their children that soon would be targeted for court-ordered integration and state-mandated closure, owed their very participation in the desegregation crisis to the spatial politics of the "City Too Busy to Hate." Implicitly designated as demographic reinforcements in Atlanta's politics of racial moderation, the white-collar families on the northside became a classic example of how the top-down and race-driven development of the metropolis could produce the neighborhood-based and class-conscious ideology at the center of suburban consciousness. Living on a suburban landscape where racial privilege took the forms of socioeconomic exclusivity and consumer abundance, and in a state where ideological divisions played out along geographic rather than partisan lines, the residents of northside Atlanta fashioned a centrist ethos of individual meritocracy that did not depend for its sustenance upon the legal boundaries of the Jim Crow system. After the *Brown* decision, when the social values of this middle-class worldview collided with the state government's turn to massive resistance, Atlanta's desegregation drama played out in public not as a racial conflict between black and white southerners but as a political showdown between public-spirited metropolitan reformers and backward-looking state politicians. Instead of a moral battle between integrationists and segregationists, Atlanta's open-schools movement recast the campaign for racial justice as an internal power struggle within the white South, matching upwardly mobile suburban families against reactionary rural demagogues.[12]

County Unit Politics

The inequitable political structure of the state of Georgia fundamentally shaped the trajectory of Atlanta's massive resistance crisis. A manifestly undemocratic feature of the one-party South, the county unit system formed the linchpin of rural dominance in state politics, governing all statewide elections as well as the apportionment of the General Assembly. The county unit formula divided Georgia's 159 counties into three categories: the 8 most populous received six unit votes each, the next 30 held four, and the 121 smallest counties enjoyed two apiece. The popular vote did not matter in the Democratic primary, where candidates for governor and the U.S. Congress only had to win a majority of the county unit votes. In the lower house of the state legislature, egregious malapportionment effectively disfranchised all metropolitan citizens, black and white. Between 1940 and 1960, the mathematic discrimination inherent in the system accelerated as the rural/agricultural sectors of Georgia lost about one million people, declining from 44 percent to barely 10 percent of the total state population. During the same period, the Atlanta metropolitan region expanded to include one-third of the state population but controlled only 26 out of 410 county unit votes, or roughly 6 percent of the seats in the legislature. Fewer than one thousand white voters in the state's three smallest counties routinely canceled out the electoral choices of more than half a million residents of Fulton County. At the height of the 1958–61 desegregation showdown, about half of Georgia's population resided in the sixteen most populous counties, but urban and suburban residents exercised less than 20 percent of formal statewide voting strength.[13]

Georgia's conservative leadership championed the county unit system as the ultimate bulwark of white supremacy, because the rural domination of state politics obscured substantial divisions based on class and geography. Rural politicians routinely linked the preservation of racial segregation to the county unit formula and campaigned against the threat of the "Negro bloc vote" and the allegedly integrationist sentiments among "silk stocking" whites in Atlanta's biracial alliance. Although the rural/metropolitan axis represented the most visible divide in state politics, the center of single-party power rested in the Black Belt region of South Georgia, the broad band of counties where blacks constituted a majority or near-majority of the population (map 2.2). The Talmadge clan—father Eugene and son Herman—controlled South Georgia through a powerful political machine that wielded disproportionate influence in state politics for three decades, from the 1930s until the judicial invalidation of the county unit system. A four-time governor, Eugene Talmadge offered rural whites a steady dose of racial demagoguery while making a separate peace with Atlanta's business

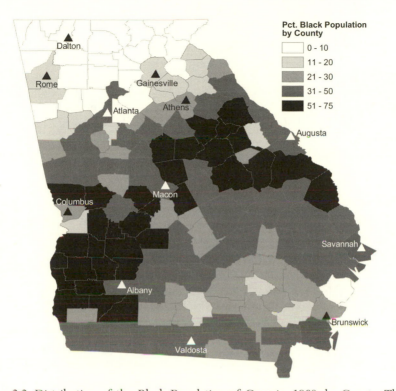

Pct. Black Population by County

- ☐ 0 - 10
- ▨ 11 - 20
- ▨ 21 - 30
- ▨ 31 - 50
- ■ 51 - 75

Map 2.2. Distribution of the Black Population of Georgia, 1960, by County. The county unit system allowed the Talmadge Democrats to exercise control over state politics through a rural base in the Black Belt region of South Georgia. Before court-ordered reapportionment in the early 1960s, Georgia's political system discriminated against metropolitan voters to a greater degree than any other state in the nation. *Sources:* U.S. Census Bureau and Historical Census Browser, University of Virginia Library.

leadership and supporting the corporate agenda of low wages, low taxes, and hostility toward organized labor. A majority of metropolitan voters consistently opposed the initiatives and candidates of the Talmadge faction, while the overwhelmingly white counties of North Georgia performed a geographic swing function in county unit politics, defecting from the rural coalition when Black Belt conservatives overplayed their hand. Between 1942 and 1954, a series of political clashes set the stage for the massive resistance showdown and revealed the absence of consensus among white Georgians when the absolute defense of racial segregation clashed with the democratic principle of public education.[14]

The county unit system failed to silence dissent but instead forced Georgia's moderates and liberals to wage defensive battles and to channel their energy into issue-oriented reform politics. Led by the League of Women Voters, metropolitan interest groups framed the reform agenda as a philosophical clash between modernizing and traditionalist worldviews, a political struggle between the American ideal of representative government and the Georgia reality of undemocratic repression. "We urban whites and blacks were locked in the same cage together," contended James Mackay, a state legislator from DeKalb County. "We were going to have rampant racism and unfairness and corruption as long as we had the county unit system and malapportionment." While reform planks such as the repeal of the poll tax and the demand for electoral reapportionment elicited fierce resistance from Black Belt conservatives, the actions of the Talmadge faction exposed an acute vulnerability on the issue of public education. In 1941, Governor Eugene Talmadge dismissed ten employees of the University of Georgia system after accusing the group of endorsing New Deal liberalism and betraying white supremacy. All ten white institutions in the system promptly lost their accreditations, and moderate Democrat Ellis Arnall led a popular uprising supported by a reform coalition of the Atlanta newspapers and middle-class metropolitan voters. In 1942, Arnall defeated Talmadge in a campaign that revolved around the value of public education, and he carried the county unit vote by combining metropolitan regions with the smaller towns and rural areas outside the Black Belt. During Arnall's progressive tenure, Georgia repealed the poll tax, increased funding for public schools, modernized the state constitution, and adjusted to the demise of the all-white primary. In the end, however, factional reform politics in a one-party state could not overcome the institutionalized constraints of the county unit system.[15]

The postwar resurgence of the Talmadge machine set Georgia on the road to massive resistance by manipulating the county unit system to exploit the racial anxieties of rural and working-class white voters. In the 1946 gubernatorial election, Eugene Talmadge concentrated almost exclusively on small rural counties, campaigning as the candidate of white supremacy and attributing black voter registration to a communist plot. Ellis Arnall's moderate protégé, a business executive from the Atlanta suburbs named James Carmichael, swept the metropolitan counties and won the most popular votes, which proved irrelevant. Talmadge won the Democratic primary with the county unit vote but died soon after the pro forma general election. In anticipation, Talmadge partisans had coordinated an extralegal write-in campaign marked by obvious ballot irregularities, and the state legislature selected Gene's son Herman as the next governor. After a period of extreme chaos and sporadic violence, the state supreme court forced Herman Talmadge to relinquish his claim to the governorship. But the younger Talmadge cemented rural control of state politics with victories in 1948 and 1950, despite losing two-thirds of the metropolitan Atlanta vote in each election and probably also losing the statewide popular vote in 1950 amid additional charges of electoral shenanigans. The second Governor Talmadge combined an uncompromising defense of the caste system with accommodation to the fiscal priorities of Atlanta's corporate establishment, a backroom alliance in which rural politicians embraced the postwar growth consensus of industrial development while business leaders enjoyed low-tax and antilabor policies and refrained from public criticism of Black Belt demagogues.[16]

As the *Brown* decision loomed on the horizon, metropolitan reform groups fought two crucial battles with the Talmadge faction: public referendums on constitutional amendments to strengthen the county unit system and to permit the replacement of public education with a system of segregated private schools. Georgia's county unit formula appeared to be immune from popular or legal attack, since the state legislature had no incentive to revise the malapportionment from which its power derived and the federal judiciary refused under the "political questions" doctrine to rule on the constitutionality of state election procedures. In the early 1950s, in recognition of growing Republican strength in the metropolitan areas, the Talmadge machine sought to incorporate the county unit system into the Georgia constitution and to extend the formula to general elections as well as Democratic primaries. In response, the LWV and other reform organizations joined an ad hoc alliance that framed the issue as a battle between representative democracy and Talmadge tyranny. Herman Talmadge campaigned for the amendments as safeguards against racial integration and the emergence of a two-party system, and he blamed opposition on "a small handful of racial equality agitators in Atlanta." But constitutional amendments required a majority of the statewide vote, meaning that electoral turnout mattered more than courthouse and countryside politics. The proposals carried South Georgia but lost overwhelmingly in the metropolitan regions and also failed to win a majority in rural North Georgia. The victorious metropolitan coalition had demonstrated grassroots strength, but the Talmadge machine's racial offensive during the 1950s also forced progressive reformers to retreat to defensive strategies and plunged the moderate bloc in state politics into disarray.[17]

The Talmadge faction designed the defense of racial segregation to be fought at the state level in large part because of suspicions of Atlanta's commitment to caste ideology. In the early 1950s, Herman Talmadge supported a program called the Minimum Foundation for Public Education that used a regressive sales tax to establish statewide standards and provide a funding baseline to rural school districts. Although the LWV had long advocated school equalization and rural uplift, Georgia's qualified commitment came only after racial conservatives recognized that the systematic underfunding of black schools would jeopardize a "separate but equal" defense in federal court. As a second line of resistance, Herman Talmadge promoted the Private School Amendment, which would remove the constitutional mandate that the state of Georgia "provide adequate education for its citizens." In the event of court-ordered desegregation, the state government would close public schools, provide tuition subsidies for private education, and lease public facilities for nominal fees. The Supreme Court handed down the *Brown* decision during the debate over the 1954 referendum, and Talmadge warned that without the Private School Amendment the city of Atlanta would begin "race-mixing" within a year. The anointed successor of the Talmadge faction, gubernatorial candidate Marvin Griffin, traveled the barbeque and catfish circuit of countryside politics pledging to preserve Georgia's "two great traditions," the county unit system and free segregated schooling.[18]

The Georgia League of Women Voters led the opposition to the Private School Amendment through a campaign that emphasized the importance of public education as the foundation of responsible citizenship and individual opportunity in a democratic society. Premiering the strategy that would shape the subsequent open-schools movement, the LWV attempted to shift the debate away from race by linking the reckless endangerment of innocent (white) children to the priorities of educational quality and economic prosperity. The literature produced by the League insisted that "THIS AMENDMENT IS A SCHOOL QUESTION, NOT A SEGREGATION QUESTION." Pamphlets warned: "If we should give up our system of public education to keep segregation in schools, it would be like giving up democracy to keep communism out of democracy. No end is so important that it justifies the use of any means." The *Atlanta Constitution* also adopted the language of Cold War freedom and New South prosperity to condemn the amendment as an assault on "the basic bulwark of this nation and its way of life—the public schools." The Atlanta Chamber of Commerce contributed a dispassionate statement that the "destruction of the public school system is not a proper or an effective means" of addressing the problem of racial integration. As the referendum neared, the Atlanta chapter of the LWV conducted a grassroots voter mobilization effort, and a coalition of church groups, educational associations, and metropolitan politicians rounded out the moderate opposition.[19]

The *Brown* decision complicated the efforts of white moderates to disentangle the issues of race and education, and the save-the-schools movement struggled to combat the emotional defense by Georgia's rural leadership of the "southern way of life." The Private School Amendment narrowly prevailed by about twenty-five thousand votes, receiving the support of 55 percent of the electorate and securing large margins across South Georgia. The predominantly white towns and rural areas of North Georgia divided almost evenly on the desirability of massive resistance, while African-American voters overwhelmingly opposed the scheme. White voters in the metropolitan regions split sharply along socioeconomic lines, as working-class precincts supported the amendment almost as heavily as Black Belt counties, while about two-thirds of the affluent voters in the northside Atlanta suburbs registered disapproval. In the upscale white neighborhoods, the percentage of votes cast against the Private School Amendment lagged behind the opposition to the 1952 county unit extension, and liberal reformers lamented that "it was hard to get the Atlanta people upset about the plan and the leadership didn't come out." Governor-elect Griffin, who won a county unit majority despite receiving only 36 percent of the ballots in the Democratic primary, declared a popular mandate for massive resistance to the Supreme Court and swore that the state would "never submit to the proposition of mixing the races in the classrooms of our schools." The General Assembly soon passed an interposition resolution that symbolically invalidated the *Brown* decision and produced a massive resistance package that empowered the governor to close public schools that fell under court-ordered desegregation.[20]

Between 1954 and 1958, white moderates and liberals appeared helpless as the Talmadge Democrats used the artificial consensus of county unit politics to neutralize popular dissent from the policy of massive resistance. The LWV continued to argue that ersatz private schools would not survive judicial scrutiny, that racial desegregation could be managed and limited in scope, and that the logic of defiance would lead to the statewide abandonment of public education. But legislators disregarded the persistent lobbying by white moderates and liberals to extricate Atlanta from massive resistance politics through adoption of a "race-neutral" local option plan based on the North Carolina model. As the inevitable showdown neared, electoral politics confirmed the impasse between the state government and the capital city. Mayor Hartsfield won reelection in 1957 on the strength of an open-schools platform that condemned massive resistance, but the formula of private negotiations favored by Atlanta's downtown establishment could not resolve this public confrontation with state policy. Civil rights lawyers, who appreciated the need for an external catalyst, seized the initiative in early 1958 by filing a class-action desegregation lawsuit against the Atlanta Board of Education. In the gubernatorial election held later that year, Ernest Vandiver of the Talmadge faction glided to victory without substantive opposition from Georgia's reeling moderates. Vandiver campaigned on the defiant standard of "no, not one" black student and repeatedly pledged that public schools throughout the state would remain completely segregated during his tenure. By the end of 1958, the city of Atlanta seemed destined to become the site of an unsolicited showdown between states' rights and federal supremacy, a New South metropolis caught in an Old South vise.[21]

The Origins of HOPE

On January 7, 1959, the NBC affiliate in Atlanta televised a community meeting conducted by HOPE, a new group of white parents based on the northside. Frances Breeden, introduced as HOPE's president, led a cadre of upper-middle-class white women who represented the public leadership and administrative staff of the organization. After an opening prayer, they listened to a message of encouragement from the Women's Emergency Committee, the group leading the grassroots struggle against massive resistance in Little Rock. Then Muriel Lokey, the wife of a former state legislator from Fulton County, explained HOPE's statement of philosophy for the television audience. She identified HOPE as "an organization of Georgia parents and the other Georgia citizens who feel that the possibility of closing any or all of the Georgia public schools is a matter of deepest concern and urgency." They had founded HOPE in order to transform and mobilize public opinion throughout the state, by disseminating the basic facts about massive resistance and convincing Georgia's political leadership that a majority of their constituents opposed the policy of defiance. Seeking to shift the debate away from race, HOPE refused "to argue the pros and cons of segregation versus desegregation, or states' rights versus federal rights." Following this declaration of purpose, four of the fathers in HOPE presented pragmatic critiques of Georgia's school-closing policy, representing the white-collar perspectives of medicine, education, business, and the law. The overall program presented a compelling case for what HOPE called its single-minded agenda: "To champion children's rights to an education within the State of Georgia, an education they can be proud of, and a public school system that the balance of the United States can look to as an example."[22]

From its inception in December 1958, HOPE promoted an image of itself as nothing more and nothing less than a collection of concerned parents who cared only about their children's futures and their state's reputation. The official version of the group's origins emphasized the spontaneous activities of a small number of middle-class housewives "in response to the demands of thousands of parents in Atlanta for leadership in the present education crisis." An early press release explained that HOPE began when two Buckhead mothers, Muriel Lokey and Maxine Friedman, organized a series of meetings in their homes, and then the open-schools message spread like wildfire across the northside suburbs. The Atlanta media—print, radio, and television—immediately began featuring in-depth interviews with HOPE's founders, and the national media closely followed (figure 2.2). In the storyline that emerged, a few suburban housewives suddenly realized that their children's public schools were in danger, and they began warning their

Figure 2.2. "We *Want* Public Schools," January 11, 1959. Four days after HOPE's public debut, newspapers across the nation picked up an Associated Press story that touted the growing strength of white moderates in Atlanta, accompanied by this photograph of Fran Breeden and Muriel Lokey, suburban mothers and open-schools activists. Courtesy of AP/Wide World Photos.

friends and neighbors through telephone trees and morning coffee gatherings. Lokey, "a petite mother of five," and Friedman, a "tall, attractive, dark-haired" mother of three, became HOPE's treasurer and vice president, respectively. They knew Fran Breeden, "a chic society matron" with four children, because all three women had seventh graders at the same public school in Buckhead. Friedman recruited executive committee member Nan Pendergrast, a West Paces Ferry resident described in the society pages as "Atlanta's best looking mother of six children," while they waited in the carpool line. This powerful iconography framed HOPE's appearance on the Georgia landscape: an organization that was public-spirited and respectable, explicitly apolitical and implicitly maternal. "We read *Better Homes and Gardens* and got recipes out of *Good Housekeeping* magazine and read Dr. Spock and had these babies," Muriel Lokey later explained. "Neither Maxine nor Fran nor I had ever started a movement."[23]

This account of HOPE's origins was less false than incomplete. Beyond the impromptu mobilization of suburban mothers and fathers lay the submerged narrative of an organization grounded in the city's legacy of female political activism and facilitated by a broad spectrum of powerful local interests. Three weeks before HOPE received its charter, the Atlanta League of Women Voters established an ad hoc steering committee to address the massive resistance crisis, and its members agreed on the need for a new citizens group to lead the open-schools campaign. Muriel Lokey and Maxine Friedman, the two women credited with founding HOPE, attended this strategy meeting, and their colleagues Fran Breeden and Nan Pendergrast were also active members of the League. During the next two years, as HOPE became the leading voice of white moderation in Georgia, the informal committee chaired by the LWV operated as a shadow organization, with secret monthly meetings attended by representatives of the NAACP, the Southern Regional Council, and a dozen other civil rights and religious organizations. The SRC played a quiet but crucial role throughout HOPE's existence, installing several contacts on the volunteer staff, coordinating communication with open-schools groups in other states, supplying strategic advice and informational literature, and providing significant financial support. Helen Bullard, a close confidant of William Hartsfield and the second most powerful figure in Atlanta politics, joined the HOPE executive committee and served as an unofficial liaison to the mayor's office. Ralph McGill, the highly respected editor of the *Atlanta Constitution*, became HOPE's most enthusiastic booster in the press. And although the business community's refusal to speak out against massive resistance would become a source of constant frustration for the parents in HOPE, several Atlanta corporations anonymously donated money, office space, and supplies. "Somebody was looking after us," as Muriel Lokey later remarked.[24]

The personal histories of the grassroots activists in HOPE illustrate the dynamic landscape of the Sunbelt South and especially the cosmopolitan ethos produced by middle-class mobility within the corporate economy. Most of the parents who formed the core leadership of the open-schools movement lived within a few miles of one another, in the recently annexed Fulton County suburbs of Buckhead and West Paces Ferry. The fathers who joined HOPE were physicians, attorneys, engineers, and midlevel managers or executives—not the wealthiest members of the so-called power structure but instead part of the postwar generation of military veterans turned white-collar professionals. The mothers who ran the day-to-day operations were college-educated women without formal careers, self-identified "house-wives" who balanced social calendars and volunteering commitments with household tasks and carpooling duties. Maxine Friedman, a Jewish woman from New York, relocated to Atlanta with her husband, the chief chemist of a manufacturing corporation. Muriel Lokey, an Episcopalian from Oregon, moved to Georgia after she married a local attorney. Fran Breeden, a self-described "white southern Protestant" from Florida, came to the city with her husband, a district manager for a sales company. Nan Pendergrast, a Catholic and the only native Atlantan among the foursome, attended college in New York and lived in Philadelphia before she and her spouse, the vice president of a small business, returned to the city of their youth. In fact, to obscure the diverse origins of HOPE's leadership, Breeden and Pendergrast made most of the early media appearances in order to prevent accusations that the group consisted of "Yankee Jewish ladies trying to tell people what to do."[25]

The upper-middle-class white women in the vanguard of HOPE stood at a generational and ideological crossroads. As an organization that entered the public arena under the rubric of parenthood, framing its rhetorical appeals around the protection of innocent children, HOPE was tapping into a political tradition with deep historical roots. Although men played key roles in the open-schools movement from the very beginning, HOPE elaborately cultivated a public image of concerned motherhood, speaking not only as respectable middle-class housewives but even more powerfully as genteel southern ladies. The news media reinforced the representation of HOPE as a fifties version of "maternalist politics," a movement of attractive and altruistic suburban mothers who could have walked right off the pages of *Life* magazine, wielding the moral authority of domesticity and femininity to influence political debate and reshape public policy. At the same time, HOPE traveled down the path paved by the League of Women Voters, where the distinctions between traditional notions of a "woman's sphere" and standard interest group politics were becoming increasingly difficult to distinguish. HOPE's reform agenda emulated the mission of the LWV and the SRC—presenting the facts in a truthful and dispassionate manner—while also charting an early version of the neighborhood-based grassroots politics that would soon appear throughout metropolitan America. In the island suburbs of northside Atlanta, the prevailing ideology of domesticity in the late 1950s and early 1960s both empowered and constrained the leading activists in HOPE's political crusade. "I have always felt that I operated on a double track," said Nan Pendergrast, who gave birth to her seventh child during the massive resistance crisis. "There was this sociable lady who went around talking about wildflowers to garden clubs and had children who went to the right schools and that sort of stuff; and then there was this fierce radical in the background."[26]

Political Culture in the Island Suburbs

The suburban topography of northside Atlanta profoundly shaped the emergence of HOPE as a grassroots organization that employed the language of children's rights and the framework of national citizenship to elevate the middle-class priority of public education above the uncompromising defense of racial caste. Daily life in Atlanta's island suburbs mirrored national patterns of middle-class domesticity and upward mobility, manifested in an automobile-based culture, the gendered division of labor within the family, the visibility of black people primarily as maids and manual laborers, the organization of society around childhood development and consumer fulfillment, and the centrality of churches, clubs, and schools (figure 2.3). The upscale neighborhoods of Fulton and DeKalb reflected the racial and socioeconomic exclusivity of the postwar wave of mass suburbanization, which submerged the structural foundation of residential inequality beneath an ethos of private accomplishment in the consumer marketplace. This political culture emphasized the priorities of family and neighborhood in the context of national citizenship and forged a value system that felt threatened rather than safeguarded by the segregationist crusades for white supremacy associated with the rural South. "We are all first *Americans*, then Georgians," HOPE proclaimed in its open-schools literature, a conscious inversion of the political mantra of the Solid South. The built environment of the new suburbs gave birth to a social creed of individual meritocracy and middle-class consciousness that flourished independently of the caste system and simultaneously created geographic buffers that appeared to guarantee that racial desegregation could be managed by whites, limited in degree, and confined to consumer spaces.[27]

The spatial landscape of northside Atlanta allowed white moderates and liberals to stake out the political center by embracing a discourse of controlled desegregation that simultaneously rejected as dangerous the policy of massive resistance and discounted as unlikely the possibility of "massive integration." In the census tracts that formed the organizational base of HOPE's open-schools movement, the racial breakdown of the population ranged from 96 to 100 percent white, and metropolitan trends ensured that the island suburbs on the northside did not face the prospect of black residential migration that inflamed white neighborhoods on the southside and westside. After the NAACP initiated litigation in 1958, PTA chapters from northside Atlanta voted overwhelmingly to accept court-ordered desegregation after

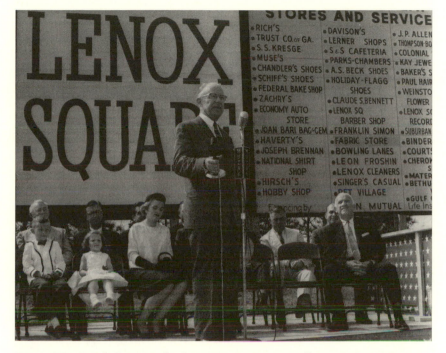

Figure 2.3. Grand Opening of Atlanta's Lenox Square Mall, August 3, 1959. Mayor William Hartsfield presiding over a "Salute to America" ceremony to mark the public unveiling of the shopping center located in the commercial heart of Buckhead, on land annexed by the city of Atlanta in 1952. Celebrated in the booster tradition of the New South, Lenox Square symbolized the postwar shift of consumer spaces from the downtown business district to the suburban fringe. Courtesy of the William Berry Hartsfield Papers, Special Collections and Archives, Robert W. Woodruff Library, Emory University.

framing the issue as a choice between closing schools and "limited integration." At Northside High School in Buckhead, which included the neighborhoods where most HOPE leaders lived, PTA members opposed massive resistance by a tally of 515 to 90. The key state legislators from the northside suburbs, Muggsy Smith of Fulton County and James Mackay of DeKalb, advocated replacement of the massive resistance program with an ostensibly race-neutral pupil placement law that they promised would bring only "token integration." In the fall of 1958, after the bombing of the Jewish Temple by white supremacists, 311 religious leaders in Atlanta signed a manifesto condemning the sin of racial hatred and charging churches and synagogues with a moral responsibility to promote open and reasoned discussion of the civil rights movement. The interfaith statement also denounced massive resistance and insisted that public schools must remain open, although it combined a call to respect the authority of the Supreme Court with explicit opposition to "massive integration."[28]

The celebration of moderation in the political culture of northside Atlanta found expression across a broad range of white institutions, including the major churches and synagogues, civic and educational associations, elected officials and media outlets. Combined with the city's underlying commitment to the politics of racial harmony, the physical boundaries of northside Atlanta shaped a dominant public discourse that elevated the class-conscious priorities of public education and economic prosperity over the absolute defense of Jim Crow and the philosophical defense of states' rights. Public statements of support for compliance with the *Brown* decision came from faculty groups at Atlanta's institutions of higher education, including Emory University, Agnes Scott College, Oglethorpe University, and Georgia Tech. A leading physicians' group released a statement deploring the possibility that young people would be deprived of educational opportunity. An association of Atlanta scientists issued a similar warning connecting the disruption of public schooling to Cold War imperatives heightened by the Soviet Union's startling launch of the *Sputnik* satellite a year earlier. Throughout the northside suburbs, a widespread public consensus formed around the viewpoint, as the former Fulton legislator and HOPE supporter Hamilton Lokey argued in a series of speeches, that the state government should not "destroy a living institution in order to preserve a dying one."[29]

HOPE had to target a statewide audience because of the county unit system, and the polarized racial climate shaped the tactical debates over whether the open-schools movement should enlist an integrated membership and positively endorse the *Brown* decision. The HOPE leaders with roots in the LWV, a group that included prominent civil rights activists Frances Pauley and Eliza Paschall, represented a progressive faction that assumed control in 1956 when the national organization mandated acceptance of black women and a large number of conservative members resigned in protest. HOPE's inner circle consisted of white liberals who believed that racial segregation was immoral and white moderates who described themselves as "liberal-minded segregationists," and the group subsumed internal uncertainty about its official stance on racial equality beneath a pragmatic decision to emphasize the ways that massive resistance threatened the self-interests of white Georgians. HOPE leaders decided to follow the recommendations of their counterparts in Virginia's open-schools movement, who advised the Atlanta group to develop a "broad enough platform to appeal to all moderates" by refusing to take a stand on the desirability of integration. "We just knew it was a total loss to make any impression on changing anybody's minds publicly by coming out with statements that segregation was wrong," Muriel Lokey later explained. "All of us really felt that way. . . . It needed to go." By the same rationale, HOPE decided to uphold a whites-only membership policy, a decision made easier after a local NAACP attorney privately assured several leaders that an integrated group would be less effective. "Everybody knew that black people wanted the schools kept open," observed Nan Pendergrast, an outspoken liberal who also belonged to the NAACP and the Southern Regional Council. "What was important was that white people wanted them open."[30]

During a series of meetings in one another's homes, the parents in HOPE mapped out the strategies and policies involved in building a social movement at the grassroots level. They created an executive committee to coordinate the work of six subcommittees: Finance, Publicity, Legal Advisory, Policy, Fundraising, and a Speakers' Bureau. The group's primary agenda revolved around the dissemination of facts—of the truth—to galvanize public opinion across the state in favor of accepting the inevitability of court-ordered desegregation and recognizing the inadequacy of private school alternatives. After some debate, HOPE decided to highlight but not specifically endorse desegregation techniques such as local option and pupil placement formulas that could serve as a compromise solution between massive resistance and massive integration. The group would emphasize the disastrous consequences of closing down public schools, including the sacrifice of children's futures, the mass exodus of good teachers, and the devastation of the business climate. HOPE planned to spread this message through news releases, brochures and flyers, telephone and letter-writing campaigns, media advertisements, reliance on favorable press coverage, and provision of speakers for community forums. Finally, to fend off anticipated attacks, HOPE would continue to "emphasize that it grew out of a spontaneous desire to retain public schools" and deny any charges that its leaders were racial integrationists, northern liberals, or allied with the NAACP and the SRC—four political liabilities that were all at least partially true. Each founding member even took a loyalty oath swearing that she or he was not a communist.[31]

Segregationist leaders responded to the rapid mobilization of Atlanta's open-schools movement with undisguised alarm. Six days after HOPE's formal debut on NBC, Ernest Vandiver promised Georgians in his inaugural address that "we have only just begun to fight." The new governor attacked the Supreme Court for imposing a second Reconstruction on the South, and he promised that Georgia would resist external threats to states' rights, "whatever the cost." Vandiver pledged an administration dedicated to fiscal responsibility, industrial growth, and "preservation of our way of life"— defined as the dual traditions of the county unit system and segregated public schools. But despite his declaration that massive resistance enjoyed the "virtually unanimous" support of the citizens of Georgia, the governor denounced the new internal threat presented by the "advocates of surrender" and "fomenters of division and discord." A few white Georgians were spreading a message of token integration, Vandiver warned, and they were beginning to delude others with this false promise. "They know, or should know, that the few raindrops of 'token integration' would become a downpour, a deluge and then a flood which would engulf our people." He offered an alternative vision of a harmonious future secured through white unanimity in the cause of massive resistance: "By our solid front and united efforts we will, under God, build a glorious and lasting commonwealth for our children and for the children of future generations."[32]

Had the Supreme Court handed down the *Baker v. Carr* decision that sparked political reapportionment before instead of eight years after the *Brown* mandate, the massive resistance crisis in Georgia probably would not have happened at all. Absent the glaring inequities of county unit politics, the city of Atlanta almost certainly would have preemptively implemented a limited desegregation plan along the North Carolina model, avoiding both massive resistance and "massive integration" for a temporary compromise based on a race-neutral facade. Instead, in January 1959 the battle was joined, between the governor's demand for white unity in service of the caste crusade and the grassroots offensive by the suburban parents of northside Atlanta to save their own children's schools by disproving the mythology of the Solid South.

CHAPTER 3

The Open-Schools Movement

> The tragedy of the South lies not only in what we have done to
> Negroes but in what we have done to ourselves. A self-imposed
> conspiracy of silence and censorship walled us off for so long not
> only from the criticism of outsiders but from that of our own
> people.
>
> —Lillian Smith (1962)

"Stand Up and Be Counted!"

On March 4, 1959, two thousand supporters of the open-schools movement gathered at Atlanta's Tower Theater, the first mass demonstration organized by the parents in HOPE. The flyers for the event urged concerned citizens to "Stand up and be counted!" and "Fill the Tower with HOPE!" The group's leaders experienced substantial anxiety after the police warned that white supremacists, including the chief suspect in the recent bombing of the Jewish Temple, planned a counterdemonstration against the "integrationists" from northside Atlanta. But the Tower rally turned out to be a peaceful and prominent display of the building grassroots opposition to Georgia's massive resistance program. The panel presentation included remarks by the two most influential white moderates in the state, Mayor William Hartsfield and *Atlanta Constitution* editor Ralph McGill. The audience also heard from Mrs. Gordon Wilson, a leader of the Women's Emergency Committee in Little Rock, who warned Atlantans to organize before the politicians closed down their schools or face the disruption of their children's education and the destruction of their city's reputation. Then Sylvan Meyer, a young newspaper editor from the city of Gainesville, called for a political uprising by white moderates to stop the state government from "turning back the clock on Georgia's advancement." With a live radio broadcast and extremely favorable publicity from local and national media, the Tower rally highlighted HOPE's strategy of framing massive resistance as a clash between the past and the future and offering itself as indisputable evidence of the vitality of the New South. The coverage in the *Atlanta Constitution* underscored "an overwhelming majority" of city residents who supported open schools, whatever their feelings about the *Brown* decision. *Time* praised the white parents in HOPE for speaking with "a fervor and eloquence" too often absent among the ranks of southern moderates. "It was the most inspirational thing you'd ever seen in your life," recalled HOPE leader Frances Pauley, a longtime liberal activist, "because [at last] you felt like there were some other people with you."[1]

In the political climate of the Deep South, where the middle ground appeared to have disintegrated, the preemptive mobilization of white moderates and liberals remained the most notable feature of Atlanta's open-schools movement. HOPE worked hard to capitalize on the momentum of the Tower rally by strengthening its Atlanta base and expanding its statewide reach through membership recruitment, information distribution, and fundraising appeals. The literature circulated at the rally urged each of the two thousand audience members to become neighborhood block captains and telephone tree organizers in the campaign to "Spread HOPE!" During the next few months, supporters from metropolitan Atlanta reported more than two hundred local initiatives, where they recruited friends and neighbors through coffee and tea gatherings, bridge parties, and evening discussion forums. This larger group then formed the basis for a petition drive and an expanded mailing list, through which HOPE distributed pamphlets and coordinated letter-writing campaigns to newspapers and elected officials. Frances Pauley, who had extensive contacts from her leadership of the Georgia LWV, assumed the difficult task of establishing affiliates in the cities and towns outside of Atlanta. While HOPE never reached its ambitious goal of fifty chapters statewide, collaboration with local women's and religious groups did produce six active affiliates by the summer of 1959: Rome, Gainesville, Marietta, Athens, Savannah, and Columbus. In Augusta and Albany, two metropolitan areas in the Black Belt, sympathetic contacts reported that the atmosphere remained too inhospitable to organize formal opposition to massive resistance.[2]

HOPE ran into a different barrier of reticence and apprehension in its efforts to recruit civic leaders throughout the state and especially the business community in Atlanta as active participants in the open-schools campaign. In the spring of 1959, the group contacted hundreds of the most powerful corporate executives in Georgia with a demand to take a public stand for compliance, coupled with a warning that their continued silence amounted to a tacit endorsement of massive resistance. HOPE also asked well-known community figures to serve on its State Advisory Board, a largely symbolic role intended to highlight the existence of open-schools sentiment beyond Atlanta. Most contacts declined any formal association with HOPE, and the most notable advisory board members turned out to be three liberal religious leaders from Atlanta who were active in the SRC through the affiliated Georgia Council on Human Relations: Rabbi Jacob Rothschild of the Temple, Reverend Harry Fifield of First Presbyterian Church, and Reverend Norman Shands of West End Baptist Church. HOPE also surveyed corporate executives and small business owners in the Atlanta metropolitan area, asking for monetary donations and endorsements of public schools. While most failed to respond, a few businessmen sent anonymous contributions along with explanations such as "I do not feel that I can afford to become affiliated with any organization regarding a subject that could be as controversial as this." Ivan Allen, Jr., soon to head the Chamber of Commerce, embodied the cautious approach of even the most supportive business moderates, rebuffing a request to serve on HOPE's State Advisory Board but quietly providing critical financial assistance to the fledgling operation.[3]

Throughout 1959, the Atlanta Chamber of Commerce remained the primary and elusive target of the suburban parents from northside Atlanta, who fully subscribed to the popular theory that involvement by the "power structure" would be the turning point in the crisis. In March, HOPE sent a direct letter to the Chamber: "This community wants and expects the business community to speak out on behalf of public education." Pointing to the "lack of foresight" by business leaders in Arkansas and Virginia, HOPE insisted that the mobilization of thousands of ordinary citizens in Georgia had already created a safe climate for the involvement of the corporate establishment. After nothing came of this request, the women in HOPE launched a futile letter-writing campaign to five hundred of the state's business leaders. Later in the year, when the SRC brought two Little Rock businessmen to Atlanta to make a public confession of the damage done by their own circumspection, HOPE issued special invitations to each member of the Chamber of Commerce. The business page of the *Atlanta Constitution* used the occasion to lecture corporate leaders on the potential consequences of their collective silence and to dismiss as unrealistic their apparent fears of an economic boycott by segregationist forces. But it would take two full years, a descent into mob violence, and an overwhelming shift in public opinion before the Atlanta Chamber of Commerce abandoned its default position of neutrality. A revealing moment came when Nan Pendergrast paid a personal visit to Harrison Jones, the chairman of the board of the Coca-Cola Company and an old family friend. In response to her request that Coca-Cola publicly endorse HOPE's mission, Jones explained that corporate leaders knew massive resistance would fail but recognized that those "out in front" would be attacked, so they would "let someone else lead, and then we will follow at a respectful distance."[4]

The political cowardice of Atlanta's corporate leadership caused HOPE to redouble its grassroots outreach by appealing to public opinion through an extensive campaign of radio and newspaper advertisements, television appearances, and public rallies. In June of 1959, District Judge Frank Hooper ordered the Atlanta Board of Education to submit a desegregation plan in compliance with *Brown*. HOPE promptly issued a press release explaining that Georgia now faced two choices: closing down public education across the state or allowing "a few Negro children" to attend white schools in Atlanta. The group produced radio commercials urging listeners throughout Georgia to contact the governor and their state legislators to demand open public schools. HOPE also paid for a full-page advertisement in Atlanta's daily newspapers that featured an evocative image of a young white child and the headline, "NOW . . . Shall We Blind These Eyes To Knowledge?" After painting a bleak portrait of a state without public education, the advertisement concluded with a membership form and the statement: "HOPE believes it is absurd to close our schools when they must inevitably reopen in accordance with the law. . . . Our schools *must* be kept open to avoid unthinkable ruin" (figure 3.1). This sense of impending tragedy also pervaded a documentary aired directly after the federal court order by WSB-TV, a network affiliate owned by the Cox family that also controlled the Atlanta newspapers. After vividly portraying the chaos in Little Rock and dismissing the option of replacement private schools, the program featured the parents in HOPE as the lonely voices of reason in the escalating crisis. The destruction of Georgia's public school system "would be . . . an unparalleled tragedy," the narrator of the documentary concluded. "Georgia's . . . laws must be changed. . . . There are a few citizens—always a few at first—who are stirring. And perhaps the few shall become many when finally people watch the doors swing shut and hear the tolling of THE LAST SCHOOL BELL."[5]

Even as the local and national news media championed HOPE as a bold exception to the prevailing dynamic of "silent moderation" in the South, the organization experienced a simmering internal dispute over its all-white membership policy and its strategic refusal to take a position on the merits of segregation versus integration. HOPE officially declined to endorse any particular method of compliance with *Brown*, but as an expedient compromise, the group implicitly promoted a pupil placement policy combined with a local option mechanism that would allow each school district to formulate its own desegregation approach. Leaders from the Virginia Committee for Public Schools advised their Atlanta counterparts to emphasize that pupil placement plans meant the transfer of "only a few well-qualified Negroes. There is no danger, if the matter is properly handled, of massive integration." As HOPE advanced this class-driven vision of pragmatic segregation, a number of insiders expressed growing discomfort with the group's willingness to extend its imprimatur to token desegregation plans that represented "another dodge which will fail as its application proves its nature." In the fall of 1959, the debates over HOPE's desegregation strategy and membership policy finally produced an open rift among members of the executive committee, and the majority faction's reaffirmation of the group's original philosophy caused several key leaders to resign in protest. Eliza Paschall of the LWV explained her decision in a passionate essay, "A Southern Point of View," that appeared a few months later in the *Atlantic Monthly*. In an

Figure 3.1. "NOW . . . Shall We Blind These Eyes To Knowledge?" HOPE placed this advertisement in the Atlanta newspapers as part of its public relations campaign during the summer of 1959. The portrayal of massive resistance as a threat to innocent white children proved to be an effective strategy for Georgia's open-schools movement. Courtesy of the Southern Regional Council and the Robert W. Woodruff Library of the Atlanta University Center.

open break with the governing approach of the open-schools movement, Paschall rebuked white liberals who believed that the evils of racial segregation could be dismantled only through a cautious strategy that avoided questions of justice and morality. "I can no longer live with my own silence," Paschall declared, while the "realistic liberals" of the white South were in danger of losing their souls.[6]

As a short-term strategy, the open-schools movement's single-minded focus on public education proved to be politically effective in securing the middle ground and marginalizing both progressive and regressive alternatives (figure 3.2). James Dorsey, the head of HOPE's legal committee, explained that the group supported the preservation and improvement of "the education of our children—*all* of our children, white and colored." After insisting that desegregation did not require "all-out racial intermixing," Dorsey observed that HOPE was being "called 'integrationists' because we recognize the Supreme Court decision as the law of the land." The editorial page of the *Atlanta Constitution* routinely came to the defense of the Buckhead parents and insisted that HOPE "is not an integrationist group. It has been careful to avoid being so." In the fall of 1959, after the U.S. Supreme Court upheld the constitutionality of North Carolina's pupil placement law, the Atlanta school board announced that it would submit a similar "race-neutral" plan to the district court. The centrist credentials of this approach appeared impeccable after Governor Vandiver promised to close any integrated school in the city and the NAACP charged that pupil placement represented a subterfuge designed to evade the *Brown* mandate. The Atlanta Council of PTAs unanimously endorsed pupil placement, and the *Constitution* assured readers that the plan would "maintain for years what would amount only to token desegregation. . . . This would be good politics," the South's leading newspaper insisted. "It is morally right. It is also the only course open if education is to be saved."[7]

By the end of 1959, Atlanta's white moderate coalition had reached a general consensus on a superficially color-blind formula that promised to minimize desegregation through implicit reliance on residential boundaries and explicit use of class-based screening policies. The insistence by open-schools supporters that Atlanta could comply with *Brown* without meaningful integration depended upon the federal judiciary's "all deliberate speed" provision that elevated the procedural path of gradualism above the constitutional principle of good-faith compliance. The school board's proposal would assign students to schools "without regard to race or color," beginning in the fall of 1960 and implemented on a grade-a-year timetable starting with seniors. The mechanics of desegregation revolved around the methodical testing of individual black students who applied for transfer to white schools, based on factors such as "scholastic aptitude and relative intelli-

Georgia's Time of Decision Is NOW!
Don't Let a Few Decide for the Many!

HOPE IS

- A state-wide non-profit organization, chartered on December 12, 1958 by 17 concerned parents and citizens "to give direction, guidance, information and program to all citizens of Georgia who desire to continue the operation of the public schools of this state."
- The only rallying point of moderate opinion on the school crisis.
- Supported voluntarily by any citizen who wants to invest in the maintenance and improvement of free education.

"HOPE asserts that public education is indispensably necessary if popular government is to function effectively; if the children of those who are not wealthy are to have a decent opportunity in life; and if our society is to continue to achieve economic progress. For these reasons, HOPE opposes the closing of the public schools of Georgia, and calls on all Georgians to unite in opposition to the closing of the schools."

–James Barrow, Attorney-At-Law, Athens.

HOPE DOES NOT

- Argue the relative merits of segregation, or de-segregation.
- Discuss whether or not the 1954 Supreme Court decision was right or wrong.
- Debate States Rights vs. Federal Rights.
- Advocate *any one* method of compliance.
- And will not at any time participate in action or litigation aimed at closing a public school in Georgia.

HOPE DOES

- Give wide distribution to the facts on the school crisis.
- Point out the high cost of private schooling, and its unavailability to the masses.
- Warn that our state will suffer drastic economic losses, *unless our schools remain open.*
- Work with individuals and groups throughout the state, by furnishing factual material and speakers. (Such work often results in HOPE chapters and committees.)
- Conduct public meetings.
- Stand ready to support any reasonable plan, acceptable to the courts, which will keep the public schools open.
- Hold that Boards of Education, Legislators, the Governor and all citizens owe allegiance to the Constitution of the U.S.A. –That we are all first *Americans*, then Georgians!
- Assert that the schools must be operated in accordance with established law, or not operated *at all* in Georgia.
- Believe that each of us has an individual responsibility to let elected officials know *now* where each of us stands: on the side of law, order, and *public schools.*

"In an era in which man has sent a rocket to the moon, it is utterly unthinkable that we could limit the education of our children. I am convinced that the *people of Georgia want public schools.* I am certain that if we remain mindful of the motto of our state: 'Wisdom, Justice, Moderation,' we shall yet find a way to conform to the law of our land and preserve our cherished system of public education."–Rabbi Jacob M. Rothschild, Atlanta.

Exercise Your Right of Citizenship NOW—
Breathe Life into Georgia's Motto—
WISDOM—JUSTICE—MODERATION

Figure 3.2. This HOPE flyer distributed in the fall of 1959 reflected the desegregation consensus among Atlanta's white open-schools activists. HOPE's refusal to endorse the *Brown* decision angered some liberal members, but the group ultimately decided to appeal to a statewide audience through a singular focus on keeping public schools open. Courtesy of the Southern Regional Council and the Robert W. Woodruff Library of the Atlanta University Center.

gence or mental energy and ability, . . . psychological qualification of the pupil, . . . morals, conduct, health, and personal standards." The Southern Regional Council condemned the imposition of onerous burdens on black families seeking their constitutional rights and denounced the pupil placement formula as "unjust and patently intended to escape the law." Judge Hooper nevertheless approved the allegedly race-neutral scheme, and he announced that the upcoming session of the state legislature offered the last chance for Georgia to change its massive resistance laws before court-ordered desegregation set off a chain reaction that closed every public school in the state. HOPE had been preparing all year for this moment, and the organization immediately announced a massive grassroots drive to high-light the only two choices available, according to the ascendant legal and po-litical discourse: token desegregation in the capital city or no public schools anywhere in Georgia.[8]

THE METROPOLITAN REVOLT

HOPE launched the first of several "last chance" grassroots campaigns with a series of coordinated public demonstrations held one month before the annual session of the General Assembly. Mayor Hartsfield proclaimed De-cember 6–12, 1959, to be "Save Our Schools Week," and HOPE publicized the events through a flurry of press releases, telephone banks, and public service announcements on radio and television stations. To kick off the week, an ecumenical group of twenty Atlanta ministers, priests, and rabbis delivered sermons in support of public education. HOPE's speakers fanned out across the state, informing a wide range of civic associations about the folly of massive resistance and the sensibility of Atlanta's pupil placement plan. Hundreds of supporters participated in a massive petition drive that ultimately gathered more than ten thousand signatures from eighty-seven different localities for an open-schools manifesto presented to the state leg-islature. The climax of the week came when HOPE celebrated its one-year anniversary with a panel discussion held at Lenox Square, the popular new shopping mall located in the commercial district of Buckhead. While heck-lers carried signs proclaiming that "Moscow Wants Integration," all four members of the Fulton delegation pledged to work for pupil placement. Save Our Schools Week highlighted the unified efforts of white moderate groups in the major metropolitan areas of Georgia, qualified only by the conspicuous absence of business elites from the open-schools coalition. In a striking departure from Atlanta's unwritten rules of etiquette, Mayor Harts-field took the occasion to demand that corporate leaders publicly repudiate massive resistance or prepare to be held responsible for the consequences of their silence. This open rebuke came after several previous, and equally unfruitful, private meetings called by the mayor's office, involving Coca-Cola, Trust Company Bank, Georgia Power, Rich's Department Store, Ford, General Motors, and other pillars of the downtown establishment.[9]

The dawn of the new decade brought the customary celebration of At-lanta Exceptionalism by the city's boosters and the political ritual of re-newed commitment to segregation and white supremacy from Georgia's rural leadership. On January 1, 1960, the *Constitution* championed Atlanta's status as the unquestioned headquarters of the New South and predicted that Jim Crow would come to an end in the near future. In his annual "State of the City" address, Mayor Hartsfield employed his best New South rhetoric to argue that Georgia had become too intricately connected with the rest of the nation to abandon public education, and he reiterated the mantra that Atlanta was "too busy building to engage in hate." Boasting thirty thousand official supporters and claiming many more sympathizers, HOPE continued to present itself as the most visible manifestation of the mayor's claim that the vast majority of Georgians opposed massive resistance. Fashionably dressed ladies affiliated with HOPE also packed the gallery of the state legislature during each day of the 1960 session, which meant that the women from the open-schools coalition witnessed their worst fear: another round of no-retreat, no-surrender speeches from politicians who seemed impervious to the metropolitan movement for compliance. Governor Vandiver established the tone in a televised address that denounced token desegregation as complete abdication to the forces that would destroy Georgia's heritage. To rousing cheers from the vast majority of lawmakers, Vandiver swore: "We are going to resist again and again and again. . . . We will exhaust every legal means and remedy available to us. . . . For the children of Georgia! For our heritage! For our fathers!" HOPE immediately issued a press release that effectively called the governor a liar, based on his repeated assurances that public schools could remain open without being desegregated.[10]

HOPE's success in mobilizing public opinion in the metropolitan areas of Georgia still left the difficult task of lobbying rural lawmakers who felt no political incentive to respond to the grassroots surge. During the winter of 1960, HOPE made a conscious decision to highlight the gendered components of its public image by drawing an explicit contrast between intransigent male politicians and the concerned mothers of the open-schools movement. After Vandiver skipped several scheduled meetings with a delegation assembled by HOPE, the open-schools coalition played up the insult in a carefully cultivated media event. National magazines and television news programs ran accounts of the Atlanta mothers waiting for the governor who never showed up, and letters to local newspapers excoriated Vandiver for his unchivalrous treatment of these sincere southern ladies. In response to the barrage of criticism, the governor warned Georgians not to be fooled by the "needless agitation and sensationalism" of groups seeking to destroy southern traditions, but he also met privately with leaders of the LWV and pledged to keep the public schools "open and segregated." A few weeks later, when Vandiver promised two thousand members of the Georgia States' Rights Council that he would never accept token integration, thirty women from HOPE disrupted his speech by waving signs that read "We Want Public Schools." HOPE also organized a delegation representing fifteen women's and religious groups that called on U.S. Senators Herman Talmadge and Richard Russell at their homes, after alerting friendly members of the news media for the Sunday afternoon photo opportunity. Again and again, HOPE's lobbying activities and public relations maneuvers emphasized that Georgia's political leaders could no longer deny that many thousands of white citizens supported compliance with the law.[11]

By the standards of the day, the open-schools movement was evolving into a full-blown political revolt organized by upper-middle-class parents from the comfortable island suburbs. HOPE quickly became a lightning rod for segregationist resentment because its high-profile activities demonstrated that conservative politicians could no longer claim to represent a united white South. State leaders who habitually attributed dissent to "outside agitators" and claimed that almost all native citizens of both races supported the status quo now faced a sizable contingent of white southerners who openly rejected segregation-at-all-costs politics. Roy Harris, the head of the Georgia States' Rights Council and the publisher of a reactionary newspaper called the *Augusta Courier*, attacked the open-schools activists as traitors to their race and region by tapping into a deep tradition of working-class hostility toward the "silk stocking" liberals in Atlanta. Editorials in the *Augusta Courier* charged that HOPE and Ralph McGill, the ringleaders of race-mixing, lived in residentially segregated neighborhoods that would never be affected by integration and could afford to escape to the ritzy private schools that remained out of reach for rural white people. At a series of massive resistance rallies in the blue-collar sections of metropolitan Atlanta, Harris called HOPE "the biggest bunch of hypocrites I ever saw. They don't care if there is murder and rape and beatings in every schoolroom in Atlanta, . . . and they don't care what their daughters' relations with Negro boys are, . . . and you know why? Because they live on the Northside." The *Atlanta Constitution* fought back with its own version of class warfare, condemning Harris as a "neurotic fanatic" who appealed to "hoodlums and white trash." HOPE responded by listing its diverse spectrum of supporters: more than fifty religious, educational, and civic associations combined with thousands of ordinary families across the state. Taking the elitism charge in stride, HOPE leaders also began referring to themselves in private as the "Northside hypocrites."[12]

While massive resisters equated HOPE with the NAACP and defended racial segregation as an all-or-nothing proposition, Atlanta's white moderates continued to adopt the discourse of pragmatic segregation to construct the broadest possible political coalition. In 1960, HOPE began to employ "controlled desegregation" as the new buzzwords in its lobbying campaign, and attorney James Dorsey defined the group's agenda as saving public schools "from destruction by segregationists and integrationists." Representative Muggsy Smith of Fulton County introduced his open-schools legislative package by insisting: "It is a lie that I am an integrationist, . . . but it is my schools they are going to close first." Atlanta superintendent Pete Latimer announced that pupil placement would have minimal impact because metropolitan patterns of residential segregation protected neighborhood schools from substantial integration. The Vandiver administration officially refused to concede any ground to the open-schools movement, but cracks were beginning to appear in the rural coalition that dominated state politics. The schism emerged in public when a group of lawmakers from North Georgia expressed unwillingness to sacrifice their own public schools, located in counties with very few black students and no indications of litigation, in order to prevent desegregation in Atlanta. After HOPE quickly added the North Georgia contingent to its list of open-schools advocates, one member of the group retracted his statement in an emotional floor speech that promised to "keep white and colored separated if I die and go to Hell!" But other legislators noted that open-schools letters were flooding their offices and suggested that the state should conduct a second referendum to gauge whether public sentiment had changed since 1954.[13]

In the winter of 1960, segregationist leaders began to recognize that the metropolitan revolt against massive resistance threatened to envelop the county unit system that formed the linchpin of rural political domination. These concerns exploded into the public sphere in mid-January when Jim Peters, the powerful chairman of the State Board of Education and a close ally of Senator Talmadge, declared that the key question was whether compliance with *Brown* would be "under control of the friends of segregation or the proponents of integration." Peters warned that massive resistance had become a political liability, and he predicted that if public schools closed throughout the state, then the counties of North Georgia would join forces with metropolitan voters and expel the Talmadge faction from power, just as they had two decades earlier during the University of Georgia debacle. Mayor Hartsfield seized the opportunity to predict that if state leaders abandoned public education in defiance of the expressed will of the majority, then citizens would blame the system of electoral malapportionment, and an open-schools candidate would emerge to rupture county unit politics forever. Ellis Arnall, the former governor whose 1942 campaign had demonstrated the vulnerability of the county unit coalition, immediately announced plans to run on an open-schools platform that would produce a political revolution in Georgia. After more than a decade of quiescence, the reinvigoration of the moderate faction in state politics presented a challenge that rural conservatives could not ignore, especially in the context of the looming judicial deadline. But rather than revise the school-closing laws before adjournment, the General Assembly instead authorized the formation of a task force, known as the Sibley Commission, to serve as a mechanism of delay while considering a new path of action.[14]

The sudden momentum behind the Sibley Commission reflected the behind-the-scenes maneuvering of the Vandiver administration and the tacit approval of Atlanta's business establishment. The proposal originated with Griffin Bell, the governor's chief of staff and also a partner in King & Spalding, the most prestigious and politically connected corporate law firm in Atlanta. A pragmatic segregationist, Bell envisioned the commission as a rearguard action that would go through the motions of soliciting public opinion, devise a less vulnerable legal policy, and provide political cover for the governor to modify his position. John Sibley, the governor's selection to lead the commission, was a distinguished Atlanta lawyer who chaired the board of directors of the Trust Company Bank and previously had been senior partner at King & Spalding and the main attorney for the Coca-Cola Company. Sibley's participation strongly suggested the existence of a quid pro quo between Vandiver and the corporate leadership of Atlanta, and the *Constitution* reported on persistent but never officially corroborated rumors that the governor had asked the Chamber of Commerce to remain silent on the massive resistance controversy in exchange for his private guarantee that the state would not abandon public education permanently. HOPE decided to turn the commission hearings into a showcase of open-schools sentiment after the group's leaders came away from an off-the-record conversation at the governor's mansion with the belief that Vandiver was seeking an escape route but would probably not act until after the arrival of a crisis. Ralph McGill summarized the new conventional wisdom in his front-page column in the *Constitution*: "We are going, apparently, to close schools. The futures of one million Georgia children and thousands of teachers are not important. The extremist forces must have their day before we act to save education."[15]

PRAGMATIC SEGREGATION

The Sibley Commission held public hearings in each of Georgia's ten congressional districts during March 1960. The members of the task force included prominent businessmen, newspaper editors, education officials, and state legislators—all representatives of the state's white male elite. As chairman, John Sibley dominated the commission's agenda and came across as the embodiment of pragmatic segregation, openly reluctant to accept the *Brown* mandate but realistic enough to concede that federal power trumped states' rights. The Atlanta attorney explained that the public hearings would determine if "the good will of the people, white and colored, . . . can modify the evils of the [Supreme Court] decision." At the commission's inaugural meeting, Sibley bluntly informed Georgians that the time had come to decide whether or not to abolish public education throughout the state on a permanent basis. In a departure from the Vandiver administration's stance that the public schools could remain "open and segregated," Sibley insisted that the state had to choose between two alternatives—minimal desegregation in a few localities or the wholesale conversion to a system of private segregated education supported by state tuition grants. This approach resembled the discursive strategy that the LWV pioneered in 1954 and that HOPE had fine-tuned since 1958, by restricting acceptable political discourse to the narrow choice of public schools with token desegregation or segregated schools through private education. Sibley's formulation rejected the caste-based argument that tokenism was impossible because integration was an all-or-nothing proposition and simultaneously excluded the proponents of good-faith compliance who protested tokenism as constitutionally inadequate and little more than massive resistance by other methods. Throughout the hearings, the chairman employed his gavel liberally whenever a witness challenged the ground rules and tried to propose an option other than minimal desegregation or massive resistance.[16]

Across the state, ordinary Georgians seized the opportunity to give political leaders advice about the road ahead. As expected, the Sibley hearings confirmed the traditional political division between metropolitan and rural areas, but they also revealed the striking reemergence of the geographic schism between the predominantly white counties of North Georgia and the heavily black counties of South Georgia. Led by rural PTA chapters and affiliates of the Citizens' Council, a majority of the witnesses who spoke at the hearings in South Georgia urged the state to close public schools rather than surrender to integration. But even in the Black Belt, the cities and towns produced appreciable support for public education from white ministers, educational associations, and black speakers. The ideological divide between rural and metropolitan Georgia was most evident in Black Belt and coastal congressional districts that contained single large cities, where the turnout by segregationists from the countryside overwhelmed the representatives of white moderate groups from Macon and Savannah. In the congressional district that included Athens, the home of the University of Georgia and a HOPE stronghold, open-schools advocates dominated the hearings. In the other two districts of North Georgia, a large majority of the witnesses endorsed the flexible policy of local option with the common refrain that court-ordered desegregation in Atlanta was not worth closing their own public schools.[17]

The Sibley Commission arrived in the capital city in late March, drawing crowds in the thousands. Assured of a media spotlight, HOPE and its allies organized a tour de force for the open-schools movement of metropolitan Atlanta. More than one hundred speakers—including ministers, university and student groups, civic organizations from the city and suburbs, and public school officials—informed the enthusiastic audience that private schools could never replace public education. Even the Atlanta Chamber of Commerce issued a brief statement in support of local option, although no representative of the organization proved willing to appear publicly. Fran Breeden presented HOPE's official testimony, which declared that all children had the right to a "free public education" and insisted that the closing of even one public school, even if only on a temporary basis, could not be justified under any circumstances (figure 3.3). HOPE's stance displayed the continuing tensions between its pragmatic strategy and progressive ideology, as the group reluctantly endorsed the local option policy as a compromise solution despite the belief that private schools would be too expensive or too deficient to function as a replacement system in any part of the state. Several African-American witnesses rejected token desegregation as an inadequate policy that did not address the root problem of racial inequality, and former HOPE official Harry Boyte, now president of the Greater Atlanta Council on Human Relations (GACHR), criticized pupil placement as a transparent ruse to maintain as much segregation as possible by evading the constitutional mandate to integrate in good faith. On the other side of the spectrum, segregationist leader Lester Maddox argued that racial integration was inspired by communism and that token desegregation was a lie, and a new group called the Metropolitan Association for Segregated Education demanded state-supported private schools in Atlanta.[18]

The Sibley hearings provided conclusive evidence for three of the central claims of the open-schools movement: that substantial diversity of opinion existed among white Georgians, that support for public education extended far beyond metropolitan Atlanta, and that the political resilience of massive resistance depended upon the undemocratic structure of the county unit system. The public forums demonstrated that a crisis involving public education had once again rearranged Georgia's political fault lines, with the potential to split the county unit coalition that facilitated rural domination of state government. The Talmadge faction's control of state politics required the constant alignment of rural counties against the effectively disfranchised residents of the metropolitan regions, but the Sibley hearings revealed that most of North Georgia and even some of the urban areas of South Georgia opposed the official state policy of sacrificing public education to maintain absolute segregation. In the spring of 1960, the direct link between massive resistance and political malapportionment became the favored explanation of white moderates who supported public education. William Hartsfield charged that the real issue at stake in the school-closing crusade was whether old-guard rural politicians would remain in power or if "we are going to have a true democracy where all votes count the same." Ralph McGill reiterated the mayor's prediction that the backlash against massive resistance would destroy the county unit system and warned that the crisis might even produce the previously unthinkable, a Republican governor. In letters

Figure 3.3. Fran Breeden, HOPE's president, expressing the group's support for open public schools during the Atlanta hearing conducted by the Sibley Commission, March 23, 1960. Courtesy of the Bill Wilson Collection, Kenan Research Center at the Atlanta History Center.

to the *Constitution*, readers from across the state complained that the county unit system prevented the election of New South leaders who would defend public education and comply with the law. Georgians suffered under "fire-breathing, emotionally hysterical political orators [who] do not really speak for most of the people," lamented a man from the town of Waycross. "If we are not to make a joke of the democratic process, then the majority should rule."[19]

The Sibley Commission released its findings at the end of April, with the judicial deadline in Atlanta barely four months away. The majority report—signed by the commission's businessmen, public educators, and two of the eight legislators—declared unequivocally that court decisions in other southern states had rendered Georgia's massive resistance laws untenable. John Sibley and his allies urged the legislature to change course rather than risk the statewide abandonment of public education. The report proposed a new "freedom of choice" formula based on the legal theory that the *Brown* decision forbade overt racial discrimination by the government but did not require active steps to achieve integration or prohibit the private right of individuals to voluntary association. The majority faction also endorsed a pupil placement law to maintain token desegregation, a local option policy to permit districts to close their own schools by popular referendum, and a private school tuition grant program for any student who objected to integrated education. The minority report—signed by the farmers and rural legislators on the commission—advocated the last-minute shift to a segregated system of state-supported private schools and a comprehensive effort to reunite Georgians behind the caste crusade. The minority faction also charged that tokenism would never work because "communist-inspired organizations"— meaning the NAACP and the Southern Regional Council—would be satisfied with nothing less than "massive and total integration on all levels." All members of the Sibley Commission agreed on the necessity of a constitutional amendment guaranteeing that no student in Georgia could ever be forced to attend an integrated school.[20]

HOPE immediately issued a statement of support for the Sibley majority report, praising the commission for acknowledging the impossibility of maintaining complete segregation in public schools and the impracticality of a statewide conversion to private education. The group also endorsed the freedom of choice program, with the qualification that "we don't see how anyone could object to a plan that permits so much." This comment reflected the increasing discomfort among the more liberal open-schools activists about how much ground they had conceded in their singular focus on saving public education in Atlanta. HOPE's leaders doubted the constitutionality of tuition grants and disapproved of the local option school-closing mechanism, but the group's long-standing policy of not supporting any particular method of compliance made it difficult to draw public distinctions between principled moderation and pragmatic segregation. Through tactics designed to sway a segregationist statewide audience and reassure self-interested suburban families in Atlanta, the white moderates and liberals in the open-schools movement had successfully narrowed public debate to a choice between "controlled desegregation" or no public schools at all. The Sibley Commission restricted the prevailing discourse even further, presenting Georgians with the option of a futile last stand for massive resistance or an ironclad assurance that any individual white student could remain in a completely segregated institution at public expense. While most black leaders expressed displeasure, the key groups in the open-schools coalition closed ranks behind the Sibley recommendations. But Governor Vandiver refused to respond to the growing pressure to call a special session of the General Assembly, which meant that the next move would come from Judge Hooper, who had already promised to close every public school in Georgia if the state government declined to repeal the massive resistance laws.[21]

Ten days after the release of the Sibley report, and more than two years after the initiation of litigation, Hooper finally set a firm date for the desegregation of the Atlanta public school system. In a ruling marked by undisguised sensitivity to the climate of political resistance, the judge approved the school board's request to delay implementation an additional year, until the fall of 1961. The NAACP attorneys protested that compliance with a Supreme Court decision should not depend on the whims of the governor or the inaction of the state legislature, since the *Brown II* mandate clearly rejected the postponement of constitutional rights because of public opposition or political defiance. Hooper responded that although Georgia's leaders had the right to repeat the disastrous school-closing experiments in Arkansas and Virginia, the next session of the General Assembly would receive one more last chance to choose a different course. In an informal statement from the bench, the judge endorsed the Sibley majority report's stance of pragmatic segregation and even pointed out that Atlanta's residential patterns would prevent "massive integration." Hooper concluded with the warning that if the legislature did not allow the city of Atlanta to desegregate its public schools, it would "risk the dam breaking and the whole state being flooded." Newell Edenfield, the president of the Georgia Bar Association, reiterated this admonition in a series of speeches arguing that Georgia's massive resistance laws hindered the cause of segregation because they encouraged class-action lawsuits and made it easy for black plaintiffs to prove discrimination. Governor Vandiver responded by calling the attorney "out of contact with reality," and he pledged that the state legislature would not repeal the massive resistance program or meet to consider the recommendations of the Sibley Commission.[22]

HOPE organized a Georgia Open School Conference in the spring of 1960, cosponsored by seven other religious and women's groups and publicized as a political convention for the supporters of public education. The five hundred white moderates and liberals invited to attend became central features of Edward R. Murrow's CBS documentary on the Georgia desegregation saga, *Who Speaks for the South?* With television cameras recording the proceedings for a national audience, the gathering produced a remarkable discussion that extended far beyond the self-censored public discourse of the moderate white South. One panel reached a consensus that racial segregation contained "moral and ethical contradictions" that demanded involvement by religious groups, while another group debating the "taboo of silence" acknowledged that the open-schools movement had made it safe to support public education but honest dialogue about integration remained difficult to achieve. Throughout the conference, participants lamented the failure of business leaders to take a forthright stand against massive resistance, and they contemplated strategies to mobilize voters in order to reshape the state legislature. HOPE warned that the recent district court ruling represented a "final reprieve" and urged its supporters to campaign against the legislators who defended massive resistance. National television viewers saw Atlanta's answer to the question *Who Speaks for the South?*

personified by the leading figures in the open-schools movement—ministers and female reformers, lawyers and college professors, prominent journalists and metropolitan politicians, led by suburban mothers turned political activists.[23]

"Operation Last Chance"

HOPE launched "Operation Last Chance" in the fall of 1960, and this time it really did seem that the day of reckoning would not be postponed. The General Assembly remained virtually unchanged after the Democratic primaries in September. While the moderate incumbents from Atlanta handily trounced their opponents, and public education supporters helped elect several new legislators from other metropolitan districts, the open-schools movement did not possess the grassroots infrastructure or the popular support to mount a serious electoral challenge in the more than one hundred small rural counties that dominated county unit politics. Instead, the open-schools movement organized "Days of Decision" forums in cities distant from HOPE's base of support, including three in the inhospitable Black Belt region: Augusta, Columbus, and Macon. To downplay the Atlanta connection, HOPE named Beverly Downing of the Athens chapter as the new head of its executive committee and coordinated the conferences through the Georgia League of Women Voters and the United Church Women. Heavily promoted with radio and television advertisements, the meetings featured workshops and speeches by leading women in the open-schools coalition, along with a keynote address by conservative Democrat Jim Peters in the South Georgia locales. As the meeting of the "Last Chance Legislature" approached, HOPE quietly finalized preparations for the January activation of its statewide network, which included almost ninety community groups and thousands of individuals. All of HOPE's substantial resources were now mobilized behind the narrow objectives of the Sibley majority report, which had become the primary emphasis of the open-schools coalition's grassroots outreach, informational literature, and lobbying activities.[24]

Then came the explosion that HOPE feared most—not in Atlanta, but five hundred miles away in New Orleans, another southern metropolis with a cosmopolitan reputation. The nationally televised mob violence that greeted court-ordered desegregation in New Orleans deeply alarmed the open-schools activists in Atlanta, and HOPE immediately sought to impress the lessons of the Louisiana tragedy upon political and corporate leaders in Georgia. "Don't Let It Happen Here!" warned HOPE's flyers and mailings, which contained pictures of white mobs and blamed the violence in New Orleans on the systematic deception of the people by state leaders who promised that schools could remain open and segregated. The Vandiver administration's unofficial response came from Frank Twitty and Carl Sanders, the governor's two floor leaders in the General Assembly. Speaking to the Georgia Chamber of Commerce during the explosions in New Orleans, the two men predicted that the governor would close Atlanta's public schools on a temporary basis, and only then would the state legislature act to modify the massive resistance program. The Vandiver administration's cavalier attitude toward the education of hundreds of thousands of students produced outrage and despair in the ranks of the open-schools movement. From HOPE headquarters, Fran Breeden sent the governor an angry telegram that called the policy a "dangerous and indefensible" assault on Georgia's children and warned that even a temporary abandonment of public education would sacrifice the state's national and international reputation. The *Constitution* reiterated HOPE's critique in an editorial observation that, more than anything else, New Orleans had lost its prestige and dignity—the most tragic fate that could befall Atlanta, at least in the minds of the city's boosters.[25]

In the final months of 1960, public debate in Georgia began shifting away from the increasingly settled question of whether public education would survive to the still uncertain matter of whether Atlanta would be humiliated by the way that desegregation arrived. For more than a year, both HOPE and the LWV had privately suspected and publicly hinted that Georgia's school-closing policies would not withstand judicial scrutiny under any scenario, a position reinforced when a federal panel in Louisiana ruled that massive resistance laws designed to evade the *Brown* decision were unconstitutional on their face. But the specter of violence and disorder continued to haunt Atlanta's open-schools coalition, especially after a rapid series of events threatened to jeopardize the city's carefully cultivated image of biracial harmony. In the fall of 1960, after several months of fruitless negotiations with business leaders, black university students launched demonstrations against Rich's Department Store, a pillar of the downtown business district. Then the arrest and eight-day imprisonment of Martin Luther King, Jr., made national headlines and contrasted Atlanta's obstructionist stance with the dozens of other New South cities that had already accepted lunch counter desegregation. Corporate leaders in Atlanta entered into secret biracial negotiations at the elite Commerce Club that produced an agreement to postpone the desegregation of downtown stores until after the resolution of the public school crisis, and their counterparts in Atlanta's black establishment pressured the students to accept the compromise. At the same time, Lester Maddox founded a new group known as GUTS (Georgians Unwilling to Surrender), which promised to defend school segregation and harass any white people considered soft on integration. When bombs subsequently damaged a black elementary school, Mayor Hartsfield blamed "an ignorant rabble inflamed by political demagogues," but he also charged that

the act of terrorism had been "encouraged by the silence of most of our substantial civic leaders."[26]

The showdown that everyone expected came in a place that no one anticipated. In early 1961, in response to a NAACP lawsuit to desegregate the
University of Georgia, District Judge W. A. Bootle lost patience with the
Vandiver administration's tactics of delay and ordered the immediate admission of two black students, Charlayne Hunter and Hamilton Holmes. The
ruling became effective on January 9, the same day that the governor was
scheduled to deliver his annual address to the General Assembly. With all
attention focused on the Atlanta situation, state leaders appeared to have
been caught completely by surprise by the swift turn of events in Athens.
On Sunday afternoon, January 8, fifty of the top politicians in the Talmadge
faction gathered at the governor's mansion for a confidential emergency
conference. While legislative leaders Frank Twitty and Carl Sanders urged
the governor to back down, most of those present called on Vandiver to shut
down the state's largest public university rather than break his promise to
prevent any and all school desegregation. HOPE's executive committee met
simultaneously and voted to unleash the direct action stage of "Operation
Last Chance." The next day, the governor ignored the pleas and demands of
open-schools supporters, including twenty-six hundred UGA students, and
closed the university in an order he called "the saddest duty of my life." But
only the most fervent segregationists believed that UGA could be converted
into an ersatz private university, and in his televised address to the legislature Vandiver made it clear that he would not accept the permanent loss of
Georgia's flagship institution. "We cannot abandon public education," the
governor declared; the time had come to replace the school-closing laws
with a new and more effective massive resistance strategy to prevent forced
integration by the federal government.[27]

One day later, Judge Bootle invalidated the massive resistance legislation
and enjoined the governor from interfering with the operations of the University of Georgia. A number of rural legislators called on Vandiver to go
to prison, but the governor promised that he would not defy the federal
courts. Ralph McGill wrote that UGA had an opportunity to undermine
communist propaganda and make up for the angry mobs of New Orleans
by showing the world an honorable picture of the South. Instead, on the
evening after the two black students began classes, violence broke out on
campus after UGA lost a basketball game to archrival Georgia Tech. An un-
ruly crowd set fires and threw rocks at the police, who used tear gas to dis-
perse two thousand demonstrators surrounding Charlayne Hunter's dormitory. The governor promptly directed the university administration to
suspend Hunter and Holmes, ostensibly for their own safety, but Judge
Bootle reinstated the students and ordered the Vandiver administration not

to obstruct their education. As the crisis settled down, HOPE commended the governor's newfound commitment to public education but blamed state leaders for the UGA riot and the extensive national coverage that had caused "irreparable harm . . . to the image of Georgia." The *Constitution* placed a different spin on the situation in a crowing editorial that encapsulated Atlanta's booster tradition of trumpeting the positive and forgetting the rest. The newspaper boasted that Georgia's "courageous" governor had not tried to close the university, glossing over the fact that Vandiver had done exactly that, albeit reluctantly and temporarily. The *Constitution* also blamed outside agitators and Klan operatives for the violence at UGA, absolving Georgia's political leaders as well as the many university students who clearly had participated in the dormitory demonstrations. "Let the nation look at us now," the editorial declared. "It is suddenly a fine feeling to be a Georgian."[28]

The state government officially retreated from the policy of massive resistance in the aftermath of the court-enforced desegregation of the University of Georgia. On January 18, 1961, Ernest Vandiver addressed another joint session of the General Assembly as well as a statewide radio and television audience. The governor called for the adoption of the Sibley recommendations to replace the "rusty and defective safeguards" of the original massive resistance program. Echoing the discourse of the open-schools movement, Vandiver defended the institution of public education in the language of children's rights and economic prosperity. He also denounced mob violence and insisted that realistic segregationists must concede that the state could not defy the superior military power of the federal government. Vandiver promised that Georgia would regroup, not surrender, with a new strategy of legal resistance that would preserve the maximum possible degree of racial segregation. The General Assembly quickly repealed the school-closing statutes and overwhelmingly ratified a new legislative package, the "Child Protection Plan," which consisted of local option, pupil placement, private school tuition grants, and a constitutional amendment guaranteeing "freedom of association." On the last day of a very tumultuous month, Vandiver signed the package into law and declared that Georgia had acted to protect the future of its children while "try[ing] to maintain our Southern traditions." Diehard segregationists continued to demand the defense of an inviolate caste line, with Georgia Democratic party chairman James Gray lambasting the governor for surrendering to the "bleeding-heart appeal to 'save our schools' by proposing to keep them open whatever the cost to principle and Southern tradition." The white moderate coalition continued to praise the governor's belated embrace of pragmatic segregation, although one of HOPE's leaders privately charged that Vandiver should be impeached for repeatedly making promises that he knew he could not keep.[29]

Leadership and Citizenship

The events of January 1961 produced two resilient myths about the denouement of massive resistance in Georgia: that the timing of the UGA crisis and
the leadership of Atlanta's business community saved the public school system in the state. According to this traditional booster narrative of top-down
male leadership, first drafted in the contemporary accounts of the Atlanta
news media, the transition away from massive resistance reflected the political courage of Ernest Vandiver combined with the corporate pragmatism of
John Sibley. Because closing the University of Georgia was politically untenable and simply unthinkable, the governor forced state leaders to embrace
the corporate exit strategy designed by the Sibley Commission. Following
the lead of contemporary revisionists, some scholarly accounts of Georgia's
desegregation crisis even have portrayed Vandiver as a "forward-looking governor on civil rights" who "accepted the inevitable with dignity and grace."
Vandiver did not have blood on his hands, and he was never a particularly
skilled demagogue, but historical assessments of the caliber of southern
leadership during the civil rights era should not use George Wallace or Ross
Barnett as the standard. Faced with undeniable evidence that an overwhelmingly majority of people in Atlanta, and tens of thousands of others
across Georgia, wanted massive resistance to end, Ernest Vandiver chose instead for a period of several years to appeal to the most bitter and reactionary segments of the political spectrum under pretense of speaking for a
unified white population.[30]

The future of public education in Georgia did indeed face a genuine
threat—not merely a manufactured emergency—from the fusion of caste
ideology and county unit politics at the foundation of the massive resistance
program. "The integration issue . . . was overwhelming," recalled Griffin
Bell, the top aide in the Vandiver administration. "It was so emotional that
economic problems were lost—totally submerged. . . . We could have had
all private schools. We could have gone without schools." But between 1959
and 1961, the grassroots mobilization of the open-schools movement and
the evolution of desegregation case law transformed the political climate of
massive resistance. Before the arrival of the UGA crisis, leading allies of the
Vandiver administration clearly had indicated that the state government
planned to wait to adopt the Sibley majority report until right after the erup-
tion of a desegregation crisis in Atlanta. And after the judicial invalidation of
massive resistance in Louisiana, Judge Hooper clearly could have, and certainly should have, ordered the immediate reopening of the Atlanta schools
instead of the alternative remedy of shutting down public education
throughout the state. Despite Ralph McGill's contention that God personally intervened to rescue the state capital, and Ernest Vandiver's claim that

Georgia changed course only to protect its flagship institution, the UGA crisis and the Sibley Commission did not save Atlanta's schools. At most, the events of January 1961 made Athens rather than Atlanta the scene of mob activity, enabled white moderates to prepare for desegregation without the uncertainty brought by school-closing laws, and prevented last-minute shenanigans by state politicians.[31]

Praising the business community for the resolution of Atlanta's desegregation crisis is incompatible with its nearly absolute failure to provide public leadership during the seven-year duration of massive resistance in Georgia. For more than two years, the middle-class parents in HOPE pleaded with the Georgia and Atlanta Chambers of Commerce to join the open-schools movement. Mayor William Hartsfield requested, lamented, and ultimately denounced the city's most powerful corporate figures for their refusal to take a public stand. In January of 1960, when the members of the Atlanta Chamber of Commerce voted not to adopt a formal position on the issue of massive resistance, a few of the city's prominent business executives did speak out as individuals for compliance, including C&S Bank president Mills B. Lane, Jr., and Lockheed Aircraft Corporation general manager W. A. Pulver. At the end of the year, Ivan Allen, Jr., the newly elected president of the Atlanta Chamber, pledged that the business group would lobby the legislature to adopt the Sibley recommendations before the looming desegregation deadline. But the first significant public action by corporate leaders came on January 22, 1961, in a statement that called on the state government to adopt the freedom of choice program and declared that the "disruption of our public school system would have a calamitous effect on the economic climate of Georgia." This anticlimactic manifesto, signed by almost one thousand businessmen affiliated with the Georgia and Atlanta Chambers of Commerce, came two weeks after the mob violence at the University of Georgia and four days after Governor Vandiver asked the state legislature to repeal the school-closing laws. It is hard to imagine who was left for the "power structure" to influence, besides the national media of the present and the historians of the future, or a few incorrigible segregationists who certainly could not have cared less about the opinion of rich businessmen from Buckhead.[32]

Atlanta's business leaders were the most conspicuous "silent moderates" during the crisis of massive resistance, the only key figures anywhere in the state of Georgia to remain officially neutral throughout the sustained showdown. The fighting moderates and dedicated liberals in HOPE spent much energy in the effort to recruit prominent businessmen to their cause, believing that the intervention of the "power structure" would turn the tide in favor of the open-schools movement. But rather than emphasizing the responsibilities of national citizenship and compliance with the law, businessmen embodied the stereotype of the passive white southerners caught in the

middle, whose circumspection encouraged the defiance of political demagogues and facilitated the segregationist myth of a Solid South. Rather than
leading their communities toward the future, businessmen forfeited a degree of public authority that they would not be able to recover during the
racial and spatial conflicts on the metropolitan horizon. Although the events
of the *Brown* era confirmed Atlanta's reputation as the nationally celebrated
capital of the New South, the city avoided the fate of Little Rock and New
Orleans in spite of, not because of, the role of its business community. The
mythology of Atlanta Exceptionalism survived massive resistance relatively
intact because of the moderate path charted by Mayor William Hartsfield
and enforced by the local news media, the controversial decision by African-
American activists to delay a frontal assault on the politics of gradualism,
and especially the three-year campaign for open schools led by the HOPE
parents from the upscale neighborhoods of northside Atlanta. Behind the
scenes, corporate leaders in Atlanta may have sought private assurances
from the governor, and they may have applauded the escape plan formulated by the Sibley Commission, but the turning points in Georgia's massive
resistance crisis did not take place in the backrooms of the Commerce Club
or the boardrooms of King & Spalding.

The most critical battles of the massive resistance era took place in the
public sphere, where citizens as well as leaders had to take sides during the
most significant moral crisis and the most pivotal political showdown in postwar southern history. Throughout much of the South, the segregationist crusade for white unity caused a profound collapse of the center, collective
silence became the equivalent of acquiescence in the politics of massive resistance, and the individual decision to take a public stand in favor of law
and order became an inherently ethical and even an existential expression of
dissent. In metropolitan Atlanta, the revitalization of the center by open-
schools activists transformed the dynamics of massive resistance, turning a
loose collection of suburban parents into a powerful movement of political
protest and making support for public education a communal expression of
public-spirited reform. During a time when many liberals carefully avoided
the language of justice and most moderates acted primarily out of self-
interest, and when almost everyone in the open-schools movement embraced or rationalized the discursive strategy of pragmatic segregation,
whether or not Atlanta should have mythologized any of its white citizens is
a certainly debatable and ultimately philosophical question. But any acco-
lades for courageous white leadership during the South's tragic descent into
massive resistance must be given to the ordinary fathers and especially the
mothers who believed in universal access to public education as the foundation of a democratic and decent society and said so over and over again.
While businessmen equivocated and politicians blustered, while African-

American citizens placed their faith in the law, a grassroots movement led by the upper-middle-class parents in HOPE filled the vacuum of leadership and convinced their communities and their state that public schools must be preserved, violence must be avoided, and federal court decisions must be respected.

CHAPTER 4

The Strange Career of Atlanta Exceptionalism

> I think all of us were disappointed at the way in which segregation had been killed, if it had been. . . . Had we been able to look down the road through the decades to see where we would be now, it would have broken our hearts.
>
> —Nan Pendergrast, (1992), former HOPE leader

OASIS

As Atlanta began intensive preparations for the August 1961 desegregation deadline, the leaders of the open-schools campaign came up with a grand proposal: a massive rally with President John F. Kennedy as the featured speaker, held just before the milestone that they had dubbed "D-Day." These citizen-boosters believed that the appearance of the president would focus the nation's attention on the "democratic conviction and goodwill" of the people of Atlanta and would guarantee international publicity for the city at the center of the "successful transition into a new era of race relations in the South." The dream of a presidential visit went unrealized, after the Kennedy administration rebuffed the initiative in another indication that the time had not yet come when national politicians were willing to expend political capital on the cause of racial integration. But the ambitiousness of the idea revealed that Atlanta's white activists believed their own accomplishment in the demise of the caste line to be the turning point of modern southern history. After the political defeat of massive resistance, open-schools groups returned their attention to the local level with an agenda that seamlessly combined peaceful compliance with the court order, protection of their children's education, and national marketing of their city's image. HOPE warned its supporters that while "responsible citizens relax in an atmosphere of self-congratulation, the extremists are increasing their activity." To mobilize Atlantans behind the desegregation mandate, HOPE and its allies launched a comprehensive public relations and community education campaign during the summer of 1961. "All that remains is this final question," the open-schools coalition declared. "Have we done all that we can to insure that Atlanta makes good her illustrious image? . . . Let us be certain that this image of a great city 'too busy to hate' will be projected before the eyes of the whole world."[1]

The leadership in the grassroots campaign to ensure peaceful compliance came from a new coalition called OASIS (Organizations Assisting Schools in September), an acronym that invoked the city's anomalous location within the Deep South and encapsulated the ideology of Atlanta Exceptionalism that reached its postwar climax with the events of 1961. The formal unveiling of OASIS brought to light the existence of the unofficial steering committee that had been meeting covertly for the previous two years, linking HOPE and the League of Women Voters together with the main civil rights organizations in Atlanta. The NAACP, the Urban League, and the Georgia and Greater Atlanta chapters of the Council on Human Relations participated in OASIS, marking the first time that HOPE publicly joined forces with African-American activists and interracial organizations committed to the moral principle of racial integration. As an umbrella organization, OASIS included more than fifty civic and religious groups, a diverse list that ranged from the Girl Scouts to the Georgia Council of Churches. Based in HOPE's headquarters and chaired by Jane Hammer of the LWV, the new alliance continued to follow the strategic path charted by the open-schools movement, under the direction of the same leadership cadre of female activists. OASIS recognized that its member organizations differed widely in philosophy but proclaimed their unanimity of purpose to prepare the community and assist city officials to achieve "peaceful and orderly desegregation." In a massive outreach, OASIS organized coffee chats with neighborhood discussion groups and provided speakers and informational literature for church and civic meetings. The citizens coalition worked closely with the mayor's office, the police department, the school administration, and the local media. The OASIS public relations committee also lobbied key members of the national media in order to highlight the good-faith commitment of the white moderates at the center of what they called the "Atlanta Story."[2]

OASIS's citywide agenda focused particular attention on the fears and anxieties of the white parents and students at the four high schools scheduled for desegregation. The fact sheets distributed by the organization offered assurances that integration would not lower academic standards, because science had determined that "race is not a factor in determining intelligence," and because the pupil placement plan restricted transfers to black students who met "demanding standards of moral, mental, and physical ability." During the summer, the youth division of OASIS conducted interracial role-playing exercises for the students who would soon be in desegregated classrooms and produced television programs to address the concerns of their parents. OASIS also moved aggressively to counter segregationist groups that tried to organize protests and promote private school alternatives. A local organization called Separate Schools warned that the second Battle of Atlanta was at hand and implored parents not to be fooled by the school board's scheme to choose "first intruders [who] will be so inoffensive" that the white community would accept defeat. Separate Schools called for a full-scale boycott of the desegregated facilities, which it blamed on the "black-bloc-controlled city administration [and] . . . Ralph McGill's Southern Regional Council . . . which are pushing the communist program for Atlanta's children." After police observed well-known white supremacists passing out racist literature in several working-class neighborhoods, OASIS recruited ten sets of "stand-by parents" to initiate preventive action at any sign of a boycott. As the start of the school year neared, OASIS sponsored discussions between the black transfer students and their future white class-mates and convened a mass meeting of parents from all four institutions to ensure that no disruptions would occur. No detail escaped the attention of the OASIS network, which even issued a stern warning that if any children came to school in blackface, as one rumor suggested, such pranks would elicit the full wrath of not only school officials but also the police depart-ment.[3]

The celebration of the moderate consensus in Atlanta overshadowed but did not defuse the growing tensions regarding the extremely limited degree of desegregation envisioned under the city's pupil placement formula. The NAACP urged black families to swamp the school system with transfer re-quests because "there is no time for patience and moderation." In an imme-diate demonstration of the priority of gradualism over the principle of good faith, the school board approved only 10 of 123 applicants (later reduced to 9), which prompted fierce criticism from black leaders and the affected fam-ilies. The members of HOPE's inner circle privately expressed acute disap-pointment at the small number of black students selected for desegregation, although the decision should not have surprised anyone who had listened to the promises of school officials and the assurances of the open-schools movement that Atlanta could achieve compliance without "massive integra-tion." When the school board systematically rejected each appeal of its decision, the frustration of many white liberals in the OASIS coalition threatened to undermine the unity platform of the open-schools movement. Ministers involved with OASIS pushed for the adoption of a statement "sup-porting the principle of desegregation and calling for more complete deseg-regation in the near future," and the GACHR released a blunt critique of the racial discrimination inherent in the pupil placement plan. Judy Neiman of HOPE directly confronted these internal divisions in a statement to the news media: "When the 'symbolic ten' go to their classrooms, segregation in Georgia's common schools will be officially over. There are those who wish the ten could be a thousand. There are many who object to even one. But whatever the views that divide them, Atlantans are united in a single hope that the story that unfolds on August 30th will be much different from the one you might have expected."[4]

As "D-Day" approached, all indicators suggested that OASIS had marginalized the opponents of controlled desegregation with the same effective techniques that HOPE had employed to discredit the politics of massive resistance. OASIS coordinated a "Weekend of Prayer for Law and Order" at the end of August, highlighted by more than 750 religious leaders who preached sermons on the moral obligation to obey the law. On the day before schools opened, Fran Breeden felt confident enough to issue a statement of gratitude to the "dedicated volunteers—housewives, lawyers, doctors, ministers—[who] are living proof that an informed public can change the climate of opinion in an entire state." "As our state gains new stature in the eyes of the world," the HOPE leader concluded, "we are indeed proud to be Georgians." To make sure, OASIS prepackaged the Atlanta Story in a handbook distributed to the two hundred visiting journalists, along with a pointed reminder that the group's name was "an acronym Atlantans feel is descriptive of their city." An introduction by Ralph McGill invoked the New South legacy of his predecessor Henry Grady to tout Atlanta as the city that "has always tried to look forward, not backward." Mayor Hartsfield instructed the press on its obligation to portray Atlanta as a "great city facing profound change with dignity, a city continuing to be a credit to the nation, a city too busy to hate." The Atlanta Chamber of Commerce declared that "the business leaders of this city have never faltered in our solid support" for the rule of law and demanded the same level of "responsible journalism" from the national media. OASIS concluded the package with a heartfelt message that asked the media not to forget that the battle for public education was won by "a bunch of starry-eyed amateurs—a strictly grassroots-type operation held together chiefly with scotch tape and imagination." The "unsung heroines" of the open-schools movement were the "ordinary housewives and mothers who left beds unmade and meals uncooked to insure their children's educational future."[5]

The image-conscious city orchestrated the events of August 30, 1961, so elaborately that it is hard to see how anything could have gone wrong. The whole world was watching, the Chamber of Commerce announced in a full-page newspaper advertisement that asked "How Great Is Atlanta?" The theme of Atlanta Exceptionalism pervaded everything, as outside commentators and local boosters joined together to pay tribute to the city as the shining leader of the New South and the enlightened oasis of the Deep South. Ernest Vandiver struck the only discordant note, with the announcement of a new massive resistance initiative that allegedly would be able to reverse the *Brown* decision, but even the governor issued firm warnings against violence. The Atlanta Police Department drew up elaborate contingency plans in case of disorder and provided a show of force that discouraged almost all segregationist demonstrators except for a self-proclaimed

Figure 4.1. Atlanta officials holding a press conference at City Hall, August 30, 1961, to announce the peaceful desegregation of four public high schools. The men addressing the national media include Mayor William Hartsfield, standing beneath the seal, Superintendent John Letson, speaking on the phone, and Police Chief Herbert Jenkins, standing immediately to Letson's left. Courtesy of the Lane Brothers Photographers Collection, Special Collections Department, Georgia State University Library.

Nazi who drove down from Virginia and four local teenagers who were arrested, tried, and sentenced before noon. Extremely favorable coverage came from the crowd of reporters quarantined at City Hall and given regular updates on the absence of news along with their complimentary Coca-Colas and later cocktails. Mayor Hartsfield, in the crowning moment of his quarter-century stewardship of his beloved city, proclaimed Atlanta to be a progressive example for the rest of the South and a global showcase of America's greatness for a Cold War audience (figure 4.1). President Kennedy praised the triumph of moderation and saluted the "vigorous efforts for months by the officials of Atlanta and by groups of citizens throughout the community." A newspaper article told of Maxine Friedman and Judy Neiman standing outside Brown High School with tears in their eyes, and for the women in HOPE who had spent three years of their lives preparing for this moment, the calm and celebrated nature of school deseg-regation in Atlanta was indeed a relief and a triumph. After several more days passed without incident, the visiting journalists left town, the schools returned to normal, and a proud city basked in the afterglow of the national spotlight.[6]

THE MODERATE BLUEPRINT

In 1961, the widespread celebration of Atlanta Exceptionalism reflected not only the public relations achievement of the open-schools movement but also the broad national approval of the politics of moderation. Most white Americans at the time could be classified as racial moderates, in the sense that they combined an abstract endorsement of equal opportunity with spe-cific support for policies of gradualism. In a 1961 Gallup survey, 61 percent of respondents agreed that "integration should be brought about gradually," and only 23 percent believed "every means should be used to bring it about in the near future." The stance that moderation represented the position of reasonable people under attack by "extremists on both sides"—a formula-tion that lumped massive resisters and civil rights activists together against the middle—emerged as a popular viewpoint in the rest of the nation before it became the dominant ideology in the metropolitan South. In the spring of 1960, a feature on the American Broadcasting Network called HOPE the leading "light of inspiration" in a region where "the passionate cries of ex-tremists drown out the voices of moderation." "Such a tortured problem as racial conflict can only be solved," the broadcast editorialized, "through the patient insistence of moderates. Paradoxically they must be bold, even mili-tant, moderates in order to make themselves heard." The *New York Times* routinely portrayed Atlanta as "an island of moderation in a sea of militantly segregationist sentiment" and praised the city's peaceful desegregation as a "new and shining example of what can be accomplished if the people of good will and intelligence, white and Negro, will cooperate to obey the law." The United States Information Agency even filmed Atlanta's school deseg-regation for a documentary on the New South to counter Soviet propaganda about the violence of Little Rock and New Orleans. Only *Newsweek* had the bad manners to point out that, despite all the hoopla, Atlanta had not ac-complished anything more than Nashville and Charlotte had done four years earlier.[7]

At the local level, the 1961 mayoral election reaffirmed the ideology of racial moderation that had resolved the caste-based massive resistance crisis and brokered the class-based desegregation formula. After Mayor Hartsfield announced his retirement, the favored candidate of the downtown establish-ment became Ivan Allen, Jr., the wealthy businessman who had quietly supported HOPE and recently headed the Chamber of Commerce. Lester Maddox, the local restaurateur who led the segregationist group GUTS, once again took up the mantle of working-class opposition to Atlanta's corporate elite. Allen's platform revolved around "Forward Atlanta," the Chamber of Commerce agenda for metropolitan development, and he linked economic growth to harmonious race relations and peaceful school desegregation. Allen also deliberately turned the election into a referendum on the politics of social class by denouncing Maddox as a race-baiting extremist who represented "redneck" violence. Maddox responded by blaming racial integration on communism and miscegenation in a series of attacks on the socialist federal government, the "black bloc" control of City Hall, and the ultraliberal Atlanta news media. He also accused the affluent whites in HOPE and OASIS of forcing race-mixing on the rest of the city while they lived in islands of suburban privilege and sent their own children to private schools. After forcing a runoff, Maddox charged that his opponent, the "Peachtree Peacock," stood for "total integration" of schools and society and a NAACP-communist takeover of municipal government. This platform of reactionary populism secured a majority of the white electorate, as Maddox easily carried the blue-collar and lower-middle-class neighborhoods of southwest and southeast Atlanta. But Ivan Allen won the election with 64 percent of the vote, based on the traditional Hartsfield formula of strong turnout in black precincts and overwhelming support from the affluent island suburbs of northside Atlanta.[8]

The biracial coalition had elected a suitable successor to William Hartsfield's long-standing priorities of the economic development of the metropolis, aggressive marketing of Atlanta's progressive image, and cautious accommodation to racial change. A few days after the mayoral election, Atlanta quietly became the 104th city in the South to integrate its lunch counters, based on the negotiated settlement that the *Constitution* called "magnificent testimony to the reason and common sense that distinguishes both races in Atlanta." A year later, after a black physician tried to move into an all-white subdivision in southwest Atlanta, Mayor Allen authorized the construction of barricades and offered a solution that would maintain residential segregation by providing land elsewhere for middle-class black neighborhoods. Immediately dubbed the "Atlanta Wall," the Berlin-style blockade provoked angry civil rights demonstrations and became a public relations debacle, and the court-ordered removal of the barricade could not disguise the confirmation that the management of residential segregation remained central to the politics of racial moderation. While the Allen administration continued to follow the national model of spatial apartheid through urban renewal and suburban development, the mayor also took the lead in pressuring the business community to accept the desegregation of restaurants and hotels, after black students launched another wave of direct action protests. With almost no support from Atlanta's corporate leaders, Allen became one of the only elected officials in the South to testify in favor of the public accommodations section of the 1964 Civil Rights Act. The mayor later called this the moment when his personal racial ideology shifted from business pragmatism to genuine liberalism, but the deepest challenges facing the city's biracial coalition were structural in nature and still on the horizon, in the intertwined areas of public school desegregation, control of municipal politics, and the spatial fragmentation produced by suburban sprawl and urban containment.[9]

Events at the state level launched a new era in Georgia's political history, as the ascendancy of racial moderation demonstrated the ripple effects of the middle-class mobilization and metropolitan revolt of the open-schools movement. Georgia's notorious county unit system barely outlasted the Black Belt campaign to maintain the caste line in the public school system. In 1962, after the Supreme Court's reapportionment ruling in *Baker v. Carr*, Governor Vandiver summoned an emergency session of the legislature in an effort to modify but preserve the basic framework of the county unit system. The federal judiciary promptly invalidated the new scheme, which meant that the next gubernatorial election would be the first decided by popular vote in a half-century. The 1962 contest matched Carl Sanders, a young lawyer from Augusta who campaigned on a New South platform of economic growth and racial moderation, against former governor Marvin Griffin, the old-style politician from South Georgia whose well-established message of white supremacy and rural hegemony seemed misplaced after the sudden shift of electoral power to the metropolitan areas. Sanders embraced the label of racial moderation, which he said "means that I am a segregationist but not a damned fool," and his media-savvy operation revolved around future-oriented themes such as progressive reform in public education and a corporate vision of economic prosperity. In a sweeping victory, Sanders won every metropolitan region, dominated the middle-class suburbs, carried the counties of North Georgia, and received almost all African-American ballots—the same combination of class, race, and geography that underlay the open-schools movement. The 1962 election verified that the sequential events of massive resistance and electoral reapportionment had produced a metropolitan realignment of state politics, although the arrival of an authentic two-party system would soon unravel the cohesion of this triumphant moderate coalition.[10]

Georgia's open-schools movement quietly demobilized in the fall of 1961, its original mission accomplished with the implementation of peaceful desegregation in Atlanta. Despite previous promises to remain active in the long-term struggle over school integration, the OASIS coalition dissolved first with an agreement that "future groups should arise from the needs of the future." A few weeks later, HOPE's board of directors voted to close the central office but maintain an inactive status, "ready to go into action when and if we are ever needed." While the progressive cadre in HOPE remained profoundly disappointed at the token nature of school desegregation, the group's broader volunteer network consisted of upper-middle-class mothers who led busy lives and whose primary concerns revolved around the education of their own children. When the immediate threat to Atlanta's public schools disappeared, HOPE's self-imposed mandate did as well. "We felt that there were things that could be done," Muriel Lokey remembered, "but we were tired." Nan Pendergrast admitted that she was "almost ashamed to say" that most members of HOPE did not remain active in the school desegregation struggle, but "I think it was total exhaustion. I really think that we felt that we were powerless to do any more at the time." In a final mailing, Beverly Downing congratulated HOPE supporters on their role in saving public education and urged them to remain active in their communities as future tests of desegregation arose. Three years after the group obtained its charter, with its stated purposes accomplished, HOPE leaders returned to their children, their spouses, their garden clubs, their law firms, their churches, and their synagogues having shown how a grassroots movement by concerned citizens and energetic parents could dramatically reshape political debate and forever alter the history of their city and state.[11]

The end of Jim Crow liberated white southerners as well as black southerners, as native liberals such as Lillian Smith had long predicted, and paved the way for the expression of racial attitudes across the ideological spectrum. While white attitudes about caste and class were in a state of flux during the postwar era, bringing these tensions to the surface required the internal catalyst of the civil rights movement and the external trigger of federal intervention. Throughout the crisis of massive resistance, HOPE's pragmatic refusal to debate the issue of integration meant that its members did not have to wrestle publicly with the question they grappled with privately: whether they were pragmatic moderates who preferred segregation but cared more about public education, or whether they were liberal reformers who believed that segregation was wrong and that racial equality in education constituted a moral imperative. Although self-interest rather than egalitarianism or altruism motivated most moderate members of the "silent majority" in Georgia that eventually turned against massive resistance, participation in the open-schools movement became a transformative event for many of HOPE's liberal activists. "I do think that those of us that worked the hardest were very much concerned about the integration issue," Muriel Lokey recalled. But HOPE "was a tremendous personal growth experience for us, and when I look back . . . I realize how far we came. We believed things we were told." Many of HOPE's leading women participated in progressive politics during the subsequent decades, especially civil rights and poverty rights, but the open embrace of racial liberalism by individual veterans of the open-schools movement only highlighted the fragmentation of the broader moderate consensus in the northside suburbs. The parents in HOPE did not know that they were part of the last generation of affluent white Atlantans to support the city's public school system as a civic imperative and a democratic obligation.[12]

In their pragmatic revolt against massive resistance, the suburban activists in HOPE played a pivotal role in the turbulent path of school desegregation in the American South. Through an unprecedented populist uprising and skillful manipulation of media imagery and public discourse, HOPE seized the moral high ground by presenting itself as a group of white parents who cared only about the education of innocent children, and a group of upright citizens who cared only about the future of their city and their state. Through the singular focus on public education, the open-schools movement made compliance with court-ordered desegregation a respectable position and turned the segregationist willingness to sacrifice public education into a political liability. HOPE's public authority revolved around its claim to speak the truth: about the inevitability of compliance with the law, the self-defeating futility of defiance, the inadequacy of private education, and the economic costs of massive resistance. But the organization's persistent refusal to discuss either segregation or integration was simultaneously the source of its short-term success and long-term failure. Most white liberals and moderates in the open-schools movement did not tell the truth about the policies of pragmatic segregation that replaced massive resistance— pupil placement schemes allowing the transfer of "a few" black students, "freedom of choice" that existed only in affluent white neighborhoods— which represented bad-faith tactics that merely postponed an eventual reckoning. "I think all of us were disappointed at the way in which segregation had been killed, if it had been," Nan Pendergrast remarked three decades later. "There was such an air of desperation . . . that we were willing to settle for less than we probably should have settled for. . . . Had we been able to look down the road through the decades to see where we would be now, it would have broken our hearts."[13]

The triumph of the open-schools movement in Atlanta demonstrated the vitality but also the limitations of the politics of moderation during an era of polarization. White liberals had successfully mobilized the "uncommitted center," HOPE activist Florence Robin wrote in a 1962 essay in *Harper's Magazine*, but only through reliance on a pragmatic strategy that circumvented the moral imperative at the heart of the *Brown* decree. "We have kept the schools open by forcing token integration," observed Robin, who had joined HOPE through the auspices of the Southern Regional Council. "Will we now allow the politicians to use token integration as a new weapon to defy the 'deliberate speed' of the Supreme Court decision?" Across the South, three distinct strains of gradualism temporarily converged around the agenda of open schools during the late 1950s and early 1960s: the pragmatic efforts by white liberals who hoped that good-faith compliance would be the first step toward genuine integration; the self-interested actions of a white moderate majority that embraced minimal desegregation as necessary to keep public schools open; and the belated recognition by diehard segregationists that tokenism represented the best legal method to maintain the ethos if not the policy of massive resistance. Although "token integration" eventually became identified with the forces of racial conservatism and white supremacy, historical verdicts of the southern accommodation to the *Brown* decision must recognize that dedicated liberals and energetic moderates initially championed and ultimately legitimated the path of gradualism and minimalism. The new desegregation formula that permitted individual exceptions to the dual school system represented a metropolitan blueprint designed to accommodate the class prejudices and residential privileges of the white-collar neighborhoods of the metropolitan South.[14]

"A Negative Peace"

As recurring rather than continuous features of the American political landscape, grassroots movements of the center emerge most often as populist responses to external threats and neighborhood defenses of local autonomy, not as active agents of social change or as progressive challenges to the status quo. In the precarious and ultimately successful campaign to revitalize the middle ground, the white activists in HOPE and OASIS became prominent exceptions to Martin Luther King, Jr.'s devastating indictment of the "appalling silence of the good people" during the era of massive resistance. But the open-schools movement in Atlanta remained vulnerable to the trenchant critique of the "Letter from a Birmingham Jail," which represented a philosophical appeal and an ethical rebuke to white moderates everywhere, from the political and business leadership of the New South to the president and the policymakers in Washington to the spectators throughout the country following the civil rights movement on their television sets and in their daily newspapers. "I have almost reached the regrettable conclusion," King wrote in 1963, "that the Negro's great stumbling block in the stride toward freedom is not the White Citizens' Councilor or the Ku Klux Klanner but the white moderate, who is more devoted to 'order' than to justice, who prefers a negative peace which is the absence of tension to a positive peace which is the presence of justice." Atlanta's open-schools movement never countered the segregationist crusade to preserve southern tradition with an alternative argument about the responsibility to atone for the injustices of the past, but instead with a color-blind vision of a prosperous future liberated entirely from the burdens of southern history. HOPE became a grassroots force in order to depoliticize the schools permanently, but the inherent inability of the politics of moderation to address squarely the historical legacies of racial inequality and the spatial patterns of residential segregation instead guaranteed the repoliticization of public education in Atlanta and the rest of the South for a long time to come.[15]

After the end of the massive resistance crisis, many of HOPE's leaders remained active in the Greater Atlanta Council on Human Relations, an interracial affiliate of the SRC that supported educational equality and meaningful integration. The moderate gospel of law and order would soon prove to be inadequate, Rabbi Jacob Rothschild of the GACHR declared during the 1961 celebration of Atlanta Exceptionalism. "Little has been said about the basic issues of human dignity and decency. We're going to have to come to grips with the problem on this basis." A few months later, the GACHR issued a press release insisting that while "Atlanta has been congratulating itself on its peaceful handling of school desegregation . . . token desegregation is creating problems we must face." The group deplored the policy of starting the transition with the oldest instead of the youngest students and demanded that the school system make a genuine commitment to integration so that "children can be brought up respecting the principles of equality and brotherhood because they see them practiced." The GACHR also called on the school administration to jettison the pupil placement plan in favor of an approach that did not apply different standards of admission to white and black students who attended the same school. In their efforts to overturn the desegregation formula of tokenism and gradualism, the several hundred white liberals involved with the GACHR rejected the politics of racial moderation at the heart of Atlanta Exceptionalism and forged open alliances with black leaders such as the Reverend Samuel Williams, an Atlanta University professor and pastor of the Friendship Baptist Church. "The whites are patting themselves on the back because nine of the city's fifty thousand Negro children are going to integrated schools without any violence," Williams told *Newsweek* in 1961. "I've never met such civic arrogance in my life."[16]

Georgia's new policy of local option meant that the city of Atlanta, the self-proclaimed epicenter of enlightened moderation in the New South, bore the full responsibility for the pace and the degree of compliance with the *Brown* mandate. During the first decade of desegregation, corporate executives dominated the Atlanta Board of Education, which included one black member and only one white liberal, an LWV activist elected during the open-schools surge of 1961. The school administration adopted a desegregation approach that openly maintained the dual school system while restricting the formal exercise of freedom of choice to a small number of highly qualified black students and occasional groups of temporarily displaced white students. In a move celebrated as evidence of moderation, Atlanta officials immediately confronted the Vandiver administration over the "freedom of association" guarantee of state-funded segregated schooling. The board denied all applications for tuition grants, and the legislature soon discontinued the program because most recipients statewide already attended private schools before desegregation. During the summer of 1961, Superintendent John Letson also announced that because of residential transition in southeast Atlanta, a white elementary school would be converted into a black institution and almost three hundred current students would be allowed to transfer to the public school of their choice. Officials defended this stark evidence that schools remained officially designated by race as a pragmatic policy designed to keep white families committed to public education and a progressive remedy for the systematic overcrowding of black facilities.[17]

The Atlanta desegregation formula did not represent a simple policy of delay through gradualism and tokenism, but instead a sophisticated combination of socioeconomic and geographic barriers designed to accommodate the class prejudices of the northside and to manage the racial anxieties of the southside. Under the tolerant supervision of Judge Hooper, who repeatedly denied NAACP challenges to Atlanta's freedom of choice scheme, the board approved 44 black applicants for the second year of desegregation and 143 transfers during 1963–64. In Atlanta's northside neighborhoods, where limited school desegregation coexisted with unlimited residential security, the initial transfer students boasted higher test scores than the average of their white classmates, and the school board carefully publicized the collegiate aspirations of the chosen few. A spokesperson for the NAACP, referring to the battery of aptitude tests and other roadblocks in the pupil placement plan, observed that "we've got a saying around here that it's easier to go to Yale than to transfer from one public school to another in Atlanta." For affluent white families in the island suburbs, "freedom of choice" resonated as an ideological synthesis of the desegregation policy that permitted high-achieving black students to break the caste line, combined with the middle-class philosophy of consumer rights that guaranteed neighborhood schools protected by residential segregation. In the unstable areas of southeast and southwest Atlanta, where thousands of white and black families lived in close proximity, the school board subverted the principle of neighborhood schools and assigned most black students to overcrowded and racially isolated institutions even when nearby white schools were below capacity in enrollment. In the breach, the district continued to flip the racial identity of schools located in transitional neighborhoods, a formal resegregation strategy that reflected the traditional moderate agenda of interracial harmony through peaceful transition.[18]

The fusion of socioeconomic and spatial discrimination at the heart of the

Atlanta approach doomed any prospect of achieving lasting integration of the public school system. While a comprehensive desegregation program distributed evenly throughout the city might at least have slowed the process of residential turnover, Atlanta officials instead made protecting the island suburbs of the northside the overriding priority through policies that repeatedly sacrificed the stability of the southside neighborhoods. The racial composition of the Atlanta school district changed dramatically during the 1960s, from a two-thirds white majority to a two-thirds black enrollment. School desegregation did not cause the massive white flight from southeast and southwest Atlanta, a residential process underway long before the city ever contemplated a substantive integration plan, but the geographic discrimination by education officials and the laissez-faire attitude of the district court certainly exacerbated an already explosive situation. In the late 1960s, after the Supreme Court invalidated freedom of choice and required the disestablishment of dual school systems, the Atlanta board finally implemented a policy that approximated neighborhood schools and then denied any further responsibility for "de facto" segregation driven by housing patterns. The new plan included substantial integration in southside Atlanta but almost completely exempted the northside from additional burdens. Demonstrations and boycotts broke out in working-class white neighborhoods, and dozens of schools in residentially transitional areas underwent the process of tipping from temporary desegregation to permanent resegregation. Liberal emissaries who asked the Atlanta Chamber of Commerce to help resolve the crisis instead met a hostile reaction, and a national media swayed by the mythology of the massive resistance era expressed unwarranted shock at the "desertion of leadership" by the businessmen from Buckhead.[19]

During the early 1970s, black and white liberals mounted two ultimately unsuccessful efforts to implement comprehensive school integration through the busing of city students and through a metropolitan consolidation plan that included the Atlanta suburbs. Even after the Supreme Court approved crosstown busing as a remedy for urban school systems, the federal judges supervising the Atlanta litigation continued to make the fear of accelerating white flight the benchmark of the city's constitutional obligations. "Atlanta now stands on the brink of becoming an all-black city," one judicial panel wrote in a 1971 ruling that granted the school district immunity from historical patterns of allegedly de facto residential segregation. "The problem is no longer how to achieve integration, but how to prevent resegregation." The legal climate remained unsettled after the Fifth Circuit Court of Appeals rejected the finding that Atlanta had eliminated all vestiges of de jure segregation and ordered the district court to reconsider its refusal to order busing out of deference to the specter of white flight. The NAACP submitted a proposal, supported by the League of Women Voters and the

Southern Regional Council, that involved the transportation of thirty thousand students and would guarantee a slight black majority at every school in the city. Black parents represented by the Georgia branch of the American Civil Liberties Union initiated separate litigation to consolidate city schools with the suburban districts in the five-county metropolitan region.[20]

The prospect of two-way busing between the southside and the island suburbs of Buckhead deeply alarmed white families and business leaders in northside Atlanta, and the threat of a metropolitan desegregation plan produced extreme hostility from the overwhelmingly white counties beyond the city limits. In this volatile climate, the white business elite initiated secret talks with local black leaders, including NAACP branch president Lonnie King, held at the downtown headquarters of the Trust Company Bank. The biracial negotiations began at the suggestion of Griffin Bell, the former Vandiver aide who lived in Buckhead and now served as a Fifth Circuit judge, and the federal courts approved the settlement produced through Atlanta's conventional method of conflict resolution. The 1973 agreement involved one-way busing of black students to ensure that all city schools contained a 30 percent minority enrollment but left untouched more than half of the district's facilities where the black population exceeded 90 percent. The African-American community also received administrative control of the school system, including the position of superintendent. The local newspapers and the Atlanta Chamber of Commerce ritually celebrated the settlement as another milestone in the city's biracial tradition of negotiated progress, but this time the hollow discourse of Atlanta Exceptionalism could not conceal the metropolitan chasms of race and class that mocked any pretense of "separate but equal" education. The city of the future had moved forward to the past.[21]

The busing deal became known as the "Atlanta Compromise," with all of the historical baggage conveyed by the allusion to Booker T. Washington's famous speech at the dawn of the Jim Crow era. The national NAACP accused Atlanta's black leadership of trading the dream of integration for a separate and unequal school system. White liberals from the SRC denounced the compromise for sacrificing the futures of poor black children for a resolution designed to stabilize the business climate and cater to the affluent families of both races. For local black leaders who were veterans of the freedom struggle, the settlement demonstrated a profound resignation about the possibility of meaningful school integration in the "City Too Busy to Hate" and a growing belief that African-American communities had to take control of the educational destinies of their own children. "What is desegregation in places like Atlanta," asked the scholar and civil rights activist Vincent Harding, "where white parents have effectively abandoned the public schools of the central city?" In a published response to liberal critics of the Atlanta Compromise, Harding declared that busing would remain a "fool's errand" as long as public schools remained under the control of white officials who "are not committed to a truly pluralistic, open and human vision of America." Black students would "continue to be victims so long as they must depend on white 'leaders' to send them on fantasy-like trips to fashionable white suburbs for their education."[22]

The Atlanta Compromise confirmed the surrender of the white and black leadership to the extreme spatial fragmentation that dominated the metropolitan landscape, the permanent hypersegregation of poor black families in the urban ghetto, and the collapse of the middle-class consensus for quality public education in the central city. By 1980, the failure to secure an egalitarian or a metropolitan remedy had left Atlanta's public schools with a 92 percent minority enrollment, a fleeing black middle class, and a lower percentage of white students than any other major city in the region. No amount of brand marketing could erase the hard truth: in the headquarters of the Sunbelt South, the spatial politics of racial moderation and class privilege had produced a school system even more segregated than the notorious Rust Belt cities of Newark and Detroit.[23]

"FORWARD ATLANTA"

The Atlanta Compromise of 1973 reflected the permanent cold war that existed between the central city and its autonomous suburbs—a direct consequence of the extraordinary growth of the metropolitan region throughout the postwar Sunbelt boom. During the 1960s, the business and political leaders in the downtown-Buckhead alliance largely succeeded in the public relations campaign to transform the capital of the New South into an undisputed national metropolis. In his first mayoral election, Ivan Allen praised the enlightened civic leadership that forged the consensus behind Forward Atlanta: a public-private partnership, secured by a multimillion-dollar marketing commitment, to attract investment capital and leverage federal funding for "new industry, new offices, and new jobs." The regional growth agenda of the corporate establishment combined suburban development and downtown redevelopment into five priorities: expressway construction, urban renewal, a municipal auditorium and a professional sports stadium, a mass transit network linking the metropolis, and a quality system of public education. By the end of the decade, an elaborate system of interstate highways connected suburban commuters to the central business district, the multiplying office parks and shopping malls, and the third-busiest airport in the nation. Federally subsidized construction projects transformed downtown Atlanta into a built environment of corporate skyscrapers, high-rise hotels, convention centers, and entertainment complexes. Atlanta achieved the cov-

Figure 4.2. Downtown Atlanta in the late 1960s, viewed from the south, with the new Atlanta Stadium in the foreground and the leafy neighborhoods of Buckhead on the distant horizon. The professional sports complex formed the centerpiece of the Forward Atlanta agenda championed by Mayor Ivan Allen, Jr. In his memoir, Allen called the stadium "the final indication to us that we had made it to the top" as a national city. The construction of the stadium, combined with the junction of the three expressways that meet in downtown Atlanta, displaced thousands of primarily poor and black residents and devastated several intown neighborhoods. Courtesy of the Edmund Hughs Collection, Kenan Research Center at the Atlanta History Center.

eted status of "major-league city" in 1965–66 when two of the South's first professional sports teams began playing in the new stadium (figure 4.2). Following the Sunbelt model, Atlanta's leaders seduced the Braves baseball franchise away from Milwaukee and secured the Falcons as an expansion team only after failing to steal professional football from other Rust Belt cities. The city soon lured the Hawks basketball team away from St. Louis and even brought professional ice hockey to the Southeast.[24]

The climactic decade of Atlanta Exceptionalism exposed the failure of imagination in the corporate vision of the city as the vibrant center of a spatially segregated but functionally integrated metropolitan region. In 1961, a *Fortune* profile of the Atlanta "power structure" portrayed several dozen middle-aged white men at a Chamber of Commerce briefing on the proposed downtown stadium, with department store magnate Richard Rich smoking his pipe in the front row. (A sidebar featured their counterparts in the black community, thirteen wealthy men from the banking, real estate, and finance industries.) The article explained that while relaxing by their Buckhead swimming pools or golfing at their exclusive country clubs, the white elite worried that the politics of racial moderation had become "caught between the younger generation of Negroes and the new red-neck community" but found comfort that deliverance would be assured through the rapid development of the metropolitan landscape. Instead the very success of suburban roads and urban redevelopment, the central priorities of Forward Atlanta, accelerated the centrifugal forces that produced the politics of metropolitan fragmentation and shattered the secondary goals of mass transit and quality urban schools. When Mayor Allen left office in 1969, he admitted that the "race problem" remained unresolved but proudly declared victory in the quest to remake Atlanta into a "national city . . . known for gleaming skyscrapers, expressways, the Atlanta Braves, and—the price you have to pay—traffic jams."[25]

The downtown establishment aggressively promoted and actively facilitated the infrastructure of the metropolitan boom, while redesigning the central business district as a safe environment and simulated urban experience for convention visitors and suburban tourists. Atlanta's powerful banks, led by Trust Company and C&S, financed the suburban office parks and middle-class subdivisions for the 1.25 million migrants who settled in the metropolitan region between 1950 and 1980, including about 70,000 refugees from residential transition inside the city limits. Rich's Department Store anchored each suburban shopping mall located by the major interstate junctions and marketed as cultural reproductions of an urban utopia—"the ultimate in shopping convenience . . . cascading fountains [and] sidewalk cafes . . . in an atmosphere of perpetual Springtime." John Portman's massive Peachtree Center became the national architectural prototype for fortifying the central business district through vertical islands of commerce and consumption. The urban renewal of the 1960s also "theme-parked" downtown with luxurious centers for the arts and venues for sports contests and rock concerts, while displacing at least 75,000 residents—primarily poor and black—through federally subsidized slum clearance programs. Presented as suburban salvation for the central city, Forward Atlanta instead intensified metropolitan patterns of residential segregation and political fragmentation, which galvanized a multifaceted grassroots revolt against the Sunbelt Synthesis of the downtown elite.[26]

The regionalist vision of the downtown establishment required the routine annexation of the affluent and almost exclusively white suburbs located north of the city limits. As residential transition on the southside foreshadowed a majority-black city population and African-American control of municipal politics, the corporate leadership attempted to replicate the 1952 incorporation of Buckhead by capturing the white voters and middle-class taxpayers who lived in the northern arc. But this time suburban homeowners fought back, with the turning point coming in the 1966 campaign to annex the upper-middle-class suburb of Sandy Springs, located just north of Buckhead in an unincorporated section of Fulton County. The Atlanta Chamber of Commerce created the Team for Tomorrow to lead the annexation drive, and the *Atlanta Constitution* relentlessly promoted the initiative. Former mayor William Hartsfield traveled the Sandy Springs civic circuit to argue that the addition of "good white citizens" would make Atlanta stronger, but "unless a city can expand, it will die." The grassroots opposition formed a homeowners movement called Save Sandy Springs that attacked annexation as a scheme to subsidize inefficient urban services with suburban property taxes and accused city leaders of a stealth agenda to force "educated, responsible . . . white citizens" into Atlanta's "melting pot [of] . . . the lowest, least educated, and most irresponsible." The decisive rejection of annexation by two-thirds of Sandy Springs voters revealed the rising view in the white suburbs that the city of Atlanta now represented a dangerous threat. In the late 1960s, when the Allen administration advocated the consolidation of the city government with Fulton County, black leaders denounced the merger as a scheme to dilute African-American political power, and the Chamber of Commerce recognized that another campaign for suburban ratification would be quixotic.[27]

The failed campaigns to annex the suburbs of the northside and the parallel racial conversion of the neighborhoods on the southside produced an urban demographic that ruptured the biracial alliance that controlled city politics throughout the postwar era. In the 1969 mayoral election, the candidate of the business establishment lost to Sam Massell, a Jewish realtor from Buckhead who clearly represented a transitional figure in a city divided almost equally between the white and black population. Massell tried to resurrect annexation with the Program for Progress, a plan to incorporate fifty thousand white suburbanites in northern Fulton County. The mayor framed the proposal as a progressive solution that would stabilize the desegregation climate in the public schools and multiply the residential and commercial tax base, a bold vision that demanded the support of "reasonable whites and blacks." He insisted that the fundamental issue was not racial but economic—not white fear of a majority-black city but interracial insurance against an "all-poor city," the only way to avoid the Rust Belt fate of Cleveland, Newark, and Detroit (three cities with new black mayors). While the corporate establishment endorsed the Program for Progress, African-American leaders denounced annexation and joined hostile white suburbanites in dismissing the claim that urban viability demanded regional cooperation rather than metropolitan divergence. In his reelection campaign, Massell responded with the racially charged slogan "Atlanta's Too Young To Die," but challenger Maynard Jackson won with overwhelming support in black precincts and about one-fifth of the white vote. In 1973, when the election of Atlanta's first black mayor closely followed the busing compromise, the African-American community gained formal control of the public school system and the municipal politics of a majority-black city surrounded by overwhelmingly white suburbs.[28]

The biracial politics of spatial fragmentation prevented the city of Atlanta from building almost any tangible connections, except for new highways and wider roads, to the autonomous suburban counties in the booming metropolitan region. The drive for a system of mass transit, which in a better world should have united a sprawling landscape of suburban commuters and urban job seekers, instead became embroiled in the spatial politics of race and class, taxation and mutual distrust. In 1968, the Allen administration mobilized business leaders behind a referendum to establish MARTA (Metropolitan Atlanta Rapid Transit Authority), a network of buses, subways, and light rail. The first MARTA referendum failed to win the approval of black voters who protested limited access in urban neighborhoods and also met defeat in suburban counties where opposition to the property tax funding mechanism prevailed. In 1971, a broad coalition of civic and environmental groups endorsed a revised mass transit proposal that promised affirmative action in MARTA employment and funding through a sales tax. Opponents predicted that rapid transit would raise property taxes anyway and warned of a MARTA conspiracy to bus black students and force public housing into the suburbs. The second referendum carried the urban precincts and the inner-ring suburban counties of Fulton and DeKalb, while voters in the outer-ring counties of Gwinnett and Clayton rejected MARTA by a four-to-one ratio. Mass transit did not even reach the proposal stage in the conservative stronghold of Cobb County, a booming Cold War suburb that wanted nothing to do with the city on the other side of the Chattahoochee River. The persistent refusal of the high-growth counties of the northern arc to participate in metropolitan ventures such as MARTA turned the Greater Atlanta region into a notorious example of the "spatial mismatch" between outer-ring job creation and inner-city unemployment and the primary rival of Los Angeles for the dubious honor of national pacesetter for unrestrained suburban sprawl.[29]

By the 1970s, the explosive metropolitan growth and celebrated downtown redevelopment that sustained the national mythology of Atlanta Exceptionalism had also produced the debilitating politics of spatial segregation and the pronounced quality-of-life crises that jeopardized the civic religion and booster ethos at the center of the city's historical consciousness. The brand marketing of Atlanta still resonated in a nation battered by a newly rediscovered "urban crisis" stretching from coast to coast: in 1971, after *Time* published a glowing cover story predicting that Atlanta and the rest of the New South might "show the U.S. the way to a truly integrated society," several nonsouthern respondents called Atlanta the "most progressive

city" in the nation, nothing less than "*the* city of the future." Less in disagreement than in resignation, a native southerner replied that the "thing
that worries some people now is not race but that the South could become
like the North." Another dismayed resident lamented that the city's progress
"cannot be celebrated by us all. The 25% native population of Atlanta cannot take any pride in the polluted air that increasingly blankets the city's
soaring buildings, in the clogged freeways for which there is no visible relief,
and in the growing transient population that causes more problems than it
cares about solving."[30]

Four years later, in the wake of the Atlanta Compromise and the collapse
of the corporate-dominated biracial alliance, even the resilient boosters at
the *Atlanta Constitution* veered sharply off script with a shrill and despon-
dent series that declared Atlanta to be "A City in Crisis." Soliciting the views
of thirty business and political leaders, the newspaper chronicled the profound distrust between a traditional white establishment that retained economic power and a new black establishment that had assumed political com-
mand. "Throughout the Sixties, Atlanta was Camelot," the *Constitution*
claimed, "spared serious racial turmoil and blessed with experienced leadership." But now Robert Woodruff was an octogenarian, Ralph McGill was
dead, and Ivan Allen and Richard Rich had withdrawn from civic affairs.
Now Mills Lane of C&S declared that the downtown banks would not fund
ventures by the black administration, and architect John Portman despaired
that residential and business flight was killing the city. Now crime was soaring, unemployment and welfare rates were escalating, metropolitan remedies appeared politically impossible, and even the most committed white
liberals were removing their children from the public schools. "What's happening to Atlanta?" the *Constitution* asked. "Will the dream survive?"[31]

"A City without Limits"

The resurrection of Atlanta Exceptionalism came through a refashioned
metropolitan consensus organized around the biracial politics of class privilege and the interracial boosterism of an internationalization project that
crested with the 1996 Summer Olympics. The logical response to "A City in
Crisis," at least at the Atlanta Chamber of Commerce, became the subordination of racial conflict and the assimilation of suburban sprawl into a new
marketing campaign to (re)create "A City without Limits." Viewed from a
historical perspective, the coexistence of the discourse of urban crisis with
the postmodern mythology of an infinite frontier represented just the latest
version of the traditional politics of moderation, less a paradox than a synthesis of the inequitable distribution of resources and rewards that has always propelled Atlanta's growth ideology. The transformation of Atlanta into

the "World's Next Great International City," the parallel corporate mission that emerged from the depths of the 1970s, allied white business leaders and black political leaders in a pragmatic rapprochement and contemporary reincarnation of the "City Too Busy to Hate."[32]

The 1980 opening of Atlanta's Hartsfield International Airport, an appropriate tribute to the modern-day prophet of the New South, announced the global debut of a metropolis where the CNN media empire and the Georgia World Congress Center soon flanked the high-rise institutions of multinational capital and the civic anchor of the Coca-Cola Company, the most visible brand on earth. The decade also included a celebrated wave of African-American suburbanization that reestablished the metropolis as America's "Black Mecca," eventually turned DeKalb into a majority-black (although still racially stratified) suburban county, and even brought more than 100,000 black residents into the outer-ring areas of the historically white northern arc by century's end (map 4.1). The improbable and audacious campaign that lured the Olympic Games to the American South revolved around the "synergy" between a globalist ethos of public-private capitalism and a consensus narrative of interracial prosperity, symbolized by the joint leadership of Billy Payne and Andrew Young, the white real estate lawyer from the north Atlanta suburbs alongside the civil rights veteran and former mayor of the New South showcase. In 1996, when the city of the future staged its triumphant international spectacle, the many critics who mocked Atlanta's shameless self-promotion or debunked its sanitized history of racial harmony spoke the truth but missed the point.[33]

The ideology of Atlanta Exceptionalism has always depended upon the collective imagination of the city as the enlightened oasis of the distinctive South and the bellwether metropolis of the Newest South—a dynamic place that embraced the ideals of national citizenship and the culture of market capitalism in order to transcend history itself, through the fusion of racial moderation and economic prosperity at the heart of the Sunbelt Synthesis. The resilience of Atlanta Exceptionalism lies in the futuristic amalgamation of pieces from across the American landscape: the Sunbelt growth ideology of Houston and Los Angeles, the Rust Belt poverty of Detroit and Newark, the elitist enclaves of Manhattan and Grosse Pointe, the consumer ethos of suburban privilege that extends from the subdivisions of Orange County to the townships of New Jersey and Connecticut. Because the architects of Atlanta Exceptionalism always aspired to transform the metropolis into a subset of American Exceptionalism, the ritual exposure of the ways that Atlanta is not after all the "City Too Busy to Hate" dissolves into just another version of the booster discourse, yet another opportunity for the Sunbelt headquarters to claim validation as the New York of the South or the Los Angeles of the East.

The politics of racial moderation in postwar Atlanta always sought peace

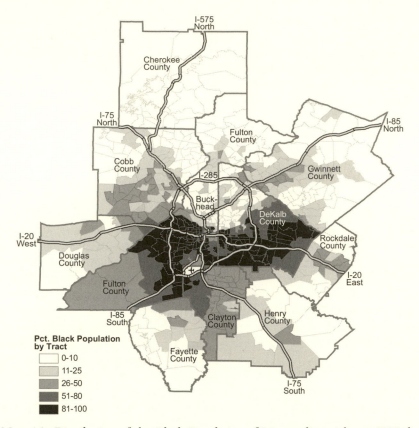

Map 4.1. Distribution of the Black Population of Metropolitan Atlanta, 2000, by Census Tract. While the black neighborhoods of westside Atlanta and the white island suburbs of Buckhead have maintained historical characteristics, the surrounding metropolis changed dramatically during the final decades of the 20th Century. The 2000 Census revealed that more than two-thirds of the black residents of metropolitan Atlanta lived in the suburbs, including the emergence of a majority-black population in DeKalb County. Residential segregation by race and class remains a prominent feature of the ten-county metropolitan region, which experienced one of the nation's fastest rates of growth during the 1980s and 1990s. *Source:* U.S. Census Bureau, 2000 Census of Population and Housing.

and progress, never justice or equality, through the conscious replication and then the triumphant enhancement of national patterns of metropolitan development and spatial segregation. While structural patterns of racial inequality provide the most visible manifestation of the lingering past in the latest New South, the mapping of the future in Atlanta remains firmly grounded in the spatial and national politics of class privilege and market capitalism. The most revealing moment of the 1996 Olympic Games was not the panoramic tribute to white city-builders that placed Reverend King in the forefront, or the animated "Whatizit" mascot ridiculed as a metaphor for Atlanta's amorphous and fabricated identity, or the bombing of the Centennial Olympic Park by a disgruntled Florida transplant from the mountains of Appalachia, or even the plastering of the Coca-Cola© logo on everything in sight. The essential chapter in the Atlanta Story happened long before the suburban spectators and international tourists arrived, when black and white leaders collaborated in the construction of the Olympic Ring right on top of fifty thousand poor and primarily African-American residents of the central city and then erased all traces of history from a spatial landscape rededicated to corporate capitalism and consumer freedom of choice.[34]

From the vantage point of Atlanta's island suburbs, a mixture of the sanguine and the sang-froid greets a remarkable half-century of transformation in the heart of the Sunbelt South. The 2000 census revealed that only one-third of Buckhead residents were natives of Georgia, which is emblematic of a metropolitan landscape where half of the 4.1 million residents were born outside the South, including hundreds of thousands of corporate transplants and Republican partisans who have migrated to the sprawling outer-ring suburbs. While luxurious gated communities and starter-home subdivisions multiply on the exurban fringe, the most prestigious addresses in metropolitan Atlanta remain the tree-lined neighborhoods of Buckhead, which the homeowners associations and business groups now call "a suburban downtown," "the Beverly Hills of the East," "the Georgetown of Atlanta," "a vibrant residential-commercial mix with the 24-hour flavor of San Francisco, New York, and Boston." Anchoring a city organized around public accommodation of private consumerism, an antihistory landscape where Lenox Square Mall is the most popular tourist destination, Buckhead boasts average home values approaching $500,000 and the exclusive restaurants and boutique chain stores that instantly evoke the geography of anywhere in America's upscale suburbs.[35]

Buckhead's graceful residential core remains an oasis of stability, with a scattering of wealthy black families now interspersed among the mansions and wooded lots. The shopping centers and nightlife districts of northside Atlanta have become substantially integrated, and new high-rise condominium towers and high-density apartment complexes have drawn a generation of younger professionals back into the (edge) city. Most children from Buckhead attend elite preparatory schools with sprawling campuses, and the former Northside High, first desegregated during the booster celebration of 1961, has been transformed into a public magnet school that contains one of the only racially diverse enrollments in the hypersegregated city system: 68 percent black, 21 percent white, 5 percent Asian and Hispanic. Although a dedicated group of white families remains committed to public education, even many white liberals openly justify the choice of private education through a color-blind vocabulary of class privilege or civic resignation, explaining that the Atlanta school system caters to students "from the lower socioeconomic status" who are not "bright and motivated."[36]

The strange career of Atlanta Exceptionalism demonstrates the centrality of the spatial landscape and the power of class ideology in shaping the fate of racial equality in the Sunbelt South. During the era of desegregation and resegregation that began with the moderate consensus brokered by the middle-class parents from the island suburbs, few citizens of Atlanta ever engaged in a genuine discussion about what integrated education in an egalitarian society might actually look like, and most families never proved willing or able to communicate honestly across the residential divides of race and class. For the liberal white activists from HOPE, who once defended public education as the foundation of equal opportunity and democratic ideals, or for the civil rights activists from the NAACP, who initiated the legal struggle for racial integration and social justice, the separate and transparently unequal school system in contemporary Atlanta might represent a tragic defeat or an unanticipated consequence of the desegregation process, but it does not represent a return to the days of Jim Crow. Today the Atlanta school district features a historically unprecedented concentration of poor minority students in the central city, a modern fusion of racial and class hypersegregation routinely overshadowed by the multiracial enrollment of almost all middle-class families in suburban public schools or selective private institutions. And while the debilitating patterns of spatial fragmentation throughout metropolitan Atlanta continue to reflect the long history of racial and class inequality, they do not represent a simple product of white flight from the central city, but instead a suburban synthesis of the gospel of growth and the ethos of individualism at the heart of the middle-class American Dream.

But the fate of the *Brown* decision in Atlanta did not provide the only path available in the Sunbelt South. Four hours north on the highway, in another booming metropolis that trumpeted its own exceptionalist mythology of interracial harmony and New South progress, the black and white citizens of Charlotte were engaged in a remarkable debate about not only racial equality but also class privilege. The lengthy showdown over court-ordered busing in Charlotte triggered a powerful revolt of the center, a grassroots uprising by a so-called Silent Majority based in the sprawling suburbs, driven by a color-blind ideology of middle-class innocence that echoed across the nation. But instead of the model of metropolitan divergence forged in Atlanta, a very different convergence of spatial and legal forces in Charlotte forced an entire community to grapple with the collective burdens of history in the Sunbelt South and ultimately produced one of the most integrated urban public school systems in the United States.

PART II

The Revolt of the Center

CHAPTER 5

The "Charlotte Way"

> I lived here twenty-four years without knowing what was going on.
> I really didn't know.
> —District Judge James B. McMillan (1971)

DURING THE WINTER of 1970, President Richard Nixon received a letter of protest and despair from Dr. Robert M. Diggs, a public school parent who lived in an upper-middle-class suburb of Charlotte, North Carolina. Two years earlier, Nixon had overwhelmingly carried the suburban Charlotte vote, and Diggs introduced himself as a "concerned member of the silent majority which has possibly remained silent too long." His decision to speak out followed a court-ordered desegregation plan that mandated busing throughout the countywide school system of Charlotte-Mecklenburg, including the two-way exchange of students from the black neighborhoods of the central city and the white subdivisions on the suburban fringe. How could it be possible in America, the physician wondered, for a federal judge to punish affluent communities simply because their residents worked hard in order to purchase a home in a respectable neighborhood and rear their children in a safe environment? Without neighborhood schools, Diggs warned, the educational and moral standards of the middle class would rapidly deteriorate, and it seemed only reasonable that citizens showing "initiative and ambition should not be penalized for possessing these qualities." In closing, the white father from an all-white subdivision pledged that his opposition to busing had "nothing to do with race or integration." This middle-class-conscious, scrupulously color-blind rhetoric mirrored the official stance of the Concerned Parents Association (CPA), the powerful antibusing organization supported by tens of thousands of white families who lived in the booming Sunbelt metropolis. In response to the NAACP's pursuit of comprehensive integration, the CPA launched a suburban resistance movement that polarized a city regarded as one of the most progressive bastions of the New South and played a leading role in the grassroots mobilization of the Silent Majority in national politics.[1]

A portion of part II was previously published in Matthew D. Lassiter, "The Suburban Origins of 'Color-Blind' Conservatism: Middle-Class Consciousness in the Charlotte Busing Crisis," *Journal of Urban History* (May 2004), 549–82. Reprinted with permission of Sage Publications.

The crucible of racial busing produced a populist revolt of the center across the metropolitan South, as white-collar families became the architects of a color-blind discourse that gained national traction as an unapologetic defense of the class privileges and consumer rights of the middle-class suburbs. In response to the civil rights movement's unprecedented assault on the structures of residential segregation that underpinned the Sunbelt politics of racial moderation, the suburban parents who joined the antibusing movement charted their own middle path between the caste framework of white supremacy and the egalitarian agenda of redistributive liberalism. A decade after the triumph of moderation over massive resistance, when the open-schools movement formulated the outlines of a class-based desegregation formula in the metropolitan South, the backlash against court-ordered busing fractured the regional consensus for quality public education and rippled upward into national politics. The leaders and foot soldiers of this energized Silent Majority included not only ideological conservatives but also many political moderates and suburban swing voters, and white-collar married couples dominated the ad hoc organizations formed at the grassroots level—physicians, dentists, insurance agents, attorneys, small business owners, middle managers, and their spouses. Many of these middle-class families already voted Republican before the arrival of busing, following the suburban trends in the postwar South, but their primary political identities turned out to be less partisan than localist: a populist mobilization of homeowners, taxpayers, and especially schoolparents. The Concerned Parents Association in Charlotte both fashioned and reflected the innovative brand of neighborhood politics spreading throughout suburban America, a movement of middle-class consciousness based in subdivision homeowners associations, shopping malls, church congregations, PTA branches, and voting booths.

As the initial testing ground for a metropolitan busing plan, Charlotte's experience represents a national as much as a southern story. First in the Sunbelt South, and then across the United States, the showdowns over court-ordered busing transcended the traditional struggle over Jim Crow to grapple with a New American Dilemma: the spatial fusion of class and racial inequality created by metropolitan structures of residential segregation. Black and white liberals in Charlotte declared that busing constituted the next stage in the fulfillment of *Brown*, the only possibility for meaningful school integration on the metropolitan landscape. The suburban parents in the antibusing movement insisted that racial patterns in Charlotte corresponded to the de facto segregation of northern cities and not the de jure segregation of the Jim Crow South. The CPA recast a legal debate over the historical burdens of racial discrimination as an ahistorical defense of meritocratic individualism by refusing even to acknowledge the public policies that created and reinforced stark patterns of residential segregation. This novel appropriation of color-blind ideology shaped an identity politics of suburban innocence that defined "freedom of choice" and "neighborhood schools" as the core elements of homeowner rights and consumer liberties, rejecting as reverse discrimination any policy designed to provide substantive integration remedies for systematic inequality of opportunity.

The trajectory of the busing crisis in Charlotte diverged from the broader national trends of metropolitan fragmentation because a fortuitous combination of spatial and legal factors forced the entire community to grapple with not only racial integration but also class discrimination. Since the consolidated public school system in Charlotte included the surrounding county of Mecklenburg, the metropolitan remedy of two-way busing meant that white flight to the outer-ring suburbs could not destroy the integration formula and that affluent neighborhoods did not escape the burdens of social change as did most of their counterparts in the rest of the nation. The original busing order by District Judge James B. McMillan produced a protracted vacuum of leadership, as Charlotte's powerful corporate establishment proved ill-equipped to deal with a populist rebellion in the white-collar suburbs and betrayed the carefully cultivated booster ethos of racial moderation at the heart of the "Charlotte Way." The eventual resolution of the five-year showdown followed an interracial movement for busing equalization by black and blue-collar white neighborhoods that revolted against the power of the wealthy island suburbs and demanded an integration formula based on the principles of racial stability and class fairness. By the mid-1970s, the exceptionalist mythology of the Charlotte Way had come to embody a New South accomplishment even more impressive than sleek skyscrapers and sprawling suburbs, as North Carolina's leading metropolis became a national model for successful school integration during the second decade after *Brown*.[2]

The Next Atlanta?

During the 1950s and 1960s, while the busing crisis remained beyond the horizon, metropolitan Charlotte celebrated the rapid economic expansion and sustained demographic growth that marked the Cold War boom across the Sunbelt. The former textile capital emerged as a high-tech magnet for white-collar professionals and cemented its reputation as one of the top banking centers in the nation, a gleaming advertisement for the latest New South. The ongoing construction of two federally funded highways promised to bring even more commerce through the major interstate trucking hub and more automobile commuters from a sprawling metropolitan region. The political and business leaders from Charlotte's downtown establishment championed the civic religion of the postwar growth consensus and defined the future through the corporate vision of new firms, more retail stores, wider roads, and white-collar migrants. Bankers and developers enjoyed nearly unfettered freedom in the construction of residential subdivisions and suburban shopping malls for the middle-class families arriving from around the state and across the country. Between 1950 and 1970, the combined population of Charlotte and Mecklenburg County nearly doubled, rising from 197,052 to 354,656 residents (an essentially biracial demographic: 76 percent white, 23.6 percent black, 0.3 percent other minority groups). The steady influx of young families turned the Charlotte-Mecklenburg public school system into the largest in the state of North Carolina, with a total enrollment of almost 85,000 students. Looking outward from the intersection of Trade and Tryon, high up in the new skyscrapers of the central business district, Charlotte's corporate leaders openly dreamed of the day when the metropolitan population would exceed one million and quietly boasted that the up-and-coming "Queen City" could soon challenge Atlanta's preeminence as the headquarters of the New South.[3]

The island suburb of Myers Park represented the unquestioned center of wealth and power in Charlotte. Almost all leading corporate executives and almost every elected and appointed official in municipal government lived in the graceful and exclusive white neighborhoods located only a few miles to the southeast of the downtown business district. Originally developed in 1910 as Charlotte's premier "garden suburb" and annexed by mutual consent in 1927, Myers Park combined the historic white-columned mansions and curvilinear oak-lined streets of the prewar era with the newer brick homes and verdant lots of the postwar automobile-based landscape. The most influential families in Charlotte pondered the implications of the social gospel at the elite Protestant churches of Myers Park, where the ministers openly endorsed the *Brown* decision and the congregations participated actively in civic affairs. Journalists casually referred to Myers Park High School, which anchored the expectations of success for the privileged white children of the island suburbs, as a "de facto private school for the fashionable Myers Park neighborhood." As in Atlanta, where the prestigious Buckhead district facilitated the explosive growth of adjacent northside suburbs, the status and influence of Myers Park channeled subsequent middle-class developments to the south and east. The outer-ring suburbs of southeast Charlotte became the primary destination for professionals sent south to manage corporate branch offices, rural and small-town North Carolinians who flourished in the white-collar economy, and prosperous white residents who remained in the city of their birth. The enviable ambiance of southeast Charlotte also reflected the heavy concentration of municipal parks and golf courses, along with desirable commercial development such as hospitals and shopping malls, while planners and politicians systematically located the interstate highways, the noxious industrial zones, the public housing sites, and the new airport on the other side of downtown (figure 5.1).[4]

Figure 5.1. The downtown Charlotte skyline in 1970, viewed from the west, with a section of Interstate-77 under construction in the foreground, beneath an unfinished interchange that would become part of the I-277 loop around downtown. The areas bisected by I-77, located to the north and west of the downtown business district, contained most of the city's African-American population as well as a heavy concentration of industry. The new suburban developments home to most white middle-class families branch out to the south and east of downtown, beyond the horizon of this photograph. Courtesy of the *Charlotte Observer* and the Robinson-Spangler Carolina Room—Public Library of Charlotte and Mecklenburg County.

The politics of racial moderation in Charlotte depended on a loose but resilient crosstown alliance between the affluent white citizens of the southeast neighborhoods and the African-American voters from the northwest
quadrant. White business leaders from the downtown establishment dominated the biracial coalition and embraced the twin pillars of racial harmony
and economic development at the core of the Sunbelt Synthesis. Stan
Brookshire and John Belk, the two mayors who served through most of the
1960s and 1970s, each used the presidency of the Charlotte Chamber of
Commerce as the stepping stone to citywide election. The annexed island
suburbs of southeast Charlotte, which contained a plurality of the city population, controlled municipal politics through an at-large electoral system that
produced a city council and county commission drawn almost exclusively
from Myers Park and surrounding neighborhoods. Deprived of district
representation, African-American voters employed the "single-shot" technique to secure the election of black businessman and civil rights leader
Fred Alexander, who joined the city council in 1965 and also received substantial support from affluent white precincts. The concentration of political
power in southeast Charlotte seemed natural and appropriate to its prime
beneficiaries, the prosperous white families who expressed pride in their
civic tradition of supplying progressive leadership for the city and the
bankers and developers who reflexively assumed that their own blueprint for
economic growth and racial peace coincided with the best interests of the
community at large. The citizens of the city were "governed by an elite minority," the *Charlotte Observer* stated in 1970 as an accepted truth, a self-
perpetuating group of corporate leaders who had guided the metropolis
through the turbulence of the civil rights era, for better and for worse.[5]

During the postwar decades, the twin processes of suburban expansion
and urban redevelopment dramatically reshaped the physical landscape of
Charlotte and Mecklenburg County, where levels of residential segregation
by race and class increased considerably between the 1940s and the 1970s.
The racial discrimination inscribed in federal mortgage subsidies and municipal planning policies governed the rapid expansion of outer-ring suburbs,
stretching farther to the south and east of Myers Park, where the white
middle-class population doubled or tripled during the farm-to-subdivision
transition of the 1960s. By the end of the decade, the ten most segregated
census tracts in southeast Charlotte-Mecklenburg contained a combined
population of 44,730 white residents, 98 nonblack minorities, and 0 black citizens. During the same period, the municipal government tapped federal urban renewal and slum clearance programs to displace at least ten thousand
intown black residents, and official planning policies combined with pervasive real estate discrimination to relocate almost all of these African-
American families in the northwest quadrant (map 5.1). The deliberate concentration of more than 90 percent of the black population and almost all

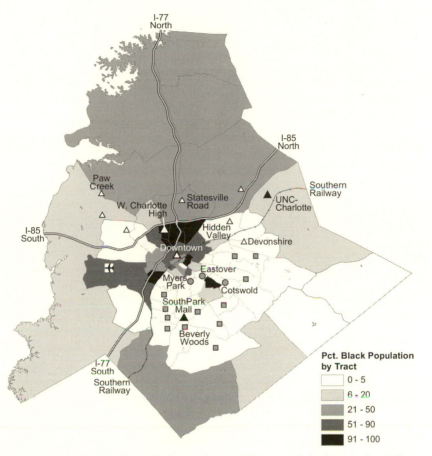

Map 5.1. Distribution of the Black Population of the City of Charlotte and Mecklenburg County, 1970, by Census Tract. The northwest quadrant contained more than
90 percent of Charlotte's black population, while ten census tracts in the southeast
suburbs included no black residents at all. Municipal planners utilized transportation
networks as racial barriers, especially I-85 on the northside and the Southern Railroad on the westside. The circles indicate the most affluent island suburbs of the
Myers Park region, including older neighborhoods developed before the postwar
growth boom. The squares denote the outer-ring southeast suburbs, constructed
during the 1950s and 1960s, that formed the base of the antibusing movement of the
Concerned Parents Association. The small triangles represent white suburbs and
school zones in north and west Charlotte-Mecklenburg that initially supported the
CPA but later defected from the antibusing coalition and began to experience racial
turnover during the battles over busing equalization. *Source:* U.S. Census Bureau,
1970 Census of Population and Housing.

low-income housing projects in northwest Charlotte created the conditions for a horizontal ghetto and deeply antagonized the white residents of the blue-collar neighborhoods clustered nearby, which began to show the predictable signs of racial turnover. Effectively disfranchised by the at-large voting system, working-class white neighborhoods persistently voted against the candidates championed by the Chamber of Commerce and denounced the "downtown establishment" for transforming their side of town into a ghetto. Although the black and white neighborhoods of north and west Charlotte shared many municipal grievances, the racial friction of geographic proximity prevented the emergence of a class alliance against the hegemony of the southeast suburbs until the mid-1970s climax of the busing saga.[6]

The civic leadership of Charlotte-Mecklenburg pursued the same objective of a spatially segregated but functionally integrated metropolis that shaped the politics of racial moderation in Atlanta. The growth agenda of the business establishment depended upon offsetting the centrifugal forces of suburban sprawl with aggressive annexation and metropolitan consolidation policies, and Charlotte enjoyed distinct advantages that the capital of Georgia did not. North Carolina's annexation laws permit the automatic incorporation of adjacent suburbs when the population density reaches a predetermined threshold, and the municipal leaders of Charlotte have persistently captured the latest migrants to the urban fringe, a nearly annual tradition that has kept a firm majority of the population of Mecklenburg County inside the city limits. Despite steady white out-migration from northwest Charlotte, the routine annexation of the middle-class suburbs proved to be the critical element in preserving the demographic stability of the city population, which remained approximately two-thirds white and one-third black throughout the postwar era. The Charlotte-Mecklenburg public school system maintained a similar racial ratio after 1960, when the Chamber of Commerce launched a consolidation initiative because annexation had decimated the county tax base and raised fears that lower academic standards would hamper the drive to recruit new industry. The black and white voters who approved the merger of city and county schools never imagined that a decade later the expansive district would become the structural basis for a two-way busing plan designed as a metropolitan remedy for the public policies that shaped the corporate agenda of racial peace through residential segregation.[7]

The white leadership's response to the civil rights movement cemented a booster ethos known as the Charlotte Way, a civic ideology that embraced the Sunbelt Synthesis of economic progress through racial moderation while managing to avoid the hubristic excesses of Atlanta Exceptionalism. In 1957, when the school district implemented a limited desegregation plan without facing a court order, the civic pride in Charlotte's racial enlightenment disintegrated after a white mob attacked a black student named Dorothy Counts.

Business leaders who had remained detached during the outbreak of working-class violence promised a "never again" philosophy toward public disorder. The city's response to the lunch counter demonstrations of 1960 established a dominant pattern of biracial negotiations held behind closed doors to avoid open conflict, a crisis-oriented dynamic in which civil rights leaders used the threat of direct action and the specter of negative publicity to secure concessions from the white elite. The Chamber of Commerce responded to the sit-in movement by establishing a biracial negotiating forum that evolved into the permanent Community Relations Committee (CRC). Three years later, as Birmingham descended into chaos, Charlotte received widespread acclaim for voluntarily desegregating its public accommodations a year before the 1964 Civil Rights Act. Mayor Stan Brookshire praised the Chamber of Commerce for leading the way out of "social consciousness, civic pride, and economic considerations"—although perhaps not exactly in that order. This fusion of pragmatism and progressivism captured the essence of the Charlotte Way, as defined by the boosters at the *Charlotte Observer*: "The highest and best example in matters of racial transition . . . resolved because of the good sense and basic good will of community leaders, white and black."[8]

The Charlotte Chamber of Commerce was "omnipotent" in local affairs, in the assessment of a Southern Regional Council report on the leadership resources that produced the 1963 breakthrough: "When the downtown elite really wants action, the city obeys." Few southern cities boasted a popular mayor such as Stan Brookshire, who publicly declared that the "current movement of Negroes to secure equal citizenship rights and opportunities is just, and . . . discrimination based on ethnic differences is wrong, both morally and legally." Business leaders in Charlotte agreed that the roots of racial inequality lay in a lack of economic opportunity, and they proudly championed the city's embrace of federal antipoverty programs without acknowledgment that "urban renewal" was concentrating black citizens in a modern ghetto. The Reverend Carlyle Marney, an outspoken supporter of civil rights, claimed that his upscale congregation at the Myers Park Baptist Church tolerated sermons about social justice so they could "brag about not firing" him for criticizing the status quo. Edward Burnside, a banker who headed the Chamber of Commerce during the desegregation of public accommodations, promised that enlightened business leadership could resolve racial conflict and predicted that most whites were ready to accept integration by their counterparts in the black middle class. The SRC report concluded that Charlotte had transcended the political culture of the Jim Crow South and "moved its racial concerns into the mainstream of American thought and activity." Since the pattern of biracial negotiations appeared to be firmly based in good faith, perhaps "not just the South but the nation might soon look to Charlotte for leadership."[9]

The Charlotte Way operated as a discourse of power that drew black leaders into the procedural politics of racial negotiation, banished segregationist extremism from the moderate public sphere, and focused attention on civil rights issues that involved individual access to consumer spaces rather than collective remedies for structural inequality. After the 1963 victory, the brothers who represented Charlotte's middle-class black leadership, NAACP president Kelly Alexander and future city councilman Fred Alexander, expressed impatience with the process of gradualism but offered sincere praise for Charlotte's white leadership as exemplary by southern standards. "Why use a fist," Fred Alexander asked, "when words will do it?" Throughout the decade, the NAACP continued to frame its requests and demands in a qualified language of Charlotte exceptionalism, arguing that while it was "somewhat true and accurate [that] Charlotte is a great city," only a genuine commitment to egalitarian reform would achieve the professed ideal of a "free society without discrimination." The most prominent militant in the black community, a dentist named Reginald Hawkins, lambasted Charlotte as "more immoral than Birmingham," an "evil system" that would respond only to concerted federal pressure. Yet even Hawkins, who openly denounced the cult of elite-negotiated progress, collaborated with Mayor Brookshire on the 1963 agreement to desegregate public accommodations after he frightened city leaders by promising a civil rights march by ten thousand people. Not until the second half of the 1960s did the Charlotte Way come under direct attack by liberal activists and full repudiation by black militants, after the NAACP finally filed a school desegregation lawsuit and the civil rights movement mobilized to combat the poverty and unemployment of the expanding westside ghetto.[10]

The intensified civil rights assault on Charlotte's pervasive patterns of educational and residential segregation revealed the spatial apartheid at the core of the politics of racial moderation and exposed the inadequacy of the Chamber of Commerce brand of conflict resolution. The hoopla surrounding the desegregation breakthrough of 1963 failed to acknowledge that business leaders had taken a default position by convincing themselves to comply with the law. Who else owned the city's restaurants, movie theaters, and department stores? Making substantial progress in the areas of schools and housing would not be possible within the current parameters of the Charlotte Way, because the same moderate ideology that facilitated the peaceful desegregation of public accommodations also shaped the growth agenda of suburban sprawl and urban containment. "We're building our future Watts right now," Fred Alexander charged in a 1966 debate with Mayor Brookshire. "Jobs and housing and education—those are the keys. Our doom is sealed without them." A few years later, the Reverend Paul Leonard contended that "with all Southern pleasantries removed . . . the present and past political and business leadership is dedicated to the (unwritten) goal of a racially and economically segregated city." Charlotte's progressive mythology flourished by allowing affluent whites to "maintain a liberal facade . . . because of their physical and social distance from the problems of race [and] poverty." Civil rights activist James Polk summed up the more confrontational attitude toward the corporate elite: "These influential people tell us inadvertently that they will do nothing unless forced to. . . . We don't have time for their hearts to change."[11]

As the Charlotte Way came under unprecedented attack, the Community Relations Committee continued to trumpet the official governing philosophy of the New South metropolis: "Almost without exception, negotiation and conciliation is easier and more successful when done privately." The exception would come soon, after black families went to court to seek justice for educational inequality shaped by residential segregation, and suburban parents went to the streets to defend neighborhood schools for their own children as a higher priority than their city's reputation for peace and progress. For five long years, the Charlotte Way would prove unable to hold.[12]

"Neighborhood Schools"

Charlotte's pragmatic ethos of racial moderation reflected the mainstream political currents in North Carolina, which did not adopt the defiant path of massive resistance taken by Virginia and the states of the Deep South. Because business interests and metropolitan voters exercised substantial influence in state politics, North Carolina's leadership responded to the *Brown* decision with a policy of pragmatic segregation that revolved around compliance with the minimum requirements of the law. The balance of power in postwar North Carolina rested in the larger cities of the central piedmont crescent, from Charlotte north to Winston-Salem and Greensboro and east to the triangle formed by Raleigh, Durham, and Chapel Hill. These metropolitan centers, located in between the predominantly white counties of the Blue Ridge mountains and the Black Belt areas of the rural eastern region, represented a New South landscape that included prestigious institutions of higher learning, explosive suburban expansion, and an urban business elite that championed the Sunbelt vision of peace and prosperity through economic development. The relatively liberal outlook of most major newspapers in the state also contributed to the construction of a public sphere that marginalized racial extremism and made the pursuit of social change a matter of pressure as much as principle. Although critics often dismissed the state's moderate reputation as merely a myth or a mirage, the vibrancy of the political center in North Carolina meant that the metropolitan priorities of protecting public education and facilitating economic growth fundamentally shaped the climate of the civil rights era.[13]

The state government's response to *Brown* devolved responsibility to local school districts through a pupil placement plan designed to allow token desegregation by carefully screened black applicants while avoiding class-action lawsuits through a race-neutral facade. In 1957, the arrival of "voluntary desegregation" in North Carolina—five transfers in Charlotte, six in Greensboro, and one in Winston-Salem—represented the South's first cautious move toward implementation of the Supreme Court's "all deliberate speed" mandate. The NAACP's desegregation petition in Charlotte predicted that "white and Negro citizens working together in good faith" would bring about a peaceful transition to equal educational opportunity, but for the next five years the school board denied almost all transfer requests by black families. In 1962, anticipating more stringent judicial requirements, the school system announced an ostensibly color-blind assignment policy based on residence rather than race, becoming one of the first districts in the South to move toward the formal doctrine of "neighborhood schools." The freedom of choice standard that accompanied the new formula allowed white students to transfer out of desegregated institutions but did not permit black students to transfer into white schools. The board also gerrymandered attendance zones by race and constructed most new facilities in the outer-ring suburbs, policies that reinforced the high degree of residential segregation in the metropolitan region. By 1964, almost five hundred black students officially attended desegregated schools, with more than 80 percent of this group assigned to a "tipping" institution in a residentially transitional area. "They say we have done as little as possible, and it may be that we haven't done all we could," David Harris, the chair of the school board, told the Southern Regional Council. "We would like to do away with segregation tomorrow. But we're convinced we couldn't get away with it. We would lose all the progress we have made."[14]

In 1965, the NAACP launched the first legal challenge to school segregation in Charlotte, and the federal judiciary responded with an official endorsement of the politics of moderation and the process of gradualism. The litigation began after the school board summarily rejected an application by college professor Darius Swann, who sought the transfer of his son to a white institution located close to his home, because "an integrated school will best prepare young people for responsibility in an integrated society." In the time-honored tradition of the Charlotte Way, the board sought a compromise rather than a battle and submitted a revised assignment formula based on unrestricted freedom of choice. After District Judge Braxton Craven approved the new plan, the plaintiffs appealed the transfer policy that allowed white students to leave integrated neighborhood schools and the dismissal of evidence regarding the racial gerrymandering of attendance zones. But in 1966, the Fourth Circuit Court of Appeals ratified Judge Craven's terse assessment that "what *can* be done in a school district is different from what *must* be done." Writing for the majority, Chief Justice Clement Haynsworth concluded that Charlotte faced no legal responsibility to "act with the conscious purpose of achieving the maximum mixture of races in the school population. . . . The School Board is under no constitutional requirement that it effectively and completely counteract all of the effects of segregated housing patterns." Civil rights activists responded by organizing protests against the Chamber of Commerce and the real estate industry, which caused the *Charlotte Observer* to retort that the city offered a decent lifestyle and progressive climate for members of both races.[15]

The NAACP revisited *Swann v. Charlotte-Mecklenburg* in the fall of 1968, after the Supreme Court ended the long era of "all deliberate speed" by declaring freedom of choice plans to be constitutionally suspect and requiring affirmative action to dismantle the dual school system. Following three years of freedom of choice, almost one-third of the black students in Charlotte attended majority-white schools, including one-eighth of the enrollment at the elite Myers Park High. Education officials also had closed sixteen historically black facilities, mainly to avoid assigning nearby white students to such institutions, which meant that several thousand African-American pupils attended unstable neighborhood schools in racially transitional areas. The thorniest issue of all remained unaddressed: the complete isolation of fourteen thousand black students in the residentially segregated sections of the central city and northwest quadrant. By the end of the decade, most white leaders in Charlotte believed with at least some justification that their city had already complied with the technical requirements of the *Brown* mandate, and they argued with equal plausibility that remaining inequities on the metropolitan landscape corresponded to the northern model of residential segregation. Most white parents also had come to imagine that they had always enjoyed freedom of choice in their children's neighborhood schools, and indeed that this educational policy represented a constitutional right in a consumer society rather than a very recent strategic response to the evolution of desegregation case law.[16]

The reopening of the case that would turn into a six-year legal saga and a landmark judicial precedent brought together three men who had grown up in rural North Carolina and attended prestigious law schools before moving to Charlotte. Julius Chambers, the plaintiff's attorney affiliated with the NAACP Legal Defense Fund (LDF), graduated from the University of North Carolina at Chapel Hill and initiated the original *Swann* litigation soon after his arrival in the city. Judge James B. McMillan, a veteran of World War II and graduate of Harvard Law, spent his youth on a farm in the eastern part of the state and rode a bus twenty-six miles daily to attend high school. McMillan currently lived in the southeast Charlotte suburbs and served as an elder in his Presbyterian church, and he had been a Democratic party activist and solid member of the downtown establishment before his appointment to the district court. William Poe, the chairman of the Charlotte-Mecklenburg Board of Education and father of six public school students, also attended Harvard and became active in Democratic politics in addition to serving as a lay leader at the Myers Park Baptist Church. Poe initially expressed anger that the NAACP had pursued litigation before giving the school board a chance to negotiate a compromise in the spirit of the Charlotte Way. "We all thought we were law-abiding people," he later remarked. Judge McMillan scheduled hearings for March 1969 and mentioned to Chambers how busy he had been "ever since you very kindly had me appointed Chairman of the County School Board." Little did the judge, much less the board members and schoolparents of Charlotte-Mecklenburg, realize how inflammatory the sentiment expressed in this joking banter would turn out to be.[17]

The NAACP case revolved around a novel contention that neither the school board nor the judge had anticipated—the proposition that residential segregation in Charlotte resulted from official policies enforced by the municipal government and subsidized by the federal government. Although in subsequent decades a scholarly consensus would emerge on the de jure roots of almost all cases of allegedly de facto segregation, civil rights advocates have always faced extreme difficulty in connecting the historical dots for white suburban audiences and for many federal jurists as well. At first, the NAACP had to convince only a single district court judge, but he too was skeptical of what he accurately recognized as a mission into uncharted territory. Early on in the proceedings, McMillan interrupted Chambers to state: "I'm a little puzzled. . . . I don't think we can sit here and try the whole community and go into all the forty thousand reasons people built houses where they did." In response, the NAACP attorney emphasized the artificiality of the de jure/de facto distinction and argued that full compliance with the *Brown* decision meant that "anything that perpetuates a segregated all black or all white school is unconstitutional." Chambers later conceded that busing seemed to be a distant possibility, because "we didn't think the court would go as far as requiring what eventually happened," but the judge underwent a genuine conversion experience during the trial. "I thought things in Charlotte were in good shape until I studied the evidence," McMillan later remarked. "I lived here twenty-four years without knowing what was going on. I really didn't know."[18]

The NAACP's historical counternarrative systematically exposed the underside of the Charlotte Way, the de jure policies that had transformed the metropolitan landscape in broad daylight but remained hidden from the collective consciousness of the white suburbs. Using federal urban renewal and highway construction funds, the city had demolished many low-income neighborhoods and relocated residents in low-rise housing projects invariably built in the identifiably black section of the city. Reports by the Charlotte-Mecklenburg Planning Commission revealed the intentional placement of transportation networks and industrial belts to create physical buffers between the working-class westside sector and the middle-class southeast suburbs. Zoning policies actively promoted resegregation by allowing commercial development in the few black census tracts located outside the northwest quadrant, which encouraged residents to move to the less noisy areas on the side of town implicitly designated for the minority population. While black areas received inadequate municipal services and suffered severely overcrowded schools, movement into white neighborhoods remained extremely difficult because of the segregationist impact of federally insured mortgage policies combined with pervasive marketplace discrimination. An expert on Charlotte's real estate market testified that local newspapers only recently discontinued the policy of listings advertisements separately by race, developers built new subdivisions specifically for black or white families, and realtors steered prospective homeowners into racially designated areas except when they occasionally "block-busted" transitional neighborhoods. By the time of the trial, about 96 percent of the black population lived in the northwest quadrant, where the highly segregated public schools directly reflected the city's prevailing spatial patterns.[19]

The board of education adopted a straightforward defense: neighborhood schools represented the soundest approach to quality education, and residential patterns remained beyond the control and the legal responsibility of the school system. "We have not built schools to perpetuate segregation," the board's attorney stated. "We have built them to serve neighborhoods." Superintendent William Self, the chief witness for the defendants, was a highly respected educator whose subsequent actions would prove him to be a firm but diplomatic supporter of meaningful integration, albeit one caught in an extremely difficult situation. Under oath, Self denied that race played any role in student or faculty assignments, and he criticized busing as an expensive violation of the concept of neighborhood schools. During cross-examination, Julius Chambers established that the board currently bused black students substantial distances to all-black schools and that about five thousand students of each race attended a more segregated institution than their closest "neighborhood school." The school board frequently used roadways separating adjacent black and white neighborhoods as attendance boundaries for primarily white schools, even though the zones of numerous black schools spanned interstate highways and busy thoroughfares. The record also revealed wide racial gaps in achievement test scores and significant physical disparities between the older inner-city schools and the newer suburban facilities. In response to a concluding query from Chambers,

William Self agreed that "in all probability" the desegregation of the all-black schools in northwest Charlotte would require the exchange of students between inner-city and suburban facilities. Two-way busing "wouldn't violate my principles," the superintendent conceded, but "it would cause a lot of problems that I would be most anxious to try to deal with."[20]

Judge McMillan began the *Swann* ruling with a simple statement: "The Charlotte-Mecklenburg schools are not yet desegregated." With unequivocal language, the judge declared that "the system of assigning pupils by 'neighborhoods,' with 'freedom of choice' for both pupils and faculty, superimposed on an urban population pattern where Negro residents have become concentrated almost entirely in one quadrant of a city of 270,000, is racially discriminatory." The carefully crafted opinion, released in late April 1969, remains one of the more remarkable federal court decisions in the massive body of desegregation case law, the product of a judge seeking to reason with his neighbors rather than to impose judgment upon the community in which he lived. McMillan began by praising the school district for having "achieved a degree and volume of desegregation of schools apparently unsurpassed in these parts," and he rejected the plaintiffs' accusation that the board had discriminated against the schools in black neighborhoods (an apparent gamble that comprehensive integration would render this issue moot). After tracing the evolution of constitutional law since *Brown*, the judge explained that the recent Supreme Court mandate to eliminate racial segregation "root and branch" meant that the policies "which in good faith the Board has followed are no longer adequate." He also reminded his audience that "when racial segregation was required by law, nobody evoked the neighborhood school theory to *permit* black children to attend white schools close to where they lived. . . . The neighborhood school theory has no standing to override the Constitution."[21]

The *Swann* order required the comprehensive integration of faculty and students in every school in the metropolitan system, an expansive remedy without precedent in any large urban district in the nation. While McMillan left the particulars of the desegregation formula to the school board, he strongly suggested that the most stable arrangement would align the enrollment of each facility with the overall district ratio of 71 percent white and 29 percent black. The judge cited the 1966 Coleman Report's finding that placing poor and minority students in classrooms with a middle-class majority represented the most effective method of achieving integration without lowering educational standards or provoking a white exodus from the public schools. Although McMillan explicitly stated that he lacked constitutional authority to require a strict racial balance, everyone involved recognized that comprehensive desegregation across the residentially segregated metropolis would mean the extensive busing of pupils. Here again the judge asked his audience to accept the hard truths of recent history that he had only recently discovered, because "the quality of public education should not depend on the economic or racial accident of the neighborhood in which a child's parents have chosen to live—or find they must live—nor on the color of his skin." The order set May 15, 1969—a mere three weeks distant—as the deadline for the school board to submit a new integration plan. "There is no reason except emotion" to oppose busing, McMillan insisted, and "I confess to having felt my own share of emotion on this subject in all the years before I studied the facts." But now the citizens of Charlotte-Mecklenburg must "think in terms of law and human rights instead of in terms of personal likes and preferences."[22]

THE POLITICS OF MIDDLE-CLASS RESPECTABILITY

Six months before Judge McMillan convened the *Swann* hearings, Richard Nixon launched the southeastern swing of his 1968 campaign in North Carolina's fastest growing city. The Republican presidential nominee appeared before an enthusiastic crowd of seven thousand people, described by the Charlotte media as well dressed, middle class, and overwhelmingly white. "A new voice is being heard in America," Nixon declared. "It's the forgotten Americans, . . . people who pay their taxes and go to work and support their churches, white people and black people, people [who] are not rioters." A local journalist observed that this populist message seemed designed not specifically for white southerners but instead as an appeal to everyone across the nation who viewed a nice "house in the suburbs" as the prerequisite of happiness and respectability. Nixon also took the opportunity to deny that the GOP had developed a Southern Strategy, and instead he lavished praise on the New South as a progressive place that had become "a lot like the rest of the country." The Republican candidate did not address civil rights until directly questioned during a television interview, and then he attempted to stake out a position in the political center by labeling *Brown* a "correct decision," endorsing freedom of choice plans unless they served as a "device to perpetuate segregation," and criticizing federal interference in local school systems as a detriment to quality education. After pointing out that segregation "isn't just a southern problem," Nixon expressed support for neighborhood schools and opposition to "forced integration," adding a personal opinion that busing ghetto children to the suburbs would backfire because of the wide gap in academic aptitude between poor and affluent students.[23]

Through his Charlotte comments, Richard Nixon was articulating nothing less than the emerging suburban blueprint on school desegregation—rhetorical support for the principle of integration combined with opposition to the methods necessary to overcome residential segregation. This nominally color-blind and explicitly class-conscious ideology revolved around the twin pillars of consumer freedom and residential privilege and resonated for white southerners who admitted that legal segregation had been wrong but believed that progress in the future need not dwell on the burdens of the past. The liberal editorial page of the *Charlotte Observer* responded that "Nixon has managed to endorse the respectable theory that America is opposed to discrimination in education, while promising Southern (and some Northern) voters that they need not struggle with the tougher demands to make that theory a fact any time soon. . . . The result of this approach is that it tends to make tokenism or glacial gradualism the major response to the educational problems of the Negro." In the 1968 election, this suburban strategy of color-blind moderation and class-driven conservatism carried Nixon to victory and revealed the grassroots Republican strength in the metropolitan regions of the Sunbelt South. Nixon won about three of every four votes cast in the sprawling outer-ring suburbs of southeast Charlotte—the respectable middle-class subdivisions that would soon lead the revolt against court-ordered busing—and he defeated George Wallace in almost every white precinct in the city and county. When they marked their ballots in 1968, the white-collar families from suburban Charlotte did not anticipate any dramatic changes in their neighborhood schools. After all, the district operated under a court-approved freedom of choice plan, and some of the most respected jurists in the South had declared that Charlotte's housing patterns constituted de facto segregation beyond the legal responsibility of the school system.[24]

Five months after the election, and barely a week after ordering his hometown to implement comprehensive integration, Judge James McMillan took the unusual step of commenting publicly on a case pending in his courtroom. In a speech to the Charlotte Kiwanis Club, the judge urged the community to choose the path of compliance and to remember that the equal protection of the law extended to all citizens regardless of race or economic status. By the same principle, McMillan sharply observed, no man stood above the law—not a federal judge, not the school board chairman, and not an insurance company executive. These were not random examples. A few days earlier, William Poe had declared himself "unequivocally opposed" to racial busing. Following the public rebuke from McMillan, the chairman explained that he did not disagree with the rule of law but instead with the judge's interpretation of the Constitution, and he insisted on the legitimacy of seeking appellate review before jettisoning the principle of neighborhood schools. The *Charlotte Observer*, which expressed unqualified editorial support for the integration mandate throughout the long crisis, responded by blasting Poe for shirking his civic duty as "a desperately needed focal point of calm leadership in the coming months." The newspaper demanded that the school board devise a busing plan that would satisfy the court and retain the support of all segments of the community, insisting that the "possibilities are limited only by the degree we are willing to apply intelligence, a sense of social justice, and democratic duty to the problem." Without forceful action by traditional leaders, the newspaper warned, the busing crisis threatened to jeopardize not only the prized public school system but also the prevailing ethos of the Charlotte Way—the "whole community's enviable record of good and humane race relations."[25]

The antibusing sentiment in the white suburbs soon coalesced in the Concerned Parents Association, an ad hoc organization without formal membership that would fill a vacuum of leadership and dominate the politics of education in Charlotte-Mecklenburg for the next year and a half. The grassroots movement began with a series of neighborhood gatherings under the direction of Thomas Harris, the insurance executive singled out by the judge. The father of three public school students, Harris played football at Duke University before buying a home in the south Charlotte suburbs and worshipping with his family at Myers Park Baptist Church. His energetic efforts proved crucial in establishing a moderate framework for the antibusing movement, as the CPA rallied around a color-blind defense of middle-class respectability and insisted that opposition to busing had nothing to do with racial prejudice. The CPA arose in the outer-ring subdivisions of Mecklenburg County, where most white-collar residents had settled within the previous decade, where the buildings of downtown Charlotte loomed on the distant horizon, and where the black neighborhoods of the northwest quadrant became essentially invisible. These all-white and exclusively middle-class subdivisions consisted of young professional couples and many first-time homeowners who possessed economic means and civic energy, but were much more likely to have coached their children's athletic teams or served as PTA leaders than to have participated in anything even approximating a social movement. CPA members were not right-wing ideologues, Tom Harris explained; indeed, few had been politically active at all before the government "started messing with our children." They were not the "upper crust" of Charlotte either, but rather "essentially the middle class, and we have every intention of maintaining the proper dignity and respect." They would act within the highest traditions of American democracy, with the belief that "our children will respect our position and, perhaps, look back upon it with pride."[26]

More than two thousand people attended the first major protest organized by the CPA (figure 5.2). A well-heeled crowd of white adults, joined by a scattering of black parents, gathered south of the city limits at a junior high school that had been all-white in 1965 and currently enrolled a 12 percent black population. Tom Harris opened the rally by declaring that the organization refused to discuss either segregation or integration, as policy and on principle, but instead would defend the family right to exercise freedom of choice and oppose the busing of any children away from their neighborhood

Figure 5.2. Thomas Harris, a grassroots leader of the antibusing movement in suburban Charlotte, prepares to address the initial rally of the Concerned Parents Association in the gymnasium of Quail Hollow Junior High, May 2, 1969. "The first thing I want to make clear," Harris told the crowd of more than two thousand parents, "is that desegregation, or integration, is not what we are here to talk about." Courtesy of the *Charlotte Observer* and the Robinson-Spangler Carolina Room—Public Library of Charlotte and Mecklenburg County.

schools. CPA petitions circulated at the meeting adopted a rights-based language of consumer liberty and socioeconomic privilege to insist on the autonomy of upwardly mobile parents who had purchased their homes based on "proximity to schools and churches of their choice." In a speech drenched with class anxiety, one father summed up the sentiments of most people in the overflow crowd. "I am not opposed to integration in any way," he announced to extensive applause. "But I was 'affluent' enough to buy a home near the school where I wanted my children to go. And I pay taxes to pay for it. They can bring in anybody they like to that school, but I don't want my children taken away from there." The CPA's immediate concern revolved around the widespread fear that the school board, with the tacit approval of the corporate establishment, would avoid legal confrontation by following the compliant path of the Charlotte Way. Members of the group forecast a taxpayers revolt if middle-class parents were going to be "pushed around" by a federal judge intent on enlisting their children in a radical social experiment. Barely two weeks after the emergence of the CPA, when a full-page reproduction of the antibusing petition appeared in the *Charlotte Observer*, more than seventeen thousand citizens had already affixed their names during public rallies and neighborhood solicitation drives.[27]

The revolt of the center by the suburban parents in the CPA propelled public debate toward a compromise position that reluctantly accepted additional one-way desegregation but fiercely rejected two-way busing. From the perspective of the placid and prosperous suburbs, it seemed only reasonable that the black families asking for more desegregation should assume the burdens of any transition, especially since the federal courts had consistently reinforced a linear understanding of integration that almost always meant the assimilation of individual black students into identifiably white schools. Parents affiliated with the CPA flooded the local media and their elected officials with letters that carefully sought to distinguish between segregated schools and neighborhood schools, imbedding racial anxieties within a middle-class discourse that professed tolerance for one-way meritocratic desegregation but reflected deep prejudice toward the spatial and racial construct of the "ghetto." Mrs. Charles Warren insisted that she would not complain if black parents worked hard and bought a house in her subdivision to send their children to the nearby school, but "if anyone thinks they're going to bus my children across town . . . without a fight, they're dreaming." Augustus Green explained that "we have accepted integration and all of its inherent problems . . . because it was the law of the land and because we are basically good citizens," but he warned that busing would force affluent families to abandon the public school system. While this father could understand the environmental benefits of bringing underprivileged students into middle-class schools, "it is likewise very difficult to understand how the reverse can therefore be true. To expect me to put my children on buses and send them across town to a school located in a predominantly black area for the sole purpose of fulfilling a mathematical equation is both ridiculous and unreasonable."[28]

Busing opponents also spoke out as aggrieved taxpayers and as harassed members of a newly awakened swath of Middle America, claiming affiliation with the group that President Nixon had called the Forgotten Americans during his 1968 campaign appearance in Charlotte. Identifying themselves as the essentially moderate representatives of the white middle-class mainstream, these suburban parents both embraced and reformulated the populist discourse of a center-right coalition that White House advisers would soon brilliantly designate the Silent Majority. The accidental activists and PTA populists from suburban Charlotte appropriated the rhetoric of the civil rights movement in their promises to take the political offensive to secure the defense of their homes and families. John Campbell articulated the feelings of many when he warned that the parents in the CPA represented "a majority that has been pushed around for the last five years by a militant minority and an aggressive bureaucracy, a majority whose chafing has been restrained only by its good manners, but also a majority which is reaching the end of its tether, and is going to bring forth its own revolution when pushed too far." William Westbrook requested that the Nixon administration fulfill the 1968 campaign pledge to prevent forced busing, after clarifying his credentials: "I am no crackpot, a good citizen in business for myself, paying combined taxes last year in excess of $4,000." Another father, claiming affiliation with the nonviolent "moderate majority" in the United States, wrote that "the white majority has civil rights too . . . and has tried to be very understanding, but we don't like having our feet stepped on repeatedly and we can't be expected to keep turning the other cheek forever."[29]

The one theme that never appeared in the CPA's defense of neighborhood schools was any acknowledgment of the finding at the heart of Judge McMillan's decision: that government policies had shaped the stark patterns of residential segregation that produced school segregation in Charlotte-Mecklenburg. The sixteen census tracts in the southeast suburbs that displayed the highest levels of activity in the Concerned Parents Association—almost all dominated by subdivisions developed after the *Brown* decision of 1954—registered a combined population of 86,183 white citizens, 160 black residents, and 149 members of other minority groups. The white families who joined the antibusing movement thought of the location of their homes and the proximity of quality public schools as nothing more and nothing less than the consumer rewards for their own willingness to work hard and make sacrifices for their children's future. This pervasive philosophy of middle-class accomplishment naturalized the glaring metropolitan inequalities in educational opportunity and finessed the internal contradictions in the meritocratic ideology through an assertive defense of the rights of children to enjoy the fruits of their parents' success. The spatial landscape and futuristic ethos of the white suburbs shaped a fundamental approval of the status quo, grounded in a historical narrative of color-blind individualism that emphasized the family privileges of class and consumerism rather than collective remedies for past discrimination. This suburban ideology of racial innocence underlay a predisposition to reject—or more often to fail even to consider—the abstract proposition that the government's culpability in concentrating black residents in a certain part of the city should have any personal impact on middle-class lifestyles.[30]

The *Charlotte Observer* initially implored suburban families to read the *Swann* opinion carefully so they would understand why the judge had issued the busing order. The editorial page sharply suggested that middle-class white parents should redirect their energy toward creating a better school system where "all children receive the equality of treatment and opportunity which is rightfully theirs, no matter where their homes may happen to be."

But with few exceptions, public discourse in the suburbs of Charlotte-Mecklenburg simply did not address the question of whether black families systematically relocated to the northwest quadrant enjoyed "freedom of choice" to live in the upscale subdivisions and attend the excellent new schools on the metropolitan fringe. It should not be surprising that like the judge, most white parents in southeast Charlotte also "didn't know," in the sense that they did not reflect upon the structural roots of racial discrimination in their city or the public policies that subsidized the expansion of their racially homogeneous neighborhoods. The "anti-bus hysteria" of the CPA seemed "more mistaken than racist," observed liberal activist Pat Watters of the Southern Regional Council, in the context of fifteen years of municipal development and federal policy based on the "hypocrisy of blinding itself to the 'de jure' nature of most 'de facto' segregation." The federal courts had permitted "leaders in a place like Charlotte to convince themselves or kid themselves into thinking that even as they continued the process of building a ghetto and a system of segregated schools, they were in compliance with the law against segregation."[31]

ONE-WAY INTEGRATION

A month of grassroots agitation in the white-collar suburbs accomplished the goal of forcing the school board to adopt a confrontational stance toward the district court. In a televised gathering on May 13, three weeks after Judge McMillan's decision, the board of education solicited advice from more than twenty community groups. The CPA, represented by Tom Harris and a physician named Don Roberson, declared that the vast majority of white families in Charlotte accepted racial integration but would never tolerate "forced busing." A majority of speakers expressed similar views, although the first substantial sentiment for full compliance came from civil rights groups and a trio of interracial organizations: the Community Relations Committee, the Charlotte-Mecklenburg League of Women Voters, and the Mecklenburg Christian Ministers Association. Jean Cook, the head of the LWV, accused parents in the antibusing movement of unwillingness to expose their children to a pluralistic society and deep-seated class prejudice that college preparation could take place only in suburban schools. The ministers association presented a resolution that endorsed integrated schools as a moral imperative and called on all Christians to "place the common good over personal preference." On the editorial page of the *Observer*, women reformers challenged CPA members to welcome black families into their neighborhoods and promised that a law-abiding if submerged majority of local citizens would support a program of comprehensive integration. But in the spring of 1969, white liberals lacked a collective voice to counter the no-longer-silent majority in the CPA, as the mobilized defenders of suburban privilege overwhelmed the isolated calls for full compliance.[32]

In late May, just a few days after the fifteenth anniversary of *Brown*, the board of education announced its intention to appeal the busing order. All five supporters of the appeal lived in southeast Charlotte, including a businessman named Herman Belk (the brother of the mayor) who reversed position to cast the deciding vote, a maneuver widely considered to reflect the unarticulated position of the corporate establishment. The four members of the board's minority faction—Julia Maulden, Betsey Kelly, Carlton Watkins, and Coleman Kerry—issued a statement that McMillan's ruling was "legally and morally sound." The group consisted of, respectively, two liberal white reformers with roots in the LWV, a progressive white physician, and the only African-American member. Although the board intentionally submitted a constitutionally suspect proposal, the judge refused to issue a specific busing order that would provide solid grounds for appeal, and instead he asked for a new plan by the beginning of August. During the interim, Charlotte officials traveled to Syracuse and Buffalo to research the one-way busing formulas employed in both places, and local officials warned their southern guests that suburban families would never tolerate the reassignment of their children into the inner city. The school board unveiled its revised desegregation plan before a gathering of black and white civic leaders in a conscious effort to reinvigorate the consensus ethos of the Charlotte Way. The approach proposed the closing of seven more historically black schools with the transportation of affected students to the outlying suburbs and left eight additional inner-city facilities open and completely segregated. Business leaders and elected officials endorsed one-way busing as a progressive resolution of a potentially explosive crisis, and they clearly expected the district court and the African-American community to accept the outcome of the traditional process of elite-sponsored compromise.[33]

The depth and intensity of the outrage expressed by thousands of black citizens had no precedent in the city's history. Throughout the spring and summer, African-American parents grew increasingly angry as they watched the school board cater to the white families in the CPA. The claim to support integration but not busing represented "contradictory double-talk," Asa Paschal charged, a smokescreen employed by suburban hypocrites who had "expended tremendous energy in assuring the all-white composition of their precious middle-class neighborhoods." At a volatile mass meeting with school board members, hundreds of black parents denounced the assumption that desegregation always meant the closing of black schools, the transportation of black students, and the demotion or termination of black faculty. The momentum against one-way busing came not from middle-class integrationist leaders but from working-class community activists such as

Figure 5.3. "We're Stopping the Shopping." Black citizens in Charlotte organized numerous consumer boycotts during the civil rights era. Participants in this downtown demonstration, conducted on August 1, 1969, were protesting the one-way busing plan endorsed by the civic and business leadership, including the closing of several historically black schools. Courtesy of the *Charlotte Observer* and the Robinson-Spangler Carolina Room—Public Library of Charlotte and Mecklenburg County.

the Reverend George Leake of the Black Solidarity Committee. Leake led a group of African-American ministers who threatened "massive resistance and civil disobedience" in order to bring "the focus of the whole world" upon Charlotte and promised that "we will not, under any circumstances, accept the closing of black schools and the busing of black children." Asking if white children were "too precious to move," black parents matched the efforts of the CPA with a petition drive that gathered twenty thousand signatures. The LWV endorsed the protests in a statement that labeled the one-way busing plan "grossly unfair," and a group of white liberals from Myers Park Baptist Church joined black parents in interracial prayer vigils and pickets of downtown businesses (figure 5.3). Summarizing the dominant stance in the African-American community, a black mother named Beverly Ford declared that "if it [integration] is going to come, it's going to come even-steven right down the line."[34]

The mobilization of Charlotte's traditional leadership behind the compromise formula of additional one-way integration demonstrated the lingering power of the Charlotte Way but also exposed the myopic belief that an elite-imposed settlement could produce a permanent resolution of the busing impasse. The plaintiffs denounced the board's plan as a product of white supremacy and a violation of the spirit of *Brown*. Taking the long view, Judge McMillan remarked that the requirements of the law had changed dramatically since the 1950s and concluded that "we are here taking part in a change that nobody here started and nobody here will see the end of." In mid-August, the judge reluctantly approved the revised plan as a temporary measure after acknowledging that one-way busing represented "an affront to the dignity and pride of the black citizens." McMillan warned that two-way busing would begin the following year, and he promised enforcement of the law without regard to public sentiment, whether the criticism came from African-American parents or from Myers Park. Borrowing President Nixon's campaign slogan and directly addressing the southeast suburbs, the judge lectured the participants in the antibusing movement on their responsibility to accept the principles of "law and order." Middle-class white citizens who appeared comfortable applying this aphorism to "the streets and slums" should consider how "it sounds hollow when it issues from people content with segregated public schools." Combining criticism of resistant white parents with a reminder to skeptical black parents, McMillan reiterated the *Brown* principle that *"segregation itself is the greatest barrier to quality education."* But after the Black Solidarity Committee organized boycotts in the inner-city areas facing long-distance busing, the judge retreated and allowed black students to exercise freedom of choice until the arrival of comprehensive integration the next year.[35]

The CPA strongholds of southeast Charlotte remained aloof during the hectic negotiations of the summer of 1969, apparently secure in the belief that the board's promise to fight two-way busing would keep suburban children in their neighborhood schools. Although minority families faced most of the burdens of the temporary formula, an outbreak of defiance also flared in the westside suburb of Paw Creek and previewed the explosive fusion of race and class prejudice that would be triggered by the reassignment of any white students to historically black schools. The population of Paw Creek included blue-collar families who represented Charlotte's textile mill past, along with a small black community and several new middle-income subdivisions. The board's plan transferred white students from the over-crowded elementary school to an abandoned black facility located on the "wrong side" of the railroad tracks. Led by a physician named Jack Scott, the homeowners in Paw Creek organized a boycott and charged that "they wouldn't do it to Myers Park." "We worked hard to be where we are," one middle-income mother said. "I don't want my kid coming down here between niggertown and the mill village to go to school." Another westside mother admitted that *"I'll be honest! . . . I do not want my teenage daughter socializing with blacks. . . .* I'll go down fighting! So will millions of us whites." The school board defused the controversy by allowing Paw Creek families the option of remaining in their current school, but the saga laid the groundwork for a broader alliance between the northwest suburbs and the southeast base of the CPA and reinforced the widespread view that concerted grassroots resistance could successfully prevent the busing of white students.[36]

After five months of busing battles, the 1969–70 school year began in a tense atmosphere marked by an uncharacteristic outbreak of violence. Unknown perpetrators firebombed the facilities of an inner-city school kept open for some of the black students who refused to be bused to the suburbs. Hundreds more black pupils scheduled for busing instead transferred to a westside high school that had been all-white four years earlier but now passed the acknowledged "tipping point" of 40 percent minority enrollment. The media emphasis on trouble spots obscured the fact that a number of majority-white schools experienced substantial desegregation increases in the fall of 1969. The board quietly reassigned teachers so that the faculty at each school contained at least 10 percent of the minority race in that facility. African-American students made up more than 25 percent of the enrollment at every high school located in the northern and western sections of the county, while counterparts in the southeast suburbs hovered around 10 percent black. The starkest racial isolation existed in the elementary schools, with their geographically smaller attendance zones, especially in the outer-ring southeast suburbs where the youngest white children remained in almost completely segregated classrooms. And now more than sixteen thousand inner-city students attended all-black institutions, the dilemma at the center of the political and legal standoff. Since the plaintiffs demanded comprehensive integration and the school board insisted that the desegregation of the remaining all-black schools was not constitutionally required or logistically possible, a lengthy and divisive showdown appeared inevitable. For the first time in Charlotte, and indeed almost anywhere in the country, an entire metropolitan region would have to grapple with the question of how to achieve a fully and fairly integrated school system. At the crossroads of the Charlotte Way, the Silent Majority spoke loudest.[37]

CHAPTER 6

Suburban Populism

> Charlotte has backed up long enough. . . . In the past, it has been
> the organizers, protesters, and demonstrators who have achieved
> the most. I say it's the silent majority's turn. Herein lies the
> purpose of the Concerned Parents Association.
>
> —Emily K. Beckham (1970), member of the
> Concerned Parents Association

"United We Stand"

The remobilization of the Concerned Parents Association during the first
months of 1970 produced a powerful revolt of the center that polarized the
moderate city of Charlotte for the next four years and pioneered the grassroots explosion of the Silent Majority onto the national political landscape.
After a period of quiescence following the initial protests during the spring
of 1969, when the CPA's petition drives and public rallies shaped the climate
of the one-way integration compromise, the renewed prospect of two-way
busing turned a defensive movement to preserve neighborhood schools
into a political offensive led by newly conscious suburban populists. "The
people of Charlotte have had it with Judge McMillan and liberal federal
courts," warned Dr. Don Roberson, the vice chairman of the CPA. "The
unorganized silent majority is about ready to take to the streets with tactics
that have seemed to work so effectively for the vocal minority groups." In
the courts and in the streets, the CPA employed a color-blind framework
that attacked "involuntary busing" as a violation of the original spirit of the
Brown decision and the race-neutral requirement of the U.S. Constitution.
Parents from the previously placid suburbs defended the class and consumer privileges of middle-class families and all-white neighborhoods
and demanded the support of elected officials at the local, state, and national levels. "A STRUGGLE FOR FREEDOM IS COMING," the CPA proclaimed.
"WHERE WILL YOU STAND?" (figure 6.1). After only four months of grassroots
agitation, the political uprising by the CPA gained control of the local
school board and convinced the Nixon administration to adopt the color-
blind platform of the antibusing movement as the formal policy of the executive branch. "Ultimately the will of the people governs," according to the
constant refrain of the suburban populists from Charlotte. "Rulings and

A STRUGGLE FOR FREEDOM IS COMING

WHERE WILL YOU STAND?

For years the Federal Courts have held that a child's color shall not prevent him from choosing where he will go to school.

Now some of the Federal Courts are ruling that a child's color does prevent him from choosing where he will go to school—and that his color alone shall determine where he must go to school—if this be necessary in order to accomplish racial integration.

Thus, they take freedom away from the child, and they impose force and compulsion upon him, and they do this solely because of his race!

They are saying that the United States Constitution requires this. They say the Constitution compels and commands that race shall control the assignment of school children — and that this is a compulsion which shall prevail over all other choices, decisions and considerations.

Eminent lawyers, scholars and Judges all over the Country say that there is not a shred of justification for such an interpretation of the Constitution.

Read the Constitution yourself. You will not find in it a single word that says anything resembling this new ruling.

There is something badly wrong when people of normal intelligence cannot see or understand what the Courts are relying on for this ruling. Nor do the Courts explain it. They simply decree it.

The plain and tragic fact is that, in this vital and major area of life, freedom of decision is being taken away from the American people!

Those who support this trend may have various purposes which they think are good. But in an effort to achieve their objectives, they are willing to destroy the free choice of everybody. No matter what their intentions may be, if they are allowed to have their way, this Nation will cease to be "a Land of Liberty"!

Rulings and decrees that are overwhelmingly opposed by the general public cannot endure. This has been proved many times throughout all history.

Ultimately the will of the people governs. They eventually determine what the law shall be. And millions of American citizens — white and black alike — are today making up their minds against this new compulsion.

Our attitude is not one of disrespect for any Court. We are trying to hold to freedom!

Why should a child's color deprive him of the opportunity of choosing where he will attend school? How can that be justified?

Taking this opportunity and this choice away from the child solely because of his race is grievously wrong. It is morally indefensible. It puts force in the place of freedom. It creates dictatorial power and undermines the American Constitution. It destroys individual liberty in an area that is close to the hearts of us all!

THE BATTLE IS FOR FREEDOM

WHERE DO YOU STAND?

CONCERNED PARENTS ASSOCIATION

P. O. Box 17733   Charlotte, North Carolina 28211

Figure 6.1. In the first months of 1970, the Concerned Parents Association distributed this "Struggle for Freedom" flyer at shopping malls, churches, and schoolgrounds rallies. The language of the flyer provides a concise portrait of the colorblind ideology and populist stance of the antibusing movement from the southeast Charlotte suburbs. In seeking to preserve "freedom of choice" and evade accusations of racism, the CPA attempted to transform the rhetoric of the civil rights movement into a race-neutral constitutional mandate. Courtesy of the Fred D. Alexander Papers, University of North Carolina at Charlotte Library.

decrees that are overwhelmingly opposed by the general public cannot endure."[1]

The CPA launched the second round of the antibusing crusade with a series of rallies in the outer-ring suburbs of southeast Charlotte, where several thousand white parents gathered on the weekend before the unveiling of the two-way integration blueprint. The January reemergence of the CPA came after Judge McMillan finally lost patience with the school board and appointed an outside consultant to devise an acceptable integration formula. The board's latest submission still refused to countenance two-way busing, insisted on the de facto nature of all remaining racial segregation, and argued that the degree of integration in Charlotte exceeded most other urban school districts in the South and the North. The judge replied that "constitutional rights will not be denied here simply because they may be denied or delayed elsewhere." While prominent business leaders quietly urged school officials to seek a nonadversarial resolution, angry white parents demanded that the board appeal the court order as the linchpin of a campaign of political resistance. At CPA demonstrations, Don Roberson told the crowds of concerned parents that they had four options: "buckle under to judicial tyranny," open private academies, organize a mass boycott, or take their children to current neighborhood schools in defiance of the court order. "Our strength can be measured only in numbers and commitment," CPA flyers proclaimed. "United we stand, divided we fall."[2]

The defiant echoes of the massive resistance era exposed the paralysis of the city's traditional leadership and illuminated the profound crisis facing the ideology of the Charlotte Way. The *Charlotte Observer* issued an extraordinary ultimatum to the city's civic and political elite, whose "greatest sin" involved the conspicuous public silence that had facilitated the rebellion of the CPA and now risked the wholesale destruction of the city's progressive reputation. In his New Year's Day address, Mayor John Belk told Charlotteans that "nothing will stop us if we all work together," but he said nothing about the escalating busing crisis. In its annual "Program of Work," the Chamber of Commerce praised itself for "prodding the consciousness of the public and its officials" to recruit industry, reduce pollution, build low-income housing, pursue urban renewal, develop mass transit—but public education went unmentioned. The League of Women Voters tried to fill the gap by insisting that "the most efficient, fairest way to desegregate our schools should be implemented as quickly as possible." Presenting its own annual report to a special gathering of the civic elite, the LWV expressed confidence that "positive and constructive leadership" could resolve the busing crisis. But both the critics and the champions of the downtown establishment were misguided in their conviction that the impasse could be resolved by the traditional formula of top-down negotiations to keep the peace. The boosters at the *Charlotte Observer* wanted to believe in the staying power of the Charlotte Way, the "good sense and basic good will of community leaders, white and black." But this time the African-American community was mobilized as never before, the district court showed no intention of backing down, and suburban parents in the CPA were adopting war metaphors to defend their children's neighborhood schools as a higher priority than their city's reputation for racial peace.[3]

When Judge McMillan convened hearings on the two-way busing formula, white parents sang verses from the civil rights anthem "We Shall Overcome" in the hallways outside the packed courtroom. The submission by the external consultant, dubbed the Finger Plan, achieved a rough 70-30 ratio across the district by pairing inner-city and outer-ring schools through satellite attendance zones and the cross-busing of five thousand elementary students of each race. The defendants tried to introduce evidence that popular opposition would make two-way busing unworkable, but the judge dismissed the line of inquiry with a brusque comment that he already had seen "ample evidence of the unpopularity of the constitution in Mecklenburg County." On February 5, McMillan ordered the school district to begin comprehensive integration on April 1, based on the "integrate now, litigate later" mandate recently announced by the Supreme Court. William Poe responded in a public statement, endorsed by Mayor Belk and county commission chairman Charles Lowe, that called upon all citizens to "respond without open defiance and disrespect for the law" but also defended the right to appeal a judicial order of dubious constitutionality. In his simultaneous insistence on the principle of peaceful compliance and the legitimacy of appellate review, Poe clearly spoke for the downtown establishment. Charting a course between calls for comprehensive integration and threats of civil disobedience, stung by the *Observer*'s criticism but even more worried about the grassroots rebellion in the middle-class suburbs, Poe's temperate antibusing stance represented the default position of moderation in a deeply polarized community.[4]

The CPA organized seven major rallies during the week following the announcement of the two-way busing deadline (figure 6.2). For the first time, the organization expanded its base beyond the southeast suburbs and established a presence in every white residential section of the metropolis, from the elite neighborhoods of Myers Park to the blue-collar sections of north and west Charlotte. Two thousand parents attended a westside protest where Dr. Jack Scott, a leader of the Paw Creek uprising the previous summer, joined Don Roberson and Tom Harris on the dais. The three men proclaimed the CPA's official policy to be a mass boycott of the public schools as soon as the busing order became operational. In the island suburb of Myers Park, a coat-and-tie crowd of more than one thousand people also pledged to support the boycott. "We're not against integration," Roberson insisted. "But to move children around from one part of the county to another to sat-

Figure 6.2. A suburban mother holds a copy of the "Struggle for Freedom" flyer during a CPA rally at Olde Providence Elementary School, February 6, 1970. The members of this almost exclusively white crowd lived in one of the most recently developed suburbs of southeast Mecklenburg County, in an upscale area that voted overwhelmingly for Richard Nixon in 1968. Claiming membership in the Silent Majority, the six hundred parents who attended this meeting resolved to borrow a tactic from the civil rights movement and boycott the public schools when busing began. Courtesy of the *Charlotte Observer* and the Robinson-Spangler Carolina Room— Public Library of Charlotte and Mecklenburg County.

isfy some judicial edict just doesn't make sense to me." The flyers distributed at CPA rallies explained that taking freedom of choice "away from the child solely because of his race is grievously wrong. It is morally indefensible. It puts force in the place of freedom. It creates dictatorial power and undermines the American Constitution. It destroys individual liberty in an area that is close to the hearts of us all!" Groups unaffiliated with the CPA extended the antibusing crusade by picketing the home of Judge McMillan and the suburban department stores owned by the family of Mayor Belk. At a massive demonstration in downtown Charlotte, parents circulated petitions demanding intervention by President Nixon, speakers called for a boycott of the *Charlotte Observer* and the city's largest corporations, and participants held signs with slogans such as "Don't Give Me the Finger" and "Impeach J. B. McMillan."[5]

While traditional leaders in Charlotte wanted resistance to come in the court of law, the organized uprising of the Silent Majority extended the battle into the sphere of public opinion and the arena of electoral politics. During the first half of 1970, the CPA established itself as a powerful grassroots force in Charlotte, an accidental social movement of suburban populism that embraced mass action techniques with remarkable speed and efficiency. Three vice chairmen—Harris, Roberson, and Scott—led a steering committee that served as the CPA's official voice and coordinated the activities of neighborhood chapters formed around churches, PTAs, and subdivision associations. The gendered division of labor within the antibusing movement reflected the dominant social patterns of the postwar suburbs, as fathers represented the CPA in public appearances and mothers performed almost all of the logistical activities such as answering queries and advertising rallies. Publicity revolved around an informal communications network that included telephone chains, distribution of flyers in carpool lines and the parking lots of churches and the SouthPark shopping mall, and word-of-mouth on subdivision streets and across backyard fences. For a membership contribution of one dollar, the central office sent supporters "No Forced Busing" bumper stickers, lapel pins, and yard signs. The CPA promised that "continuing expression of public opinion is the answer," and with not even two months remaining before the busing deadline, its multifaceted approach sought above all else to forge a solid community front through an antibusing consensus that would stiffen the resolve of elected officials. "Politicians—We Parents VOTE" read a sign at one rally, and despite the warnings of sympathetic leaders that the legal appeal represented the only viable option, Charlotte's no-longer-silent majority insisted that surely something more could be done.[6]

The "Color-Blind" Crusade

Almost sixteen years after the *Brown* decision, the citizens of Charlotte-Mecklenburg found themselves in the middle of an unprecedented debate about what a fully desegregated public school system ought to look like. The activities of the CPA during the winter of 1970 prompted an extraordinary community-wide dialogue that converged on the editorial pages of the *Charlotte Observer*, which became the primary forum for ideological disputes in the New South metropolis. The most common refrain from suburban correspondents remained the defense of freedom of choice to attend neighborhood schools, expressed in the prevailing language of middle-class meritocracy and color-blind innocence. In the race-neutral rhetoric of "quality education," many opponents warned that busing would mean higher taxes, longer traffic jams, disrupted family schedules, and declining popular support for public schools. White parents routinely argued that they could not possibly be racists, pointing to their children's current enrollment in schools with black students and the CPA's willingness to accept even more one-way integration. CPA leaders also tried to recruit black families to the neighborhood schools movement in order to counter accusations that segregationist sympathies shaped the antibusing stance. This fruitless strategy elicited a fierce round of criticism from African-American parents who confidently assumed the moral high ground. "Where were the cries of indignation when millions of blacks were bused daily . . . to lesser schools?" asked one father. "Where were the cries of 'unconstitutional'?" Other black parents reprimanded the CPA for lacking faith that white children could succeed in a genuinely meritocratic environment and for the inability to "adjust to a democratic society or to the teachings of Jesus."[7]

The CPA claimed to represent a united front, a cohesive Silent Majority throughout the suburbs, but public debate in Charlotte revealed deep fissures within the white community regarding the proper response to the court order. While some far-right ideologues linked integration with communism and miscegenation, and conservative partisans frequently attacked civil rights groups and federal judges in strident terms, mainstream antibusing sentiment combined a fledgling rights-based language of middle-class victimization with the uncertain ethos of white-collar civil disobedience. Distraught suburban mothers lamented that their children had become "martyr[s] at such an early age," mere "sheep" and "pawns" in a radical social experiment. Many white parents warned that they would boycott or transfer their children to private schools, but a backlash against the CPA's calls for defiance displayed the considerable diversity of opinion within the ranks of the antibusing movement. Several correspondents who criticized the court order expressed even more hostility toward a mass boycott or private school movement that would undermine community support for public education. In the all-white subdivision of Beverly Woods, a southeast Charlotte neighborhood paired with an inner-city elementary school, several parents asked the CPA leadership "how can you say you're for the best for our children when you preach lawlessness?" (figure 6.3). In letters to the newspaper, liberal opponents of the boycott gambled on appeals to class conscience, expressing shock that physicians, businessmen, and their "college-educated wives" would advocate breaking the compulsory attendance law and deploring the bad example that "intelligent, well-provided for, middle-class white Americans" were setting for their own children.[8]

The debates in the public sphere revealed a reservoir of support for immediate compliance and demonstrated the substantial diversification of the racial attitudes of white southerners during the course of the previous decade. Almost 40 percent of the letters published in the *Observer* openly endorsed the busing decision, often accompanied by harsh criticism of the

WE IN BEVERLY WOODS DO NOT WANT OUR SCHOOL CHILDREN BUSED !!

IS FREEDOM OF CHOICE DEAD?   ARE "NEIGHBORHOOD SCHOOLS" DEAD?

Are you going to allow judicial tyranny?

Are you going to allow a Rhode Island "midwife" to determine the fate of your child?

If freedom of choice and neighborhood schools die, does not public education die?

Do you want your child involved in a social experiment?

The necessity for having uniformed policemen patroling school halls is abhorrent to Americans.

Will Mecklenburg County tax payers tolerate the expense of court requirements?

Will you vote for the next school bond?

If courts can determine which school your child must attend and what your child is taught, what is their next step?

How has forced racial mixing succeeded in our nation?

Will you support a PTA on another side of town?

Are your elected officials expressing your views as voters? Call them and urge support for preservation of our neighborhood schools and freedom of choice.

How will the children be selected who are to be forcibly bused?

GOALS AND OBJECTIVES

1. Quality education for all children
2. Freedom of choice
3. Neighborhood schools
4. Improved neighborhood school facilities

5. Better equipment in all schools
6. Better Teacher pay for quality teachers
7. Innovative program for all who need them.

YOU HAVE FOUR CHOICES:

1. Buckle under to judicial tyranny.
2. Put your child in private school.
3. Keep your child at home until an educationally sound program is developed.

4. Return your child, in person, to his original neighborhood school classroom.

OUR STRENGTH CAN BE MEASURED ONLY IN NUMBERS AND COMMITMENT--

UNITED WE STAND, DIVIDED WE FALL.

Figure 6.3. Members of the CPA chapter from the Beverly Woods subdivision, located near SouthPark Mall in the south Charlotte suburbs, circulated this flyer during recruitment drives in 1970. Under the proposed two-way busing plan, fifth- and sixth-grade students from Beverly Woods would be transported to First Ward Elementary, an all-black school located ten miles away in downtown Charlotte. The theme of strength through unity shaped the political strategy of the antibusing movement, but a substantial number of white families in Beverly Woods denounced the boycott and refused to support the CPA. Courtesy of the Fred D. Alexander Papers, University of North Carolina at Charlotte Library.

CPA. White liberals explained that busing represented the only practical way to extend the principle of equal opportunity to all neighborhoods and emphasized the need for children of both races to attend integrated schools if they were to thrive in a pluralistic society. The League of Women Voters continued to lead the way, offering discussion facilitators to church groups and community gatherings in order to "get the facts about urban problems to our friends in middle class suburbia." Several prominent pastors, including Eugene Owens of Myers Park Baptist, picketed the school administration building with signs reading "Calm Our Fears" and "Forgive Our Sins and Heal Us, O Lord." The Mecklenburg Christian Ministers Association issued a statement that denounced the boycott and portrayed comprehensive integration as a challenge demanded by the law and "our collective conscience." The interracial leadership of the Charlotte Student Coordinating Council asked the school board for "a chance to make the plan work" and added that "we expect our parents to set the correct example for us." The most ambitious effort to counter the CPA's claim to represent a broad antibusing consensus came from the Interested Citizens Association (ICA), a new interracial group of more than four hundred parents that circulated petitions in support of two-way integration and held public rallies to lobby against an appeal of the court order.[9]

When elected officials sought the measure of public sentiment in Charlotte, the collective voice of the CPA drowned out the calls for compliance from the progressive coalition of ministers, black parents, women reformers, and white liberals. In late February, with the overt blessing of the downtown establishment, the school board formally appealed the two-way busing requirement of the Finger Plan. During a tense and emotional meeting before a full gallery, three of the six members who voted to appeal expressed deep reluctance and attributed their decision to the intense community opposition rather than personal disagreement with the court order. In a coordinated action on the same day, the Charlotte Chamber of Commerce released its first official pronouncement since the beginning of the ten-month crisis. Clearly sensitive to criticism of its failure to play a public leadership role, the business alliance tried hard to reclaim the center by announcing a vote of confidence in the school board while urging the community to maintain its traditional commitment to public education. The vaguely worded statement admitted that Charlotte had "not done all that we might have done to improve educational opportunities," but insisted that the city had "done more than most" comparable urban centers. The Chamber concluded with a resolution urging the legislative and executive branches of the federal government to establish a national desegregation standard, which in current political parlance meant a formal doctrine of neighborhood schools. Predicting victory at the appellate level, the school board sought a stay of the April 1 deadline on the grounds that two-way busing would be financially prohibitive, logistically impossible, and educationally disastrous. Charlotte needed answers, William Poe declared, and "it's high time we got them from the highest court in the land."[10]

The developments during the volatile winter of 1970 demonstrated that from the local to the national levels, politicians were following rather than leading their organized and outraged suburban constituents. Bob Scott, the Democratic governor of North Carolina, had forged a reputation as a racial moderate and previously taken uncompromising stands for compliance with federal court orders. But in February, after the CPA fiercely attacked him for inaction, Scott pledged to invoke a state law cutting off funds for "involuntary busing," enacted a year earlier at the instigation of Mecklenburg legislators. In Washington, Democratic Senator Sam Ervin and Republican Representative Charles Jonas introduced bills to ban "forced busing" and establish freedom of choice as national educational policy. The two politicians also escorted a group of CPA leaders who flew to the nation's capital for private conferences with Vice President Spiro Agnew and Harry Dent, the powerful southern affairs adviser in the Nixon administration. The delegation reported that the White House was "eager to help," especially since more than 700,000 students in eight southern states faced midyear desegregation deadlines and antibusing movements had emerged in Denver and Los Angeles. A few days later, HEW secretary Robert Finch released a blistering statement that labeled Judge McMillan's decision constitutionally misguided and "totally unrealistic." One of the NAACP attorneys in the *Swann* litigation protested the "cruel irony that when an able and conscientious Southern federal judge has the courage to apply the Constitution to his home town, federal officials encourage defiance." The mobilized members of the Silent Majority believed that to the contrary, elected officials finally were beginning to respond to their pleas and demands.[11]

The suburban parents in Charlotte's antibusing movement sent a deluge of letters and telegrams to the White House, following the CPA directive to "write the President every day." During the first two weeks of February alone, Richard Nixon received more than five thousand pieces of correspondence from residents of metropolitan Charlotte, many of whom directed the Silent Majority trope back at the politician they had voted for two years earlier. These white parents combined racial and class anxieties into a volatile outpouring of frustration, anger, confusion, and despair. "Mr. President, I need your leadership," wrote Reverend Edwin Byrd of the Third Presbyterian Church in east Charlotte, which hosted one of the recent CPA rallies. "I love my country and I do not want to be a party of participating in a movement that would show disrespect to the principles of our great country, but . . . [the court order] is not fair and I do not believe that it is morally right." A married couple from the southeast suburbs informed the president that they supported integration and believed that high-achieving black students deserved to attend the best schools, but they warned that two-way busing would drive away affluent families and "bankrupt our school system." Another southeast Charlotte resident clarified that he was neither crazy nor a segregationist, but instead a law-abiding parent upset that his daughter "will be being excluded illegally because of her race" from the neighborhood school. After reminding Nixon of his campaign promise in Charlotte, this father demanded that the White House "come to the rescue of the silent majority who may not be silent much longer. The silent majority has been pushed about as far as it will tolerate." Finally, a telegram from an antibusing activist contained a pithy warning: "You can't force the black race down the majority of the Americans' throats. We don't like a president that speaks out of both sides of his mouth at the same time."[12]

The White House responded with a major policy address on school desegregation, issued under Richard Nixon's signature on March 24, 1970. Although he reaffirmed the administration's commitment to the *Brown* decision, Nixon embraced an inviolable principle of neighborhood schools and declared mandatory racial busing to be a violation of constitutional standards. "There is a constitutional mandate that dual school systems and other forms of *de jure* segregation be eliminated totally," the president explained. But "*de facto* segregation, which exists in many [metropolitan] areas both North and South," resulted from residential forces beyond the proper jurisdiction of the federal courts. Like the grassroots antibusing movement, the Republican administration refused to accept the legal finding that the artificial de jure/de facto distinction obscured the official policies that produced educational and residential segregation and the logical remedy that a fully integrated school district should contain no single-race facilities. The White House policy statement, a political agenda presented in constitutional wrapping, closely echoed the color-blind stance of the CPA and clearly represented a direct response to the suburban constituents in the Silent Majority. While civil rights groups responded with outrage, the administration promised to intervene in the *Swann* litigation on the side of the Charlotte-Mecklenburg school board. Chairman William Poe called the address a "fine, comprehensive statement that ought to get the nation back on the road to a workable integration policy." The *Charlotte Observer* accused the president of improperly pressuring the federal judiciary and formulating a cynical policy designed to shift the political heat for desegregation enforcement from the executive branch to the courts.[13]

One day after the White House announcement, Judge McMillan abruptly postponed implementation of the busing order until the start of the next academic year in September. The Fourth Circuit Court of Appeals had already issued a temporary stay of the Finger Plan, and although McMillan denied that the president's address had influenced his decision, the judge did acknowledge that he had never considered a midsemester transition to be preferable. While the plaintiffs filed an unsuccessful appeal of the deferred timetable, based on the claim that local hostility had influenced judicial deliberations, the relief throughout most of the metropolis was palpable. Both buses and boycotts would be avoided, at least in the short term, and even many liberals agreed with William Poe's assessment that the delay was necessary "to keep the community reasonably settled down." The CPA leadership responded with cautious optimism based on the reasonable interpretation that two months of grassroots protest by the Silent Majority had resounded all the way to the White House and the Supreme Court. "The order itself has not been changed one word," Don Roberson observed. "But it does show public opinion of the masses does make a difference, politically and judicially." For the second year in a row, the antibusing uprising in Charlotte's middle-class suburbs had played a critical role in the postponement of two-way integration, and the recent sequence of events strengthened the CPA's confidence that Judge McMillan had exceeded his constitutional mandate. To intensify the political pressure, the CPA leadership began plotting with antibusing counterparts from Atlanta to Houston to form a regional alliance of the Silent Majority. And closer to home, the upcoming school board election offered a golden opportunity to convert the CPA's formidable grassroots base into formal municipal power.[14]

THE CRISIS OF LEADERSHIP

The school board election held during the spring of 1970 demonstrated that a majority of white voters in Charlotte-Mecklenburg supported the antibusing movement of the Concerned Parents Association. Of the three incumbents who faced reelection, liberals Coleman Kerry and Betsey Kelly actively championed comprehensive integration and moderate Ben Huntley had supported the legal appeal with open reluctance. The CPA assembled a slate of challengers who combined the organization's color-blind crusade for neighborhood schools with a reform platform that called for higher teacher salaries, the establishment of kindergartens, and the upgrading of historically black facilities. Vice chairman Tom Harris continued to emphasize the moderate antibusing stance of the respectable suburbs, while his two running mates represented more conservative voices on the political spectrum. William Booe, an attorney with a public record of hostility toward the *Brown* decision, was a lifelong Charlotte resident who lived in Myers Park and had two school-age daughters. Jane Scott, a homemaker married to CPA vice chairman Jack Scott, had relocated from Philadelphia and lived in the westside suburb of Paw Creek with their three children. The CPA slate relied on extensive advertising in the local media and a grassroots network of hundreds of volunteers who passed out flyers in suburban neighborhoods, churches, and shopping malls. The Interested Citizens Association actively worked to defeat the antibusing threesome, and the *Charlotte Observer* covered the campaign with undisguised hostility toward the CPA, portrayed as a right-wing political machine seeking power by exploiting the busing crisis. In response, the CPA candidates distanced themselves from fundamentalist Christian attacks against sex education and pledged to fight the "force and compulsion" of busing for racial balance while making quality education a reality for all children throughout the district.[15]

The CPA prevailed in the election by constructing an antibusing coalition that temporarily bridged the considerable class and geographic divisions of metropolitan Charlotte. Tom Harris and William Booe won seats on the school board with overwhelming support in the white precincts of the northern and western sections of Mecklenburg County, but only narrow margins of victory in the southeast subdivisions that formed their group's base. The CPA candidates failed to carry the affluent island suburbs of the Myers Park area, where the antibusing slate received fewer votes than Coleman Kerry, the board's only African-American member. White residents of southeast Charlotte also favored Kerry in his runoff with Jane Scott, but she completed the CPA sweep with a heavy westside turnout and 51 percent of the vote, followed by bitter controversy because her husband installed armed guards at polling areas in black precincts. The election returns ensured antibusing resistance from the school board but also revealed the absence of political consensus in southeast Charlotte and the broader geographic instability of the CPA alliance. Future events would illustrate the difficulty of the CPA to maintain a confederation with two disparate groups: blue-collar families from north and west Charlotte who had placed their hopes in an organization dominated by white-collar professionals from the other side of town, and upper-middle-class moderates from southeast Charlotte who disapproved of busing but hesitated to support an organization that countenanced boycott and reached out to right-wing ideologues. As legal developments during the summer of 1970 brought the crisis to a climax, the suburban parents in the antibusing majority found that they could no longer avoid the choice between maintaining the city's traditionally deep commitment to public education and resisting through a self-destructive boycott or a self-interested retreat to private schools.[16]

Everyone in Charlotte assumed that the Supreme Court would ultimately decide the constitutionality of two-way busing, but the political strategy of the CPA depended on a judicial resolution before the deadline in September. As the Fourth Circuit Court of Appeals considered the *Swann* litigation, all sides pleaded for guidance on the question of exactly what constituted a unitary school system that had eradicated all vestiges of de jure segregation. In late May, the appellate panel ruled that unitary status did not require the desegregation of every school in the district and concluded that

Charlotte-Mecklenburg faced no legal obligation to address "an intractable remnant of segregation" in the inner-city ghetto. "Busing is a permissible tool for achieving integration," the Fourth Circuit determined, "but it is not a panacea." The majority opinion vacated the Finger Plan and ordered McMillan to balance the goal of racial integration against a "test of reasonableness" that included factors such as the cost, distance, and traffic involved in crosstown busing. In a fierce dissent, Judge Simon Sobeloff accused his colleagues of making "an abstract, unexplicated judgment . . . [that] desegregation of this school system is not worth the price." Both the plaintiffs and the defendants immediately asked the Supreme Court to clarify the situation before summer's end, but the justices deferred a decision on an expedited hearing pending reargument in the district court. The CPA sent another delegation to Washington to lobby administration officials for an emergency session and mailed sixty thousand flyers urging members to demand that the White House and Congress prevent implementation until the Supreme Court rendered its decision. If not a supreme irony, it was at the least a notable turnabout for white southerners to be placing their last-chance hopes in the highest court in the land.[17]

The climate of uncertainty in Charlotte, combined with the CPA's continued preparations for a school boycott, produced an emotional debate about the responsibilities of leadership in a community faced with the likely implementation of an unpopular integration plan. In early July, editor C. A. "Pete" McKnight of the *Charlotte Observer* rebuked leading politicians and businessmen by name and demanded forceful action by the downtown establishment to prepare citizens to meet the challenge "calmly and constructively" in the time-honored tradition of the Charlotte Way. The city faced the greatest crisis in its history, McKnight declared in his weekly column, and "the alternatives to complete compliance . . . are unthinkable." A few days later, the school board, city council, and county commission responded with an extraordinary joint resolution: "Once the Supreme Court speaks out loud and clear and the community is told what is required of it, uncertainties will be dispelled and its leadership can effectively assert itself by uniting the people in support of our public schools." The Chamber of Commerce released a similar statement explaining that "no leadership, regardless of strength or good intentions," could prevent the civic chaos and racial conflict that would result from the forced transition to a busing plan of suspect constitutionality. Charlotte's business leaders did promise to support the Supreme Court decision, "whatever it might be," but they also urged Judge McMillan as a distinguished local citizen to stay his order pending appellate review. Charles Crutchfield of the Chamber of Commerce soon met with President Nixon in the quest for a last-minute reprieve, and the three top elected officials in Charlotte—William Poe, John Belk, and Charles Lowe—chartered a flight to Washington to maintain the pressure on the administration. "We are the community leaders," Lowe insisted, "but how can we lead until we know where we're going?"[18]

Defiance was neither in the nature nor the twenty-year economic blue-prints of Charlotte's political and business elite. The collective pledge of the downtown establishment to assume the responsibilities of leadership as soon as, but not until, the Supreme Court rendered a judgment underlined the extent to which the metropolis had been rudderless during the sustained crisis of the last year and a half. These wealthy and pragmatic men had smoothly guided their city through the turbulence of the 1960s, but at the same time they had supervised construction of the starkly segregated metro-politan landscape that now haunted them as the evidentiary basis of the ex-pansive busing remedy. They reflexively equated their own outlook with the interests of the community at large, and celebrated their civic activism as they drove from their comfortable Myers Park homes to the corporate sky-scrapers they had built in the central business district or to the office parks and shopping centers they had developed in the booming suburbs. They be-lieved deeply in the Charlotte Way, but they circumscribed its progressive potential through the parochial and paternalistic ethos of Myers Park. They subscribed to the New South gospel of economic growth, and the essential corollary of negotiated racial harmony, but they had never before faced a populist uprising led by the same middle-class white families who embodied the future in their vision of metropolitan prosperity. In the summer of 1970, the desperate decision by the downtown elite to suspend their own cele-brated responsibility for providing community leadership amounted to a high-stakes gamble that the Supreme Court would rescue their city before the busing deadline. They were businessmen who had always assumed they could transcend the past and control the future, but this time they were wrong.

On August 3, in a stubborn and principled message to all of his critics, James McMillan ruled that the two-way busing plan in Charlotte was "ex-pressly found to be reasonable" and issued a finding of fact that "there is no 'intractable remnant of segregation' in this school system." The judge made clear his own distaste for the entire exercise of applying a standard of rea-sonableness in an evocative section that implicitly addressed the Supreme Court as well as the Charlotte-Mecklenburg community. "If a constitutional right has been denied, this court believes that it is the constitutional right that should prevail against the cry of 'unreasonableness.' . . . The cost and inconvenience of restoring those rights is no reason under the Constitution for continuing to deny them." In a passage explaining his refusal to take pop-ular opposition into account, McMillan assumed an audience that reached all the way to the White House. "Civil rights are seldom threatened except by majorities," the judge observed, and his courtroom would operate under the precept that "constitutional rights of people should not be swept away by temporary local or national public opinion or political manipulation." McMillan specifically denounced as both unconstitutional and unreasonable the plan submitted by HEW, which concentrated school integration in racially transitional areas and would have guaranteed massive white flight. While noting that "a judge would ordinarily like to decide cases to suit his neighbors," McMillan again urged leaders and citizens to study Charlotte's history of residential segregation in order to understand why they faced this constitutional burden. A lengthy coda offered recommendations to local officials on how to mobilize the community behind the task of compliance, including a biracial citizens advisory committee to assist civic and political leaders in fulfilling their responsibilities under the law. The deadline was less than one month away.[19]

Tens of thousands of white families in Charlotte continued to hope that somehow political pressure and popular resistance could persuade the Supreme Court to intercede. On the weekend of August 15–16, the CPA published a full-page petition in the *Charlotte Observer* under the headline "FREEDOM IS ABOUT TO BE LOST." Addressed to Richard Nixon, the petition quoted from the president's recent policy statement on neighborhood schools and demanded emergency action before a renegade judge punished innocent children in violation of the color-blind guarantee of the Constitution. In late August, when CPA leaders formally presented the petition to White House officials, almost 20 percent of the residents of Mecklenburg County had affixed their signatures. Within a month, the total would nearly double to 104,000 people, representing more than half of the white adults in the metropolis. When the Fourth Circuit Court of Appeals and the U.S. Supreme Court each denied the school board's request for a stay, stunned CPA leaders blamed Nixon personally for the turn of events. During another round of antibusing rallies, Don Roberson charged that the president had "not lifted a finger to help us" and promised payback in 1972. Tom Harris expressed genuine confusion that the administration had betrayed the "hard-core, solid bedrock Americans" who formed its base of support. Rank-and-file CPA members called for a middle-class march on Washington, and closer to home the organization unleashed a campaign of letters and telephone calls to pressure the board to postpone the reopening of schools indefinitely (figure 6.4).[20]

The failure to secure judicial salvation narrowed the political debate in Charlotte to a choice between compliance with the busing mandate or defiance through a public school boycott. The ICA, which now boasted one thousand active members, denounced the CPA's boycott movement and conducted its own rallies to mobilize support for public education. Black and white religious leaders endorsed compliance and warned that Charlotte's long-standing commitment to its public school system hung in the balance. And for the first time, most leaders of the downtown establishment

Figure 6.4. "Integration, Yes! Busing, No!" One week before the two-way busing program began, white teenagers from suburban Charlotte carry signs that capture the color-blind strategy and freedom of choice agenda of the Concerned Parents Association. Members of the NAACP Youth Council, holding placards that read "Make Desegregation Work," watch their white counterparts in front of the headquarters of the Charlotte-Mecklenburg Public Schools, Sept. 2, 1970. Courtesy of the *Charlotte Observer* and the Robinson-Spangler Carolina Room—Public Library of Charlotte and Mecklenburg County.

issued calls for the acceptance of the busing order. Charles Lowe explained that the time had come to obey the law whether families were "mad, sad, or glad." George Broadrick of First Citizens Bank, the current head of the Chamber of Commerce, declared that the "eyes of the nation are focused on Charlotte. This community has a history of progress and . . . will face this matter in a calm and rational manner." Chamber vice president Charles Crutchfield editorialized in favor of compliance on the radio and television stations owned by his broadcasting corporation, although he also labeled the court order unfair and probably unconstitutional. Mayor Belk remained notable for his passive leadership, including a prediction that busing would be "dynamite" and a suggestion that all students should "just walk to the neighborhood school." After initially warning that successful integration might harm the appeal, William Poe asked the community to "put aside personal feelings" and make the best of the situation. It remained to be seen, however, whether the tardy and reluctant consensus for compliance from the top would be able to overcome the CPA's angry populism of the center. The *Charlotte Observer* chided political and business leaders for their protracted default of civic responsibility, but the editorial page explained that there was no time to dwell on the mistakes of the past because "the moment of truth is here."[21]

D-Day

The Concerned Parents Association embraced the mass boycott as a weapon of political unity, but the day of reckoning divided rather than strengthened the broad but loose antibusing coalition. During late August and early September, the CPA organized nightly rallies throughout the white suburbs and advised all parents to keep their children at home in order to demonstrate to the Supreme Court the unworkability of busing. At a protest in northern Mecklenburg, the Reverend Jack Hudson of the giant Northside Baptist Church urged white families to draw inspiration from the Bible and sacrifice for their beliefs. At other gatherings, Tom Harris explained that his "children are not up for adoption by the federal government" and urged parents to stay the course for as long as it took to win the war. Of the CPA's most visible leaders, incoming school board members Harris and Jane Scott pledged to boycott the busing plan, while vice chairman Don Roberson and board member-elect William Booe placed their children in private schools. "I hope it makes no difference, because I believe in the cause," Roberson said after enrolling his children in the Charlotte Latin School, a preparatory academy located in the southeast suburbs. "I've simply taken my children off the battlefield while I fight the battle." But it did make a difference, as the foursome immediately came under a two-sided attack from moderate CPA members who opposed the boycott and blue-collar parents who could not afford private schools. One suburban mother praised the CPA for its valiant efforts in the past but condemned the boycott as an illegal action that would damage white children and undermine public education. Several working-class parents complained bitterly about the private schools being organized "on the rich side of town" and asked if the CPA leaders from southeast Charlotte really cared about the rest of the city at all.[22]

The two-way busing deadline produced a reprise of the community-wide debate held six months earlier, except that this time there would be no reprieve. Many parents in the CPA warned that two-way busing would destroy public education through massive white flight, pointing to a half-dozen new private academies in the planning stages and long waiting lists at all of the established parochial and preparatory schools in the county. White families who desperately wanted their children to remain in current facilities expressed great anxiety about the safety of historically black schools in northwest Charlotte. "How in heaven's name," one distraught suburban woman asked, "do you think you are going to force me to send my little girl into an area . . . that I wouldn't even drive through in broad daylight with locked doors and a gun?" "Black people aren't savages," replied an outraged African-American mother. "We're human like you and it's time for you to wake up to reality . . . [and] be mature enough to accept the law of the land." George Leake and other working-class black leaders who remained skeptical of busing nonetheless harshly questioned the suburban resistance movement and insisted that the entire community must comply with the court order. White liberals charged that the CPA "functions out of irrational fear and a fundamental if subtle racism" and lambasted the antibusing campaign for transforming the progressive city of Charlotte into a place "where ignorance now seems to flourish and hate has the green light." A number of white liberals and moderates also predicted that local parents in the genuine silent majority would protect their children and redeem their city by organizing a countermovement for peaceful compliance.[23]

Beneath the surface of the antibusing revolt, Charlotte's deep-seated commitment to public education and legal compliance came to the fore during September 1970. More than four thousand parents and students volunteered to assist the administrative staff in the massive transition. The Charlotte-Mecklenburg PTA recruited parents to chaperone each bus and assigned volunteers to paint classrooms and clean school grounds. The *Charlotte Observer* established a special hotline to answer questions from anxious families, and the Chamber of Commerce organized a public relations committee to assist the district. Individual schools held open houses to introduce transfer students and their parents to new classmates, and the board launched a last-minute initiative to improve the physical plants of the historically black institutions. West Charlotte High, scheduled to switch from all-black to majority-white, hosted five hundred incoming students and parents who expressed surprise at the excellent condition of the facilities and excitement about the prospects of the football team. The Charlotte Student Coordinating Council and the NAACP Youth Council called on all parents to obey the law and allow young people the opportunity to demonstrate that integration could succeed. The *Observer* praised the grassroots movement to "make school integration work for education" and counseled CPA members to "do much soul-searching before using their children as instruments of protest." The boycott would not last very long, the newspaper predicted, because "most parents love their children too much to deny them an equal start with their classmates."[24]

The CPA sponsored a huge rally on the evening before schools opened, bringing almost ten thousand people to the county fairgrounds north of Charlotte. The last major demonstration that the antibusing alliance would ever organize displayed in full the powerful fusion of populism, patriotism,

Protestantism, and pessimism about two-way integration. The fairgrounds rally opened with prayer and the playing of "Dixie" and "The Star-Spangled Banner." CPA vice chairman Jack Scott told the crowd that "D-Day" had arrived and urged parents to make the "decision for freedom" by choosing to boycott. Jane Scott followed her husband on the stage and pledged to keep their sons at home out of respect for the color-blind principle of the Constitution and the higher moral law of parental protection of innocent children. Dressed in red, white, and blue, she closed by leading the crowd in a rousing version of "God Bless America." William Booe denounced President Nixon and portrayed the boycott as a symbol of unity, although a resentful member of the audience shouted "out of the private school or off the platform" in reference to the CPA leader's decision to exercise the Myers Park version of freedom of choice. CPA vice chairmen Tom Harris and Don Roberson avoided the fiery fairgrounds protest and spoke to a more genteel group of five hundred parents in the southeast suburbs. Roberson predicted that widespread participation in the boycott would influence the deliberations of the Supreme Court by demonstrating the failure of racial busing. Harris guaranteed that "we will . . . win this battle—maybe not tomorrow, but we hope to gain the attention of the United States on this tyrannical act perpetuated upon us." In a final exhortation, the CPA founder swore that "we didn't come this far to look at D-Day and turn chicken."[25]

On September 9, after more than a year and a half of legal maneuvering and political drama, the buses finally rolled both ways in Charlotte, from the suburbs to the inner city and back again. The desperate school district borrowed buses from Trailways and the city transit network, but many ran their routes either completely or nearly empty because worried parents drove their children to school or withheld them altogether. The integration formula involved massive dislocations, with more than thirty thousand students assigned to new facilities and the heaviest burdens falling on the paired elementary schools that exchanged black children in grades 1–4 and white children in grades 5–6. About one-fifth of the eighty-two thousand pupils enrolled in the system did not attend orientation, with the boycott most evident in the suburban neighborhoods reassigned to formerly all-black schools. Education officials and the *Charlotte Observer* emphasized the smoothness of the transition, a version of events hotly disputed by CPA leaders who alleged a conspiracy by the news media and the downtown elite to cover up the success of the antibusing boycott. The divergent experiences of two ten-year-old children from an affluent subdivision in southeast Charlotte symbolized the hopes and fears of the white families on the latest integration frontier. Gerald Reynolds opposed the boycott and sent his daughter Lisa on the twelve-mile trip to a westside elementary school, but after one day she returned home in such distress that he immediately began shopping for a private alternative. Their neighbors down the street, James and Jane

Love, sent their son John on the same bus after praying about the decision, and several weeks into the semester he continued to enjoy his new teachers and classmates. By mid-September, districtwide attendance averaged 92 percent, not much different from a typical school day, although white enrollment remained depressed in the facilities located in black neighborhoods. While Charlotte's saga was still far from over, the center had held after all.[26]

The dire predictions that busing would shatter the moderate consensus for public education proved to be false, and white flight turned out to be minimal in the suburban schools where the black population now represented between one-fifth and one-third of the total enrollment. At the end of the first week, CPA leaders announced that while the boycott of crosstown busing would continue, families whose own children remained in neighborhood schools should feel free to return to class. Tom Harris allowed his son to go back to South Mecklenburg High but enrolled his fifth-grade daughter in a private school rather than permit her to be bused downtown. Although a number of critics rejoiced that "the CPA is dead," Don Roberson promised that "the war's not over yet." The antibusing movement's claim to have achieved a 30 percent boycott rate proved to be roughly accurate if restricted to the formerly all-black schools. Between one-third and one-half of the white students assigned to West Charlotte High and six other westside schools did not appear, and soon each facility either contained a black majority or rapidly approached such status. A well-established maxim held that most white students would remain in desegregated schools if the minority enrollment did not exceed a tipping point of approximately 40 percent. While many suburban families in Charlotte obviously objected to long-distance transportation, it soon became clear that substantial prejudice also existed toward the physical construct of historically black schools that many white citizens reflexively assumed to be inferior. In the fall of 1970, the fundamental threat to the integration formula came not from the short-lived collective boycott of the CPA but from the thousands of individual decisions by suburban parents about whether to stay in the unstable schools of northwest Charlotte.[27]

The resegregation trends in the westside public schools and the growth of private academies in the southeast suburbs represented a double-sided danger for the long-term future of public education in Charlotte. The district court order expressly forbade the operation of any majority-black facilities, but the board of education refused to accept any legal obligation to address the tipping phenomenon, and the judge postponed redress pending the Supreme Court ruling. The most volatile situations arose in the residentially transitional areas of the westside, where white parents repeatedly accused the school board of protecting southeast Charlotte and sacrificing their side of town in order to create a showcase of failure for the Supreme Court. The opening of several new low-income housing projects exacerbated the racial imbalance and convinced many westside white families to sell their homes and move away. At least two thousand white students, mainly from the southeast suburbs, switched to private schools in order to avoid two-way busing. Hundreds of families applied to Charlotte Country Day, an elite preparatory school with little room that did accept its first black student in an effort to distinguish itself from hastily assembled "white flight" academies. Charlotte's parochial schools announced that families seeking to escape integration were not welcome, although a few managed to find space anyway. The three main Christian schools in the metropolitan region took advantage of the crisis to boost enrollment, as did a new preparatory academy called Charlotte Latin (in planning before the busing order). Several members of the CPA's leadership circle helped start Providence Day as an antibusing refuge, and neighborhood groups from the southeast suburbs also opened four temporary private schools for the fifth and sixth graders reassigned to inner-city facilities. After the Supreme Court reversed the busing order, one organizer promised, "my child will be back in public school next year, because we support the public schools 100 percent."[28]

The trajectory of the busing crisis in Charlotte from 1969 to 1970 reveals a dynamic portrait of the evolving attitudes toward racial integration in the middle-class suburbs of the Sunbelt South. Sixteen years after the *Brown* decision, white liberals in the New South metropolis openly championed the principle of comprehensive racial integration and sharply criticized the antibusing movement without fear of social retribution. The most progressive activists in Charlotte endorsed the cultural benefits of pluralism and the moral imperative of redistributive racial policies with a confidence that would have been impossible a decade earlier. The much larger number of white moderates strongly preferred neighborhood schools and supported the appeal of the court order, but most refused to countenance defiance of the law and chose compliance after the tactics of delay failed. The nearly complete marginalization of open segregationist sentiment owed much to the public sphere constructed by the *Charlotte Observer* but also to the politics of color-blind respectability embraced by white-collar CPA leaders who banished racial extremists to the fringes of the antibusing movement. The local and national critics who charged that all antibusing families were simply segregationists misunderstood the spatial interplay between race and class among the many white parents who accepted one-way desegregation of suburban neighborhood schools but remained hostile toward two-way integration in black residential areas. But racial conservatives also had learned to couch their distaste for integration in a color-blind interpretation of *Brown* and had begun to mobilize against what they considered a full-scale assault by federal judges and liberal bureaucrats to turn local schools into laboratories for social experimentation. The first stage of Charlotte's busing crisis demonstrated that the era of political consensus for legal segregation had definitely ended but that the debate over the meaning of racial integration had only just begun.

SWANN AND THE "REASONABLENESS" STANDARD

As Charlotte awaited the Supreme Court review of *Swann*, the CPA pursued a two-pronged strategy designed to exert political and legal pressure on the federal judiciary. The antibusing movement sincerely believed that local sentiment could influence desegregation case law, which represented a reasonable interpretation of the haphazard and decentralized enforcement of the *Brown* decree throughout the previous decade and a half. In the political arena, a CPA delegation helped found the Unified Concerned Citizens of America, a coalition of antibusing organizations that claimed one million members across the nation and designated the upcoming Supreme Court hearings as national days of prayer. On the legal front, the CPA executed an obstructionist strategy that forced Judge McMillan to name the organization as a defendant in the *Swann* litigation and guaranteed that the group's color-blind interpretation of the U.S. Constitution would receive full appellate consideration. In its brief to the Supreme Court, the CPA argued that busing innocent children for racial balance violated the Civil Rights Act of 1964 and constituted a "complete and amazing reversal of *Brown v. Board of Education*." With flowery language, the suburban antibusing movement insisted that the "true and essential meaning" of the landmark school desegregation decision guaranteed that "children shall be free to attend public schools without regard to their race or color. . . . Does not this case present a clear and appropriate context in which to lift high again that guiding light?"[29]

Civil rights organizations and urban school districts considered *Swann* to be the most important case to reach the Supreme Court since the *Brown* decision and the best vehicle for the elaboration of a national desegregation standard. The NAACP Legal Defense Fund told supporters that if the high court approved busing to overcome residential segregation in Charlotte, then "an already tested, *and operating*, plan for full desegregation can become a model to city school systems all over the country, and not just in the South." A broad coalition of progressive groups, including the National Education Association and the League of Women Voters, filed amicus briefs imploring the Supreme Court to reject the Fourth Circuit's vague "reasonableness" doctrine and issue a clear national standard for the comprehensive integration of urban school systems. The brief by the Charlotte-Mecklenburg Board of Education accused Judge McMillan of launching a "crusade for social reform" through an unconstitutional regime of racial busing that had proven "unnecessary, impractical, costly, disruptive, [and] educationally unsound." The school board denied any legal responsibility for

Charlotte's patterns of residential segregation and argued that the prevailing de jure/de facto distinction improperly applied a unique judicial standard to the South. "It is inescapable that an all-black school in Washington or Baltimore is just as unequal as an all-black school in Charlotte or Atlanta. People are pretty much the same everywhere and race prejudice now and in the past has not been confined to the southern part of the United States." The board's submission closely mirrored the White House brief, which endorsed a national antibusing standard that revolved around a laissez-faire approach to residential segregation and a constitutional defense of neighborhood schools.[30]

On April 20, 1971, Charlotte found out that Judge McMillan had been right all along, while the rest of the nation's urban school districts faced only confusion. The Supreme Court decision authored by Chief Justice Warren Burger conceded that those who desired a clear definition of a unitary school system would find the guidelines in *Swann* "incomplete and imperfect." A more precise characterization would be that the text was intentionally vague and riddled with internal contradictions. The opinion muddied the recent *Green* mandate that school boards must take "whatever steps might be necessary" to eliminate the dual school system "root and branch" and contained enough qualifications to assure an avalanche of appeals. While *Swann* rejected an absolute color-blind doctrine and sanctioned "affirmative action" when necessary to eliminate de jure segregation, it noted explicitly that district courts could not order a strict racial balance in the public schools. The decision approved busing as a remedial tool but adopted the "reasonableness" standard advanced by the Fourth Circuit and specifically concurred that factors such as the length and distance of bus rides should be weighed against the goal of integration. The Supreme Court also embraced the Nixon administration's contention that the existence of all-black schools did not constitute prima facie evidence of racial discrimination. And the justices plainly stated that upon achievement of unitary status, school districts no longer had any constitutional obligation to prevent resegregation. The *Swann* opinion concluded with a statement framed revealingly in the double negative: "On the facts of this case, we are unable to conclude that the order of the District Court is not reasonable, feasible, and workable."[31]

The *Swann* decision represented an uneasy compromise forged by a deeply divided Supreme Court that decided to sacrifice intellectual coherence for the tradition of maintaining unanimity in the volatile field of southern school desegregation. Burger's initial draft philosophically reflected the Nixon administration's antibusing platform and specifically reversed the district court finding that Charlotte's history of de jure residential segregation mandated affirmative action to achieve school integration. To preserve the unanimous facade, centrist justices brokered a compromise that retained

Burger's framework but modified the text to uphold McMillan's order. In retrospect, the waning liberal bloc should have precipitated an open break with the chief justice and constructed a more expansive opinion. The liberal justices hoped that lower courts would rely on McMillan's comprehensive remedy instead of their own vague guidelines, but the highly subjective "reasonableness" formula allowed busing opponents to complain with accuracy that the Constitution had different meanings in different political jurisdictions. Along with many other observers, the *New York Times* concluded erroneously that *Swann* applied only to the South, based on the misguided but still prevalent notion that racial segregation in the rest of the nation resulted only from de facto housing patterns. The NAACP knew better and celebrated the milestone in the battle against residential segregation, but the drive for metropolitan remedies would soon founder on the political and judicial opposition that lurked between the lines of *Swann*. The justices had achieved unanimity for the last time in desegregation case law, and Burger's opinion foreshadowed the path he would soon take in leading a reconstituted Supreme Court to a formal policy of suburban protection in almost all metropolitan regions except the already consolidated school districts of the Sunbelt South.[32]

Although elusive as a national standard, the *Swann* decision unambiguously validated Judge McMillan's discretionary authority to supervise comprehensive integration in Charlotte-Mecklenburg. The *Observer* responded by issuing an ultimatum to local leaders to "create a new climate of compliance with the law that will overcome the negativism of the past two years." Charles Crutchfield, the new president of the Chamber of Commerce, promised that the business alliance would serve as the "catalyst for positive and constructive action" until the community stabilized around a recommitment to quality public education. The CPA warned that the Supreme Court had guaranteed the destruction of public education, and antibusing leaders endorsed a national campaign to secure a freedom of choice amendment to the U.S. Constitution. The reactions of white suburban families who supported the antibusing movement ranged across the spectrum, from angry defiance to grudging acceptance to qualified optimism. A westside mother declared that she and her husband had saved and struggled to move into a middle-class subdivision for nothing: "It appears we would be better off to quit work, sit down do nothing, draw welfare and live in a low income housing development. . . . Then our daughter would be bussed into a good neighborhood school!" A "heartbroken" woman from north Charlotte lamented the ruling but promised that her family would remain faithful to public education. In the affluent CPA stronghold of Lansdowne, a white mother admitted that the busing of her fifth grader to the inner city "hasn't upset my child like I expected, and though I'm surprised to hear myself say this, I think in years to come we'll see that it's something that had to be done. Desegregation would never have happened if it had been left to the people."[33]

The *Swann* decision arrived near the end of a difficult but not disastrous year in Charlotte, which weathered with mixed success an unprecedented transition to two-way integration in a large metropolitan school system. The popularity of the CPA diminished after the antibusing leadership joined the school board, because William Booe launched a right-wing assault that included efforts to fire the highly respected superintendent and terminate popular programs such as sex education and Head Start. Numerous antibusing parents and all eight other members of the board denounced Booe, who had misread both the community's moderation and the CPA's mandate, and he soon rivaled Judge McMillan as the most unpopular person in the county. Many white families reported that busing had produced unanticipated positive experiences, strengthening the hopes of civil rights activists that actual integration could change hearts as well as minds. But sporadic outbursts of violence in the junior and senior highs disrupted the learning process, and the NAACP condemned the school administration because black students received more than 90 percent of about four thousand disciplinary suspensions. Black families also protested the discriminatory application of ability tracking, demanded the banishment of "Dixie" and the Rebel flag at athletic contests, and called for the incorporation of African-American history and literature in the curriculum. After white and black students at three senior highs organized "friendship rallies/love-ins," the Southern Regional Council filed an optimistic report that praised Charlotte for making genuine integration a real possibility and highlighted the broad reservoir of community support for public education. As the long year came to a close, however, the administration canceled the final week of classes at all ten senior highs following a new outbreak of racial violence.[34]

During the two-year period between Judge McMillan's original busing order and the Supreme Court's *Swann* decision, a defensive movement of suburban populism produced a protracted crisis of leadership in one of the most economically dynamic and racially moderate metropolises in the entire nation. The powerful revolt of the center created a political vacuum filled by the defiant and desperate voices of middle-class white parents who demanded that local and national leaders come to the rescue of the Silent Majority. While an alternative and overlapping silent majority of Charlotte's citizens eventually chose to comply with the judicial mandate, the Supreme Court decision would prove to be not a resolution of the busing conflict but instead the catalyst for a remarkable struggle over how—rather than whether—the deeply divided community would integrate its public schools. In May 1971, when Judge McMillan again charged the school board with an affirmative obligation to prevent resegregation by maintaining a majority-white enrollment in every facility, the *Charlotte Observer* called for a new approach that would evenly distribute "the burdens and opportunities of desegregation" to all sections of the metropolis. The CPA soon faded from the scene as a political force, but it would take three more arduous years and an interracial grassroots movement to overcome the legacies of the antibusing uprising and break the impasse between the district court and the school board. After education officials switched to an integration formula that revolved around the accommodation of the privileges and prejudices of the affluent white families in the southeast suburbs, the disfranchised citizens of north and west Charlotte organized their own version of neighborhood politics to demand busing equalization through geographic fairness. Between 1971 and 1974, the intricate quest for desegregation stability forced the New South metropolis to come to terms with a rough form of socioeconomic, as well as racial, justice in the public schools.[35]

CHAPTER 7

Neighborhood Politics

> We have been told by some black people that this [busing formula]
> is a similar type of discrimination to what they experienced over a
> period of years.
> > —Wilson Bryan (1971), Citizens United for Fairness

RACE + GEOGRAPHY = CLASS

A few weeks before the two-way busing deadline in 1970, a white mother
who lived in one of Charlotte's northside suburbs announced that her part of
town had "borne the full burden of integration for several years now." In a
letter published in the *Charlotte Observer*, Ann Wood acknowledged her
own opposition to busing but then complained bitterly that the Concerned
Parents Association represented only affluent families from southeast Charlotte who wanted to escape their obligation to participate in "some of what
we have been doing for a long time." In a sarcastic conclusion, she explained
that her family and their neighbors were "ready to share 'social progress'
with all the citizens of Mecklenburg. We shouldn't just keep it for ourselves
in the northern part of the county." Another white mother who also resented
the privilege and power of southeast Charlotte portrayed an even greater
awakening of working-class consciousness in a private letter to Julius Chambers, the lead attorney in the *Swann* litigation. Mrs. T. L. Paige confessed
her previous support for the CPA but then expressed gratitude to the
NAACP for demanding a comprehensive plan that would spread the burdens of integration fairly throughout the metropolis. There came a point in
time, this former antibusing activist observed, when ordinary working people experienced what it meant not to be wealthy, a feeling that must be similar to the moment when black people discovered the consequences of not
being white. Along with many other white residents of the racially mixed
sectors of north and west Charlotte-Mecklenburg, these two parents were in
the process of rethinking the relationship between race and class in their
political outlook, and beginning to view the district court and nearby black
neighborhoods as potential allies in a fairness campaign against their mutual
enemies in the southeast suburbs.[1]

The intermediate phase of Charlotte's desegregation crisis revolved
around an interracial version of neighborhood politics that shattered the

suburban antibusing coalition assembled by the Concerned Parents Association. During the initial stage of the busing saga, the civil rights challenge to racial segregation in neighborhood schools became the crucible for a suburban politics of middle-class consciousness and color-blind ideology, embodied in the white-collar populism of the CPA. Affluent parents from southeast Charlotte defended the educational and residential landscape of class and racial privilege by organizing a powerful social movement at the grassroots level and joining a political uprising by the Silent Majority at the national level. Elected officials and policymakers responded by exempting affluent white families from most of the burdens of two-way integration and concentrating the consequences of social change in struggling working-class and lower-middle-class neighborhoods in north and west Charlotte. In many urban areas, this fusion of racial integration and class discrimination created a debilitating chain reaction: the defense of the integrity of white neighborhoods, followed by the destabilization of school desegregation through residential transition, and then a political consensus on the policy failure of court-ordered busing. In Charlotte-Mecklenburg, the leverage provided by Judge McMillan's refusal to permit resegregation eventually transformed the populist ethos of the blue-collar suburbs on the northside and westside from a reactionary defense of residential segregation into a progressive demand for socioeconomic equality. Between 1971 and 1974, the political mobilization of north and west Charlotte fundamentally challenged the spatial arrangements of municipal power and metropolitan development and ultimately forced the New South metropolis to seek stable racial desegregation through conscious class fairness.[2]

The northern and western sections of Charlotte-Mecklenburg included older textile mill towns, newer blue-collar and middle-income suburbs, almost all of the city's public housing projects, and about 96 percent of the African-American population. In the spring of 1970, at the height of Charlotte's antibusing revolt, a white minister and liberal activist named Paul Leonard circulated a grassroots manifesto calling for an interracial movement to challenge the domination of municipal politics by the corporate elite and the wealthy southeast suburbs. In a comprehensive deconstruction of the Charlotte Way, Leonard declared that the "development and protection of the southeast has been and is the controlling factor in every decision affecting the life of this city." Municipal policies actively diminished the quality of life in the disfranchised black and white neighborhoods of north and west Charlotte, while the corporate establishment depended on racial tensions to prevent a geographic alliance against the hegemony of Myers Park. "The problems of law and order, housing, and schools are very real to these people [in north and west Charlotte] because of the physical nearness of blacks," Leonard observed. "Out of a blindness engendered by fear, the low-moderate income whites in reality vote consistently against their self-interest." The manifesto concluded by outlining a new version of neighbor-hood politics based on class solidarity and interracial cooperation, in order to spread resources throughout the metropolis on an equitable basis and halt the ongoing conversion of northwest Charlotte into a racially segregated and impoverished ghetto. "What has happened to the west side of Charlotte has happened to whites and blacks alike who live there," Leonard warned, "and it will continue to happen until they stand together on common is-sues."[3]

Many white and black citizens who did not live in the southeast suburbs believed that the policies of the downtown establishment systematically dis-franchised their neighborhoods and intentionally diminished their quality of life. The antibusing coalition forged by the CPA, which recruited blue-collar families from the northside and westside into an organization dominated by white-collar leaders from the southeast suburbs, turned out to be a tempo-rary exception to the prevailing pattern of class conflict over the metropoli-tan distribution of political power and economic resources. During the late 1960s and early 1970s, a series of energetic homeowners revolts based in northwest Charlotte launched a direct assault on the traditional authority of the Myers Park elite. The Charlotte Chamber of Commerce called its politi-cal action committee "Let's Keep Moving Forward 70's," but every munici-pal election, bond referendum, and zoning decision generated fierce opposi-tion from neighborhoods that demanded a change of direction. Reflecting on the first year of the new decade, the *Charlotte Observer* warned that the antibusing movement represented only the most visible element in the broad collapse of the Charlotte Way and lamented the "whole tenor of a year marked by citizen protest, anger, distrust, and flat rejection of some things that pointed toward a better community." But this time, instead of the ritual call for strong guidance from the downtown establishment, the *Observer* demanded that municipal leaders begin to listen to the neighbor-hood groups mobilized against the structural inequities of the at-large voting system, the site placement of low-income housing, and the geographic im-balance of municipal planning and development. If southeast Charlotte con-tinued to refuse to share power with the rest of the metropolis, the newspa-per predicted that "there is little indication that the discontent, the protests, the disappointments and the alienation of many citizens will go away."[4]

The most volatile conflict in municipal politics revolved around the sys-tematic concentration of low-income housing in northwest Charlotte. "Lo-cation of public housing," a civil rights report concluded, "represents [the] city's official stamp that particular neighborhoods have gone down and will never come back." In the spring of 1969, white homeowners groups on the westside staged protests against the "planned segregation of the poor" and accused city leaders of an open conspiracy to trigger white flight and trans-form their side of the city into an all-black ghetto. An umbrella organization of homeowners associations called Citizens for Orderly Development collected more than eight thousand signatures on a petition that labeled residential segregation immoral and demanded that city planners construct all future low-income projects in other sections of the metropolis. With limited success, the Citizens for Orderly Development also attempted to forge a biracial alliance with several thousand black homeowners who were also protesting the destabilization of their neighborhoods and overcrowding of their schools by the city's site selection for public housing. In the municipal elections of 1969, a massive turnout by westside whites almost defeated businessman John Belk in the mayoral contest and made Joe Withrow of the Citizens for Orderly Development only the second member of the city council who lived outside the southeast suburbs (after black leader Fred Alexander). The chastened city council promised to scatter low-income housing outside the northwest sector, and reformers escalated calls for a citizens advisory committee to give a voice to the less affluent neighborhoods that "seem to feel the Chamber of Commerce is running the city."[5]

Although the at-large voting system secured the disproportionate power of southeast Charlotte in both city and county government, the era when the corporate establishment simply imposed its version of progress on the rest of the metropolis had ended. In the late 1960s and early 1970s, voters from north and west Charlotte-Mecklenburg joined with fiscal conservatives from the southeast suburbs to reject a series of referendums to fund civic ventures championed by the Chamber of Commerce. Westside residents launched quality-of-life protests against industrial zoning policies, while homeowners on the northside stopped a landfill and unsuccessfully proposed Myers Park as an alternative site. One hundred families from textile villages formed the North Charlotte Action Committee to protest inadequate municipal services and bring a hospital to their side of town. The leaders of the group—a truck driver, a church secretary, and a retired mill worker—proclaimed that north Charlotte needed a representative on the city council, and it did not matter "if he's black or white." In 1971, a white northsider named Jim McDuffie won a council seat with advertisements that highlighted the Myers Park addresses of most incumbents and promised instead to "represent ALL areas of Charlotte." Mobilized westsiders also elected a second champion of scattered-site public housing, but the city council's vacillating commitment to residential integration galvanized homeowner opposition everywhere else. An affordable housing proposal in southeast Charlotte prompted white homeowners to organize a shopping mall "park-in" to demonstrate the traffic jams that allegedly would follow, while plans for a low-income development in the northeast suburbs elicited an intense campaign by neighborhood associations against "economic integration." Build all new low-income projects in Myers Park, one protest leader told the corporate executives who dominated the housing authority. "Let them come over on your side. . . . We have our quota. We have far more than you do."[6]

During a 1970 meeting of the Mecklenburg County Commission, a white westsider named Jeanne Bohn shouted a warning: "You have no idea how angry we are. Not discontented but angry." Along with thousands of other black and white residents from north and west Charlotte, Bohn wanted the county to build a medical center on her side of town, and she promised a taxpayers revolt against every bond referendum until it happened. Shared grievances produced a geographic alliance between black and white neighborhood groups during the two-year dispute over the site of the new medical center, which the hospital authority planned to locate on Randolph Road near Myers Park. Fierce opposition came from the predominantly white North Charlotte Action Committee and the Mecklenburg Citizens for Fair Taxation, as well as the Black Solidarity Committee and a new coalition called the Citizens for the Complete Development of Charlotte-Mecklenburg. County commissioners twice canceled bond referendums because of the political uncertainty, but the hospital authority refused to endorse an alternative site, and physicians who lived in southeast Charlotte expressed unwillingness to commute or relocate. Opponents then lobbied for geographic diversity on the hospital authority, because business executives from the Myers Park area made up 90 percent of the appointees, but the chairman declared publicly that no qualified candidates from other parts of town appeared to exist. County leaders acknowledged the eventual need for a new hospital location because of suburban growth north of Charlotte, but by the end of 1971 they had effectively abandoned the controversy because of indications that the neighborhood movement was expanding into a broader political revolt. Enraged grassroots activists proclaimed that they would no longer live under a political system that sentenced north and west Charlotte to be "neglected and ruled by a few people" from Myers Park.[7]

The traditional leadership from southeast Charlotte believed that the electoral system of at-large representation produced good government by "outstanding public-spirited citizens" who selflessly acted in the best interests of the entire metropolitan area. In January 1971, at the unveiling of its annual "Leadership Is the Answer" report, the Chamber of Commerce did acknowledge the wide-ranging assault on its authority by admitting that "we perhaps have not taken the time to look beyond our own interests to those of the community." The business coalition promised to promote the citywide distribution of low-income housing as part of a "visionary" agenda of metropolitan expansion and downtown revitalization. A scathing rebuttal came immediately from neighborhood activist Jesse Riley, the head of another new reform organization called the Charlotte Citizens for Independent Political Action. Riley charged that the guiding principle of municipal government could be easily summarized: "What's good for the Chamber of Commerce and realtors is good for Charlotte." He conceded that the corporate growth ideology had "made Charlotte what it is" but argued that the celebrated landscape of the New South looked very different from the perspective of the black families displaced by urban renewal, the low-income neighborhoods bisected by interstate highways, the westsiders and northsiders deprived of medical care, the municipal employees fired for union organizing, and the children who played in deteriorating public parks instead of ritzy country clubs. Charlotte desperately needed a new "people-centered" growth philosophy promoted by a very different leadership "dedicated to the well-being of the entire community rather than to one small, advantageously placed segment." While the Chamber of Commerce did not "invent the affluent society," Riley concluded, "they do worship at that shrine. They just aren't the kind of men to get us out of the hole they helped dig."[8]

THE CHARTER DEBACLE

The widening grassroots revolt against the power of southeast Charlotte coalesced around a drive to replace the at-large voting formula with a political system based on district representation. During 1970–71, an elite-sponsored initiative to consolidate the city of Charlotte with the county government of Mecklenburg became the unlikely reform vehicle for a diverse coalition of civil rights activists, progressive groups, and neighborhood movements. The Chamber of Commerce unwittingly created the opening by lobbying the state legislature to create the Charlotte-Mecklenburg Charter Commission. As in the earlier consolidation of the city and county school systems, business leaders championed the merger of governments for reasons such as efficiency in social services, equalization of tax burdens, and centralized metropolitan planning. In private, members of the downtown establishment also recognized that city-county consolidation would circumvent the growing grassroots resistance to suburban annexation and avoid the trends of metropolitan fragmentation currently undermining the power of their counterparts in Atlanta. The unintended consequences of the consolidation initiative began with the makeup of the Charter Commission, which included far more racial, gender, and geographic diversity than any other policymaking body in local history. Urged by ordinary citizens and policy experts to think imaginatively about the future, most members of the Charter Commission agreed in principle that a majority of officials in the consolidated government should represent geographic districts. The charter deliberations immediately became a flashpoint for antibusing activists who blamed the countywide school system for two-way integration and neighborhood movements that viewed merger as the mechanism for a genuine redistribution of political power.[9]

The Charter Commission held the initial public hearings during the summer of 1970, and neighborhood groups from north and west Charlotte organized a show of force for district elections. The debate became racialized after commission member Fred Alexander endorsed geographic districts as the only way for the black community to achieve equal representation in a countywide government, and CPA leader William Booe attacked him for supporting a "guaranteed racial balance" in politics as in the public schools. "If you think your rights are being trampled on" by racial busing, Booe warned the crowds at CPA rallies, "it's even worse with that Charter Commission. Join with me to defeat it." Civil rights leaders responded by pointing out that Charlotte had adopted at-large representation several decades earlier in order to prevent the election of black candidates. Interracial and religious groups that supported a district plan cautioned that refusal to modify the at-large formula would send a message to thousands of alienated citizens of both races that "only upper-income whites qualified" for leadership positions. Westside activists warned that failure to reform municipal politics would mean "all low-cost housing going to one part of the city and all the hospitals going to another part." George Leake of the Black Solidarity Committee framed the issue in stark terms: "Governmental control of this community is in the hands of a very select few, and districts are necessary because the way things are now we don't have a democracy." In a pragmatic decision that reflected sensitivity to the strong feelings on all sides of the issue, the Charter Commission proposed a consolidated governing body with twelve districts and three at-large members, a school board with six districts and three at-large seats, and geographic diversity without fixed ratios in appointments to planning commissions.[10]

The unanticipated linkage between electoral reform and metropolitan consolidation alarmed most city and county politicians and galvanized the leaders of the Chamber of Commerce, who opposed any revision of the at-large system and quietly maneuvered for changes that would preserve the municipal power of southeast Charlotte. At the beginning of 1971, the Chamber submitted a counterproposal for a roughly equal mixture of at-large and district representatives on the governing council and the school board. Chamber president Charles Crutchfield publicly defended the formula as a public-spirited effort to save consolidation, although it clearly included calculations to ensure a political majority for southeast Charlotte. The *Observer* condemned the scheme as a public "disservice" undertaken by "out-of-touch" businessmen, "consistent with the Chamber's tendency in recent years to sit tight when it should be leading." At the next charter hearing, neighborhood groups from north and west Charlotte denounced the compromise, and civil rights leaders framed the issue as a simple question of racial equality and economic justice. The LWV and the National Conference of Christians and Jews asked for nothing less than genuine democracy and warned that the "credibility of the present leadership in this community is dangerously low." A few days later, the Chamber of Commerce exercised the privileges of power and met privately to cut a deal with the reluctant members of the Charter Commission, who believed that the consolidation initiative could not succeed without the financial support of the business community. The commission scheduled a March referendum on a consolidated governing body with twelve district and six at-large members, and the *Observer* endorsed the revised formula as a necessary if distasteful compromise between the elite leaders of southeast Charlotte and the disfranchised citizens who lived everywhere else.[11]

Later it would seem convenient for business leaders to deflect blame by attributing the defeat of the merger referendum to the climate of unrest created by the busing crisis. But the grassroots resentment extended far beyond the situation in the schools, and the downtown establishment had lost the confidence of a large cross-section of citizens throughout Charlotte-Mecklenburg. The Chamber of Commerce wavered for more than a month before endorsing the charter, and then its campaign arm touted merger through ironic advertisements that highlighted the Myers Park residences of most elected and appointed officials and promised that "consolidation will remedy this imbalance by allowing YOU to elect a representative from YOUR district." The CPA denounced the charter government as a racial and socioeconomic quota system, and antibusing leaders played central roles in the two ad hoc organizations that orchestrated the antimerger campaign. The Committee to Insure Good Government, a bipartisan coalition of white-collar professionals from southeast Charlotte, endorsed the principle of city-county consolidation but opposed replacement of at-large elections. The group ran anticharter advertisements warning that district representation would "eliminate many able people" from public service and bring the corruption of ward politics to Charlotte. CPA leader William Booe also organized the Mecklenburg Conservatives, a smaller collection of right-wing ideologues who denounced the charter as a conspiracy to bring racial balance in neighborhoods as well as schools, a "device by which the liberals can continue their drive toward socialism in this country."[12]

The voters of Charlotte-Mecklenburg decisively rejected the charter by a two-to-one margin in a referendum held on March 22, 1971. The key blow to consolidation came from the white neighborhood groups of north and west Charlotte, which either remained neutral or actively campaigned against the compromise formula demanded by the Chamber of Commerce. The liberal reformers in the LWV tried to mobilize support by sending speakers to churches and neighborhood gatherings and setting up informational booths in suburban shopping malls. But in the end the elite negotiations that produced the backroom compromise reinforced the alienation of blue-collar neighborhoods in north and west Charlotte without assuaging the fears of white-collar homeowners in the southeast suburbs. In an exceptionally high turnout, three-fourths of white voters opposed the charter and only the black precincts rallied in firm support. Middle-class homeowners in the unincorporated suburbs overwhelmingly rejected metropolitan government, and 95 percent of voters in the westside suburb of Paw Creek opposed the referendum. "There was a big silent majority voting against something today," the banker who headed the charter campaign remarked. "I don't know what." White voters throughout Charlotte-Mecklenburg expressed attitudes ranging from anger about higher taxes and court-ordered busing to resentment and distrust of the power of the Chamber of Commerce. The metropolitan vision of the corporate leadership no longer commanded the respect or guaranteed the support of the political center.[13]

The Charlotte Chamber of Commerce did not—and probably could not—make an effective case for the fundamental rationale behind the city-county consolidation drive: as a structural remedy to control the political consequences of suburban sprawl and to ensure that Charlotte would never become a majority-black city. The downtown establishment's metropolitan synthesis of racial moderation in politics and spatial segregation in planning created the conditions for white flight from northwest Charlotte and required the routine antidote of suburban annexation. While maintaining the allegiance of all citizens to the same municipal system represented astute public policy, the Myers Park elite also championed consolidation to reinforce their own electoral base through the wholesale incorporation of every white family that resided outside the city limits. During the course of the charter debacle, the businessmen-politicians from southeast Charlotte revealed the intrinsic racial paternalism and overt class prejudice that underlay the ethos of white moderation in the Sunbelt South. In a speech delivered soon after the merger defeat, Charles Crutchfield explained that metropolitan government remained essential because black people were not "economically or mentally qualified to run large cities such as Charlotte." Under a firestorm of criticism, the president of the Chamber of Commerce retreated to the position that because of historical discrimination, "poorly educated and inexperienced blacks and whites . . . are not now equipped to run a city." The most illuminating aspect of this clarification involved the signal that business leaders felt threatened not only by the political mobilization of the African-American community but also by the simultaneous explosion of blue-collar populism in north and west Charlotte and the antiurban revolt of white-collar homeowners in the unincorporated suburbs.[14]

Soon after the crushing defeat of city-county consolidation, Charlotte leaders launched a new campaign to annex the outer-ring southeast suburbs along with additional middle-income subdivisions recently developed on the northside. The annexation initiative targeted forty-four thousand residents of Mecklenburg County, an overwhelmingly white population that included many of the prosperous neighborhoods at the center of the CPA's antibusing revolt. Suburban homeowners responded with legal challenges and political pressure to repeal North Carolina's automatic annexation laws. The Charlotte Chamber of Commerce aggressively fought an effort in the state legislature to make annexation contingent on approval by suburban voters, arguing that the "greatest bargain in America today is the economic and cultural benefits enjoyed by perimeter residents who live near one of our large cities . . . without having to bear financial responsibility." Civil rights attorneys also intervened with a class-action lawsuit against suburban annexation as an unconstitutional dilution of black voting power, but the federal courts refused to order the requested remedy of district elections. Charlotte finally did annex its outer-ring suburbs in 1974, gaining a new booster slogan as the fiftieth-largest city in the United States. Although the metropolitan school district remained the city's greatest advantage in the ongoing busing crisis, municipal planning policies also continued to destabilize the desegregation formula by channeling residential development to the southeast suburbs and creating faraway havens from two-way integration. A resolution would not be possible until the school system addressed the protests by people whom the business elite considered incapable of sharing political power: white and black citizens who lived in north and west Charlotte.[15]

"Class Discrimination"

After the Supreme Court's ruling in *Swann*, the Charlotte-Mecklenburg school board devised a new busing formula that openly favored the affluent families in the southeast suburbs and extensively burdened the black and white neighborhoods on the northside and westside. During the summer of 1971, as the community awaited the revisions to the desegregation plan, a profound dispute emerged over two competing narratives of white flight. The majority on the board remained obsessed with the fear that two-way busing would drive prosperous families from southeast Charlotte to private education, and the arrival of the threesome from the CPA reinforced the resolve to keep suburban children in their neighborhood schools. The NAACP and many westside activists warned that unless the board stabilized the tipping schools in northwest Charlotte, the foreseeable flaws in the desegregation formula would continue to accelerate racial turnover in nearby white neighborhoods. Many white parents from the westside believed that the school board had intentionally sabotaged their children's schools in an attempt to present an unworkable plan to the Supreme Court, and they demanded the redress of severe racial imbalances such as the 508 black students and 68 white students at one elementary school. "I'm surprised there are even a few on the school board who even know where the westside is," remarked one neighborhood leader who had shifted his attention from the hospital protests to the busing controversy. One year after white families in north and west Charlotte overwhelmingly voted for the CPA candidates, the conflict over which students should be transported to black neighborhoods produced a permanent geographic schism in the antibusing movement and engulfed the public schools in the same class conflicts that roiled municipal politics and metropolitan development.[16]

The school board initially attempted to appease white families across the geographic spectrum through a one-way busing plan that closely resembled the contentious compromise of 1969. The proposal would have closed several more historically black schools and bused inner-city students to overcrowded suburban facilities supplemented by new mobile classrooms. The local television station run by Charles Crutchfield editorialized that unless the transportation burdens fell almost exclusively on minority students, integration would fail and the public schools would become "almost totally black." After Judge McMillan rejected the scheme, the superintendent's office drew up a "feeder plan" that sought long-term stability by keeping elementary classmates together through graduation and shifted almost all two-way integration reassignments to north and west Charlotte. The judge eventually approved a revised version of the feeder plan and forbade the operation of any majority-black school, which meant that the board would have to police the racial ratio of each facility and reassign white students to combat the tipping point phenomenon. A divided school board voted to implement the feeder plan but also to appeal the judge's authority to supervise resegregation trends. An enraged William Booe denounced the moderate antibusing faction, including fellow CPA leader Tom Harris and chairman William Poe, for refusing to obstruct the court-authorized plan, and he promised that true conservatives would sweep the next election and bring "a complete change in the school administration . . . from the superintendent on down."[17]

Judge McMillan acknowledged that the feeder plan revolved around "class discrimination" and created neighborhood schooling "protectorates" in the affluent sections of southeast Charlotte, but he suspended judgment on the question of whether obvious socioeconomic inequality would produce unconstitutional racial resegregation. The feeder plan sent black students to suburban schools for an average of ten out of twelve years and bused many white students from north and west Charlotte to historically black schools for either six or eight years. Residents of the Myers Park area would remain in their own neighborhood schools for the duration of their academic careers, and with few exceptions the middle-class children from the southeast suburbs that had launched the CPA also would stay close to home. The superintendent's office defended the disproportionate burdens

on white neighborhoods in north and west Charlotte by explaining that busing trips would be shorter because of the proximity of black areas. This approach displayed blindness toward the deep resentments that already existed in the neighborhood movement and failed to appreciate how rapidly
an uneven desegregation policy could destabilize a fragile residential landscape, especially when safe havens existed on the sprawling fringe of southeast Charlotte. "To sell out and move is a whole lot cheaper than sending a
child to a private school," exclaimed one white father during a speech warning the school board that the feeder plan would transform the westside into
an all-black ghetto. "I have long since stopped complaining about integration and have accepted this as humanly right," explained another parent who
had just moved his family from northwest Charlotte to a northeast suburb
because of the school situation, "but I do not and will not accept the fact
that my children must be bused through city traffic from a very desirable
neighborhood to an extremely undesirable neighborhood."[18]

The class and geographic inequities at the heart of the feeder plan became the catalyst for a new coalition called the Citizens United for Fairness
(CUFF), which cemented an informal alliance between white neighborhoods in northwest and northeast Charlotte that had emerged during the recent battles over planning policies and district representation. CUFF represented more than one thousand parents from five predominantly white
subdivisions, including many families that had played active roles in the
Concerned Parents Association a year earlier (figure 7.1). During the summer of 1971, CUFF petitioned the school board for busing equalization, declaring that "we are willing to bear a fair portion of school assignment burdens" and asking only that all white neighborhoods "be in the same boat."
Wilson Bryan, the leader of the CUFF alliance, explained that "we have
been told by some black people that this is a similar type of discrimination to
what they experienced over a period of years." The school board rejected
the equalization request at a raucous meeting where weeping teenagers and
shouting parents denounced Tom Harris as a "sell-out" after the CPA leader
provided the swing vote. CUFF then filed a class-action lawsuit asking
Judge McMillan to invalidate the feeder plan on equal protection grounds
and requesting permission to intervene on the side of the plaintiffs in the
Swann litigation. As the school year approached, students from the five
neighborhoods held a car wash to raise money for the fairness campaign,
and parents in CUFF organized a peaceful demonstration on the first day of
classes.[19]

The board recognized in advance that the feeder plan would destabilize
the schools and neighborhoods of north and west Charlotte, but education
officials continued to make the political accommodation of the southeast
suburbs the overriding priority. A few weeks after the majority faction denied the CUFF petition, a group of white families from southeast Charlotte

Figure 7.1. The Concerned Parents Association organized a massive rally at the county fairgrounds in the northern section of Mecklenburg County, Sept. 8, 1970. On the eve of the busing deadline, thousands of working-class white families promised to boycott the public schools, but the schisms within the suburban antibusing movement also moved quickly to the surface. During the next four years, many of the parents from north and west Charlotte in attendance at this rally joined the Citizens United for Fairness, a group that promoted busing equalization among white neighborhoods. Courtesy of the *Charlotte Observer* and the Robinson-Spangler Carolina Room—Public Library of Charlotte and Mecklenburg County.

protested their own reassignments to West Charlotte High, and the board quickly voted to allow the rising seniors from these affluent neighborhoods to remain in their current schools. Although many CUFF families followed the rules and hoped for a favorable outcome in the equalization lawsuit, a number of parents changed their children's legal guardianships, falsified their addresses, or rented temporary apartments and trailers in other attendance zones. Fewer than half of the white students assigned to West Charlotte High appeared when the new school year began, and the five westside and northside neighborhoods in CUFF began to portray the classic signs of residential transition. Julius Chambers denounced the feeder plan as an unconstitutional scheme "designed by southeast Charlotte" and a transparent blueprint for resegregation that "discriminat[es] against both blacks and whites." Wilson Bryan of CUFF, whose three children remained in the public schools, pleaded with Judge McMillan to intercede before north Charlotte became all-black. The judge instead responded that if the school board would accept its legal responsibility to ensure a white majority in the westside schools, then "it is within the realm of reason to hope that white adults will quit thinking of them as undesirable."[20]

CUFF's neighborhood-based populism demonstrated the potential but also the powerful obstacles facing an interracial coalition between the white and black families of north and west Charlotte. While geographic proximity created a shared resentment of the privileges and the power of the southeast suburbs, the same spatial landscape inflamed racial tensions that hampered an alliance of class interests. Both of the fairness policies demanded by the parents in CUFF—the equalization of the busing burden among white neighborhoods, and the stabilization of the integration ratio in the westside schools—revolved around fears that the feeder plan would trigger the racial turnover of their formerly all-white subdivisions. CUFF simultaneously represented a reactionary crusade against the reassignment of white children to schools in black neighborhoods, a progressive demand for lasting school integration through class fairness, and a desperate effort by white homeowners to stick together against the encroachment of black suburbanization. One white liberal who observed the chain reaction blamed the busing formula for white flight from the northeast suburb of Hidden Valley: "After a year of patience, whites began to leave to escape [busing] and some blacks moved in. . . . Most of the people here had a tolerance level, the number of blacks that would have to be on their block before they would move. . . . Shady real estate operators were going from door to door soliciting business. . . . Only when the influx of blacks was sudden did real problems arise." As black middle-class suburbanization brought neighborhoods such as Hidden Valley to the tipping point, residents who moved away candidly explained their motives in a media survey: "We just had to go. . . . We were the only white family left on the block"; "We had some neighbors moving in that we did not particularly like, and we have a teenage daughter [so] we had to get out of there"; "I moved out here [to the outer-ring suburbs] because my kids were being bused."[21]

The Revival of Moderation

In the fall of 1971, the *Charlotte Observer* announced the arrival of a "new and better era" and claimed that most citizens now viewed busing "as a challenge instead of a threat, an opportunity instead of a death sentence." The second year of comprehensive desegregation began smoothly, though the relative calm reflected the fact that the feeder plan catered to the privileges and prejudices of the southeast suburbs, while former CPA families from north and west Charlotte were now demanding fairness in court rather than organizing boycotts in the streets. The most dedicated busing opponents had also abandoned the conflict and transferred their children to private schools, which enrolled about two thousand additional white students during the 1971–72 academic year. But several troubled areas threatened to undermine the fragile consensus for quality education, including the tipping enrollments in the westside schools and another outbreak of racial violence in the traditionally white institutions. In late October, almost two hundred students took part in brawls at three high schools, and 96 percent of those arrested by the police and disciplined by the board were African-American (figure 7.2). The NAACP prepared an extensive report that focused on the underlying causes of the turmoil, including findings that many black students resented lengthy bus rides to hostile suburban schools, that informal quotas limited the number of minorities on sports teams, that security forces covered up disruptions started by white students, that discrimination pervaded the ability tracking programs, and that teachers remained ill-equipped to educate a new mixture of pupils from diverse racial and socioeconomic backgrounds. "Desegregation is one of those problems which cannot be solved by the schools alone," the NAACP concluded. "It is evident that the community as a whole must work together to achieve a truly integrated society."[22]

After the racial turbulence in the suburban schools, establishment leaders in Charlotte asked the Community Relations Committee to explore the root causes of citizen anger in an effort to resolve the protracted busing crisis. More than four thousand people—black and white, parents and students, rich and poor—answered the CRC's request for public input. The forums allowed a local silent majority to vent widespread frustrations against the traditional leadership, and hundreds of speakers castigated the Concerned Parents Association, the school board, the Chamber of Commerce, and the wealthy suburbs. "A lot of white people in Charlotte would like to do something in relation to their better instincts," maintained one father of four who formerly supported the CPA but now expressed anger about the favoritism extended to southeast Charlotte. "They don't quite know what to do and they are resentful and alienated from the traditional leadership. . . . They feel that the busing system that we now have is unjust and inequitable. That some neighborhoods where the rich and powerful live you don't have to be bused at all." A westside parent active in CUFF pledged that his neighborhood remained "willing to bear our part of the burden, our part of the opportunity, but we're just not going to take the present situation. We'll just move away or form private schools." Another white father described how his initial opposition to busing had evolved into an appreciation of the need for compliance with the law and an awareness of the discrimination faced by the black community. "I can't afford private schools," he admitted. "It's this or

Figure 7.2. During 1971, racial brawls and civil rights demonstrations spread through the high schools of Charlotte-Mecklenburg on several different occasions. At this suburban facility, police officers watch a group of black students who walked out of class to protest racial discrimination in disciplinary procedures and to demand courses in African-American history and a holiday to honor Martin Luther King, Jr. Courtesy of the *Charlotte Observer* and the Robinson-Spangler Carolina Room—Public Library of Charlotte and Mecklenburg County.

nothing else. . . . I'm not asking everybody to love my child or my child to love everybody, but he can respect their life and they can respect his. Usually as you get to know people, you do begin to like them better and respect them more. I don't know what else I can contribute, but I am trying. I may be against it, but I am trying."[23]

The heartfelt responses revealed a community in transition, still deeply divided in many respects but largely united in the desire to end the permanent politicization of public education. The CRC—a highly respected group that included establishment figures of both races and a heavy representation of white liberals from southeast Charlotte—presented its findings in March 1972. The report reinforced the accusations of inadequate leadership leveled by thousands of ordinary parents and concluded that the school board should include a diverse cross-section of the community in the search for a resolution. The CRC acknowledged the fundamental obstacle to desegregation stability: many black and white families in north and west Charlotte believed that they "are somehow less favored as citizens in this community and that citizens in other neighborhoods are better treated because of personal favoritism by those in power." In a notable plea for the reinvigoration of the Charlotte Way, the CRC predicted that if elected officials and prominent businessmen made quality education their top priority, then "the vast majority of the citizens of this community" would follow their leaders. The report also endorsed a broad range of reforms, from fairness in disciplinary proceedings to formal procedures to facilitate interracial dialogue among parents and students. Although the CRC did not recommend any specific guidelines for revision of the controversial feeder plan, the report forcefully concluded that "we need to involve the total community in a radical rethinking of what our schools are all about and what we expect of them. . . . Action, positive action, is needed to turn the tide strongly for public education."[24]

The school board election in the spring of 1972 provided convincing evidence that business leaders were determined to recapture the center. The downtown establishment mobilized behind three candidates who promised to shift the focus from busing to quality education: incumbent chairman William Poe; Dick Spangler, a resident of the elite island suburb of Eastover who owned a real estate brokerage and a construction company; and Phil Berry, an African-American executive at a major downtown bank. The unofficial slate received backing from the Committee for Better Government, the campaign arm of a powerful group of Democratic politicians and corporate executives, which ran advertisements and funded get-out-the-vote drives in black precincts. The establishment candidates also received the endorsement of the *Charlotte Observer* and the grassroots assistance of the Citizens for a Positive School Board, a new coalition started by white moderates in the southeast suburbs. The most progressive candidate, an LWV activist named Marylyn Huff, openly endorsed two-way integration and mobilized a network of liberal female reformers from southeast Charlotte. The westside and northside parents in CUFF supported an antibusing slate of neighborhood activists but also urged consideration of Phil Berry, on the grounds that the black community deserved representation on the school board. The Mecklenburg Conservatives, the anticharter group founded by William Booe, sponsored right-wing extremists who demanded a confrontation with the federal judiciary and denounced curriculum innovations such as sex education and reading through phonics. Two years after riding a populist backlash to power, the CPA endorsed stalwart opponents of busing but found it difficult to rally suburban parents in the evolving political climate. As one leader of the fading group acknowledged, "the people realize that they've gone as far as they can on the local level."[25]

The election restored the moderate tradition of leadership and confirmed the collapse of the organized antibusing resistance. The top four finishers, in descending order, were William Poe, Dick Spangler, Marylyn Huff, and Phil

Berry. The chairman avoided the runoff with overwhelming support in the southeast suburbs that spanned the ideological spectrum, from CPA members who still resented busing to white moderates who approved of his record of complying with the law and protecting affluent neighborhoods whenever possible. Spangler and Huff, the establishment moderate and the progressive reformer, carried the island suburbs of Myers Park and the subdivisions of southeast Charlotte that had voted for the CPA slate two years earlier. Black candidate Phil Berry received extensive single-shot voting in minority precincts, solid support in the affluent white suburbs, and a surprisingly strong showing in the white areas of north and west Charlotte (where blue-collar voters also chose George Wallace in the presidential primary). In an amiable runoff, business executives Spangler and Berry narrowly defeated Marilyn Huff, who lost out to the transparent desire of the downtown establishment to refill the semiofficial "black seat" on the board of education. The election returns validated the decisive intervention of the business community and marked the end of the CPA's three-year antibusing crusade. Reflecting on the hazy community consensus for quality education, one religious leader suggested that Charlotte's acceptance of the court order was "more likely the product of collective social fatigue than of moral awakening." But beneath the revival of moderation lurked the same unresolved dilemma: the inequitable distribution of busing burdens along lines of race and class.[26]

The professional educators in the school administration took advantage of the shifting community currents to propose a fundamental reassessment of the feeder plan. In the fall of 1972, schools reopened without major revisions in the desegregation formula for the first time in four years, but West Charlotte High again teetered on the brink of forbidden territory with a black enrollment of 49.4 percent. After the new year, the administrative staff released a Pupil Assignment Study shaped by advice solicited from students, teachers, parents, and civic organizations. The report declared bluntly that the inequitable burden of busing in the "self-destroying" feeder plan had caused white flight from north and west Charlotte. Because the integration formula had become the primary determinant of neighborhood selection for new arrivals and local migrants, an "equitable and stable assignment plan is hardly possible as long as school assignments are based on residence." The Pupil Assignment Study also recommended the formation of a diverse advisory committee to provide citizen input by bringing together business leaders, religious and civic groups, and neighborhood associations. Presenting the plan to the general public, assistant superintendent John Phillips drew the obvious but unpopular conclusion that two-way busing would remain necessary until Charlotte-Mecklenburg made a firm commitment to housing integration and reoriented population growth away from the southeast suburbs. He also warned that the time had come to stabilize the westside

schools with students from the symbolically powerful and residentially secure neighborhoods of southeast Charlotte: "The day of reckoning is at
hand."[27]

"Socioeconomic Integration"

During 1973, the neighborhood movements in north and west Charlotte finally forged an effective interracial alliance that demanded class and geographic fairness through the elimination of the antibusing sanctuaries in the
southeast suburbs. Despite the resurgence of moderation in the recent election and the call for a new desegregation formula in the Pupil Assignment
Study, the standoff between the school board and the judge continued to
revolve around the legal obligation to prevent resegregation in northwest
Charlotte. A terrible outbreak of violence also spread through a dozen junior and senior highs, resulting in campus patrols by police in full riot gear
and the hospitalization of several pupils and teachers. A large group of black
students from West Mecklenburg High received ten-day suspensions without formal hearings, even though a NAACP report charged that several hundred white students provoked the confrontation by chanting racial slurs and
throwing rocks at the buses taking their classmates home. The *Charlotte
Observer* blamed the unrest on the refusal of many in the white community
to reconsider their definition of desegregation as a "one-way street in which
blacks are required to meet whites' terms." The school board provided the
latest evidence of this bias with a new proposal to bus even more black students out to the suburbs, along with a resolution endorsing a neighborhood
schools amendment to the U.S. Constitution. Judge McMillan sharply accused the majority faction of a pattern of behavior that "tends to induce people to think or hope that desegregation of schools will 'go away' and that
without 'bussing' segregation can be restored." School officials responded
with an amended plan that met the district court halfway but also triggered
a fateful round of outrage from white and black parents on the northside
and westside.[28]

The busing revisions proposed in the spring of 1973 created a political
opening for the fairness movement and forced the judge to reassess his previous tolerance of "class discrimination." In a significant concession, the
school board offered to stabilize the tipping problem in several inner-city
schools with white students from the southeast suburbs. But the board also
needed to increase the white enrollment at West Charlotte High, because
of racial turnover in the subdivisions represented by CUFF, and education
officials chose the northside suburbs of Devonshire and Statesville Road.
A group of white liberals from north Charlotte, including an eloquent
spokesman named Julian Mason, decided that the time had come to take a

stand. A humanities professor at UNC-Charlotte, Mason lived in one of the new middle-income subdivisions in the Devonshire zone and had three children in the public schools. Under the feeder plan, one of his daughters rode the bus to a formerly black elementary school, where his wife Elsie served as co-president of the PTA. Both of the Masons believed firmly in racial integration, and three years earlier they had watched in dismay as many of their neighbors joined the CPA. But in 1973, Julian Mason sympathized with the widespread opposition against busing Devonshire students to West Charlotte, and he forcefully stated the case to the school board and in a private audience with the judge. "Feeling is running high and growing in this section that it is being unfairly discriminated against in these matters in favor of the more affluent," he warned. Many of his neighbors were threatening to sell their homes and move to the safe havens in southeast Charlotte. "Real good has been accomplished in changing attitudes" because of two-way integration, Mason believed, but now "ugly overt racism has begun to show itself again, and the feeling of having been treated unfairly gives it too fertile ground to grow in."[29]

Julian Mason represented a progressive cadre of ministers and college professors who urged their neighbors in northeast Charlotte to organize a protest movement around the themes of class and racial fairness rather than antibusing hostility. They reminded white parents that the feeder plan discriminated against black families more than anyone else, and they argued that an interracial neighborhood alliance could enlist the judge as an ally against the school board. "Stand up and be counted before it's too late," the ad hoc group urged in a flyer distributed to families in the Devonshire district. "Our children have borne the brunt of an unfair and unfeeling school board, a board who is afraid to create a stable school situation. Since we cannot all move to the southeast where such stability is assured, we must try to influence this board to create stability for us all." At a school board meeting on May 30, hundreds of black and white parents denounced the policy of protecting the affluent suburbs at the expense of everyone else. Julian Mason declared that "until all of the community is involved in busing there will be no stability in our school system. . . . The black community and the northern part of the community have done their share." The high point of the meeting came when Kathleen Crosby, a black activist and elementary school principal, criticized the heavy burden on minority students bused to overcrowded suburban schools while inner-city facilities remained far below capacity. The white parents from northeast Charlotte responded with rousing applause. "I said to myself, 'Honey, this can't be happening,'" Crosby told the news media afterward, as black and white parents huddled to plot strategy and formalize the new geographic alliance.[30]

Four years in the making, the interracial breakthrough represented an extraordinary development in the Charlotte saga, as suburban neighborhoods that had recently been fertile ground for the CPA's antibusing crusade now demanded comprehensive integration based on class and racial fairness. At the next school board meeting, a blue-collar leader of the northside parents unveiled a map demonstrating that two-thirds of board members, four-fifths of the administrative staff, and three-fourths of the city council and county commission lived in southeast areas that enjoyed complete immunity from two-way busing. Adopting the new interracial discourse of the neighborhood movement, construction worker Bruce Patterson declared that he was "not asking, not pleading, . . . I am demanding that the board take immediate action to insure fair busing for all citizens—black and white." In an informal conference with board members, Judge McMillan announced that he would not approve the reassignment of white students from northeast Charlotte, and instead he recommended that all additional transfers come from Myers Park—the city's real and symbolic embodiment of wealth, prestige, and power. "There is an unconscious assumption on the part of a lot of people on the board that folks with big lawns and spreading houses are more intolerant," the judge told his audience. "I don't think that's true." But the busing of Myers Park students to northwest Charlotte remained anathema to William Poe, who promised another appeal and forecast a doomsday scenario in which upper-middle-class families abandoned the public schools en masse. "Originally, the judge was talking about racial integration," the chairman told the press. "Now he is talking about socioeconomic integration, and the law says nothing about that. . . . It's just the judge's idea of how society ought to be."[31]

McMillan struck back with a remarkable appeal to the collective conscience of southeast Charlotte, tapping into a growing refrain that the white residents of the island suburbs were "limousine liberals" unwilling to accept their fair share of social change. The judge began by quoting from his original 1969 opinion, which recommended racial stability through a formula that would "equalize the benefits and burdens of desegregation over the whole county, instead of leaving them resting largely upon the people of the northwestern, western, and southwestern parts." He drew a sardonic comparison between the feeder plan and the ancient astronomical belief in an "earth-centered universe" to charge that a majority on the school board remained in denial of the legal obligation to prevent resegregation. For two years, McMillan had resisted the "class discrimination" claims by the NAACP plaintiffs and the CUFF interveners, but now he found as a matter of law that the unequal treatment of white neighborhoods thwarted the constitutional mandate to maintain racial desegregation. The judge issued an ethical appeal as well as a legal directive on the immediate problem of stabilizing the westside facilities with white students from the southeast suburbs that "continue to enjoy substantial immunity from having children transported to 'black' schools." He rejected predictions of upper-middle-class flight as an "apparent assumption that the people who live in south and east Mecklenburg are more self-centered or racially intolerant than the people who are already experiencing 'bussing.'" Directly addressing his own neighbors, the rural-born judge concluded: "I can not and will not make such a gloomy and defeatist and uncomplimentary presumption about such a large number of progressive citizens."[32]

The judge ordered public school officials to develop a completely new integration formula, based on class fairness and racial stability, in time for the 1974–75 academic year. The *Observer* embraced McMillan's stance with a piercing editorial that accused the school board of "blatant discrimination against many whites and blacks" and criticized predictions of mass defections to private schools as "an insult to the fair-minded people" who lived in southeast Charlotte. Charges that the privileged families of the island suburbs were not only selfish but also racially prejudiced stung many people who "held their own civic-mindedness in the highest esteem," in the words of one local journalist. In a survey conducted by the *Observer*, a large majority of business and political leaders, including Chamber of Commerce president C. C. Cameron and county commission chairman W. T. Harris, called on the school board to extend the additional busing burdens to southeast Charlotte. A group of upper-middle-class parents from the island suburb of Eastover transformed the proposal to send their children to Piedmont Junior High in downtown Charlotte into a conspicuous opportunity to demonstrate their own good faith. Once all-white, Piedmont had become associated with the crime and poverty of nearby housing projects, although the school remained only a few miles away from Eastover's pretty tree-lined streets. After a tour by the white parents, organizer Bob Culbertson reported: "Sure, I would rather the school be in a high-income neighborhood, but I think the move can be a favorable one for my children and for others."[33]

As the 1973 school year approached, the school board employed a random lottery to assign almost six hundred southeast students to West Charlotte High and voted to appeal the constitutionality of court-ordered "socioeconomic integration." While protests came from some white families that "won" the lottery, the transfers affected only a small percentage of suburban students, and the latest antibusing crusaders were left lamenting the resignation of the community to the tyranny of the judge. West Charlotte held an open house to display its refurbished football stadium and enhanced curriculum, and one white parent remarked that "they're trying to make a showcase out of it. It may end up being the best school in town." In the fall, 68 percent of the lottery students showed up at West Charlotte, and the high school's chronic instability gave way to a comfortable white majority. Optimists could note that two-thirds of suburban families had remained faithful to public education despite the presumed inconveniences of transportation to a historically black school. Pessimists could point to the fourth straight year of declining enrollment throughout the system, an aggregate departure of about ten thousand white students. Charlotte-Mecklenburg nevertheless continued to fare better than most other urban districts undergoing court-ordered busing, thanks to the consolidated school district and the judge's passionate refusal to tolerate residential segregation as natural or school resegregation as inevitable. The interracial neighborhood movement for class fairness and racial stability had created the political opening for a good-faith resolution, which would have to await the new busing formula required for 1974–75 and the decisive grassroots intervention by a group of dedicated white liberals from southeast Charlotte.[34]

CHAPTER 8

Class Fairness and Racial Stability

For integration to really work you've got to have a good
socioeconomic mix as well as a black and white mix.
—Robert Davis (1974), African-American principal,
Charlotte-Mecklenburg Public Schools

FORGING CONSENSUS

On the national stage, the mobilization of the Silent Majority depended
upon a populist discourse that obscured the divisions between working-
class and middle-class white voters and defined Middle America through a
suburban identity politics based on consumer status, taxpayer rights, and
meritocratic individualism. In both the political and judicial arenas, the
busing battles of the 1970s appeared to represent a clear confrontation between "color-blind" conservatism and "race-based" liberalism. But at the
metropolitan level, the links between social class and residential geography
shaped not only the initial emergence of color-blind populism but also the
ultimate outcome of race-conscious legal mandates. The *Swann* era revealed that the long-term viability of urban school systems under court-
ordered desegregation plans depended upon spatial and socioeconomic
remedies that encompassed the suburbs and pursued racial stability
through policies sensitive to the demands of class fairness. Judge McMillan's 1973 order to prevent racial resegregation by removing the class-based
inequalities among white neighborhoods represented a legal doctrine even
more innovative than his original mandate to overcome residential segregation by employing two-way busing throughout the consolidated school district. The court order presumed that "socioeconomic integration" of the
suburbs could arrest trends of white flight by eliminating antibusing sanctuaries through a comprehensive metropolitan remedy. In the short term,
the interracial movement for busing equalization culminated in a genuine
political settlement to Charlotte's constitutional impasse, proving the
power of the law to transform educational patterns but also the myriad
ways in which local people could shape the implementation of a judicial
decree. In the long term, the relentless march of suburban sprawl, combined with the failure to pursue a collective housing remedy that addressed
the causes instead of the symptoms of residential segregation, jeopard-

ized the most progressive accomplishment in the history of the Charlotte Way.

A political solution to the protracted busing crisis became possible because liberal activists and business leaders expanded the traditional framework of the Charlotte Way to address the neighborhood movement's demands for class fairness and geographic representation. The breakthrough originated in a collaboration between the League of Women Voters and the Chamber of Commerce, a convergence of the grassroots energy of the female reform tradition and the civic authority of corporate pragmatism. For almost three years, the LWV had lobbied municipal leaders for the establishment of a representative citizens committee to broker a desegregation compromise. In the spring of 1972, the Chamber of Commerce finally accepted the request to launch a community-wide alliance called the Quality Education Committee (QEC). A banking executive named Gene Cathey chaired the organization, and other founders included future Chamber president Don Bryant, progressive school board candidate Marylyn Huff, and Myers Park activist Margaret Ray. Although the QEC included parents from across the school district, LWV veterans and liberal white women from the affluent churches and island suburbs of southeast Charlotte were the driving force. In the fall of 1973, QEC leaders seized the opportunity to build on the momentum created by the interracial fairness movement by organizing a "Schools in Focus Week," sponsored by WBTV and the *Charlotte Observer* and highlighted by the participation of several thousand parents in community forums. Framing racial desegregation in the broader context of educational reform, and borrowing the language of the Community Relations Committee, the QEC reiterated that "we need to involve the total community in a radical rethinking of what our schools are all about and what we expect of them."[1]

The gateway to a grassroots resolution opened in November, when the school board held a special session to solicit advice on the new desegregation formula scheduled for unveiling in the spring of 1974. In the weeks preceding the public hearing, the QEC organized three closed-door gatherings of the invited speakers, including representatives from the NAACP, the Chamber of Commerce, the League of Women Voters, the Citizens United for Fairness, and the remnants of the Concerned Parents Association. "Southerners are usually trained to be polite at the table," observed Maggie Ray of the QEC, and so the initial meeting took place over a potluck dinner. The behind-the-scenes breakthrough came when participants agreed in principle that the burdens of busing must be spread more evenly throughout the district and that a racially and geographically diverse citizens committee would be necessary to bring the crisis to an end. At the televised meeting on November 20, most of the twenty-one community leaders embraced the ascendant consensus for "fairness and stability." Wilson Bryan of

CUFF demanded that all students in the district ride the buses for the same number of years, and a leader of the CPA's most conservative faction admitted that "we're tired of fighting" and agreed that everyone should "work together tighter, colored and white." Kelly Alexander of the NAACP reaffirmed the civil rights commitment to a pluralistic and egalitarian society and declared that "the schools are a good place to begin" the process of overcoming the racial divide between cities and suburbs. All of the speakers at the forum then jointly petitioned the board for recognition as an official advisory committee to help devise the new busing plan.[2]

Convincing the school board of the virtues of participatory democracy, and of the need for elected officials to be rescued by their constituents, remained a difficult task. After several weeks of resistance, and considerable behind-the-scenes pressure from the superintendent's office, William Poe announced the formation of the Citizens Advisory Group (CAG). The credibility of the new coalition lay in its broad-based membership, probably as representative as possible of the geographic, racial, and ideological spectrums in Charlotte-Mecklenburg. One parent from each feeder zone served on CAG, along with delegates from the LWV, the PTA Council, the Charlotte Area Clergy Association, the American Association of University Women, the Community Relations Committee, and the Knight Publishing Company (corporate owner of the *Charlotte Observer*). Other members included CUFF's Wilson Bryan, who claimed to represent thirty thousand "liberals and conservatives" from north Charlotte, two leaders of the remnants of the CPA, and the head of a new ultraconservative antibusing group from Mecklenburg County. Two women from the QEC assumed key roles: Sarah Stevenson, an African-American activist and former head of the PTA Council, and Elizabeth Bennett, a southeast Charlotte liberal who taught at a school for academically troubled youth. All of the CAG members were college graduates active in their PTAs, churches, and other civic organizations; most of the men were white-collar professionals or midlevel business executives, and most of the women were mothers and homemakers with a strong tradition of engagement in community affairs.[3]

CAG's public voice and private leader was Margaret Ray, a liberal reformer in her early thirties who grew up and still lived in the elite section of Myers Park (figure 8.1). Along with her husband, Tom, an attorney who often represented civil rights plaintiffs, Maggie Ray embodied the deep commitment to progressive activism common in the older island suburbs. As a member of the housing authority, Tom Ray championed the cause of residential integration through planned communities of racial and class diversity and the scattering of public housing projects throughout the suburbs. In 1969, the Rays proposed a two-way busing plan between the wealthiest neighborhoods in southeast Charlotte and the lower-income schools of the northwest quadrant, based on the prescient recognition that a desegregation

Figure 8.1. Maggie Ray, the chair of the Citizens Advisory Group, with her two children in front of their Myers Park home, May 30, 1974. Courtesy of the *Charlotte Observer* and the Robinson-Spangler Carolina Room—Public Library of Charlotte and Mecklenburg County.

formula perceived to favor Myers Park would destabilize the entire integration process. A former teacher, Maggie helped to found the Street Academy for students expelled from regular public schools. Her involvement with the QEC began after she volunteered in Marylyn Huff's school board campaign, and she delivered her second child one day after the runoff election. QEC colleagues recommended her for leadership of the Citizens Advisory Group because of her consensus-building skills and her extensive contacts throughout the Charlotte establishment. She was a personal friend of Judge McMillan, acquainted with William Poe through mutual membership at Myers Park Baptist Church, and a political ally of new county commission chairman W. T. Harris. She was fiercely committed to the full and fair integration of the public schools but patient and diplomatic in steering CAG in that direction. Her associates from across the ideological spectrum offered almost nothing but praise for her leadership during the hectic days of 1974.[4]

Throughout the winter, CAG struggled to devise guidelines that would satisfy the community and circumvent the "integration paradox," revealed in both local and national public opinion polls, where white parents expressed support for the principle of diversity but opposed the methods necessary to overcome residential segregation. CAG relied heavily on a scientific survey of schoolparents in order to "help the board get a better reading on exactly what people mean when they say 'fair' and 'stable.'" Two decades after the *Brown* decision, 69 percent of respondents expressed a preference for integrated schools if academic quality remained constant, while 22 percent favored a return to racial segregation. Two-thirds of community members opposed busing away from neighborhood schools, but an even greater three-fourths majority agreed that transportation burdens should be equalized across the district. The poll also revealed that two-thirds of parents preferred assignment to the closest school for as many years as possible instead of keeping classmates together throughout their academic careers, a rejection of the fundamental feature of the feeder plan. Using this redefinition of stability, CAG endorsed radically redrawn attendance zones through an approach dubbed the "proximity plan," including a fairness recommendation of busing equalization and an affirmative commitment to guard against resegregation. CAG also advocated the stabilization of racially integrated neighborhoods through assignment to the nearest school and a policy of constructing all new facilities in areas that would maximize integration and minimize transportation.[5]

Resolution at Last

At the beginning of 1974, when Bob Dylan came to town as part of his long-awaited comeback tour, Judge McMillan told a local gathering of educators that in Charlotte too, "the times they are a-changin'." In a speech that advanced a progressive and pluralist vision of public education and argued that exposure to racial and class diversity would prepare students for "the world and the future," the judge contended that "true education doesn't begin until we leave the neighborhood school." A few days earlier, the Fourth Circuit had dismissed the latest appeal by the school board, leaving in place the mandate to prevent resegregation in northwest Charlotte and equalize busing in southeast Charlotte. McMillan proclaimed his eagerness to close the *Swann* litigation, but when asked to define unitary status he replied, "I know it when I see it." The racial demographics in the district illustrated the clear failure of the feeder plan, with four majority-black facilities in direct violation of the court order and projections that one-third of the schools would soon exceed the tipping point of 40 percent black. But the majority faction on the school board rejected pleas to adopt CAG's "fairness and stability" guidelines and instead submitted a plainly unacceptable plan that increased the busing burden on the black and white neighborhoods of north and west Charlotte. When the judge ordered a new formula based on CAG's proximity model, the board promised another appeal and insisted that Charlotte-Mecklenburg had eliminated all vestiges of de jure segregation. In the political abstract, they had a solid argument that Charlotte faced a much stricter constitutional standard than many other cities that had achieved unitary status without dismantling all-black schools. But the judge held the legal trump card, and he had never wavered in his determination that desegregation be comprehensive and permanent.[6]

During the spring, Judge McMillan executed a shrewd strategy that empowered CAG as the legitimate voice of the community and thwarted the school board's transparent desire to seek appellate review. The board's defiant stance deeply angered the CAG members who had spent months working on desegregation guidelines, and they decided to submit their own plan to the district court. Maggie Ray bluntly informed the school board that the "community is ready and willing to undergo change in order to achieve some long range fairness and stability." From one end of the spectrum, antibusing leader James Postell said that participation in CAG had convinced him that "we'll have a better society if we assure everyone an equal education." From the other, black insurance agent Bill Smith reported that after "yelling at each other for the first couple of meetings, we discovered . . . we wanted the same things for our children—good education at the closest school possible, a minimum of time spent on the bus, an end to these constant changes and tipping schools." The judge promptly blasted the board for having "again defaulted in an obligation to the community and to the school patrons (in addition to the long-standing default in compliance with the orders of the court)." McMillan had always believed that a successful desegregation formula would have to come from within the community, and he ordered school officials to provide technical assistance for CAG's proximity formula. It seems clear that the judge intentionally postponed a legal showdown until after the upcoming school board elections, because all leading candidates were praising CAG's search for a resolution. "The public is ahead of the school board on the busing issue," declared Bob Culbertson, a former CAG member campaigning for fairness and stability. "The board seems more concerned with going back to court and fighting legal issues than it is with our kids."[7]

CAG unveiled the proximity plan in late May and prompted another contentious debate about the specter of white flight. By refusing to insulate southeast Charlotte from two-way integration, the proximity approach actually decreased the overall amount of busing across the school district. To achieve fairness, CAG's plan reduced the average transportation requirement for black students to six years and roughly equalized the busing for white students at three years (the racial disparity proved mathematically necessary because of the two-thirds white majority in the school system). On the crucial issue of stability, CAG recommended the vigilant maintenance of a 20–45 percent range of black students in each school for at least five years. CAG also called for racial quotas to govern admission to magnet schools and promised to locate six K–4 facilities in black neighborhoods, a symbolic break from the general policy of busing the youngest black children to the suburbs. To fill West Charlotte High, CAG selected five of the most prestigious island suburbs in southeast Charlotte—Myers Park, Oakhurst, Winterfield, Eastover, and Cotswold. More than anything else, these measures represented political solutions, designed to address the concerns of black parents about the survival of community institutions and defuse the charges of class discrimination from the white neighborhoods of north and west Charlotte. William Poe responded by branding the CAG plan "potentially a disaster," and other officials warned of a doomsday scenario where Charlotte-Mecklenburg reached a systemwide tipping point that would trigger massive middle-class flight from a majority-black and majority-poor district.[8]

But this was Charlotte, not Atlanta, and a loud chorus immediately insisted that the fundamental obstacle was not white flight but instead unimaginative leadership. After Poe conceded that a guiding principle had always been reluctance to place a "heavy busing burden on whites who can afford to send their children to private school," Maggie Ray accused the chairman of exaggerating the potential for white flight and insisted that southeast Charlotte would accept the requirements of fairness. The PTA presidents from the affluent island suburbs scheduled for reassignment to West Charlotte also expressed indignation and predicted that a majority of their neighbors would tolerate the new plan. "I don't like it," one PTA leader said, "but I realize I haven't paid any burden on this." On the other side of town, a north Charlotte parent named Robert Vermillion predicted that "fair-minded people will not abandon the school system just because everything isn't favorable to their special interests. I believe most people are fair if given the chance, and that our leaders have failed in their responsibility to encourage the best of our instincts and have sometimes inflamed the worst." The most critical intervention came from W. T. Harris, the owner of a local supermarket chain and the powerful chairman of the county commission, who expressed his "confidence in the good will of the people of this county to . . . support a plan which is fair." After a confidential lunch with the judge, Harris privately informed Poe that the time had come to accept a compromise that would satisfy the court and the community. Then Julius Chambers issued an unconditional endorsement of the proximity formula as "a fair and effective approach for desegregation." This convinced corporate allies on the board, led by businessman Dick Spangler, to call for negotiations with CAG in order to reach an accommodation that would be "fair to black students as well as preserving the confidence of the white community so they'll stay in the public schools."[9]

The school board elections of 1974 provided conclusive evidence that community sentiment favored the CAG approach of class fairness and racial stability. Two members of the Quality Education Committee quickly emerged as front-runners. Marylyn Huff galvanized a grassroots army of one thousand female volunteers who handed out cookies at suburban shopping centers and staked signs in yards across town. For half a decade, the southeast Charlotte liberal had raised an often lonely voice to insist that busing represented an opportunity and not a burden. During the 1974 campaign, Huff declared that educational opportunity should not depend on racial or economic status and said that "the time has come to focus our attention . . . on what happens in the classroom after the bus ride is over." Bob Culbertson, an insurance executive funded by the business establishment, endorsed the CAG plan that reassigned all three of his children to westside schools and pointed out that "integration is the law of the land, . . . and busing is the only answer to integration as long as we don't have integrated housing patterns." The *Charlotte Observer* endorsed liberal candidates Huff and Culbertson as well as John McLaughlin, a northern Mecklenburg resident who campaigned for geographic fairness. Marylyn Huff easily won the first round of voting, and in the runoff Culbertson and McLaughlin defeated an African-American challenger and unseated a conservative antibusing incumbent. The election of three supporters of "fairness and stability" revealed signs of a new progressive spirit but even more the reinvigoration of the Charlotte Way in a community that traditionally valued pragmatism over ideology and recognized that quality education would best be served by ending the long legal conflict.[10]

Could it really be over at last? The victory of three candidates who pledged to support the CAG approach seemed to assure a school board majority in favor of the elusive commitments to equalize busing and prevent resegregation. Representatives from CAG and the superintendent's office hammered out the details of the new desegregation plan in negotiations that were often heated and always complex. Maggie Ray refused to retreat on the long-term stability ratios, the assignment of affluent southeast neighborhoods to West Charlotte High, and the assurance that no black students would be bused to the suburbs throughout their careers. The formula also paired several inner-city black neighborhoods with outer-ring suburbs of southeast Charlotte—the same areas that five years earlier had formed the base of the Concerned Parents Association. CAG leaders reluctantly agreed to the retention of most of the K–4 grades in the suburban schools, a trade-off denounced by black community leaders and demanded by the school administration in order to diminish the threat of white flight. Almost no one embraced all aspects of the plan, but its diverse supporters recognized that the new approach would satisfy the court and probably the community. "I think school is for education and not for social experimentation," said one

Myers Park mother whose teenage daughter would soon attend West Charlotte. "The integration does not bother me—it's this idiot bus riding. We bought this house because of the neighborhood and the schools." Another Myers Park mother admitted that "I really think this is a more fair plan, but I don't like it. . . . I didn't think it was fair that the young black children got most of the busing in the past, while ours haven't been bused. . . . My son, I guess, has accepted it more than I have."[11]

On July 9, 1974, the new school board voted 6-2 to approve the joint proposal negotiated by CAG and the administrative staff. Chairman William Poe called on his Myers Park neighbors to accept reassignments to the westside but also reiterated his charge that the increased burden on southeast Charlotte came not from the law but instead "social, economic, or political reasons." Tom Harris, the former leader of the moderate wing of the Concerned Parents Association, refused on principle to vote for a plan that mandated "racial balance" but promised to work hard for successful implementation. The recalcitrant William Booe, representing the most conservative faction of the antibusing movement, guaranteed "extreme white flight" and insisted that the formula violated the color-blind requirement of the Constitution—an argument five years behind and several decades ahead of its time. A few weeks later, Judge McMillan issued a ruling that applauded the affirmative commitment to maintain desegregation as "a clean break with the essentially 'reluctant' attitude which dominated Board actions for many years." Assuming that the school board continued to demonstrate good-faith compliance, McMillan promised that he would soon close the case and declare the Charlotte-Mecklenburg school system to be " 'unitary' (whatever that is)." The judge had always refused to define desegregation in merely technical terms, and he had always insisted that the *Brown* decision meant that racially segregated schools inherently violated the Constitution, regardless of what the White House or the new Supreme Court majority or his neighbors in southeast Charlotte thought (figure 8.2). In conclusion, McMillan observed that just as *Brown* had recognized the injuries caused by racial segregation to the "hearts and minds" of black students, it took a change in the hearts and minds of Charlotte's leaders and citizens to reach the point when judicial supervision could end.[12]

CHARLOTTE EXCEPTIONALISM

The public schools of Charlotte-Mecklenburg opened without great fanfare in the fall of 1974, and every facility in the district remained within the court-mandated racial ratios. Most of the southeast students reassigned to West Charlotte showed up for classes, and the high school reached full capacity with a 61 percent white enrollment. William Poe conceded that

Figure 8.2. District Judge James B. McMillan, in an undated photograph. In 1969, editor Pete McKnight of the *Charlotte Observer* wrote that McMillan appeared to be "running for the office of s.o.b. without opposition." The judge, who endured numerous death threats in addition to antibusing demonstrations outside of his home, always maintained that he had no choice but to follow the legal principles set forth in the *Brown* decision. Courtesy of the Robinson-Spangler Carolina Room—Public Library of Charlotte and Mecklenburg County.

CAG's fairness formula had exceeded his expectations: "We have frankly sought stability by consciously giving to every neighborhood some reason to be unhappy about its school assignment at some point between kindergarten and graduation. It's an odd way to gain stability, but it does show some promise." At the end of a relatively quiet year, Judge McMillan deactivated the litigation in a final order titled "Swann Song." The NAACP did not contest the ruling, although Julius Chambers expressed lingering concern about the lack of K–4 grades in black residential areas and the in-school segregation trends in ability tracking programs. McMillan praised the new school board, which had "at last openly supported affirmative action" to combat resegregation, and he offered a final retort to the perennial critics who charged that busing represented nothing more than a liberal social experiment conducted by an unelected judge. "Ghosts continue to walk," he noted, most recently in sociological studies that blamed court-ordered busing for white flight from urban school systems, but all of his decisions had been based on the *Brown* ruling that racial segregation in public education was unconstitutional and "inherently unequal." More than two decades after that landmark ruling, six years after McMillan's first order in *Swann,* Charlotte's epic busing crisis had finally come to an official resolution.[13]

When Judge McMillan removed *Swann* from the active docket, the *Charlotte Observer* remarked that "the community has stumbled its way toward an emotional cease-fire, a kind of grudging community consensus" that fairness and stability were preferable to turmoil and uncertainty. The city's largest newspaper played a crucial role throughout the sustained crisis and guaranteed itself a prominent place in the annals of the progressive South. By never wavering in its support for the district court, the *Observer* established the boundaries of a public sphere that celebrated compliance, marginalized defiance, and pushed readers to think hard about the deeper meanings of racial integration and equal opportunity. "We had a strong source of support in the *Charlotte Observer,*" the judge reflected some years later. "It was informative, intelligent, and consistent. The *Observer* helped to shape the public's attitudes about the facts of the case. What they did was simply good journalism." It was even more than that. A southern newspaper, run by white southern liberals, insisted on the moral imperative as well as the legal inevitability of comprehensive integration in Charlotte, whether or not the rest of the nation remained committed to the task. The editorial page spoke a secular language of sin and redemption, calling on white families to view busing not only as a burden made necessary by the wrongs of the past but also as an opportunity for all children to grow up in a pluralistic and egalitarian society. The *Observer* often had more faith in the citizens of Charlotte-Mecklenburg than they had in themselves, and in the end much of that faith proved to be justified.[14]

The outcome of the busing battles in Charlotte also validated the essential wisdom of the founding principle of the Southern Regional Council: "Southerners themselves must ultimately work out democratic solutions to the South's problems." The extended impasse in a New South city dedicated to the peaceful resolution of racial conflict resulted in large part from the widespread perception that Charlotte had become the national test case for a radical desegregation experiment: first through the two-way busing program to overcome residential segregation, and then through the mandate to prevent white flight by pursuing "socioeconomic integration." Despite the suburban uprising of the CPA and the lengthy default of leadership by the downtown establishment, a potent reservoir of moderation and a powerful commitment to public education always existed in Charlotte-Mecklenburg. The key breakthrough came through the efforts of the grassroots delegates to the Citizens Advisory Group, led by liberal white women who brokered a compromise that revitalized the ethos of the Charlotte Way: "the highest and best example in matters of racial transition . . . resolved because of the good sense and basic good will of community leaders, white and black." But the catalysts in this process were the neighborhood movements from north and west Charlotte that restructured the framework of the Charlotte Way by demanding the involvement of the entire community in the desegregation plan, which forced the metropolitan region to face squarely the issue of class discrimination as well as racial inequality. Ten years of litigation did not accomplish everything that the NAACP wanted, but in the end it accomplished a lot. During the bleakest decade in contemporary urban history, the Charlotte-Mecklenburg school system attained a greater degree of racial integration and retained a higher degree of popular support than most of its counterparts among the large cities of the South and in the rest of the nation.[15]

As early as 1973, the *Charlotte Observer* predicted that the city would one day realize that "the painful dismantling of forced segregation in its school system may turn out to be its greatest asset for the future." That same year, when a metropolitan busing plan for Richmond, Virginia, failed on appeal, the *Observer* warned that "if the Supreme Court is becoming a protector of the suburbs and in effect a force for resegregation, the losers will be the cities—not simply because they are turning black but because they will be collecting places for disadvantaged peoples and inferior, segregated schools." By middecade, as the tumultuous busing battles in Boston dominated the headlines and the Supreme Court's *Milliken* decision foreclosed the possibility of metropolitan solutions in most major cities, the consolidated school system in Charlotte-Mecklenburg provided contrasting evidence that successful desegregation plans required suburban inclusion through spatial and socioeconomic integration remedies. "For integration to really work," African-American principal Robert Davis said in the summer of 1974, "you've got to have a good socioeconomic mix as well as a black and white mix." Even William Poe, who resisted class integration in Charlotte far more fiercely than he opposed racial busing, acknowledged in retrospect that "it has surprised me in a way that the school case could have had that much impact on almost everything in the Charlotte-Mecklenburg community, but strangely enough, and gladly enough, it has really seemed to me to sort of resolve race issues in Charlotte-Mecklenburg for the present time and to the foreseeable future. There had to be a struggle somewhere. It was fought at the level that impacted a great many people in a very emotional environment, . . . and it just had the effect of saying, well, this is the way things are going to be in Charlotte."[16]

After the end of the litigation, a school board dominated by white and black liberals became one of Charlotte's foremost champions of comprehensive and permanent integration. African-American incumbent Phil Berry easily led a crowded field in the 1976 election, and every victorious candidate (including former CPA leader Tom Harris) pledged to defend the "fairness and stability" formula. The assignment plan devised by CAG required only minor adjustments until 1978, when the school board transferred al-most five thousand students to remain within the court-approved racial ratios and to combat resegregation trends in northside and westside neigh-borhoods. The board's willingness to take affirmative action against resegre-gation prompted another "color-blind" lawsuit by the same attorneys who had represented the CPA eight years earlier, in an effort to use the Supreme Court's ambiguous *Bakke* ruling for a claim of "reverse discrimination" through a racial quota system. The school board aggressively defended its race-conscious assignment policies, and Judge McMillan upheld the trans-fers as appropriate under the *Swann* guidelines and permissible as an inde-pendent decision by school authorities that racially diverse classrooms pro-duced educational benefits. During each of the next seven years, under the interracial leadership of CAG veterans and liberal women activists such as Sarah Stevenson, Elizabeth Bennett, and Carrie Winter, the school board reassigned between one thousand and two thousand students for the express purpose of preventing resegregation. Between the mid-1970s and the mid-1980s, private schools registered only slight increases and the district's over-all enrollment stabilized at a 60-40 white-black ratio, providing compelling evidence that a metropolitan desegregation formula could neutralize white flight.[17]

Eventually, and not at all surprisingly, corporate boosters incorporated the achievement forged during the divisive struggles over court-ordered busing into the national marketing of Charlotte as the prosperous and pro-gressive embodiment of the latest New South. The Chamber of Commerce began touting the high quality of the integrated school system as part of its unrelenting drive to recruit corporations and white-collar migrants to its corner of the Sunbelt. The NAACP continued to express concern about lin-gering racial disparities in achievement test scores and lengthy bus rides for the youngest black children, but the civil rights organization strongly main-tained its commitment to systemwide desegregation in majority-white schools. Charlotte also received a burst of favorable publicity as the antithe-sis of the Boston disaster, highlighted by a CBS television special news re-port that contrasted the experiences of the two cities in a southern versus northern morality play. By the early 1980s, the city was basking in a spotlight of Charlotte exceptionalism, praised in the national media as proof that in the right place busing could succeed. A glowing profile in the *New York Times Magazine* featured numerous black and white students from Char-lotte who praised the racial diversity of their educational experiences, and the author then accused the Reagan administration of distorting the positive benefits of busing through its call for a return to neighborhood schools.[18]

Two leading actors in the Charlotte drama, Julius Chambers and James McMillan, became outspoken champions of the city that each had always believed possessed the resources and the character to do the right thing, if pushed hard enough. At a Senate hearing in 1981, both men testified that court-ordered desegregation had made Charlotte a better place to live, increasing opportunity in the schools and improving race relations in the community at large. North Carolina Senator Jesse Helms responded by denouncing "forced busing" as a liberal experiment in "social engineering [that] has had a devastating impact on the people of my state of all races." But a different message could be heard from William Poe, who embodied the boundaries of moderation and the potential for change in the New South city that never wanted conflict but found itself under the firm mandate of an indefatigable civil rights attorney and a very stubborn federal judge. By 1983, the former chairman of the board of education had reconsidered a central argument of the antibusing movement, that the "social experiment" of integration should not be conducted on schoolchildren: "If society's objective is to basically expose everybody to all there is in the environment and to hope that they will deal with conflicting forces, differences in people and all this, which I guess really is the overriding goal we ought to accomplish in society, then I suspect we are closer to the right track than we were before."[19]

The climactic moment in the chronicle of Charlotte exceptionalism occurred during a 1984 episode that quickly entered the progressive mythology of the New South metropolis. On a fall campaign swing, President Ronald Reagan spoke at a political rally at the SouthPark shopping mall, located in the heart of the affluent southeast suburbs. Fifteen years earlier, the Concerned Parents Association had passed out antibusing bumper stickers and gathered petition signatures at SouthPark, already a sprawling symbol of the growth priorities and consumer ethos of the Sunbelt South. Reagan delivered his standard stump speech for the overwhelmingly white audience, touting his administration's efforts to "encourage the values by which our nation has flourished," including the return of prayer to the public schools and provision of tax credits for private education. Then the president turned to what he and his advisers certainly expected to be an automatic applause line. The Democratic party, Reagan charged, supported "busing that takes innocent children out of the neighborhood school and makes them pawns in a social experiment that nobody wants. We found out it failed." The Republican crowd responded with an awkward silence. Local leaders from both parties criticized Reagan's remarks, and Superintendent Jay Robinson warned that a return to neighborhood schools "would tear the conscience out of this community." The *Charlotte Observer* summed up the prevailing mood in an editorial headlined "You Were Wrong, Mr. President." "Charlotte-Mecklenburg's proudest achievement of the past 20 years is not the city's impressive new skyline or its strong, growing economy," the

Observer declared. "Its proudest achievement is its fully integrated public school system, . . . shaped by caring citizens who refused to see their schools and their community torn apart by racial conflict."[20]

SPRAWL AND SEGREGATION

The local and national celebrations of Charlotte exceptionalism deflected attention from the persistent patterns of residential segregation that caused and outlasted the busing crisis of the 1970s. The direct connection between sprawl and segregation always represented the central obstacle to integrating the countywide school system, since almost all black families lived in the northwest quadrant and the majority of the white population lived in the southeast suburbs. The court-ordered remedy of two-way busing addressed the symptom of racial segregation in neighborhood schools but never directly challenged the structural foundations of housing segregation by race and class that dominated the metropolitan region. Most parents and leaders in Charlotte came to accept the necessity of a "fairness and stability" resolution in order to satisfy the judge and end the long standoff, not out of any genuine acknowledgment of the public policies that simultaneously subsidized the white suburbs and constructed the black ghetto. But the schools would be fighting a constant battle against resegregation as long as suburban sprawl continued to be created by developers, pursued by homeowners, and actively subsidized by the municipal, state, and federal governments through policies ranging from mortgage interest deductions to utilities extensions and highway construction. Although the countywide desegregation formula mitigated white flight by removing incentives to purchase homes based on the racial demographics of the nearest school, most residents of metropolitan Charlotte continued to reside in neighborhoods segregated by a fusion of race and income. By the end of the 1970s, 93 percent of the African-American population remained in a compact area encompassing 9 percent of the land in the northwest quadrant, while the suburban boom had spread throughout Mecklenburg County and beyond into a sprawling metropolitan region.[21]

The developer-dominated political culture in Charlotte, driven by the growth agenda of the city's banking, retail, real estate, and construction industries, exerted constant stress on the "fairness and stability" desegregation blueprint. Longtime mayor John Belk, the president of the family corporation whose department stores anchored every major suburban shopping mall, openly symbolized Charlotte's overriding priority of unrestrained growth. But Allen Tate, a wealthy real estate developer who served as chairman of the Charlotte-Mecklenburg Planning Commission during the busing crisis, provided the clearest example of the downtown establishment's casual conflicts of interest and reflexive conflation of corporate profits with the civic good. As the community struggled to resolve the desegregation conflict, Tate's real estate company began a new project transforming four hundred acres of farmland in southern Mecklenburg County into a one-thousand-home subdivision called Walnut Creek. In the mid-1970s, Walnut Creek represented only one of six new residential subdivisions under construction on the exurban fringe of southeast Charlotte, encompassing more than six thousand homes and requisite amenities such as strip malls and golf courses. Summing up his own philosophy, Tate explained that citizens were willing to accept inconveniences such as traffic congestion and a more impersonal city in exchange for the "good, sound growth" that provided homeowners with the suburban dream and guaranteed Charlotte a future of economic prosperity. The NAACP countered with demands that planners and politicians actively curtail residential expansion in the southeast suburbs by refusing to extend water and sewer services to new subdivision developments that would exacerbate housing segregation and require long-distance busing to desegregate nearby schools. "Let us not forget," NAACP leader Kelly Alexander said, "that the total community should be working toward the common goal of not only developing an integrated school system, but also an integrated society."[22]

During the 1970s, the corporate growth agenda across the Sunbelt South came under unprecedented attack from quality-of-life revolts at the neighborhood level. The antisprawl movement in Charlotte included a diverse spectrum of civil rights activists, disfranchised northside and westside neighborhoods, and affluent suburban homeowners. "Is there no place in Charlotte, not even in the perimeter, where a residential area is sacred?" lamented one suburban mother frustrated by traffic jams and overcrowded schools. Another white-collar couple from southeast Charlotte charged that "it has become a continuing battle for suburban homeowners to protect themselves against developers who would desecrate remaining open land with crowded apartment complexes and unnecessary shopping centers." During the 1973 municipal elections, northside activist Jim McDuffie almost unseated John Belk by deriding the mayor as the front man for the "downtown business–Chamber of Commerce establishment." Although the *Charlotte Observer* traditionally embraced the growth-is-good mantra of the Sunbelt South, the editorial page broke ranks during the election and declared runaway suburbanization to be the most urgent issue facing the metropolitan region. After acknowledging that Charlotte's bankers and developers had transformed the city into a national metropolis, the newspaper charged that their vision of progress equaled "the downtown of Atlanta combined with the suburbanized world of Los Angeles, . . . an all-commercial skyscraper downtown, supplied with automobile escape lanes to outlying areas of ersatz 'country living.'" The *Observer* demanded a system of mass transit and insisted that the time had come to pursue "growth intelligently directed in the public interest, not growth controlled only by the natural laws of the marketplace."[23]

The formation of the Dimensions project, promoted by neighborhood activists who argued for a more inclusive approach to metropolitan planning, represented another conspicuous sign of the dissolution of popular deference to the corporate leadership. Under pressure on multiple fronts, the Chamber of Commerce agreed to establish the Charlotte-Mecklenburg Dimensions Committee, a racially and geographically diverse group of citizens charged with the task of mapping the city's future. The Dimensions delegates endorsed a new city-county consolidation drive, district representation in municipal politics, geographic diversity on the planning commission, medical facilities located throughout the county, a system of mass transit, and a commitment to permanent school integration. In a concurrent development, city and county planners unveiled a twenty-year blueprint, "Comprehensive Plan 1995," designed to address quality-of-life crises such as traffic congestion, air pollution, and suburban sprawl. The document promised geographically balanced suburban growth through the use of sewer and water utilities as leverage to encourage residential developments to the north and west of the city. Subdivisions would cluster around five new "Metropolitan Service Centers," modeled on the giant SouthPark shopping mall and office complex and connected to downtown by mass transit and to one another by an outer-belt interstate highway. Although the blueprint ducked the fundamental issue of residential segregation, Comprehensive Plan 1995 represented an ambitious regionalism strategy based on attracting young professionals to the downtown district while channeling suburban growth more evenly throughout the county.[24]

The interracial neighborhood movement that forced a class-based resolution of the busing crisis and demanded a balanced approach to metropolitan planning also played the critical role in the demise of Charlotte's undemocratic system of at-large elections. A successful petition drive by civic groups from north and west Charlotte resulted in a 1977 ballot referendum to replace the current city council with seven districts and four at-large seats. Mayor John Belk and a majority of the council members opposed the initiative and raised the familiar specter of "machine politics" in an open effort to preserve the power and privilege of southeast Charlotte. Support for the referendum came from Harvey Gantt, an African-American architect who won a seat on the council after heading a committee that called for city planners to redirect growth away from the southeast suburbs and focus instead on revitalizing urban neighborhoods. The *Charlotte Observer* endorsed the district plan as essential to making progress in addressing the sprawl crisis and overdue in distributing power beyond the southeast base of the business establishment. In the spring of 1977, an interracial electorate based in north and west Charlotte provided the narrow margin of victory for district representation and altered forever the allocation of political power in municipal government. Six years later, black and white voters who supported the "neighborhood planning" movement placed Harvey Gantt in the mayor's office, a progressive black leader in a majority-white southern city. Although a symbolic end to the hegemony of Myers Park, the arrival of district representation and the election of an African-American mayor refined rather than shattered the Charlotte Way, as the crosstown alliance between corporate executives and black professionals remained intact. The more significant sign of political transformation came in 1987, when Republican Sue Myrick defeated Gantt in an election decided by middle-class white voters in recently annexed suburbs that the mayor had actively pursued, in the city's interest if not his own.[25]

The central dilemma of Charlotte's recent history is that the busing crisis empowered a neighborhood movement that demanded fairness in planning and stability in the schools, but the dynamic growth of the Sunbelt metropolis has increasingly strained the civic allegiance to comprehensive desegregation. Absent an aggressive and systematic municipal commitment to residential integration, including mandatory mixed-income zoning for all new developments and formal coordination between metropolitan planning and school desegregation policies, suburban sprawl has offered individual remedies rather than a collective antidote for a historical landscape of de jure housing segregation. In a 1973 consent decree that settled a civil rights lawsuit, the city council did agree to locate all new public housing projects in majority-white neighborhoods, but fifteen years later the controversial scattered-site program had produced fewer than one thousand apartment units. Black residential patterns also increasingly reflected socioeconomic differences with the suburbanization of the African-American middle class and an influx of minority professionals from the North. During the 1980s and 1990s, indices of residential segregation in Charlotte declined to a level significantly below the national average, but about half of all black students continued to live in a hypersegregated and high-poverty section of the northwest quadrant (map 8.1). At the same time, a large percentage of white middle-class migrants settled in outer-ring subdivisions on the exurban fringe of southeast Charlotte or in new residential suburbs located in the northern part of the county near UNC-Charlotte and along the I-77 corridor. Barely a decade after the "fairness and stability" resolution, the political repercussions of suburban sprawl reignited the dormant debate between defenders of affirmative action to maintain racial integration and supporters of neighborhood schools to safeguard class privilege.[26]

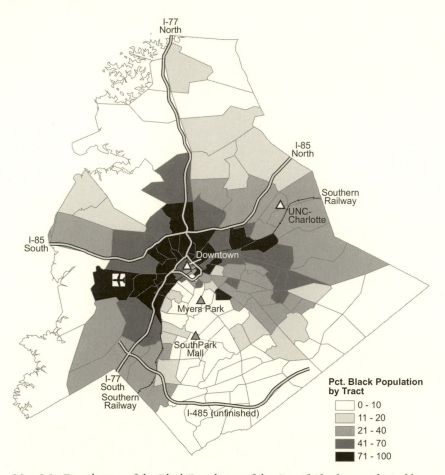

Map 8.1. Distribution of the Black Population of the City of Charlotte and Mecklenburg County, 2000, by Census Tract. Thirty years after the busing crisis began, the
northwest Charlotte ghetto continued to display high levels of residential segregation, but suburban migration by middle-class black families also produced a substantial degree of housing integration in the northern, eastern, and western sections of
Mecklenburg County. The island suburbs of southeast Charlotte remain overwhelmingly white and affluent. The I-485 beltway, scheduled to encircle the city by 2010
and modeled on Atlanta's perimeter highway, symbolizes the public policies that
have encouraged the spread of suburban sprawl throughout Mecklenburg County
and into the metropolitan region beyond. *Source:* U.S. Census Bureau, 2000 Census
of Population and Housing.

BACK TO THE FUTURE?

The meritocratic ethos celebrated throughout America's upper-middle-class suburbs has always contained two central contradictions: the refusal to acknowledge that any historical forces greater than individual accomplishment shaped the spatial patterns of the metropolitan landscape and the "neighborhood schools" presumption that children of privilege should receive every advantage of the consumer affluence accumulated by their parents instead of competing on an egalitarian playing field. In the era of the Silent Majority, court-ordered busing evoked intense grassroots opposition precisely because the redistributive policy severed the link between residence and education that white suburban families viewed as the consumer reward of a free-market meritocracy—an essentially inalienable middle-class right secured through individual perseverance and paid for by hard-earned taxes. In this sense, the antibusing protests that revolved around "color-blind" justifications and "reverse discrimination" charges resembled the political and philosophical opposition to affirmative action policies much more than the initial segregationist resistance to the *Brown* decision, except that for white suburban families the stakes were far higher than in the emerging debates over racial preferences in employment or college admissions. In Charlotte-Mecklenburg, affirmative action in the form of court-ordered busing transported individual white students to inner-city neighborhoods that suburban parents imagined to be dangerous and impoverished, to schools that they knew had never been "separate but equal."

Two-way integration constituted a frontal assault on the consensus among the white middle class that a nice home in a safe and segregated suburban neighborhood served by quality public schools was critical to living the good life and the key to their children's futures. Over the course of the five-year legal struggle, however, a large majority of white families in Charlotte-Mecklenburg decided that they could reconcile their own versions of the American Dream with enrollment in a comprehensively integrated school system. Although an acceptance of the benefits of diversity generally eclipsed acknowledgment of the de jure roots of housing segregation, in time many of these parents and students came to believe that integrated schools were both desirable and essential in a multiracial and decent society. Whether white families made these decisions out of egalitarian ideals, financial constraints, simple resignation, or evolving priorities as actual experiences in desegregated environments altered racial attitudes, the outcome of Charlotte's long busing saga demonstrated the possibilities of progress toward genuine integration and equal educational opportunity in the second generation after the *Brown* decision. Over time, the civic pride in Charlotte's accomplishment became so entrenched among many longtime residents that when a neighborhood schools movement finally resurfaced in the white-collar suburbs, conventional wisdom blamed self-centered newcomers and especially "Yankee transplants" who did not understand the burdens of history in the New South metropolis.[27]

Suburban sprawl in the Sunbelt South has not proved to be compatible with either racial stability or class fairness. By 1990, a remarkable one-fifth of the 473,133 residents of Charlotte-Mecklenburg had moved to the county from out of state during the previous half-decade. Drawn by civic anchors such as NationsBank (now Bank of America) and the surge of corporate relocations and regional branch offices that turned Charlotte into one of the nation's premier financial centers, most of these white-collar migrants bought homes in the sprawling suburbs on the southeast fringe or the distant new subdivisions of northern Mecklenburg County. In the late 1980s, transplanted middle-class parents became the driving force behind a revitalized neighborhood schools movement that blamed "forced busing" for the creation of a mediocre school system that inconvenienced children with long-distance transportation and damaged educational quality by mixing students of vastly different academic abilities. "We can't get anyone to admit that there are any problems in this district," lamented a real estate agent who moved down from New Jersey and joined a group of parents from an affluent southeast subdivision to oppose the placement of "slow and quick learners" in the same classrooms. "Because ability levels pretty much go down black-white lines," another mother in the group explained, "it's frustrating to have the issue muddied by a label of racism. This is not a busing issue. This is not an integration issue. This is a quality-of-education issue." The class-driven expression of antibusing sentiment also appeared among some black families in the suburbs, as an African-American parent recently transferred to Charlotte explained that "if I wanted my children to attend school with kids from the projects, I'd have moved next to one."[28]

In the resilient tradition of the Charlotte Way, the corporate establishment intervened to forge a middle path between the political demands for class resegregation and the existing program of two-way busing, without sacrificing the city's national reputation for progressive race relations and its direct link to the local economic boom. The Chamber of Commerce has always viewed school integration through the lens of the business climate, and during the late 1980s and early 1990s prominent figures such as NationsBank CEO Hugh McColl and First Union CEO Ed Crutchfield exerted critical behind-the-scenes influence that led to a major reorganization of the desegregation plan. During an era of national anxiety over the perceived failure of public schools to prepare students for the global economy, high-level executives of corporations that had relocated to Charlotte began exerting considerable pressure for the termination of the busing program. In 1987, the public relations emergency convinced the Chamber of Commerce to establish a task force to address the "problem of quality education" in order to ensure that the metropolitan region would not be "disadvantaged as a community in attracting and keeping good industry." One year later, candidates funded by major corporate interests won the school board election by unseating a group of incumbents that included Carrie Winter and Sarah Stevenson, two veterans of CAG and longtime champions of comprehensive integration. The Chamber of Commerce also backed the hiring of a new superintendent who promised to phase out two-way busing between inner-city and suburban schools in favor of "voluntary desegregation" through magnet programs, against the opposition of the NAACP and the LWV. In the spring of 1992, the school board converted more than twenty inner-city facilities into magnet schools, with admission governed by a racial percentage formula, while committing Charlotte-Mecklenburg to "become the premier integrated urban school system in the nation."[29]

The 1990s demonstrated once again that grassroots backlash against comprehensive integration is inevitable in a metropolitan school district that includes a hypersegregated ghetto marked by a high concentration of poor minority students along with multiplying exurban subdivisions home to predominantly white and overwhelmingly middle-class families. The population of Charlotte-Mecklenburg increased by more than 200,000 residents during the decade, as the metropolitan region remained an exemplar of the growth boom across the Sunbelt. Enrollment in the public school system also soared to nearly 100,000 students (50 percent white, 42 percent black, 4 percent Hispanic, 4 percent Asian). Most schools maintained stability in a range between 30 and 60 percent black, but a number of facilities in the inner city and the outer-ring suburbs became racially isolated, and many magnet programs also reflected patterns of in-school segregation. In a series of hard-fought contests, a new suburban organization called Citizens for a Neighborhood School System elected several antibusing representatives, but a majority on the school board remained committed to the race-conscious desegregation formula. A growing number of African-American parents also joined the call for a return to neighborhood schools as an alternative to the long-distance busing of black students to the suburbs and discriminatory ability tracking in the magnet schools. Faced with clear evidence of a divided community, political and business leaders in Charlotte returned to the formula that had resolved the original busing crisis by establishing a diverse citizens group to devise new desegregation guidelines. The 1997 report of the Citizens Task Force for Future School Planning announced a vision of "a community where equity and educational excellence define our schools, while racial integration and reduced reliance on busing naturally occur." How all of these priorities could be achieved simultaneously remained unclear and quickly became the source of an escalating debate.[30]

The central refrain of Charlotte's latest neighborhood schools movement revolves around an unapologetic defense of class privilege, expressed as a "quality education" demand for socioeconomic segregation, that extends far beyond the rhetoric of the Concerned Parents Association in the 1970s. While Charlotte's original antibusing movement denounced two-way integration but reluctantly endorsed the one-way transportation of black students to suburban facilities, the participants in the 1990s incarnation advanced a color-blind demand that students of different income levels and achievement test scores should not learn together in the same classrooms or even attend the same schools. In an updated fusion of overt class prejudice and submerged racial sentiment, the neighborhood schools revolt of the late 1990s insisted that the one-way busing of low-income students into affluent areas damaged the self-confidence of poor pupils and hampered the educational opportunities of their high-scoring suburban classmates. A historian, or a resident with a long memory, might be forgiven a sense of déjà vu as the color-blind echoes of the Silent Majority spread across the southeast suburbs. "Our taxes should cover us to go to the public school of our choice," an angry white father told the school board. A real estate agent who recently relocated to Charlotte complained that middle-class families "felt that when we chose to settle in our various neighborhoods, we also chose our schools." The *Charlotte Observer* responded that since new arrivals had not lived through the hardest struggle in the city's history or experienced meaningful desegregation "in the suburbs of the North," they did not understand the depth of the community's commitment to school integration or the moral burdens that made racial equality a civic imperative. "As a long-time resident who remembers what life was like in this part of the world before desegregation," a liberal white activist remarked, "I have no patience with the current crop of carpetbaggers seeking to undo thirty years of progress for their own convenience."[31]

Despite the judicial approval of resegregation in many southern cities and the color-blind retreat encouraged by the Reagan and Bush administrations, a firm commitment to the principle if not always the practice of racial integration infused Charlotte's political culture throughout the 1980s and 1990s. The failure of the neighborhood schools movement to secure color-blind assignments through municipal politics led to a new round of class-action litigation charging that the race-conscious desegregation plan constituted reverse discrimination against white students. As metropolitan Charlotte closed out the twentieth century with another landmark trial on the horizon, vacillating between the booster celebrations of Sunbelt prosperity and the destabilizing consequences of suburban sprawl, the most significant feature of the busing battle was that the community remained in a position to have this debate at all. Unlike their counterparts in Atlanta, and in so many other major metropolitan regions, most suburban families in Charlotte-

Mecklenburg have not escaped the question of what it means to attend integrated public schools in an increasingly multiracial society. Through the 1990s, the metropolitan remedy effectively prevented an irreparable cleavage between the suburbs and the central city and created the spatial framework for stable racial demographics, grassroots citizen engagement, and a resilient civic consensus to pursue both integration and quality education in a large urban school district. But despite Charlotte's structural advantages and the eventual "fairness and stability" resolution, the powerful antibusing movement of the 1970s played a leading role in the political revolt of the Silent Majority during the Nixon era, and many former members of the Concerned Parents Association might reasonably have concluded that they lost the local battle but won the national war.

At the grassroots level, supporters of comprehensive integration turned out to be correct in their insistence that the citizens of Charlotte-Mecklenburg could not defy the authority of Judge McMillan. But in the broader arena, the reliance on the NAACP and the judicial branch to devise and enforce the nation's desegregation policies illustrated the absence of a political coalition willing to address the structural legacies of residential segregation or challenge the historical amnesia of color-blind meritocracy. In a reflective speech delivered one year after the end of the *Swann* litigation, the decade-long chairman of the Charlotte-Mecklenburg school board lamented the absence of a coherent national desegregation standard, which had allowed "judicial policymaking to fill a legislative vacuum." William Poe criticized the outcome as "indefensible and unfair," based on broad discrepancies in the legal requirements faced by large cities "because different judges have read different shades of meaning and have injected their widely varying personal philosophies into the Constitution." Whether or not observers agreed with the political philosophy of the veteran of Charlotte's busing crisis, it would be hard to dispute the fundamental assessment that the constitutional mandate of *Brown* did not mean the same thing across the South or throughout the nation, or even within separate political jurisdictions located in the same metropolitan region. The national commitment to the principle of racial equality would be sorely tested during the polarized era of the Silent Majority, as the suburbanization of southern politics and society accelerated, the battles over court-ordered busing and metropolitan remedies enveloped the Sunbelt, and the politics of neighborhood schools and housing integration exploded above the Mason-Dixon line.[32]

PART III

Suburban Strategies

CHAPTER 9

The Suburbanization of Southern Politics

> Is our party the party of Lincoln or the party of Thurmond? . . .
> The Republican Party must respond to the challenge of change in
> the South by stepping forward boldly and offering Southerners of
> all races hope for a new tomorrow.
>
> —The Ripon Society (1967)

IN THE SUMMER of 1970, delegations from suburban antibusing movements in seven southern states gathered in Atlanta to forge a political alliance called the Unified Concerned Citizens of America (UCCA). The leaders of the grassroots uprising spreading across the metropolitan South included physicians, attorneys, and other upper-middle-class professionals—the most affluent tier of the broad swath of Middle America mobilizing under the banner of the Silent Majority. Although President Richard Nixon had popularized the political label in the fall of 1969, when he called on the "great silent majority of my fellow Americans" to rally behind his military policies in Vietnam, the founders of the UCCA expressed anger that the White House had failed to rescue their children from the domestic threat of "forced busing." The coalition demanded intervention by the Nixon administration to ensure that school districts in the South faced the same desegregation requirements as their counterparts outside the region. "Time for lip service is over," the UCCA's statement of principles declared. "We want action." Taking matters into their own hands, the leaders of the populist rebellion in the white-collar suburbs promised to establish a "Legal Offense Fund" to counter the Legal Defense Fund affiliated with the NAACP. Spokesmen for the UCCA claimed to represent one million neighborhood schools supporters in twenty-seven states, and they called on all Americans to support their "great crusade." "It is time, long overdue, that we take a stand," declared Dr. Mitchell Young of Texas, the chairman of the fledgling organization. "We are going on the offensive," warned a Miami Beach attorney named Ellis Rubin. "We are going to organize the largest, most effective lobby this country has ever seen."[1]

Two weeks later, more than one hundred antibusing leaders from three dozen metropolitan regions reconvened in Norfolk, Virginia, to launch a national campaign of grassroots protest with the slogan "Go for Neighborhood Schools." Adopting the color-blind discourse of the suburban antibusing movement, the UCCA insisted that members of the confederation "are not opposed to integration and are not a racist organization." The group's manifesto denounced "government tyranny in our public schools" and called for control of public education to be returned to local communities. The UCCA leadership predicted that if white middle-class families across the nation exerted sufficient pressure on the White House and the U.S. Congress, a bipartisan political movement would prevent the federal courts from violating the Constitution by busing students away from neighborhood schools for racial balance. In pursuit of regional fairness, the group demanded that the metropolitan South receive "the same treatment as northern cities" because residential patterns in urban centers throughout the United States resulted from "de facto as opposed to de jure segregation." To demonstrate the national solidarity of the Silent Majority, the UCCA touted delegates from Mississippi to Michigan and scheduled its third meeting in Chicago on the weekend before the Supreme Court hearing in the *Swann v. Charlotte-Mecklenburg* case. The antibusing confederation also announced a nationwide membership drive and threatened to hold a political convention of the Silent Majority on the eve of the 1970 fall elections.[2]

The suburban strategies evident in the grassroots mobilization of the Silent Majority, not a Southern Strategy implemented from the top-down by conservative GOP politicians, paved the way toward the center-right dynamic that has dominated regional and national politics since the late 1960s. Building on Kevin Phillips's thesis in *The Emerging Republican Majority*, influential scholars and journalists have explained southern political realignment through a reductionist narrative that portrays Barry Goldwater and George Wallace as the prophets of a conservative racial backlash that laid the groundwork for the winning Southern Strategy employed by Richard Nixon and his Republican successors. While numerous GOP campaigns have featured "dirty tricks" and veiled appeals to the racial resentments of a subset of the white electorate, accounts of regional transformation that highlight these stories often conflate the fringe with the middle and invert the sequence of political change in the South. According to one historian of postwar conservatism, "Nixon's odes to the 'silent majority' in 1968 echoed Goldwater's 'forgotten man,' and his 'Southern Strategy' courted the same white 'backlash' voters that gave Dixie to Goldwater by huge margins." According to the most prominent biographer of Wallace, the segregationist Alabama governor provided the road map for opportunistic Republican politicians from Richard Nixon to Ronald Reagan to Newt Gingrich. Through a process that the Southern Strategy school has dubbed the "Southernization of American politics," the race-based realignment that began in the Deep South expanded into a national backlash against liberalism, as the Republican party constructed a populist white conservatism that transcended class lines and regional borders.[3]

A grassroots approach to the political transformation of the South reveals that the regional base of the Republican party always depended more on the middle-class corporate economy than on the working-class politics of racial backlash. As political rhetoric, the populist label of the Silent Majority concealed the socioeconomic and geographic divisions among white voters, but corporate executives and white-collar professionals and blue-collar laborers have not fit comfortably into a racially constructed electoral coalition at either the regional or the national level. Richard Nixon's triumph in 1968 depended upon a de facto suburban strategy that targeted middle-class voters in the metropolitan South and positioned the GOP as the centrist alternative to the racial extremism of George Wallace and the racial liberalism of Hubert Humphrey. In the midterm elections two years later, when the White House did pursue a genuine Southern Strategy designed to steal Wallace's thunder by exploiting the desegregation climate, the top-down attempt to re-create the Solid South through racial demagoguery turned into a political disaster. The GOP's abandonment of the middle ground created an opening for a new breed of moderate Democrats who dominated southern politics during the 1970s and assumed the leadership of the national party during the 1990s. The "third way" championed by President Bill Clinton, combining fiscal and social moderation with populist appeals to Middle America, represented the Democratic version of a centrist suburban strategy forged during the divisive showdowns of the Nixon era.

Although the Republican party benefited most from the suburban ethos of the Silent Majority, the populist revolt of the center transcended the conservative mobilization of the New Right. During the late 1960s and early 1970s, in response to the civil rights movement's concerted attack on metropolitan patterns of residential segregation and educational inequality, the neighborhood-based mobilization of the Silent Majority propelled a powerful politics of middle-class warfare into the national arena. The suburban strategies that revolved around a color-blind defense of the consumer rights and residential privileges of middle-class white families ultimately succeeded where the overtly racialized tactics of the Southern Strategy had failed. By the mid-1970s, the grassroots protests of middle-class suburbs and the transparent responsiveness of political and judicial institutions had produced a new public policy framework that circumscribed civil rights reform on the metropolitan landscape and effectively redefined state-sponsored residential segregation as "de facto" economic stratification. The suburban realignment of American politics ultimately helped to establish an underlying consensus in a postliberal order, a bipartisan defense of middle-class entitlement programs and residential boundaries combined with the futuristic ethos of color-blind moderation and full-throttled capitalism at the center of the Sunbelt Synthesis.

THE SUBURBAN ORIGINS OF SOUTHERN REPUBLICANISM

Demographics played a much more important role than demagoguery in the emergence of a two-party system in the American South. As a top-down and race-dominated account of electoral realignment, the Southern Strategy framework obscures a more compelling narrative that revolves around the class-stratified and grassroots-driven politics produced by the spatial land-scapes of suburban development and the ideological triumph of the Sunbelt growth consensus. During the three decades after World War II, the politi-cal center of gravity shifted to the sprawling metropolises of the Sunbelt South, and the middle-class residents of the booming suburbs became the most influential swing voters in a region traditionally divided between the cities and the countryside. Steady depopulation underlay the fading power of the rural Black Belt, a subregion whose share of the presidential vote de-clined from 43 to 23 percent of the Deep South between 1920 and 1980, and from 22 to 4 percent in the states of the Outer South. The explosive population growth in the metropolitan centers reflected the economic revo-lution launched by the Keynesian fiscal policies of New Deal liberalism and cemented by the militarization of the regional economy through Cold War spending patterns. During the postwar decades, the suburban residents of the metropolitan regions and the white-collar migrants to the Sunbelt South increasingly converged with the class-based and issue-oriented voting trends in the rest of the nation and diverged from the single-party politics of white supremacy that dominated the Black Belt and the rural strongholds of the Deep South.[4]

The Dixiecrat revolt of 1948 represented the opening gambit of the Black Belt campaign of massive resistance, not the segregationist spark that cre-ated the southern wing of the Republican party. After the national Demo-crats endorsed a strong civil rights platform, racial conservatives from the Deep South renounced Harry Truman and formed the alternative States' Rights Democratic party. Led by Governor Strom Thurmond of South Car-olina, the Dixiecrat agenda sought to deny Truman a majority in the elec-toral college by sweeping a Solid South. Instead Thurmond's third-party candidacy carried only four Lower South states—Louisiana, Mississippi, Al-abama, and South Carolina—and electoral shenanigans kept Truman's name off the ballot in each of these Dixiecrat conquests. Truman easily defeated Thurmond in every southern state that offered the electorate the opportu-nity to select the national Democratic ticket. In the six states of the Outer South, between 83 and 91 percent of white voters rejected the Dixiecrat option, with fidelity to the two-party system strongest in the metropolitan regions and the mountains. The strain within political history that ap-proaches the dissolution of the Solid South from the geographic perspective

TABLE 9.1

Percentage of the White Southern Vote Received by Segregationist/States' Rights Candidates in Three Presidential Elections, 1948–1968, by State and Subregion.

Candidate	Thurmond (1948)	Goldwater (1964)	Wallace (1968)
Mississippi	92	91	83
Alabama	84	77	78
South Carolina	76	70	41
Louisiana	52	65	60
Georgia	22	65	51
Deep South	56	71	63
Arkansas	17	49	46
Tennessee	14	51	39
North Carolina	9	49	37
Florida	16	56	32
Virginia	11	52	28
Texas	10	44	22
Outer South	12	49	31
Total South	23	55	40

Source: Earl Black and Merle Black, The Vital South: How Presidents Are Elected (Cambridge: Harvard Univ. Press, 1992), 147.

of the Black Belt and the top-down machinations of conservative elites downplays the consistent failure of the Dixiecrats and their various Southern Strategy successors to achieve the goal of regional unity throughout the civil rights era. Beginning in 1948, the states of the Deep South diverged from broader regional and national trends and supported the losing candidate in every presidential election for the next two decades, with the sole exception of the Kennedy-Nixon contest in 1960 (table 9.1).[5]

The Republican surge during the 1950s revealed the substantial differences in political outlook between white-collar voters in the metropolitan regions and Dixiecrat stalwarts in the rural countryside. According to the leading observers of southern political trends, "the rise of cities and suburbs increasingly led by a new middle class committed to economic development was creating an electorate more sympathetic to Republican economic views." In 1952, moderate Republican Dwight Eisenhower campaigned in the no-longer-solid South and won half of the white vote regionwide, including the high-growth states of Virginia, Tennessee, Texas, and Florida. A turning point in the trajectory of Sunbelt realignment, the Eisenhower breakthrough "clearly established the GOP as the respectable party of the urban and suburban affluent whites." The Republican base revealed a high correlation with economic status, as Eisenhower received about three-fourths of the vote in upper-middle-class and wealthy metropolitan precincts across the region, including the affluent corners of the Deep South. In 1956, two years after the *Brown* decision, Eisenhower's reelection campaign secured a majority of the region's electoral votes and added Louisiana to his existing Outer South coalition. Although the grassroots party infrastructure lagged behind the presidential returns, the fiscal conservatism and social moderation of the national Republicans appealed strongly to upwardly mobile white voters who placed economic priorities over "the primacy of strict racial segregation" and rejected the single-party mantras of the Solid South.[6]

In the fall of 1960, 200,000 people in Atlanta turned out to hear Vice President Richard Nixon announce that "it is time for the Republican candidates to quit conceding the South to the Democrats." After the middle-class crowd mobbed his motorcade, Nixon delivered a campaign speech that promised military strength in the Cold War and advocated limited government and individual initiative in the domestic economy. He also defended the Eisenhower administration's civil rights record and the national commitment to ending racial discrimination under the law, while telling the audience that "I recognize it is not just a southern problem." Although Nixon lost the election, the Outer South states of Florida, Virginia, and Tennessee remained in the Republican column, and middle-class white voters in metropolitan centers such as Atlanta and Charlotte continued the trend toward the GOP. John F. Kennedy barely edged Nixon in four other states—Texas, Arkansas, North Carolina, and South Carolina—where the Republican ticket garnered between 46 and 48 percent of the ballots. As the depopulation of rural areas and the explosive growth of metropolitan centers altered the regional balance of power, the long-term outlook in the Sunbelt states of the Outer South and the booming suburbs throughout the region clearly favored the economic conservatism and relative racial moderation of the national Republican party. Between 1950 and 1970, the ratio of southerners living in metropolitan regions increased from 34.5 to 55.2 percent, including about half of the population in four states (Georgia, Alabama, Louisiana, Tennessee) and around two-thirds of the total in three of the largest states (Virginia, Florida, Texas). During the same period, a majority of the states in the Outer South aligned with the victorious side in the quadrennial national elections.[7]

The Goldwater debacle of 1964 fundamentally misread the long-term trends in southern politics and flipped the Republican base in the region inside-out. Senator Barry Goldwater of Arizona updated the genuine Southern Strategy of the Dixiecrats by campaigning as a states' rights conservative who opposed the Civil Rights Act and openly appealed to the segregationist wing of the Democratic party. But "hunting where the ducks are," as Goldwater labeled his racial backlash strategy, succeeded in forfeiting 63 percent of the electoral votes in the South. By winning only his home state and the hard-core base of racial resentment in the Lower South, Goldwater inadvertently reaffirmed the wisdom of the Eisenhower-Nixon strategy of running nationally oriented rather than southern-specific campaigns aimed at the suburban electorate. The GOP won 87.1 percent of the Mississippi vote and carried four other Lower South states, small consolation for a devastating defeat in the national returns that included the loss of Texas, Florida, Virginia, North Carolina, Tennessee, and Arkansas. The Goldwater forces marginalized centrist Republicans who had been struggling to build the party at the grassroots and alienated moderate swing voters as well as the increasingly powerful black electorate. The Ripon Society, a progressive GOP policy group formed two years earlier, mocked Goldwater's predictions of a Solid Republican South and pointed out that the ticket performed much worse than Eisenhower's record in the 1950s and lost ground among middle-class white voters in the major metropolitan areas. Ripon urged the party to return to its well-tested New South strategy and reminded GOP leaders that "until 1964, Republican growth in the South was centered in the urban and suburban communities, which enjoyed an atmosphere of more racial moderation, higher educational attainment and greater economic prosperity."[8]

The ascendancy of the metropolitan South reflected the increasing convergence of regional trends with the suburban outlook of national politics and the Sunbelt agenda of economic conservatism. In their pioneering work on electoral realignment, political scientists Earl and Merle Black concluded that the "main winners in the new southern politics have been the growing middle classes," a product of the economic modernization of a "region whose social structure is no longer distinctive." During the postwar decades, the fusion of racial moderation and fiscal conservatism represented by the power of Sunbelt corporations and the values of suburban taxpayers supplanted the political culture of the New Deal era. The suburban priorities of the New South simultaneously rejected the race-baiting politics of the Black Belt and the progressive social programs of the Great Society, resulting in a "region energetically committed to rapid economic development" but organized around faith in the "primacy of individual, not governmental, responsibility for economic well-being." In the aftermath of the Goldwater setback, the Ripon Society demanded the restoration of moderation over extremism and declared that "the Republican Party must respond to the challenge of change in the South by stepping forward boldly and offering Southerners of all races hope for a new tomorrow." The GOP faced a clear choice, Ripon announced: "Is our party the party of Lincoln or the party of Thurmond?" The answer to this question, from the grassroots mobilization of the Silent Majority to the Sunbelt agenda championed by the New Nixon, split the difference down the middle. The modern

Republicans turned out to be neither the defenders of civil rights nor the demagogues of white supremacy, but instead the regional and national party of middle-class entitlement, corporate power, and suburban protectionism.[9]

NIXON'S SUBURBAN STRATEGY

Richard Nixon won the 1968 presidential election on the strength of an implicit suburban strategy that targeted white voters who identified themselves as Middle Americans and capitalized on the political convergence of the metropolitan South with the prevailing patterns in the nation at large. For many Americans, the tumultuous events of 1968 raised fundamental fears about the future of their nation, as a half-decade of political violence spread from the backwoods of Mississippi to the inner cities of Los Angeles and Detroit, from the streets of Dallas to the assassinations of Robert Kennedy and Martin Luther King, Jr., from the jungles of Vietnam to the climactic confrontation between antiwar activists and the Chicago police at the Democratic National Convention. During the most polarized era of the century, the Republican candidate's populist appeals to the Forgotten Americans simultaneously cast white-collar and blue-collar families as the unsung heroes of the nation and the undeserving victims of the liberal War on Poverty, the military stalemate in Vietnam, the militancy of the Black Power movement, and the disorder in the cities and on the college campuses. In his convention speech, Nixon promised "an honorable end" to the war in Vietnam and the restoration of "law and order" in domestic affairs, and he reassured Middle American voters that "the dark long night for America is about to end."[10]

The three-way contest allowed Nixon to stake out the political center, by design and by default, as the respectable choice for middle-class voters who rejected the Great Society liberalism of Hubert Humphrey and the reactionary racial populism of George Wallace. In the first national election in which suburban residents constituted a plurality of the electorate, the Nixon campaign reached out to disaffected blue-collar Democrats but aimed primarily at white-collar Republicans and moderate swing voters in the metropolitan centers of the Sunbelt South and West and the upwardly mobile suburbs of the Midwest and Northeast. Nixon forfeited the African-American vote to the Democratic party and conceded the Deep South to the Wallace insurgency, in recognition that the Goldwater debacle of 1964 had reversed Republican trends in the high-growth states of the Outer South. The third-party candidacy of George Wallace revolved around a blue-collar populism that championed "the average man on the street, . . . the bus driver, the truck driver, the beautician, the firemen, the policeman, and the steelworker, the plumber." Nixon's broader embrace of Middle America emphasized the white-collar suburban subdivision more than the working-class urban neighborhood, the middle-class nuclear family over the beauticians and barbers, and the Sunbelt South instead of the Deep South. During a televised appearance in North Carolina, Nixon explicitly denied charges that his campaign was employing a Southern Strategy to steal Wallace's segregationist base and conspicuously commended the citizens of the New South for their progressive racial attitudes and full embrace of national ideals.[11]

The Nixon campaign understood that an open appeal to the Wallace insurgency would backfire by alienating moderate Republicans and middle-class swing voters in the suburban South and in the rest of the nation. The Republican candidate claimed in his memoirs that he could not have won the Deep South in 1968 without reversing his long-standing support for the *Brown* decision. Nixon's most widely circulated comments regarding civil rights came after the campaign rally in Charlotte, when he endorsed school desegregation but expressed opposition to busing for racial balance and counseled against class-based integration between ghettoes and suburbs. This color-blind stance did not represent a play for the working-class voters of the Deep South and the rural countryside, where the politics of white supremacy and massive resistance still resonated. Nixon's platform aimed instead at the white-collar voters in the residentially segregated suburbs of the Sunbelt South, where the political culture of middle-class respectability shunned Wallace as a lower-class rabble-rouser, and the prevailing ethos of individual meritocracy accepted the principle of racial equality under the law. Nixon's suburban strategy in 1968 revolved around the incisive recognition that an insurance agent in Charlotte or a middle manager in Atlanta welcomed the same combination of conservative economic policies and moderate racial rhetoric that resonated for an aerospace engineer in southern California, a homemaker in Omaha, or an accountant in New Jersey.[12]

Political consultant Harry Dent, a close ally of Senator Strom Thurmond and the adviser for southern affairs in the Nixon White House, later revealed that campaign leaders vetoed efforts by the most conservative faction in the GOP camp to reach out to white segregationists through a full-blown Southern Strategy. Behind the scenes, Nixon certainly attempted to finesse the race issue, and his public commitment to *Brown* was always more perfunctory than enthusiastic. At the Republican National Convention in Miami, Nixon quietly appeased the racial conservatives from the Goldwater wing of the party, led by Thurmond and Governor Ronald Reagan of California, by choosing backlash hero Spiro Agnew as his running mate and promising to keep federal enforcement of school desegregation and open housing to the minimum required by the law. Thurmond stumped across South Carolina to assure white voters that Nixon backed the local control of public schools, and the campaign publicized the candidate's Charlotte comments against forced busing in flyers circulated throughout the state (figure 9.1). The GOP also bombarded the South with advertisements warning that a wasted vote for Wallace would help elect Humphrey. The clearest example of this balancing act came during a regionally televised appearance in Atlanta when journalists forced Nixon to address Hubert Humphrey's charge that Wallace was "the apostle of hate and racism." George Wallace "is against a lot of things Americans are frustrated about," Nixon responded. "He's against the rise in crime. He's against the conduct of foreign policy. . . . I'm against a lot of these things. The difference is I'm for a lot of things, and that's what we need now."[13]

The law-and-order platform at the center of Nixon's suburban strategy tapped into Middle American resentment toward antiwar demonstrators and black militants but consciously employed a color-blind discourse that deflected charges of racial demagoguery and insulated the Republican from direct comparisons to Wallace. In his Miami convention speech, Nixon pledged to reverse the "failed" Great Society programs that he claimed had squandered billions of dollars in the War on Poverty and vowed to conduct an aggressive war on crime to guarantee all citizens their right to enjoy "freedom from fear." Then he directly addressed accusations that the "law and order" slogan represented a coded appeal to white racism by declaring that his agenda involved nothing less than "justice for every American." In a national radio address pledging to "win the war against crime and disorder," Nixon again raised the charge that his emphasis on law and order was "secretly anti-Negro" in order to assure audiences that "nothing could be less true." At a rally in Norfolk, Virginia, he promised that hardworking Americans would flourish and the "lazy" would falter under a Nixon administration, with equal opportunity for all "no matter what their background or heritage or the color of their skin." After a predominantly middle-class crowd of 150,000 greeted Nixon's motorcade in Atlanta, the candidate again denied that law and order was "a code word for racism," denounced George Wallace as unqualified for the White House because of his confrontational style, and equated the New South with the values and priorities of the rest of the nation.[14]

The television commercials produced by the Nixon campaign also adopted racially inclusive words and images, not in a genuine attempt to win black votes but instead in order to reassure the target audience of white moderates. "I see the face of a child," Nixon's voice opened one television commercial. "What his color is, what his ancestry is, doesn't matter. . . . This child must not have his dream become a living nightmare of poverty, neglect, and despair." Black as well as white representatives of Middle America appeared throughout these advertisements, which contrasted the productive citizens of both races with hedonistic youth and angry protesters who almost always appeared as white figures. The most controversial commercial

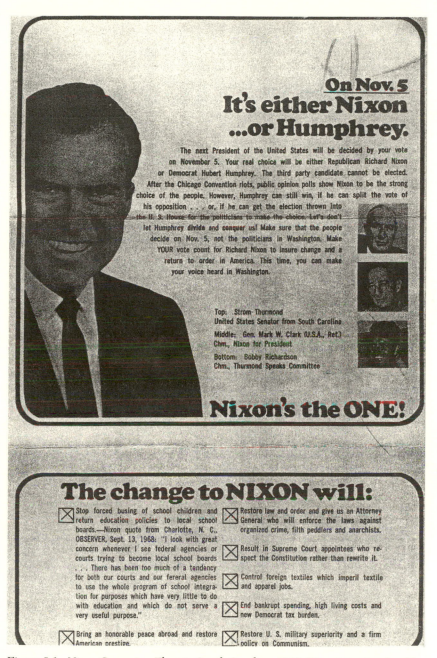

Figure 9.1. Nixon Campaign Flyer in South Carolina, 1968. Literature circulated by the Republican party and endorsed by Senator Strom Thurmond quoted Richard Nixon's Charlotte commentary against "forced busing" and warned South Carolinians not to waste their votes on George Wallace. Courtesy of the Harry S. Dent Papers, Special Collections, Clemson University Libraries.

sought to exploit fears of urban crime by portraying a middle-aged white woman walking nervously down a deserted city street as heavy footsteps sounded behind her, leaving the color of the stalker to the imagination of the viewer in a revealing example of the visible invisibility of race in Nixon's suburban strategy. A more typical advertisement flashed a discordant mixture of distant shots of burning cities and close-up images of bloodied white students before concluding with Nixon's assurance that "the first civil right of every American is to be free from domestic violence, so I pledge to you: We shall have order in the United States."[15]

The Nixon campaign's most evocative television commercial directly contrasted the campus radicals and urban militants of the sixties with a mélange of racially inclusive and patriotically iconographic scenes that celebrated the quiet heroes of Middle America by invoking the placid memories associated with fifties suburbia. The four-minute advertisement opened with jarring music and disturbing images of armed troops in the nation's cities, defiant student protesters, Vietnam War casualties, and a row of missiles. In words drawn from the convention speech, Nixon's voiceover told viewers that "America is in trouble today not because her people have failed but because her leaders have failed. We see Americans dying on distant battlefields abroad. We see Americans hating each other, fighting each other, killing each other at home." Then the tone suddenly shifted to soothing music and tranquil scenes of a nuclear family on a pretty beach, a white mother raking leaves in front of a typical suburban home, a black man hard at work, a group of happy shoppers at the mall, a middle-class white family making homemade ice cream. "Let us listen now to . . . the voice of the great majority of Americans, the forgotten Americans, the non-shouters, the non-demonstrators," implored the Republican candidate. "They are not racists or sick. They are not guilty of the crime that plagues the land. They are black and they are white, native-born and foreign-born, young and old. They work in America's factories; . . . they run America's businesses; they provide most of the soldiers who died to keep us free. They give drive to the spirit of America; . . . they give lift to the American dream. . . . They work, they save, they pay their taxes, they care." After defining Middle America as a stoic and heroic group that included the industrious members of every race and ranged from corporate executives to blue-collar steelworkers, Nixon reminded viewers that the nation deserved "leaders to match the greatness of her people."[16]

Praising the essential decency and quiet heroism of Middle America has always been a shrewd electoral strategy, but Nixon's reaffirmation of the moral innocence of "the great majority" also represented a carefully calibrated response to the civil rights movement and an implicit repudiation of the 1968 Kerner Report. Nixon's convention address featured the ostensibly compassionate sentiment that racial reconciliation could only happen in people's hearts if the nation were to "build bridges to human dignity across the gulf that separates black America from white America." This prescription of psychological transformation as the primary remedy for racial segregation invoked and then deflected the Kerner Commission's structural indictment of the public policies that had created "two societies, one black, one white—separate and unequal." And the moral descriptions of the Forgotten Americans found throughout Nixon's stump speeches and television advertisements—"they are not racist," "they are not guilty," "they care"—invoked and then rejected the Kerner Report's blunt conclusion that "white racism is essentially responsible for the explosive mixture which has been accumulating in our cities." Nixon's color-blind populism celebrated the hardworking and taxpaying Forgotten Americans in order to evade the call for forceful government action to address residential segregation in the suburbs and combat racial inequality in the cities, a political blueprint that resonated for white middle-class voters in the metropolitan South and throughout the nation.[17]

THE "EXTREME CENTER"

In national returns, Richard Nixon barely edged Hubert Humphrey in the popular vote, with George Wallace finishing a distant third. The Republican electoral calculus depended upon a geographic coalition based in the Sunbelt and the lower Midwest. In the South, Nixon won a narrow 34.7 percent plurality, followed by Wallace with 34.3 percent and Humphrey with 31 percent. This "tripartite southern electorate" revealed the presence of three unusually distinct voting blocs with strong correlations to class status and residential geography—a Republican base among middle-class and upper-income whites in the cities and suburbs, the Wallace coalition of rural and working-class whites, and the Democratic reliance upon African-Americans. Nixon received a 45 percent plurality in the Outer South and won the states of Virginia, North and South Carolina, Tennessee, and Florida. He secured a clear majority of white-collar professionals, middle-class suburbanites, political independents, and self-identified racial moderates. The Wallace fusion of economic populism and racial demagoguery received 31 percent of the vote in the Outer South, with the bulk of his support coming from white residents of working-class urban neighborhoods and rural precincts. Wallace handily carried the states of the Deep South with a 63 percent white majority that resembled the Goldwater patterns of 1964. Nixon received less than one-third of the white vote in the Deep South, with GOP inroads heavily concentrated in the affluent metropolitan precincts. African-American voters overwhelmingly supported Hubert Humphrey, who edged Nixon in Texas through the resilience of New Deal alliances, but otherwise the

Democratic ticket appealed mainly to prosperous white liberals. Although far from a conservative realignment, the 1968 election demonstrated that around three-fourths of white southern voters and a solid majority of their counterparts outside the region had decisively rejected the party of Great Society liberalism.[18]

Nixon dominated the white-collar suburbs of the metropolitan South in an election that demonstrated the grassroots strength of the Republican party in the Sunbelt economy. In the bellwether state of Virginia, Nixon carried the fast-growing suburbs outside Washington and won nearly 60 percent of the ballots in the suburban Richmond counties of Chesterfield and Henrico, two overwhelmingly white enclaves where 25 percent of the voters supported Wallace and only 15 percent preferred Humphrey. In North Carolina, Nixon received more than two-thirds of the vote in the upper-middle-class suburbs of Charlotte and about half of the equivalent vote in Raleigh and Greensboro, with the remainder divided evenly between his two competitors. The returns in Georgia, which Wallace carried decisively, illustrated the class and geographic divisions within the white South more than any other state. In metropolitan Atlanta, Nixon secured half of the suburban vote in DeKalb County, while Humphrey edged Wallace for second place. In adjacent Fulton County, Nixon easily won the affluent white precincts in the northside suburbs, Humphrey triumphed in the black precincts inside the city, and Wallace carried the blue-collar southside neighborhoods. The GOP campaign successfully targeted the "affluent urban and suburban whites throughout the region," according to a statistical analysis of the southern electorate, revealing that "the economic conservatism of the affluent whites was substantially different from the social conservatism of the common white folks."[19]

Nixon's moderate rhetoric on civil rights issues reflected a political balancing act that effectively sanctioned the status quo in race relations and roughly captured the evolving, and at times contradictory, expressions of white sentiment across the country. In the fall of 1968, two-thirds of white respondents in a national survey criticized African-Americans for "asking for more than [they are] ready for," and fewer than one-third believed that "progress in civil rights should be speeded up." At the same time, more than half endorsed the statement that "America has discriminated against Negroes for too long" and agreed that law and order required more "justice for minorities." When asked which candidate shared their racial views, survey participants identified Wallace with a reversal of civil rights and Humphrey with an acceleration of racial progress, while a plurality associated Nixon with maintenance of the status quo. Mutually contradictory attacks by his opponents cemented Nixon's firm occupancy of the political center, as Wallace labeled the Republican a closet liberal on civil rights while Humphrey accused the GOP of courting far-right segregationists. Election surveys also demonstrated the moderate appeal of Nixon's suburban strategy, as the GOP received the votes of 44 percent of white southerners who supported additional racial desegregation and 56 percent of those who preferred the status quo, but only 23 percent of the unreconstructed segregationists (who overwhelmingly backed Wallace).[20]

The suburbanization of southern politics reflected in the 1968 election, combined with the dramatic growth of the black electorate and the uncertain future of the Wallace partisans, ushered in an era of substantial fluidity in the regional climate. The tripartite electorate guaranteed political instability because the two-party system could not adequately represent the region's three distinct voting blocs. On the strength of the middle-class suburbs, Richard Nixon carried the Upper and Outer South states that had reliably supported the Republican ticket in every presidential election for two decades, excluding the Goldwater disaster of 1964. With his working-class base, George Wallace carried the same Deep South states that had been on the losing side of all but one national election during the postwar period. The dealignment of a majority of the white southern electorate from the Democratic party did not guarantee a new version of the Solid South or an inexorable Republican realignment. While the percentage of white southerners who identified as Democrats dropped below half by 1970, political independents outnumbered Republicans by a two-to-one ratio. Voter surveys revealed that 47 percent of middle-class whites and 42 percent of working-class whites labeled themselves conservatives, 38 percent of middle-class whites and 49 percent of working-class whites called themselves moderates, and 14 percent of middle-class whites and 10 percent of working-class whites characterized themselves as liberals. This competitive environment meant that the political center remained up for grabs, in the South as in the nation, because middle-class suburbanites (racially moderate, fiscally conservative) and working-class whites (racially conservative, fiscally liberal) each represented a potential swing vote in any two-party election.[21]

The contentious debate over the lessons of 1968 intensified with the appearance of two influential books that offered conflicting interpretations of the location of Middle America on the ideological spectrum. A year after the presidential election, Kevin Phillips published *The Emerging Republican Majority*, an enthusiastic obituary for the New Deal Order and a racialized forecast of conservative realignment. Phillips, who made his mark in the ethnic cauldron of New York City politics and then worked as a GOP strategist during the 1968 campaign, boasted openly to the media that he understood "the whole secret of politics—knowing who hates who." In the backlash scenario of *The Emerging Republican Majority*, the association of the Democratic party with the civil rights movement and the urban riots had produced a "new popular majority [that] is white and conservative." Phillips

recognized that the Republican base had shifted from the Northeast establishment to the "tax-revolt centers of middle-class suburbia" and the southern and western states that formed the booming Sunbelt (a label he coined).
He highlighted the political repercussions of the three major demographic
transformations of the postwar era, accurately observing that "the interrelated Negro, suburban, and Sun Belt migrations have all but destroyed the
old New Deal coalition." But in the most questionable thesis of the book,
Phillips argued that Nixon's performance in the South built on Goldwater's
inroads in 1964, and he effectively guaranteed that the working-class Walla-
ceites would soon combine with middle-class suburban voters to form a cohesive Republican majority. Instead of acknowledging the class and geographic divisions within the white southern electorate, the Phillips formula
simply added the revolt against racial liberalism by the Wallace partisans to
the GOP's demographic foundation in the suburban Sunbelt and then proclaimed an inevitable conservative realignment.[22]

The tactical implications of *The Emerging Republican Majority*, which
implicitly counseled the Nixon administration to recruit Wallace voters
through a race-based backlash strategy, drew a sharp rebuke from two moderate Democrats. In *The Real Majority*, political consultants Richard Scammon and Ben Wattenberg argued that the central lesson of the 1968 election
was a time-honored truth: the party that occupied the political center gained
the presidency. They labeled as "preposterous" the charge that the Republicans had employed a Southern Strategy and emphasized that Richard Nixon
won by campaigning as the moderate champion of Middle America. *The
Real Majority* pointed out that the average voter was middle income and living in the suburbs, a blue-collar member of the "extreme center" rather
than an ideological conservative: "Middle Voter is a forty-seven-year-old
housewife from the outskirts of Dayton, Ohio, whose husband is a machin-
ist." Scammon and Wattenberg urged the Democratic party to address
forthrightly the fears and anxieties of Middle Americans regarding the "Social Issue," a constellation that included crime, racial integration, patriotism,
and taxes. They advised liberals not to dismiss the politics of law and order
as simple racism, since more than 80 percent of the electorate listed crime
as a top concern, and since working-class white families who lived near black
neighborhoods believed they were bearing the full costs of social change.
The Real Majority warned that "if Republicans capture the center as Democrats go to the extreme, we may well see Republican Presidents in the White
House for a generation." At the same time, the authors predicted a repeat
of the Goldwater fiasco if the GOP followed the advice of Kevin Phillips,
and they flatly concluded that "there is no inevitable emerging Republican
majority."[23]

Conservative strategists in the Nixon administration dreamed of translating the 1968 election into a Republican version of the Solid South, but the

political fluidity revealed by the region's tripartite electorate raised serious doubts about the race-driven calculus of Kevin Phillips. On one occasion, after the president ordered aides to implement the Phillips strategy of building a conservative majority by exploiting racial backlash, domestic policy adviser John Ehrlichman responded by endorsing the arguments of *The Real Majority* and warning that "the Social Issue strategy is a centerist strategy, not a liberal or conservative strategy." Political counselor Harry Dent outlined the public stance that the White House ultimately adopted: "We should disavow Phillips' book as party policy" and instead "stick with the silent majority theme," in order to champion a populist coalition of the center rather than a conservative realignment or a regional backlash too closely associated with the charges of a Southern Strategy. With the president's approval, Dent instructed White House officials and state party chairmen that "in answer to the question of a Nixon administration so-called Southern Strategy, we are responding . . . that this administration has no Southern Strategy but rather a national strategy which, for the first time in modern times, *includes* the South, rather than *excludes* the South from full and equal participation in national affairs." In a sign of the fundamental tensions in the administration's regional approach, Dent warned that following the Phillips strategy "could cost us what we won in 1968" and might well alienate the "growing body of moderate whites developing in the South," but he also proposed that the GOP recruit racial conservatives by retreating from aggressive civil rights enforcement and making sure that voters blamed the Democrats for "massive integration."[24]

"THE POLITICS OF SCHOOLS"

In the wake of the Goldwater debacle, the Ripon Society issued a warning to the Sunbelt wing of the GOP that "the future alignments of Southern politics will depend heavily upon the type of Southern strategy which the Republican party pursues." The progressive think tank urged party leaders to renounce the failed Southern Strategy of the Goldwater campaign: "a deliberate attempt to trade away Republican strength among the rapidly growing Negro and moderate white electorates of the South in return for the support of dissatisfied segregationist Democrats." After the 1968 election, Ripon praised Nixon for returning to the suburban strategy aimed at the corporate centers of the New South but lamented the lost opportunity to gain African-American support because the candidate "allow[ed] his once strong civil-rights image to be blurred and scrambled." A critical analysis called *The Lessons of Victory* counseled the Republican party to maintain the middle ground and demanded that Nixon's "support of civil rights must be strong and unequivocal." Ripon denounced the Kevin Phillips scheme to create a "lily-white GOP in the South" and urged Republicans to expand their regional base through a centrist strategy aimed at an interracial coalition of moderate suburbanites and upwardly mobile black voters. "Republicans who try to out-segregate the Democrats seldom win," the group warned in another special report on the GOP future in southern politics. The Ripon Society implored the Nixon White House to reject the conservative advice to build the party from the top down through racial backlash, a "suicidal . . . relapse into the negativism and extreme conservatism that characterized the Goldwater campaign."[25]

Richard Nixon initially promised to defuse the polarized climate of 1968 through an administration dedicated to an overriding goal: "bring the American people together." Instead, in an era of upheaval at home and quagmire abroad, his administration quickly adopted a backlash strategy of reactionary populism based on the calculated exploitation of racial resentments and cultural conflicts for political gain. For a president elected with a narrow plurality instead of a popular majority, the central dilemma involved the choice between expanding the Republican base without abandoning the political center or following the advice of Kevin Phillips to capitalize on the racial backlash among blue-collar Catholics in the North and Wallace independents in the South. During the first two years of the Nixon administration, the conservative political advisers in the backlash camp won a fierce internal battle over civil rights enforcement with the policymakers from the moderate and liberal wings of the Republican party. In one memorandum, speechwriter Patrick Buchanan proclaimed that "the second era of Reconstruction is over; the ship of integration is going down; it is not our ship; it belongs to national liberalism—and we cannot salvage it; and we ought not to be aboard." In another internal communiqué, Harry Dent argued that if the executive branch could implement school desegregation "without blame being attached to this administration," while convincing the public to hold the Democratic party and the federal courts responsible, "then we will have achieved the miracle of this age." The president himself ultimately declared that on the issue of integration, "this is politics, and I'm the judge of the politics of schools." He ordered executive branch officials to stay "in step with my express policy—do what the law requires and not *one bit* more."[26]

The White House approach to the South favored the Republican base in the white-collar suburbs through a protectionist policy of neighborhood schools while seeking to recruit the Wallace voters in the rural and blue-collar areas with a therapeutic rhetoric of reactionary populism. "The Nixon winning margin came in the metropolitan areas," Harry Dent reminded his administration colleagues. "The practical effect [of a neighborhood schools policy] seems to be little difference for rural and small town areas because of their integrated housing. . . . However, the metropolitan areas will have less [desegregation] than anticipated." The first major civil rights test for the new administration came as the federal courts began to apply the Supreme Court's 1968 ruling in *Green v. New Kent County*, which required affirmative action to achieve comprehensive desegregation and invalidated freedom of choice plans that perpetuated racial segregation. In the summer of 1969, Attorney General John Mitchell and HEW secretary Robert Finch released a joint policy statement on school desegregation that represented an uneasy compromise between the southern strategists and civil rights advocates inside the White House. They pledged that "this administration is unequivocally committed to the goal of finally ending racial discrimination in schools, steadily and speedily, in accordance with the law of the land." But the policy also promised "to induce compliance rather than compel submission" and contended that "in some districts there may be sound reasons for some limited delay . . . [for] bona fide educational and administrative problems."[27]

The administration decision to politicize civil rights enforcement emerged clearly in a case involving thirty-three school districts in Mississippi under court order to desegregate in the fall of 1969. Within weeks of the deadline, and following direct instructions from the president, Secretary Finch petitioned the federal courts for postponement in order to prevent "chaos, confusion, and a catastrophic educational setback." The NAACP responded through a full-page advertisement in the *New York Times* with the image of a young black student and a banner headline: "On August 25, 1969, the United States Government broke its promise to the children of Mississippi." The U.S. Civil Rights Commission condemned the administration for turning its back on school integration, and the SRC charged that the policy of delay "cynically held out hope to southern segregationists that the law of the land would not really have to be obeyed." Senator Strom Thurmond confirmed this political agenda by expressing gratitude that the White House had bolstered southern efforts to minimize integration. Portraying himself as the true moderate, Nixon proclaimed that "there are those who want instant integration and those who want segregation forever. I believe that we need to have a middle course between those two extremes." In an emergency appeal to the Supreme Court, the LDF pointed out that fifteen years of evasion and obstruction of the *Brown* decision in Mississippi hardly qualified as "instant integration." In *Alexander v. Holmes*, handed down in October, a unanimous Court rejected the administration's position and officially repudiated its own infamous doctrine of "all deliberate speed." The landmark ruling, authored by Nixon appointee and new chief justice Warren Burger, established the principle that every district in the South must "terminate dual school systems at once and to operate only unitary schools."[28]

The Mississippi controversy inaugurated a cynical scheme designed by the political operatives in the White House to shift the public perception of desegregation enforcement from the executive to the judicial branch.

Richard Nixon openly expressed his disapproval of the *Holmes* decision but pledged to enforce the law. Privately the president and his political staff believed that their tactics had won points with the white segregationists who formed the Wallace base in the Deep South. "The President is looking good down in Dixie," White House adviser John Ehrlichman observed in an internal memorandum, "because the Supreme Court shot him down with the state of Mississippi." In a private meeting with southern education officials, Attorney General John Mitchell told the group to "watch what we do instead of what we say." As the lower courts implemented the *Holmes* mandate, Nixon reinforced this emerging Southern Strategy by firing or reassigning the most aggressive civil rights enforcers in the executive branch, including Robert Finch at HEW and Office of Civil Rights head Leon Panetta. Under pressure from Goldwater Republicans, the White House also purged HEW's regional headquarters in Atlanta by removing four top officials whose tenure predated the administration and whose enthusiasm for civil rights rendered them vulnerable. In truth, the administration was offering little more than rhetorical comfort and temporary delay to white parents in the rural South, holding out false hope that racial segregation could be maintained. The most significant consequences of the "politics of schools" came in the metropolitan South, where the presidential directive that HEW shift to a "no busing" standard had the effect of insulating affluent suburbs while concentrating desegregation burdens in the white working-class neighborhoods that bordered black residential areas.[29]

The neighborhood schools policy represented a suburban strategy that evolved through the political interplay between the White House and the grassroots antibusing movements in the metropolitan South. The administration's initial desegregation statement in the summer of 1969 addressed the issue of urban residential patterns by premiering a new, although still embryonic, theme of southern and northern convergence. "Racial discrimination is prevalent in our industrial metropolitan areas," announced the joint report by HEW and Justice. "The educational situation in the North, the Midwest and the West requires immediate and massive attention." The statement argued that "segregation and discrimination in areas outside the South are generally de facto problems stemming from housing patterns . . . but the result is just as unsatisfactory as the results of the de jure segregation." Behind the scenes, Harry Dent explained that the administration never intended to take meaningful action against de facto segregation but instead offered the equation as a message to the South that it "would be treated like the rest of the country and no longer as a stepchild or whipping boy." By the early months of 1970, when the arrival of court-ordered busing shifted the administration's attention from the rural to the metropolitan South, the neighborhood schools campaign by the suburban antibusing movement transformed the dynamics of the desegregation debate. Shortly before being replaced as HEW secretary, and again under direct presidential order, Robert Finch declared the legal distinction between de jure and de facto segregation "no longer valid." But instead of calling for enforcement nationwide, Finch contended that federal judges could not require the busing of students for racial balance because housing patterns in Charlotte and Atlanta were identical to major cities outside the South.[30]

In March 1970, through the most substantial policy statement on school desegregation ever delivered by an American president, Richard Nixon confirmed that suburban protectionism represented the official civil rights policy of his administration. The address began with a forceful declaration of support for the *Brown* decision and committed the administration to the elimination of de jure segregation where it remained in the public schools of the South. The White House rejected the view that rural school districts could escape their obligations under the law and promised $1.5 billion in emergency funding to assist local communities in the transition. Seeking a middle ground between the segregationist ultimatums of the rural South and the affirmative integration mandate of the *Green* decision, Nixon embraced the suburban vision of color-blind assignments to neighborhood schools demanded by the antibusing movements in the metropolitan centers. The president's calculated appeal to the white-collar suburbs drew a sharp constitutional distinction between the illegal (de jure) segregation evident in rural school districts and the market-based (de facto) version prevalent in metropolitan regions, a formula that superseded the traditional emphasis on the regional divide between the South and the North. This color-blind policy effectively endorsed a national standard of neighborhood schools that revolved around a laissez-faire approach to residential segregation and an overt defense of the spatial and socioeconomic privileges of middle-class suburbs throughout the country. Nixon also adopted the conservative mantra that unelected judges should not use public education for liberal social experimentation, defined as a "tragically futile effort to achieve in the schools the kind of a multiracial society which the adult community has failed to achieve for itself."[31]

The Republican administration's distinction between de facto and de jure segregation was both politically motivated and artificially constructed. "When in doubt," the president personally instructed the officials at HEW and Justice, "call segregation *de facto*, not *de jure*." The NAACP responded by accusing Nixon of paying "lip service to integrated schools and an integrated society" while pursuing policies that emboldened opponents of the civil rights movement. While the "politics of schools" in the South clearly shaped the administration's antibusing platform, the new de facto policy also reflected the prescient recognition that suburban hostility toward racial busing transcended partisan, class, and regional boundaries. A major public opinion survey in the spring of 1970 revealed that 65 percent of respondents across the nation opposed busing students outside of their neighborhoods for the purpose of racial desegregation, with only 22 percent expressing approval. In the wake of Nixon's pronouncement, the LDF announced a campaign to desegregate the public schools of the urban North on the grounds that the de jure/de facto distinction misrepresented the pervasive public policies that had created metropolitan segregation throughout the United States. By the spring of 1970, administration officials and civil rights critics essentially agreed with the regional convergence theory of metropolitan segregation but sharply diverged on the question of whether the Constitution required or forbade a judicial remedy. At a political fundraiser in South Carolina, Vice President Agnew denied that the antibusing stance represented a calculated Southern Strategy and instead portrayed the administration's desegregation policy as a decision to treat southerners the same as all other Americans. As the busing crisis moved to center stage, the Republican base in the residentially segregated suburbs stood to reap the benefits of this formal policy of protecting neighborhood schools, while working-class whites who lived in residentially transitional areas received little more than racially charged words.[32]

The Regional Fairness Campaign

During the explosive desegregation climate of 1969–70, as the metropolitan South embraced a suburban strategy of neighborhood schools, the political leadership of the Deep South resurrected the rhetoric of massive resistance. Since the antibusing policy of the executive branch offered little relief for rural segregationist movements and could not halt court-ordered integration in urban districts, charges of national bias against the South moved to the center of political discourse. Two distinct regional fairness campaigns emerged from the southern political landscape. The color-blind platform of the suburban antibusing movement, which drew heavily from the white-collar Republican base, equated the metropolitan South with northern-style de facto segregation and demanded a national standard of neighborhood schools. Meanwhile a segregationist rebellion based in the Deep South, led by Democratic governors in the mold of George Wallace, called for the termination of civil rights enforcement on the grounds of national hypocrisy. Nixon responded by trying to finesse the class and geographic divisions within the region through a message that praised white southerners as identical to the rest of America but condemned the national bias against the South that victimized them unjustly. During the fall of 1969, the president told advisers to "go as far south and as far conservative as we can" after a bipartisan coalition in the U.S. Senate rejected the Supreme Court nomination of Clement F. Haynsworth, Jr., the conservative chief judge of the

Fourth Circuit Court of Appeals. G. Harrold Carswell, an appellate judge from Florida who became the product of this dubious search, immediately faced fierce attacks for personal racism and professional incompetence. When the Senate also rejected Carswell's nomination, Nixon issued a press release expressing his sympathy toward "the bitter feeling of millions of Americans who live in the South about the act of regional discrimination that took place in the Senate."[33]

Charges of a double standard for the South moved to center stage as all hell broke loose during the winter of 1969–70, with hundreds of recalcitrant school districts scheduled to implement desegregation plans in the largest single transition of the *Brown* era. The midyear changeovers required by the *Holmes* "immediate integration" mandate made an already difficult situation even more explosive, with local boycotts and segregated private school movements dotting the educational landscape of the Lower South. In the five-state region stretching from Florida to Louisiana, each governor revived the political demagoguery of massive resistance and encouraged popular defiance of the federal courts. At the same time, Deep South politicians went on the attack with the promise that northern liberals would retreat from desegregation enforcement if forced to taste their own integrationist medicine. Governor John Bell Williams of Mississippi urged white parents to boycott public schools or enroll in segregated private academies and then wait until his scheme to file integration lawsuits in the North convinced the Supreme Court to retreat. "These punitive decrees are directed against our people while those in the North and East have enjoyed immunity," he charged. "We have been made victims of the rawest kind of discrimination. . . . It is time for states outside the South to begin enjoying the benefits of the so-called 'Law of the Land.'" Governor John McKeithen of Louisiana also encouraged popular defiance of court-ordered desegregation and denounced the "hypocrites of the North" for destroying public education in his state. "We cry out for justice," the governor exclaimed. "Why is the South still treated like some conquered province?"[34]

Tapping into a potent historical tradition, the regional fairness campaign in the Deep South portrayed white southerners as the innocent victims of the civil rights movement, the tyrannical federal government, and the limousine liberals of the North. In January, the state of Georgia initiated an equal protection lawsuit against Nixon officials for discriminating against its citizens by failing to enforce school desegregation throughout the nation. A month later, the attorneys general of three Deep South states filed a legal brief asking for "immediate integration" in Pasadena, California. Always popular, the accusations of a double standard practiced by "Yankee integrationists" enjoyed especially wide circulation in the southern media during the desegregation transition of 1970. News articles listed the expensive private schools in Washington attended by the children of many of the same congressional liberals who forced integration on the South. The reactionary editorial page of the *Mobile Register* charged that "while the federal government swings an integration blackjack against Southern states, the flight in the North from integrated schools is taking on the likeness of a stampede." Mississippi newspapers chronicled the exploits of Attorney General Albioun Summer, who conducted a surprise investigation that caught the white suburbs of Minneapolis–St. Paul in the act of operating neighborhood schools and concluded that the de facto/de jure distinction was a myth because "segregation is segregation." The archconservative *Jackson Clarion-Ledger* found that the "supreme irony of the situation is that many Southern families seeking segregated public schools for their children might find it necessary to emigrate North . . . where segregation survives unruffled by Supreme Court decisions." "We have more blacks in integrated schools in Mississippi," imagined one white woman from the small town of Lucedale, "than you have in the entire Northeast."[35]

The demand for a uniform desegregation standard represented a transparent effort by politicians in the Deep South to maintain segregated schools, but the national political dynamics also had shifted since the initial round of massive resistance in the 1950s. While southern charges of northern hypocrisy had a long history on the floors of Congress, Senator John Stennis of Mississippi threw traditional alliances into disarray when he introduced two regional fairness measures in February 1970. The first amendment mandated an equitable federal desegregation policy toward northern and southern public schools, and the second proposed a national antibusing standard that replicated the language of a law recently signed by Governor Nelson Rockefeller, the liberal Republican from New York. Stennis promised that "when the North feels the pinch as it has been felt in the South, the harsh regulations and demands will be moderated." To widespread surprise, Senator Abraham A. Ribicoff of Connecticut spoke in favor of the first Stennis amendment and charged the North with "monumental hypocrisy." One of the stalwarts of the liberal wing of the Democratic party, Ribicoff proclaimed that "we're just as racist in the North as they are in the South" and warned that "we cannot solve our 'urban crisis' unless we include the suburbs in the solution." President Nixon indirectly endorsed the Stennis proposals, which both houses of Congress approved on the strength of bipartisan support from the South and West, but northern liberals defused the crisis by removing the amendments in conference committee. As a compromise path, liberals established a special Senate committee on equal educational opportunity with a mandate to investigate racial segregation throughout the nation, but the hearings held throughout 1970 only exacerbated the charges of regional discrimination emanating from almost every corner of the South, from the rural countryside to the upscale suburbs.[36]

The demands for regional fairness remained a potent issue in the South as both parties prepared for the fall elections, but the civil rights climate also revealed that the days of massive resistance and overt racism were fading, and that the fate of the *Brown* decision would be determined primarily by the metropolitan showdowns over court-ordered busing and neighborhood schools. In May 1970, a survey by the Gallup organization revealed that on the issue of school desegregation, the trajectory of white southern attitudes during the previous decade demonstrated one of the most pronounced shifts in the history of opinion polling. Only 16 percent of white parents expressed opposition to sending their children to school with a small number of black students, compared to 61 percent in 1963. Forty-three percent would refuse to send their children to a school where half of the students were black, compared to 78 percent seven years earlier. This racial sentiment closely mirrored Richard Nixon's middle-ground stance in the 1968 election, combining rhetorical support for the principle of racial integration with public policies that defended the sanctity of neighborhood schools. In the first two years of the Nixon administration, the mobilization of the suburban South established the busing controversy as an urgent and unavoidable crisis in national politics, advancing a color-blind agenda that accepted the abstract authority of the *Brown* decision but recast a metropolitan landscape of de jure racial segregation as the innocent outcome of de facto class stratification. The grassroots uprising of the Silent Majority signaled an explosive new stage in the history of suburban populism, a free-market defense of middle-class consumer meritocracy and white residential privilege, marked by the increasing convergence of southern and national politics.[37]

In the midterm elections of 1970, instead of expanding the suburban strategies that secured the metropolitan South in the recent presidential campaign, the White House embraced a racially polarizing Southern Strategy designed to consolidate the region's white voters into a cohesive Republican majority. Aiming for the Goldwater converts and the Wallace partisans, GOP strategists launched a top-down experiment to reconstitute the Solid South through a reprisal of the era of massive resistance, not simply by capitalizing on the desegregation crisis but also by inflaming racial resentment in the blue-collar neighborhoods and the countryside. Instead of a Republican surge, the pivotal election cycle of 1970 sabotaged the centrist GOP tradition in regional politics and paved the way for the ascendance of a group of "New South Democrats" who championed legal compliance and color-blind progress. Just as the extremism of massive resistance had divided rather than united white southerners a decade earlier, the top-down politicization of desegregation in the early 1970s highlighted the socioeconomic and geographic differences between the Outer and the Deep South, the white-collar suburbs and the rural countryside, the Sunbelt and the Black Belt, the racial moderates and the diehard segregationists. By counting on a monolithic white South obsessively focused on racial integration, by courting an imaginary Silent Majority that transcended class and ideological boundaries, the fundamental premise of the Southern Strategy proved to be deeply flawed. During an era of social crisis and racial turmoil, the GOP voters in the suburbs and the Wallace voters in the countryside would not fit comfortably into a stable political coalition.

CHAPTER 10

The Failure of the Southern Strategy

> The Southern Strategy won't work. The only way to outflank
> George Wallace is to go into the Gulf of Mexico.
> —Charles Morgan (1970), director of the Southern
> Regional Office, American Civil Liberties Union

The Wallace Challenge

Kevin Phillips was the false prophet of reactionary populism. After the 1968 election, the Nixon administration abandoned its centrist suburban strategy and embraced a genuine race-based Southern Strategy as a defensive maneuver to neutralize George Wallace and a top-down offensive to transform the presidential base into a Republican majority in regional politics. During 1969–70, as the pace and scope of court-ordered school desegregation accelerated dramatically throughout the South, the administration responded by aligning the GOP with reactionary politicians who preached defiance of the federal judiciary. The White House aggressively recruited and financed candidates across the region, rejecting moderate GOP leaders for segregationist former Democrats, many of whom had switched parties as Goldwater Republicans. But instead of the next stage in an inexorable Republican realignment, the midterm elections of 1970 demonstrated the intellectual bankruptcy of the Southern Strategy in the electoral climate of the Sunbelt South. The hard shift to the right orchestrated by the White House opened the political center for a group of New South Democrats who rejected the divisive racial politics of the past, championed the principle of color-blind nondiscrimination, endorsed compliance with court-ordered desegregation, and projected a regional future of interracial progress. The midterm elections turned out to be the last stand for massive resistance, the epitaph for open race-baiting in the political culture of the New South. "The Southern Strategy won't work," longtime liberal activist Charles Morgan warned President Nixon in the spring of 1970. "The only way to outflank George Wallace is to go into the Gulf of Mexico."[1]

The Wallace challenge shaped the contours of the race-based Southern Strategy outlined by Kevin Phillips and developed by the White House for the midterm elections. In the late summer of 1969, as comprehensive court-ordered desegregation arrived in many Deep South school districts, the former governor of Alabama returned to the political stage with a familiar message of grassroots resistance against federal tyranny. Wallace's personal backlash strategy involved the exploitation of the civil rights climate to recapture his old job, primarily for a platform from which to launch another presidential bid. The opening gambit of his gubernatorial campaign came at a Labor Day rally in a blue-collar Mobile suburb, sponsored by neighborhood groups that threatened to boycott public schools and open segregated private alternatives. The countywide school system in Mobile faced an appellate court order to implement a limited busing plan that revolved around the one-way transportation of black students and the transfer of a small number of white students. Wallace told the parents in the Labor Day audience that freedom of choice remained legal, no matter what federal judges or Washington bureaucrats said, because "your children belong to you." Then he called for a "mothers and fathers march on the schools" and recommended that parents take their children "to the [former] school and see what happens."[2]

Wallace's intervention in the politics of school desegregation led to a direct clash with Albert Brewer, the current governor of Alabama and a racial moderate by the constricted standards of the Deep South. After the Labor Day speech, Brewer rebuked his predecessor and declared that "I don't think there is any responsible person in Alabama who would use the school children of the state as a political issue." Wallace responded by amplifying his calls for defiance at a Birmingham protest organized by a local freedom of choice group. With the Confederate flag as a backdrop, he denounced the "lawbreakers" on the Fifth Circuit Court of Appeals and warned that federal judges would soon order the busing of white students to black schools. As the desegregation crisis increasingly overlapped with the gubernatorial contest, Albert Brewer tried to compete by lambasting federal judges, urging school boards to resist "diabolical" busing orders, and announcing a regional fairness scheme to sue the federal government for failing to enforce the *Brown* decision in the North. But the governor was neither an accomplished nor an enthusiastic demagogue, and the Mobile newspapers observed that he had staked out the position of "moderation and responsibility" in Alabama politics. When Brewer discouraged citizen boycotts of desegregated schools, Wallace questioned the manhood of a "sissy britches" governor who refused to defy the federal courts.[3]

In January 1970, as school districts throughout the Deep South prepared for midyear desegregation, George Wallace launched a direct attack on the civil rights enforcement policies of the Nixon administration. On the CBS program *Face the Nation*, he accused the White House of a "counter-Southern strategy which is going to be the strategy of defeat for any administration that destroys the security and safety of the children of our region and every other region." Concerned parents were mobilizing across the

South, Wallace told the national television audience, and they would punish Richard Nixon unless he saved public education from the dangers of forced integration. At a series of antibusing rallies in suburban Birmingham, Wallace taunted Nixon as a one-term president, barring immediate action to limit the scope of federal court decisions. In front of fifteen thousand parents, the Alabama firebrand made it clear that he would run for president in 1972 unless the Nixon administration fixed "the mess our schools are in." The White House responded with a concerted behind-the-scenes effort to assist the reelection campaign of Albert Brewer, including the extralegal distribution of $400,000 in cash, at the same time that its politicization of desegregation enforcement sought to blunt Wallace's charges of regional bias. "If Wallace is defeated," a GOP leader from Alabama explained privately, "it would be the one thing that could bring about a Republican South for there would be no place for them [white working-class voters] to go."[4]

The Democratic primary between Wallace and Brewer matched the nation's leading opponent of the civil rights movement against the Alabama version of a New South campaign for the future. Wallace nationalized the election by declaring that "if I lose, it will be a signal that the people of Alabama have surrendered to the very forces I have been fighting." Brewer sought to defuse the race issue by preaching the gospel of Sunbelt development and stating that government should provide equal opportunity to all citizens. The incumbent governor led Wallace in the primary with strong support from white-collar metropolitan voters and a solid black turnout. For the runoff, Wallace returned to the race-baiting campaigns of the past, accusing Brewer of soliciting the black "bloc vote" and being the "tool of black militants." Inflammatory newspaper advertisements portrayed the governor's supporters as a "spotted alliance [of] . . . Negroes and their white friends." Flyers circulated in rural and working-class precincts pictured a white girl surrounded by black boys as the potential future of Alabama and superimposed Muhammad Ali's image on a photograph of country singer Johnny Cash greeting Governor Brewer. Wallace won the runoff with 51.6 percent of the vote, narrowly surviving the secret efforts of the Nixon administration and the open desire of almost half of the Alabama electorate to keep him out of office. The governor-elect portrayed his victory as a personal message to Richard Nixon to stop busing, and he advised the White House to "undercut me by treating the South right."[5]

Watching from Washington as events unfolded in Alabama, having failed to defeat Wallace on his home turf, the southern strategists in the Nixon administration decided that a policy of imitation would be the sincerest form of flattery. But the voting returns from the gubernatorial runoff in Alabama suggested that an electoral strategy that revolved around demagoguery and defiance would be unlikely to succeed outside of the Deep South. With the exception of Mobile, Brewer carried the major metropolitan regions, including decisive margins in the middle-class suburbs of Montgomery and Birmingham. Political journalists observed that Brewer proved to be especially popular in the "Republican suburban neighborhoods" where many residents viewed Wallace as an embarrassment to their state. Wallace's combination of strident racism and economic populism did produce a powerful turnout among blue-collar and rural white voters throughout Alabama, from the Black Belt to the northern highlands. Looking ahead to the fall elections, White House operatives calculated that busing controversies and desegregation resentment had weakened the traditional divergence between the Outer and the Deep South, the suburbs and the countryside, and that a large majority of white voters would rally behind a regional strategy of racial backlash. The Ripon Society sharply disputed this assessment in a special report warning that the Wallace victory had "killed the Southern strategy as a national tactic" and imploring the administration to recognize that the segregationist politics of the Deep South did not represent the region's future. "The party must cultivate the moderate parts of the South," Ripon concluded. "Racism will fail, as it has in the past."[6]

"The Important Thing Is Education!"

White House strategists believed that South Carolina offered the ideal conditions for a Southern Strategy designed to expand the Republican base from the top down through the politicization of desegregation enforcement and the exploitation of racial backlash. In the 1968 election, Richard Nixon won a narrow plurality in the state after Strom Thurmond guaranteed that the GOP would preserve freedom of choice. In early 1970, following the Supreme Court's "immediate integration" mandate, the Fourth Circuit Court of Appeals ordered midyear desegregation in two South Carolina localities, the upstate school system of metropolitan Greenville and the lowcountry district of rural Darlington County. As grassroots resistance erupted in both communities, the desegregation saga quickly became embroiled in a fierce gubernatorial contest between Republican Congressman Albert Watson and Democratic Lieutenant Governor John West. The White House recruited Watson, an ultraconservative segregationist who had switched parties during the Goldwater campaign, with the calculation that racial demagoguery would carry the GOP to the governor's mansion for the first time since Reconstruction. But the Goldwater Republicans in South Carolina had a mixed record of translating the GOP base in presidential elections into success at the state level. Governor Robert McNair, a moderate Democrat from the New South wing of the party, defeated a segregationist Goldwater Republican in the gubernatorial contest of 1966. Four years later, as Thurmond and Watson encouraged South Carolinians to return to the days of massive resistance, McNair promised that "we're not going to defy the courts, defy the law of the land, regardless of our personal feelings."[7]

In the winter of 1970, Greenville became the largest city outside of the Gulf Coast states to undergo comprehensive desegregation in the middle of the academic year. A fast-growing piedmont metropolis of 240,000, Greenville represented both the textile past and the Sunbelt future of South Carolina. The city and surrounding Greenville County operated a consolidated school system serving 58,000 students, 80 percent white and 20 percent black. Under court order, the school board devised a countywide busing formula that approximated the 80-20 ratio in every facility. In stark contrast to the concurrent vacuum of leadership in Charlotte, a broad coalition of civic and political leaders in Greenville aggressively intervened to assure a peaceful desegregation transition. The board established a Citizens Committee that included corporate executives, prominent ministers, white-collar professionals, middle-class black leaders, and LWV activists. R. Cooper White, the first Republican mayor in the city's history, appealed to constituents to obey the law and promised that his four children would "remain in the public schools and attend the schools assigned." The Greater Greenville Chamber of Commerce launched a massive public relations campaign revolving around a simple slogan displayed on television, radio, newspapers, billboards, and lapel pins: "THE IMPORTANT THING IS EDUCATION!"[8]

Antibusing parents in Greenville rapidly mobilized under the banner of the Silent Majority to demand that political leaders preserve freedom of choice and neighborhood schools. One working-class father, speaking for the "average citizens with an average textile income," promised to vote for Wallace if Nixon broke his promise to prevent forced busing. Another blue-collar resident asked that "good, average Christian Americans, . . . the so-called silent majority, now rise up like Americans should and speak out." A grassroots network called Silent Americans Speak Out launched a mass telegram campaign targeting President Nixon and Governor McNair: "Prevent disaster in our schools, support freedom of choice, prevent busing, consider quality of education." White-collar families from more affluent neighborhoods organized the Citizens Committee to Prevent Busing, led by a Republican businessman named Carroll A. Campbell, Jr. (who would later serve two terms as governor of South Carolina). Campbell promised that "we are not against integration" and invited parents of all races to join the antibusing movement. In an uneasy juxtaposition of massive resistance and color-blind rhetoric, the group petitioned McNair to declare recent Supreme Court decisions null and void in order to guarantee the constitutional right "to educate our children irrespective of race, color, or creed." In late January, the Citizens Committee to Prevent Busing organized a motorcade of several thousand parents who drove to the state capitol in Columbia for a boisterous rally. Protest leaders presented a petition with more than 100,000 signatures, while members of the crowd booed the governor for refusing to obstruct the court order.[9]

Governor McNair asked the demonstrators to accept the authority of the law and promised that South Carolina would not revisit the days of massive resistance. "We're going to have to maintain, support, and strengthen our public school system," he told a statewide television audience. "We've run out of courts, and we've run out of time, and we must adjust to new circumstances." Leaders from the Goldwater wing of the state GOP immediately moved to exploit the desegregation crisis, which they viewed as a golden political opportunity to undermine the moderate Democrats. Strom Thurmond traveled to Greenville to attack "forced integration" and assure his audience that "we will eventually end up under the freedom of choice plan." The senator also criticized McNair's call for compliance: "Public statements indicating acquiescence to Supreme Court decisions, however well intentioned, . . . serve only to encourage the rabid integrationists to push further for total domination of our schools." Congressman Albert Watson demanded "determination and courage" from state leaders and contrasted his own steadfastness to the governor's "vacillation" in the "fight against judicial tyranny." In an opening strike of his gubernatorial campaign, Watson encouraged grassroots resistance against the courts and endorsed the massive resistance mechanism of defunding districts that complied with busing orders. As the Greenville deadline approached, the local antibusing movement warned that "preservation of public education for our children" hung in the balance and called on families throughout the county to "Stand United!"[10]

On a winter day in mid-February, the real majority of white citizens in Greenville garnered national attention for implementing comprehensive desegregation in a peaceful and efficient manner. Less than a week before the Greenville transition, President Nixon released a memorandum of opposition to court-ordered busing and declared his administration's support for a national desegregation standard of neighborhood schools. But mainstream sentiment in Greenville recognized that the politicization of civil rights enforcement at the national level did not negate the legal obligation at the local level, and community leaders mobilized to avoid an outbreak of violence that would tarnish their city's reputation. In a school board election held just before the transition, voters selected a group of business executives and white-collar professionals who endorsed full compliance with the law and portrayed desegregation as an opportunity to improve quality education. The Christian Ministers Association of Greenville called on all families to accept integration with "an attitude of cooperation, understanding, and good will." Wade Hampton High School hung welcome banners for the three hundred black students transferring to an institution named after the famous Confederate general. The Republican mayor bluntly informed white families that separate had never been equal and pointed out that metropolitan patterns of housing segregation made busing the only way to achieve meaningful school integration.[11]

The broad civic consensus for compliance with the law eclipsed the considerable discontent expressed by black as well as white critics of the Greenville formula. A group called the Concerned Black Parents Committee protested two specific elements of the desegregation plan: the systematic busing of the youngest African-American students to white schools and the decision to close or downgrade all five historically black high schools in the county. The school board compromised by assigning white fifth and sixth graders to undercrowded elementary schools in black residential areas, but overall the burdens of reassignment still fell heaviest on African-American families. Hundreds of white students avoided two-way busing by transferring to segregated private alternatives hastily established by conservative churches, with several more Christian elementary schools scheduled to open in the fall. Local antibusing leaders promised that "by September we'll have the freedom-of-choice plan back again" and traveled to Washington as part of a Southeast delegation that met with presidential adviser Harry Dent and members of Congress from both parties. Although the repercussions of the events in Greenville would shape the administration's backlash strategy in the fall elections, the local desegregation verdict revealed the resilience of racial moderation in one of South Carolina's major metropolitan regions. The center held in Greenville, thanks to favorable racial demographics in a countywide school system, a comprehensive busing plan that kept most white students in their current facilities, preemptive action by local civic and business leaders determined to avoid disorder and defiance, and a silent majority of white families who looked to the future and maintained their allegiance to public education.[12]

"THE HIGH ROAD TO PROGRESS"

The calm transition in Greenville contrasted sharply with the breakdown of public order in Darlington County, the scene of a protracted crisis that led to a partisan showdown over civil rights enforcement. The court order to implement midyear desegregation produced a widespread backlash in the rural school district, including the opening of several private schools and a Mothers March for Freedom of Choice. The publisher of a local newspaper explained that integration could not work in his agricultural community as it had in Greenville, because "they only have a 20 percent colored population over there. Here it's more like 50-50. . . . The Nigras have too far to go to catch up with the whites." The Darlington County Freedom of Choice

Committee organized a public school boycott that revolved around a hotbed of resistance in the town of Lamar. Although a majority of county students remained in the public schools after desegregation, a group in Lamar moved toward open confrontation through skirmishes with law enforcement and schemes to block bus routes. The climax came in early March, when a band of one hundred white men captured national headlines by assaulting two school buses loaded with young black children. Officers from the state highway patrol rescued the students by dispersing the mob with tear gas, and Governor McNair mobilized the National Guard to restore order. The state arrested twenty-nine participants, mainly farmers and factory workers, and county schools closed for a week as clashes between locals and law enforcement continued to flare.[13]

A few days before the outbreak of racial violence, Albert Watson delivered a defiant address to a segregationist rally of twenty-five hundred white citizens in Lamar. The Republican gubernatorial candidate urged the crowd to "stand up and use every means at your disposal" to prevent illegal orders from the federal courts. Watson also told the gathering not to be intimidated by "people who call you racist, bigot, and hard-core rednecks." After the assault on the buses, Governor McNair denounced the instigators of mob violence but placed primary blame on elected officials "who have helped to create the type of dangerous and inflammatory public attitude which makes such an act possible." In a forceful statement holding Watson and Thurmond responsible for a return to the days of massive resistance, the Democratic governor charged that "we now see the consequences which result from an open defiance of the law; we now pay the penalty for the type of disrespect and disregard for authority which has been publicly advocated by many in recent days." Both Republicans responded by attributing the violence in Lamar to the frustrations of white parents who believed that the McNair administration had surrendered to the tyranny of the federal government. In an echo of the Southern Manifesto, Thurmond charged that "people are less likely to resort to violence if they have faith that their leaders will stand up for them by using every legal resource provided within our system." With a word of advice from the White House, Harry Dent advised Watson to "go hard for the country music–working man vote" because "the Wallace-type voter just resents this [school desegregation] to no end."[14]

The racial demagoguery of the Goldwater Republicans and the White House collusion in Watson's reactionary campaign led to a critical showdown over the values and the future of the GOP in South Carolina. Thurmond and Watson imagined a conservative Republican party constructed from the top down by capitalizing on segregationist resentment against the racial liberalism of the national Democrats and tapping into white anxiety about the rapid expansion of the state's black electorate. In the opposing camp, moderate GOP leaders such as Mayor White of Greenville and real estate developer Arthur Ravenal of Charleston envisioned a centrist party that would combine the grassroots Republican base in the suburbs with political outreach to black voters. In the winter of 1970, Ravenal opened his own gubernatorial campaign by criticizing Watson's role in fomenting the violence in Lamar and imploring the GOP to choose the path of racial moderation. Ravenal privately informed White House strategists that the effort to secure South Carolina's "seg and racist vote" would backfire because Watson "can get absolutely no black vote and very little support from the white moderates." His campaign faced a formidable obstacle, however, because the state Republicans selected candidates at a malapportioned convention dominated by rural counties. Following Thurmond's lead, the convention rejected Ravenal's call for a primary election and awarded the gubernatorial nomination to Albert Watson. The Greenville delegation overwhelmingly supported Ravenal's doomed candidacy, and one moderate party activist denounced Watson as "Nixon's own personal envoy of bigotry."[15]

As the Republican leadership in South Carolina rejected the center for the Southern Strategy, the state Democratic convention embraced an interracial New South agenda and defined itself as "the party of moderation and responsibility." The Democratic platform endorsed full compliance with federal court orders and repudiated "all forms of extremism and demagoguery that seemingly motivate our opposition." African-Americans represented almost one-fifth of the Democratic delegates, an indication of the party's increasing dependence on the black electorate, and they played a crucial role in the abandonment of a plank that originally supported freedom of choice. Lieutenant Governor John West, the consensus choice for the gubernatorial nomination, enjoyed a reputation as a racial moderate and a deeply religious man who subscribed to the philosophy of the social gospel. In a speech during the Greenville crisis, West called for obedience to court orders and criticized the "voices of extremism" represented by Watson and Thurmond. The nominee portrayed the election as a contest between the reactionary race-based conservatism of the Republicans and the progressive color-blind alternative offered by the new Democrats. In rhetoric designed to divide the electorate into those stuck in the past and those looking to the future, and in an effective appeal to suburban moderates as well as African-American voters, West argued that his victory would demonstrate to the nation that South Carolina was no longer "a land of magnolias, segregation, and discrimination."[16]

The civil rights climate turned the gubernatorial campaign between Albert Watson and John West into a referendum on the Southern Strategy of the Nixon administration. Two months before the election, most of the remaining school districts in South Carolina implemented substantial desegregation plans under federal court order. An outraged Strom Thurmond

denounced the Nixon administration for abandoning "the great silent majority," although he placed the blame on "ultraliberal" policymakers in the
executive branch. In an openly racist campaign, Watson aired television
commercials that pictured African-American rioters in Watts and asked omi-
nously: "Are we going to be ruled by the bloc?" Vice President Spiro Agnew
joined Strom Thurmond at campaign rallies for the Republican nominee,
who also touted Nixon's public endorsement. A dismayed resident of suburban Greenville responded by inverting Nixon's 1968 campaign slogan to
argue that a vote against Watson represented a vote for "law and order."
Watson also sought to exploit a fall outbreak of racial violence in the capital
city of Columbia, where the acceleration of white flight had followed implementation of an unstable desegregation plan scaled back by HEW after the
political intervention of Harry Dent. When racial disturbances flared again
one day after Watson condemned school integration, John West blamed his
opponent for encouraging disorder and reminded voters of the violence
in Lamar six months earlier. The Democratic candidate assured South
Carolinians that his administration would not "by word or deed or action do
anything to inflame or polarize class against class, rich against poor, color
against color."[17]

The outcome of the election represented a major blow to the Nixon administration's Southern Strategy of creating a majority party in South Carolina by pandering to the segregationist Wallace-Thurmond base. John West
outpolled Albert Watson by a margin of 250,551 to 221,233, including a substantial number of white moderates who had supported Nixon in 1968 but
rejected the Republican embrace of massive resistance. West also benefited
from a very high turnout among African-American voters, who demonstrated forcefully that GOP extremism would bring a strong counterpunch.
The Democrats recaptured many of the textile mill communities of the upstate, where working-class white voters in the Wallace camp resented the
economic policies of the Nixon administration (and also lived in school districts with very few black students). Although Watson did win a majority of
the white electorate, the combination of black voters and white moderates
revealed the potential for an interracial coalition of the center in the two-
party South. A key swing vote came from white-collar professionals in the
cities and suburbs who typically leaned Republican but responded favorably
to the New South platform of economic growth and quality public education
advanced by John West. A civil rights analysis concluded that the Democratic ticket also "won support from much of the conservative 'establishment' leadership who . . . viewed Rep. Watson as a rabble-rouser who
threatened stability." Mayor White of Greenville, who repeatedly criticized
the racist tactics of the Watson campaign, called for the resignation of the
entire leadership of the South Carolina Republican party. In his victory
speech, celebrating statewide support that cut across class and racial lines,

John West rejoiced that "the silent majority said loud and clear that South Carolina will take the high road to progress."[18]

The South Carolina election, in the contemporary assessment of two political journalists, symbolized "the extreme failure of Nixon's Southern approach." The Republican strategy to run a campaign of Wallace-style defiance galvanized black voters, alienated white moderates, and allowed an interracial Democratic party to reclaim the center in state politics. At the end of a year of persistent racial conflict, during the most substantial desegregation transition in the history of the state, voters rejected a Republican party taking its cues from Washington operatives and a segregationist leadership based in the lowcountry and the rural Black Belt. After the election, John West rendered his judgment on the legacy of Senator Strom Thurmond: "The old man is a racist. He is one of the most negative, obstructive forces in America." Thurmond's own belated recognition of the power of the black vote and the divided nature of the white electorate meant that the 1970 contest would be the last display of overt race-baiting in the career of the longest-serving stalwart of the Dixiecrat South. The new political dynamic in South Carolina meant that moderate Democrats could win elections with a high black turnout and slightly more than one-third of the white electorate, while a GOP backlash strategy required an overwhelming percentage of the white vote. The progressive tenure of John West included increased resources for public education and antipoverty programs, appointment of civil rights leaders to posts in state government, and the creation of a regulatory agency to oversee affirmative action and investigate racial discrimination. "We are each one God's people," the governor declared in his inaugural address, as he promised minority groups "no special status other than full-fledged responsibility in a government that is totally color-blind."[19]

THE VIRGINIA BETRAYAL

In Virginia, the Southern Strategy pursued by the Nixon administration set off a struggle for the soul of the Republican party between racially moderate grassroots activists from the metropolitan regions and segregationist former Democrats from the rural strongholds. The White House intervention came as the collapse of the Byrd Organization and the arrival of a competitive two-party system threw the traditional arrangements of state politics into disarray and ushered in a fluid era of uncertain realignment. The segregationist Byrd Organization, once the dominant force in a single-party state, faded rapidly during the 1960s after federal voting rights legislation and court-ordered reapportionment led to the empowerment of the African-American electorate and the rise of the middle-class suburbs as a new power base. The 1965 gubernatorial campaign matched Linwood Holton, a pro-

gressive Republican from Roanoke, against Mills Godwin, Jr., a former architect of massive resistance who abandoned segregationist politics in recognition of the growing strength of the black vote. After Holton lost the election, he pledged to expand the GOP through an interracial coalition of the
middle-class suburbs, the mountain counties, and the black electorate. In
the 1966 primary, two suburban Democrats launched a campaign to destroy
the Byrd Organization by defeating the state's ultraconservative senators, A.
Willis Robertson and Harry F. Byrd, Jr. William Spong of Portsmouth unseated Robertson in a spirited battle over the modernization of the Democratic party, while the successor to the Byrd dynasty narrowly survived the
challenge from Armistead Boothe of Alexandria. The 1968 presidential election, which produced a secure plurality for Richard Nixon and revealed that
Virginia's six largest metropolitan regions contained a majority of the
statewide electorate, confirmed the end of the era of segregationist politics
in the Old Dominion.[20]

The gubernatorial election in 1969 wrote the epitaph for the Byrd Organization and established the Republican party as a powerful force in Virginia
politics. In his second campaign, Linwood Holton adopted the slogan "Time
for a Change" and constructed an unprecedented electoral coalition to end
eighty-four years of Democratic occupation of the governor's mansion. A
longtime racial progressive, Holton courted the black electorate by condemning the massive resistance policies of the 1950s and promising a "color-
blind administration" with equal opportunity for all. He received 40 percent
of the statewide black vote and 63 percent in Richmond, far exceeding
Nixon's recent performance. In addition to his home base in the Shenan-
doah Valley, Holton displayed formidable strength in the booming tidewater
suburbs of Virginia Beach and the Chesapeake region, the metropolitan
Richmond counties of Chesterfield and Henrico, and Fairfax County in
northern Virginia. Holton's interracial base refuted the election eve forecast
of Kevin Phillips, who warned Nixon that an appeal to the center "is not going to work down South. It also is not in accord with the true Southern Strategy" (figure 10.1). After the election, Phillips produced a revised analysis
that attributed Holton's victory to the abandonment of the Democratic party
by racial conservatives and Wallace segregationists, a verdict the governor
promptly labeled "utter nonsense." The Ripon Society also repudiated the
Phillips interpretation in a report urging the GOP to adopt Holton's "winning and progressive" outreach to suburban moderates and black voters, a
New South strategy "not based on race but on economic and class interests."[21]

Linwood Holton believed that the Republican party should expand its
southern wing from the grassroots up rather than the top down, with appeals to a color-blind future rather than a bitter past. In his inaugural address, the governor promised to usher in a new era of individual meritocracy

MEMORANDUM

THE WHITE HOUSE
WASHINGTON

OCTOBER 31, 1969

CONFIDENTIAL

TO: HARRY S. DENT

FROM: GORDON S. BROWNELL

Our expert on the Southern Strategy in the Justice Dept. has
passed along a suggestion for a memorandum to the President
if Lin Holton goes down (as he feels he will) on Tuesday.

The attached article from today's WASHINGTON POST has Holton
calling for "the old, the young and the black" to join the GOP
in Virginia. Such a policy, as you mentioned to the President
in regards to Rodney Cook, is not going to work down South.
It also is not in accord with the true Southern Strategy.

Thus Mr. Phillips feels the Virginia defeat, when and if it
comes, should not be considered a defeat for the Strategy
down South and feels the President should be informed that
this is not a valid test. Of course, if Holton wins this
is proof that the Southern Strategy is valid and the GOP should
look below the Potomac for more votes in the future.

cc: Kevin Phillips

Figure 10.1. Memorandum on the Southern Strategy, 1969. Harry Dent, the southern affairs adviser in the Nixon administration, received this memorandum a few
days before Linwood Holton won the gubernatorial election in Virginia. Kevin
Phillips predicted Holton's defeat because the progressive Republican had deviated
from the "true Southern Strategy," but Nixon's advisers also hedged their bets. Courtesy of the Harry S. Dent Papers, Special Collections, Clemson University Libraries.

and equal opportunity, "an aristocracy of ability, regardless of race, color, or
creed." Quoting Abraham Lincoln in the former capital of the Confederacy,
Holton told Virginians that they had a duty to "achieve an open society that
operates with malice toward none, with charity for all." During 1970, when
court-ordered busing came to Virginia's largest cities, Holton parted ways
with the president by refusing to exploit the crisis for political gain. As Deep
South governors resurrected the rhetoric of massive resistance, Holton proclaimed: "No more must the slogan of states' rights sound a recalcitrant and

Figure 10.2. Governor Linwood Holton of Virginia accompanying his thirteen-year-old daughter, Tayloe, to John F. Kennedy High School, August 31, 1970. State policy permitted the governor to send his children to any public school in the city, and Holton transferred all three of his children from prestigious facilities in Richmond's upscale West End to formerly all-black schools located in the East End. John F. Kennedy shifted from 100 percent black to 29 percent white under Richmond's controversial court-ordered busing plan. Courtesy of the Virginia Historical Society, Richmond, Virginia.

defensive note for the South, . . . for the era of defiance is behind us." The governor called on all Virginians to obey the law in recognition that freedom of choice had not produced meaningful school integration. Holton also voluntarily transferred his three children to majority-black public schools in Richmond, a gesture that drew national attention and widespread praise as an exceptional example of responsible leadership from a prominent politician in the midst of a busing crisis (figure 10.2). Although the governor publicly maintained his support for Nixon, the political media increasingly contrasted the Holton vision of an inclusive and interracial party with the "lily-white" backlash strategy at the heart of the White House plan for the realignment of the South.[22]

In the midterm election of 1970, the Nixon administration betrayed Linwood Holton and played a decisive role in wrecking his lifelong ambition to transform the GOP into the interracial party of the center in Virginia. With antibusing movements active throughout the metropolitan regions, and segregationist Democrats without a home in state politics, the White House jettisoned the suburban strategy of 1968 and regrouped around the Southern Strategy of the Goldwater Republicans. The key showdown came in the reelection campaign of Senator Harry F. Byrd, Jr., the target of numerous White House entreaties to switch parties. Instead Byrd decided to run as an independent, based on the probability that he would lose a primary contest in the increasingly liberal Democratic party. Nixon's political team held out hope that Byrd would convert after the election, and the administration provided substantial support for the segregationist scion of the former Democratic dynasty, including bankrolling a group called "Republicans for Byrd" that operated under Harry Dent's control. The administration's southern strategists pressured Holton to endorse the senator, but the governor refused in a principled objection to a GOP "built on the remnants of the Byrd Organization." Behind the scenes, the governor accused White House officials of "hampering our efforts to build a strong Republican party in Virginia" through a foolhardy plan to abandon the middle for the fringe. In public, Holton declared that under his leadership the Virginia GOP had "no desire to befoul its ranks with white supremacists."[23]

The interference of the White House guaranteed the reelection of Senator Byrd and empowered the conservative wing of Virginia's Republican party. The intraparty dispute boiled over at the state GOP convention in the summer of 1970, when Linwood Holton led the resistance to the Republicans for Byrd. Harry Dent appeared personally to press the convention not to nominate a challenger, but instead delegates selected a progressive but little-known candidate named Ray Garland. The Nixon administration and the Republican National Committee refused to provide financial assistance to the party's nominee, tacit support for Byrd that enraged many grassroots GOP activists. At one Garland rally in the Norfolk suburbs, members of the crowd spoke of "treason" and waved signs demanding White House support. Byrd capitalized on the desegregation climate by calling for local control of public schools, conservative justices on the Supreme Court, and grassroots opposition to "compulsory busing for the purpose of achieving an artificial racial balance." Garland echoed the Holton platform of racial moderation and legal compliance, and he reminded voters of Byrd's energetic efforts to abandon public education during the now discredited era of massive resistance. The three-way election split the anti-Byrd vote between the two major parties and allowed the incumbent to win with a 54 percent majority. Byrd maintained his traditional Southside base, received an overwhelming percentage of the Wallace vote, and also polled well in the middle-class suburbs of Richmond where many conservative Republicans lived. Although the GOP never won Byrd's partisan allegiance, his voting record remained consistently conservative, and he repaid Nixon with an endorsement in the 1972 election.[24]

The interracial coalition of Linwood Holton became the genuine casualty of the Southern Strategy in Virginia. As in South Carolina, the reliance on a convention process rather than a primary system facilitated the takeover of the party leadership by the Goldwater Republicans. At the state GOP convention in 1972, Holton fought unsuccessfully as the Nixon administration enlisted right-wing Congressman William Scott in a challenge to Democratic Senator William Spong. The delegates ousted a Holton ally as party chairman in favor of a Byrd conservative, and Spong lost the election after a misleading television campaign orchestrated by the White House that accused the moderate Democrat of supporting mandatory busing and gun control. A year later, the conservative delegates who dominated the malapportioned state convention chose former massive resister Mills Godwin as their gubernatorial nominee, and the brand-new Republican narrowly edged liberal Democrat Henry Howell. The realignment of state politics along racial and ideological lines during the 1970s produced not a new GOP hegemony, but instead a competitive landscape matching a conservative and overwhelmingly white Republican party against an interracial and increasingly progressive Democratic alternative. Voter surveys in the early 1970s revealed that 43 percent of Virginians classified themselves as moderates, with one-third conservative and one-fourth liberal. The metropolitan regions held the swing vote in statewide contests, with the suburban electorate split between the conservative Republican strongholds outside Richmond and the more moderate communities in the tidewater and northern Virginia. As Linwood Holton had predicted, the GOP's top-down shift to the right "postpone[d] into the indefinite future the opportunity to make Virginia a solid Republican state." Because of, not in spite of, the Southern Strategy, the middle remained up for grabs in Virginia politics and across the Sunbelt South.[25]

THE "NEW SOUTH GOVERNORS"

In Florida, where suburban growth and the Sunbelt boom brought substantial Republican inroads during the 1950s and 1960s, the miscalculated resort to a race-based Southern Strategy reversed the trends of partisan realignment and reinvigorated the Democratic party as the interracial champion of the New South. In the mid-1960s, Republican Claude Kirk won the gubernatorial election with a strong base in the middle-class suburbs, and long overdue political reapportionment shifted power to the metropolitan regions and brought a considerable GOP increase in the state legislature. In his reelection campaign, Kirk made a disastrous decision to embrace the politics of massive resistance, in sharp contrast to the moderate stance of his predecessor, LeRoy Collins, after the *Brown* decision. During the early months of 1970, Kirk ordered school districts not to surrender to federal desegregation mandates and promised that "we can have complete resistance to forced busing and still be in compliance with the law of the land." The governor then seized control of the Manatee County school system in order to prevent the implementation of court-ordered integration. Kirk defied an injunction to stand down and promised to go to jail if necessary, and before the crisis ended the governor's aides blocked his arrest by threatening to fire upon federal marshals. During the fall campaign, Kirk continued his demagogic attacks on the federal courts and charged that "Florida's school children are being bused around like pawns in an insane numbers game."[26]

The White House enthusiastically supported the Republican strategy in Florida, including personal campaign visits by Spiro Agnew and Richard Nixon. The vice president visited Florida in the fall as part of a national tour to denounce the forces of "radical liberalism"—a political enemies list that included progressive Democrats, busing judges, antiwar protesters, long-haired students, permissive pornographers, and violent criminals. At an Orlando rally, Governor Kirk praised Agnew as "our gladiator . . . going into the fields all across this nation to do battle with the Philistines, the ultraliberals and the wild radicals and we love you for it." President Nixon traveled to Tallahassee, barely a month after the school district implemented a controversial desegregation plan, to praise Kirk as a "man who has fought hard for these principles" of neighborhood schools and opposition to forced busing. Urging voters in the Silent Majority to "forget party labels," the president proclaimed that his administration had no Southern Strategy except the belief that "there are no second-class regions in America." The theme of regional fairness dominated a series of campaign rallies in cities and suburbs across the sunshine state, as Nixon declared that "the same standard that applies in Florida should apply . . . in Michigan or New York. . . . Let's just stop this hypocrisy that the problem in our schools is only in the South. . . . The time has come to quit kicking the South around."[27]

The Republican effort to ride antibusing sentiment and reactionary populism to victory in Florida "went jarringly awry," according to an analysis by the *Washington Post*. The massive resistance bravado of Governor Kirk cleared a wide path for Reubin Askew, a forty-two-year-old attorney from the panhandle city of Pensacola. While Kirk labeled the Democratic nominee a "permissive liberal" and a "patsy powderpuff," Askew asked voters to restore "seriousness in the governor's office." He rejected the politics of defiance and also reached out simultaneously to Wallace voters and the African-American electorate with an economic platform that promised higher taxes on corporations and lower taxes on working families. In the concurrent election for the U.S. Senate, Republican William Cramer hammered the busing issue and appealed to "the discerning Democrats of this state to join us in our fight to stop the cop killers, the bombers, the burners, the racial revolutionaries who would destroy America." The Democratic candidate, another young New South progressive named Lawton Chiles, followed Askew's lead in shifting the debate to an economic agenda and contrasted his own fried-chicken rallies with the black-tie fundraisers and cocktail parties of the country-club Republicans. Genuine rather than fair-weather populists, both Democrats trounced their Republican opponents with a broad coalition of African-Americans, working-class whites from the panhandle, and moderates and liberals from the suburbs. In Miami, Reubin Askew won 62 percent of the upper-middle-class white vote and 56 percent of the most affluent precincts, as Claude Kirk suffered a ten-point decline from his base in 1966. In the north Florida city of Jacksonville, where Kirk won more than two-thirds of the white vote in his first gubernatorial campaign, the GOP showing in 1970 dropped between 15 and 20 percentage points in every socioeconomic category of the white electorate.[28]

Reubin Askew quickly emerged as a leading voice of the regional wave of progressive Democrats and moderate Republicans celebrated in the national media as the political triumph of the New South. A devout Presbyterian, Askew implemented affirmative action in state government and openly censured the segregated private school movement. In the fall of 1971, in the face of a fierce antibusing revolt, Askew offered the most powerful endorsement of comprehensive integration ever heard from a southern governor to date. "Busing is an artificial and inadequate instrument of change," the governor told a statewide television audience. "Yet the law demands, and rightly so, that we put an end to segregation in our society." In the progressive version of the color-blind ideology, Askew urged Floridians to "put the divisive and self-defeating issue of race behind us once and for all, and . . . redirect our energies to our real quest—that of providing an equal opportunity for quality education to all of our children." He also told voters that the only morally acceptable alternative to busing would be meaningful changes in housing patterns so that "every neighborhood school is . . . a desegregated school." This stance of racial liberalism cost Askew some support in his re-election effort, especially among conservative Democrats who responded to a GOP campaign blaming the governor for "forced busing." But Askew won a second term with 61.2 percent of the vote, including massive support from racial minorities and a strong showing in white-collar suburbs that typically leaned Republican.[29]

In Arkansas, the gubernatorial election of 1970 produced a bipartisan consensus for the politics of racial moderation and ended the career of one of the original architects of massive resistance. After closing Little Rock's public high schools, Orval Faubus won biannual reelection on a segregationist platform until he stepped down in 1966. His successor in office, Winthrop Rockefeller, became the first Republican governor of Arkansas during the modern era. Like his brother Nelson in New York, Winthrop Rockefeller was a wealthy businessman who positioned the GOP as an interracial party of the center. He withstood challenges from segregationist Democrats in 1966 and 1968, winning strong majorities in the affluent white precincts of Little Rock and more than 90 percent of the African-American vote statewide (as Richard Nixon simultaneously forfeited the same ratio). Rockefeller publicly broke with Nixon over busing, which he called a "useful tool" to be used "judiciously," and he criticized the administration's politicization of desegregation enforcement as "an insult, not only to blacks, but to the thousands of whites who have gone ahead and dealt with it." As an antibusing movement in Little Rock attacked the Republican governor, Orval Faubus abandoned retirement in an effort to turn the racial climate into a comeback campaign. On the stump, Faubus labeled court-ordered busing "idiotic" and "insane," and he compared the "lawlessness" in Little Rock's integrated high schools to the minority crime rate in Washington, D.C.[30]

Rockefeller denounced his predecessor as an unreconstructed segregationist, while Faubus appealed to the working-class and rural voters who had given Wallace a plurality in 1968. To widespread surprise, Faubus lost the Democratic primary to Dale Bumpers, a self-described "country lawyer" and the most progressive candidate in a crowded field. Bumpers promised voters that he would "be a governor you don't have to apologize for. I want to create an image for Arkansas that you'll be proud of." He easily defeated Faubus with a coalition of the mountain counties and the metropolitan regions, including nearly three-fourths of the vote in the middle-class and affluent neighborhoods of Little Rock. In the general election campaign, both candidates endorsed racial nondiscrimination in public policy and openly pursued the African-American electorate. Although a majority of black voters remained loyal to the GOP, Bumpers handily defeated Rockefeller with an agenda of economic populism that resonated for working-class whites and a Sunbelt development platform that reassured the affluent suburbs. As governor his accomplishments included a more progressive tax system, increased access to health care in rural areas, and the establishment of kindergartens and community colleges. Celebrated as another New South Democrat in the ascendant tradition of racial moderation, Bumpers overwhelmingly won reelection in 1972 before embarking upon a distinguished career in the U.S. Senate.[31]

In Georgia, another country politician in the Bumpers mold launched his meteoric rise to national prominence in 1970. Jimmy Carter's gubernatorial campaign managed to bridge the traditional divisions in the state Democratic party between the segregationist rural counties and the moderate metropolitan wing. Lester Maddox, the flamboyant demagogue and longtime champion of racial segregation, entered the governor's office in 1966 through a disputed loophole despite winning fewer votes than his Republican opponent. In the 1970 election, moderate and liberal Democrats rallied behind Carl Sanders, a New South progressive who served a term as governor in the aftermath of the Atlanta massive resistance crisis. Sanders called for calm and compliance during the busing battles of 1969–70, while Maddox linked busing to communism and urged white families to boycott the public schools. In the Democratic primary, Carter skirted close to the line of segregationist politics with a freedom of choice outreach that included explicit appeals for support from Maddox and Wallace voters. Playing the class card more openly than the race card, the peanut farmer labeled Sanders a country-club elitist and cocktail-party liberal. Sanders possessed a formidable statewide network but could not overcome two cross-currents in the 1970 election: many voters in the white-collar suburbs who previously supported him had moved firmly into the GOP camp in a two-party state, and his remaining alliance of minorities and affluent liberals could not match Carter's class-based coalition from the small towns, rural districts of South Georgia, and blue-collar urban precincts.[32]

In the general election, Jimmy Carter consolidated the diverse factions within the Democratic party and overcame the suburban base of his moderate Republican opponent. The GOP's first primary election of the century featured a showdown between the grassroots centrist wing and the Goldwater Republicans. Atlanta television newscaster Hal Suit defeated Jimmy Bentley, a segregationist Democrat who switched parties to run for governor, with a wide victory margin in the suburbs of Fulton and DeKalb. Atlanta's white-collar suburbs stayed in the Republican column in the general election, but Carter won a decisive victory with the class-based coalition of Wallace populists and black Democrats. In his inaugural address, Carter garnered national attention with a firm declaration that "the time for racial discrimination is over. . . . No poor, rural, weak, or black person should ever have to bear the additional burden of being deprived of the opportunity of an education, a job, or simple justice." Once in office, Carter encouraged white parents to protest busing orders, but he also symbolized the new era of Georgia politics by hanging the portrait of Martin Luther King, Jr., in the state capitol. In the spring of 1971, a *Time* magazine cover story profiled Carter as the leader of the rising tide of "New South Governors" whose racial moderation had discredited the Nixon backlash strategy: John West of South Carolina, Linwood Holton of Virginia, Reubin Askew of Florida, and Dale Bumpers of Arkansas (figure 10.3). Later that fall, the New South impulse arrived in Louisiana and Mississippi, as moderate Democrats Edwin Edwards and William Waller succeeded segregationist governors on the Gulf Coast. "There is a new dynamic, a new freedom that exists throughout the South," Carter proclaimed. "The South is ready," Reubin Askew agreed, "to adjust and become part of the nation."[33]

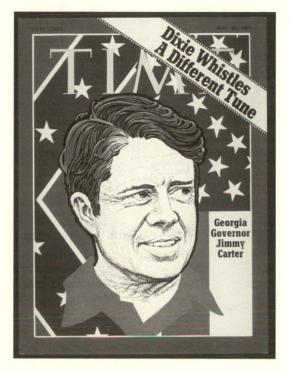

Figure 10.3. Governor Jimmy Carter of Georgia on the cover of *Time*, May 31, 1971. The *Time* feature, headlined "New Day A'Coming in the South," celebrated the rise of the New South Governors as evidence of the regional triumph of racial moderation. The article concluded that the South "has a chance to shed its old hatreds and show the U.S. the way to a truly integrated society." Courtesy of Time Life Pictures/Getty Images.

THE LEGACY OF 1970

The midterm elections of 1970 must be viewed as a smashing defeat for the Southern Strategy promoted by Kevin Phillips and orchestrated by the White House. In an era of national polarization, with school desegregation conflicts raging across the South, the candidate positioned in the political center won the gubernatorial election in every state except for Alabama. "Democrats Void Nixon Administration's 'Southern Strategy,'" read the banner in the *New York Times*, which lamented the "near death of the once promising progressive Republican tradition" in the region and warned of the expansion of the "reactionary" wing led by Strom Thurmond. "Electorate Rejects Appeal to Extremism," headlined the *Washington Post*, which highlighted the interracial coalitions assembled by the "new breed" of moderate Democrats. The White House decision to veer hard to the right backfired across the national landscape, as the Democratic party picked up ten gover-norships and thwarted Nixon's pleas for Republican control of the U.S. Sen-ate. Gallup reported that the GOP "went after the wrong group," repelling suburban moderates without attracting enough working-class Democrats to make up the difference. The Ripon Society observed that the racial backlash strategy "alienated progressive suburbanites from the GOP" and proved to be especially short-sighted during a worsening economic recession, failing to recruit Wallace partisans in the downscale South or blue-collar voters in the urban North. The Democratic party managed to "steal the center," Ripon concluded in its special report on the election, because the GOP's misguided mission of electoral polarization abandoned the politics of mod-eration in the South and throughout the nation.[34]

Only in Tennessee, one of the most Republican states in the South, did the Nixon administration find small cause for celebration in the 1970 returns. The White House heavily financed a campaign to unseat three-term Senator Albert Gore, a New Deal liberal who voted against Nixon's Supreme Court nominees and vocally opposed the Vietnam War. During a rally in Memphis, Vice President Agnew branded Gore the "Southern re-gional chairman of the Eastern liberal establishment." GOP candidate Bill Brock, a wealthy businessman from Chattanooga, saturated the state with television commercials blasting Gore for his liberal stance on busing, gun control, public school prayer, and Vietnam. The counties of west Tennessee proved decisive in the close election, as Brock defeated Gore by 52 to 48 percent with a strong showing among middle-class voters in suburban Memphis and Wallace supporters in the rural and working-class precincts. Memphis dentist Winfield Dunn also won the gubernatorial election for the GOP over the Nashville base of liberal Democrat John Jay Hooker. While pundits credited Gore's defeat to the Southern Strategy, longtime observers of Tennessee politics offered a different version of events. Journalist David Halberstam blamed Nixon and Agnew personally for "the most disreputable and scurrilous race I have ever covered in Tennessee, . . . hitting away daily at the most emotional issues they can touch." But Halberstam concluded that "the credit should go to the TVA and the prosperity it brought to the area. Tennessee is becoming a Republican state anyway. If the Republicans had run a more decent, more liberal, more honest campaign, I think they would have won even more votes, and more important, built the basis for a strong party in the future."[35]

In North Carolina, a bitter showdown between moderates and conserva-tives highlighted the divergent paths facing the Republican party in the Up-per South. During the 1968 gubernatorial election, Democrat Bob Scott de-feated a reactionary GOP challenger with an interracial coalition of black voters and middle-class whites from the metropolitan regions. Scott champi-oned industrial development and educational reform, and during the busing crisis he declared that "no legislation or court decree can erase centuries of discrimination in education, in housing, and in employment." In 1972, James Holshouser became the state's first Republican governor during the modern era by following Linwood Holton's centrist strategy: combining the white-collar base in the suburbs, solid black support in the cities, and traditional GOP strength in the mountains. At the same time, Jesse Helms won election to the U.S. Senate with a fiercely ideological campaign of antibusing fervor and far-right extremism that carried the rural Wallace counties of eastern North Carolina and alienated African-American voters and moderate suburbanites. At the state convention a year later, the centrist Republicans who rallied around Holshouser's leadership defeated the Helms wing for control of the party. In the mid-1970s, Senator Helms turned the tables and consolidated power over the party machinery, a maneuver that enhanced his personal career more than the statewide prospects of the GOP. The Democrats never succeeded in unseating their nemesis Helms, but they remained the leading party in state politics as four-term governor Jim Hunt succeeded Holshouser through an interracial base of support and a commitment to progressive reform.[36]

The Southern Strategy of 1970 squandered a golden opportunity to forge a centrist GOP alternative in the new two-party South and facilitated the ascendance of an interracial Democratic party that retained the balance of power in regional politics throughout the decade. Moderate Republicans struggled to maintain their party's traditional interracial base, with temporary successes in Virginia and North Carolina, and dignified defeats in Arkansas and Georgia. The unsuccessful GOP candidates believed they could ride racial backlash to power by presenting themselves as a retrograde fusion of Barry Goldwater, George Wallace, and Spiro Agnew. Instead the top-down reprisal of massive resistance turned off moderate swing voters in the suburbs, failed to entice many working-class whites into the GOP, and galvanized a massive black turnout for the Democrats. Assessing the landscape at middecade, the *Charlotte Observer* remarked that across the region, "a new wave of moderate Democrats . . . captured the political center that might have gone to Republicans," who made the fateful decision to chase after Wallace segregationists. Kevin Phillips offered the opposite interpretation in an election postmortem that tried to salvage his prophetic reputation by claiming that the analysis in *The Emerging Republican Majority* applied only to presidential contests. The leading exponent of the Southern Strategy promised that "a new hegemony still can be established," but only if President Nixon reigned in federal policies of forced integration and embraced the conservative principles espoused by Governor Ronald Reagan of California. "The New Right wants to replace the current White House pseudoconservatism—negative rhetoric wrapped around warmed-over Great Society programming—with creative positive programming."[37]

The public schools of the South rapidly shifted from the most segregated to the most integrated in the nation during the late 1960s and early 1970s. By expressing solidarity with the grassroots antibusing movement and purging policymakers who favored full compliance with the law, Richard Nixon committed the executive branch to a two-tiered approach of protecting the affluent white suburbs with its policies and inflaming working-class resentment with its rhetoric. Two campaign trips during the 1970 election cycle illustrate the fundamentally political orientation of the administration's approach to civil rights enforcement. During an August appearance before civic and educational leaders in Louisiana, Nixon became the first president to visit the Deep South in order to issue a personal plea for "orderly and peaceful" desegregation. Then he promptly told a cheering crowd in New Orleans that the federal courts were "treating the South as basically a second-class part of the nation." A week before the election, Nixon traveled to the North Carolina city of Asheville, which had smoothly implemented a comprehensive busing plan earlier in the year. The president congratulated white southerners for complying with the law, but then he reminded the audience of his opposition to "the use of busing solely for the purpose of achieving racial balance. . . . The important thing for us to remember is let us not destroy the quality education of our children." Nixon and his political strategists always insisted that the administration never received due credit for supervising the end of Jim Crow in the South, and they demanded that the civil rights record of the White House be evaluated separately from the "politics of schools." A white southerner who voted for the Nixon-Agnew ticket in 1968 offered a different verdict: "After promising to 'bring us together,' . . . they have tried to divide the North against the South, black against white, haves against have-nots. While talking 'law and order,' . . . [Nixon] has not had the moral courage and commitment to lead us to obey the Constitution of the United States."[38]

The key lesson of the underappreciated 1970 election cycle is the persistent competitiveness of the two-party system in the American South, not simply during an era of political realignment but during any era when the center is legitimately contested. The futility of the Nixon administration's Southern Strategy reveals a political truth that New Right strategists have discovered again and again: rural white residents, working-class voters, and affluent suburban professionals do not fit smoothly into a stable political coalition, especially in times of social crisis or economic downturn. During the two climactic episodes of the civil rights era—the massive resistance showdowns of the late 1950s and the busing battles of the early 1970s—racial crises exposed rather than submerged the class and geographic and ideological divisions among white southerners. The four-time failure of the Southern Strategy to unify a Solid South—from the Dixiecrat revolt, to the Goldwater and Wallace campaigns, to Nixon's debacle in 1970—should caution against the monocausal interpretation of the racial backlash thesis and the unwarranted conclusion that the civil rights movement destroyed Democratic prospects in the region. This teleological view of southern political history necessitates a denial of the vitality of the center, including the continued potential for an interracial Democratic party to occupy the region's middle ground. At the same time, a critical perspective on the failure of the Southern Strategy reveals the political success of the color-blind suburban strategies targeted at the racial and class privileges of white-collar homeowners, from the national impact of the grassroots antibusing movement to the federal judiciary's retreat from metropolitan remedies for school and residential segregation.

CHAPTER 11

Metropolitan Divergence

> The City of Richmond's present pattern of residential housing . . .
> is a reflection of past racial discrimination contributed in part by
> local, state, and federal government. . . . Negroes in Richmond live
> where they do because they have no choice.
> —*Bradley v. Richmond* (1972),
> District Judge Robert R. Merhige, Jr.

> We think that the root causes of the concentration of blacks in the
> inner cities of America are simply not known.
> —*Bradley v. Richmond* (1972),
> Fourth Circuit Court of Appeals

METROPOLITAN REMEDIES

As the political and racial foundations of southern exceptionalism crumbled, the metropolitan centers of the region stood at a fateful crossroads during the late 1960s and early 1970s. The bitter battles over court-ordered busing represented only the most visible of the metropolitan showdowns that would shape the spatial landscapes of the Sunbelt South: homeowners revolts against policies of suburban annexation, civil rights litigation to merge city and county school systems, urban conflicts surrounding the inequities of at-large political representation, and struggles over the placement of low-income housing, the distribution of tax burdens, and the impact of urban renewal and exurban sprawl. The Sunbelt Synthesis of racial moderation and economic growth, championed by the downtown business coalitions that governed most southern cities during the civil rights era, came under two-sided assault from white suburbs that demanded political independence and black urban neighborhoods that sought formal power. Would the Sunbelt South adopt the Charlotte path of metropolitan convergence and regional cooperation, based on the class-based desegregation remedy, consolidated city-county school system, automatic annexation of suburbs, interracial alliance for electoral reform, and stable racial demographics? Or would the Sunbelt South follow the Atlanta model of metropolitan divergence and regional fragmentation, emulating the national pattern of increasingly poor and heavily minority urban populations surrounded by overwhelmingly white and politically autonomous suburbs? The future of the New South would be determined by the political and legal showdowns over the pursuit of metropolitan remedies and class-based resolutions for the historical burdens of residential segregation and racial inequality.

During the postwar decades, the corporate leadership of the Sunbelt South embraced a regional planning framework in order to manage the consequences of suburban sprawl, including growth policies that efficiently segregated the metropolis by race and class and an annexation agenda to maintain a white majority in municipal politics. With the advent of court-ordered busing in the 1970s, the NAACP sought to turn regionalism to the cause of racial integration through metropolitan remedies that would force the middle-class suburbs to take part in desegregation and therefore diminish the sanctuaries for white flight from urban schools. In the metropolitan South, three interrelated factors decisively shaped the outcome of successful cases of court-ordered desegregation: the prior existence of a consolidated countywide school system, the presence of a substantial white majority in the overall district enrollment, and the implementation of a comprehensive formula that achieved class as well as racial integration. The most important development in the NAACP's landmark busing victory in Charlotte happened in 1960, when the business leadership pushed through the consolidation of the city and county school systems, inadvertently making possible the metropolitan remedy that included the suburbs. A critical turning point in the NAACP's failure to integrate the Atlanta public schools came in 1966, several years before almost anyone anticipated the *Swann* precedent, when affluent homeowners in the northside suburb of Sandy Springs vetoed annexation by the city. The "relative elasticity" of a metropolitan region—a land-use index that includes favorable annexation laws, city-county governmental consolidation, and unified city-suburban school systems—became the primary structural determinant of the degree of school desegregation achieved in the urban South.[1]

During the era of widespread court-ordered busing, which lasted from the late 1960s until the mid-1980s, the largest city-suburban consolidated districts in the South displayed a much higher level of racial integration and suffered a much lower degree of white flight than almost all urban school systems across the nation (table 11.1). With few exceptions, the favorable desegregation conditions in these metropolitan districts included an enrollment breakdown of about three-fourths white students before busing began and a comprehensive integration formula that maintained a white majority in most of the individual facilities. More than half of the most populous countywide districts were located in the state of Florida, where business leaders aggressively pursued suburban annexation and engineered the merger of city and county governmental functions during the postwar growth boom. The city of Jacksonville joined together with surrounding Duval County in 1967, only a few years before the implementation of a sys-

TABLE 11.1
Decline in White Enrollment, 1968–1986, and Percentage of Black Students in
Majority-White and Racially Isolated Schools, 1986, Large City-Suburban
Consolidated (Countywide) School Districts in the South.

City/County	%White (1968)	%White (1986)	%Black/Maj. White Schools	%Black/Racially Isolated Schools
Greenville, SC/ Greenville Co.	78	72	87.4	1.8
Raleigh, NC/ Wake Co.	74°	71	N/A	N/A
Tampa, FL/ Hillsboro Co.	74	69	80.8	1.5
Orlando, FL/ Orange Co.	83	67	53.2	7.4
Ft. Lauderdale, FL/ Broward Co.	75	65	41.6	23.9
Nashville, TN/ Davidson Co.	76	63	62.0	2.1
W. Palm Beach, FL/ Palm Beach Co.	70	62	36.4	27.9
Jacksonville, FL/ Duval Co.	72	60	50.9	14.9
Charlotte, NC/ Mecklenburg Co.	71	58	65.2	3.2
Mobile, AL/ Mobile Co.	58	55	34.0	43.1
Miami, FL/ Dade Co.	58	24	8.2	59.2

Sources: Gary Orfield and Franklin Monfort, *Racial Change and Desegregation in Large School Districts* (Alexandria: NSBA, 1988), 7–9, 11–13, 20–23; *Raleigh News and Observer*, Aug. 7, 1970.
°City schools only (consolidation in 1976)

temwide desegregation plan. The metropolitan districts that included Tampa and Orlando produced some of the lowest percentages of minority students in racially isolated schools anywhere in the nation. In Tennessee, the unification of the school systems and governments of Nashville and Davidson County during the early 1960s minimized white flight despite a protracted busing conflict a decade later. The metropolitan formula in Greenville, South Carolina, placed almost all black students in predominantly white schools that retained the support of the vast majority of families in the county. The comprehensively integrated schools of Charlotte-Mecklenburg continued to lead the way in demonstrating the structural efficacy of metropolitan remedies in curtailing white flight during the *Swann* era, especially in the younger midsized cities of the Sunbelt South.[2]

A number of southern school districts experienced significant white flight and rapid resegregation because of unstable plans devised by HEW and partial approaches approved by federal judges. The Nixon administration's mandate that HEW avoid "racial busing" and preserve neighborhood schools resulted in ill-conceived formulas that consistently imposed the desegregation burden on transitional working-class neighborhoods and therefore turned antibusing propaganda into self-fulfilling prophesy. In several major districts—including Charlotte, Greenville, Greensboro, and Raleigh—school boards rejected HEW formulas as recipes for resegregation because of the proposed reassignment of substantial numbers of white students to majority-black schools. In Miami-Dade County, the only consolidated system to experience considerable decline in white enrollment, the HEW plan avoided busing and the courts permitted desegregation based on geographic proximity that left one-fourth of black students in racially isolated schools and placed many others in tipping situations. In Mobile, the combination of a minimalist HEW formula and an obstructionist federal judge produced the only other metropolitan district with a high degree of racial segregation, although the location of most new suburban developments within the expansive county boundaries limited overall white flight. In Columbia, South Carolina, direct pressure from the White House resulted in a self-destructive HEW plan that left twenty-three schools racially segregated and reassigned many working-class white students to majority-black institutions. Business leaders launched a campaign asking white families to "keep your cool—support our schools," but public relations proved no match for the tipping point phenomenon, and within a few years the Columbia system became majority-black.[3]

Metropolitan remedies often faced skepticism from African-American parents who questioned the assimilationist philosophy of one-way desegregation and protested the persistent pattern of closing black schools and demoting black teachers that accompanied integration into majority-white facilities. The necessity of maintaining white control in order to avoid the tipping point appealed to a broad range of education officials, public policymakers, federal judges, and municipal leaders. The two-way busing resolution in Charlotte turned out to be a rare (and only partial) exception that proved the general rule of the "fate of black schools in the South," in the urban centers and the rural countryside alike, and black families frequently organized boycotts and protests against inequitable desegregation plans that sacrificed neighborhood institutions and denigrated community pride. In the summer of 1970, the Congress of Racial Equality (CORE) held a convention in Mobile to promote its new agenda: "A True Alternative to Segregation—a Proposal for Community School Districts." The Black Power advocates in CORE traveled to several southern cities to promote the philosophy that white racism made equality unattainable in integrated schools, with the only solution the establishment of an "autonomous and truly equal" system of racial separation. Most black parents in the South instead appeared to agree with the sentiments of a mother caught up in Greenville's metropolitan desegregation plan. "I don't care to have my children bused to a school three or four miles away from my home, when there is one less than a block from my house," remarked Lillie Wright. "Nor do I really care if they ever sit next to a little white girl or boy. But what I do care about is that they have the best education possible. . . . If it is in a society area, upper middle class or slum area, if that's where it is, then that is where I want them to go."[4]

After the victory in *Swann*, the NAACP launched a major drive to secure metropolitan integration remedies in the major cities of the South and North. Building on the relatively successful model of countywide districts in the Southeast, the Legal Defense Fund developed a strategy to overcome trends of metropolitan fragmentation through the court-ordered consolidation of city and suburban school systems. The NAACP fought for two-way busing plans but ultimately believed that white-majority school districts and white-majority facilities represented the essential features of a meaningful and stable integration climate. The Leadership Conference on Civil Rights (LCCR), representing more than one hundred member organizations, also portrayed metropolitan remedies as the only way to fulfill the promise of *Brown* and avoid the dire "two societies" forecast of the Kerner Report. "Most black people and their leaders are solidly for busing as a method to desegregate the schools," the LCCR proclaimed in 1970, because they understood that "the only way to make certain that black Americans receive an equal educational opportunity is to put them in the same classrooms with whites." The LCCR's "Facts about Busing" pamphlet conceded that "there is no inherent virtue in having a black child sit next to a white child" but concluded that in a majority-white nation "separate but equal schools have never been equal and are not now equal." Before the Atlanta Compromise of 1973 exempted the suburbs of the capital of the Sunbelt South, before the Supreme Court's landmark 1974 verdict on city-suburban consolidation in the Rust Belt city of Detroit, the NAACP's quest for metropolitan remedies took a decisive turn in the older southern city of Richmond, Virginia.[5]

SUBURBAN ANNEXATION IN VIRGINIA

The James River that now bisects the capital of Virginia once marked the border between the city of Richmond and the suburbs of Chesterfield County. The interstate corridors that bring suburban commuters to the central business district also displaced thousands of minority families and accelerated the centrifugal forces of black residential expansion within the city and white settlement on the metropolitan fringe. The postwar population of metropolitan Richmond expanded more slowly than many of the upstart centers of the New South, as the tobacco center shifted from the blue-collar past of river-based industry to the white-collar future of Sunbelt banking and automobile-driven suburbanization. Following the trend throughout the Southeast, metropolitan Richmond became much more residentially segregated during the postwar era, as federal funds for urban renewal and highway construction subsidized suburban decentralization, and city planners and politicians explicitly pursued spatial separation by race and class. Between 1950 and 1970, the population inside the Richmond city limits declined steadily and the demographic ratio shifted from more than two-thirds white to an equal number of white and black residents. During the same period, the suburban population tripled in the adjacent counties of Chesterfield and Henrico, including white migration to the new subdivisions in the southern and western parts of the metropolis as black families moved into the older neighborhoods in the northern and eastern sections of the city (map 11.1). Faced with the prospect of a majority-black city, the corporate leadership of Richmond sponsored a series of annexation and consolidation initiatives designed to maintain elite control of municipal politics by capturing suburban sprawl.[6]

Richmond Forward, the lobbying arm of the business leadership in municipal politics, fervently supported metropolitan government as the best way to control white flight and maintain the white-collar tax base. But in 1961, when civic leaders initiated an effort to merge the city with Henrico County, suburban homeowners and urban black coalitions launched parallel challenges to the regionalist agenda of the downtown establishment. The Crusade for Voters, a black political organization dominated by middle-class professionals, made support for consolidation conditional upon replacement of the city's at-large voting system with district representation. When their counterparts in Richmond Forward refused to compromise, the Crusade for Voters campaigned against the merger as a scheme to dilute black power. The referendum secured a narrow majority within the city but failed after more than 60 percent of Henrico voters rejected consolidation. Municipal leaders then shifted tactics from the electoral to the legal arena, because Virginia's land-use policies permitted cities to file annexation lawsuits against adjacent counties, resulting in a judicial determination of financial compensation for the transfer of suburban residents and infrastructure. Hostility toward annexation became a defining feature of suburban politics in Virginia during the 1960s, with the outlying areas of metropolitan Norfolk adopting the strategy of defensive incorporation to become the overwhelmingly white "cities" of Virginia Beach and Chesapeake, and the emergence

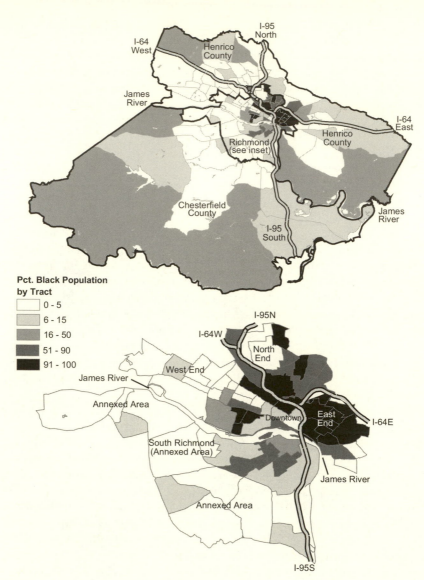

Map 11.1. Distribution of the Black Population of the City of Richmond, Henrico County, and Chesterfield County, 1970, by Census Tract. Planners and politicians in postwar Richmond used interstate highways and urban renewal to fortify the downtown business district, setting off a chain reaction as middle-class black families moved out of the East End ghetto into formerly all-white North End neighborhoods. In 1970, the annexation of forty-four thousand residents of the white suburbs of northern Chesterfield County, designated South Richmond on the inset map, temporarily returned the city to majority-white status. After antibusing movements emerged in the white neighborhoods of the West End and the annexed area, the NAACP attempted to include the suburban counties of Henrico and Chesterfield in a metropolitan integration plan. *Source:* U.S. Census Bureau, 1970 Census of Population and Housing.

of fierce resistance throughout the middle-class subdivisions of Henrico and Chesterfield. After Richmond received an unfavorable ruling in the Henrico litigation, city leaders concentrated on legal proceedings to annex more than sixty thousand residents of northern Chesterfield, while suburban families demanded to be left alone and rejected any responsibility to share in the urban "problems" across the river.[7]

Richmond and Chesterfield leaders secretly negotiated a compromise in the late 1960s, after some version of court-ordered annexation appeared inevitable. Under the bargain, Chesterfield ceded forty-four thousand residents and twenty-three square miles in exchange for $27 million. The settlement included less than half of the county land originally sought by the city and exempted eighteen thousand suburban residents who lived inside the target area but beyond the compromise line. Eleven civic associations in Chesterfield filed legal petitions to halt the annexation agreement, and few white suburbanites appreciated Richmond's plan to purchase them for $616.63 apiece. Raucous crowds at judicial hearings compared forced annexation to the recent Soviet invasion of Czechoslovakia and drew analogies between Neville Chamberlain at Munich and Chesterfield's decision to sacrifice them to save the rest of the county. Antiannexation leaders also lamented their negligence to incorporate the neighborhoods south of the James River as a suburban city, following the preemptive path of Virginia Beach and Chesapeake. In the summer of 1969, the special annexation court approved the compromise with a declaration that "the exodus of productive citizens and the influx of the economically underprivileged create an intolerable condition that must have some means of amelioration." The judicial panel informed the Chesterfield homeowners that "people who establish their residences near a large city must anticipate that eventually they will become a part of that municipality."[8]

Neighborhood associations in Chesterfield appealed the annexation decree, and many suburban homeowners denounced the ruling in bitter terms. The most frequently voiced complaint concerned the projected doubling of property taxes following absorption by the city, although the racialized nature of the annexation debate always lurked near the surface. The proannexation forces avoided public discussion of racial politics, but opposition leaders accused the power brokers in Richmond Forward of coveting suburban homeowners because of the color of their skin. A state legislator from northern Chesterfield charged that the "single issue of the annexation trial was to dilute the black vote." Antiurban sentiments emerged in denunciations of "this cancer called Richmond," and many homeowners despaired that hardworking families had lost control of their lives, "herded together like sheep" into the city. A more sanguine suburban resident reminded her "self-centered" neighbors that most of them worked and shopped downtown, and therefore higher taxes seemed a fair price to pay for the benefits of metropolitan citizenship. The *Richmond Times-Dispatch* praised the residents of newly designated south Richmond as a "tremendous asset" that would make the city a "stronger, more vibrant municipality." After state and federal courts refused to consider appeals of the annexation order, the forty-four thousand suburbanites from Chesterfield became residents of Richmond on the first day of 1970, and the city population suddenly dropped from 52 to 42 percent black.[9]

Suburban annexation allowed the corporate leadership to retain control of municipal politics in the short term, but within a few years the racial undercurrents of the Chesterfield case provided the unanticipated leverage for a legal remedy for voting discrimination. In the 1970 municipal elections, the newly acquired residents of south Richmond enabled the white candidates endorsed by Team of Progress, the corporate arm that supplanted Richmond Forward, to maintain a two-thirds majority on the city council. One year later, a working-class black Richmonder named Curtis Holt filed a federal lawsuit seeking to reverse the Chesterfield annexation as a violation of the Voting Rights Act of 1965. District Judge Robert R. Merhige, Jr., acknowledged the many public policy arguments in favor of regional government but also found that racial considerations played a central role in the annexation decision, including the intentional dilution of black influence in municipal politics. Several white homeowners associations provided financial support for the *Holt v. Richmond* litigation, and many residents of south Richmond anticipated court-ordered repatriation to Chesterfield County. Instead of a deannexation remedy, the federal courts and the Justice Department required the replacement of Richmond's at-large formula with a system of district representation. The next municipal election in 1977 resulted in a black majority on the city council and the appointment of Richmond's first African-American mayor, NAACP attorney Henry Marsh III.[10]

Richmond's experience during the 1960s and 1970s reveals the double-sided nature of metropolitan remedies, because the longtime corporate mission to institute regional government ultimately intersected with the new civil rights strategy to pursue a suburban solution for urban school segregation. Business leaders feared that Richmond would follow the national trend toward central cities with a majority-black population and a declining tax base—a dynamic that their own development policies of segregation-based sprawl had helped to set in motion. Civil rights leaders demanded full participation in municipal politics but also came to recognize that the same demographic trends that forecast black power in city government would make it impossible to achieve meaningful school integration without a metropolitan remedy. A crucial failure of the corporate executives in Richmond Forward/Team of Progress resulted from their paternalistic refusal to strike a power-sharing bargain with their counterparts in the Crusade for Voters, trading white backing of district elections for black support of regional government. In the early 1970s, the simultaneous revolts by suburban whites and urban blacks against the annexation agenda doomed the business coalition's last-ditch attempt to create a metropolitan government through a renewed effort to merge with Henrico County and incorporate most of the remainder of Chesterfield. Under pressure from suburban constituents, the Virginia legislature intervened to block Richmond's latest expansion initiative and effectively granted permanent immunity from involuntary annexation to the unincorporated areas of the state's metropolitan regions. By then the political context of metropolitan remedies had changed dramatically, because of the massive grassroots backlash against the concurrent drive to merge the Richmond city schools with the suburban districts of Henrico and Chesterfield.[11]

Showdown across the James

Two months after the suburban residents of northern Chesterfield became citizens of Richmond, the NAACP filed a motion to replace the current freedom of choice assignment plan with comprehensive desegregation of every school in the city district. The antiannexation movement had not expressed overt concern about the prospect of school integration, but crosstown busing suddenly replaced higher taxes as the salient issue for the reluctant Richmonders who lived south of the James River. Neighborhood associations from south Richmond intervened in the desegregation lawsuit and demanded the retention of freedom of choice for the twelve thousand white students who had until recently attended Chesterfield public schools. Mothers from the annexed area picketed the courthouse, explaining that "our children are not cattle" and warning of the dangerous rush-hour traffic on the main bridge across the river. "The collar of governmental control has tightened around my neck so that I am about to strangle," one woman exclaimed. "Patrick Henry's words ring all too clear: 'Give me liberty or give me death.'" The Richmond school board submitted a plan devised by HEW that paired black and white schools in geographic proximity while leaving untouched the two most residentially segregated sections of the city, the predominantly black East End and the almost exclusively white suburbs in the annexed section. District Judge Robert Merhige rejected the HEW approach and ordered the board to submit a constitutional formula that made meaningful integration, not neighborhood schooling, its highest priority.[12]

Antibusing groups formed throughout the city during the summer of 1970, with the fiercest protests coming from the annexed subdivisions of south Richmond, where more than one thousand parents organized the Citizens against Busing (CAB). Led by a fundamentalist minister named John Book, who declared publicly that "the combining of all races by force is communism," CAB occupied the most conservative place on the antibusing spectrum. The group advocated the establishment of a network of private Christian schools and demanded that Governor Linwood Holton call an emergency session of the legislature to repeal the compulsory attendance law. Holton expressed his personal opposition to busing but asked the parents to remain calm and accept the authority of the federal courts. Instead CAB organized events such as a "drive-in" where motorists repeatedly circled Capitol Square and a freedom of choice rally at the Richmond Arena with a Dixieland band providing entertainment. Several thousand white citizens attended the rally, where CAB adopted the slogans "Busing—Never!" and "United We Stand—Divided We Fall." The protest coincided with the release of the school board's revised desegregation plan, which proposed busing five thousand students from south Richmond to the East End. Reverend Book urged CAB supporters to participate in a mass boycott and appropriated civil rights language to complain that white southerners "are tired of being treated like second-class citizens."[13]

In the older neighborhoods of the city, affluent white parents formed a more temperate organization called the West End Concerned Parents and Friends (WECPF), which gathered fifteen thousand signatures on antibusing petitions to the governor and the U.S. Congress. The position statement of the WECPF proclaimed opposition to "busing without parental consent" and support for "the preservation of a strong neighborhood public school system." Adopting the class-based rhetoric of color-blind moderation, one West End mother of three expressed her support for "reasonable integration" but not the mixture of students with "different socioeconomic values." She preferred the middle-class black students who attended her neighborhood school under the freedom of choice program but worried that the busing plan would bring her children into contact with "a different type of black child." In an emotional letter to the judge, a father from the West End wrote: "I have never resisted the logical integration of public schools. . . . Although raised and educated in the South, I have always tried to judge a man on his merits." But the court order had left him with three unwelcome choices: moving to the suburbs, switching to a private school, or busing his daughter in dereliction of parental responsibility. James Doherty, the chairman of the WECPF, explained to the school board that "if the Supreme Court distinguishes between de jure and de facto segregation, we would like to be placed in the latter category and treated like . . . the major cities in the North and Midwest." The WECPF refused to join the boycott called by the south Richmonders in CAB, but the West End group also warned that if left unaltered, the busing plan would destroy public education.[14]

The business leadership of Richmond remained silent throughout the summer, while grassroots support for comprehensive integration came from an unusual mixture of black integrationists, West End liberals, and desperate working-class white families who still lived in the East End. "Our group is *in favor of busing*," announced the PTA that represented the last remnant of white East End families. "We know that the neighborhood school plan will not possibly work in our area due to the racial ratio [660 white and 14,000 black pupils]. We do not want to move out of the city as many people from other areas have suggested and we want our children to attend public schools but on an equal basis." In a letter to the *Times-Dispatch*, an African-American father declared that the real issue was not busing but whether whites would accept blacks "as fellow humans. . . . We do request and again ask WASP Richmond—give it a try." In midsummer, an interracial group of liberal activists and religious leaders formed the Ad Hoc Committee for Education, which launched a public relations campaign behind the slogan "Our Public Schools Need Our Support!" Members of the Ad Hoc Committee repeatedly asked the business community to join the movement for compliance, but leaders of the Chamber of Commerce were unable to reach agreement on a public statement supporting "the peaceful reopening of the schools." Notwithstanding the conspicuous default of the downtown establishment, the Ad Hoc Committee warned that the negative stance of the local media represented the greatest obstacle to a smooth transition.[15]

The city's two main newspapers played a significant role in exacerbating racial tensions in Richmond and confirmed their reputation as the region's most conservative media institutions outside of the Deep South. In an extension of their enthusiasm for defiance during the massive resistance era of the 1950s, the *Richmond Times-Dispatch* and the *Richmond News Leader* maintained a shrill tone and encouraged an obstructionist stance throughout the three-year busing crisis. Expressing open hostility toward the black plaintiffs and the federal courts, the *Times-Dispatch* repeatedly invoked a doomsday scenario of coercive integration where "thousands of children would be hauled from their own neighborhoods to strange schools in strange communities miles away." The *News Leader* called for grassroots resistance to the "Orwellian" decisions of federal judges, the reverse discrimination and liberal social engineering that would surely provoke an "incipient race war in the public schools . . . [and] tear the social fabric of this nation apart." The editorial pages launched a campaign of personal vituperation against Linwood Holton after his refusal to exploit the crisis, which the *Times-Dispatch* attributed to the governor's solicitation of black voters for the Republican party. The *News Leader* actively participated in the antibusing movement by circulating its own freedom of choice petition, signed by 29,122 readers and delivered to the steps of the Supreme Court by editor Ross Mackenzie and Senator Harry F. Byrd, Jr. Executives at both newspapers insisted that they were only exercising the constitutional right to protest a busing decree not yet approved by the Supreme Court. A community study of the Richmond crisis concluded that the editorial pages jointly created "an atmosphere of mass hysteria and defiance by fanning the flames of emotionalism and racial bigotry, which only served to poison race relations between blacks and whites at a time when understanding and mutual cooperation were desperately needed."[16]

The implementation of a limited busing formula in Richmond demonstrated that racial instability would inevitably follow the assignment of white students to majority-black schools. In late August, Judge Merhige approved the board's revised proposal on a temporary basis and ordered the submission of a comprehensive formula within three months. Linwood Holton issued a televised appeal for the community to "play it cool" and called for responsible guidance from the business establishment and the local media. Court decisions "must be obeyed," the governor insisted. "There is no reasonable alternative." After Holton enrolled his three children in majority-black East End schools, even his enemies at the *Times-Dispatch* praised his "political leadership of the highest order." Business leaders in the city never took a public stand for compliance, although at the last minute the Richmond newspapers and Mayor Thomas J. Bliley, Jr., did urge citizens to avoid violence. Almost four thousand students boycotted the busing plan, representing nearly one-fifth of the overall white enrollment in the district. More than two-thirds of the reassigned pupils refused to attend the formerly all-black schools of the East End, and most of the missing students came from the annexed suburbs of south Richmond or the affluent neighborhoods of the West End. A group of families in the annexed area opened the James River Schools as an antibusing haven, and numerous white parents falsified their addresses or rented apartments in other attendance zones to avoid sending their children into black neighborhoods. Barely two weeks into the academic year, the *Times-Dispatch* pronounced busing a disastrous failure that would soon produce an all-black school system.[17]

Many middle-class families in Richmond invoked the specter of the nation's capital and lamented the discrimination against white children who suddenly found themselves in an intolerable role reversal as racial minorities. "We would hate to see Richmond become another Washington, D.C.— an empty shell of welfare cases," warned a West End mother who predicted "a mass exodus of young families out of the city." A parent who did comply with the busing program informed the school administration that his children were the "token integrators" in a 92 percent black facility, and he demanded meaningful integration in accordance with *Brown*. "Before I was occupied by the city of Richmond, I was relatively happy and had no serious problems," remembered a suburban father from the annexed area. But now his "children are members of the white minority and their civil rights appear to be violated." The Richmond media highlighted reports of violence and intensified the fears of white families who did accept transfer to the East End, including a week-long WRVA radio series on the plight of the Listrom children, who were "accosted by a group of young hoodlums" at the bus stop and subjected to "roving bands of non-students or dropouts" inside their majority-black school. "I am not a racist and I am not opposed to integration," Mrs. Listrom told the audience. "All I want is an atmosphere that is conducive to learning and where my child will be physically safe." Another mother who openly supported integration warned that the current busing approach threatened to polarize the city between wealthy families seeking private education and poor students abandoned in public schools as middle-class homeowners of both races "flee to the suburbs and so avoid the problems."[18]

THE RICHMOND CONSOLIDATION SAGA

A regional desegregation plan achieved through the consolidation of urban and suburban school systems offered the most viable solution to this New American Dilemma, but the failure to achieve a metropolitan remedy instead tore Richmond apart and brought the NAACP a crushing legal defeat with national implications. The original proposal for the merger of the Richmond system with its neighboring suburban districts came from the Sartain Report, a federally funded study by a group of university professors on the causes of resegregation on the city's northside. Released in 1969, the Sartain Report recognized that stable school desegregation ultimately required an expansive housing remedy and called for public policies to increase residential integration through the genuine enforcement of open-housing laws and the scattering of low-income projects throughout the metropolis. The study blamed white flight on the chain reaction set off by urban renewal programs, orchestrated by the corporate "establishment," that obliterated black neighborhoods to make way for expressways and downtown redevelopment. Thousands of middle-class black families were "fleeing from certain aspects of the city, . . . looking for better homes in better neighborhoods with 'better' schools," and the illegal blockbusting widely practiced by the real estate industry guaranteed the resegregation of the northside neighborhoods that had come to represent "Negro suburbia." To combat white flight, the Sartain Report recommended that Richmond leaders seek a metropolitan government and the consolidation of the city and county school systems, based on the finding that racial stability required a white and a middle-class majority in each individual facility. The *News Leader* ridiculed the merger proposal as an "academic excursion into some liberal wonderland, where complex racial problems and attitudes can be permanently resolved through forced housing laws and the dispersal of slums throughout the suburbs."[19]

Despite the annexation of northern Chesterfield, the Richmond school system contained a majority-black enrollment when court-ordered busing began, and the ensuing white flight from the piecemeal desegregation plan only increased the racial imbalance. The city schools threatened to reach a systemwide tipping point in the fall of 1970, with an overall enrollment of 64 percent black and 36 percent white. On the other side of the municipal boundary, the suburban districts of Henrico and Chesterfield each exceeded 90 percent white. The reintroduction of the consolidation proposal came from Judge Merhige, who suggested in an informal letter to the NAACP plaintiffs that a metropolitan remedy might be necessary to achieve effective desegregation. The *Times-Dispatch*, an avid proponent of annexing the "tremendous assets" who lived in the suburbs, attacked the judge for suggesting that "if free citizens exercise their right to move from a troubled community to one that offers peace, then the troubles they fled should be packed up and sent to them." But steady white flight from the city schools convinced both the Richmond board of education and the civil rights plaintiffs that only a regional solution would work. In the fall of 1970, the school board formally asked the district court to mandate the merger of the three districts in metropolitan Richmond as the only available technique to achieve stable integration. A month later, the NAACP filed its own petition for metropolitan consolidation as an appropriate remedy for the state of Virginia's long history of perpetuating racial segregation in public education.[20]

The prospect of a metropolitan busing remedy produced an explosive backlash throughout the Richmond suburbs. The Chesterfield County Board of Supervisors immediately voted to begin the process of defensive incorporation as a suburban city, and its chairman promised to lead a "people's revolt" against the menace of consolidation. "Richmond can rot in hell," declared another politician on the Henrico Board of Supervisors. Homeowners associations in the suburbs formed the Richmond Federation of Concerned Citizens and Parents to coordinate the anticonsolidation campaign. The Richmond newspapers launched ferocious attacks against the school board for surrendering to the unreasonable demands of civil rights agitators and embracing a reverse racism regime of "busing and quotas." The state of Virginia also opposed the merger, with Governor Holton explaining that he supported "regional cooperation and not legal coercion." CORE attacked consolidation as inconsistent with its philosophy of community control, and the Black Power organization entered into an ad hoc alliance of strange bedfellows with the antimerger movement in Henrico and Chesterfield. Judge Merhige spent more than two years under the protection of federal marshals because of frequent death threats and recurring demonstrations outside of his Henrico home.[21]

A countervailing grassroots movement also emerged to prepare the community for compliance with a metropolitan consolidation mandate. In the fall of 1970, the League of Women Voters took the lead in assembling an interracial organization based inside the city, the Citizens for Excellent Public

Schools (CEPS). Updating a tactic from the massive resistance era, the liberal leaders of CEPS defined themselves as a "moderate group" and refused to take a stand on the issues of busing and merger. Instead the alliance promised to work for "smooth transition in the event of consolidation" and proclaimed that "Richmond has a golden opportunity to set the pattern for the rest of the country in stabilizing urban school systems." The group distributed buttons and bumper stickers reading "I'm a CEPS Miracle Worker" in an effort "to boost morale and change the negative attitude of many of our citizens," while warning that without a suburban remedy "we may develop into another sad urban cemetery like Newark." White parents who lived inside the city and supported consolidation as the remedy for their children's racially imbalanced schools reinforced the CEPS message in often desperate tones. From the annexed area, a father announced that the new border separating the city from the suburbs "should not protect them any more than the artificial boundary that has in the past year forced me to share in the problem." A man who recently moved down from New York City reported that he had "seen quite vividly the results of middle- and upper-class exodus" and endorsed countywide integration as the only way to avoid disaster. Another Richmond resident called merger the last chance to "keep our beautiful and wonderful capital city from becoming a ghetto city as many northern cities have become when white citizens rush to the counties to avoid desegregation."[22]

In January 1972, after more than a year of legal maneuvering, Judge Merhige ordered the consolidation of the Richmond schools with Henrico and Chesterfield, a single metropolitan system that would serve more than 100,000 students. *Bradley v. Richmond* mandated the two-way busing of inner-city and suburban students to ensure a white majority in every facility, a novel application of the *Swann* precedent across separate political jurisdictions. The wages of massive resistance pervaded the ruling, as the judge exhaustively reviewed the state government's culpability in establishing the dual school system and actively resisting racial desegregation in all three districts. In addition to detailing the history of Jim Crow, Judge Merhige explored the modern version of structural racism that shaped metropolitan regions throughout the country, and he found the city of Richmond and its suburbs responsible for de jure—not de facto—practices of residential segregation. The decision specifically charged Henrico and Chesterfield with zoning policies to exclude low-income and minority housing, in the past and the present, and listed numerous other intentional public and private actions to prevent African-American suburbanization. Merhige declared the antimerger sentiment in the suburban counties to be "explicable principally in terms of racial hostility," and he suggested with substantial optimism that public resistance might dissolve if "fair-minded" white families learned the truth about the government policies that had created residential segregation. In a frontal challenge to the color-blind ideology of suburban innocence, the judge concluded that "the present is simply a culmination of the past and, unless affirmative action is taken, a prophesy of the future."[23]

Bradley v. Richmond resounded throughout the nation's white suburbs and represented the most important school desegregation landmark since *Brown*—if confirmed on appeal. As a matter of law, Judge Merhige had constructed an intricate evidentiary base and a compelling rationale, driven by the conclusion that the equal protection clause of the Fourteenth Amendment applied broadly to state governments and not separately to each individual political jurisdiction. But as a matter of politics, the prevailing winds cast doubt on the judge's reiteration of the decades-old judicial warning that "the mandate of the Constitution will not, of course, cede to hostility to its dictates." The anticonsolidation movement wrapped itself in the ascendant discourse of color-blind innocence and never even acknowledged the finding of state-sponsored residential segregation. The *News Leader* blasted the "reverse racism" at the heart of the court order and declared: "It is profoundly wrong. It is profoundly sad. And it must not stand." Syndicated columnist James J. Kilpatrick, one of Virginia's original architects of massive resistance, accused Merhige of "doctrinaire racism" in the establishment of forced integration by group quotas. The *Times-Dispatch* found a sliver of hope in the consolidation decree, which it denounced as "pernicious gibberish," a "malignant precedent," and a "nauseating mixture of vacuous sociological theories and legal contradictions." The newspaper predicted that if the appellate courts did not reverse Merhige's mandate, a grassroots suburban rebellion throughout the nation "would put an end to destructive federal court attacks upon public schools, once and for all."[24]

The antibusing movements in Henrico and Chesterfield believed that mobilization of public opinion would influence the appellate process, and more than twenty groups consolidated their strength in the Richmond Area Coordinating Committee. The umbrella organization conducted a protest march at the State Capitol and sponsored a motorcade of thirty-five hundred automobiles that traveled to Washington to maximize the pressure on the Supreme Court and the White House. President Nixon responded by proposing a busing moratorium and threatening to support a constitutional amendment if the appellate courts did not overturn the merger decree. Local supporters of consolidation struggled to gain traction as Richmond remained in a profound crisis of leadership. The CEPS warned the corporate establishment that without metropolitan desegregation, "a public confidence crisis of considerable proportion is forecasted as the black and white middle class have not received assurances from the power structure that those who control this city intend to make especially strong efforts to preserve quality education." Jarrell Raper, a physician active in CEPS, lashed out at suburban families content to "enjoy all the advantages of life in a large metropolitan area while isolating themselves from its problems." He guaranteed that without consolidation, middle-class families of both races would abandon the city and "the largely black lower-class children of Richmond would be doomed permanently to second-class citizenship." In the spring of 1972, a CEPS survey revealed that more than three-fourths of black families in Richmond supported the metropolitan busing plan, while 87 percent of Chesterfield and Henrico parents promised to keep their children in a consolidated district if quality education did not decline. But in the end, the white families from the Richmond suburbs did not have to face this choice.[25]

After a month of grassroots agitation by the antibusing movement, the Fourth Circuit Court of Appeals defused the tensions with a stay of Merhige's order. In June, a five-to-one majority on the appellate court reversed the consolidation decree with the finding that "the last vestiges of state-imposed segregation have been wiped out" in all three school systems. Mischaracterizing the metropolitan remedy as a "fixed racial quota" in violation of the *Swann* precedent, the Fourth Circuit ruled that Judge Merhige had no constitutional authority to force the state of Virginia "to restructure its internal government for the purpose of achieving racial balance." The majority opinion also declared that neither the state nor the suburban counties bore any legal responsibility for patterns of school and housing segregation inside the city of Richmond. In an evasion of the substantial evidentiary basis for Merhige's finding of de jure housing segregation, the Fourth Circuit asserted that "what little action, if any, the counties may seem to have taken to keep blacks out is slight." The appellate decision compared Richmond's overwhelmingly white suburbs and increasingly black urban core to the landscapes of the metropolitan North and concluded that "a school case, like a vehicle, can carry only a limited amount of baggage." In the most striking sentence of the decision, a judicial validation of the ideology of suburban innocence, the Fourth Circuit held: "We think that the root causes of the concentration of blacks in the inner cities of America are simply not known."[26]

The political escape of the Richmond suburbs through appellate reversal of consolidation guaranteed an urban system debilitated by a fusion of race and class hypersegregation. The Supreme Court heard the Richmond appeal in 1973, but the recusal of Justice Lewis Powell because of his prior involvement with the city schools left the remaining eight members deadlocked. The Court's inability to issue an opinion let stand the appellate decision and postponed the judicial showdown over metropolitan remedies to the Detroit litigation. By the mid-1970s, the white enrollment in the Richmond district had dropped below 20 percent, and most affluent families still living in the city patronized private schools. Thousands of middle-

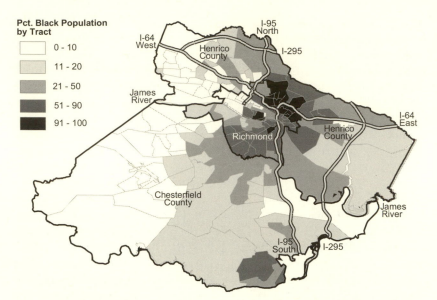

Map 11.2. Distribution of the Black Population of the City of Richmond, Henrico County, and Chesterfield County, 2000, by Census Tract. Three decades after the failure of metropolitan school consolidation, the impoverished East End and the prosperous West End remain segregated by race and class, while middle-income black families have moved into the annexed suburbs of South Richmond and throughout much of northern and eastern Henrico County. The departure of most middle-class families to the suburbs or private education has left the city of Richmond with one of the most hypersegregated school systems in the nation. *Source:* U.S. Census Bureau, 2000 Census of Population and Housing.

class black families also pursued the individual remedies of moving into the inner-ring subdivisions of Henrico and Chesterfield, and by 1980 more than one-third of the African-American population of metropolitan Richmond lived in the suburbs. In 1986, the city's majority-black board of education requested a return to neighborhood schools, and Judge Merhige approved the termination of busing for racial desegregation. By the end of the century, many of the annexed neighborhoods south of the James River had experienced transition to predominantly black status, and African-American families made up 24.7 percent of the Henrico population and 17.8 percent in Chesterfield (map 11.2). In the Richmond district, despite voluntary desegregation techniques such as magnet schools, middle-class flight by families of all races had left a student enrollment nearly 90 percent black and overwhelmingly poor.[27]

Two Paths to the Future

The landmark defeat of consolidation in Richmond revealed the ascending pattern of metropolitan divergence between central cities and surrounding suburbs in many of the largest population centers of the Sunbelt South. During the 1960s, urban business coalitions enjoyed considerable success in advancing the regionalist agenda of suburban annexation, countywide school districts, and metropolitan government. The legal power to incorporate outlying suburbs and the civic tradition of city-county consolidation provided structural advantages in many Sunbelt centers that favorably distinguished them from their Rust Belt counterparts. Metropolitan remedies greatly eased the transition to comprehensive desegregation in countywide school districts, but the arrival of court-ordered busing made it nearly impossible to secure popular support for consolidation initiatives in the future. Timing was everything. In 1971–72, suburban voters rejected city-county government consolidation in Charlotte, Memphis, Augusta, and Columbia. The corporate leadership of the urban South had to acknowledge that the regionalism agenda could no longer overcome taxpayer and homeowner resistance and a deepening grassroots distrust of the Chamber of Commerce style of leadership. The experiences of two older southern cities, Raleigh and Memphis, reveal the divergent paths available during the era of court-ordered busing: a stable metropolitan remedy in the capital of North Carolina made possible by the state's progressive land-use policies, and a disastrous desegregation saga in Tennessee that aligned the state's largest school district with the dominant patterns of the Rust Belt.[28]

Three hours south of Richmond on Interstate 85, the regional vision of Raleigh's business leadership produced a double-sided backlash by urban neighborhoods and suburban subdivisions during the early 1970s. Class divisions among white neighborhoods marked Raleigh's spatial landscape, which included affluent annexed suburbs in the northern and western parts of the city and almost all black families and blue-collar white subdivisions situated in the eastern and southern quadrants. In 1970, when the battle over comprehensive desegregation began, HEW designed a proximity plan that systematically burdened the black and working-class white families of east Raleigh and guaranteed resegregation by concentrating reassignments in transitional neighborhoods. The NAACP proposed a two-way busing exchange of black students from east Raleigh and upper-middle-class white students from north Raleigh. A group of working-class white families from east Raleigh also called for a stability approach that would balance every facility along the 74–26 percent districtwide ratio, combined with the citywide scattering of low-income housing to stem the racial transition of their neighborhoods. Charles Holloman, the leader of the east Raleigh parents, blamed municipal leaders for concentrating an African-American ghetto in one quadrant of the city and announced that "we understand the black man's problems for the first time." After a year of partial desegregation, the school board implemented a busing formula that sought a white majority in every school but distributed the burdens of reassignment very unevenly. As in Charlotte, an interracial alliance emerged to denounce the protectionist policy for the powerful island suburbs and called for busing equalization as the only way to prevent white flight to havens that enjoyed neighborhood schools.[29]

The bankers and developers who dominated Raleigh's political leadership pursued the Sunbelt agenda of annexation and consolidation to manage the forces set in motion by their growth policies of suburban sprawl and residential segregation. In 1969, a team of education specialists recommended the merger of the Raleigh schools with the surrounding district of Wake County as an antidote for the "sprawl and decay of the contemporary scene." After the arrival of court-ordered busing, the *Raleigh News and Observer* endorsed consolidation as the best way to ameliorate the "trend toward a predominantly black city surrounded by predominantly white suburbs." The state legislature authorized a referendum in the fall of 1972, and pro-merger forces mounted an apocalyptic campaign that asked: "Do You Want a Black Raleigh School System?" Advertisements and leaflets warned that without a countywide district, "the exodus of whites to the suburbs will continue until only blacks are left in Raleigh. We will then find ourselves in the same situation as Richmond or Washington." The affluent suburban township of Cary formed the base of the leading antimerger organization, the Wake County Citizens Committee, which conducted a door-to-door operation emphasizing the double threat of higher taxes and crosstown busing. In addition to widespread suburban opposition, many black voters inside the city objected to the racially charged pro-merger campaign and the prospect of long-distance transportation to desegregate unfriendly county schools. In the end, 59 percent of Raleigh voters and 77 percent of the Wake electorate rejected consolidation.[30]

Two progressive reforms in the mid-1970s ended the political monopoly of the island suburbs of north Raleigh and established a metropolitan remedy for school desegregation—the first a result of grassroots democracy and the second quite the opposite. The interracial neighborhood coalition forged during the busing crisis expanded into a "planned growth" revolt against the business leadership and successfully dismantled the city's at-large system of political representation. In 1973, after pushing through district elections over the opposition of the Raleigh Chamber of Commerce, the neighborhood movement took control of the city council and elected Clarence E. Lightner the first African-American mayor of a large majority-

white city in the South. In a concurrent development, the corporate establishment managed to engineer city-county school consolidation without a
popular vote by taking advantage of a provision in state law that permitted
merger with the approval of both school boards. Raleigh leaders touted a
countywide system as the long-term remedy for white flight, with the overriding priority that the city "remain an attractive climate for business." Wake
officials consented to the merger plan despite deep suburban resistance because they shared the booster agenda of the corporate establishment. The
1976 creation of the Wake County Public School System stabilized the racial
enrollment through comprehensive desegregation in majority-white schools
in a rough approximation of the Charlotte model. During subsequent decades, Raleigh's metropolitan remedy provided a major marketing advantage for civic boosters as the quality urban school system and the high-tech
boom surrounding the Research Triangle Park turned the region into a celebrated example of Sunbelt prosperity.[31]

In Memphis, the tenth-largest school district in the nation, the failure of
court-ordered desegregation revealed the inadequacy of a partial busing formula in a majority-black system marked by intense residential segregation.
During the postwar decades, Memphis leaders pursued regional planning
through an apartheid agenda of channeling new black housing south of the
city while annexing the white middle-class subdivisions to the east. The city
incorporated more than 150,000 residents of adjacent Shelby County during
the 1960s and early 1970s, thanks to Tennessee's automatic annexation laws,
but suburban voters twice rejected referendums to consolidate the city and
county governments. After the second defeat, with court-ordered busing on
the horizon, the Chamber of Commerce launched a public relations campaign called "Believe in Memphis!" Through therapeutic techniques ranging from bumper stickers to church sermons, the civic leadership hoped to
overcome "hearing nothing but negative attitudes in our city, . . . a kind of
community inferiority complex which is not justified." While the Chamber
offered a psychological diagnosis, another group called the Citizens Study
Committee released a forceful report labeling "institutional racism" the fundamental cause of the acknowledged Memphis crisis: "resistance by groups
of common interest—churches, education, business, professions, residential
areas—to the entrance of the black man as an equal member." The Citizens
Study Committee called for a metropolitan approach to racial integration,
including reversal of the zoning policies that prevented black families from
moving to the east Memphis suburbs and a civic commitment to educational
and economic opportunity for minorities living in neighborhoods of concentrated poverty.[32]

In the initial response to NAACP litigation to desegregate the Memphis
schools, District Judge Robert M. McRae, Jr., ruled that "the solution is not
to be found in transporting an undetermined number of Negro or white stu-

dents to distant parts of the city." During the 1971–72 academic year, Memphis operated one of the least expansive desegregation plans anywhere in the urban South, with 88 percent of black students and 76 percent of white students attending racially isolated schools. After the *Swann* verdict, the appellate courts instructed McRae to revisit the Memphis case, and the district judge responded with a very limited busing plan anchored in the vague "reasonableness" standard endorsed by the Supreme Court. "It is not practical," McRae found without elaboration, "to provide the citywide transportation necessary to relieve the problem of isolated minorities." The desegregation formula, which the NAACP condemned as a recipe for white flight, relied heavily upon geographic proximity reassignments in transitional neighborhoods and left untouched dozens of single-race schools in the inner city and the annexed suburbs. Tens of thousands of white families formed a group called Citizens against Busing (CAB), which called for a total boycott of the public schools and began planning an emergency system of private academies. In the months before the January 1973 implementation of the revised desegregation plan, CAB members picketed the headquarters of the school board, fed their reassignment forms to a goat, and denounced the "liberal do-gooders" and wealthy businessmen who urged other people's children to comply with the law.[33]

The Memphis Chamber of Commerce took a leading role in the formation of IMPACT (Involved Memphis Parents Assisting Children and Teachers), a procompliance coalition that included civil rights organizations, the LWV, moderate religious groups, and experts from the Southern Regional Council. IMPACT launched a public relations campaign featuring interracial images of happy students and warning that "disruptive and unlawful activities are no solution to the problem. . . . The Memphis city schools and the children of this city need our support, now and for the future." Despite these efforts, more than ten thousand white students boycotted the public schools during the midyear transition, and at least half switched to private academies hastily launched by CAB. Around fifteen thousand more pupils abandoned the public schools the next fall, when the second phase of the piecemeal desegregation plan doubled the amount of busing but still left 25 inner-city schools unaffected. Conservative churches also started dozens of Christian academies, and overall about thirty-seven thousand white students attended 125 private schools in metropolitan Memphis. By the end of the decade, the city system served a 75 percent black and substantially poor population. The energetic efforts of public school supporters could not overcome the structural forces of residential segregation, the instability caused by an inadequate desegregation approach, and the local mobilization of a newly awakened Religious Right. Without a metropolitan remedy, the suburban annexation agenda alone could not counteract three decades of growth policies that divided the metropolis by race and class, and by the

time that business leaders finally accepted some responsibility for the fragmented landscape it was already too late for many white families that did
not "Believe in Memphis!" any more.[34]

Contrary to charges that "forced busing" inevitably caused massive white
flight and destroyed urban public schools, the most expansive integration
remedies consistently produced the highest levels of racial stability across
the metropolitan South. Although all three cities actively pursued suburban
annexation, Raleigh avoided the hypersegregated fates of Richmond and
Memphis because of more favorable racial demographics and a comprehensive integration plan in a countywide school district. New Orleans entered
the busing era with a 31 percent white enrollment, which as a rule made desegregation unworkable without a suburban remedy, and by the mid-1980s
the city schools had shifted to more than 90 percent black. In the largest
cities of Texas, aggressive suburban annexation expanded municipal boundaries but often failed to incorporate affluent suburbs that preemptively established their own separate school districts, such as the municipal islands of
Highland Park and University Park that are encircled by Dallas. The separate populations of African-American and Latino students each exceeded
the white remnants in Dallas and Houston, two cities that never pursued
meaningful school desegregation and nevertheless lost a combined total of
more than 140,000 white students during the 1970s. The New South capital
of Atlanta continued to blaze the trail of extreme spatial fragmentation and
hypersegregation with a 7 percent white enrollment by the mid-1980s,
lower than every major city in the nation except Washington, D.C. The
structural forces of residential segregation played an even greater role than
the specific policies of school desegregation as many of the largest cities in
the South succumbed first to the northern pattern of majority-black systems
surrounded by unfriendly white suburbs, followed by the ultramodern formula of overwhelmingly poor districts marked by the middle-class exodus of
families of all races (table 11.2).[35]

Metropolitan problems require metropolitan solutions. The NAACP's
consolidation strategy recognized that if the *Brown* decision ultimately
would have any genuine consequence in urban public schools, only metropolitan remedies could ameliorate the de jure landscapes of spatial fragmentation created by the public policies of suburban sprawl and residential
segregation. When the Fourth Circuit Court of Appeals reversed the Richmond consolidation decree, Judge Harrison L. Winter asked in his lone dissent: "How then, in an area which constitutes a single community of interest, can schools racially identifiable as black be permitted to exist a short
distance within the boundary of Richmond and schools racially identifiable
as white be permitted to exist a short distance without? To me, this result is
manifest frustration of the teaching of *Brown*." The majority on the Fourth
Circuit evaded this question with an affirmation of suburban innocence

TABLE 11.2
Decline in White Enrollment, 1968–1986, and Percentage of Black Students in
Majority-White and Racially Isolated Schools, 1986, Large Urban Districts in the
South without Metropolitan Integration Plans.

City	%White (1968)	%White (1986)	%Black/Maj. White Schools	%Black/Racially Isolated Schools
Atlanta	38	7	1.6	90.8
New Orleans	31	8	0.7	84.2
Richmond	36	13.6	0.1	56.6
Houston	53	17	3.4	69.6
Dallas	61	21	4.6	65.7
El Paso	42	23	9.8	3.1
Memphis	46	24	12.0	66.0
Ft. Worth	67	37	22.1	36.4
Austin	81	47	21.8	6.9

Sources: Gary Orfield and Franklin Monfort, *Racial Change and Desegregation in Large School Districts*, 7–9, 11–13, 20–21; *Bradley v. Baliles*, 639 F. Supp 680 (1986).

from the burdens of history, a political response that signaled the absence of any judicial remedy for the constitutional wrong of racial segregation in large portions of the divided American metropolis.[36]

The contingent fate of the *Brown* decision in the metropolitan South depended upon the structural elasticity of the spatial landscape and the metropolitan scope of the desegregation remedy, even more than the leadership resources of the community and the individual racial attitudes of the school-parents. "There can be little doubt that many metropolitan plans have provided high and relatively durable levels of desegregation for a generation," an academic study critical of the emerging antibusing consensus observed in 1988, in the wake of the national retreat from affirmative action to achieve school integration. As the busing backlash extended beyond the South, and the nation's commitment to the principle of *Brown* hung in the balance, most major American cities followed the path of metropolitan fragmentation taken by Atlanta and Richmond and Memphis, instead of the suburban remedies pioneered by Greenville and Charlotte and Raleigh. The national mobilization of the Silent Majority during the 1970s revealed the parallel suburbanization of southern and American politics, a dominant pattern of regional convergence as the color-blind ideology of white racial innocence and middle-class residential privilege shaped the underlying consensus of a new postliberal order.[37]

CHAPTER 12

Regional Convergence

> The South and the nation are not exchanging strengths as much as they are exchanging sins. . . . For good and ill, the South is just about over as a separate and distinct place.
>
> —John Egerton (1974), *The Americanization of Dixie: The Southernization of America*

MIDDLE AMERICANS

At the end of 1969, *Time* magazine recognized the middle-class victims and suburban heroes of the Silent Majority as "Man and Woman of the Year: The Middle Americans." The editors of *Time* defined this amorphous yet formidable group in the language of whiteness and populism, rather than partisan ideology or social class: a broad cross-section that firmly occupied the political center, marked by a "contradictory mixture of liberal and conservative impulses." Neither wealthy nor poor, the ordinary men and women in the no-longer Silent Majority "feared that they were beginning to lose their grip on the country . . . [but] still want to believe in America and the American dream." Half of the nation's population fell within these boundaries of Middle America, which apparently included teenagers who watched football and John Wayne films, mothers who worried about rising crime rates and declining moral standards, the National Confederation of American Ethnic Groups, *Apollo* astronaut Neil Armstrong, the working-class policemen who beat antiwar protesters at the Chicago convention, the evangelical Protestants who followed the Reverend Billy Graham, and the executive director of the Atlanta Chamber of Commerce. From the sprawling suburbs of the Sunbelt South to the ethnic enclaves of the urban North, *Time* discovered an aggressively but anxiously patriotic mixture of white-collar professionals and blue-collar hard hats that culminated in President Nixon himself—"the embodiment of Middle America." In the most perceptive passages of the article, *Time* observed that the White House "was pursuing not so much a 'Southern strategy' as a Middle American strategy" and concluded that Nixon "is riding the crest of the huge wave called Middle America, but he is reacting to it rather than leading it."[1]

The unprecedented award given to an estimated 100 million citizens validated a political rediscovery of the Silent Majority shaped by Nixon's appeals to the Forgotten Americans in the 1968 election and confirmed by the grass-roots revolts ranging from the law-and-order backlash in blue-collar urban neighborhoods to the antibusing movements in white-collar suburban sub-divisions. *Newsweek*'s lengthy 1969 examination of the "Troubled American" discovered a similar "vast white middle-class majority," from the tract homes outside Atlanta and Los Angeles to the industrial suburbs of the Midwest, in full-scale revolt against the redistributive agenda of racial liberalism. Millions of Middle Americans who had lost faith in the future of their country now embraced an ethos of victimization in the face of urban riots, campus demonstrations, rising inflation, and a general sense of breakdown in traditional moral values. *Newsweek*'s scientific survey of middle-income white Americans revealed that almost 80 percent believed that a typical racial minority on welfare had chosen not to work and more than 40 percent claimed that blacks now had a "better chance" than their own families to obtain good jobs and decent educations, despite substantial statistical evidence to the contrary. Only 25 percent supported government policies to accelerate school integration, and a mere 2 percent endorsed the technique of busing to overcome residential segregation. Despite the president's calculated celebrations of the Silent Majority and his well-publicized remark that "these are my people," fewer than half of middle-income white voters expressed approval of Richard Nixon's performance in the White House. The *Newsweek* report concluded with individual portraits of Middle Americans who believed that their tax dollars subsidized both the rich and the poor and who denounced the liberal elites and the welfare cheats with equal fervor.[2]

As the theme of the radical center moved to the forefront of political analysis, the most perceptive investigations of Middle America placed the unrest and uncertainty among middle-income families within a broader story of the structural limitations of Great Society liberalism and the class-based inequality that animated reactionary populism. In an article called "The Forgotten American," published in the August 1969 edition of *Harper's Magazine*, Peter Schrag warned of the growing anger and alienation among the 80 million white citizens who resided in the psychological and geographical spaces found in between the impoverished ghettoes and the affluent suburbs. Instead of glossing over the socioeconomic differences within a so-called Silent Majority, Schrag identified a more specific revolt of the white lower-middle class, whose transparent racism on social issues and genuine progressivism on economic issues formed a volatile combination unfavorably disposed toward both limousine liberals in their lily-white suburbs and corporate conservatives with their country-club populism. In late 1969, Hubert Humphrey offered a similar assessment when interviewed by *U.S. News and World Report* for an otherwise conventional cover story titled the "Revolt of the Middle Class." The former vice president criticized the disdain for Middle Americans expressed by many affluent liberals, and he warned that the Democratic party must address the perception among blue-collar white families that the government had singled out their schools and neighborhoods for racial integration while their hard-earned tax payments subsidized the lifestyles of the rich and the poor.[3]

The dominant backlash narrative that emerged from the late 1960s and early 1970s glossed over the spatial and socioeconomic disparities among Middle Americans at the grassroots level by condensing the retreat from Great Society liberalism to a strictly racialized phenomenon encompassing the "vast white middle-class majority." This mainstream validation of the populist formulations of the Nixon administration has obscured some basic political facts about the elusive Silent Majority and about American suburbia more generally: white-collar professionals and blue-collar laborers do not have the same class interests, do not generally live in the same neighborhoods, and have never realigned into a permanent electoral coalition. As the sociologist Jonathan Rieder observed about working-class white Democrats: "The Right gained their votes more than it gained their hearts. Despite all its bathos about silent and moral majorities, the Right's 'populism' never entirely converged with the people's. After all, there is a big difference between speaking populist words and offering populist policies." In a provocative reassessment of the media rediscovery of Middle America, the social critic Barbara Ehrenreich pointed out that the racial backlash thesis glossed over the inconvenient fact that among the white electorate, one-half of blue-collar voters but only one-third of white-collar counterparts cast their ballots for Hubert Humphrey in 1968. A sizable majority of upper-middle-class and wealthy citizens throughout the nation voted for Nixon, while only in the South did George Wallace draw substantially more blue-collar than white-collar support. Ehrenreich concluded that "working-class anger should have shown that middle-class liberalism had not gone far enough," but the popular interpretation of blue-collar backlash allowed "middle-class observers . . . to seek legitimation for their own more conservative impulses."[4]

The recurring fixation on working-class backlash and the resilient framework of the Southern Strategy have operated in parallel fashion to present a distorted story of political transformation in modern America. Explanatory models of working-class prejudice have consistently overshadowed the persistent insulation of affluent neighborhoods from the reach of civil rights reform, while the durable narrative of southern exceptionalism has long served to reaffirm the de facto racial innocence that is central to the national mythology of American Exceptionalism. In the mid-1970s, as busing battles polarized the urban North and suburban sprawl destabilized the metropolitan South, one of the shrewdest chroniclers of the region observed that "the South and the nation are not exchanging strengths as much as they are exchanging sins." Liberal journalist John Egerton captured the convergence of southern and national politics in his assessment that the dominant trends in both regions included "deep divisions along race and class lines, an obsession with growth and acquisition and consumption, a headlong rush to the cities and suburbs, diminution and waste of natural resources, . . . and a steady erosion of the sense of place, of community, of belonging." The suburbanization of the New South had produced a Sunbelt Synthesis that managed to transcend the region's history by avoiding an ethical reckoning with the past, a political culture of white innocence and collective amnesia firmly grounded in the ideology of American Exceptionalism. "For good and ill," Egerton concluded, "the South is just about over as a separate and distinct place."[5]

The United States became a definitively suburban nation during the final decades of the twentieth century, with the regional convergence of metropolitan trends and the reconfiguration of national politics around programs to protect the consumer privileges of affluent white neighborhoods and policies to reproduce the postindustrial economy of the corporate Sunbelt. Since the rediscovery of Middle America during the Nixon era, the suburban orientation of the bipartisan battle for the political center has remained persistently unreceptive to civil rights initiatives designed to address the structural disadvantages facing central cities and impoverished communities. Despite the ritual declarations that the federal courts would not permit public opposition to influence the enforcement of constitutional principles, the historical fate of collective integration remedies for educational and residential segregation demonstrated the responsiveness of the judicial and policymaking branches to the grassroots protests of affluent suburban families. The color-blind and class-driven discourse popularized in the Sunbelt South helped create a suburban blueprint that ultimately resonated from the "conservative" subdivisions of southern California to the "liberal" townships of New England: a bipartisan political language of private property values, individual taxpayer rights, children's educational privileges, family residential security, and white racial innocence.

"Forced Integration of the Suburbs"

The Kerner Report of 1968 urged the United States to choose the path of residential integration as formal public policy in order to reverse the movement of the nation "toward two societies, one black, one white—separate and unequal." Despite the explosive impact of court-ordered busing, the transportation remedy addressed only the symptoms and not the causes of school segregation in metropolitan regions: the public policies that simultaneously constructed the white suburbs and the urban ghettoes. In the early 1970s, the black freedom struggle launched a multifaceted assault on suburban exclusion as "the next frontier of the civil rights movement," from schools to housing to employment. But federal civil rights policy never seriously addressed the structural forces undergirding residential segregation, and the enduring suburban resistance to "forced busing" and "forced housing integration" has spanned regional boundaries and partisan affiliations. By the middle of the decade, the national insurgency embodied in the Silent Majority successfully pushed all three branches of the federal government to adopt explicit policies of suburban protection that rejected metropolitan remedies for metropolitan inequities and reimagined state-sponsored residential segregation as de facto "economic segregation" beyond the reach of constitutional law. If Kerner represented the last gasp of the progressive impulse during the era of the Great Society, the ensuing decades have demonstrated the inability and the unwillingness of a broad and bipartisan spectrum of political institutions to confront the spatial and socioeconomic boundaries placed on the reach of race-conscious liberalism by the grassroots revolt of the Silent Majority.[6]

For a brief period during the late 1960s and early 1970s, the "Open Communities" initiative of the Department of Housing and Urban Development contemplated the withholding of federal highway funds and infrastructure subsidies from suburban jurisdictions that employed exclusionary zoning policies to ban low-income housing and maintain residential segregation. HUD Secretary George Romney, a liberal Republican from Michigan, warned of the "ominous trend toward stratification of our society by race and by income" and pushed a suburban integration agenda that would give genuine meaning to the affirmative action requirements of the Fair Housing Act of 1968. As leverage for the extremely unpopular program, Romney threatened financial consequences "if the suburbanites refuse to see their obligations, their opportunity," by adopting open-housing policies and rezoning for low-income developments. In 1970, HUD negotiated an agreement to scatter fourteen thousand units of public housing throughout the five predominantly white suburban counties surrounding Dayton, Ohio. Using this Dayton Plan as a model, HUD asked Congress to pass legislation making highway and sewer funding for the suburbs contingent on open-housing policies and acceptance of a fair share of low-income projects. The Open Communities agenda prompted scorn and dismay from the president and his top political advisers, and one journalist remarked that the HUD secretary appeared to operate in "an orbit all his own" within the administration. Romney "keeps loudly talking about it [suburban integration] in spite of our efforts to shut him up," domestic policy adviser John Ehrlichman wrote in a memorandum to Nixon, who responded with a blunt comment in the margin: "Stop this one."[7]

The official federal retreat from affirmative action to integrate suburban housing came in response to a grassroots homeowners rebellion that spread throughout metropolitan Detroit. In the spring of 1970, the working-class suburb of Warren, which included only 28 black families in a population of 180,000, chose to forfeit $20 million in federal urban renewal funds rather than adopt a fair housing ordinance mandated by HUD. That summer, the *Detroit News* ran an explosive weeklong series charging that the "federal government intends to use its vast power to force integration of America's white suburbs—and it is using the Detroit suburbs as a key starting point." The immediate targets would be Warren and Dearborn, "blatant offenders" of the Fair Housing Act because each suburban municipality included tens of thousands of black workers employed in automobile factories but remained almost completely segregated in residential patterns. Under fire from within the administration, Romney traveled to Michigan to reassure the mayors of thirty-nine communities outside Detroit that while the law required "affirmative action to prevent discrimination," HUD did not have a policy of "forced integration of the suburbs." Hostile white residents jeered their former governor during the visit and waved signs recommending the construction of low-income housing in Bloomfield Hills, the elite suburb where the Romneys lived. As the backlash intensified, Kevin Phillips issued a strident warning in his syndicated column that HUD liberals planned to "produce a racial balance in America's suburbs." When asked to clarify administration policy during a press conference, President Nixon replied that "forced integration of the suburbs is not in the national interest."[8]

In June 1971, the White House released a major statement on "equal housing opportunity" that sharply distinguished between illegal racial discrimination resulting from private action and legal class segregation produced by natural market forces. After a paean to the frontier mythology of suburbia—"through the ages, men have fought to defend their homes; they have struggled and often dared the wilderness"—the president promised prosecution of individual violations of open-housing laws. But Nixon also pledged that the federal government "will not seek to impose economic integration" or destabilize suburban neighborhoods "with a flood of low-income families." The policy statement observed that "quite apart from racial considerations, residents of outlying areas may and often do object to the building in their communities of subsidized housing which they fear may have the effect of lowering property values and bringing in . . . a contagion of crime, violence, drugs, and other conditions." Nixon did suggest that suburban communities might voluntarily choose to provide housing options for low-income families, but he informed Americans that "we cannot be free, and at the same time be required to fit our lives into prescribed places on a racial grid—whether segregated or integrated, and whether by some mathematical formula or by automatic assignment." The rhetoric was forceful: administration policy would ostensibly guarantee "equal housing opportunity for people of all income levels on a metropolitan areawide basis." But the policy was also clear: the executive branch would extend the same protection to "economic segregation" in suburban neighborhoods that the previous year's antibusing manifesto had extended to suburban neighborhood schools.[9]

The Nixon administration's redefinition of structural racism in suburban housing as the market-based outcome of benign economic segregation drew a sharp rebuke from civil rights organizations. The National Coalition against Discrimination in Housing accused the White House of pursuing a national "suburban strategy" and condemned the effort to distinguish between de jure and de facto segregation as "a meaningless charade." The Leadership Conference on Civil Rights lambasted the "artificial distinctions" between racial and economic segregation and called for the termination of all federal funding for suburban communities that refused to comply with the affirmative action procedures of the Fair Housing Act. The Civil Rights Commission rebuked HUD's retreat from its own Open Communities program and declared that "racial integration cannot be achieved unless economic integration is also achieved." Later in 1971, during an appearance in Detroit, the president reiterated his opposition to "a forced housing policy" and instead envisioned the end of residential segregation "on a voluntary basis by having an open housing program in which any individual who has the opportunity can move where he wants." Two years later, as protests against proposed low-income housing raged in the affluent Westchester suburbs outside of New York City, the Nixon administration announced a moratorium on the construction of federally subsidized projects and impounded almost $13 billion in congressionally authorized funding. The president also fired Romney and instructed his replacement at HUD to curtail programs that challenged exclusionary zoning in suburbia.[10]

The civil rights movement responded by launching a concerted legal assault against exclusionary zoning policies that enforced racial and class segregation in suburban housing markets. At the next NAACP convention, delegates ratified a drive to open up the suburbs by scattering low-income housing throughout the metropolis. Executive director Roy Wilkins declared that the national commitment to racial integration hung in the balance because "the big question for the 1970s is where shall the Negro live? Will he live in the suburbs?" The Supreme Court's rejection of metropolitan remedies came through a series of decisions that extended constitutional protection to municipal housing discrimination on the basis of class and approved exclusionary zoning in the suburbs as long as the policies remained ostensibly race-neutral. In *James v. Valtierra* (1971), the Court upheld a California law that empowered localities to veto low-income housing by voter referendum because the policy did not depend upon "distinctions based on race" but instead banned all poor people in color-blind fashion. The dissent by Justice Thurgood Marshall argued that the equal protection clause of the Fourteenth Amendment covered low-income citizens and therefore any "explicit classification on the basis of poverty" should represent a constitutional violation. Four years later, in *Warth v. Seldin* (1975), the Supreme Court found that although the exclusionary zoning policies of a Rochester suburb intentionally "excluded persons of low and moderate income," the failure of the plaintiffs to obtain housing resulted from the race-neutral "consequence of the economics of the area housing market." The convoluted decision, issued by a majority dominated by Nixon appointees, effectively eliminated the standing of civil rights plaintiffs to bring federal class-action litigation against residential segregation in suburban municipalities.[11]

"A New American Majority"

The color-blind retreat from metropolitan remedies and the de facto defense of class segregation appealed to a broad political spectrum during the early 1970s, as northern liberalism underwent a crisis of purpose in response to the civil rights assault on suburban residential patterns. In the winter of 1970, Alexander Bickel of Yale Law School published an influential article in the *New Republic* called "Desegregation: Where Do We Go from Here?" The professor defined white flight and school resegregation as the central dilemma facing the nation, from the rural districts of Mississippi to the major cities of the North and Midwest. "Can we any longer fail to acknowledge," Bickel asked, "that the federal government is attempting to create in the rural South conditions that cannot in the foreseeable future be attained in large or medium urban centers in the South or in the rest of the country?" He concluded that "massive school integration is not going to be attained in this country very soon, in good part because no one is certain that it is worth the cost. Let us, therefore, try to proceed with education." In the *New York Times*, Pat Watters of the SRC responded with a scathing critique headlined "Southern Integrationists Feel Betrayed—by the North." The busing crisis represented the "ultimate confrontation with racism," Watters believed, because "regardless of how it [segregation] comes about, de jure or de facto, it is wrong and hurts both races . . . and it must be ended because the cost of not ending it will be the life of the nation." Charles Morgan, another white liberal activist from the Deep South, warned that the Bickel thesis symbolized a "national retreat: a convenient, if gossamer, cover under which bona fide racists, black and white, and the merely mistaken men of South and North might respectably gather prior to an all-out and undisguised attack on desegregation."[12]

Busing escalated from a regional issue to a full-blown national controversy in 1971, after black parents filed class-action lawsuits in San Francisco

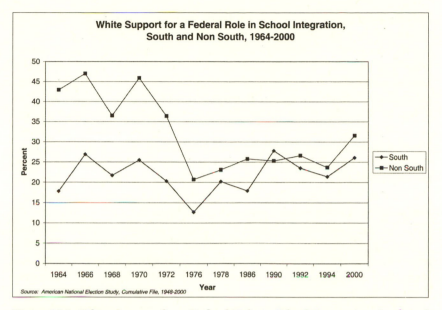

Figure 12.1. White Support for a Federal Role in School Integration, South and Non-South, 1964–2000. *Source*: Marc J. Hetherington, *Why Trust Matters: Declining Political Trust and the Demise of American Liberalism* (Princeton: Princeton Univ. Press, 2004), 104.

and Los Angeles, and NAACP litigation alleged de jure segregation in New York City, Denver, and Detroit. Public support for federal policies that promoted school integration declined throughout the nation but began to plummet among white families outside the South (figure 12.1). In the spring, a bipartisan coalition in the U.S. Senate rejected proposals by Abraham Ribicoff of Connecticut to mandate the construction of low-income housing in the suburbs and to achieve integration through consolidation of all school districts in metropolitan regions. Ribicoff condemned the de jure/de facto distinction and informed liberal politicians that they "can no longer be hypocritical and tell the South how to achieve desegregation and do nothing about the North." When the Supreme Court issued the *Swann* opinion, Richard Nixon clarified the stance of his administration: "Where it [segregation] is de jure, we comply with the Court; where it is de facto, . . . I do not believe that busing to achieve racial balance is in the interests of better education." In the summer, Nixon announced that the administration would "hold busing to the minimum required by law" and directed HEW to jettison its own plan for two-way integration in Austin, Texas. Since almost all smaller southern districts had implemented full desegregation a year earlier, the minimal busing policy effectively targeted the largest cities in the South and their counterparts in the North and West. As another tense academic year began, racial extremists bombed ten school buses in Pontiac, Michigan, the site of the first court-ordered busing program outside the South, and working-class white mothers in the factory town launched NAG (National Action Group against Busing).[13]

The most explosive development came in Detroit, when District Judge Stephen J. Roth ruled that "governmental actions and inaction at all levels, federal, state, and local, have combined with those of private organizations . . . to establish and to maintain the pattern of residential segregation throughout the Detroit metropolitan area." Citing the de jure segregation enforced by public institutions ranging from the Federal Housing Administration to the Detroit school board, Roth ordered the state of Michigan to devise a metropolitan remedy as the only way to achieve meaningful integration in the majority-black city system. Roy Wilkins of the NAACP celebrated the "significant breakthrough in the struggle to eliminate northern-style Jim Crow education." Resistance movements immediately mobilized throughout Detroit's overwhelmingly white suburbs, from the blue-collar subdivisions of Warren and Dearborn to the upscale neighborhoods of Grosse Pointe and Bloomfield Hills. All five of the white liberal Democrats who represented metropolitan Detroit promptly reversed their previous stances and voted for antibusing legislation hurriedly passed by the U.S. House of Representatives. In mid-1972, Judge Roth ordered the most expansive busing program in the history of desegregation case law, a three-county formula that involved fifty-four independent school districts and nearly 800,000 students. If confirmed on appeal, the consolidation plan would employ two-way busing to integrate every school in a rough approximation of the 80-20 white-black ratio of the metropolitan region.[14]

The grassroots backlash spreading across the nation turned "forced busing" into one of the central issues of the 1972 presidential election. George Wallace fired the opening shots of his campaign for the Democratic nomination by accusing Nixon of "trying to stand forthrightly on both sides of the issue." Although the president "just keeps saying he's against busing," Wallace charged, "our children keep on getting bused." The Alabama governor selected the Florida primary to begin his populist crusade to take the Democratic party back from the "intellectual snobs who feel that big government should control the lives of American citizens from the cradle to the grave." With the slogan "Send Them a Message," Wallace predicted that "if the people of Florida vote for me, Mr. Nixon . . . will end busing" within two months. Among the other Democratic candidates, Hubert Humphrey expressed opposition to "forced busing" and "quota systems," and Senator Henry Jackson of Washington proposed a constitutional amendment to protect neighborhood schools. In mid-March, three-fourths of Florida voters ratified a nonbinding resolution to ban court-ordered busing, and Wallace dominated a crowded field with 42 percent of the ballots. The governor won with the support of working-class men and rural north Floridians, and he promised that the victory marked the beginning of a national movement that would reach Washington.[15]

Two days after the Florida primary, President Nixon appeared on national television and asked Congress to impose a moratorium that would "call an immediate halt to all new busing orders by federal courts," a gambit of dubious constitutionality that eclipsed his former pledge to enforce *Swann*. The White House began devising its latest suburban strategy after the consolidation decrees in the Detroit and Richmond cases, but the timing of the presidential address appeared to validate the impact of the Wallace victory. To counterbalance the moratorium, the president proposed a multibillion dollar commitment to improve inner-city schools "so that the children who go there will have just as good a chance to get quality education as do the children who go to school in the suburbs." The administration promise to uplift urban education as a substitute for integration resembled the emerging stance of many northern liberal politicians who were touting the equalization of funding among school districts as an alternative to metropolitan busing plans in Detroit and elsewhere. The SRC compared the retreat of northern liberals to the southern era of massive resistance—a return to the doctrine of separate but equal supported by "respectable whites" in both regions. "Hysteria over school busing is sweeping the nation," proclaimed the LCCR, which warned that the United States "is on the verge of the gravest racial crisis since the Civil War. . . . We are seriously concerned that we are witnessing the beginning of the end of the Second Reconstruction. We soon will know whether the moral fervor of the sixties will give way to the moral cowardice of the seventies, and whether the faith and dreams of Black people will be sabotaged once more."[16]

The grassroots anger of the Silent Majority fused with the civil rights retreat of leading politicians in both parties during the spring of 1972. The crucial showdown came once again in Michigan, where the Democratic contenders competed to demonstrate their opposition to the metropolitan busing plan. Former vice president Hubert Humphrey applauded Nixon's moratorium legislation while campaigning in the Detroit suburbs and claimed that the president finally had said "amen to some of the things that some of the rest of us have been trying to do." From the left, Senator George McGovern initially denounced the president for caving in to the extremism of George Wallace and observed that Middle Americans who supported the Alabama governor were "deeply frustrated and disgusted with the way their government is ignoring their concerns and interest." The South Dakotan received unpleasant confirmation of the depth of blue-collar resentment during an appearance at an automobile plant in suburban Detroit, when a factory worker shouted "get out of here, McGovern! You're in Wallace country now!" In the days before the primary, McGovern suggested that the federal courts had gone "too far" and expressed sympathy for parents in the suburbs "who are concerned about their children being sent to inferior schools." Unburdened by ambiguity, Wallace denounced busing as "the most asinine, callous, ludicrous, cruel, and plain mean thing any pointy-headed intellectual can do to little children." Riding a populist backlash against busing and welfare, Wallace won the Michigan primary with a resounding 51 percent of the vote, including a heavy turnout in blue-collar precincts and substantial crossover support from Republicans in the white-collar suburbs.[17]

The presidential campaign matched Nixon against McGovern, who secured the Democratic nomination on a platform of immediate withdrawal from Vietnam combined with renewed dedication to "justice and jobs" at home. Wallace won primaries in three additional states dominated by the busing backlash—Maryland, North Carolina, and Tennessee—but severe wounds suffered during an assassination attempt in May prevented him from mounting another third-party challenge. Soon after the Michigan contest, President Nixon singled out Detroit as "the most flagrant example" of busing plans that sacrificed quality education for racial balance, and he warned that if Congress did not enact his moratorium scheme then "we will have no choice but to seek a constitutional amendment." Nixon later traveled to Macomb County, a blue-collar hotbed of the grassroots resistance, to condemn busing as reverse discrimination and demand "uniform national standards for school desegregation." The White House also released a list of metropolitan school districts in the South that might be allowed to return to neighborhood schools under the administration's proposed antibusing legislation. During the fall campaign, Nixon straddled the political center of a nation in upheaval as he leveled a barrage of populist attacks against McGovern as the candidate of income redistribution, higher taxes, racial quotas, forced busing, runaway crime, permissive morality, and weak national defense. Casting the election as a showdown between "the work ethic and the welfare ethic," a choice between the Republican belief in color-blind equality and the liberal doctrine of reverse racism, Nixon appealed to "those millions who have been driven out of their home in the Democratic Party . . . to join us as members of a new American majority."[18]

Nixon won forty-nine states in the 1972 election and received 60.7 percent of the popular vote. About one-third of Democrats nationwide defected to the Republican ticket, which also attracted a large majority of the Wallace supporters from 1968. The GOP reconstructed a solid South for the first time since World War II, winning 71 percent of the ballots in the region. But interpretations of the Republican landslide that revolve around a rehashed version of the Southern Strategy rely on a fundamental misperception of the full-scale repudiation of race-based and rights-based liberalism by the white electorate throughout the nation. McGovern did not even compete in most southern states, marking the advent of a dubious strategem by the national party, and many moderate Democrats in the region followed Governor Edwin Edwards of Louisiana in renouncing the nominee as the representative of the "non-American left-wing fringe." Richard Nixon did not always tell the truth in his political career, but he spoke with accuracy a few weeks before the election to an audience of southern Republican leaders in the Sunbelt metropolis of Atlanta. After half a million people watched the presidential motorcade down Peachtree Street, Nixon told the crowd that southern issues and national issues were identical: parents from Georgia to Michigan opposed the busing of their children away from neighborhood schools, and all members of the Silent Majority wanted peace with honor, decent jobs, law and order, justice for all citizens, and preservation of traditional moral values. "It has been suggested that . . . I have a so-called Southern strategy," Nixon observed. "It is not a Southern strategy; it is an American strategy. . . . That is what the South believes in and that is what America believes in. . . . We seek what I call a new American majority."[19]

Separate and Unequal

The suburban strategy of the Nixon administration dovetailed with the reconstitution of the Supreme Court in the early 1970s, as the executive and judicial branches jointly rejected metropolitan remedies for racial segregation in public schools and residential segregation in suburban housing. In the fall of 1971, the president appeared on national television to announce two Supreme Court nominations, Richmond corporate lawyer Lewis F. Powell, Jr., and Assistant Attorney General William H. Rehnquist. Nixon praised both men as constitutional conservatives who would help reorient the federal judiciary away from the liberal activism of the Warren era. The Senate easily approved Powell, a moderate Democrat who had personally signed a brief urging the Supreme Court to grant Richmond a reprieve from busing orders. The nomination of Rehnquist proved more controversial because the Goldwater Republican had left a lengthy paper trail of hostility toward racial integration, including states' rights arguments against the *Brown* decision and the Civil Rights Act of 1964. Just one year earlier, Rehnquist authored a memorandum urging the administration to introduce a constitutional amendment that would outlaw busing and protect neighborhood schools. The confirmation of the two nominees, combined with the previous appointments of Warren Burger and Harry Blackmun, meant that Nixon had named four members of the Supreme Court in a single term of office. When the president elected by the Silent Majority decisively altered the ideological direction of the Supreme Court, the political and legal resistance against affirmative action to integrate the suburbs converged.[20]

The judicial evolution of the de jure/de facto debate ultimately overturned the long-standing distinction between southern-style segregation and its northern counterpart but confined the remedy within urban school districts. In *Keyes v. Denver* (1973), the Supreme Court for the first time charged a large nonsouthern district with an "affirmative duty" to disestablish a dual school system. *Keyes* applied a standard of "segregative intent" to find Denver guilty of gerrymandered assignment zones and other de jure methods of deliberate discrimination. In his concurrence, Justice William Douglas urged the Court to move beyond the investigation of racial versus nonracial motives and articulate a national standard that "there is no constitutional difference between *de jure* and *de facto* segregation, for each is the product of state actions or policies." Lewis Powell also called for the abandonment of the "*de facto/de jure* distinction nurtured by the courts and accepted complacently by many of the same voices which denounced the evils of segregated schools in the South." But his concurring opinion endorsed limited remedies that respected the "legitimate community interests in neighborhood school systems," and Justice Rehnquist's dissent rejected any application of an "affirmative duty to integrate" to urban districts segregated by residential patterns. As legal scholars such as Alexander Bickel claimed that "there is a moral difference" between de jure and de facto segregation, antibusing leaders from thirteen states gathered in Memphis to launch the National Council for the Preservation of Our Educational Freedoms. The coalition pledged to enact a constitutional amendment to preserve neighborhood schools, and a delegate from suburban Detroit predicted a "national boycott—we'll pull it off if there's any way we can."[21]

In 1974, in the landmark case of *Milliken v. Bradley*, a narrow majority on the Burger Court rejected the civil rights drive for metropolitan remedies through the consolidation of city and suburban school districts. Two decades after *Brown*, it was less ironic than fitting that the NAACP's devastating legal defeat came in a Rust Belt metropolis whose racial politics—like the nation's—changed forever as a result of the Great Migration of black southerners to the North. The majority opinion by Warren Burger elided the clear evidence that a history of pervasive state-sponsored housing segregation had shaped the landscapes of metropolitan Detroit and sarcastically mischaracterized the suburban remedy as the personal preference of judges who worried that a city-only plan "would not produce the racial balance which they perceived as desirable." The chief justice declared that "no single tradition in public education is more deeply rooted than local control over the operation of schools," rejecting the trial court's finding that "district lines are simply matters of political convenience and may not be used to deny constitutional rights." *Milliken* reversed the consolidation decree and restricted the desegregation remedy to the city of Detroit, based on the absence of rigorous proof that suburban policies had directly caused "a significant segregative effect" in the urban schools. Justice Potter Stewart provided the swing vote and filed a concurrence that circumvented the factual findings of the trial court by attributing the segregation of black students in Detroit to "unknown and perhaps unknowable factors such as in-migration, birth rates, economic changes, or cumulative acts of private racial fears." All three of the other Nixon appointees joined Burger's majority opinion in *Milliken*, which effectively divided metropolitan Detroit between the unconstitutional (de jure) segregation located inside the city and the innocent (de facto) variation found throughout the suburbs.[22]

From Richmond to Detroit, from Atlanta to Los Angeles, the interplay between the political revolt of the Silent Majority and the judicial accommodation of suburban resistance transformed state-sponsored residential segregation into a historical wrong without a constitutional antidote. "Deliberate acts of segregation and their consequences will go unremedied," Justice Byron White argued in his dissent, because the majority "fashions out of whole cloth an arbitrary rule that remedies for constitutional violations . . . must stop at the school district line." The scathing dissent by William Douglas predicted that if the "'separate' but 'inferior'" schools in Detroit did not violate the Fourteenth Amendment, then the impact of *Milliken* "will likely put the problems of the blacks and our society back to the period that antedated the 'separate but equal' regime of *Plessy v. Ferguson*." Thurgood Marshall's eloquent dissent charged that "the Court today takes a giant step backwards" after two decades of gradual and arduous progress toward the constitutional promise of *Brown*. The former chief legal counsel of the NAACP observed that a city-only remedy would inevitably fail and accused the Court of making "a solemn mockery of *Brown I's* holding that separate educational facilities are inherently unequal and of *Swann's* unequivocal mandate that the answer to *de jure* segregation is the greatest possible degree of actual desegregation." Alluding to the antibusing movement that stretched from the suburbs to the White House, Marshall portrayed *Milliken* as "a reflection of a perceived public mood that we have gone far enough in enforcing the Constitution's guarantee of equal justice" and warned that "public opposition, no matter how strident, cannot be permitted to divert this Court" from its obligation to follow the rule of law. "In the short run, it may seem to be the easier course to allow our great metropolitan areas to be divided up each into two cities—one white, the other black—but it is a course, I predict, our people will ultimately regret."[23]

Milliken immunized most suburbs throughout the nation from the burdens and opportunities of meaningful integration and sentenced most minority students who lived in urban centers to attend public schools hypersegregated by a fusion of race and family income. Piecemeal desegregation plans applied within the largest urban districts of the North and West imposed the requirements of social change on working-class families and accelerated residential flight from cities that had already experienced massive white out-migration long before the advent of busing. During the 1970s, New York and Los Angeles each lost more than 200,000 white students, and by decade's end most major cities throughout the nation operated school systems that contained a substantial majority of African-American and Latino pupils. Although the consolidated districts of the Sunbelt South demonstrated that expansive metropolitan remedies could overcome suburban opposition and mitigate white flight, by the mid-1970s a powerful mythology had emerged that court-ordered busing caused the decline of urban schools. This political consensus ignored the necessity of metropolitan approaches to stabilize racial integration and misapplied the lessons of cities such as Boston, where secure suburban spectators watched as struggling white communities fought reassignment to poor black neighborhoods. "To understand reactionary populism," a scholar of the Boston saga concluded, "we must recognize the role of class and its consequences in the formation of public policy, particularly policies designed to alleviate racial injustice. If class is ignored, as it was in Boston and consistently tends to be in dealing with desegregation, then those policies have little chance of success."[24]

Forty-six percent of black students in the South attended majority-white schools at the time of the *Milliken* decision, in contrast with only 28 percent in the rest of the nation. By the end of the 1970s, only 23 percent of southern black students attended racially isolated schools, with 48.7 percent of African-American pupils in the Northeast and 43.6 percent in the Midwest enrolled in intensely segregated institutions. Outside the South, the conspicuous exceptions to the debilitating trends of metropolitan fragmentation and inner-city hypersegregation involved three different types of urban school districts. In northern cities with very small minority populations—such as Seattle, Portland, and Minneapolis—white flight remained minimal and stark racial isolation almost nonexistent. Several Southwestern metropolises with countywide school systems, such as Albuquerque and Las Vegas, also exhibited high levels of desegregation and racial stability. And in the most revealing development, a small number of metropolitan regions that underwent court-ordered city-suburban consolidation after 1974—most notably Louisville, Wilmington, and Indianapolis—each stemmed white flight and attained a substantial degree of racial integration. Civil rights plaintiffs in these cases surmounted the difficult barriers raised by *Milliken* and demonstrated the responsibility of state policies ranging from highway construction to the site placement of low-income housing for the establishment and maintenance of residential segregation. But the broader elusiveness of metropolitan remedies meant that most large urban districts in the North and Midwest resembled the southern cities of Atlanta and Richmond—

TABLE 12.1
Decline in White Enrollment, 1968–1986, and Percentage of Black Students in
Majority-White and Racially Isolated Schools, 1986, Large Urban School Districts
outside the South.

City	%White (1968)	%White (1986)	%Black/Maj. White Schools	%Black/Racially Isolated Schools
Washington	6	4	0.5	94.1
Detroit	39	9	0.6	76.1
Newark	18	9	1.0	96.6
Chicago	38	14	2.4	81.3
San Francisco	41	15	0	49.3
Los Angeles	54	18	4.9	70.0
Baltimore	35	19	5.1	68.3
New York	44	22	6.8	74.1
Cleveland	43	25	0.9	5.2
Philadelphia	39	25	10.6	73.7
Boston	68	26	4.0	13.3
Milwaukee	73	36	11.8	23.6
Denver	66	37	19.0	0
San Diego	76	44	26.5	8.5
Portland	89	73	47.7	0
Minneapolis	N/A	N/A	57.2	0.3
Seattle	N/A	N/A	25.8	4.5
Albuquerque	60	55	51.8	2.5
Las Vegas/Clark Co.	84	73	79.3	3.5
Louisville/Jefferson Co.°	80°	69	93.3	0
Indianapolis°°	66	51	44.6	0

Source: Gary Orfield and Franklin Monfort, *Racial Change and Desegregation in Large
School Districts*, 7–9, 11–13, 19–23.
°Consolidated by court order in 1975
°°Metropolitan desegregation plan

predominantly nonwhite and increasingly impoverished, racially separate
and transparently unequal (table 12.1).[25]

In the absence of a federal commitment to tackle metropolitan structures
of "economic segregation" and residential inequality, civil rights organizations and low-income plaintiffs increasingly turned to state courts to challenge discriminatory features in suburban zoning policies and school funding formulas. In the *Mount Laurel* case that began in the 1970s, the New
Jersey Supreme Court found that "economic discrimination" enforced by
exclusionary zoning violated the equal protection clause of the state constitution and ordered suburban municipalities to provide a "fair share" affordable housing remedy. The immediate political backlash included grassroots
resistance by affluent homeowners, obstructionist tactics by the legislature,

and a powerful wedge issue for the suburban Republicans who gained control of state government. While developers in New Jersey eventually built numerous affordable housing units, the litigation has lasted for decades and barely dented the prevailing patterns of residential segregation. A concurrent class-action lawsuit securing court-ordered equalization of school funding galvanized fierce opposition by residents of New Jersey's wealthy suburbs, which systematically delayed legal compliance and denied any obligation even to achieve "separate but equal" educational opportunity. The chastened Democrats regained power only through reinvention as a culturally liberal party that would hold the line on property taxes and defend suburban quality of life at all costs. As New Jersey began moving away from the GOP in the 1990s, it was not incidental but intrinsic to the Democrats' suburban strategy that it represented one of the most racially segregated and income-stratified states in the nation.[26]

In the campaign for school funding equalization, the elusiveness of good-faith compliance with judicial decrees recalls the stratagems of the southern era of "all deliberate speed" without the violence. In 1971, the California Supreme Court invalidated the system of financing public schools through local property taxes, followed by similar action in six other states where distribution formulas also advantaged affluent suburbs and shortchanged rural and urban districts. Two years later, in *San Antonio v. Rodriguez* (1973), the Burger Court overturned a Texas ruling that massive funding disparities between urban and suburban school systems violated the Fourteenth Amendment. The five-to-four decision formalized the doctrine that federal equal protection guarantees did not forbid state-sponsored "wealth discrimination" and found that public education did not constitute a fundamental right of national citizenship. The school reform movement at the grassroots level proved more successful through litigation that paired the equal protection and public education guarantees found in most state constitutions. Courts in twenty states ranging from Alabama to Massachusetts overturned property tax formulas between 1971 and 2001, but as a general rule the grudging legislative responses increased funding contributions to poorer districts without achieving actual equalization. In New York, where some of the wealthy suburbs of Westchester County and Long Island spend as much as $10,000 more per student than public schools in the city, an equalization order issued in 2001 produced an apparent political consensus that the state government simply would not comply in good faith. "Having long since turned its back on the moral implications of *Brown v. Board of Education*," the social critic Jonathan Kozol charged, "the nation's largest and now uncontested bastion of apartheid education does not even seem prepared to live up to the tarnished promises of *Plessy v. Ferguson*."[27]

THE VOLATILE CENTER

The grassroots revolt of the Silent Majority reshaped national politics and established durable spatial constraints on civil rights remedies for racial inequality, but the white electorate's repudiation of Great Society liberalism did not translate into a cohesive conservative majority or an enduring Republican realignment. The power of the populist vocabulary that dominated the Nixon era—Middle America, the Forgotten Americans, the Silent Majority, the New American Majority—arose from its ability to transcend the substantial divisions between working-class and upper-middle-class voters, but never more than temporarily. During the three decades following the national disintegration of the New Deal Order, both political parties have grappled with an unstable class dynamic at the center of their electoral strategies. The Republicans have depended upon the upward mobility facilitated by suburban expansion and Sunbelt development, and they have capitalized on the blue-collar revolts against liberal "special interests" evident in the McGovern disaster of 1972, the Reagan ascendance during the 1980s, and the Gingrich surprise of 1994. The Democrats have won back working-class defectors during periods of economic turmoil—most notably the Carter election in 1976, the Reagan recession of 1982, and the Clinton triumph a decade later—and the party's migration to the center has increasingly attracted white-collar professionals and suburban swing voters who dislike the social conservatism of the Religious Right. Neither party has proved capable of maintaining the allegiance of the broad but elusive group that Richard Nixon (mis)labeled the Silent Majority. Since the 1970s, the bipartisan battle for the volatile center has increasingly revolved around the pursuit of shifting groups of Middle American swing voters in the sprawling metropolises of a self-consciously suburban nation.[28]

The casual analysis that the Solid South simply shifted from the Democratic to the Republican column in direct backlash against the civil rights movement underestimates the ideological breadth and Sunbelt base of the New Right and overlooks the resilience of the interracial tradition of moderate New South Democrats. After the failure of the Southern Strategy in 1970, the SRC observed that "the Republicans cannot win the South *on their own* in 1972. The Democrats may *give* them the South, but it is the Democrats who have the initiative in determining where the region . . . will go." The overwhelming white support for Nixon's reelection transcended partisan lines but provided almost no coattails for the GOP's southern wing, which suffered a steady decline in office holders for the rest of the decade, from the U.S. Senate down to the state legislatures. Economic divisions reemerged in the 1976 election, when Gerald Ford received the support of the white-collar suburbs and native son Jimmy Carter won back the Wallace faction and swept every southern state except Virginia with a coalition of black voters and the white working class. Kevin Phillips lamented the GOP's inability to maintain the allegiance of blue-collar Democrats and predicted that "the Republican party does not have a long-term future." But the inventor of the Sunbelt label should have had more confidence in the most compelling insight of his realignment manual, the long-term demographic trends that forecast Republican power in the middle-class suburbs and the high-growth Sunbelt states of the South and West. The rejuvenation of the southern Republicans in the 1980s mirrored the national triumph of the Reagan coalition, including the tax revolts in the white-collar suburbs, the grassroots mobilization of the Religious Right, and the conservative populism that encouraged downwardly mobile voters to blame the government and not the market for the collapse of the middle-class social contract.[29]

As population growth and electoral power shifted to the South and West, the dominant wing of each political party emerged from the political culture of the Sunbelt, the booming region from Virginia to California that produced every American president elected between 1964 and 2004. The Reagan ascendance within the Republican party moved the priorities of Sunbelt corporations to the center of the national agenda and rewarded the upper-middle-class suburbs that strongly supported the fiscal conservatism of the GOP, from Orange County in California to Cobb County outside Atlanta, from Bergen County in New Jersey to Fairfield County in Connecticut. The rise of the Religious Right revealed the grassroots impact of evangelical Protestants whose organizational base rested in Sunbelt "edge cities" such as Colorado Springs and Virginia Beach, and the GOP's social conservatism accompanied the takeover of the party apparatus in many states by the offshoots of the Moral Majority and the Christian Coalition. Reagan's reelection in 1984 with an electoral coalition of forty-nine states exposed the national crisis of identity facing the Democratic party, especially the blue-collar revolt against liberalism in the Catholic suburbs of the Midwest and the working-class precincts of the South. But despite a defeatist tendency among liberals to lament as permanent the loss of the "Reagan Democrats" and (mis)read a new Solid Republican South into specific presidential election cycles, lower-middle-class white voters and southern swing states proved to be critical constituencies in the reinvigoration of the Democratic party in the 1990s. Building on his foundation in the interracial New South politics of the seventies, Bill Clinton launched a populist "third way" drive for the White House with an unattributed homage to the Nixon era and the Silent Majority: a "campaign for the future, for the forgotten hard-working middle-class families of America."[30]

The reinvention of the "New Democrats" as the champions of quality-of-life issues in suburban swing districts and the fiscally responsible managers of the high-tech economy revitalized the competitiveness of the center in a postliberal political order. The ideological transformation of the party engineered by the Democratic Leadership Council (DLC) identified the suburbs and the South as key political battlegrounds and then "triangulated" the difference between the New Right agenda of the GOP and the fading remnants of Great Society liberalism. "The way to win the South," counseled DLC founder Al From, is "by changing the center of political gravity within the party. The South is very much where the mainstream of the country is." Clinton's victory in the 1992 election, the first in which suburban voters represented an outright majority of the electorate, won back crucial states in the South and Midwest while maintaining Democratic strength in the Northeast and on the West Coast. The Democratic agenda during the 1990s revolved around an operational suburban strategy that included targeted entitlement programs for "soccer moms" and working women, an ethic of tolerance for upscale moderates alienated by the culture wars of the Christian Right, probusiness management of the high-tech economy shaped by the Sunbelt boom, and fiscal policies selected for their acceptability in middle-class focus groups. Throughout the decade, DLC strategists reminded the party that "sprawl is where the voters are" and touted the politics of moderation as key to "staying competitive in suburban areas." The new century ushers in an "emerging Democratic majority" in American politics, at least according to the manifesto of the New Democratic movement, because the party understands that "America's future lies in places like Silicon Valley and North Carolina's Research Triangle." But the Republicans have countered with their own time-tested suburban strategy, including sophisticated voter mobilization campaigns targeting the white families moving to the exurban fringes in key battleground states such as Florida and Ohio.[31]

In the South, the ardent conservatism of the overwhelmingly white Republican party and the determination of the New Democrats to occupy the center with a coalition of black voters and white moderates means that regional politics have remained competitive in the aftermath of the civil rights era and the explosive growth of the metropolitan Sunbelt. "The old solid Democratic South has vanished," the leading analysts of regional political trends observed in 2002. "A comparably solid Republican South has not developed. Nor is one likely to emerge." The Republican decision to forfeit the substantial black vote, combined with the rapid expansion of the Latino population and the swing function performed at different times by suburban moderates and working-class populists, effectively guarantees that the GOP cannot reproduce a Solid South on a permanent and grassroots basis. Electoral reapportionment and the racial gerrymandering of congressional districts helped polarize the region's delegation to the House of Representatives, with national consequences during the Republican surge of 1994. But the politics of moderation still resonate in statewide contests—every southern state elected at least one Democratic governor between 1989 and 1999—and the Democrats can also be competitive in the region during presidential elections, when they actually try. George W. Bush's embrace of "compassionate conservatism" during the 2000 campaign represented nothing so much as an updated version of Richard Nixon's color-blind appeals to the Silent Majority, an inclusive rhetorical device aimed at suburban swing voters in the South and across the nation turned off by the politics of racial extremism and religious intolerance. The genuine political realignment in contemporary America—beyond the fallacy of "red state/blue state" national polarization, symbolized by the corporate conservatism of the Republicans and the suburban moderation of the New Democrats—is the disappearance of a party that represents the interests of the working class and champions the plight of the poor.[32]

In an era that demonstrates the vitality and the limitations of the political center, the most ambitious proposals to address the lingering inequities of the metropolitan landscape revolve around explicit class-over-race appeals to the self-interest of the suburban majority. The "hidden agenda" developed by William Julius Wilson distinguishes between the historical racial discrimination that created the urban underclass and the primacy of economic structures such as deindustrialization and a spatial mismatch between jobs and housing in the contemporary perpetuation of cycles of poverty. In the context of rapid suburbanization by millions of minority families, and the collapse of moral authority in the liberal discourse surrounding inequality, Wilson advocates broadening race-specific individual remedies into a macroeconomic agenda of universal programs such as full employment policy, guaranteed health insurance, and affordable housing subsidies. The "metropolitanist" platform advanced by the Brookings Institution seeks to capitalize on the current sprawl crisis and rethink the traditional urban-suburban dichotomy by mobilizing a political coalition behind public policies that provide mutual benefits to all metropolitan residents and forge new structural links between the core and the fringe. Since traffic jams and school crowding have replaced crime and taxes as primary anxieties in the sprawling exurbs, and as the racial and socioeconomic challenges of central cities have penetrated many inner-ring suburbs, metropolitanism seeks to connect smart growth and social justice in a spatial agenda of mass transit, mixed-income zoning, revenue equalization, and land-use reform. If middle-class Americans accept the need for metropolitan institutions to address the quality-of-life crisis caused by suburban sprawl, then perhaps policymakers can use regional structures as leverage to overcome fragmented political governance and ameliorate persistent patterns of employment discrimination, housing segregation, and educational inequality.[33]

The dominant ethos of American suburbia has always idealized the present and celebrated the future at the expense of any critical reflection on the past. For more than three decades, from the grassroots revolt of the Silent Majority in the 1970s to the bipartisan pursuit of middle-class swing voters in the 1990s and beyond, suburban homeowners and their political and judicial champions have naturalized residential segregation and defended metropolitan inequality through a powerful discourse of socioeconomic privilege and free-market meritocracy. For just as long, civil rights activists and progressive scholars have challenged the foundational mythology of suburban racial innocence and the color-blind ideology of middle-class individualism by exposing the de jure roots of almost all cases of allegedly de facto segregation—a historical verdict based on overwhelming evidence that has proved to be singularly unpersuasive in the political and legal arenas. The population shift to the middle-class suburbs and the power shift to the Sunbelt economy requires a new metropolitan framework for political history and public policy that transcends the urban-suburban dichotomy and confronts instead of obscures the pervasive politics of class in the suburban strategies of the volatile center. Surely an honest assessment of the nation's collective responsibility in creating the contemporary metropolitan landscape remains an essential prerequisite for grappling with the spatial fusion of racial and class politics that ultimately produced an underlying suburban consensus in the electoral arena. If "the problem of the color line" represented the fundamental crisis of the twentieth century, the foremost challenge of the twenty-first has evolved into the suburban synthesis of racial inequality and class segregation at the heart of what may or may not be the New American Dilemma.[34]

Epilogue

Forced busing . . . is doomed to failure because people in a
democracy will, in the end, have the final word.
                                    —Thomas Harris (1970), vice chairman,
                                    Concerned Parents Association, Charlotte

IN THE LATE 1990s, the racially integrated public school system of
Charlotte-Mecklenburg, once the national landmark for busing to overcome
residential segregation, returned to the headlines as a turning point in the
conservative campaign to dismantle affirmative action through the federal
courts. The agenda of color-blind conservatism began gathering steam under the Reagan administration, which aggressively promoted a race-neutral
interpretation of the Constitution and sought the termination of busing
plans through a return to neighborhood schools. During the civil rights era,
as a rising political star in the nation's most populous state, Ronald Reagan denounced open-housing legislation as a violation of the private property right "to discriminate against Negroes" and promised "to vigorously
oppose—by all legal means—the forced busing of California school children." The Republican platform in 1980 included a similar pledge to overturn "forced busing," and the Reagan administration intervened to test its
color-blind theory in a crucial case involving the city of Norfolk, Virginia. In
the *Riddick* decision of 1986, the Fourth Circuit Court of Appeals permitted
Norfolk to discontinue crosstown busing and reassign students to neighborhood schools. The appellate panel dismissed the NAACP's arguments about
the continued impact of state-sponsored housing discrimination with a finding that the school system had "succeeded in eradicating all vestiges of de
jure segregation." The Supreme Court declined to review the decision, and
Assistant Attorney General William Bradford Reynolds, the architect of the
administration's color-blind strategy, called *Riddick* "a model for the future
and for other school districts to follow." A number of southern cities that
had attained substantial integration under court order began to undergo the
process of resegregation as they exchanged busing plans for a combination
of neighborhood schools and magnet programs.[1]

In 1997, a white parent and corporate transplant named Bill Capacchione
filed a lawsuit challenging the admissions formula in Charlotte-Mecklenburg's
magnet schools, after his daughter failed to gain entrance to a facility designed

to achieve voluntary integration without mandatory busing. The case came before District Judge Robert Potter, appointed to the federal bench by President Reagan at the behest of Republican Senator Jesse Helms. Three decades earlier, Potter had participated actively in the grassroots campaign of the Concerned Parents Association, including the provision of legal advice to the city's initial antibusing movement. Instead of recusing himself, the judge reactivated the *Swann* case and expanded the *Capacchione* litigation into a wide-ranging review of whether Charlotte-Mecklenburg's race-conscious desegregation formula violated the equal protection clause of the Fourteenth Amendment. NAACP attorneys intervened as a class action for black students and contended that race-conscious assignments remained necessary to redress the vestiges of de jure segregation still evident in metropolitan housing patterns. The school board joined this defense and also cited the diversity rationale (the Supreme Court's *Swann* ruling in 1971 forbade racial balance if ordered by judges but acknowledged that public education officials "might well conclude . . . that in order to prepare students to live in a pluralistic society, each school should have a prescribed ratio of Negro to white students reflecting the proportion for the district as a whole"). A fierce debate raged throughout metropolitan Charlotte as citizens awaited the desegregation trial scheduled for the spring of 1999, ranging from conservative appropriations of Martin Luther King, Jr.'s sentence that children no longer be judged "by the color of their skin" to the liberal rejoinder written on a sign held by a white woman at a crowded school board gathering: "Separate will never be equal."[2]

On September 9, 1999, Judge Potter enjoined Charlotte-Mecklenburg "from assigning children to schools or allocating educational opportunities and benefits through race-based lotteries, preferences, set-asides, or other means that deny students an equal footing based on race." The judge dismissed the NAACP claim that the legacies of state-sponsored residential segregation remained evident with the observation that "Charlotte has become one of the most racially integrated cities in America." He rejected the school board's employment of the *Bakke* rationale in a declaration that "achieving diversity is not a proper grounds for race-conscious action." In a deliberate inversion of the moral categories of the civil rights era, Potter accused the school district of " 'standing in the schoolhouse door' and turning students away from its magnet programs based on race, which is inconsistent with the movement towards race neutrality envisioned in *Brown*." With rhetoric that echoed the original antibusing movement of the Silent Majority, the judge invalidated the entire student assignment plan as "a numbers game of non-remedial racial balancing goals . . . [in which] children are not viewed as individual students but as cogs in a social experimentation machine." In a circular trap, the race-conscious remedies pursued in Charlotte for thirty years became the evidence that the school district finally had achieved the elusive unitary status and therefore could no longer exercise an "affirmative obligation to actively desegregate."[3]

The NAACP appealed the color-blind mandate, and the Fourth Circuit, sitting *en banc*, issued a convoluted split decision in the fall of 2001. A narrow majority in *Belk v. Charlotte-Mecklenburg* affirmed the designation of unitary status because "the dual system has been dismantled and the vestiges of prior discrimination have been eliminated to the extent practicable." This controlling opinion rejected the NAACP's contention that de jure racial discrimination remained in evidence, including school board policies that had located almost all recently constructed facilities in the primarily white outer-ring suburbs marked by dramatic population growth. At the same time, a separate majority reversed the lower court finding that Charlotte-Mecklenburg's previous use of race in formulating magnet school assignments violated the equal protection clause, based on the argument that the district had been operating under a court-approved desegregation plan and therefore no constitutional violation could have occurred before the judicial designation of unitary status. This element of the opinion vacated Judge Potter's blanket injunction against any use of race in the magnet programs, although with the oblique warning that "certain race-conscious policies might no longer be permissible" after transition to a unitary system. The appellate judges who dissented from the declaration of unitary status charged that the philosophy of color-blind absolutism had established a false dichotomy "between 'countering demographic change' on the one hand and 'remedying past discrimination' on the other. . . . *Swann's* basic teaching is that the Constitution sometimes requires schools to 'counter demography' in order to achieve desegregation." As the future of Charlotte-Mecklenburg's public schools became even more entangled in the murky case law surrounding affirmative action, the dissenters declared that "we must be willing to acknowledge and confront our history, . . . [or] we risk falling into a mode that equates the cure with the disease: civil rights with favoritism, desegregation with segregation. As American citizens, we know better."[4]

Before the completion of the 1999 trial, a *Charlotte Observer* analysis of residential patterns revealed that a policy of color-blind assignments to neighborhood schools would result in the immediate resegregation of half of the facilities in the countywide district. In an even more striking feature, the report concluded that the suburbanization of the black middle class combined with the geographic isolation of low-income African-American and Latino families would leave the vast majority of poor minority students in hypersegregated inner-city schools. A policy of neighborhood schools in Charlotte would not re-create the patterns of the Jim Crow era, desegregation expert Gary Orfield warned, but instead "schools of the sort that they've never seen before, . . . much more virulent than the ones you had historically because they're segregated by race and class. . . . People will suddenly see those schools on the lists as worst schools." In the fall of 2002, Charlotte-Mecklenburg implemented its new race-neutral plan, a complex formula of neighborhood school assignments subject to family choice through transfer applications and lotteries for open spaces in desirable facilities. Resisting progressive calls to devise a comprehensive class-based integration policy, the district explained that "diversity will no longer be mandated . . . but rather will be based on the decisions of the family." About half of the public schools retained meaningful integration levels, especially the majority-white facilities in the inner-ring suburbs, but hypersegregation by race and family income accelerated dramatically in the black and Latino neighborhoods of the inner city. By 2004, 66 of the 134 schools in Charlotte-Mecklenburg contained enrollments that exceeded 75 percent nonwhite, and minority students represented more than 90 percent of the population in 38 of these facilities. In the local manifestation of the New American Dilemma, the racial diversification of the Charlotte suburbs continues to rise, and so does the economic segregation and spatial isolation of poor minority students.[5]

At the beginning of the twenty-first century, Charlotte continues to embody the possibilities and the perils of the latest New South, perhaps more than any other metropolis found across the booming Sunbelt. Los Angeles and Atlanta might have burnished their international reputations by hosting the Olympic Games, but Charlotte once seemed to possess the resources and the commitment to forge a more egalitarian alternative to the dominant patterns of the Sunbelt Synthesis. The civic dedication to an integrated public school system has not disappeared, but in the end corporate leaders and their political allies always chose growth over equality, suburban sprawl over social justice. Charlotte now boasts its own professional sports teams, long a rite of passage for any southern city seeking recognition as a truly national metropolis. The bars and restaurants of the downtown cultural district (rechristened "Uptown") serve an upscale and multiracial clientele of young professionals who work in monuments to capitalism such as the Bank of America skyscraper, visible sometimes through breaks in the pretty trees that line the streets of the island suburbs. The unmistakable aura of prosperity pervades SouthPark and the other shopping malls located nearby the white-collar subdivisions, where upmarket retail chains cater to the cosmopolitan tastes of families drawn from all over the nation. SouthPark stands as a testament to the developer-dominated vision of Charlotte's future, a semipublic space where the professional classes still interact with the laborers in the service economy, a bustling if ultimately sterile showcase of the consumer values of the ascendant New South. And SouthPark—where the Concerned Parents Association once circulated flyers to fight court-ordered busing, where President Reagan later promised Charlotte a return to neighborhood schools—could be anywhere in America, interchangeable with all of the other affluent sprawlscapes that signify wealth and power in this suburban nation.[6]

Compared to the extravagant mansions appearing beside golf courses and inside gated communities on Charlotte's ever-expanding suburban fringe, the modest ranch houses in the middle-class subdivisions that produced the city's original antibusing movement seem like relics from a postwar era that happened a long time ago. The island suburb of Myers Park no longer monopolizes the fate of the metropolis, but its graceful neighborhoods symbolize the traditional privilege that lingers on, even as commercial development and high-density construction now press at their borders. In the 1990s, Charlotte-Mecklenburg began construction of an outer-ring beltway—another asphalt dream for bankers and developers and a promise of relief for the suburban homeowners who still subscribe to the illusion that more roads will ease the consequences of sprawl. The traffic jams and air pollution throughout the region are terrible, notwithstanding limited attempts to establish mass transit, and in the arena of growth it is now clear that Charlotte has repeated rather than learned from the mistakes made in Atlanta. From the "new urbanist" villages surrounding UNC-Charlotte in the northern part of the county, an automobile can speed downtown, and beyond to the international airport and the southeast suburbs, on an intricate network of interstate highways and multilane thoroughfares, named for Mayors John Belk and Stan Brookshire and the Reverend Billy Graham, but not for Julius Chambers or James McMillan or Margaret Ray. And in a celebrated metropolis where suburbanization now exacerbates class segregation more than racial isolation, a commuter cannot even see the once vibrant inner-city neighborhoods now bisected by the federal highways, or the economically depressed areas that still exist beyond the trees and the concrete walls.[7]

The unitary designation and the color-blind catalysts that accelerated the resegregation of the public school system of Charlotte-Mecklenburg—including the central role played by conservative judges appointed by Republican presidents elected by the Silent Majority—represent less an ironic example of desegregation case law coming full circle and more an illustration of the permanent politicization of the law itself. In 1971, the Supreme Court decision in *Swann* defined unitary status as the vague, magical moment when all vestiges of state-sponsored racial segregation vanished. At some point during the subsequent three decades, the patterns of residential segregation still clearly evident in metropolitan Charlotte simply became de facto and natural rather than de jure and justiciable, at least in terms of constitutional law. Beginning in 1999, the federal courts withdrew permission to take affirmative action to combat housing segregation and ushered in a new era of "race-neutral" policy for a metropolis that struggled for years to dismantle racial discrimination in its public schools and remained committed to the principles of integrated education and equal opportunity. But the citizens and leaders of Charlotte-Mecklenburg also bear substantial responsibility for the contemporary resegregation of the school system, because of the long-term failure to adopt inclusionary mixed-income zoning policies to spread residential integration across the metropolis, and through the recent refusal to implement a class-based desegregation formula in the aftermath of the judicial decree.

When Judge Potter issued his color-blind directive, a noted commentator on racial policy took the opportunity to offer the eulogy. "It's the end of an era in American social policy," Glenn C. Loury concluded. "The weight that was borne by school desegregation as the vehicle for trying to equalize opportunity will now have to be borne elsewhere." If the Charlotte decision marked the end of an era, during which the civil rights movement relied upon the federal courts to bring about social change, and the nation committed itself to the goals of racial integration and equal opportunity in public education, then it is an era that has been in the process of ending for at least three decades. "Forced busing . . . is doomed to failure," the leader of the Concerned Parents Association promised in 1970, "because people in a democracy will, in the end, have the final word." The events in Charlotte during that turbulent time sparked the NAACP's drive for metropolitan school integration and propelled the suburban backlash of the Silent Majority onto the national stage. Thirty years later, the waves that once rippled outward came crashing back.[8]

Notes

Abbreviations

Newspapers and Magazines

Atlanta Constitution (AC)
Atlanta Journal (AJ)
Atlanta Journal and Constitution (AJC)
Atlantic Monthly (AM)
Charlotte News (CN)
Charlotte Observer (CO)
Christian Century (CC)
Detroit Free Press (DFP)
Detroit News (DN)
Georgia Voter (GV)
Greenville News (GN)
Harper's Magazine (HM)
Jackson Clarion-Ledger (JCL)
Memphis Commercial Appeal (MCA)
Mobile Register (MR)
New South (NS)
New Yorker (NY)
Norfolk Virginian-Pilot (NVP)
Raleigh News and Observer (RNO)
Richmond News Leader (RNL)
Richmond Times-Dispatch (RTD)
Saturday Review (SR)
South Today (ST)
Southern School News (SSN)
Southern Voices (SV)
The New Democrat (TND)
The New Republic (TNR)
U.S. News and World Report (USN)
Wall Street Journal (WSJ)
Washington Post (WP)
Weekly Compilation of Presidential Documents (WC)

Archival Collections

Arthur Jarrell Raper Papers, Virginia Historical Society, Richmond, Va. (AJR/VHS)
Benjamin Muse Papers, 1934–66, Accession #10031, Special Collections Department, University of Virginia Library, Charlottesville, Va. (MUSE/UVA)
Benjamin S. Horack Papers, University of North Carolina at Charlotte Library (BSH/UNCC)

Charles Raper Jonas Papers, Southern History Collection, University of North Carolina at Chapel Hill (CRJ/SHC)

Charlotte-Mecklenburg Charter Commission Records, University of North Carolina at Charlotte Library (CCR/UNCC)

Community Relations Committee Papers, University of North Carolina at Charlotte Library (CRC/UNCC)

Eliza Paschall Papers, Special Collections and Archives, Robert W. Woodruff Library, Emory University (EP/RWW)

Frances Freeborn Pauley Papers, Special Collections and Archives, Robert W. Woodruff Library, Emory University (FFP/RWW)

Fred D. Alexander Papers, University of North Carolina at Charlotte Library (FDA/UNCC)

Frye Gaillard Papers, Southern History Collection, University of North Carolina at Chapel Hill (FG/SHC)

Georgia Government Documentation Project, Special Collections Department, William Russell Pullen Library, Georgia State University (GGDP)

Harry S. Dent Papers, Strom Thurmond Institute, Special Collections, Clemson University Libraries (HSD/STI)

HOPE/Muriel Lokey Papers, Atlanta History Center (HOPE/AHC)

Horace H. Edwards Papers, M246, Special Collections and Archives, James Branch Cabell Library, Virginia Commonwealth University (HHE/VCU)

James Auxford Sartain Papers, Virginia Historical Society, Richmond, Va. (JAS/VHS)

James L. Doherty Papers, Virginia Historical Society, Richmond, Va. (JLD/VHS)

Julian Mason Papers, Private Collection, Charlotte, North Carolina (JM)

Julius L. Chambers Papers, University of North Carolina at Charlotte Library (JLC/UNCC)

Kelly Miller Alexander, Sr., Papers, University of North Carolina at Charlotte Library (KMA/UNCC)

League of Women Voters of Charlotte, North Carolina Papers, Robinson-Spangler Carolina Room, Public Library of Charlotte and Mecklenburg County (LWV/RSCR)

Margaret Whitton Ray Papers, University of North Carolina at Charlotte Library (MWR/UNCC)

Nan Pendergrast Papers, Special Collections and Archives, Robert W. Woodruff Library, Emory University (NP/RWW)

Reginald Hawkins Papers, University of North Carolina at Charlotte Library (RH/UNCC)

Robert Pendleton Hilldrup Papers, Virginia Historical Society, Richmond, Va. (RPH/VHS)

Southern Regional Council Papers, 1944–68, University Microfilms International (SRC/UMI)

U.S. Supreme Court Records and Briefs, *School Board of City of Richmond v. State Board of Education of Virginia*, 412 U.S. 92, No. 72-549, Congressional Information Service, Microfiche (RICH/USSC)

U.S. Supreme Court Records and Briefs, *Swann v. Charlotte-Mecklenburg*, 402 U.S. 1, No. 281, Congressional Information Service, Microfiche (SWANN/USSC)

Virginia Crockford Papers, M283, Special Collections and Archives, James Branch Cabell Library, Virginia Commonwealth University (VC/VCU)

W. Thomas Ray Papers, University of North Carolina at Charlotte Library (WTR/UNC)

William B. Spong Papers, Accession #9838, Special Collections Department, University of Virginia Library, Charlottesville, Va. (WBS/UVA)

William Berry Hartsfield Papers, Special Collections and Archives, Robert W. Woodruff Library, Emory University (WBH/RWW)

William R. Overhultz Papers, Private Collection, Charlotte, North Carolina (WRO)

William Waggoner Papers, University of North Carolina at Charlotte Library (WW/UNCC)

INTRODUCTION

1. James E. McDavid, Jr., to Charles R. Jonas, Feb. 5, 1970, folder 494, series 1.1, CRJ/SHC.

2. *CO*, July 12, 1975.

3. *Report of the National Advisory Commission on Civil Disorders* (New York: New York Times Co., 1968), 2, 22. For a sampling of the busing literature, see Gary Orfield, *Must We Bus? Segregated Schools and National Policy* (Washington, DC: Brookings, 1978); J. Harvie Wilkinson III, *From Brown to Bakke: The Supreme Court and School Integration, 1954–1978* (New York: Oxford Univ. Press, 1979); Raymond Wolters, *The Burden of Brown: Thirty Years of School Desegregation* (Knoxville: Univ. of Tennessee Press, 1984); Davison M. Douglas, ed., *School Busing: Constitutional and Political Developments*, vols. 1–2 (New York: Garland, 1994); Gary Orfield, Susan E. Eaton, and the Harvard Project on School Desegregation, *Dismantling Desegregation: The Quiet Reversal of Brown v. Board of Education* (New York: New Press, 1996). On the "American Dilemma," see Gunnar Myrdal, *An American Dilemma: The Negro Problem and Modern Democracy* (New York: Harper and Bros., 1944); Jennifer L. Hochschild, *The New American Dilemma: Liberal Democracy and School Desegregation* (New Haven: Yale Univ. Press, 1984).

4. On public policies and residential segregation, see Douglas S. Massey and Nancy A. Denton, *American Apartheid: Segregation and the Making of the Underclass* (Cambridge: Harvard Univ. Press, 1993); Michael B. Katz, ed., *The "Underclass" Debate: Views from History* (Princeton: Princeton Univ. Press, 1993); John Charles Boger and Judith Welch Wegner, eds., *Race, Poverty, and American Cities* (Chapel Hill: Univ. of North Carolina Press, 1996).

5. George Lipsitz, *The Possessive Investment in Whiteness: How White People Profit from Identity Politics* (Philadelphia: Temple Univ. Press, 1998). The "color-blind" concept has a complex and lengthy genealogy in American political culture and constitutional law, dating back to the period before the *Plessy v. Ferguson* decision of 1896, appearing at different times on almost all parts of the ideological spectrum, and generally advanced in strategic opposition to "race-conscious" public policies. For a perceptive account of the liberal and conservative roots of the color-blind campaign against race-based affirmative action, see Nancy MacLean, *Freedom Is*

Not Enough: The Opening of the American Workplace (Cambridge: Harvard Univ. Press and the Russell Sage Foundation, forthcoming 2005). Academic critiques of color-blind ideology and rhetoric include Orlando Patterson, *The Ordeal of Integration: Progress and Resentment in America's "Racial" Crisis* (Washington: Civitas, 1997); David R. Roediger, *Colored White: Transcending the Racial Past* (Berkeley and Los Angeles: Univ. of California Press, 2002); Michael K. Brown, et al., *Whitewashing Race: The Myth of a Color-blind Society* (Berkeley and Los Angeles: Univ. of California Press, 2003).

6. Richard Nixon, "The Philosophy of Government," Oct. 21, 1972, *WC*, 1546–48; Nixon, "Remarks at a Reception in Atlanta," Oct. 12, 1972, *WC*, 1512–15.

7. Kevin P. Phillips, *The Emerging Republican Majority* (New Rochelle, N.Y.: Arlington House, 1969); Dan T. Carter, *The Politics of Rage: George Wallace, the Origins of the New Conservatism, and the Transformation of American Politics* (New York: Simon and Schuster, 1995); Carter, *From George Wallace to Newt Gingrich: Race in the Conservative Counterrevolution, 1963–1994* (Baton Rouge: Louisiana State Univ. Press, 1996); Joseph A. Aistrup, *The Southern Strategy Revisited: Republican Top-Down Advancement in the South* (Lexington: Univ. Press of Kentucky, 1996); Peter Applebome, *Dixie Rising: How the South Is Shaping American Values, Politics, and Culture* (New York: Harcourt Brace, 1996); Thomas Byrne Edsall with Mary D. Edsall, *Chain Reaction: The Impact of Race, Rights, and Taxes on American Politics* (New York: Norton, 1991).

8. Bruce J. Schulman, *The Seventies: The Great Shift in American Culture, Society, and Politics* (New York: Free Press, 2001); Earl Black and Merle Black, *Politics and Society in the South* (Cambridge: Harvard Univ. Press, 1987); Numan V. Bartley and Hugh D. Graham, *Southern Politics and the Second Reconstruction* (Baltimore: Johns Hopkins Univ. Press, 1975); Jack Bass and Walter De Vries, *The Transformation of Southern Politics: Social Change and Political Consequence since 1945*, 2d ed. (Athens: Univ. of Georgia Press, 1995); David Lublin, *The Republican South: Democratization and Partisan Change* (Princeton: Princeton Univ. Press, 2004); Alexander P. Lamis, *The Two-Party South* (New York: Oxford Univ. Press, 1984).

9. Thomas J. Sugrue, *The Origins of the Urban Crisis: Race and Inequality in Postwar Detroit* (Princeton: Princeton Univ. Press, 1996); Arnold R. Hirsch, *Making the Second Ghetto: Race and Housing in Chicago, 1940–1960* (Cambridge: Cambridge Univ. Press, 1983); Jonathan Rieder, *Canarsie: The Jews and Italians of Brooklyn against Liberalism* (Cambridge: Harvard Univ. Press, 1985); Ronald P. Formisano, *Boston against Busing: Race, Class, and Ethnicity in the 1960s and 1970s* (Chapel Hill: Univ. of North Carolina Press, 1991); J. Anthony Lukas, *Common Ground: A Turbulent Decade in the Lives of Three American Families* (New York: Knopf, 1985); Kenneth D. Durr, *Behind the Backlash: White Working-Class Politics in Baltimore, 1940–1980* (Chapel Hill: Univ. of North Carolina Press, 2003). Stanley B. Greenberg adopts a suburban perspective on the "Reagan Democrats" in *Middle Class Dreams: The Politics and Power of the New American Majority* (New Haven: Yale Univ. Press, 1996), rev. and updated edition. On recent trends in political history, see Steve Fraser and Gary Gerstle, eds., *The Rise and Fall of the New Deal Order, 1930–1980* (Princeton: Princeton Univ. Press, 1989); Meg Jacobs, William J. Novak, and Julian E. Zelizer, eds., *The Democratic Experiment: New Directions in American Political History* (Princeton: Princeton Univ. Press, 2003).

10. The best accounts of Sunbelt conservatism are Lisa McGirr, *Suburban Warriors: The Origins of the New American Right* (Princeton: Princeton Univ. Press, 2001); Rick Perlstein, *Before the Storm: Barry Goldwater and the Unmaking of the American Consensus* (New York: Hill and Wang, 2001); Mary C. Brennan, *Turning Right in the Sixties: The Conservative Capture of the GOP* (Chapel Hill: Univ. Of North Carolina Press, 1995); William C. Martin, *With God on Our Side: The Rise of the Religious Right in America* (New York: Broadway, 1996). My emphasis on a suburban political culture that is broader than the story of the New Right follows in the tradition of Mike Davis, *City of Quartz: Excavating the Future in Los Angeles* (London: Verso, 1990); Peter Schrag, *Paradise Lost: California's Experience, America's Future* (Berkeley and Los Angeles: Univ. of California Press, 1999); Robert O. Self, *American Babylon: Race and the Struggle for Postwar Oakland* (Princeton: Princeton University Press, 2003). For recent explorations of postwar consumer culture, see Lizabeth Cohen, *A Consumers' Republic: The Politics of Mass Consumption in Postwar America* (New York: Knopf, 2003); Meg Jacobs, *Pocketbook Politics: Economic Citizenship in Twentieth-Century America* (Princeton: Princeton University Press, 2004).

11. Michael Kazin, *The Populist Persuasion: An American History* (New York: Basic Books, 1995); David Brooks, *On Paradise Drive: How We Live Now (and Always Have) in the Future Tense* (New York: Simon and Schuster, 2004), 3.

12. Kenneth T. Jackson, *Crabgrass Frontier: The Suburbanization of the United States* (New York: Oxford Univ. Press, 1985), 290, 293; Carl Abbott, *The New Urban America: Growth and Politics in Sunbelt Cities* (Chapel Hill: Univ. of North Carolina Press, 1981), 184–85; Kevin M. Kruse, *White Flight: Atlanta and the Making of Modern Conservatism* (Princeton: Princeton Univ. Press, forthcoming); U.S. Commission on Civil Rights, *School Desegregation: The Courts and Suburban Migration* (Washington: GPO, 1975). The seminal work on school desegregation policy is Orfield, *Must We Bus?*

13. Sugrue, *Origins*, 9. Theoretical models of spatial analysis include Edward W. Soja, *Postmetropolis: Critical Studies of Cities and Regions* (Oxford: Blackwell, 2000); David Harvey, *Justice, Nature, and the Geography of Difference* (Oxford: Blackwell, 1996); Sharon Zukin, *Landscapes of Power: From Detroit to Disney World* (Berkeley and Los Angeles: Univ. of California Press, 1991).

14. On growth liberalism, see Alan Brinkley, *The End of Reform: New Deal Liberalism in Recession and War* (New York: Knopf, 1995); Robert M. Collins, *More: The Politics of Economic Growth in Postwar America* (New York: Oxford Univ. Press, 2000). On the rise of the Sunbelt, see Bruce J. Schulman, *From Cotton Belt to Sunbelt: Federal Policy, Economic Development, and the Transformation of the South, 1938–1980* (New York: Oxford Univ. Press, 1991); Ann Markusen, ed., *The Rise of the Gunbelt: The Military Remapping of Industrial America* (New York: Oxford Univ. Press, 1991); Sunbelt series in *NYT*, Feb. 8–12, 1976. For synthetic treatments of suburbanization, see Jackson, *Crabgrass Frontier*; Cohen, *Consumer's Republic*; Joel Garreau, *Edge City: Life on the New Frontier* (New York: Doubleday, 1991).

15. Numan V. Bartley, *The New South, 1945–1980* (Baton Rouge: Louisiana State Univ. Press, 1995); James C. Cobb, *The Selling of the South: The Southern Crusade for Industrial Development, 1936–1980* (Baton Rouge: Louisiana State Univ. Press, 1982); Bradley R. Rice, "If Dixie Were Atlanta," in *Sunbelt Cities: Politics and*

Growth since World War II, ed. Richard M. Bernard and Bradley R. Rice (Austin: Univ. of Texas Press, 1983), 37.

16. David R. Goldfield, *Black, White, and Southern: Race Relations and Southern Culture, 1940 to the Present* (Baton Rouge: Louisiana State Univ. Press, 1990); Elizabeth Jacoway and David R. Colburn, eds., *Southern Businessmen and Desegregation* (Baton Rouge: Louisiana State Univ. Press, 1982); J. Douglas Smith, *Managing White Supremacy: Race, Politics and Citizenship in Jim Crow Virginia* (Chapel Hill: Univ. of North Carolina Press, 2002). The Sunbelt Synthesis framework is deeply indebted to William H. Chafe's concept of the "Progressive Mystique," although my exploration of residential segregation expands on his model; see *Civilities and Civil Rights: Greensboro, North Carolina, and the Black Struggle for Freedom* (New York: Oxford Univ. Press, 1980). The postwar Sunbelt Synthesis represented an updated version of the original New South ideology of the late 1800s; see Paul M. Gaston, *The New South Creed: A Study in Southern Mythmaking* (New York: Knopf, 1970); Edward L. Ayers, *The Promise of the New South: Life after Reconstruction* (New York: Oxford Univ. Press, 1992).

17. On municipal politics, see J. Mills Thornton III, *Dividing Lines: Municipal Politics and the Struggle for Civil Rights in Montgomery, Birmingham, and Selma* (Tuscaloosa: Univ. of Alabama Press, 2002); Ronald H. Bayor, *Race and the Shaping of Twentieth-Century Atlanta* (Chapel Hill: Univ. of North Carolina Press, 1996); Chafe, *Civilities*.

18. Abbott, *New Urban America*; Bernard and Rice, *Sunbelt Cities*; David C. Perry and Alfred J. Watkins, eds., *The Rise of the Sunbelt Cities* (Beverly Hills: Sage, 1977).

19. David L. Chappell, *Inside Agitators: White Southerners in the Civil Rights Movement* (Baltimore: Johns Hopkins Univ. Press, 1994). Scholars have conducted a lively debate about the meaning and the impact of *Brown*. For an introduction, see James T. Patterson, *Brown v. Board of Education: A Civil Rights Milestone and Its Troubled Legacy* (New York: Oxford Univ. Press, 2001); Derrick Bell, *Silent Covenants: Brown v. Board of Education and the Unfulfilled Hopes for Racial Reform* (New York: Oxford Univ. Press, 2004); Michael J. Klarman, *From Jim Crow to Civil Rights: The Supreme Court and the Struggle for Racial Equality* (New York: Oxford Univ. Press, 2004).

20. *RNO*, Oct. 21, 1972; Randall M. Miller and George E. Pozzetta eds., *Shades of the Sunbelt: Essays on Ethnicity, Race, and the Urban South* (New York: Greenwood, 1988).

21. V. O. Key, Jr., *Southern Politics in State and Nation*, new ed. (Knoxville: Univ. of Tennessee Press, 1984), 11; John Egerton, *The Americanization of Dixie: The Southernization of America* (New York: Harper's Magazine Press, 1974), 20; Black and Black, *Politics and Society*, 34–43. On political change, also see Dewey W. Grantham, *The Life and Death of the Solid South: A Political History* (Lexington: Univ. Press of Kentucky, 1988); Earl Black and Merle Black, *The Rise of Southern Republicans* (Cambridge: Harvard Univ. Press, 2002). On the relationship between urban/metropolitan growth and regional transformation, see David R. Goldfield, *Cotton Fields and Skyscrapers: Southern City and Region, 1607–1980* (Baton Rouge: Louisiana State Univ. Press, 1982); Goldfield, *Region, Race, and Cities: Interpreting the Urban South* (Baton Rouge: Louisiana State Univ. Press, 1997).

22. Black and Black, *Politics and Society*, 12–14. On electoral trends, see Gordon E. Baker, *The Reapportionment Revolution: Representation, Political Power, and the Supreme Court* (New York: Random House, 1966); Bernard Grofman, *Voting Rights, Voting Wrongs: The Legacy of Baker v. Carr* (New York: Priority Press, 1990); Steven F. Lawson, *Black Ballots: Voting Rights in the South, 1944–1969* (New York: Columbia Univ. Press, 1976); Lawson, *In Pursuit of Power: Southern Blacks and Electoral Politics, 1965–1982* (New York: Columbia Univ. Press, 1985); Chandler Davidson and Bernard Grofman, eds., *Quiet Revolution in the South: The Impact of the Voting Rights Act, 1965–1990* (Princeton: Princeton Univ. Press, 1994).

23. *NYT*, Sept. 4, 1963; *Bell v. School City of Gary*, 324 F.2d 209 (1963); *Downs v. Board of Education*, 336 F.2d 988 (1964); *Deal v. Cincinnati Board of Education*, 369 F.2d 55 (1966); Civil Rights Act of 1964 <http://usinfo.state.gov/usa/infousa/laws/majorlaw/civilr19.htm>; Sugrue, *Origins*, 224–29; Self, *American Babylon*, 260–72.

24. Nixon, "President's News Conference," July 20, 1970, *WC*, 967; *NYT*, March 10, 1970.

25. Benjamin Green Braswell to Virginia Crockford, May 5, 1970, Robert C. Hall, Jr., to David E. Satterfield III, April 6, 1972, box 1, VC/VCU.

CHAPTER 1: THE DIVIDED SOUTH

1. Muse Memo, July 3, 1959, reel 56, frames 1179–80, SRC/UMI (hereinafter cited as 56:1179–80, SRC/UMI); *SSN*, Oct. 1958, Feb. 1959. On the history of the SRC, see Morton Sosna, *In Search of the Silent South: Southern Liberals and the Race Issue* (New York: Columbia Univ. Press, 1977); John T. Kneebone, *Southern Liberal Journalists and the Issue of Race, 1920–1944* (Chapel Hill: Univ. of North Carolina Press, 1985); John Egerton, *Speak Now against the Day: The Generation before the Civil Rights Movement in the South* (New York: Knopf, 1994).

2. Muse, "The Southern Leadership Project—after Five Months," Sept. 1, 1959, 56:0827, Muse Arkansas Memo, July 6, 1959, 56:1181-82, SRC/UMI; *Arkansas Gazette*, March 1, 3, 1959; Nat Griswold, "Arkansans Organize for Public Schools," *NS* (June 1959), 3–7; "Chamber of Commerce Seeks Open Schools," *NS* (June 1959), 8–10.

3. WEC, "Policy and Purpose," Sept. 1959, 74:1728, "What Is the Women's Emergency Committee?" n.d., 74:1727, "Little Rock Report: The City, Its People, Its Business, 1957–1959," Aug. 1959, 74:1651–1727, SRC/UMI; Griswold, "Arkansans Organize for Public Schools," 3–7; *SSN*, Sept. 1959.

4. Harry Ashmore, "The Easy Chair: The Untold Story behind Little Rock," *HM* (June 1958), 10–19; Chappell, *Inside Agitators*.

5. SRC, "News Release," Dec. 6, 1959, 9:0307–10, SRC/UMI.

6. James C. Cobb, *Industrialization and Southern Society, 1877–1984* (Lexington: Univ. Press of Kentucky, 1984); Gavin Wright, *Old South, New South: Revolutions in the Southern Economy since the Civil War* (New York: Basic Books, 1986).

7. Bartley and Graham, *Southern Politics*, 81–110; Lawson, *Black Ballots*; Baker, *Reapportionment Revolution*.

8. Key, *Southern Politics*; Black and Black, *Politics and Society*.

9. "Toward the South of the Future: A Statement of Policy and Aims of the Southern Regional Council," *NS* (Dec. 1951), 1–2; Numan V. Bartley, *The Rise of Massive Resistance: Race and Politics in the South during the 1950's* (Baton Rouge: Louisiana State Univ. Press, 1969); Richard Kluger, *Simple Justice: The History of Brown v. Board of Education and Black America's Struggle for Equality* (New York: Vintage, 1975); Cobb, *Selling*; Neil R. McMillen, *The Citizens' Council: Organized Resistance to the Second Reconstruction, 1954–1964* (Urbana: Univ. of Illinois Press, 1971).

10. Bartley, *New South*, 187–260.

11. Gaston, *New South Creed*.

12. C. Vann Woodward, *The Strange Career of Jim Crow*, 3d rev. ed. (New York: Oxford Univ. Press, 1974), 165–66; Walter A. Jackson, "White Liberal Intellectuals, Civil Rights and Gradualism, 1954–1960," in *The Making of Martin Luther King and the Civil Rights Movement*, ed. Brian Ward and Tony Badger (New York: New York Univ. Press, 1996), 102; Martin Luther King, Jr., "The Negro Is Your Brother," *AM* (Aug. 1963), 78–88.

13. *WP*, Feb. 10, June 1, 1952, Nov. 28, 1954, Feb. 5, 1956, March 24, Aug. 25, Oct. 13, 1957; Benjamin Muse, "The Durability of Harry Flood Byrd," *Reporter* (Oct. 3, 1957), 26–30; Muse, "Virginia: How Long Can Defiance Last?," *TNR* (Jan. 23, 1956), 10–11; Muse, "Byrd's 'Massive Resistance,'" *Nation* (Sept. 20, 1958), 150–52; Muse, Speech to Charlottesville Council on Human Relations, July 20, 1957, box 3, MUSE/UVA.

14. *WP*, Sept. 9, 1956; Benjamin Muse, "The NAACP's Responsibility," *TNR* (April 2, 1956), 80–10; Muse, "The Submerged Moderates," *TNR* (May 28, 1956), 14–15.

15. William M. Lightsey, "Organizing to Save Public Schools," 71:1899–1932, SRC/UMI; Matthew D. Lassiter and Andrew B. Lewis, eds., *The Moderates' Dilemma: Massive Resistance to School Desegregation in Virginia* (Charlottesville: Univ. Press of Virginia, 1998).

16. Lightsey, "Organizing to Save Public Schools"; "Special Report: Background Summary on Charlottesville, Arlington, Norfolk, and Newport News," Aug. 11, 1958, 220:0947–70, "A Public Petition to the Norfolk City Council," n.d., 71:1869, Lightsey to Harold C. Fleming, March 10, 1959, 71:1820–26, SRC/UMI; Muse, Speech to Charlottesville Council on Human Relations; John C. Jeffries, Jr., *Justice Lewis F. Powell, Jr.* (New York: Charles Scribner's Sons, 1994), 145–52; James H. Hershman, Jr., "A Rumbling in the Museum: The Opponents of Virginia's Massive Resistance" (Ph.D. diss., Univ. of Virginia, 1977).

17. VCPS, "Report on the School Situation," Jan. 9, 1959, 71:1797–1801, "Questions and Answers," March 20, 1959, 71:1864–65, "Summary of Legislative Activity," April 30, 1959, 71:1856–60, SRC/UMI; Lightsey, "Organizing to Save Public Schools."

18. *WP*, Jan. 8, 1956, Sept. 21, 1958, Feb. 15, 1959; J. Harvie Wilkinson III, *Harry Byrd and the Changing Face of Virginia Politics, 1945–1966* (Charlottesville: Univ. Press of Virginia, 1968); Robert A. Pratt, *The Color of Their Skin: Education and Race in Richmond, Virginia, 1954–1989* (Charlottesville: Univ. Press of Virginia, 1992).

19. "Resistance Growing to School Closings," *NS* (Nov. 1958), 3–7; Lorin A. Thompson, "Virginia Education Crisis and Its Economic Aspects," *NS* (Feb. 1959),

3–8; "Desegregation—or No Public Schools," *NS* (March 1959), 3–6; Benjamin Muse, *Virginia's Massive Resistance* (Bloomington: Indiana Univ. Press, 1961), 175–77.

20. Muse, "The Southern Leadership Project—after Five Months," Sept. 1, 1959, 56:1489–93, "Research Reports," April 10, 1959, 56:1062–63, L-2 through L-13, 221:0878–0932, Muse Memo, April 10, 1959, 56:1062–63, "Effective Services Rendered by SRC," n.d., 56:0653, SRC/UMI; Chappell, *Inside Agitators*, 190–95; Leslie W. Dunbar to the author, May 11, 1994.

21. Muse Florida Memos, 56:1197–1203, Tennessee Memos, 56:1353–63, Atlanta Memos, 56:1067–74, Muse to Boyd Ridgeway, Aug. 31, 1959, 56:1695, SRC/UMI; Bartley, *New South*, 213–20.

22. Muse to James M. Dabbs, June 8, 1959, 56:0759–61, Muse Sit-In Memos, 56:1077–90, 1193–96, 1301–20, 1390–94, 1770–71, SRC/UMI; Leslie W. Dunbar, "The Annealing of the South," *Virginia Quarterly Review* (Autumn 1961), 499–502.

23. Muse New Orleans Memos, 56:1205–16, 1737–38, Mrs. Moise S. Cahn to Paul Rilling, Nov. 10, 1959, Rilling to Cahn, Nov. 16, 1959, SOS, "Our Stake in New Orleans Schools: A Study of Education and Economics," Aug. 1, 1960, 137:1675–94, "Close Our Schools?" 137:1876–85, SOS Pamphlet, 1960, "A Statement by Clergymen of New Orleans," July 16, 1960, 137:1671–73, SRC/UMI; Adam Fairclough, *Race and Democracy: The Civil Rights Struggle in Louisiana, 1915–1972* (Athens: Univ. of Georgia Press, 1995), 234–64.

24. Muse Alabama Memos, 56:1094–96, 1132–76, SRC/UMI.

25. Muse Mississippi Memos, 56:1097–1101, 1222–94, SRC/UMI; James W. Silver, *Mississippi: The Closed Society* (New York: Harcourt, Brace, and World, 1964); Pat Watters and Reese Cleghorn, *Climbing Jacob's Ladder: The Arrival of Negroes in Southern Politics* (New York: Harcourt, Brace, and World, 1967); Benjamin Muse, *Ten Years of Prelude: The Story of Integration since the Supreme Court's 1954 Decision* (New York: Viking, 1964); Muse, *The American Negro Revolution: From Nonviolence to Black Power, 1963–1967* (Bloomington: Indiana Univ. Press, 1968).

26. Bartley, *Massive Resistance*, 342–43 (first quotation); *RNL*, August 27, 1963 (Kilpatrick); Pat Watters, *The South and the Nation* (New York: Pantheon, 1969), 239–41; Calvin Trillin, "Reflections: Remembrance of Moderates Past," *NY* (March 21, 1977), 85–97. More recently, Bartley has written that "metropolitan elites emerged as the arbiters of the regional political agenda" in the wake of the massive resistance era; see *New South*, 260.

27. Davidson and Grofman, *Quiet Revolution*; Grofman, *Voting Rights*.

28. Florence Robin, "Transition without Tragedy: A Community Preparation Handbook," Dec. 1963, 219:0306–0437, Dunbar, "Report of Program Activities," 1964, 6:2020–43, ABLE, "Keep Mobile Schools Open," n.d., 137:1887–92, Paul Anthony, ABLE Memos, 59:0431–38, SRC/UMI. Quotations from Cobb, *Industrialization*, 111; Elizabeth Jacoway, "An Introduction: Civil Rights and the Changing South," in Jacoway and Colburn, *Southern Businessmen*, 9. On the business thesis, also see Bartley, *Massive Resistance*, 315–39; Goldfield, *Black, White, and Southern*, 118–48.

29. Dunbar, "Report of Program Activities"; Leslie W. Dunbar, *A Republic of Equals* (Ann Arbor: Univ. of Michigan Press, 1966).

30. Muse, Speech to Fairfax County Unitarian Center, May 29, 1955, Speech to Alexandria LWV, April 16, 1955, box 3, MUSE/UVA; "The Southern Regional Council—Its Origins and Aims," 221:0876–77, SRC/UMI; *Statistical Summary of School Segregation-Desegregation in the Southern and Border States, 1964–65* (Nashville: SERS, 1964), 2–3.

31. Dunbar, "Report of Program Activities."

CHAPTER 2: HOPE IN THE NEW SOUTH

1. Nan Pendergrast Interview, June 24, 1992, GGDP, 58, 61; Pendergrast biographical information, box 1, NP/RWW; Joseph F. Thompson and Robert Isbell, *Atlanta: A City of Neighborhoods* (Columbia: Univ. of South Carolina Press, 1994); Susan Kessler Barnard, *Buckhead: A Place for All Time* (Athens, Ga.: Hill Street Press, 1996); Garreau, *Edge City*, 139–78.

2. Pendergrast Interview, 63.

3. Gaston, *New South Creed*; Frederick Allen, *Atlanta Rising: The Invention of an International City, 1946–1996* (Atlanta: Longstreet Press, 1996).

4. David L. Sjoquist, "The Atlanta Paradox: Introduction," in *The Atlanta Paradox*, ed. David L. Sjoquist (New York: Russell Sage Foundation, 2000), 1–2. My thinking about urban ecology and metropolitan space is indebted to Soja, *Postmetropolis*; Davis, *City of Quartz*; Charles Rutheiser, *Imagineering Atlanta: The Politics of Place in the City of Dreams* (New York: Verso, 1996).

5. William A. Emerson, Jr., "Surge in the South: The Long Reach of Atlanta," *Newsweek* (March 15, 1954), 59–62; Seymour Freedgood, "Life in Buckhead," *Fortune* (Sept. 1961), 108–12, 180–90; *AC*, Jan. 1, 1960; Rice, "If Dixie Were Atlanta," 31–40; Watters, *South and the Nation*, 138–43; Bartley, *New South*, 134–40; Harold H. Martin, *Atlanta and Environs: A Chronicle of Its People and Events; Years of Change and Challenge, 1940–1976*, vol. 3 (Athens: Univ. of Georgia Press, 1987); Larry Keating, *Atlanta: Race, Class, and Urban Expansion* (Philadelphia: Temple Univ. Press, 2001), 12.

6. Bayor, *Twentieth-Century Atlanta*, 29–30; Watters, *South and the Nation*, 215; Harold H. Martin, *William Berry Hartsfield: Mayor of Atlanta* (Athens: Univ. of Georgia Press, 1978); *NYT*, Sept. 29, 1961.

7. Clarence N. Stone, *Regime Politics: Governing Atlanta, 1946–1988* (Lawrence: Univ. Press of Kansas, 1989); Floyd Hunter, *Community Power Structure: A Study of Decision Makers* (Chapel Hill: Univ. of North Carolina Press, 1953); Gary M. Pomerantz, *Where Peachtree Meets Sweet Auburn: The Saga of Two Families and the Making of Atlanta* (New York: Scribner, 1996); Bayor, *Twentieth-Century Atlanta*, 17–29; Watters, *South and the Nation*, 215; Chafe, *Civilities*, 8.

8. Numan V. Bartley, *From Thurmond to Wallace: Political Tendencies in Georgia, 1948–1968* (Baltimore: Johns Hopkins Univ. Press, 1970), 47; Stone, *Regime Politics*, 25–30; Bayor, *Twentieth-Century Atlanta*, 29–32.

9. Metropolitan Planning Commission, *Up Ahead: A Regional Land Use Plan for Metropolitan Atlanta* (1952), 51–61; Metropolitan Planning Commission, *Atlanta Standard Metropolitan Statistical Area: Population—Housing* (1960), 27–30; Bayor,

Twentieth-Century Atlanta, 53–92; Stone, *Regime Politics*, 25–42; Samuel L. Adams, "Blueprint for Segregation: A Survey of Atlanta Housing," *NS* (Spring 1967), 73–84.

10. Metropolitan Planning Commission, *Up Ahead*, 88–90; Kruse, *White Flight*.

11. *Plan of Improvement for the Governments of Atlanta and Fulton County, Georgia* (1950); William Hartsfield, Speech to Buckhead Civitan Club, March 24, 1941, box 29, WBH/RWW; Bradley R. Rice, "The Battle for Buckhead: The Plan of Improvement and Atlanta's Last Big Annexation," *Atlanta Historical Society Journal* (Winter 1981), 5–22; Stone, *Regime Politics*, 30–35; Bayor, *Twentieth-Century Atlanta*, 85–87.

12. Hartsfield quoted in Bayor, *Twentieth-Century Atlanta*, 87.

13. "The County Unit System," *GV* (April 1959), box 1, HOPE/AHC; Georgia LWV, "Is It a Mystery to You? The County Unit System," 1959, box 16, EP/RWW; *AC*, Nov. 30, 1960; Key, *Southern Politics*, 117–24; Numan V. Bartley, *The Creation of Modern Georgia*, 2d ed. (Athens: Univ. of Georgia Press, 1990), 161–78, 224–25.

14. Key, *Southern Politics*, 106–29.

15. "LWV of Georgia—1920–1957," *GV* (April 1957), box 21, EP/RWW; James Mackay Interview, March 31, 1986, GGDP, 1–9; Bartley, *Creation*, 193–201; Harold P. Henderson, "Ellis Arnall and the Politics of Progress," in *Georgia Governors in an Age of Change: From Ellis Arnall to George Busbee*, ed. Harold P. Henderson and Gary L. Roberts (Athens: Univ. of Georgia Press, 1988), 25–39.

16. Harold P. Henderson, *The Politics of Change in Georgia: A Political Biography of Ellis Arnall* (Athens: Univ. of Georgia Press, 1991), 171–89; Bartley, *Creation*, 201–7; Bartley, *Thurmond to Wallace*, 28; Robert Sherrill, *Gothic Politics in the Deep South: Stars of the New Confederacy* (New York: Ballantine, 1969), 41–78.

17. LWV Press Release, Sept. 7, 1950, box 5, "Brief History of Matters Affecting the County Unit Fight," box 16, EP/RWW; *AC*, n.d. [1952], folder 16, box 5, FFP/RWW; Bartley, *Thurmond to Wallace*, 22–23.

18. "1951–61—Decade of Decision: The League and the Schools," *Facts* (Oct. 1961); *AC*, Nov. 2, 1954; Gary L. Roberts, "Tradition and Consensus: An Introduction to Gubernatorial Leadership in Georgia, 1943–1983," in Henderson and Roberts, *Georgia Governors*, 8.

19. "Georgia's Schools: Public or Private?" *GV* (Feb. 1954), box 21, EP/RWW; Georgia LWV, "The Private School Amendment," 1954, folder 13, Atlanta LWV Newsletter, Oct. 1954, folder 7, box 5, FFP/RWW; *AJC*, Oct. 17, 31, 1954; *AJ*, Oct. 26, 1954; *AC*, Nov. 2, 1954.

20. *AC*, Nov. 2–5, 1954, Jan. 26, 1956; Bartley, *Thurmond to Wallace*, 22–23, 41; Osgood Williams Interview, June 6, 1988, GGDP, 30–31; "LWV of Georgia—1920–1957."

21. LWV, "This Is What We Mean and Think You Mean," 1954, folder 7, box 5, FFP/RWW; Charles Pyles, "S. Ernest Vandiver and the Politics of Change," in Henderson and Roberts, *Georgia Governors*, 144–47.

22. HOPE Minutes, Jan. 7, 1959, 212:1457, Policy Statement, Jan. 1959, 212:1399, SRC/UMI.

23. HOPE Minutes, Dec. 17, 1958, 212:1453, Press Release, Jan. 19, 1959, 212:1747–48, SRC/UMI; *AC*, Dec. 15, 1958; "Organized Hope," *Time* (March 16, 1959), 71–72; Gerald Walker, "How Women Won the Quiet Battle of Atlanta," *Good*

Housekeeping (May 1962), 76–77, 194–96, 202; Florence B. Robin, "Honeychile at the Barricades," *HM* (Oct. 1962), 175; "Around Town" column, n.d., folder 6, box 1, NP/RWW; Pendergrast Interview, 71–73; Hamilton and Muriel Lokey Interview, Jan. 26, 1989, GGDP, 55–63.

24. Atlanta LWV Minutes, Nov. 25, 1958, box 21, EP/RWW; HOPE Minutes, Dec. 9, 1958, 212:1455–56, April 30, 1959, 212:1463, Grace Hamilton, "The Beginning of HOPE: The Story of the Struggle for Open Schools in Georgia," April 1960, 137:1783–87, Hamilton, "A Record of Process—Community Preparation for Desegregation of Public Schools in Atlanta, Georgia," July 28, 1961, 213:0267, Harold C. Fleming to Harry Boyte, Feb. 13, 1959, 212:0011, SRC/UMI; Pendergrast Interview, 65, 72–75, 80; Lokey Interview, 17, 64–78.

25. HOPE Incorporation Petition, Dec. 12, 1958, 212:1377–80, SRC/UMI; Lokey Interview; Pendergrast Interview, 71; Pendergrast biographical information, box 1, NP/RWW; Walker, "How Women Won the Quiet Battle of Atlanta"; 1959 editions of the *Atlanta, Georgia, City Directory* and *Atlanta, Georgia, Suburban Directory*.

26. Pendergrast Interview, 61; Kathryn Nasstrom, "Women, the Civil Rights Movement, and the Politics of Historical Memory in Atlanta, 1946–1973" (Ph.D. diss., Univ. of North Carolina at Chapel Hill, 1993); Susan Lynn, *Progressive Women in Conservative Times: Racial Justice, Peace, and Feminism, 1945 to the 1960s* (New Brunswick, N.J.: Rutgers Univ. Press, 1992); Elaine Tyler May, *Homeward Bound: American Families in the Cold War Era* (New York: Basic Books, 1988); Louise M. Young, *In the Public Interest: The League of Women Voters, 1920–1970* (New York: Greenwood, 1989).

27. HOPE pamphlet, Fall 1959, 212:1417–18, SRC/UMI. Metropolitan Planning Commission.

28. *Atlanta Standard Metropolitan Statistical Area: Population—Housing* (1960), 27–30; *AC*, Jan. 8–9, 13, 1959; Georgia Council of Churches, " 'Out of Conviction': A Second Statement on the South's Racial Crisis," Nov. 22, 1958, box 21, EP/RWW.

29. "Closing Public Schools Would Constitute Catastrophe," Dec. 21, 1958, folder 9, box 8, FFP/RWW; "Scientists' Statement," Dec. 10, 1958, 212:0001, SRC/UMI; *AJC*, Dec. 14, 1958, Feb. 1, 1959; Lokey Interview, 26.

30. Robert Stern to Hamilton Lokey, Dec. 13, 1958, box 1, HOPE/AHC; Frances Pauley Interview #1, April 11, 1988, GGDP, 24; Lokey Interview, 58, 65–69; Pendergrast Interview, 73–75; *AC*, Feb. 17, 1960. On the integration of the LWV, see *AJ*, March 31, 1956; Sara Mitchell Parsons, *From Southern Wrongs to Civil Rights: The Memoir of a White Civil Rights Activist* (Tuscaloosa: Univ. of Alabama Press, 2000), 18–27.

31. HOPE Minutes, Dec. 14, 1958, 212:1454, Dec. 29, 1958, 212:1452, Policy Committee Plan, Dec. 18, 1958, 212:1391–92, Publicity Committee Plan, Dec. 22, 1958, 212:1433–36, Speakers' Bureau Report, April 27, 1959, 212:1784, SRC/UMI.

32. *AC*, Jan. 12, 14, 16, 1959.

CHAPTER 3: THE OPEN-SCHOOLS MOVEMENT

1. Tower Rally Program, March 4, 1959, 212:1762–64, Leaflet, 212:1772, Mrs. Gordon Wilson speech, 212:1765–69, Press Release, n.d., 212:1745, SRC/UMI; *AC*,

March 5–6, 1959; *Time* (March 16, 1959), 71–72; Pendergrast Interview, 66–67; Pauley Interview #1, 58–59.

2. "Here's How You Can Help Spread *HOPE!*," 1959, 212:1763, "Progress Report," 1959, 212:1443, HOPE Minutes, April 19, 1959, 212:1461–62, Aug. 6, 1959, 212:1481, Lucile Kennan to Frances Pauley, March 17, 1959, 212:0069–74, SRC/UMI.

3. State Advisory Board correspondence, 212:1827–1900, Press Release, n.d., 212:1750–51, HOPE-businessmen correspondence, 212:0019–0075, Ivan Allen to Fran Breeden, Sept. 18, 1959, 212:1848, HOPE Minutes, Aug. 13, 1959, 212:1483, SRC/UMI.

4. Harry Boyte to Jack Adair, March 18, 1959, 212:0076, HOPE Minutes, Oct. 1, 1959, 212:1495, Press Release, Oct. 28, 1959, 212:1649, SRC/UMI; *AC*, Nov. 5, Dec. 8, 1959; Pendergrast Interview, 78–79.

5. HOPE Minutes, June 4, 1959, 212:1470, June 11, 1959, 212:1471, Press Release, June 8, 1959, 212:1627–28, Newspaper advertisement, 212:1629, Radio transcripts, 212:1650–53, SRC/UMI; *AC*, June 8, 1959; WSB-TV, "The Last School Bell," box 24, EP/RWW.

6. Warren Cox to Muriel Lokey, Feb. 3, 1959, box 1, HOPE/AHC; Nathaniel Polster to Pauley, July 12, 1959, folder 7, box 6, FFP/RWW; HOPE Minutes, Sept. 10, 1959, 212:1488–89, Oct. 9, 1959, 212:1497–98, SRC/UMI; Eliza Paschall, "A Southern Point of View," *AM* (May 1960), 66–67.

7. James W. Dorsey, "There is 'HOPE' for the Public Schools," *Emory Alumnus* (Dec. 1959), 10–11, 37, folder 5, box 8, FFP/RWW; *AC*, Oct. 27, Dec. 2, 4, 8, 15, 1959.

8. HOPE Press Release, Dec. 14, 1959, 212:1668, SRC/UMI; *AC*, Dec. 15, 31, 1959; *AJ*, Dec. 14, 1959; *NYT*, Dec. 6, 1959.

9. "Save Our Schools Week" documents, 212:1658–67, HOPE Petition, Jan. 26, 1960, 212:1688–92, SRC/UMI; *AC*, Dec. 5–12, 1959; Helen Fuller, "Atlanta Is Different," *TNR* (Jan. 2, 1959), 8–11.

10. HOPE Minutes, Feb. 25, 1960, 212:1506, Press Release, Jan. 12, 1960, 212:1678–79, SRC/UMI; *AC*, Jan. 1, 5, 11–12, 1960.

11. *AC*, Dec. 16, 21–22, 1959, Feb. 8–9, 1960.

12. HOPE Minutes, Jan. 26, 1960, 212:1505, Press Release, Feb. 14, 1960, 212:1696–97, SRC/UMI; *Augusta Courier*, Feb. 22, 1960, box 2, HOPE/AHC; *AC*, Jan. 26, Feb. 2, 5–6, 1960.

13. HOPE Press Release, Feb. 14, 1960, 212:1696–97, SRC/UMI; *AC*, Jan. 9, 12–15, Feb. 17, 19, 1960.

14. *AC*, Jan. 17–19, Feb. 5, 1960.

15. HOPE Press Release, Feb. 8, 1960, 212:1694, SRC/UMI; *AC*, Jan. 22, Feb. 25, 1960; Griffin Bell Interview #1, June 12, 1990, GGDP, 31–37; Lokey Interview, 78–85; Trillin, "Remembrance of Moderates Past," 87–88; Allen, *Atlanta Rising*, 86–111.

16. *AC*, Feb. 18, March 4, 1960; Jeff Roche, *Restructured Resistance: The Sibley Commission and the Politics of Desegregation in Georgia* (Athens: Univ. of Georgia Press, 1998); Paul E. Mertz, " 'Mind Changing Time All Over Georgia': HOPE, Inc. and School Desegregation, 1958–1961," *Georgia Historical Quarterly* (Spring 1993), 41–61.

17. *AC*, March 4–22, 25, 1960.

18. "HOPE Statement for the Georgia Study Commission," March 23, 1960, 212:1704, HOPE Memo, March 1960, 212:1741, SRC/UMI; GACHR, "Notes and News," July 1961, box 1, EP/RWW; *AC*, March 24, April 1, 1960.

19. *AC*, April 1–2, 6, 21, 1960.

20. *AC*, April 28–29, 1960.

21. HOPE Press Release, April 28, 1960, 212:1707, HOPE Minutes, May 25, 1960, 212:1511, "HOPE Asks Some Unanswered Questions," Feb. 15, 1960, 212:1695, SRC/UMI; *AC*, April 29, 1960.

22. *AC*, April 30, May 10, 27, 1960.

23. CBS, *Who Speaks for the South?* broadcast May 27, 1960 (Films for the Humanities and Sciences, 2002); Georgia Open School Conference documents, 212:1708–12, 1910–57, SRC/UMI.

24. *HOPE Bulletin* (Fall 1960), folder 1, box 8, FFP/RWW; Georgia LWV, "Countdown for Schools," Fall 1960, box 21, EP/RWW; "Operation Last Chance" documents, 212:1589–1616, 1716–31, 1934–46, SRC/UMI; *AC*, Sept. 6–16, Oct. 10, 18–19, 1960.

25. HOPE Flyer, n.d., 212:1570, Mass Mailing, Nov. 28, 1960, 212:1569, Breeden to Ernest Vandiver, Nov. 11, 1960, 212:1731–32, SRC/UMI; *AC*, Nov. 11–15, 1960.

26. HOPE Minutes, Aug. 13, 1959, 212:1483–84, SRC/UMI; *AC*, Oct. 20, 24–28, Nov. 2, Dec. 13, 1960, March 8, 1961; Ivan Allen, Jr., *Mayor: Notes on the Sixties* (New York: Simon and Schuster, 1971), 34–42; Stone, *Regime Politics*, 52–55; David J. Garrow, ed., *Atlanta, Georgia, 1960–1961: Sit-ins and Student Activism* (Brooklyn, N.Y.: Carlson, 1989).

27. HOPE Minutes, Jan. 8, 1961, 212:1563, SRC/UMI; *AC*, Jan. 7–10, 1961; Bell Interview #1, 41.

28. HOPE, "Statement of Concern," Jan. 12, 1961, 212:1734–35, SRC/UMI; *AC*, Jan. 10–14, 1961; Calvin Trillin, *An Education in Georgia: The Integration of Charlayne Hunter and Hamilton Holmes* (New York: Viking, 1964).

29. HOPE Telegram, Jan. 17, 1961, 212:1737–39, SRC/UMI; W. C. Henson to Pauley, Jan. 25, 1961, folder 8, box 7, FFP/RWW; *AC*, Jan. 17–21, 28, Feb. 1, 1961.

30. Defenders of the governor include Charles Pyles, "S. Ernest Vandiver and the Politics of Change," in Henderson and Roberts, *Georgia Governors*, 143–56 (first quotation); Harold Paulk Henderson, *Ernest Vandiver: Governor of Georgia* (Athens: Univ. of Georgia Press, 2000), 237 (second quotation). Uncritical accounts of corporate leadership include Allen, *Atlanta Rising*, 86–111; Alton Hornsby, Jr., "A City That Was Too Busy to Hate: Atlanta Businessmen and Desegregation," in Jacoway and Colburn, *Southern Businessmen*, 120–36. For more nuanced versions that still primarily credit business leaders, see Bartley, *Creation*, 211–16; Stone, *Regime Politics*, 46–50; Roche, *Restructured Resistance*. For a critique of Atlanta's booster celebration of male leadership, see Nasstrom, "Politics of Historical Memory," 172–94.

31. Griffin Bell Interview #2, Sept. 19, 1990, GGDP, 10–11; Bell Interview #1, 30; *AC*, Jan. 12, Feb. 1, 1961.

32. *AC*, Nov, 29, 1960, Jan. 10, 21–23, 1961; Draft Statement by Atlanta Chamber of Commerce, Dec. 6, 1960, 137:1756, Open-Schools Newsletter, Dec. 1960, 212:1613, SRC/UMI.

CHAPTER 4: THE STRANGE CAREER OF ATLANTA EXCEPTIONALISM

1. HOPE Mailing, April 8, 1961, 212:1773, OASIS Proposal, May 15, 1961, 213:0140, OASIS Minutes, July 11, 1961, 213:0111–12, OASIS Mailing, July 13, 1961, 213:0104–05, SRC/UMI.

2. OASIS Minutes, July 11, 1961, 213:0111–12, Press Release, May 17, 1961, 213:0873–75, "The Purpose of OASIS," n.d., 213:0006–12, "History of OASIS," June 12, 1961, 213:0163–64, OASIS Membership, 212:1425, Memo to Supporters, June 1961, 213:0064, SRC/UMI.

3. "How Will Desegregation Affect Our Atlanta Public Schools?" n.d., 213: 0456–63, Discussion Sheet, May 22, 1961, 213:0048, OASIS Memo, June 1961, 213:0052, Report of Contingency Planning Committee, Aug. 17, 1961, 213:0751–52, Mass Mailing, Aug. 1, 1961, 213:0102, OASIS Minutes, Aug. 21, 1961, 213:0117–18, OASIS Memo, Aug. 29, 1961, 213:0202, Mass Meeting, Aug. 28, 1961, 213:0203, SRC/UMI; *AC*, Aug. 29–30, 1961; Separate Schools, Inc., Newsletter, April 1961, box 3, WBH/RWW.

4. GACHR Memo, June, Aug. 17, 1961, GACHR Minutes, July 11, 1961, box 1, OASIS, "Background: A Handbook for Reporters Covering the Desegregation of Atlanta's Public Schools," box 22, EP/RWW; Beverly Harris to Anne Sawyer, June 12, 1961, 213:0160, OASIS Minutes, Aug. 14, 1961, 213:0517–18, SRC/UMI; *AC*, May 1, 16, June 6, 14, July 7, 1961.

5. "Weekend of Prayer" documents, 213:0551–69, 0725–26, 0878–79, Press Release, Aug. 29, 1961, 213:1065, SRC/UMI; OASIS, "Background."

6. OASIS Memo, Aug. 18, 1961, 213:0753–54, SRC/UMI; *AC*, Aug. 30–31, Sept. 1–2, 16, 1961; *NYT*, Aug. 28, 31, 1961.

7. ABN Newscast, April 11, 1960, 212:1706, OASIS Mailing, July 13, 1961, 213:0104–05, SRC/UMI; Trillin, "Remembrance of Moderates Past," 85–97; *NYT*, Aug. 27, 31, 1961; "Integration: A Proud City," *Newsweek* (Sept. 11, 1961), 31–32; George H. Gallup, *The Gallup Poll: Public Opinion, 1935–1971* (New York: Random House, 1972), 1724.

8. *AC*, June 27, Sept. 14, 19, 21, 23, 1961; Bartley, *Thurmond to Wallace*, 47; Allen, *Mayor*, 43–63.

9. *AC*, March 8, Sept. 29, 1961; "Ivan Allen," *ST* (Sept. 1969), 8; Adams, "Blueprint for Segregation," 73–84; Stone, *Regime Politics*, 55–76; Allen, *Mayor*, 64–116; Bayor, *Twentieth-Century Atlanta*, 65–85.

10. Bartley, *Creation*, 222–23; Pyles, "S. Ernest Vandiver," 150–52; James F. Cook, *Carl Sanders: Spokesman of the New South* (Macon, Ga.: Mercer Univ. Press, 1993).

11. OASIS Minutes, Sept. 27, 1961, 213:0500, HOPE Minutes, Oct. 6, 1961, 212:1561, SRC/UMI; HOPE Mailing, Oct. 16, 1961, box 1, HOPE/AHC; *NYT*, July 2, 1961; Lokey Interview, 86–88; Pendergrast Interview, 92–94.

12. Lillian Smith, "Now, the Lonely Decision for Right or Wrong," *Life* (Oct. 12, 1962), 32; Lokey Interview, 65–66, 87–90; Pendergrast Interview, 41–43, 52, 87–88; Pauley Interview #1, 76–81.

13. Pendergrast Interview, 92–94.

14. Robin, "Honeychile at the Barricades," 173–77.

15. King, "Negro Is Your Brother," 78–88.

16. GACHR, "The Immorality of Racial Segregation," April 29, 1960, Press Release, Dec. 4, 1961, "Report on Atlanta School Desegregation," Dec. 7, 1961, Minutes, Feb. 14, April 11, Dec. 7, 1961, Jan. 8, 1963, Eliza Paschall to Samuel Williams, April 30, 1961, box 1, EP/RWW; *NYT*, Aug. 28, 1961; "Education: As the South Turns the Corner on Integration," *Newsweek* (Sept. 18, 1961), 71–73.

17. *AC*, Feb. 4, 9, June 20, Aug. 8–16, 1961; Trillin, *Education in Georgia*, 47–48; Parsons, *Southern Wrongs*, 73–90, 104–13.

18. Research Atlanta, "School Desegregation in Metro Atlanta, 1954–1973," folder 4, box 29, FFP/RWW; *NYT*, Aug. 27, 1962; Calvin Trillin, "U.S. Journal: Atlanta Settlement," *NY* (March 17, 1973), 101; Stone, *Regime Politics*, 103 (quotation); Bayor, *Twentieth-Century Atlanta*, 226–35.

19. HEW, "Atlanta Metropolitan School Enrollment, 1951–1973," folder 4, box 18, FFP/RWW; Research Atlanta, "School Desegregation"; Georgia LWV, "Report on Atlanta Schools," *Facts* (Feb. 1968), box 21, EP/RWW; Gary Orfield and Carole Ashkinaze, *The Closing Door: Conservative Policy and Black Opportunity* (Chicago: Univ. of Chicago Press, 1991), 103–12; *NYT*, Feb. 23, 1970; William Winn, "Atlanta: Schools Order Reveals a Crisis of Leadership," *ST* (Feb. 1970), 4–5.

20. *Calhoun v. Cook*, 332 F. Supp. 804 (1971), 806, 808; *WP*, Oct. 22, 1971; Research Atlanta, "School Desegregation"; Roger Mills, "The Atlanta School Case," folder 6, box 29, FFP/RWW.

21. Mills, "Atlanta School Case"; Research Atlanta, "Analysis of the Atlanta Compromise," March 18, 1973, folder 5, box 29, FFP/RWW; Trillin, "Atlanta Settlement," 101–5.

22. Pat Watters, "Atlanta's Questionable Compromise," *CC* (Aug. 29, 1973), 819–20; Vincent Harding, "The Atlanta Compromise: Other Questions, Other Hopes," *CC* (Oct. 3, 1973), 988–90; Trillin, "Atlanta Settlement," 101–5.

23. Gary Orfield, *Public School Desegregation in the United States, 1968–1980* (Washington: Joint Center for Political Studies, 1983), 22–31.

24. *AC*, Aug. 10, 1961; Allen, *Mayor*, 32–34, 145–64.

25. Freedgood, "Life in Buckhead," 108–14, 180–90; "Ivan Allen," *ST* (Sept. 1964), 8; Allen, *Mayor*, 145–46; Rutheiser, *Imagineering*, 49–50.

26. Roger M. Williams, "Saving Our Cities," *SR* (May 14, 1977), 6–11; William G. Conway, "The Case against Urban Dinosaurs," *SR* (May 14, 1977), 12–15; Rutheiser, *Imagineering*, 58–61, 161–66; *AC*, Sept. 8, 1971; *Report on the Relocation of Individuals, Families, and Businesses: Atlanta Community Improvement Program* (Atlanta: Eric Hill Associates, 1966); Rice, "If Dixie Were Atlanta," 53; Martin, *Atlanta and Environs*, 535–36; Allen, *Atlanta Rising*, 152–53. Also see Michael Sorkin, ed., *Variations on a Theme Park: The New American City and the End of Public Space* (New York: Hill and Wang, 1992).

27. Save Sandy Springs, "A Few Reasons Why Sandy Springs Should Vote *Against* Annexation," March 7, 1966, box 29, WBH/RWW; Annexation campaign coverage in *AC*, March 15–May 13, 1966; Bayor, *Twentieth-Century Atlanta*, 85–92; Abbot, *New Urban America*, 50–51, 174–75, 228–29; David R. Goldfield and Blaine A. Brownell, *Urban America: A History*, 2d ed. (Boston: Houghton Mifflin, 1990), 369, 406; Garreau, *Edge City*, 141–78.

28. Charles S. Rooks, "The Atlanta Elections of 1969," Voter Education Project Report, 220:0307–92, SRC/UMI; *AC*, Dec. 28–30, 1971; Allen, *Mayor*, 219–36; Stone, *Regime Politics*, 80–94.

29. *AC*, Nov. 6–8, 1968, Nov. 5–11, 1971; Bayor, *Twentieth-Century Atlanta*, 188–96; Stone, *Regime Politics*, 98–102; Abbott, *New Urban America*, 192–93; Applebome, *Dixie Rising*, 23–55; Robert D. Bullard, Glenn S. Johnson, and Angel O. Torres, eds., *Sprawl City: Race, Politics, and Planning in Atlanta* (Washington: Island Press, 2000).

30. "New Day A'Coming in the South," *Time* (May 31, 1971), 14–20; Letters To the Editor, *Time* (June 21, 1971), 2.

31. "A City in Crisis" series, *AC*, March 23–30, 1975.

32. Rutheiser, *Imagineering*, 65–66, 74–75.

33. *AJC*, June 16, 1996; Rutheiser, *Imagineering*, 62–110, 227–88; Black suburbanization in DeKalb series, *AJ*, May 26–29, 1980; Charles Jaret, Elizabeth P. Ruddiman, and Kurt Phillips, "The Legacy of Residential Segregation," in Bullard, Johnson, and Torres, *Sprawl City*, 111–38; Garreau, *Edge City*, 143–78. The expansion of the black middle class in Atlanta and in other metropolitan regions reflects the substantial progress accelerated by the civil rights movement, but the historical legacies and contemporary forces of racial inequality have continued to distinguish the experiences of many black suburbanites from their white counterparts, from educational resources to home equity to the persistence of residential segregation patterns beyond the city limits. See Andrew Wiese, *Places of Their Own: African American Suburbanization in the Twentieth Century* (Chicago: Univ. of Chicago Press, 2004).

34. Preston Quesenberry, "The Disposable Olympics Meets the City of Hype," *Southern Changes* (Summer 1996), 3–15; Rutheiser, *Imagineering*, 1–3, 13–14; *AJC*, June 16, 1996.

35. Buckhead Web <www.buckhead.org/>; BATMA <www.batma.org/>; Emily Graham, "Buckhead," *Creative Loafing*, April 18, 2001; Rutheiser, *Imagineering*, 122–29; *AJC*, March 23, 2001.

36. Georgia Department of Education, "1999–2000 Georgia Public Education Report Card" <http://accountability.doe.k12.ga.us/report2000/Educ/7610192.pdf>; *WP*, May 24, 1993.

CHAPTER 5: THE "CHARLOTTE WAY"

1. Robert M. Diggs to Richard Nixon, Jan. 31, 1970, folder 494, series 1.1, CRJ/SHC.

2. Community studies of busing in Charlotte include Davison M. Douglas, *Reading, Writing, and Race: The Desegregation of the Charlotte Schools* (Chapel Hill: Univ. of North Carolina Press, 1995); Frye Gaillard, *The Dream Long Deferred* (Chapel Hill: Univ. of North Carolina Press, 1988); Stephen Samuel Smith, *Boom for Whom? Education, Desegregation, and Development in Charlotte* (Albany: State Univ. of New York Press, 2004).

3. Pat Watters, "Charlotte" (Atlanta: SRC, 1964), 1–3, 12–14, 75–76; *CO*, May 20, 1971; "Enrollment in Charlotte-Mecklenburg Schools," folder 13, box 2, FG/SHC; Chamber of Commerce, "Research Report," 1972, folder 12, box 3, JLC/UNCC; *1970 Census of Population and Housing*.

4. *CO*, Aug. 22, 1969, Aug. 16, 1970, May 2, 1971; Howard Maniloff, "Busing No Longer Bothers Charlotte," *ST* (Jan.–Feb. 1973), 8; Thomas W. Hanchett, *Sorting*

Out the New South City: Race, Class, and Urban Development in Charlotte, 1875–1975 (Chapel Hill: Univ. of North Carolina Press, 1998), 145–81, 201–56.

5. *CO*, March 8, 1970, May 2, 1971; Watters, *Charlotte*, 3–6, 32–41.

6. *1970 Census of Population and Housing*; *CO*, July 7, 1970, June 10, July 6, 1971; Hanchett, *New South City*.

7. *CO*, May 13, 27, 1971; Margaret Claiborne, "The History and Organization of the Charlotte-Mecklenburg School System, 1957–1984," folder 15, box 2, FG/SHC; Charlotte Annexation Table, 1960–2004, provided by Charlotte–Mecklenburg Planning Commission.

8. *CO*, Jan. 30, 1970; Watters, "Charlotte," 3–13, 26–32, 45–52, 77; Gaillard, *Deferred*, 3–12.

9. Watters, "Charlotte," 3, 7–13, 21–32, 60–62, 70–91.

10. Watters, "Charlotte," 15–21, 32–44; NAACP Petition, June 3, 1968, folder 26, box 28, KMA/UNCC.

11. CRC Symposium, "Can Charlotte Have a Race Riot?" Nov. 8, 1966, folder 5, box 39, FDA/UNCC; Paul Leonard, "A Working Paper: Charlotte, an Equalization of Power through Unified Action," April 22, 1970, folder 19, box 3, JLC/UNCC; Watters, "Charlotte," 81–84.

12. CRC Report, 1968, folder 12, box 1, CRC/UNCC.

13. On the myth/paradox trope, see Key, *Southern Politics*, 205–28; Bass and De Vries, *Transformation*, 218–47; Thad L. Beyle and Merle Black, eds., *Politics and Policy in North Carolina* (New York: MSS, 1975). My interpretation of metropolitan moderation in North Carolina as a coherent synthesis rather than a paradox builds on Chafe's "progressive mystique" thesis in *Civilities and Civil Rights*.

14. NAACP Petition, Sept. 1, 1955, folder 18, box 30, Memo, March 29, 1957, folder 21, box 30, KMA/UNCC; "Desegregation of Charlotte-Mecklenburg Schools," folder 13, box 2, FG/SHC; Julius Chambers to Kelly Alexander, Nov. 23, 1964, folder 13, box 3, JLC/UNCC; Watters, "Charlotte," 62–70; Muse, *Prelude*, 112–45; Douglas, *Reading*, 25–83.

15. *Swann v. Charlotte-Mecklenburg*, 243 F. Supp. 667 (1965), 668; *Swann v. Charlotte Mecklenburg*, 369 F.2d 29 (1966), 32; Darius L. Swann to Charlotte-Mecklenburg Board of Education, Sept. 2, 1964, folder 13, box 3, JLC/UNCC; protest clippings in box 1, RH/UNCC.

16. "Motion for Further Relief," Sept. 6, 1968, 2a-8a, "Supplemental Findings of Fact," June 24, 1969, 459a, SWANN/USSC; "Desegregation of Charlotte-Mecklenburg Schools"; *Green v. New Kent County*, 391 U.S. 430 (1968); *CO*, Jan. 30, March 11, 1969.

17. James B. McMillan Interview, March 1986, William Poe Interview, Aug. 1986, folder 19, box 2, FG/SHC; McMillan to Chambers, Jan. 9, 1969, folder 15, box 3, JLC/UNCC; Gaillard, *Deferred*, 29–43; *CO*, Nov. 20, 1969, Jan. 29, 1970, July 17, 1974.

18. "Transcript of Hearing," March 10, 13, 1969, 1a–45a, 189a–92a, SWANN/USSC; McMillan to Mordecai C. Johnson, April 2, 1970, folder 19, box 3, JLC/UNCC; Julius Chambers Interview, March 1986, folder 19, box 2, FG/SHC; Pat Watters, "Charlotte, North Carolina: 'A Little Child Shall Lead Them,'" in *The South and Her Children: School Desegregation, 1970–1971* (Atlanta: SRC, 1971), 29–30.

19. "Transcript of Hearing," March 10, 13, 1969, 29a–64a, 173a–219a, SWANN/USSC; *CO*, June 26, 1968; "Minutes of Building and Sites Committee," May 13, 1968, folder 14, box 3, Paul Leonard, "Research Report," March 1970, folder 5, box 9, JLC/UNCC; Douglas, *Reading*, 50–57.

20. "Transcript of Hearing," March 10, 13, 1969, 65a–173a, SWANN/USSC; Deposition of William Poe, Jan. 1969, folder 15, box 4, JLC/UNCC; *CO*, March 11, 1969; John Phillips Interview, Sept. 1986, folder 19, box 2, FG/SHC.

21. *Swann v. Charlotte-Mecklenburg*, 300 F. Supp. 1358 (1969), 1360, 1369, 1372.

22. *Swann v. Charlotte-Mecklenburg*, 300 F. Supp. 1358 (1969), 1360, 1370.

23. "Nixon Campaign Statements on School Desegregation," Oct. 8, 1968, folder 87, box 3, HSD/STI; *CO*, Sept. 12–13, 1968.

24. *CO*, Sept. 15, Nov. 6, 1968.

25. *CO*, March 14, April 24–25, May 1–2, 1969.

26. *CO*, May 6, 1969, March 7, 1970; *CN*, May 3, 10, 1969; William R. Overhultz Interview, Aug. 20, 1997, Charlotte, North Carolina; Sharon McGinn Interview, Aug. 20, 1997, Charlotte, North Carolina.

27. *CN*, May 3, 1969; *CO*, May 3, 19, 1969; McGinn Interview; "Defendants' Response," Oct. 11, 1969, 609a–15a, SWANN/USSC.

28. *CO*, May 14, 1969; Augustus E. Green to Charles R. Jonas, May 12, 1969, folder 827, series 2, CRJ/SHC.

29. *CO*, May 6, July 8, 1969; William C. Westbrook to Jonas, May 7, 1969, folder 827, series 2, CRJ/SHC.

30. Author's calculations based on *1970 Census of Population and Housing*.

31. *CO*, May 1, 1969; Watters, "Little Child," 29–33.

32. *CO*, May 8, 14, 26, June 18, 27, 1969.

33. "Plan for Desegregation of Schools," May 28, 1969, 330a–63a, "Opinion and Order," June 20, 1969, 448a–58a, "Amendment to Plan," July 29, 1969, 480a–524a, SWANN/USSC; *CO*, May 20, July 10, 24, 1969.

34. *CO*, May 28, July 26–28, Aug. 1–4, 1969; *LWV Bulletin* (Aug. 1969), box 5, LWV/RSCR.

35. "Transcript of Proceedings," Aug. 5, 1969, 525a–74a, "Order," August 15, 1969, 579a–92a, "Order," August 29, 1969, 593a–95a, SWANN/USSC; *CO*, Aug. 6, 11, 27, 30, 1969.

36. *CO*, Aug. 19, 24, Sept. 3, 1969; Mrs. William A. Cox to Jonas, July 28, 1969, folder 827, series 2, CRJ/SHC.

37. *CO*, Sept. 3, 8, 1969; "Motion for Further Relief," Sept. 2, 1968, 596a–600a, "Defendants' Response," Oct. 11, 1969, 609a–15a, "Defendants' Report," Oct. 30, 1969, 616a–54a, SWANN/USSC.

CHAPTER 6: SUBURBAN POPULISM

1. CPA, "A Struggle for Freedom Is Coming," 1970, folder 20, box 14, FDA/UNCC; Don Roberson to Jonas, Dec. 5, 1969, folder 827, series 2, CRJ/SHC.

2. "Amendment to Plan," Nov. 17, 1969, 670a–90a, "Opinion and Order," Dec. 1, 1969, 698a–716a, SWANN/USSC; *CO*, Nov. 6, 8, Dec. 2, 1969, Jan. 1, 28–29, Feb. 2, 1970; CPA, "Beverly Woods Bulletin," Feb. 26, 1970, folder 20, box 14, FDA/UNCC.

3. *CO*, Jan. 2, 16, 30, 1970; LWV, "School Committee Report," Jan. 1970, folder 1, box 9, JLC/UNCC.

4. "Transcripts of Proceedings," February 2, 5, 1970, 749a–804a, "Plan for Desegregation of Schools," Feb. 2, 1970, 726a–48a, "Order," Feb. 5, 1970, 819a–39a, SWANN/USSC; *CO*, Feb. 3–6, 1970.

5. "A Struggle for Freedom Is Coming"; *CO*, Feb. 6–9, 13, 1970.

6. "Beverly Woods Bulletin"; CPA Flyer, n.d., WRO; *CO*, Feb. 9–10, 13, 1970; Overhultz Interview; McGinn Interview.

7. *CO*, Feb. 8, 11–14, 25, 1970. The evidence in this and the following two paragraphs is based on a content analysis of 127 letters published in the *Charlotte Observer* during February 1970. Sixty-one percent of the letters expressed opposition to busing, and 39 percent supported compliance and/or criticized the CPA.

8. *CO*, Feb. 3, 7–8, 10–13, March 2, 1970; McGinn Interview.

9. *CO*, Jan. 31, Feb. 6, 11–12, 15, 1970; *LWV Bulletin* (Nov./Dec. 1969), box 5, LWV/RSCR.

10. "Notice of Appeal," Feb. 25, 1970, 904a–5a, SWANN/USSC; *CO*, Feb. 25, 1970.

11. Governor Bob Scott, Public Statement, Feb. 11, 1970, folder 14, box 1, BSH/UNCC; Adam Stein to Robert Finch, Feb. 25, 1970, folder 17, box 3, JLC/UNCC; *CO*, Feb. 7, 12, 20, March 2, 1970.

12. Edwin O. Byrd to Nixon, Feb. 2, 1970, Mr. and Mrs. Isaac Falkner to Nixon, Feb. 2, 1970, Thomas E. Conder to Nixon, Feb. 5, 1970, Jonas to Conder, Feb. 10, 1970, A. D. Prentiss to Jonas, Feb. 13, 1970, folder 494, series 1.1, CRJ/SHC; *CO*, Feb. 2, 1970; CPA Flyer, WRO.

13. Richard Nixon, "Desegregation of America's Elementary and Secondary Schools," March 24, 1970, *WC*, 424–40; *NYT*, March 25–26, 1970; *CO*, March 25, 31, 1970; *CN*, March 25, 1970.

14. "Court of Appeals Granting Stay Order," March 5, 1970, 922a–24a, "Order," March 25, 1970, 1255a–58a, SWANN/USSC; *CO*, March 17, 22, 26–28, 1970; *WP*, March 30, 1970.

15. CPA Election Flyer, WRO; *CO*, May 18, 1969, March 8, 14, April 3–4, 21–24, 1970.

16. *CO*, May 3, 31, June 1, 1970.

17. *Swann v. Charlotte-Mecklenburg*, 431 F.2d 138 (1970), 142–43, 145, 152; *CO*, May 19, 28, June 9–10, 30, July 22, 1970; *NYT*, April 9–10, 1970.

18. Joint Governing Bodies of Charlotte-Mecklenburg, "Statement and Resolution," July 13, 1970, folder 22, box 17, FDA/UNCC; *CO*, July 5, 14–15, Aug. 16, 1970.

19. *Swann v. Charlotte-Mecklenburg*, 318 F. Supp. 786 (1970), 793, 795, 801.

20. *CO*, Aug. 16, 22, 26, 28, Sept. 22, 1970; *CN*, Aug. 15, 1970; Overhultz Interview.

21. *CO*, Aug. 4–5, 13, 26–27, 29, 31, Sept. 10, 1970.

22. *CO*, Aug. 9, 26, 28, 31, Sept. 2–3, 8–9, 1970.

23. *CO*, Aug. 24–28, Sept. 4, 7–10, 1970.

24. *CO*, Aug. 27–31, Sept. 1–6, 1970.

25. *CO*, Sept. 9, 13, 1970; *NYT*, Sept. 10, 1970; Tom Harris Interview, 1986, folder 7, box 2, FG/SHC.

26. *CO*, Sept. 10–16, Oct. 15, 1970; *NYT*, Oct. 7, 1970.

27. "Interim Report on Desegregation," Sept. 23, 1970, SWANN/USSC; *CO*, Sept. 17–19, 23–24, Dec. 7, 1970.

28. *CO*, April 16, Sept. 18, 23, Oct. 1, 6, 11, 15, 1970; McGinn Interview; Overhultz Interview.

29. *CO*, Sept. 13, 1970; "Motion for Expediting of Case," July 28, 1970, and other CPA legal documents in folders 14–15, box 1, BSH/UNCC.

30. LDF, Memorandum to Contributors, n.d., folder 23, box 3, JLC/UNCC; briefs in microfiches 22–30, SWANN/USSC.

31. *Swann v. Charlotte-Mecklenburg*, 402 U.S. 1 (1971), 14–15, 28, 31.

32. *CO*, April 23, 1971; *NYT*, April 21–22, 1971; Bernard Schwartz, *Swann's Way: The School Busing Case and the Supreme Court* (New York: Oxford Univ. Press, 1986); Bob Woodward and Scott Armstrong, *The Brethren: Inside the Supreme Court* (New York: Avon, 1981); Wilkinson, *Brown to Bakke*, 134–50.

33. *CO*, April 21–22, 29–30, 1971; Mrs. A. J. Woodle to Jonas, April 22, 1971, folder 906, series 2, CRJ/SHC.

34. NAACP Youth Council, "Basic Position Statement," Aug. 13, 1970, folder 19, box 30, KMA/UNCC; Watters, "Little Child," 21–22, 33–37; *CO*, Feb. 18–26, March 12, 30, April 16, June 5, 1971.

35. *CO*, May 19, June 3, 1971.

CHAPTER 7: NEIGHBORHOOD POLITICS

1. *CO*, Aug. 3, 1970; Mrs. T. L. Paige to Chambers, Nov. 19, 1969, folder 16, box 3, JLC/UNCC.

2. *CO*, Jan. 6, 1974.

3. Leonard, "Equalization of Power."

4. *CO*, May 29, 1970, Jan. 3, 1971.

5. Leonard, "Research Report"; *CO*, March 3–5, 8, May 10–11, 27, 1969.

6. *CO*, Nov. 5, May 31, July 14, Aug. 2, Oct. 1, 6, 1970, Feb. 14, May 2, 8, June 15, 1971; *CN*, Aug. 18, 1969, May 26, 1970.

7. *CO*, Jan. 18, 22, Feb. 16, March 6, April 10, May 12, 20, 1971; *CN*, Feb. 20, April 6, 1970.

8. Charles E. Knox, Memo to Charlotte Chamber of Commerce Board of Directors, Dec. 30, 1970, folder 21, box 4, CCR/UNCC; Charlotte Chamber of Commerce, "Leadership Is the Answer: 1971 Program of Work," folder 1, box 37, FDA/UNCC; *CO*, Jan. 14, 21, 1971.

9. Charter Commission, "Questions and Answers—Charlotte-Mecklenburg Government Consolidation," 1971, folder 18, box 4, CCR/UNCC.

10. Committee on Elected Representation, "Report to the Charter Commission," Aug. 18, 1970, folder 27, box 28, KMA/UNCC; National Conference of Christians and Jews, Statement to the Charter Commission, July 9, 1970, folder 18, box 4, CCR/UNCC; *CO*, June 17, 20, 24, Sept. 3, Oct. 26, 1970.

11. LWV, Statement to the Charter Commission, Jan. 5, 1971, National Conference of Christians and Jews, Statement to the Charter Commission, Jan. 6, 1971, folder 18, box 4, CCR/UNCC; *CO*, Dec. 31, 1970, Jan. 2, 6, 13, 1971.

12. Fair Open Representative Government, "Why Consolidation?" 1971, folder 18, box 4, CCR/UNCC; *CO*, Feb. 8, 12, 26, March 5, 21, 1971.

13. LWV, "City-County Consolidation," 1971, folder 18, box 4, CCR/UNCC; *LWV Bulletin* (March 1971), box 5, LWV/RSCR; *CO*, March 21–24, 29, 1971.

14. *CO*, May 29, 1971.

15. *CO*, May 13, 27, 1971, Jan. 16, 26, Feb. 26, 1974.

16. "Plaintiffs' Preliminary Response," June 17, 1971, folder 22, box 2, JLC/UNCC; *CO*, April 30, June 19, 1971.

17. "Pupil Assignment Plan, 1971–1972," June 25, 1971, folders 23-24, box 5, WW/UNCC; WBTV Editorial, "The School Assignment Plan," broadcast June 17–18, 1971, folder 27, box 3, JLC/UNCC; *Swann v. Charlotte-Mecklenburg*, 328 F. Supp. 1346 (1971); *CO*, June 17–18, July 14–15, 23, 1971.

18. *Swann v. Charlotte-Mecklenburg*, 328 F. Supp. 1346 (1971), 1349; L. T. Hovis, Sr., to Jonas, July 28, 1971, folder 906, series 2, CRJ/SHC; *CO*, June 29–30, July 15, 1971.

19. CUFF Petition, Aug. 1971, folder 8, box 9, JLC/UNCC; *Swann v. Charlotte-Mecklenburg*, 334 F. Supp. 623 (1971); *CO*, July 28, Aug. 3–4, 26, Sept. 4, 1971.

20. "Factors Affecting the Transfer of Seniors," Aug. 16, 1971, "Report with Respect to West Charlotte High School," Jan. 20, 1972, folder 16, box 4, WW/UNCC; *Swann v. Charlotte-Mecklenburg*, 334 F. Supp. 623 (1971), 625; *CO*, Aug. 18, 22, Sept. 23, 25, 1971.

21. Cloyd Goodrum, Jr., to Rolland Jones, March 29, 1974, folder 3, box 4, Hidden Valley PTA Committee, Homeowner Survey, 1973, folder 7, box 3, JLC/UNCC; *CO*, Aug. 6, 1971, Jan. 6, 1974.

22. NAACP, "Position Paper on School Disruptions," Dec. 10, 1971, "Statement to Board of Education," Dec. 14, 1971, folder 19, box 30, KMA/UNCC; *Givens v. Poe*, 346 F. Supp. 202 (1972); *CO*, Sept. 3, 9, 14, 1971.

23. CRC Hearings, Transcript Nos. 1–4, Nov. 21, 28, Dec. 5, 10, folders 5–6, box 39, FDA/UNCC; Maniloff, "Busing No Longer Bothers Charlotte," 1, 8–9.

24. CRC Report, March 14, 1972, folder 7, box 39, FDA/UNCC.

25. *CO*, Sept. 3, 1971, May 4–6, 1972; Marylyn Huff Interview, April 27, 1998, Black Mountain, North Carolina.

26. *CO*, May 7–8, June 1, 4, 1972; Frye Gaillard, "Charlotte's Road to Busing," *Christianity and Crisis* (Oct. 29, 1973), 216; Frank Barrows, "School Busing: Charlotte, N.C.," *AM* (Nov. 1972), 17–22.

27. "Pupil Assignment Plan Study," March 6, 1973 (revised Sept. 27, 1973), folder 14, box 29, KMA/UNCC; *CO*, March 7, 1973.

28. NAACP Youth Council, "Report on Investigation of Racial Disorder," March 13, 1973, folder 19, box 30, KMA/UNCC; "Memorandum on Charlotte School Disorders," March 20, 1973, folder 2, box 4, JLC/UNCC; *Swann v. Charlotte-Mecklenburg*, 362 F. Supp. 1223 (1973), 1232–33; *CO*, March 7–12, May 2, 1973.

29. Julian Mason to Chambers, May 10, 1973, Mason to McMillan, May 21, 1973, folder 2, box 4, JLC/UNCC; *CO*, May 19, 1973; Julian and Elsie Mason Interview, Charlotte, North Carolina, April 29, 1998.

30. Northeast Concerned Parents Flyer, May 21, 1973, JM; Mason, Statement to Board of Education, May 30, 1973, Mason to Chambers, June 15, 1973, folder 2, box

4, JLC/UNCC; Mason Interview; Gaillard, "Charlotte's Road to Busing," 218; Gaillard, *Deferred*, 114–19; *CO*, May 23, 31, June 2, 4, 1973.

31. *CO*, June 11, 13, 15–16, 1973.

32. *Swann v. Charlotte-Mecklenburg*, 362 F. Supp. 1223 (1973), 1224, 1233, 1237.

33. *CO*, May 24, June 20–24, 1973; Gaillard, *Deferred*, 121–23.

34. "Report Pursuant to the Order of the Court," Sept. 5, 1973, folder 8, box 3, JLC/UNCC; *CO*, July 7, 17, 21, Aug. 9, 20, 24, Sept. 1, 1973.

CHAPTER 8: CLASS FAIRNESS AND RACIAL STABILITY

1. LWV Minutes, Jan. 6, 1972, box 8, LWV/RSCR; "Annual Report of the Charlotte-Mecklenburg Schools," 1972–73, folder 22, box 17, FDA/UNCC; Gaillard, *Deferred*, 133–34; *CO*, Sept. 2–4, 7, 1973.

2. *CO*, Nov. 13, 21, 23, 1973; Claiborne, "Charlotte-Mecklenburg School System"; Gaillard, *Deferred*, 134–38; NAACP Statement, Nov. 20, 1973, folder 19, box 30, KMA/UNCC.

3. "CAG Exhibit 1," folder 11, box 3, JLC/UNCC; *CO*, Nov. 23, Dec. 2, 5, 1973.

4. "Plan for Integration of the Charlotte-Mecklenburg School System," Aug. 1969, folder 3, box 3, WW/UNCC; "CAG Exhibit 1"; *CO*, Feb. 16, 1971, May 31, 1974; Gaillard, *Deferred*, 133–45; Thomas Ray, "Living with the Scattered Site Concept," folder 1, box 3, WTR/UNCC.

5. CAG, "Suggested Pupil Assignment Guidelines," 1974, folder 9, box 3, JLC/UNCC; *CO*, Dec. 1, 1973, Jan. 9, Feb. 12, 1974.

6. *Swann v. Charlotte-Mecklenburg*, 489 F.2d 966 (1974); "Motion to Approve Plan and to Dismiss Case," March 1, 1974, folder 9, "Report," April 1, 1974, folder 10, box 3, JLC/UNCC; "Order," March 20, 1974, folder 7, box 1, MWR/UNCC; *CO*, Jan. 18, 30, Feb. 1, 28, 1974.

7. Margaret Ray to Members of Charlotte-Mecklenburg School Board, Feb. 7, 1974, folder 4, "Order," April 3, 1974, folder 7, box 1, MWR/UNCC; *CO*, April 5, 10, 1974.

8. CAG, "Report to Court," April 22, 1974, folder 11, box 3, JLC/UNCC; CAG legal documents, folder 5, box 1, MWR/UNCC; *CO*, May 21–22, 29, June 9, 1974.

9. "Plaintiffs' Response," June 7, 1974, folder 7, box 1, MWR/UNCC; Gaillard, *Deferred*, 143–49; *CO*, May 22–23, June 9–10, July 10, 1974.

10. *CO*, April 10, 28, May 1, 5, 8–9, June 5, 1974; Huff Interview.

11. "Joint Proposal for School Assignment of Students," July 9, 1974, folder 6, box 1, MWR/UNCC; *CO*, July 10–12, 1974.

12. *Swann v. Charlotte-Mecklenburg*, 379 F. Supp. 1102 (1974), 1103, 1105; *CO*, July 10–11, 1974.

13. William Poe, "Five Years of Busing in Charlotte," Sept. 25, 1974, "Plaintiffs' Response," n.d. (1975), folder 12, box 2, FG/SHC; *Swann v. Charlotte-Mecklenburg*, 67 F.R.D. 648 (1975), 649–50; *CO*, Aug. 27, Sept. 12, 1974, July 12, 1975.

14. *CO*, July 12, 1975; Claiborne, "Charlotte-Mecklenburg School System."

15. SRC, "News Release," Dec. 6, 1959, 9:0307–10, SRC/UMI; *CO*, Jan. 30, 1970.

16. *CO*, June 1, 1973, May 31, 1974; Poe Interview.

17. Jay Robinson, "Memorandum to Members of the Board of Education," Nov. 28, 1977, folder 19, box 30, KMA/UNCC; "Desegregation of Charlotte-Mecklenburg Schools"; *Martin v. Charlotte-Mecklenburg*, 475 F. Supp. 1318 (1979); *1985 Directory of North Carolina Non-public Schools* (Raleigh: Office of the Governor, 1985), 34–38; Gaillard, *Deferred*, 166–71; *CO*, Aug. 18, Sept. 14–15, 1976; Huff Interview.

18. CBS, *Busing: Complying with Swann in 1976*, broadcast May 28, 1976 (Films for the Humanities and Sciences, 2002); *CO*, Dec. 5–6, 1983; NAACP Statement, Jan. 17, 1978, Feb. 13, 1979, folder 19, box 30, KMA/UNCC; Lee A. Daniels, "In Defense of Busing," *NYT Magazine* (April 17, 1983), 34–37, 92–93, 97–98.

19. *The 14th Amendment and School Busing*, Hearings before the Subcommittee on the Constitution of the Committee on the Judiciary, U.S. Senate, May 14, 1981, 153–63; *Court-Ordered School Busing*, Hearings before the Subcommittee on Separation of Powers of the Committee on the Judiciary, U.S. Senate, Oct. 16, 1981, 436–53, 511–54, 563–65, 611–17; Poe Interview.

20. *CO*, Oct. 9, 1984.

21. Robinson Memorandum; *CO*, Jan. 6–8, 1974.

22. NAACP Statement, Jan. 17, 1978, folder 19, box 30, KMA/UNCC; *CO*, April 25, 1971, May 5, 1973, Feb. 26, 1974.

23. *CO*, June 18, 1970, Nov. 4, 7, 1973.

24. *CO*, March 4, 9, 23, May 19, 22, 1974.

25. *CO*, April 15, 1974, Feb. 2, 1975, April 17, 20, 1977; Gaillard, *Deferred*, 155–59; Hanchett, *New South City*, 253–56; Goldfield, *Black, White, and Southern*, 228–29; Stephen Samuel Smith, "Hugh Governs? Regime and Education Policy in Charlotte, North Carolina," *Journal of Urban Affairs* (1997), 253–56.

26. *CO*, May 1, 1973, Oct. 19, 1987, March 21, 1992; Gary Orfield, *Toward a Strategy for Urban Integration: Lessons in School and Housing Policy from Twelve Cities* (New York: Ford Foundation, 1981); Erica Frankenberg, "The Impact of School Segregation on Residential Patterns: Mobile, AL and Charlotte, NC," a paper presented to the 2002 conference "Resegregation of Southern Schools? A Crucial Moment in the History (and the Future) of Public Schooling in America." Montgomery County, Maryland, is the national pacesetter in the establishment of policies of mandatory mixed-income zoning in pursuit of stable levels of residential and school integration. See David Rusk, *Inside Game/Outside Game: Winning Strategies for Saving Urban America* (Washington, DC: Brookings, 1999), 178–200.

27. *CO*, April 19, 1986; Alison Morantz, "Desegregation at Risk: Threat and Reaffirmation in Charlotte," in Orfield and Eaton, *Dismantling Desegregation*, 179–206.

28. *CO*, April 19, 1986, Nov. 29, Dec. 9, 1987, Jan. 28, 1988, April 6, 1997; Morantz, "Desegregation at Risk," 182–86; Roslyn Arlin Mickelson and Carol Axtell Ray, "Fear of Falling from Grace: The Middle Class, Downward Mobility, and School Desegregation," *Research in Sociology of Education and Socialization* (1994), 207–38; Mickelson, "The Academic Consequences of Desegregation and Resegregation: Evidence from the Charlotte-Mecklenburg Schools," *North Carolina Law Review* (May 2003), 1520.

29. *CO*, May 4, June 1, 28, 1988, March 25, April 1, 1992, Feb. 8, 1994; Morantz, "Desegregation at Risk," 188–206; Mickelson and Ray, "Fear of Falling," 231; Smith, *Boom for Whom?*

30. *CO*, Jan. 19, April 6, Oct. 25, 1997; Jan. 13–17, 1999; Frankenberg, "Impact of School Segregation"; Mickelson, "Academic Consequences," 1513–62.

31. *CO*, April 6, 1997, Jan. 14–16, 1998; "Linda" posting, "Deciding Desegregation" forum, Jan. 11, 1999 <http://www.charlotte.com/observer/special/deseg/guest book/>.

32. William Poe, Speech to Charlotte Rotary Club, Sept. 21, 1976, folder 13, box 2, FG/SHC.

CHAPTER 9: THE SUBURBANIZATION OF SOUTHERN POLITICS

1. UCCA, "General Statement," Aug. 1970, sec. 2, JLD/VHS; *AC*, Aug 31, 1970; *CO*, Aug. 31, 1970; *NVP*, Sept. 1, 1970; Nixon, "The War in Vietnam," Nov. 3, 1969, *WC*, 1546–54.

2. WECPF Memo, Sept. 1970, sec. 2, JLD/VHS; *CO*, Sept. 13, Oct. 7, 1970; *NVP*, Sept. 13, 1970.

3. Phillips, *Emerging*; Sam Tanenhaus, "The GOP, or Goldwater's Old Party," *TNR* (June 11, 2001), 40; Perlstein, *Storm*; Carter, *Rage*; Carter, *George Wallace to Newt Gingrich*.

4. Black and Black, *Politics and Society*, 42; Schulman, *Sunbelt*.

5. Kari Frederickson, *The Dixiecrat Revolt and the End of the Solid South, 1932–1968* (Chapel Hill: Univ. of North Carolina Press, 2001); Grantham, *Life and Death*; Earl Black and Merle Black, *The Vital South: How Presidents are Elected* (Cambridge: Harvard Univ. Press, 1992), 141–49; Bartley, *Massive Resistance*, 28–46.

6. Black and Black, *Vital South*, 176–89 (quotation 177); Bartley and Graham, *Southern Politics*, 81–110 (quotation 86); Black and Black, *Politics and Society*, 22 (third quotation); Bass and De Vries, *Transformation*, 23–27.

7. *AC*, Aug. 27, 1960; *NYT*, Aug. 27, 1960; Bass and De Vries, *Transformation*, 403, 499.

8. George Brown Tindall, *The Disruption of the Solid South* (Athens: Univ. of Georgia Press, 1972), 47–72; Bass and De Vries, *Transformation*, 27–29, 403; Ripon Society, "Southern Republicanism and the New South," Fall 1966, in *The Ripon Papers, 1963–1968*, ed. Lee W. Huebner and Thomas E. Petri (Washington: National Press, 1968), 19–24.

9. Black and Black, *Politics and Society*, 48–49, 72, 194; Ripon Society, "Can We Bridge the Ideological Gap?" June 1967, in Huebner and Petri, *Ripon Papers*, 25–45.

10. Richard M. Nixon, "Acceptance Speech," Aug. 8, 1968, in *Campaign Speeches of American Presidential Candidates, 1948–1984*, ed. Gregory Bush (New York: Frederick Ungar, 1985), 153–63.

11. Richard M. Scammon and Ben J. Wattenberg, *The Real Majority* (New York: Coward-McCann, 1970), 67–68; Kazin, *Populist Persuasion*, 221–42; Edsall and Edsall, *Chain Reaction*, 77; *CO*, Sept. 12–13, 1968.

12. "Nixon Campaign Statements on School Desegregation," Oct. 8, 1968, folder 87, box 3, HSD/STI; Richard M. Nixon, *RN: The Memoirs of Richard Nixon* (New York: Simon and Schuster, 1990), 316–17.

13. "Nixon's the One," 1968, folder 58, box 2, HSD/STI; *NYT*, Oct. 4–5, 1968; Harry S. Dent, *The Prodigal South Returns to Power* (New York: Wiley, 1978), 57–117; Garry Wills, *Nixon Agonistes: The Crisis of the Self-Made Man* (Boston: Houghton Mifflin, 1970), 246–75; Carter, *Rage*, 324–31.

14. Nixon, "Acceptance Speech"; *NYT*, Sept. 30, Oct. 3–5, 1968; *WP*, Oct. 4, 1968.

15. *Nixon/Wallace 1968 TV Election Spots* (International Historic Films, 1985); Joe McGinnis, *The Selling of the President, 1968* (New York: Trident, 1969).

16. *Nixon/Wallace*.

17. Nixon, "Acceptance Speech"; *Report of the National Advisory Commission*, 1, 10.

18. Bartley and Graham, *Southern Politics*, 126–35; Black and Black, *Vital South*, 302–3; Phillips, *Emerging*, 206–7, 229–32.

19. *AC*, Nov. 7, 1968; *RNL*, Nov. 7, 1968; Bartley and Graham, *Southern Politics*, 126–35.

20. Scammon and Wattenberg, *Real Majority*, 97–100; Black and Black, *Vital South*, 298–303.

21. Black and Black, *Politics and Society*, 58–59; Bartley and Graham, *Southern Politics*, 137–41.

22. Phillips, *Emerging* (quotations 31–32, 39); Wills, *Nixon Agonistes*, 264–68.

23. Scammon and Wattenberg, *Real Majority* (quotations 20–22, 70, 184, 203).

24. John Ehrlichman to Nixon, Oct. 21, 1970, reprinted in Ehrlichman, *Witness to Power: The Nixon Years* (New York: Simon and Schuster, 1982), 215–20; Harry Dent to Nixon, Oct. 13, Dec. 8, 1969, folder 45, box 2, March 13, 1970, folder 153, box 5, July 21, 1970, folder 210, box 7, Dent to John Brown, Feb. 25, 1970, folder 157, box 5, HSD/STI.

25. Ripon Society, "Southern Republicanism," 19–24; Ripon Society, *The Lessons of Victory* (New York: Dial, 1969), 8, 182, 268; "The GOP and the South," *Ripon Forum* (July/Aug. 1970), 3–16.

26. Dent to Bob Haldeman, Jan 13, 1970, folder 210, box 7, HSD/STI; Buchanan memorandum in *NYT*, March 19, 1972; Ehrlichman, *Witness*, 227 (Nixon quotation); *AC*, Nov. 7, 1968. On internal debates, see Leon E. Panetta and Peter Gall, *Bring Us Together: The Nixon Team and the Civil Rights Retreat* (Philadelphia: Lippincott, 1971); Tom Wicker, *One of Us: Richard Nixon and the American Dream* (New York: Random House, 1991), 484–94.

27. Dent to Nixon, March 25, 1970, folder 202, box 6, HSD/STI; *Green v. New Kent County*, 391 U.S. 430 (1968); *NYT*, July 4, 1969.

28. *NYT*, Sept. 3, 13, Oct. 30–31, 1969; Wicker, *One of Us*, 493; *The Federal Retreat in School Desegregation* (Atlanta: SRC, 1969); *Alexander v. Holmes*, 396 U.S. 19 (1969).

29. Ehrlichman to Dent, Nov. 13, 1969, folder 20, box 1, HSD/STI; Kenneth O'Reilly, *Nixon's Piano: Presidents and Racial Politics from Washington to Clinton* (New York: Free Press, 1995), 277–329 (Mitchell quotation 290); Reg Murphy and Hal Gulliver, *The Southern Strategy* (New York: Charles Scribner's Sons, 1971), 21–77; Ehrlichman, *Witness*, 224–27.

30. Dent to Nixon, July 8, 1969, folder 82, box 3, HSD/STI; *NYT*, July 4, 1969; *JCL*, March 2, 1970.

31. Nixon, "Desegregation of America's Elementary and Secondary Schools," March 24, 1970, *WC*, 424–40.

32. *NYT*, March 25–26, April 20, May 15, 1970; Ehrlichman, *Witness*, 233.

33. Wicker, *One of Us*, 492–506, 635.

34. *MR*, Jan. 16, 20, 1970; *JCL*, Nov. 8, Dec. 11, 1969; *NYT*, Feb. 2–3, 1970.

35. *GN*, Jan. 21, 1970; *JCL*, June 4, July 23, Sept. 2–3, 28, 1970; *NYT*, Feb. 14, 1970; *MR*, Jan. 31, 1970.

36. *JCL*, Oct. 18, 1969; *NYT*, Feb. 5–6, 10–13, 19–20, March 1, 1970.

37. *Gallup Poll: Public Opinion, 1935–1971*, 2248; *NYT*, May 3, 1970.

CHAPTER 10: THE FAILURE OF THE SOUTHERN STRATEGY

1. *NYT*, Feb. 15, 1970. Kevin P. Phillips accurately recognized the significance of the Sunbelt but has spent most of his career in a disguised retreat from the failure to grapple with class politics in *The Emerging Republican Majority*. See *Post-conservative America: People, Politics, and Ideology in a Time of Crisis* (New York: Random House, 1982); *The Politics of Rich and Poor: Wealth and the American Electorate in the Reagan Aftermath* (New York: Random House, 1990); *Boiling Point: Democrats, Republicans, and the Decline of Middle-Class Prosperity* (New York: Random House, 1993); *Wealth and Democracy: A Political History of the American Rich* (New York: Broadway, 2002).

2. *MR*, Aug. 13, Sept. 3–4, 1969.

3. *MR*, Sept. 7–8, 21, 1969, Jan. 17, 22, 1970; *NYT*, Feb. 9, 1970; Carter, *Rage*, 391.

4. James D. Martin to Dent, Aug. 7, 1969, folder 1, box 1, HSD/STI; *JCL*, Jan. 19, 1970; *MR*, Jan. 27, 1970; *NYT*, Feb. 9, 1970; Dent, *Prodigal*, 159–64; Carter, *Rage*, 387–92.

5. *NYT*, April 24, June 3–5, 1970; Murphy and Gulliver, *Southern Strategy*, 78–106; Bartley and Graham, *Southern Politics*, 164–66; Carter, *Rage*, 381–96; Earl Black, *Southern Governors and Civil Rights: Racial Segregation as a Campaign Issue in the Second Reconstruction* (Cambridge: Harvard Univ. Press, 1976), 56–57.

6. *RTD*, July 23, 1970; Numan V. Bartley and Hugh D. Graham, *Southern Elections: County and Precinct Data, 1950–1972* (Baton Rouge: Louisiana State Univ. Press, 1978), 21–22, 347–50; Murphy and Gulliver, *Southern Strategy*, 86.

7. *GN*, Jan. 22, 1970; Black, *Governors*, 83; Bass and De Vries, *Transformation*, 248–65.

8. *GN*, Jan. 20–21, 30–31, Feb. 3, 13, 1970; *NYT*, March 2, 1970.

9. *GN*, Jan. 22–27, 1970.

10. *GN*, Jan. 24–25, 28, 31, 1970; *NYT*, Jan. 28, 1970.

11. *GN*, Feb. 3, 8, 11–13, 17–18, 1970.

12. *GN*, Jan. 24, Feb. 8–9, 20, 1970; *CO*, Feb. 18, 1970.

13. *GN*, Feb. 4, 15, March 3–11, 1970; *NYT*, March 2, 1970.

14. Strom Thurmond, "News Release," March 5, 1970, Dent to Albert Watson, April 27, 1970, folder 207, box 6, Dent to Nixon, March 13, 1970, folder 153, box 5, HSD/STI; *GN*, March 4–7, 1970; *NYT*, March 4, 1970.

15. Spiro Agnew to Nixon, n.d., Arthur Ravenal, Jr., to Dent, Jan. 13, 1970, folder 207, box 6, HSD/STI; *GN*, March 6, 21–22, 26, 1970.

16. *GN*, Feb. 23–24, March 26, 1970; Black, *Governors*, 85.

17. Dent to Nixon, Oct. 27, 1970, folder 181, box 6, HSD/STI; *NVP*, July 18, 1970; *NYT*, Aug. 27, Nov. 1, 1970; Bartley and Graham, *Southern Politics*, 151; Murphy and Gulliver, *Southern Strategy*, 171–72.

18. *NYT*, Nov. 4, 1970; Jack Bass, "John C. West," *ST* (July/Aug. 1972), 9; Murphy and Gulliver, *Southern Strategy*, 156–72; Bass and De Vries, *Transformation*, 262–63; Bartley and Graham, *Southern Politics*, 152–53.

19. *CO*, Jan. 20, Aug. 25, 1971; Murphy and Gulliver, *Southern Strategy*, 171; Bass, "Thurmond Thawing?" *ST* (May 1971), 3, 7; Bass, "John C. West," 9–10.

20. Bass and De Vries, *Transformation*, 348–54; Lamis, *Two-Party South*, 145–53.

21. Gordon S. Brownell to Dent, Oct. 31, 1969, folder 29, box 1, HSD/STI; "The GOP and the South," *Ripon Forum* (July/Aug. 1970), 6; *RTD*, July 13, 1969, July 23, 1970; *WP*, Nov. 5–6, 1969, May 16, 1970; Black, *Governors*, 117; Bartley and Graham, *Southern Elections*, 405–7; James R. Sweeney, "Southern Strategies: The 1970 Election for the United States Senate in Virginia," *Virginia Magazine of History and Biography* (Spring 1998), 178–79.

22. *RNO*, Feb. 1, 1970; "Four Men for the New Season," *Time* (May 31, 1971), 18.

23. Dent to Nixon, Dec. 3, 1969, folder 39, box 1, Dent to Nixon, June 9, 1970, Linwood Holton to Dent, Oct. 22, 1970, folder 225, box 7, HSD/STI; Sweeney, "Southern Strategies," 165–200.

24. Dent to Nixon, June 29, 1970, folder 225, box 7, HSD/STI; *NVP*, June 28, Sept. 11, 1970; *RTD*, Oct. 29, 1970; *WP*, Nov. 4, 1970; Sweeney, "Southern Strategies."

25. "Survey of the Political Climate in Virginia," Oct. 1971, box 12, WBS/UVA; Holton to Dent, Oct. 22, 1970, folder 225, box 7, HSD/STI; *WP*, May 16, 1970; *RNO*, Oct. 15, 1972; Lamis, *Two-Party South*, 151–57; Bartley and Graham, *Southern Politics*, 177–78.

26. *GN*, Jan. 21, 1970; *CO*, April 6, 9–10, 1970; Lamis, *Two-Party South*, 184; Bass and De Vries, *Transformation*, 107–35.

27. Nixon, "Remarks at the Tallahassee Municipal Airport," Oct. 20, 1970, *WC*, 1484–85; Dent to Nixon, Sept. 18, 1970, folder 130, box 4, HSD/STI; *NYT*, Oct. 23, 1970; *WP*, Oct. 29, 1970.

28. James Clotfelter and William R. Hamilton, "But Which Southern Strategy?" *ST* (April 1971), 1, 6–7; Bartley and Graham, *Southern Elections*, 357–60; Murphy and Gulliver, *Southern Strategy*, 131–55; Bass and De Vries, *Transformation*, 124; *WP*, Nov. 4, 1970.

29. Reubin Askew Address, *ST* (May 1972), 2–3; Larry Vickers, "'Equal Opportunity,'" *ST* (Oct. 1971), 1, 6; Lamis, *Two-Party South*, 186–87; *CO*, Sept. 3, 1971.

30. *GN*, Feb. 14, 1970; *NYT*, July 28, 1970; *WP*, Aug. 24, 26, 1970; Bass and De Vries, *Transformation*, 87–97; Black, *Governors*, 98–105, 269–71; Bartley and Graham, *Southern Elections*, 353.

31. *WP*, Nov. 1, 1970; Bartley and Graham, *Southern Politics*, 147–49; Bartley and Graham, *Southern Elections*, 353; Lamis, *Two-Party South*, 122–26; Black, *Governors*, 105–6; Ed Stanfield, "Arkansas' Bumpers," *ST* (May 1972), 6–7.

32. *AC*, Sept. 2, 10–11, 1970; Murphy and Gulliver, *Southern Strategy*, 173–97; Bartley and Graham, *Southern Politics*, 112–17, 148–50; Winn, "Atlanta," 4–5.

33. "New Day A'Coming in the South," *Time* (May 31, 1971), 14–20; *AC*, Sept. 10–11, 1970, Jan. 13, 1971; *NYT*, Nov. 4, 1970, Sept. 5, 1971; Lamis, *Two-Party South*, 96–99; Murphy and Gulliver, *Southern Strategy*, 190–97; Ferrell Guillory, "Edwards of Louisiana," *ST* (April 1973), 5–7; Bass and De Vries, *Transformation*, 211–14.

34. *WP*, Nov. 4–6, 8, 1970; *NYT*, Nov. 4–5, 1970. Also see Randy Sanders, *Mighty Peculiar Elections: The New South Gubernatorial Campaigns of 1970 and the Changing Politics of Race* (Gainesville: Univ. Press of Florida, 2002).

35. David Halberstam, "The End of a Populist," *HM* (Jan. 1971), 35–45; Bass and De Vries, *Transformation*, 284–96; Murphy and Gulliver, *Southern Strategy*, 107–30; Lamis, *Two-Party South*, 163–78; *JCL*, Sept. 23, 1970; *WP*, Nov. 4, 1970.

36. *RNO*, Aug. 21, 1970, Nov. 8–9, 1972; *CO*, Nov. 6, 1973; Black, *Governors*, 106–13; Bass and De Vries, *Transformation*, 218–47; Lamis, *Two-Party South*, 131–44; Ferrell Guillory, "North Carolina," *ST* (Oct. 1973), 7–8.

37. *CO*, Sept. 5, 1974; *WP*, Nov. 7, 1970; Clotfelter and Hamilton, "Which Southern Strategy?" 6; Lamis, *Two-Party South*, 22–43.

38. Nixon, "Remarks in Front of Buncombe County Courthouse," Oct. 20, 1970, *WC*, 1423–24; *WP*, Aug. 15, 1970; *MCA*, Nov. 5, 1972. Insider defenses of Nixon's desegregation record include Dent, *Prodigal*, 121–56; Ehrlichman, *Witness*, 207–43. Although few scholars would concur, academic support for this thesis has come from Joan Hoff, *Nixon Reconsidered* (New York: Basic Books, 1994).

CHAPTER 11: METROPOLITAN DIVERGENCE

1. On the concept of "relative elasticity," see Rusk, *Inside Game/Outside Game*, 3–11; David Rusk, *Cities without Suburbs*, 3d. ed. (Washington: Woodrow Wilson Center, 2003).

2. Gary Orfield and Franklin Monfort, *Racial Change and Desegregation in Large School Districts* (Alexandria: NSBA, 1988), 7–9, 11–13, 21–23; Abbott, *New Urban America*, 52; Brett W. Hawkins, *Nashville Metro: The Politics of City-County Consolidation* (Nashville: Vanderbilt Univ. Press, 1966); Richard A. Pride and J. David Woodard, *The Burden of Busing: The Politics of Desegregation in Nashville, Tennessee* (Knoxville: Univ. of Tenn. Press, 1985).

3. *Pate v. Dade County*, 434 F.2d 1151 (1970); *NYT*, Sept. 2, 1970; *CO*, June 30, 1970; *RNO*, Aug. 12, Sept. 3, 1970; Egerton, *Americanization*, 156–57; Robert E. Anderson, Jr., "Mobile, Alabama: The Essence of Survival," in *The South and Her Children*, 38–49; Orfield, *Must We Bus?* 279–360.

4. David S. Cecelski, *Along Freedom Road: Hyde County, North Carolina, and the Fate of Black Schools in the South* (Chapel Hill: Univ. of North Carolina Press, 1994); CORE, "A True Alternative to Segregation—a Proposal for Community School Districts," Feb. 1970, folder 2, box 9, JLC/UNCC; *GN*, Jan. 21, Feb. 19, 1970; *CO*, Sept. 8, 1970.

5. LCCR, "Facts about Busing," 1970, LCCR Statement, Sept. 1972, folder 21, box 15, FDA/UNCC.

6. City Manager, "Urban Renewal in Richmond," May 24, 1962, box 6, HHE/VCU; *RTD*, July 3, 1970; Christopher Silver, "The Changing Face of Neighborhoods in Memphis and Richmond, 1940–1985," in Miller and Pozzetta, *Shades of*

the Sunbelt, 93–126; John V. Moeser and Rutledge M. Dennis, *The Politics of Annexation: Oligarchic Power in a Southern City* (Cambridge: Schenkman, 1982), 29–31.

7. Citizens for Merger, "The Important Facts about the Proposed Merger of Henrico County and Richmond," 1961, box 1, VC/VCU; *NYT*, June 5, 1955, Feb. 18, 1962; *RTD*, Oct. 27, 1967; Moeser and Dennis, *Annexation*, 35–109; Abbott, *New Urban America*, 52, 200–209.

8. "Order of Annexation," July 12, 1969, box 1, VC/VCU; *RNL*, June 23, 1969; *RTD*, July 2, 1969; Moeser and Dennis, *Annexation*, 110–34.

9. *RTD*, July 2–3, 9, 1969, Sept. 6, 1970.

10. *Holt v. City of Richmond*, 334 F. Supp. 228 (1971); Moeser and Dennis, *Annexation*, 134–85.

11. Moeser and Dennis, *Annexation*, 185–87.

12. *RTD*, June 20–28, July 10, 1970.

13. *RTD*, July 17–18, Aug. 11–12, 20, 29, 1970.

14. WECPF, "Statement of Position," Aug. 14, 1970, sec. 2, JLD/VHS; J. C. Moss, Jr., to Robert R. Merhige, Jr., May 19, 1970, James L. Doherty to Virginia Crockford, Sept. 21, 1970, box 1, VC/VCU; *RTD*, July 26, Aug. 4, 1970.

15. Mrs. W. G. Mize to Crockford, July 16, 1970, box 1, VC/VCU; Ad Hoc Committee Memo, July 31, 1970, sec. 2, Doherty to Bob Holland, Oct. 15, 1970, sec. 1, JLD/VHS; *RTD*, July 30, Aug. 8, 20, 1970.

16. *RTD*, July 29–31, Aug. 11, 19, 1970; *RNL*, July 22, 1970; Pratt, *Color*, 101.

17. *RTD*, Aug. 18, 26–30, Sept. 9, 13–15, 1970; Pratt, *Color*, 49–53.

18. Mary Pantele to Crockford, April 23, 1970, Paul T. Bassett to L. D. Adams, Sept. 10, 1970, T. Stevens Daugherty to Thomas J. Bliley, Aug. 20, 1970, box 1, VC/VCU; WRVA, "A Reasonable Request," Nov. 2–6, 1970, sec. 2, JLD/VHS; *RTD*, Sept. 14, 1970.

19. Urban Team, "Study on Resegregation of Northside Schools," Feb. 20, 1969, sec. 5, RPH/VHS; Urban Team, "The Northside: Negro Suburbia?" June 17, 1968, sec. 1, JAS/VHS; *RTD*, Nov. 22–24, 1968; *RNL* editorial in Moeser and Dennis, *Annexation*, 119.

20. "Motion for Joinder," Nov. 4, 1970, 90a–98a, "Amended Complaint," Dec. 14, 1970, 99a–109a, RICH/USSC; *RTD*, July 7–8, 1970.

21. Richmond Federation to Member Groups, May 5, 1971, sec. 2, JLD/VHS; *RTD*, Nov. 10–15, 1970, Jan. 16, 1972; *NVP*, Nov. 24, 1970; *CO*, Aug. 17, 1971; *RNL*, Jan. 19, 1972.

22. "Miracle Worker Campaign Report," March 7, 1971, sec. 2, JLD/VHS; CEPS Newsletter, Jan. 1972, Archie B. Ellis to Crockford, Nov. 20, 1970, William G. Colby, Jr., to Crockford, Nov. 18, 1970, Mrs. Murray Lowenstein to Crockford, Nov. 18, 1970, box 1, VC/VCU; CEPS Sample Speech, n.d., sec. 4, AJR/VHS.

23. *Bradley v. Richmond*, 338 F. Supp. 67 (1972), 100, 115, 178.

24. *Bradley v. Richmond*, 338 F. Supp. 67 (1972), 177; *RNL*, Jan. 11, 15, 1972; *RTD*, Jan. 11, 1972.

25. CEPS Report, Nov. 11, 1971, sec. 4, Mass Mailing, June 8, 1972, sec. 1, Arthur Raper to *RTD*, Jan. 15, 1971, sec. 2, AJR/VHS; CEPS Survey, March 22, 1972, box 1, VC/VCU; *RTD*, Jan. 11–13, 1972; *RNL*, Jan. 21, Feb. 10, 1972; *WP*, Feb. 18, March 18, 1972.

26. *Bradley v. Richmond*, 462 F.2d 1058 (1972), 1060, 1063, 1066, 1070; *RNL*, Feb. 9, 1972.

27. *City of Richmond v. State Board of Education*, 412 U.S. 92 (1973); *Bradley v. Baliles*, 639 F. Supp 680 (1986); Pratt, *Color*, 83–110; Robert P. Hilldrup, "After the Richmond Decision," *SV* (March/April 1974), 76–79. Population data from American FactFinder, U.S. Census Bureau <http://factfinder.census.gov/>.

28. Goldfield and Brownell, *Urban America*, 370–72; Egerton, *Americanization*, 151–71; *AJC*, July 11, 1971.

29. *RNO*, Aug. 5–7, Sept. 2–3, 1970, July 21, 1971, Oct. 6, 1972; *NYT*, Aug. 24, 1970.

30. *RNO*, April 25–27, 1969, Oct. 11–12, 16, 29, Nov. 2–4, 8–9, 1972.

31. *RNO*, Aug. 2, 1970, Oct. 1, 21, 1972; *CO*, Nov. 9, 1973; Ferrell Guillory, "In Raleigh, N.C., Something of a Miracle," *SV* (March/April 1974), 80; "History of the Wake County Public School System" <http://www.wcpss.net/history/>; Clifford V. Jones, *A History of Merger* (Raleigh: WCPSS, 1980).

32. *MCA*, Nov. 22, 26, Dec. 19, 1972, Jan. 5, 1973; *AJC*, July 11, 1971; Silver, "Changing Face," 93–126.

33. *Northcross v. Board of Education*, 312 F. Supp. 1150 (1970), 1157; *Northcross v. Board of Education*, 341 F. Supp. 583 (1972), 596; *MCA*, Nov. 2, 29, Dec. 8, 1972, Jan. 6, 1973; John Egerton, *Promise of Progress: Memphis School Desegregation, 1972–1973* (Atlanta: SRC, 1973).

34. *MCA*, Nov. 5, Dec. 5, 14, 1972, Jan. 14, 25–28, Aug. 15, Sept. 23, 1973; Egerton, *Promise*; David Nevin and Robert E. Bills, *The Schools That Fear Built: Segregationist Academies in the South* (Washington: Acropolis, 1976), 11, 26–36, 75–77; Orfield, *Public School Desegregation*, 24, 28.

35. Orfield, *Public School Desegregation*, 22–49; Orfield and Monfort, *Racial Change*, 7–9, 11–13, 20–21; Abbott, *New Urban America*, 51–54; Garreau, *Edge City*, 209–59.

36. *Bradley v. Richmond*, 462 F.2d 1058 (1972), 1078.

37. Orfield and Monfort, *Racial Change*, 23.

CHAPTER 12: REGIONAL CONVERGENCE

1. "Man and Woman of the Year: The Middle Americans," *Time* (Jan. 5, 1970), 10–17.

2. "The Troubled American: A Special Report on the White Majority," *Newsweek* (Oct. 6, 1969), 28–59.

3. Peter Schrag, "The Forgotten American," *HM* (Aug. 1969), 134–41; "Revolt of the Middle Class," *USN* (Nov. 24, 1969), 52–58.

4. Jonathan Rieder, "The Rise of the 'Silent Majority,'" in Fraser and Gerstle, *Rise and Fall of the New Deal Order*, 243–68; Barbara Ehrenreich, *Fear of Falling: The Inner Life of the Middle Class* (New York: HarperPerennial, 1990), 97–143.

5. Egerton, *Americanization*, xix–xxi.

6. *Report of the National Advisory Commission*, 1; NAACP, "Suburbia: The Next Frontier of the Civil Rights Movement?" 241:0902, SRC/UMI.

7. "Battle to Open the Suburbs: New Attack on Zoning Laws," *USN* (June 22, 1970), 39–40; *NYT*, June 3, 7, 1970; Ehrlichman to Nixon, Oct. 21, 1970, reprinted in Ehrlichman, *Witness*, 218; W. Dennis Keating, *The Suburban Racial Dilemma: Housing and Neighborhoods* (Philadelphia: Temple Univ. Press, 1994), 40–44.

8. "Furor over a Drive to Integrate the Suburbs," *USN* (Aug. 10, 1970), 23–24; *DFP*, May 28, 1970; *DN*, June 21–26, 1970; *WP*, July 27, Nov. 6, 1970; Nixon, "President's News Conference," Dec. 10, 1970, *WC*, 1653.

9. Nixon, "Federal Policies Relative to Equal Housing Opportunity," June 11, 1971, *WC*, 892–905.

10. Nixon, "Remarks at Economic Club of Detroit," Sept. 23, 1971, *WC*, 1315; *NYT*, Dec. 10, 1970, May 11, July 14, 1971, Jan. 9, 28, 1973; H. R. Haldeman, *The Haldeman Diaries: Inside the Nixon White House* (New York: Putnam's Sons, 1994), 210–11, 491–92.

11. *James v. Valtierra*, 402 U.S. 137 (1971), 141, 144–45; *Warth v. Seldin*, 422 U.S. 490 (1975), 491–93; *WP*, July 5, 1971; *NYT*, July 11, 1971.

12. Alexander M. Bickel, "Desegregation: Where Do We Go from Here?" *TNR* (Feb. 7, 1970), 20–22; Pat Watters, "Southern Integrationists Feel Betrayed—by the North," *NYT Magazine* (May 3, 1970), 26–27, 104–8; Charles Morgan, Jr., "Schools: Bickel's 'New Paternalism' Masks a National Retreat," *ST* (March 1970), 9.

13. Nixon, "President's News Conference," April 29, 1971, *WC*, 698–99; *NYT*, March 21, April 21–22, Aug. 4, 24, 1971; *CO*, Aug. 30, Sept. 19, 1971.

14. *Bradley v. Milliken*, 338 F. Supp. 582 (1971), 587; *Bradley v. Milliken*, 345 F. Supp. 914 (1972); *NYT*, Sept. 28, Oct. 18, 1971; *WSJ*, Nov. 24, 1971, June 15, 1972.

15. *CO*, Aug. 30, 1971; *NYT*, Sept. 5, 1971, Jan. 14, Feb. 16, March 15–16, 21, 1972; *RNL*, Jan. 13, 1972.

16. Nixon, "Educational Opportunity and Busing," March 16, 1972, *WC*, 590–93; *NYT*, Oct. 4, 1971, Feb. 15, March 18–19, 1972; Pat Watters, "That Big Old Busing Bamboozle," *ST* (April 1972), 2; LCCR Statement, May 25, 1972, folder 19, box 30, KMA/UNCC; LCCR Statement on Busing, Sept. 1972, folder 21, box 15, FDA/UNCC.

17. *NYT*, March 18, 24, May 12, 14–18, 1972.

18. Nixon, "Remarks on the Education Bill," June 23, 1972, *WC*, 1082–85; Nixon, "Remarks Accepting the Nomination," Aug. 23, 1972, *WC*, 1263–70; Nixon, "School Busing," Aug. 24, 1972, *WC*, 1279; Nixon, "Labor Day Radio Address," Sept. 2, 1972, *WC*, 1344; CO, May 2, June 2, 1972; *NYT*, May 17, July 14, Aug. 24–25, 1972; Bartley and Graham, *Southern Politics*, 164–68.

19. Nixon, "Remarks at a Reception in Atlanta," Oct. 12, 1972, *WC*, 1512–15; *NYT*, Oct. 13, Nov. 6–8, 1972; Guillory, "Edwards," 5; Lamis, *Two-Party South*, 28–30; Bartley and Graham, *Southern Politics*, 172–83.

20. *WP*, Oct. 22, 1971; *RTD*, Aug. 20, 1970; *NYT*, March 17, 1972; Kluger, *Simple Justice*, 604–9.

21. *Keyes v. Denver*, 413 U.S. 189 (1973), 200, 206, 216, 218–19, 251, 258; Alexander M. Bickel, "Busing: What's to Be Done?" *TNR* (Sept. 30, 1972), 21–23; *MCA*, Jan. 21–22, 1973.

22. *Milliken v. Bradley*, 418 U.S. 717 (1974), 733, 740–41, 745, 756.

23. *Milliken v. Bradley*, 418 U.S. 717 (1974), 759, 761, 763, 768, 782, 808, 814–15.

24. Orfield, *Must We Bus?*; Orfield, *Public School Desegregation*, 22–31; Hochschild, *New American Dilemma*; Formisano, *Boston against Busing*, 237–38.

25. Gary Orfield and Franklin Monfort, *Status of School Desegregation: The Next Generation* (Alexandria: NSBA, 1992); Orfield, *Urban Integration*; Jeffrey A. Raffel, *The Politics of School Desegregation: The Metropolitan Remedy in Delaware* (Philadelphia: Temple Univ. Press, 1980).

26. *Southern Burlington County NAACP v. Mount Laurel*, 67 N.J. 151 (1975); *Robinson v. Cahill*, 118 N.J. Super. 223 (1972); David L. Kirp, John P. Dwyer, and Larry A. Rosenthal, *Our Town: Race, Housing, and the Soul of Suburbia* (New Brunswick, N.J.: Rutgers Univ. Press, 1995); *NYT*, Aug. 19, Nov. 8, 2001; *Newark Star-Ledger*, Nov. 7, 2001.

27. *Serrano v. Priest*, 5 Cal. 3d 584 (1971); *San Antonio v. Rodriguez*, 411 U.S. 1 (1973), 18; "In Search of School Financing," *Time* (Feb. 19, 1973), 73; Cohen, *Consumers' Republic*, 240–51; Peter Schrag, "What's Good Enough?" *Nation* (May 3, 2004), 41–44; Jonathan Kozol, *Savage Inequalities: Children in America's Schools* (New York: HarperPerennial, 1992); Kozol, "Malign Neglect," *Nation* (June 10, 2002), 20–23.

28. Greenberg, *Middle Class Dreams*; Rieder, "'Silent Majority'"; "Suburbs Rule: How the Suburban Majority is Changing America," *NYT Magazine* (April 9, 2000).

29. Clotfelter and Hamilton, "Which Southern Strategy?"; Lamis, *Two-Party South*, 22–43; Bass and De Vries, *Transformation*, 32–40; *NYT*, Feb. 10, 1976; Thomas Frank, *What's the Matter with Kansas? How Conservatives Won the Heart of America* (New York: Metropolitan Books, 2004).

30. Marc Cooper, "God and Man in Colorado Springs," *Nation* (Jan. 2, 1995), 9–12; Peter Beinart, "Battle for the 'Burbs," *TNR* (Oct. 19, 1998), 25–29; Greenberg, *Middle Class Dreams*, 182.

31. William Schneider, "The Suburban Century Begins," *AM* (July 1992), 33–44; *NYT*, Jan. 16, 1986 (From quotation); Richard Moe and Carter Wilkie, "Sprawl Is Where the Voters Are," *TND* (March 1, 1999); Jennifer Veiga, "Winning in the Suburbs," *TND* (July 1, 1998); John B. Judis and Ruy Teixeira, "Majority Rules: The Coming Democratic Dominance," *TNR* (Aug 5 and 12, 2002), 18–23; Judis and Teixeira, *The Emerging Democratic Majority* (New York: Scribner, 2002); Matt Bai, "The Multilevel Marketing of the President," *NYT Magazine* (April 25, 2004), 42–49, 68, 126–29.

32. Black and Black, *Southern Republicans*, 3; Black and Black, *Vital South*; James M. Glaser, *Race, Campaign Politics, and the Realignment in the South* (New Haven: Yale Univ. Press, 1996); Ruy Teixeira and Joel Rogers, *America's Forgotten Majority: Why the White Working Class Still Matters* (New York: Basic Books, 2000); Nicholas Lemann, "The New American Consensus: Government of, by and for the Comfortable," *NYT Magazine* (Nov. 1, 1998), 37–42.

33. William Julius Wilson, *The Truly Disadvantaged: The Inner City, the Underclass, and Public Policy* (Chicago: Univ. of Chicago Press, 1997); Bruce Katz and Jennifer Bradley, "Divided We Sprawl," *AM* (Dec. 1999), 26–42; Myron Orfield, *American Metropolitics: The New Suburban Reality* (Washington: Brookings, 2002).

34. W.E.B. Du Bois, *The Souls of Black Folk* 1903; reprint, (New York: Bantam, 1989), xxxi.

EPILOGUE

1. *Riddick v. School Board of City of Norfolk*, 784 F.2d 521 (1986), 543; *NYT*, Feb. 18, 1970, Nov. 9, 1986; Raymond Wolters, *Right Turn: William Bradford Reynolds, the Reagan Administration, and Black Civil Rights* (New Brunswick, N.J.: Transaction, 1996); McGirr, *Suburban Warriors*, 187–216; Orfield and Eaton, *Dismantling Desegregation*.

2. "Deciding Desegregation" series, *CO*, Jan. 13–17, 1999; *CO*, May 3, 1969, March 31, 1999; *NYT*, Sept. 11, 1999; *Swann v. Charlotte-Mecklenburg*, 402 U.S. 1 (1971), 16.

3. *Capacchione v. Charlotte-Mecklenburg*, 57 F. Supp. 2d 228 (1999), 237, 290–91, 293–94.

4. *Belk v. Charlotte-Mecklenburg*, 269 F.3d 305 (2001), 335, 409, 415, 418. Although the appellate decision left room for differing interpretations, the concurring opinion by Chief Judge J. Harvie Wilkinson III appeared to capture the majority sentiment: "This holding puts the school district on a race-neutral footing going forward, thereby granting it a truly fresh start." The Supreme Court declined to review the Fourth Circuit ruling; *Capacchione v. Charlotte-Mecklenburg*, 535 U.S. 986 (2002); *Belk v. Charlotte-Mecklenburg*, 535 U.S. 986 (2002). Through 2004, the Supreme Court had neither issued a categorical color-blind mandate in the field of secondary school education nor clarified the constitutional scope and permissibility of race-conscious assignment policies in unitary districts, leaving the case law in the lower courts ambiguous and contradictory. Also see John Charles Boger, "Willful Colorblindness: The New Racial Piety and the Resegregation of Public Schools," *North Carolina Law Review* (Sept. 2000), 1719–96.

5. "Deciding Desegregation"; "The Face of Choice," *Educate!* (Sept. 26, 2002), 1–19; "2002–03 Adopted Student Assignment Plan" <http://www.cms.k12.nc.us/studentassignment02-03/introduction.asp>; "The Changing Face of CMS," *Educate!* (Sept. 17, 2004), 3.

6. Applebome, *Dixie Rising*, 148–81, and my personal observations in this and the following paragraph.

7. "Outerbelt: Coming Our Way" series, *CO*, July 20–25, 1997.

8. *NYT*, Sept. 11, 1999; *CO*, Feb. 6, 1970.

Index

Page numbers in italics refer to illustrations and tables.

Ad Hoc Committee for Education (Richmond), 287

affirmative action, 113, 261, 268; attacked as "reverse discrimination," 4–5, 210, 217; and "color-blind" conservatism, 324–26; as open-housing policy, 305–8; as school integration policy, 133, 171, 173–74, 202, 206–7, 215, 243, 245, 292, 300, 314, 328. *See also* busing; "color-blind" ideology

African Americans, 7; and biracial alliances in cities, 27, 48–53, 87, 100–1, 108–9, 112–14, 126, 129–31, 150–51, 215; and busing, 2, 107–9, 122–23, 139, 144–47, 154, 163, *164*, 166–68, 184–85, 203–7, 209–10, 219, 252, 255–57, 277–80, 285–87, 295–98, 308–11; and civil rights activism, 37, 39–40, 42, 59, 87–89, 92–93, 133, *145*; and discrimination within integrated schools, 173, 189, *190*, 193, 210, 219; electoral power of, 15, 27, 34, 41, 53–54, 101, 111–15, 214–15, 231–32, 237–39, 241–42, 253, 259–62, 267–73, 284, 296–97, 319–21; and homeowner politics, 178–79; in interracial movements, 14, 23, 95, 105, 123, 143, *145*, 156, 175–79, 193–95, 197–204, 210, 214–15, 287, 290–91, 295–97; living in suburbs, 52–53, 115, *116*, 117–18, 146, 188, 215, *216*, 218, 293, *294*, 304–8, 326, 347n.33; in middle class, 12, 14, 48, 100, 109–11, 129–30, 215, 255, 281, 286, 289, 292–94; portrayed as Middle Americans, 137, 234, 236; and residential segregation, 1–2, 9–12, 50–52, 64, 100, 126–28, 135, 142–43, 176, 212–13, 215, *282*, 297, 325; as students in segregated/integrated schools, 43, 105–9, 132–35, 147, 167–68, *278*, *279*, 290, 293–94, 298–99, *300*, 316, *317*; and suburban annexation, 52–53, 112, 184, 215, 281, 284–85; support for open-schools movement by, 58–59, 62, 67, 81, 95; and urban hypersegregation, 14, 109, *116*, 117–18, 215, *216*, 219, 293–94, 298–99, *300*, 315–16, *317*, 326–27; and voting rights, 11, 28, 39, 56, 181–83; and white violence, 38, 128, 258. *See also* Black Power; civil rights movement; NAACP; residential segregation; school desegregation; urban renewal; *specific cities and organizations*

Agnew, Spiro, 17, 157, 233, 246, 260, 267, 272–74

Alabama, 16, *27*, 230, 318; massive resistance in, 38, 41; political developments in, 228, *229*, 252–54, 271. *See also* Wallace, George

Alabamians behind Local Education, 41

Albany, Ga., 55, 70

Albuquerque, N.M., 316, *317*

Alexander, Fred D., 126, 130, 178, 181

Alexander, Kelly M., 130, 200, 213

Alexander v. Holmes, 243–44, 247

Ali, Muhammad, 253

"all deliberate speed," 25, 32, 74, 85, 103, 132–33, 243, 318. See also *Brown v. Board of Education*; school desegregation

Allen, Ivan, Jr., *49*, 71, 91, 99–101, 109–14

Almond, J. Lindsay, Jr., 33

American Civil Liberties Union, 108, 251

"American Dilemma," 2, 30, 47. *See also* "New American Dilemma"

"American Dream": in the New South, 17, 118; and racial exclusion, 1–2, 10; and school integration, 217; as suburban ideal, 213, 236, 301

American Exceptionalism: and mythology of racial innocence, 16, 303–4; and the Sunbelt South, 47, 115

annexation. *See* suburban annexation

antibusing movement, 108, *140*, *152*, *155*, *164*, 252–57, 264–70, 298, 302; in Charlotte, 139–74, *187*, 191–92, 200, 203, 206, 218–20, 329; color-blind platform of, 1–2, 14, 121–23, 142–43, *149*, 217, 246, 249; divisions within, 10, 14, 154–55, 165, 167, 175–77, 184–90, 193–97, 295–96; as national revolt, 4, 18, 157, 170, 221, 225–26,

antibusing movement (*continued*)
245–46, 248, 275, 300, 308–15; in Richmond, 285–93; supported by Nixon administration, 5–6, 137–38, 157–58, 244–45, 274, 279, 311–13; supported by Ronald Reagan, 211, 324. *See also* busing; Concerned Parents Association; Silent Majority

anticommunism: and open-schools movement, 58, 67, 88; and segregationist ideology, 56, 76, 82, 84, 96, 100, 154, 270, 285–86

antisprawl movement, 113–14, 213–15, 296–97, 322

apportionment. *See* political apportionment

Arkansas, 16, 27; massive resistance in, 23–25, 29, 35, 41, 71–72; political developments in, 229, 230–31, 268–69, 273. *See also* Little Rock

Arlington Committee to Preserve Public Schools, 33

Arnall, Ellis, 56, 79

Asheville, N.C., 274

Asian-Americans, 117, 219

Ashmore, Harry, 23, 25

Askew, Reubin, 267–68, 270

Athens, Ga., 55, 70, 81, 86, 88–89, 91

Atlanta Board of Education, 59, 71, 74, 85, 95–96, 105–7

Atlanta Chamber of Commerce, 301; boosterism of, 108, 114; municipal power of, 48, 99–100, 110–11; and school desegregation, 58, 107; silence during massive resistance of, 71, 80, 82, 90–92, 97; and suburban annexation, 52, 112

"Atlanta Compromise," 108–9, 114, 280

Atlanta Constitution, 36, 69, 78, 80, 83, 112, 114; boosterism of, 76, 87, 89, 100; endorsement of token desegregation by, 74; opposition to massive resistance of, 58, 62, 71

Atlanta Exceptionalism, 118, 128; as booster ethos, 45–46, 76; as "City Too Busy to Hate," 11, 47–48, 50, 53, 77, 94, 108; as growth ideology, 109–11, 113–15; and school desegregation, 92, 95, 97–98, 105, 108; as subset of American Exceptionalism, 47–48, 99, 115. *See also* "Charlotte Way"; Sunbelt Synthesis

Atlanta, Ga., 3–4, *51*, *110*, *116*, 245, 315–17; antibusing movement in, 108–9, 159,

225, 270; biracial alliance in, 48–54, 87, 100–1, 108–9, 112–14; black suburbanites in, 52–53, 115, *116*, 117–18, 347n.33; business leadership of, 11–13, 36–37, 48, *49*, 50–53, 57–58, 62, 70–71, 76, 79–80, 82–83, 87, 90–92, 97, 99–101, 105, 107–17; civil rights activism in, 23, 35, 48–49, 56, 59, 62, 66, 82, 87–89, 92–93, 95–96, 100, 105–9, 118; compared to Charlotte, 14, 99, 118, 124, 128, 171, 180, 204, 213, 220, 276, 327–28; economic development/urban renewal in, 44, 46–48, 50–53, 65, 109–17; elections in, 50, 56–59, 86, 99–101, 112–13, 238, 270; as headquarters of New South, 18, 45–47, 76, 92, 97, 105, 109–10, 113–15, 124, 280; mass transit in, 109, 111, 113; news media in, 36, 45, 56, 58, 60–63, 66, 69, 71–72, 74, 76–78, 80–81, 87, 89, 92, 95, 100, 108, 112, 114; northside "island suburbs" of, 13, 18, 44–45, 50–53, 59–66, 78, 100, 103, 106–8, 111–13, 117–18; Olympic Games in, 47, 114–15, 117, 327; open-schools movement in, 17–18, 36, 45–46, 53, 58–99, 101–5, 118; outer-ring suburbs of, 44, 47, 107–17, 277, 280, 300, 302; "pragmatic segregation," 72, 74–76, 78–85, 88–89, 92, 96, 103–4; private schools in, 78, 95, 100, 117–18; professional sports in, 110–11; and racial moderation, 46–50, 53, 64–66, 74–76, 91–93, 96, 99–106, 109, 111, 114–16; racial/residential transition in, 51–52, 64, 106–7, 109, 111–13, 118; religious groups in, 45, 58, 62, 65–66, 70, 77–78, 85, 95, 97; Republican politics in, 5, 57, 117, 230, 233–34, 238, 270, 313, 320; residential segregation in, 4, 12, 46–47, 50–53, 64, 79, 85, 100, 104–11, 115–18; school desegregation in, 94–99, 105–9, 118, 299, *300*; segregationist groups in, 82, 87, 95–96, 100; southside region of, 52, 64, 100, 106–8, 111–12, 238; and suburban annexation, 52–53, 111–12, 277; as Sunbelt metropolis, 6–7, 11, 16, 44–48, 51–52, 62, 109–11, 115–18; westside region of, *51*, 52–53, 64, *116*. *See also* Atlanta Exceptionalism; Buckhead; DeKalb County, Ga.; Fulton County, Ga.; Help Our Public Education; New South; Sunbelt Synthesis; *specific people and organizations*

Atlanta League of Women Voters, 52, 58, 62–63, 66, 95, 105, 107

Atlanta Negro Voters League, 48–50, 52–53
Atlanta University Center, 48, 105
at-large electoral systems. *See* political apportionment
Augusta Courier, 78
Augusta, Ga., 55, 70, 86, 101, 295
Austin, Tex., *300*, 309

backlash thesis: 3–7, 226–27, 239–41, 254, 262, 271–72, 274–75, 301–3, 319. *See also* conservatism; Southern Strategy
Baker v. Carr, 15, 28, 41, 68, 101
Bakke decision, 210, 325
Baltimore, Md., 171, *317*
Bank of America (Charlotte), 218, 327
Barnett, Ross, 90
Belk, Herman, 144
Belk, John, 126, 150–52, 161, 164, 178, 212–14, 328
Belk v. Charlotte-Mecklenburg, 326, 364n.4
Bell, Griffin, 80, 90, 108
Bennett, Elizabeth, 200, 210
Bentley, Jimmy, 270
Bergen County, N.J., 320
Berry, Phil, 191–92, 209
Beverly Woods (Charlotte), *127*, 154, *155*
Bickel, Alexander M., 308, 314
Birmingham, Ala., 12, 38, 129–30, 252–54
Black Belt: contrasted with Sunbelt South, 6–7, 15, 28, 45–46, 249; defined, 16, 27; in Georgia, 55; political influence of, 3, 27, 34, 41, 101, 228–29; segregationist sentiment in, 29, 32, 54–57, 70, 86, 131, 231, 254, 261; and support for massive resistance, 30, 39, 58–59, 81. *See also* Deep South
Black, Earl and Merle, 16, 231
Black Power, 14, 108–9, 113, 232, 279–80, 290
Black Solidarity Committee (Charlotte), 145–46, 179, 181
Blackmun, Harry, 313
Blacks. *See* African Americans
Bliley, Thomas J., Jr., 288
Bloomfield Hills, Mich., 306, 310
Booe, William, 159–60, 165, 167, 173, 181–82, 185, 191, 206
Book, John, 285–86
boosters. *See* business community; New South
Boothe, Armistead, 262

Bootle, W. A., 88
Boston, Mass., 13, 117, 209–10, 316, *317*
Boyte, Harry, 82
Bradley v. Richmond, 276, 285, 288–93, 299–300
Braswell, Benjamin G., 19
Breeden, Frances (Fran), 60, *61*, 62–63, 82, *83*, 87, 97
Brewer, Albert, 252–54
Broadrick, George, 164
Brock, Bill, 272
Brookings Institution, 322
Brooks, David, 8
Brookshire, Stan, 126, 129–30, 328
Brown v. Board of Education, 3, 43, 118, 146, 221, 249, 252, 313, 318, 336n.19; and "color-blind" formulas, 14, 45–46, 74, 148, *149*, 169–70, 217, 233, 325; and comprehensive integration, 122–23, 134, 136, 153, 206–8, 243, 247, 280, 288, 292; and "de facto" segregation, 16, 158, 245; and divided white South, 17, 26–28, 30, 39–40, 45, 53, 79; and exemption of suburbs, 18, 107–9, 299–300, 293–94, 314–16; and "freedom of choice" plans, 105–7, 132–33, 137; and massive resistance, 23–24, 29, 57–59, 87, 97; and political malapportionment, 28, 68; and southern leadership, 25; and token desegregation, 24, 74, 80–84, 96, 131–32; and transformation of the South, 15, 169, 202; and white liberals, 32, 34–35, 103–4, 124; and white moderates, 13, 31, 64–66, 69, 71–72, 75, 91–93, 266. *See also* busing; civil rights movement; massive resistance; neighborhood schools; open-schools movement; school desegregation; Supreme Court
Brown II. *See* "all deliberate speed"
Bryan, Wilson, 175, 186–88, 199–200
Bryant, Don, 199
Buckhead, 13, 44, 112, 124; annexed by Atlanta, 52–53; as elite enclave, 91, 107–9, 111; open-schools movement in, 60–62, 74, 76; political culture of, 63–65, 117–18; residential segregation in, 50, *51*, 64. *See also* Atlanta; Help Our Public Education; "island suburbs"
Buffalo, N.Y., 144
Bullard, Helen, 62
Bumpers, Dale, 269–70
Burger, Warren, 171–72, 243, 313–15, 318

Burnside, Edward, 129
Bush, George H., 6, 220
Bush, George W., 322
business leaders: control of municipal politics by, 11–14; growth ideology of, 26, 42, 48, 109–12, 114–17, 123–24, 212–13, 277, 296–97, 327; historical debates about, 11, 41, 90–92, 339n.28, 344n.30; and racial desegregation, 24, 29–30, 35–39, 129–31, 255–56, 279, 297–99; silence during busing by, 107, 150–51, 161–62, 286–88; silence during massive resistance by, 24–26, 33, 36–42, 70–71, 90–92; as target of grassroots revolts, 14, 112–14, 175–84, 213–15, 276, 281–85, 295; and urban renewal, 51–52, 126–28, 289. *See also* Atlanta, business leadership of; Chamber of Commerce, *specific chapters*; Charlotte, business leadership of; Southern Leadership Project; Sunbelt Synthesis
busing, 1–3, 221, 249, 295, 304, 324, 329; black attitudes toward, 108–9, 144–47, 154, *164*, 170, 189, *190*, 194, 200, 209–11, 219, 279–80, 293, 311; in Charlotte, 18, 118, 121–23, 134, 136–39, 151–56, 160–70, 173–76, 184–212, 217–19; in Greenville, 255–57; in Memphis, 297–99; in Mobile, 252; and "New South" governors, 259–61, 263–65, 267–70, 272–73; and Nixon administration policy, 157–58, 244–46, 279, 309–11; in the North and West, 16, 144, 247–48, 300, 302–3, 308–16; in Raleigh, 295–97; in Richmond, 19–20, 285–94; and suburban/metropolitan remedies, 9, 14, 107–9, 209, 276–80, 299–300, 310, 314–17; and the Supreme Court, 170–72, 293, 313–16; and transformation of southern education, 15, 274. *See also* affirmative action; antibusing movement; NAACP; residential segregation; school desegregation; *Swann v. Charlotte-Mecklenburg*
Byrd, Edwin O., 157
Byrd, Harry F., Jr., 262, 265, 287
Byrd Organization, 31–34, 261–62, 265

C&S Bank (Atlanta), 91, 111, 114
California, 10, 16, 233, 247, 273, 304, 307, 318, 320, 324
Cameron, C. C., 196
Campbell, Carroll A., Jr., 255
Capacchione, Bill, 324–25

Capacchione v. Charlotte-Mecklenburg, 220, 324–26, 329
Carmichael, James, 56
Carswell, G. Harrold, 247
Carter, Jimmy, 269–270, *271*, 319–20
Cash, Johnny, 253
caste system: as "American Dilemma," 2; and civil rights movement, 3, 42, 76; contrasted with class ideology, 26–30, 40–43, 45–46, 64, 66, 102, 122, 231–33; contrasted with residential segregation/spatial inequality, 4, 11, 15, 53, 118, 122, 291, 310, 326–27; and massive resistance, 23, 30, 57, 68, 81, 84, 89–90, 101; and politics of white supremacy, 13, 15, 26, 28, 34, 54, 56, 76, 101, 228; and school desegregation, 34, 104, 106, 146; and transformation of South, 17–18, 25, 40, 94, 274; and white liberals, 29, 40, 94, 274; and white liberals, 29, 102; and white moderates, 24, 41, 66, 99, 129. *See also* racial segregation
Cathey, Gene, 199
Chafe, William H., 49, 336n.16
Chamber of Commerce, 11, 295. *See also* business leaders; *specific cities and chapters*
Chambers, Julius, 133–35, 175, 187, 204, 207, 210–11, 328
Chapel Hill, N.C., 131
Charlotte Chamber of Commerce: and busing, 150, 156, 161–62, 164, 166, 172, 189, 196, 199, 210, 218–19; municipal power of, 126, 129–30, 133, 177–80, 213–14; support for countywide schools/government by, 128, 180–84
Charlotte Citizens for Independent Political Action, 179
Charlotte City Council, 126, 161, 178, 195, 214–15
Charlotte Country Day School, 169
Charlotte Housing Authority, 177–78, 200
Charlotte Latin School, 165, 169
Charlotte, N.C., 4, 12, *125*, *127*, *216*, *278*; antibusing movement in, 139–74, *187*, 191–92, 200, 203, 206, 218–20, 329; biracial alliance in, 126, 129–31, 144, 150–51, 215; black suburbanites in, 146, 188, 215, *216*, 218, 326; business leadership of, 123–31, 144, 150–51, 156, 161–66, 172, 176–84, 191–92, 196, 199, 210, 212–15, 218–19, 255, 327; civil rights activism in, 128–31, 133, 144–46; compared to Atlanta,

14, 99, 118, 124, 128, 171, 180, 204, 213, 220, 276, 327–28; economic development/urban renewal in, 123–24, *125*, 126–28, 129–31, 134–35, 162, 176–80, 210–15, 218–19, 327–28; elections in, 138, 159–60, 178, 182–83, 191–92, 205, 209, 219; failure of city-county consolidation in, 180–83, 295; interracial movements in, 123, 143, 145, 156, 160, 163, 175–79, 193–95, 197–204, 210, 214–15, 296; "island suburbs" of, 13, 123–24, 126, 151, 160, 176, 191–92, 195–96, 200, 204, 327–28; metropolitan integration remedy in, 122–23, 128, 136–37, 172, 175–76, 195–98, 209, 220–21, 276–79, 297, 300; as New South metropolis, 11, 121, 123–24, 131, 137, 162, 169, 174, 176, 179–80, 208, 210–11, 218, 327–28; north/west sections of, 126–28, 135, 146–47, 151, 160, 165–66, 168–69, 174–95, 209, 212–15; one-way busing in, 144–47; private schools in, 150, 154, 165, 167–69, 184, 186, 189, 196, 204, 210; professional sports in, 327; racial violence in, 128–29, 147, 173, 189, *190*, 193; racial/residential transition in, 126, 128, 132, 168–69, 176–78, 183–84, 186–89, 192, 194, 198, 204, 210, 212, *216*; religious groups in, 124, 129, 143, 145, 156–57, 165, 169, 181, 200; Republican politics in, 121–22, 137–38, 211, 230, 233, 238; residential segregation in, 1, 122, 126, *127*, 128, 130–37, 142–43, 150, 162–63, 170–71, 176–78, 202, 212–13, 215–17, 245, 326–29; Silent Majority in, 1–2, 18, 121–22, 141–42, 147–50, 153–54, 157–59, 163, 173, 176, 198, 217, 220–21, 325, 328–29; southeast (outer-ring) suburbs of, 124, 126, *127*, 138, 142–43, 146–47, 150–51, *152*, 154, *155*, 157–58, 160, 167–69, 174–78, 183–86, 192, 195–96, 205, 212–13, 215; suburban annexation in, 124, 128, 180, 183–84, 215, 276; suburban sprawl and, 123–24, 128, 130, 183, 198–99, 212–16, 218–220, 327–28; as Sunbelt metropolis, 3–4, 14, 121–23, 126, 128, 138, 169, 183, 210–15, 218–20, 327; two-way busing in, 151, 158–70, 174–76, 185–88, 192–209, 217, 220–21. *See also* "Charlotte Way"; Concerned Parents Association; Mecklenburg County, N.C.; Myers Park; New South; Sunbelt Synthesis; *Swann v.*

Charlotte-Mecklenburg; *specific people and organizations*

Charlotte Observer, 126, 220, 326; boosterism of, 129, 133; criticism of municipal leaders by, 150–51, 161, 165, 172, 177, 181–82; criticism of Richard Nixon by, 138, 158, 273; criticism of Ronald Reagan by, 211–12; as public sphere, 141, 143, 153–54, 163, 169, 175, 191, 205; support for antisprawl movement by, 213–14; support for busing by, 138–39, 142, 152, 160, 166–67, 188, 199–200, 208–9; support for fair desegregation by, 174, 193, 196

Charlotte Student Coordinating Council, 156, 166

"Charlotte Way": as booster ethos, 11, 123, 218; challenged by civil rights activists, 176–77; defined, 129, 131, 139; endangered by busing crisis, 144–47, 150–51, 161–62, 191; and racial moderation, 128, 130, 132, 140, 205; redefined, 208–9, 215; and residential segregation, 134–35, 198–99. *See also* Atlanta Exceptionalism; Sunbelt Synthesis

Chattanooga, Tenn., 36, 272

Charlotte-Mecklenburg Board of Education: and busing, 138, 140, 143–47, 150, 156–58, 161, 163, 166, 170–71, 199–200, 204, 206; elections to, 159–60, 181, 191–92, 205, 209, 219; favoritism toward southeast Charlotte by, 184–91, 193–96, 202–3; neighborhood schools policy of, 132–37; and resegregation, 168, 173–74, 207, 210, 325–26. *See also* Charlotte-Mecklenburg Public Schools

Charlotte-Mecklenburg Charter Commission, 180–82

Charlotte-Mecklenburg Community Relations Committee (CRC), 129, 131, 143, 189–91, 199–200

Charlotte-Mecklenburg Dimensions Committee, 214

Charlotte-Mecklenburg Hospital Authority, 179

Charlotte-Mecklenburg League of Women Voters, 143–45, 150, 156, 181–82, 191, 199–200, 219

Charlotte-Mecklenburg Planning Commission, 135, 181, 212, 214

Charlotte-Mecklenburg PTA Council, 166, 200

Charlotte-Mecklenburg Public Schools, 278; and busing litigation, 121, 134–37, 142, 170–72; city-county consolidation of, 123, 128, 277; class-based integration in, 174–76, 193–209, 220–21; closing of black facilities in, 133, 144–45; enrollment in, 124, 210, 219; initial desegregation of, 128, 132–33; as integration model, 14, 118, 210–12, 276, 278–79, 300; magnet programs in, 218–19, 324; one-way busing in, 144–47; racial violence in, 173, 189, *190*, 193; resegregation of, 325–29; two-way busing in, 151, 158–70, 185–88, 192, 217; "white flight" from, 168–69, 174, 197, 212. *See also* Charlotte-Mecklenburg Board of Education; Concerned Parents Association; *Swann v. Charlotte-Mecklenburg*; West Charlotte High School
Charlottesville, Va., 33
Chesapeake, Va., 281, 283
Chesterfield County, Va., *282, 294*; black suburbanites in, 293–94; controversy over metropolitan busing in, 289–93; controversy over suburban annexation in, 280–85; Republican gains in, 238, 262. *See also* Richmond
Chicago, Ill., 226, 232, 301, *317*
Chiles, Lawton, 268
Christian Right. *See* Religious Right
Citizens Advisory Group (CAG), 200–10, 219
Citizens against Busing (CAB), Memphis, 298
Citizens against Busing (CAB), Richmond, 285–86
Citizens Committee (Greenville), 255
Citizens Committee to Prevent Busing (Greenville), 255–56
Citizens' Council, 29, 81, 104
Citizens for a Neighborhood School System (Charlotte), 219
Citizens for a Positive School Board (Charlotte), 191
Citizens for Excellent Public Schools (CEPS), 290–93
Citizens for Orderly Development (Charlotte), 177–78
Citizens for the Complete Development of Charlotte-Mecklenburg, 179
Citizens Task Force for Future School Planning (Charlotte), 219
Citizens United for Fairness (CUFF), 175, 186–89, 191, 193, 195, 199–200

"City Too Busy to Hate." *See* Atlanta Exceptionalism
Civil Rights Act of 1964, 8, 15–17, 19, 101, 129, 170, 230, 313
civil rights movement, 4, 7, 14, 37, 239, 323, 329; challenge to residential segregation by, 2, 9, 16, 122, 130, 134, 158, 170–72, 176, 213, 227, 280, 304–10, 317–18; defeat of Jim Crow by, 3; marginalized by white moderates, 30, 45–46, 99, 104; and massive resistance, 26–30; and municipal politics, 12; in the North and West, 16, 221, 247–48, 301–18; and Richard Nixon/Nixon administration, 137–38, 232–38, 241–47, 274, 305–7, 309–13; suburban constraints on, 6, 209, 275, 303–8, 313–19; and transformation of the South, 15, 19, 41, 102, 118, 274, 316, 319, 321; and white southern liberals, 25–26, 37, 42–43, 308. *See also* African Americans; *Brown v. Board of Education*; busing; massive resistance; NAACP; school desegregation; *specific cities*
class: as analytical category, 4, 9–10; and busing formulas, 9, 123, 176, 184–88, 193–98, 208–9, 276–77, 286; and "color-blind" individualism, 1–5, 8, 42, 46, 53, 137–40, 142, 217, 300, 323; contrasted with caste ideology, 26–29, 42–43, 45–46, 66, 102, 122; and divisions among white southerners, 13–15, 18, 26, 28, 39, 50–52, 54, 100–1, 128, 160, 246, 249–50; fusion with racial ideology of, 40, 47; and interracial working-class movements, 14, 123, 175–79, 193–95, 214–15, 295–97; and middle-class consciousness, 18, 25, 30, 40, 42–43, 64, 121–22, 176; and political realignment in South, 226–33, 237–39, 262, 274; and reactionary populism, 9, 302–3, 316; and school desegregation formulas, 9, 13–14, 36, 45–46, 72, 74–75, 99, 104, 106–7; and socioeconomic prejudice, 143, 146, 183, 218, 220; and suburban politics, 3–4, 6–8, 39–40, 122, 275, 304, 319, 322–23; and suburban residential segregation, 2, 4, 10, 13, 17, 44, 64, 126, 148, 169, 212, 215, 233, 245, 306–8, 328–29; and spatial inequality, 114, 116, 118, 122, 281; and urban hypersegregation, 109, 118, 293–94, 298–99, 315–17, 326–27. *See also* integration (class-based)

Clayton County, Ga., 113, *116*
Cleveland, Ohio, 112, *317*
Clinton, Bill, 227, 319–21
Cobb County, Ga., 47, 113, *116*, 320
Coca-Cola Company, 48–49, 71, 76, 80, 115, 117
Cold War, 230; New South as showcase in, 98–99; and opposition to massive resistance, 58, 66; and rise of Sunbelt South, 10, 26, 47, 113, 123, 228
Coleman Report, 136
Collins, LeRoy, 36, 266
Colorado Springs, Col., 320
"color-blind" ideology: advanced by antibusing movement, 121–22, 139–41, 148, *149*, 153–54, *155*, 159, 163, *164*, 167, 169–70, 206, 225–26, 255, 286; challenged by Kerner Commission, 3, 237; and class privilege, 118, 220; as defense of "de facto" segregation, 10, 14, 17–18, 122–23, 170–71, 249, 305; and George W. Bush, 322; as product of massive resistance era, 13–14, 30, 40, 42–43, 45–46, 59, 65, 68, 74–75, 104–5, 132; progressive version of, 249–50, 259, 261–63, 268; and public policy, 171, 293, 307–8, 314–18, 325–29; and Reagan administration, 220, 324; and residential segregation, 4–5, 8, 16, 142–43, 221, 291–92, 304–8; and "reverse discrimination" charges, 210, 217, 220; and Richard Nixon/Nixon administration, 5, 17, 137–38, 158, 233–37, 244–45, 306–7, 312; and Silent Majority, 1–3, 19, 118, 157–58, 198, 328; and suburban politics, 6, 176, 227, 246, 275, 300, 304, 323; and whiteness, 4, 10, 333n5. *See also* affirmative action; antibusing movement; class; Concerned Parents Association; conservatism; constitutional law; meritocratic individualism
Columbia, S.C., 255–56, 260, 279, 295
Columbus, Ga., 55, 70, 86
Commerce Club (Atlanta), 87, 92
Committee to Insure Good Government (Charlotte), 182
Concerned Black Parents Committee (Greenville), 257
Concerned Parents Association (CPA), *140*, *152*, *155*, *187*, 324–25; "color-blind" ideology of, 1, 148, *149*, 169–70, 182, 210, 217; criticized by black parents, 144–45, 154,

166; decline of, 174, 191–92, 200; defense of southeast Charlotte suburbs by, 184–85; grassroots techniques of, 153, 159–60, 167–68, 211; as part of national antibusing movement, 170, 172, 225–26; as part of Silent Majority, 1–2, 121–22, 141–42, 148, 157–58, 173, 176, 221; pressure on Nixon administration by, 157–59, 161, 163; rallies organized by, 139–40, 150–52, 165–67, 181; and Republican politics, 138; residential segregation and, 122–23, 142–43; schisms within, 154, 165, 175–77, 186, 188–89, 194–95; suburban origins of, *127*, 139–41, 146–47, 327–28; support for one-way integration by, 141, 143, 220. *See also* antibusing movement; Charlotte; Silent Majority
Congress, U.S.: and antibusing movement, 157, 161, 211, 226, 257, 286, 310–12; and civil rights legislation, 15–16, 32, 39, 43; and midterm elections of 1970, 264–65, 267–68, 271–72; northern liberals in, 247–48; protection of suburban residential segregation by, 4, 305, 309; Republican trends in, 319, 321; southern segregationists in, 29; and Supreme Court nominees, 246–47, 313. See also *specific members*
Congress of Racial Equality (CORE), 279–80, 290
Connecticut, 115, 248, 309, 320
conservatism: and "color-blind" ideology, 2, 5, 198, 206, 245, 324–26, 328–29; and backlash thesis, 3, 5–6, 8–9, 226, 239–42, 251, 262, 273, 301–3; and grassroots politics, 7–8, 159–60, 178, 182, 185, 191, 200, 298; and growth liberalism, 7–8, 10; and racial/segregationist politics, 26, 29, 54–59, 104, 154, 169, 228, 230, 241–42, 246–48, 252–53, 258–61, 268, 272–73, 285–87; and suburban/Sunbelt politics, 3, 6–8, 15, 18, 28, 113, 122, 227–39, 265–66, 304, 312–13, 319–22. *See also* antibusing movement; New Right; Nixon, Richard M.; Religious Right; Republican party; Silent Majority
consolidation. *See* metropolitan consolidation
constitutional law: and de jure/de facto school segregation, 14, 16–17, 107, 133–37, 158, 170–72, 244–45, 308–10, 314–15; inconsistent application of in-school integration cases, 203, 221, 299–300; and permissibility of "economic

constitutional law (*continued*)
  segregation" in housing, 10, 304–8,
    317–18; and political apportionment, 15,
    28, 57; responsiveness to grassroots pres-
    sure of, 3–4, 291–93, 304–5, 315, 328–29;
    and school resegregation, 209, 220, 324–27;
    and socioeconomic discrimination, 198,
    318; and suburban protectionism, 2–4, 293,
    308, 313, 315, 323. *See also* busing; "color-
    blind" ideology"; school desegregation;
    Supreme Court; *specific cases*
consumer politics: and civil rights movement,
    64, 130; as defense of middle-class rights,
    3, 8, 14, 122–23, 140, 148, 198, 217; as
    ethos of meritocratic individualism, 26, 46;
    as ethos of New South, 30, 115–17, 211,
    304, 327–28; and school desegregation
    policies, 45–46, 106, 133, 137–38, 245; and
    suburban politics, 39–42, 227, 249, 304;
    and suburban residential segregation, 1–2,
    53, 64, 142–43, 217, 306–7, 323. *See also*
    antibusing movement; homeowner poli-
    tics; neighborhood schools
Cook, Jean, 143
corporate leaders. *See* business leaders
Cotswold (Charlotte), *127*, 204
Counts, Dorothy, 128
county unit system (Georgia), 44, 54–59,
    66–68, 79, 82–83, 86, 90, 101. *See also*
    political apportionment
Cramer, William, 267–68
Craven, Braxton, 132–33
Crosby, Kathleen, 194
Crusade for Voters (Richmond), 281, 284
Crutchfield, Charles, 161, 164, 172, 181,
    183, 185
Crutchfield, Ed, 218
Culbertson, Bob, 196, 203, 205

Dallas, Tex., 48, 232, 299, *300*
Darlington County Freedom of Choice Com-
    mittee, 257–58
Darlington County, S.C., 254, 257–58
Davidson County, Tenn., 278
Davis, Jimmie, 37
Davis, Mike, 8, 335n.10
Davis, Robert, 198, 209
Dayton, Ohio, 240, 305
"de facto" segregation: in artificial dichotomy
    with "de jure" segregation, 4, 14, 16, 134,
    143, 158, 245–46, 291, 307–10, 314, 323;

and city-suburban dichotomy, 315; and
    "color-blind" ideology, 17, 249; as defense
    of neighborhood schools, 107, 122, 133,
    138, 150, 226, 246, 286; and framework of
    southern exceptionalism, 4, 16–17,
    170–72, 244–45, 248, 314; as redefinition
    of state-sponsored residential segregation,
    10, 14, 227, 305–8, 328. *See also* antibus-
    ing movement; constitutional law; Nixon
    administration; North; racial segregation;
    residential segregation
"de jure" segregation. *See* caste system;
    "de facto" segregation; racial segregation
Dearborn, Mich., 306, 310
Deep South: contrasted with Sunbelt South,
    6–7, 28, 47–48, 95, 97, 131, 233, 249–50,
    263–64; and debate about political realign-
    ment, 6–7, 226–27; defined, 16; massive
    resistance in, 35, 37–39, 41, 70; regional
    fairness campaign in, 246–48, 274; Repub-
    lican gains in, 229–31; segregationist poli-
    tics in, 228, 229, 244; support for George
    Wallace in, 232, 237–39, 251–54. *See also*
    Black Belt; *specific states and cities*
DeKalb County, Ga.: black suburbanites in,
    115, *116*; mass transit in, 113; open-
    schools movement in, 64–65; political de-
    velopments in, 56, 238, 270; residential
    segregation in, *51*. *See also* Atlanta
Democratic Leadership Council (DLC), 321
Democratic party, 7–8, 242, 275; attacked by
    Ronald Reagan, 211; and black voters, 232,
    260, 273; and election of 1968, 237–40;
    and election of 1972, 310–13; and election
    of 1976, 319–20; and elections of 1970,
    271–72; New South wing of, 27, 48, 101,
    157, 249, 251, 259–62, 266–70, 273, 319;
    retreat from suburban integration by,
    310–12, 318; and rise of "New Demo-
    crats," 18, 227, 320–22; segregationist wing
    of, 28, 54–59, 89, 228–30, 241, 246–48,
    251, 253, 261, 264–65; and working-class
    white voters, 302–3, 319. *See also* Dix-
    iecrats; liberalism; New Deal Order; *spe-
    cific politicians*
Dent, Harry, 157, 233, 241–42, 244, 257–58,
    260, *263*, 265
Denver, Col., 157, 309, 314, *317*
Department of Health, Education, and Wel-
    fare (HEW), 157, 163, 243–45, 260, 279,
    285, 295, 309

Department of Housing and Urban Development (HUD), 305–7
desegregation: of low-income housing, 177–79, 200, 215, 289, 295–96, 305–8, 317–18, 329, 354n.26; of public accommodations, 12, 37, 50, 87, 100–1, 129–30. *See also* school desegregation
Detroit, Mich., 3, 9, 12–13, 16, 109, 112, 115, 232, *317*; busing controversy in, 18, 280, 293, 309–12, 314–15; open-housing controversy in, 16, 305–7
Detroit News, 306
Diggs, Robert M., 121
Dixiecrats, 6, 28, 41, 228–30, 261, 274
Doherty, James, 286
Dorsey, James, 74, 78
Douglas, William O., 314–15
Downing, Beverly, 86, 102
Druid Hills (Atlanta), 44, *51*
Dunbar, Leslie, 37, 42–43
Dunn, Winfield, 272
Durham, N.C., 131
Duval County, Fla., 277, *278*
Dylan, Bob, 202

Eastover (Charlotte), *127*, 191, 196, 204
economic development: of metropolitan South, 11–14, 26–28, 32, 40, 42, 46–53, *65*, 109–18, 123–28, 143, 176–80, 210–15, 218–19, 276–77, 280–81, 296–97, 327–28; and moderate opposition to massive resistance, 24–25, 30–31, 35–36, 39, 45–46, 58, 66, 75, 91; and "New South" Democrats, 36, 101, 260–61, 269; and political transformation of South, 6–9, 15–17, 41, 227–32, 237–38, 319–21; and suburbanization, 9–10; of Sunbelt, 10–11, 304. *See also* New South; Sunbelt Synthesis; urban renewal; *specific cities*
economic discrimination. *See* class; "de facto" segregation
economic integration. *See* integration (class-based)
Edenfield, Newell, 85
education, private. *See* private schools
education, public. *See* public schools
Edwards, Edwin, 270, 313
Egerton, John, 15, 301, 303–4
Ehrenreich, Barbara, 303
Ehrlichman, John, 241, 244, 305
Eisenhower, Dwight D., 32, 229–31

El Paso, Tex., *300*
elections (congressional): and failure of Richard Nixon's Southern Strategy in 1970, 6, 271–75; in Florida (1970), 267–68; in North Carolina (1972), 273; and Republican losses in 1970s, 319; and Republican takeover in 1996, 319, 321; in Tennessee (1970), 272; in Virginia (1966), 262; in Virginia (1970), 264–65; in Virginia (1972), 266
elections (gubernatorial): in Alabama (1970), 252–54; in Arkansas (1970), 268–69; and failure of Nixon's Southern Strategy in 1970, 6, 249–51, 271–75; in Florida (1966), 266; in Florida (1970), 267–68; in Florida (1974), 268; in Georgia (1942–50), 56; in Georgia (1954–58), 58–59; in Georgia (1962), 101; in Georgia (1970), 269–70; in Louisiana (1971), 270; in Mississippi (1971), 270; in North Carolina (1968), 272; in North Carolina (1972), 273; in South Carolina (1966), 254; in South Carolina (1970), 258–61; in Tennessee (1970), 272; in Virginia (1965), 261–62; in Virginia (1969), 262, *263*; in Virginia (1973), 266. *See also* Democratic party, New South wing of; Southern Strategy
elections (municipal): in Atlanta (1957), 50, 59; in Atlanta (1961), 99–100, 109; in Atlanta (1969), 112; in Atlanta (1973), 112–13; in Charlotte (1969), 178; in Charlotte (1970), 159–60; in Charlotte (1971), 178, 180–83; in Charlotte (1972), 191–92; in Charlotte (1973), 213; in Charlotte (1974), 205; in Charlotte (1976), 209; in Charlotte (1977–87), 214–15; in Little Rock (1958), *25*; in Raleigh (1972–73), 296–97; in Richmond (1970–77), 284
elections (presidential), 5–6, 27, 226–27, *229*, 319; in 1948, 28, 228; in 1952, 229–30; in 1956, 230; in 1960, 230; in 1964, 230–31; in 1968, 28, 137–38, 232–40, 254; in 1972, 310–13; in 1976, 319–20; in 1980–84, 320; in 1992, 320–21; in 2000, 322
electoral apportionment. *See* political apportionment
Emerging Republican Majority, The, 5, 226, 239–41, 273, 320. *See also* Phillips, Kevin P.
Ervin, Sam, 157
exclusionary zoning. *See* zoning

fair housing. *See* open-housing movement

Fair Housing Act of 1968, 305–7

Fairfax County, Va., 262

Fairfield County, Conn., 320

Faubus, Orval, 23–24, 268–69

federal courts: approval of gradual/token desegregation by, 74–75, 84–85, 106, 132–33; attacked by antibusing movement, 1–2, 139–42, 148–58, 166–67, 170, 225–26, 255–56, 285–87, 290; attacked by northern politicians, 310–12; attacked by Richard Nixon/Nixon administration, 157–58, 242–45, 274, 311–12; attacked by southern politicians, 23–24, 58–59, 77, 247–48, 252–53, 256, 258–60, 267, 269–70; busing ordered by, 108, 136–37, 151, 162–63, 171–72, 185, 285, 291–92, 295–96, 310; city-suburban consolidation overturned by, 209, 293–94, 299–300, 314–16; and civil rights movement, 37, 40–41, 221; "de facto" segregation/economic discrimination upheld by, 17, 107, 143, 307–8, 314, 317–18; invalidation of school-closing legislation by, 34, 38, 88, 90; and politicization of law, 3–4, 304–5, 315, 328–29; reconstituted by Republican presidents, 313–14, 328; and school resegregation, 176, 187–88, 207–8, 220, 324–27; and "socio-economic integration," 195–98, 202–6; and suburban annexation, 184, 284; supported by white southern moderates and liberals, 74, 93, 103–4, 255–56, 259, 263–64, 268–69, 272–73, 288, 290–91; unstable integration plans ordered by, 279, 297–98. *See also* busing; constitutional law; massive resistance; school desegregation; Supreme Court; *specific cases and judges*

federal government: attacked by Silent Majority, 1–2, 8, 139, 148–49, 165, 169, 225–26, 285, 303, 320; attacked by southern segregationists, 247–48, 251–53, 258–60, 310; cautious enforcement of *Brown* by, 25, 31–32, 39; civil rights intervention in South by, 15, 23, 36, 38–43, 49, 59, 80, 89, 101–2, 130, 261; criticized by Richard Nixon, 5, 137; policies establishing residential segregation of, 1, 3, 10–12, 16, 50, 126, 129, 134–35, 142–43, 276, 291–92, 310; spending programs in metropolitan/Sunbelt South of, 10, 15, 26–27, 47, 109–11, 123, 228; subsidies for

suburban homeowners by, 1–2, 8–10, 212, 281; retreat from remedies for metropolitan inequality by, 4, 237, 275, 304–18, 324. *See also* Congress; federal courts; Nixon administration; Supreme Court

Federal Housing Administration, 10, 310

Fifield, Harry, 70

Fifth Circuit Court of Appeals, 107–8, 252

Finch, Robert, 157, 243–45

Finger Plan (Charlotte-Mecklenburg), 151–2, 156, 158, 161

Florida, 16, 27, 63, 117; city-county consolidation in, 277–79; metropolitan growth in, 230; political developments in, 229–31, 237, 247, 266–68, 270, 310–11, 321; school desegregation in, 29–30, 36, 278

Ford, Gerald R., 319

"Forgotten Americans," 5, 137, 141, 232, 236–37, 302, 319. *See also* Middle Americans; Silent Majority

Fort Lauderdale, Fla., 278

Fort Worth, Tex. *300*

Fourth Circuit Court of Appeals, 246–47; and Charlotte litigation, 133, 158, 160–61, 163, 170–71, 202, 326, 364n.4; and Greenville litigation, 254; and Norfolk litigation, 324; and Richmond litigation, 276, 293, 299–30

"freedom of choice." *See* school desegregation

Friedman, Maxine, 60–63, 98

From, Al, 321

Front Royal, Va., 33

Fulton County, Ga.: mass transit in, 113; open-schools movement in, 60–66, 76, 78; political developments in, 54, 238, 270; residential segregation in, 50, *51*, *116*; and suburban annexation 52–53, 111–12. *See also* Atlanta; Buckhead

Gainesville, Ga., *55*, 69–70

Gantt, Harvey, 214–15

Garland, Ray, 265

General Assembly of Georgia, 54, 59, 76–77, 79, 84–89

Georgia, 16, *55*; county unit system/segregationist politics in, 44, 54–59, 79; massive resistance program of, 53, 59, 67–69, 77; metropolitan growth in, 230; and North Georgia/South Georgia divisions, 54–58, 79, 81–82, 101; open-schools movement

in, 36, 41, 45, 60–79, 85–87, 101–4; political developments in, 17, 101, 229, 238, 269–70, *271*, 273, 313; and regional fairness campaign, 247; Republican gains in, 57, 238, 270; shift to token desegregation in, 79–85, 88–99, 105–6. *See also* Atlanta
Georgia Chamber of Commerce, 87, 91
Georgia Council on Human Relations, 70, 95
Georgia Institute of Technology (Georgia Tech), 66, 88
Georgia League of Women Voters, 56–59, 66, 70, 72, 77, 81, 86–87
Georgia States' Rights Council, 77–78
Georgians Unwilling to Surrender (GUTS), 87, 100
Gingrich, Newt, 6, 226, 319
Godwin, Mills, Jr., 262, 266
Goldwater, Barry, 5–7, 226, 230–32, 237, 239–42, 274
"Goldwater Republicans," 233, 244, 249, 251, 254, 256, 258–59, 265–66, 270, 273, 313
Gore, Albert, 272
gradual desegregation. *See* school desegregation
Grady, Henry, 97
Graham, Billy, 301, 328
grassroots politics, 63, 104, 122, 198, 208–9; as counterpoint to top-down political history, 3, 5–10, 41–43, 90–93, 226–28, 315; as neighborhood-based revolt against downtown leadership, 14, 111–13, 176–84, 189–90, 213–15, 276–77, 281–85, 295–97; as suburban backlash against racial liberalism, 1–5, 16, 121–23, 148–59, 217–20, 225–26, 249, 275, 301–6, 310–12, 319, 323; and transformation of South, 13, 17–19, 25–26, 30, 39–41, 102–4, 138, 227–28, 238, 320–22. *See also* antibusing movement; civil rights movement; Concerned Parents Association; Help Our Public Education; open-schools movement; Silent Majority; *specific cities*
Gray, James, 89
Great Migration, 7, 314
Great Society, 7, 231–32, 234, 238, 273, 302–3, 305, 319, 321
Greater Atlanta Council on Human Relations (GACHR), 82, 95–96, 105
Green v. New Kent County, 171, 243, 245
Greensboro, N.C., 37, 49, 131–32, 238, 279

Greenville Christian Ministers Association, 256
Greenville, S.C., 254–57, 259–60, 278–80, 300
Griffin, Marvin, 58–59, 101
Grosse Pointe, Mich., 13, 115, 310
growth liberalism, 7–8, 10, 47, 228
Gwinnett County, Ga., 113, *116*

Halberstam, David, 272
Hall, Robert C., Jr., 19
Hammer, Jane, 95
Harding, Vincent, 108–9
Harper's Magazine, 103, 302
Harris, David, 132
Harris, Roy, 78
Harris, Thomas (Tom), 2, 139, *140*, 143, 151, 153, 159–60, 163, 165, 167–68, 185–86, 206, 209, 324, 329. *See also* Concerned Parents Association
Harris, W. T., 196, 201, 204
Hartsfield, William B., 11, 48, *49*, 50–53, 59, 62, *65*, 69, 76–77, 79, 82, 87–88, 91–92, 97–100, 112, 115. *See also* Atlanta
Hawkins, Reginald, 130
Haynsworth, Clement F., Jr., 133, 246
Helms, Jesse, 211, 273, 325
Help Our Public Education. *See* HOPE
Henrico County, Va., *282*, *294*; black suburbanites in, 293–94; controversy over suburban annexation in, 281, 283, 285; controversy over metropolitan busing in, 289–93; Republican gains in, 238, 262. *See also* Richmond
Hidden Valley (Charlotte), *127*, 188
Hirsch, Arnold R., 7
Hispanics. *See* Latinos
Holloman, Charles, 296
Holmes, Hamilton, 88
Holshouser, James E., Jr., 273
Holt, Curtis, 284
Holt v. Richmond, 284
Holton, Linwood, 261–63, *264*, 265–66, 270, 273, 286–88, 290
homeowner politics: and backlash thesis, 301–3; and class identity, 9–10; and conflicts over municipal power, 175–80, 184–88, 193–95, 213–15, 295–96; as defense of residential segregation/neighborhood schools, 1–2, 4, 121–23, 139–42, 148–58, 285–93, 298–99, 305–7, 310–12,

homeowner politics (*continued*)
317–18, 323; and opposition to suburban
annexation, 14, 111–12, 180–84, 276,
281–85; as populist suburban identity, 7–8,
122; and suburban entitlement programs,
9–10. *See also* antibusing movement; consumer politics; grassroots politics; Silent
Majority
Hooker, John Jay, 272
Hooper, Frank, 71, 75, 84–85, 90, 106
HOPE (Help Our Public Education), *61, 73,
75, 83*; attacked by segregationists, 67–68,
77–78, 100; based in northside "island suburbs," *51*, 62–66; and business community,
36, 41, 70–71, 91–93; deployment of gendered imagery by, 63, 77–78; endorsement
of "controlled desegregation" by, 71–76,
78–79, 81–82, 84; legacies of, 45–46,
101–5, 118; open-schools strategies of,
66–70; origins of, 60–63; preparation for
desegregation by, 89, 94–98; statewide
outreach of, 70, 76–77, 85–89. *See also*
Atlanta; Buckhead; liberalism;
moderates (white); open-schools
movement
housing. *See* open-housing movement; public
housing; residential segregation
Houston, Tex., 48, 115, 159, 299, *300*
Howell, Henry, 266
Hudson, Jack, 165
Huff, Marylyn, 191–92, 199, 201, 205
Humphrey, Hubert, 227, 232, 234, 237–38,
302–3, 310–11
Hunt, James B., Jr. (Jim), 273
Hunter, Charlayne, 88
Huntley, Ben, 159
hypersegregation. *See* racial segregation

Indianapolis, Ind., 316, *317*
industrial development. *See* economic
development
integration (class-based): and busing fairness,
174–75, 193–97, 203–8, 295–96, 316; and
formulas encompassing suburbs, 9, 123,
198, 209, 276–77, *278*, 300, 327, 329; and
resistance to "economic integration," 17,
118, 178–79, 195, 220, 233, 286, 305–8,
317–18; and school desegregation policies,
13–14, 18, 36, 74–75, 104–7, 129, 157–58.
See also class; "de facto" segregation; "New
American Dilemma"

integration (racial): and "American
Dilemma," 30; and antibusing movement,
121, 139–44, 151–54, 157–58, 226–27, 255;
attacked as "forced integration"/"forced
busing," 5, 16, 29, 88, 137, 211, 247–48,
252–53, 256, 273, 287, 292, 299, 305–6,
310, 312; as civil rights agenda, 2, 12, 32,
38, 40–43, 82, 96, 105, 118, 121–22,
132–34, 156, 242–43, 268, 304–5, 307; and
class inequality, 10, 106–7, 123, 175–76,
184–97, 279, 302–3, 316; and evolution of
white attitudes, 169–70, 173, 211, 217; and
exclusionary zoning, 13; and fears of "massive integration," 28, 64–68, 72, 84–85, 90,
100, 241, 257, 308; and "integration paradox," 137–38, 201–2; and Nixon administration policies, 157–58, 171, 242–46, 274,
305–7, 311, 359n.38; and open-schools
movement, 24–26, 33–35, 45–46, 53,
66–67, 74, 75, 78, 95, 102–4; and public
opinion polls, 99, 239, 245–46, 249, 302,
309; and southern public schools, 15, 274,
278, *300*, 316; and suburban/metropolitan
remedies, 3, 9, 14, 18–19, 107–9, 123,
136–37, 147, 198, 220–21, 276–80, 284,
289–300, 309–10, 313–18. *See also* affirmative action; *Brown v. Board of Education*;
busing; open-housing movement; school
desegregation; *Swann v. Charlotte-
Mecklenburg*
Interested Citizens Association (ICA), 156,
160, 163
Interstate Highway Act of 1956, 10
Involved Memphis Parents Assisting Children and Teachers (IMPACT), 298
"island suburbs," 14, 18, 24, 296; in Atlanta,
18, 44–45, 50–53, 59–66, 78, 100, 103,
106–8, 111–13, 117–18; in Charlotte,
123–24, 126, *127*, 151, 160, 176, 191–92,
195–96, 200, 204, 327–28; defined, 13. *See
also* Buckhead; Myers Park

Jackson Clarion-Ledger, 248
Jackson, Henry, 310
Jackson, Kenneth T., 9
Jackson, Maynard, 112–13
Jackson, Miss., 39, 41
Jacksonville, Fla., 268, 277, *278*
James v. Valtierra, 307
Jenkins, Herbert, *98*
Jim Crow. *See* caste system

Johnson, Lyndon B., 8, 39
Jonas, Charles R., 157
Jones, Harrison, 71

Kazin, Michael, 8
Kelly, Betsey, 144, 159
Kennedy, John F., 36, 38, 94, 98, 229–30
Kennedy, Robert F., 232
Kerner Commission, 2, 5, 18, 236–37, 280, 304–5
Kerry, Coleman, 144, 159–60
Key, V. O., Jr., 15
Keyes v. Denver, 314
Kilpatrick, James J., 40, 292
King & Spalding (Atlanta), 80, 92
King, Lonnie, 108
King, Martin Luther, Jr., 31, 87, 104, 117, *190*, 232, 270, 325
Kirk, Claude, 266–68
Knoxville, Tenn., 36
Kozol, Jonathan, 318
Ku Klux Klan, 89, 104

Lamar, S.C., 257–60
Lane, Mills B., Jr., 91, 114
Las Vegas, Nev., 316, *317*
Latimer, Pete, 78–79
Latinos, 117, 219, 299, 316, 321, 326–27
"law and order": and open-schools movement, 24, 92, 97, 105; and Richard Nixon, 5–6, 146, 232, 234, 236, 260, 274, 313; and white attitudes, 238; and white neighborhoods, 176–77, 240, 302
Leadership Conference on Civil Rights (LCCR), 280, 307, 311
League of Women Voters (LWV), 66; in Greenville, 255; and massive resistance, 29; in Memphis, 298; national organization of, 66, 107, 170; in Virginia, 33, 290. *See also* Atlanta League of Women Voters; Georgia League of Women Voters; Charlotte-Mecklenburg League of Women Voters
Leake, George, 145, 166, 181
Legal Defense Fund (LDF): 133, 170, 225, 243, 246, 280. *See also* NAACP
Lenox Square Mall (Atlanta), 65, 76, 117
Leonard, Paul, 130–31, 176–77
Letson, John, *98*, 106
liberalism: and *Brown v. Board of Education*, 13–14, 17–18, 23, 25–26, 30–32, 35–43, 66,
85; and busing, 107–8, 122, 143–45, 156, 166, 169, 194, 199–201, 205, 208–9, 268, 286–87, 290; criticized by Republican politicians, 5, 211, 232, 245, 260, 267, 272, 312; failure to confront class/suburban privilege by, 10, 131, 176–77, 195, 227, 240, 248, 300, 302–4, 308–12, 318, 322–23; and New Deal Order, 6, 8; and open-schools movement/token desegregation, 45–46, 64, 70, 74, 84, 91–93, 96, 102–5, 118; and political realignment, 8–9, 226–27, 237–40, 258–59, 266, 319–22; and private schools, 114, 118, 247–48; as "race-conscious" liberalism, 2, 198, 242, 289, 302, 305; racial contradictions of, 7; and segregationist politics, 28. *See also* affirmative action; civil rights movement; Democratic party; Great Society; growth liberalism; Kerner Commission; Southern Regional Council
Life, 63
Lightner, Clarence E., 296
Lincoln, Abraham, 225, 231, 263
Little Rock, Ark.: massive resistance in, 23, 38, 50, 72, 92, 99; open-schools movement in, 24–25, 60, 69; political developments in, 268–69
Little Rock Chamber of Commerce, 24, 36–37, 71
Lockheed Corporation, 47, 91
Lokey, Hamilton, 66
Lokey, Muriel, 60, *61*, 62–63, 66, 102
Los Angeles, Cal., 327; busing controversy in, 157, 308–9, 315; racial segregation in, 317, *317*; racial unrest in, 130, 232, 260; suburban politics in, 8, 302; suburban sprawl in, 113, 115, 213
Louisiana, 16, *27*, 274; massive resistance in, 37–38, 41, 86–87, 90, 247; political developments in, 228, *229*, 230, 270, 313
Louisville, Ky. 316, *317*
Loury, Glenn C., 329
Lowe, Charles, 151, 161–62, 164
Lower South. *See* Deep South
low-income housing. *See* public housing

Mackay, James, 44, 56, 65
Mackenzie, Ross, 287
Macomb County, Mich., 312
Macon, Ga., 55, 81, 86
Maddox, Lester, 50, 82, 87, 100, 269–70

Manatee County, Fla., 267
Marietta, Ga., 70
Marney, Carlyle, 129
Marsh, Henry III, 284
Marshall, Burke, 35
Marshall, Thurgood, 35, 307, 315
Maryland, 312
Mason, Elsie, 194
Mason, Julian, 193–94
Massachusetts, 318
Massell, Sam, 112
massive resistance, 3, 7, 17–18; in Alabama,
  38; in Arkansas, 23–25; and "color-blind"
  desegregation strategies, 13–14, 30, 40,
  42–43, 45–46, 59, 65, 68, 74–75, 104–5,
  132; in Georgia, 56–93; legacies of, 30,
  45–46, 103–4, 122, 274–75; in Louisiana,
  37–38, 86–87; in Mississippi, 38–39; ori-
  gins of, 25–29; resurrected in 1970, 247,
  249–52, 258, 266–67, 273; silence of busi-
  ness leaders during, 24–26, 33, 40–42,
  70–71, 90–92; in Virginia, 32–34; and
  white liberals, 26, 31, 35–43, 102–4. See
  also *Brown v. Board of Education*; open-
  schools movement; school desegregation;
  Southern Leadership Project
Maulden, Julia, 144
McColl, Hugh, 218
McDavid, James E., Jr., 1
McDuffie, Jim, 178, 213
McGill, Ralph, 36, 62, 69, 78, 80, 82, 88, 90,
  96–97, 114
McGovern, George, 311–13, 319
McKeithen, John, 247
McKnight, C. A. "Pete," 161, 207
McLaughlin, John, 205
McMillan, James B., 121, 201, *207*, 208, 328;
  background of, 133–34; comprehensive
  busing ordered by, 123, 136–37, 142, 151,
  158–59, 161–63, 171–72, 221; criticism of
  antibusing movement by, 138, 146; criti-
  cized by antibusing movement, 148, 152,
  170; criticized by Nixon administration,
  157; orders to prevent school resegregation by, 173–74, 176, 185, 188, 193,
  202–3, 206–7, 210; orders to pursue
  "socioeconomic integration" by, 194–96,
  198. See also *Swann v. Charlotte-
  Mecklenburg*
McNair, Robert, 254–56, 258
McRae, Robert M., Jr., 297–98

Mecklenburg Christian Ministers Association, 143, 156
Mecklenburg Citizens for Fair Taxation, 179
Mecklenburg Conservatives, 182, 191
Mecklenburg County Commission, 126, 151,
  161, 179, 195–96, 201, 204
Mecklenburg County, N.C., *127, 216*; antibusing movement in, 139, 165; failure
  of city-county consolidation in, 180–83;
  neighborhood politics in, 175–80; residential segregation in, 126, 134–35, 212; suburban annexation in, 128, 183–84, 215;
  suburban growth in, 123–24, 213–15, 219,
  328. *See also* Charlotte; Charlotte-
  Mecklenburg Public Schools; *Swann v.
  Charlotte-Mecklenburg*
Memphis Chamber of Commerce, 297–99
Memphis, Tenn., 13, *300*, 314; busing controversy in, 297–300; failure of city-county
  consolidation in, 295, 297; political developments in, 272
Merhige, Robert R., Jr., 276, 284–85, 288,
  290–94
meritocratic individualism: as defense of residential segregation, 1, 8–9, 46, 122, 153,
  323; as ideology of white innocence, 2,
  142–43, 221; and middle-class suburban
  politics, 3, 26, 28, 30, 42–43, 53, 64, 118,
  198, 231, 233, 249, 323; and opposition to
  affirmative action, 4–5, 122–23, 217, 325;
  and Republican politics, 230, 262–63. *See
  also* class; color-blind ideology; Silent
  Majority
Metropolitan Association for Segregated
  Education (Atlanta), 82
Metropolitan Atlanta Rapid Transit Authority
  (MARTA), 113
metropolitan consolidation: of city and
  county school systems, 123, 128, 252,
  277–79, 296–97, 316; as civil rights strategy, 19, 108–9, 276–77, 280, 289–93, 299,
  310, 314–15; and efforts to merge city and
  county governments, 13, 112, 180–83, 214,
  281–85, 295, 297; and stable school integration plans, 172, 197–98, 209, 212,
  255–57, *278*, 300, 316. *See also* Charlotte-
  Mecklenburg Public Schools
metropolitan growth. *See* South, metropolitan growth in
Metropolitan Planning Commission
  (Atlanta), 52

Meyer, Sylvan, 69
Miami, Fla., 233–34, 278; busing controversy in, 225, 279; political developments in, 268; school desegregation in, 36
Michigan, 267; busing controversy in, 226, 310–11, 313–15; open-housing conflict in, 305–7; political developments in, 311–12
Middle Americans: and antibusing movement, 225–26; and backlash thesis, 301–4, 311; Bill Clinton's appeals to, 227, 320; debate about, 239–40; populist defenses of, 8; Richard Nixon's appeals to, 5, 232–34, 236; and suburban identity politics, 141, 198, 319. *See also* Forgotten Americans; Silent Majority
middle class (black). *See* African Americans
middle class (white): and government entitlement programs, 10; and mobilization of Silent Majority, 1–2, 121–22, 141–42, 148, 157–58, 198, 225–26; and political transformation of South, 6–7, 15, 25–30, 39–43, 45–46, 226–40, 274–75, 319–22; and suburban politics, 3–5, 7–8, 13–14, 17–18, 322–23. *See also* antibusing movement; "color-blind" ideology; Concerned Parents Association; Help Our Public Education; meritocratic individualism; moderates (white); open-schools movement; *specific cities*
middle-class consciousness. *See* class
Midwest: migration to South from, 15, 44; political developments in, 232, 237, 320–21; racial segregation in, 244, 286, 308, 316–17; white backlash in, 7, 302. *See also* North; Rust Belt; *specific states and cities*
Milliken v. Bradley, 209, 314–16
Milwaukee, Wis., 110, *317*
Minneapolis, Minn., 248, 316, *317*
Mississippi, 16, 27, 40, 226, 232, 308; massive resistance in, 38–30; political developments in, 6, 228, 229, 231, 270; school desegregation in, 41, 243–44, 247–48
Mississippi Economic Council, 39
Mississippians for Public Education, 41
Mitchell, John, 243–44
mixed-income zoning. *See* zoning
Mobile, Ala., 252–53, 278, 279
Mobile Register, 248
moderates (white): in Atlanta, 48–50, 58–86, 94–109, 115–16; and *Brown v. Board of Education*, 64–66, 69, 71–72, 75, 91–93; in Charlotte, 126–33, 139, 141–42, 151, 159–60, 165–66, 169, 188–92, 208, 211; and civil rights movement, 45–46, 99, 104; defined, 13–14, 28; establishment of residential segregation by, 11–12, 50–53, 100, 122, 126–28, 183; historical debates about, 40–41, 91–93, 339n.26; in Little Rock, 24–25; national approval of, 99; opposition to massive resistance by, 17–18, 30; and political transformation of South, 229–33, 237–39, 241–42, 249–50, 259–73, 320–22; as "silent moderates," 25–26, 31, 35–39; in Virginia, 32–34. *See also* business leaders; Help Our Public Education; New South; open-schools movement; Sunbelt Synthesis
Montgomery, Ala., 50, 254
Montgomery County, Md., 354n.26
Morgan, Charles, Jr., 251, 308
Mount Laurel, 317–18
Mount Laurel litigation, 317–18
municipal politics: and biracial alliances, 27, 48–50, 99–100, 111–13, 126, 128–31; and massive resistance, 25; and neighborhood-based revolts, 113–14, 175–84, 213–15, 281–85; and residential segregation, 12, 50–53, 127–28, 212–13, 281, 289, 296–97; in Sunbelt South, 11–15, 123–24. *See also* specific cities
Murrow, Edward R., 85
Muse, Benjamin (Ben), 23–24, 31–39, 43. *See also* Southern Leadership Project
Myers Park, 13, *127*; annexed by Charlotte, 124; antibusing movement in, 151, 159; as center of municipal power, 126, 162, 176–79, 182–83, 215; and controversy over busing equalization, 185, 195, 201, 204–6; as elite enclave, 124, 146, 167, 328; support for busing compliance in, 160, 192, 199–200. *See also* Charlotte; "island suburbs"
Myers Park Baptist Church, 129, 134, 139, 145, 156, 201
Myers Park High School, 124, *133*
Myrick, Sue, 215

NAACP (National Association for the Advancement of Colored People), 221; and activism by local chapters, 39, 130; in alliances with white liberal/moderate groups,

NAACP (*continued*)

35, 62, 67, 95, 199; attacked by segregationists, 50, 78, 84, 100; campaign against
Plessy v. Ferguson by, 29; challenge to residential segregation by, 172, 213, 307; challenge to school segregation in North by,
16, 246, 309–10, 314–15; criticism of discrimination within integrated schools by,
173, 189, 193, 207, 210; criticism of gradual/
token desegregation by, 74, 85, 96, 106;
criticism of Nixon administration by, 157,
243, 245; opposition to one-way integration by, 146; opposition to school resegregation by, 324–26; pursuit of metropolitan
integration remedies by, 14, 18–19, 107–8,
121, 133–35, 175, 200, 209, 277, 280, 282,
289–90, 299, 310, 314–15, 329; and school
desegregation litigation, 64, 88, 118, 132,
285, 297–98; support for busing by, 166,
170, 175, 184, 219, 295; support for "socioeconomic integration" by, 187, 195, 204.
See also *Brown v. Board of Education*;
civil rights movement; Legal Defense
Fund; *Swann v. Charlotte-Mecklenburg*
NAACP Youth Council (Charlotte-
Mecklenburg), *164*, 166
Nashville, Tenn., 36, 99, 272, 278
National Action Group against Busing
(NAG), 310
National Advisory Commission on Civil
Disorders. *See* Kerner Commission
National Coalition against Discrimination in
Housing, 307
National Conference of Christians and Jews,
181–82
National Council for the Preservation of Our
Educational Freedoms, 314
National Education Association, 170
Nationsbank (Charlotte), 218
neighborhood politics, 175–97. *See also*
antibusing movement; grassroots politics;
homeowner politics; *specific cities and
organizations*
neighborhood schools: as "color-blind" response to *Brown*, 13–14, 41, 46, 106–7,
132–36; defended by Richard Nixon/Nixon
administration, 5, 137, 158, 171, 242–46,
249, 256, 267, 270, 307, 312–13; defended
by Ronald Reagan, 210–11, 324, 327–28;
defended by Silent Majority, 1, 17–18,
121–23, 139–40, 148–53, *155*, 157–58, 176,

225–26, 255; as middle-class ideal, 40, 42,
217; and proposed constitutional amendment to protect, 193, 292, 310, 312–14;
and resegregation, 215, 218–20, 294,
324–27; and residential segregation,
142–43, 212. *See also* antibusing move-
ment; busing; school desegregation
Neiman, Judy, 96, 98
"New American Dilemma," 19, 289, 323,
327; defined, 2, 122
"New American Majority," 5, 312–313, 319.
See also Nixon, Richard M.; Silent Majority
New Deal, 6–7, 10, 26, 28, 56, 228, 231,
237, 272
New Deal Order, 3, 8, 239–40, 319
"New Democrats," 18, 227, 318, 320–22. *See
also* Democratic party
New Jersey, 115, 218, 233, 317–18, 320
New Orleans, La., 37–38, 86–88, 92, 99, 274,
299, *300*
New Republic, 32, 308
New Right, 5, 7–8, 227, 273–74, 303, 319,
321, 335n.10. *See also* conservatism; Religious Right
New South, 14, 37, 42; as booster ethos, 11,
45–47, 336n.16; and end of regional distinctiveness, 15–16; racial moderation of,
12, 48–50, 128–31; residential segregation
in, 11–12, 50–52, 126–28, 303–4; response
to *Brown* decision in, 13–14, 17–18, 30,
105–7, 131–33. *See also* Atlanta; Charlotte;
South, metropolitan/Sunbelt development
in; South, political transformation of; Sunbelt Synthesis; *specific cities*
"New South Democrats." *See* Democratic
party, New South wing of
New York, 63, 248, 267, 269, 318
New York City, N.Y., 16, 115, 117, 239, 291,
307, 309, 316, *317*
New York Times, 16, 99, 172, 210, 243,
271, 308
Newark, N.J., 109, 112, 115, 291, *317*
Newsweek, 99, 105, 302
Nixon administration: antibusing policies of,
148, 157–58, 171, 244–46, 279, 309–13;
backlash strategy in 1970 elections of,
253–54, 258–74; defense of suburban "de
facto" segregation by, 17, 244–46; housing
policies of, 305–7; retreat from civil rights
enforcement by, 242–44. *See also* busing;
neighborhood schools; Nixon, Richard M.

Nixon, Richard M.: antibusing platform of, 5–6, 137, 158, 233–34, 235, 245, 248–49, 256, 274, 292, 309, 311–12; attacked by George Wallace, 252–53, 310; criticism of federal courts by, 243–44; declaration of southern/northern convergence by, 5, 17, 137, 246, 267, 313; defense of suburban "economic segregation" by, 305–7; and election of 1960, 229–30; and election of 1968, 138, 231–42, 303; and election of 1972, 312–13; and failure of Southern Strategy, 18, 249–51, 259–61, 271–72; historical debates about, 5–6, 8, 226–27, 359n.38; "law and order" platform of, 5–6, 146, 232, 234, 236, 313; nominations to Supreme Court by, 246–47, 313; and Silent Majority/Middle Americans, 5, 121, 141–42, 148, 152, 157–58, 163, 167, 221, 225–26, 233, 236–37, 301–2, 319, 322. *See also* busing; "color-blind" ideology; Nixon administration

Norfolk, Va., 33, 225, 234, 265, 281, 324

North, 221; attacked for racial double standard, 247–48, 252, 309; busing controversies in, 310–12, 314–17; compared to Sunbelt, 10, 13, 52; migration to South from, 11, 15, 44, 63, 67, 124, 215, 218, 220; open-housing conflicts in, 305–8, 317–18; political convergence thesis and, 300–1, 304; political developments in, 232, 240, 272, 311–13, 319–21; racial segregation defended as "de facto" in, 16, 150, 308; and regional variations in school integration, 210, 316; southern convergence with metropolitan patterns of, 4, 15–17, 114–15, 117, 122, 133, 158, 226, 244–45, 267, 286, 291, 293, 299, 303–4; targeted by civil rights movement, 246, 280, 309–10; white backlash in, 6–7, 242, 301–2, 309. See also Midwest; Rust Belt; *specific states and cities*

North Carolina, 16, 27, 348n.13; gradual/token desegregation in, 24, 29–30, 36, 59, 68, 74, 131–32; political developments in, 137–38, 157, 211, 229, 230–31, 233, 237–38, 272–74, 312, 321; suburban annexation policies of, 128, 184. *See also* Charlotte; Raleigh

North Charlotte Action Committee, 178–79

Northside Baptist Church (Charlotte), 165

Northside High School (Atlanta), 65, 117

Ohio, 240, 305, 321

Olympic Games, 47, 114–15, 117, 327

open-housing movement, 16, 130, 176, 289, 297, 304–8, 317–18, 324, 354n.26

open-schools movement: in Atlanta, 36, 45–46, 53, 58–99, 101–5, 118; desegregation solution of, 13–14, 17–18; in Little Rock, 24–25, 60, 69; and transformation of South, 25–26, 30, 35, 39–43; in Virginia, 32–24. See also *Brown v. Board of Education*; Help Our Public Education; massive resistance; moderates (white); Southern Leadership Project

Orange County, Cal., 115, 320

Orfield, Gary, 326–27, 335n.12

Organizations Assisting Schools in September (OASIS), 94–97, 100–1, 104

Orlando, Fla., 267, 278

Outer South, 37; defined, 16; open-schools sentiment in, 29, 36; political developments in, 6, 28, 228, 229, 230–32, 237–39. *See also* Upper South; *specific states and cities*

Owens, Eugene, 156

Panetta, Leon, 244

Pasadena, Cal., 247

Paschall, Eliza, 66, 72, 74

Patterson, Bruce, 195

Pauley, Frances, 66, 70

Paw Creek (Charlotte), *127*, 146–47, 151, 159, 183

Payne, Billy, 115

Peachtree Center (Atlanta), 111

Pendergrast, Nan, 44–45, 61–64, 67, 71, 94, 102–3

Peters, James (Jim), 79, 86

Philadelphia, Pa., 63, *317*

Phillips, John, 192–93

Phillips, Kevin P., 5, 226, 239–42, 251, *262*, *263*, 271, 273, 306, 320, 357n.1. *See also* Southern Strategy

Plessy v. Ferguson, 29, 315, 318

Poe, William, 134, 138, 151, 157–59, 161, 164, 185, 191–92, 195, 200–1, 204, 206–7, 209, 211, 221. *See also* Charlotte-Mecklenburg Board of Education

political apportionment: and at-large systems in municipal politics, 11, 126, 128, 177–82, 214–15, 276, 281, 284, 296–97; and effects of court-ordered reapportionment, 15–16,

political apportionment (*continued*)
41, 101, 261, 266, 321; and links between
malapportionment and massive resistance,
27–28, 33, 68, 82–83; and links between
malapportionment and one-party
system/rural power, 26, 31–32, 44, 54–59.
See also *Baker v. Carr*; county unit system
politics. *See* class, and suburban politics;
"color-blind" ideology, and suburban politics; consumer politics; Democratic Party;
grassroots politics; homeowner politics;
neighborhood politics; populism; Republican Party; Silent Majority; taxpayer politics; *specific places and people*
Polk, James, 2, 131
Pontiac, Mich., 310
populism: and class divisions among white
voters, 10, 14, 227, 303; and conservatism,
226, 303, 320; and George Wallace's
appeals, 232, 237, 254, 310–12; as localist
political identity, 7, 122; and "New South
Democrats," 227, 268–70, 320; as politics
of center, 8, 104, 122, 173, 227, 241; and
Richard Nixon's appeals, 5, 137, 232–37,
312–13; and Silent Majority/Middle Americans, 2, 141, 148, 176, 198, 225–26, 249,
301–2, 319; and suburban politics, 4, 18,
103, 123, 148–67. *See also* grassroots
politics; "reactionary populism"
Populist movement, 28
Portland, Ore., 316, *317*
Portman, John, 111, 114
Postell, James, 203
Potter, Robert, 325–26, 329
Powell, Lewis F., Jr., 293, 313–14
Prince Edward County, Va., 34
private schools: as antibusing sanctuaries,
252, 257, 298; in Atlanta, 78, 95, 100,
117–18; in Charlotte, 150, 154, 165,
167–69, 176, 184, 186, 189, 196, 204, 210;
in Richmond, 286, 289, 293–94; as segregationist academies, 23–24, 29, 33–34, 38,
40, 57–59, 67, 72, 75, 81–84, 89–90, 106,
247, 268
"Progressive Mystique," 49, 336n.16, 348n.13
public housing: in Charlotte, 124, 126, 128,
135, 150, 168, 177–79, 200, 215; and Nixon
administration policies, 305–7; suburban
exclusion of, 113, 289, 291, 295, 306–7,
309, 316–18; and Sunbelt growth policies,
12, 52, 276; and Supreme Court, 307–8.

See also open-housing movement; residential segregation; urban renewal
public schools. See *Brown v. Board of Education*; busing; massive resistance; neighborhood schools; open-schools movement;
school desegregation; *specific cities*
Pulver, W. A., 91

Quality Education Committee (QEC),
199–201, 205

racial backlash. *See* antibusing movement;
backlash thesis; grassroots politics; massive
resistance
racial caste. *See* caste system
racial integration. *See* integration (racial)
racial segregation: as "American Dilemma,"
2, 30; and artificial de jure/de facto dichotomy, 4, 14, 16, 134, 143, 158, 245–46,
291, 307–10, 314, 323; as urban hypersegregation, 14, 109, 117–18, 215, 219,
293–94, 298–99, 315–17, 326–27; and
white southern liberals, 29, 42–43, 66, 74,
85, 102–4. *See also* African Americans;
Brown v. Board of Education; caste system;
"de facto" segregation; massive resistance;
residential segregation; school desegregation; *Swann v. Charlotte-Mecklenburg*
racism, 240, 248, 280, 302–3; and antibusing
movement, 143, 166; denial of by whites,
154, 218, 226, 236, 289; evolution of, 3–4;
in political campaigns, 6, 226, 234, 253–54,
259–60; as structural racism, 1, 42, 237,
291, 297, 307–8; and "white flight," 9, 194.
See also African Americans; caste system;
civil rights movement; "color-blind"
ideology; massive resistance; racial segregation; residential segregation
Raleigh Chamber of Commerce, 296
Raleigh, N.C., 13, 131, 278, 300; busing controversy in, 279, 295–96; city-county
school consolidation in, 296–97, 299; political developments in, 238
Raleigh News and Observer, 14, 296
Raper, Arthur Jarrell, 293
Ravenal, Arthur, 259
Ray, Margaret (Maggie), 199–200, *201*,
203–5, 328
Ray, W. Thomas (Tom), 200
"reactionary populism," 6–7, 9, 100, 176, 188,
232, 242, 251, 267, 302, 316

Reagan administration, 210, 220, 324
"Reagan Democrats," 7, 320, 334n.9
Reagan, Ronald W., 6, 211, 226, 233, 273, 319–20, 324–25, 327
Real Majority, The, 240–41
Rehnquist, William H., 313–14
religious groups. See *specific cities and organizations*
Religious Right, 160, 285–86, 298, 303, 319–21
Republican Party (GOP): and debate about political realignment, 3–8, 226–27; and election of 1968, 138, 232–40; and election of 1972, 312–13; and elections of 1970, 253–54, 258–70, 272–73; and failure of Southern Strategy, 6, 249–50, 271–75; growth in metropolitan South of, 3, 15, 17–18, 27, 32, 57, 117, 122, 215, 227–31, 238; and success of suburban strategy, 5, 137, 232–37, 241–42, 312–13, 318–22. *See also* conservatism; Nixon administration; Phillips, Kevin P.; Ripon Society; Southern Strategy; *specific politicians*
Research Triangle Park (North Carolina), 297, 321
residential integration. See open-housing movement
residential segregation, 9, 221; in Atlanta, 46–47, 50, *51*, 52–53, 64, 78, 100, 111, *116*; challenged by civil rights movement, 2, 9, 16, 122, 130, 134, *158*, 170–72, 176, 213, 227, 280, 304–10, 317–18; in Charlotte, 126, *127*, 128, 130–31, 134–37, 142–43, 162–63, 170–71, 176–78, 212–13, 215, *216*, 326–29; contrasted with caste system, 4, 11, 15, 53, 118, 122, 291, 310, 326–27; established by government policies, 1, 3, 10–12, 16, 50, 126, 129, 134–35, 142–43, 276, 291–92, 310; in metropolitan South, 11–13, 42, 276–77, 297, 299; retreat from metropolitan remedies for, 227, 275, 299–300, 304–18; in Richmond, 281, *282*, 285, 289–93, *294*; and school desegregation formulas, 13–14, 30, 34, 45–46, 74, 79, 85, 104–9, 132–33; and southern/northern convergence, 4, 15–17, 122, 158, 170–72, 226, 244–46, 314; and suburban/Silent Majority politics, 1–4, 26, 28, 122–23, 137–38, 217, 227, 233, 237, 305–7, 323. *See also* busing; class; "color-blind" ideology; "de facto" segregation; homeowner politics; "New American Dilemma"; open-housing movement

"reverse discrimination," 1, 17, 123, 210, 217, 220, 287, 290, 292, 312, 325. *See also* affirmative action; "color-blind" ideology
Reynolds, William Bradford, 324
Ribicoff, Abraham A., 248, 309
Rich, Richard, 110, 114
Richmond News Leader, 287, 289, 292
Richmond Times-Dispatch, 284, 287–88, 290, 292
Richmond, Va., 3–4, 13, 276, 295–96, *300*, 315–16; busing controversy in, 18–19, 209, *264*, 280–94, 299–300, 311, 313; political developments in, 238, 262, 265–66; private schools in, 286, 289, 293–94; residential segregation in, 281, *282*, 285, 289–93, *294*; suburban annexation in, 280–85. See also *Bradley v. Richmond*; Chesterfield County, Va.; Henrico County, Va.
Rich's Department Store (Atlanta), 76, 87, 111
Riddick v. School Board of City of Norfolk, 324
Rieder, Jonathan, 303
Riley, Jesse, 179–80
Ripon Society, 225, 231, 241–42, 254, 262, 272
Roberson, Don, 1–2, 143, 148, 150–53, 159, 163, 165, 167–68. *See also* Concerned Parents Association
Robertson, A. Willis, 262
Robin, Florence, 103
Robinson, Jay, 211
Rockefeller, Nelson, 248, 269
Rockefeller, Winthrop, 268–69
Rome, Ga., 55, 70
Romney, George, 305–7
Roth, Stephen J., 310
Rothschild, Jacob, 70, 105
Russell, Richard B., Jr., 77
Rust Belt, 10, 109–10, 112, 115, 280, 295, 314. *See also* Midwest; North; *specific states and cities*

San Antonio v. Rodriguez, 318
San Diego, Cal., *317*
San Francisco, Cal., 117, 308, *317*
Sanders, Carl, 87–88, 101, 270
Sandy Springs (Atlanta), *51*, 112, 277
Savannah, Ga., 55, 70, 81

Save Our Schools (SOS), 37–38, 41

Scammon, Richard, 240

school desegregation, 17–18; and "freedom of choice" plans, 13–14, 41, 45–46, 83, 89, 105–7, 132–33; and gradual/token desegregation plans, 23–25, 30–32, 36, 38, 40, 72, 74–75, 96, 103–5, 132; and local option plans, 34, 84, 89; and magnet schools, 219, 294, 324–26; and metropolitan remedies, 277–80, 290–94, 297–300, 310, 314–17; and neighborhood schools plans, 13–14, 41, 107, 135–36, 244–45, 279, 324; and one-way busing plans, 108–9, 144–47, 185, 252, 326–27; and two-way busing plans, 136–37, 151, 162–63, 167–69, 185–97, 202–7, 255–57, 285–89, 295–96. *See also* African Americans; *Brown v. Board of Education*; busing; integration (racial); massive resistance; NAACP; open-schools movement; *specific cities*

school funding equalization, 311, 317–18

Schrag, Peter, 302

Scott, Jack, 146, 151, 153, 159–60, 167

Scott, Jane, 159–160, 165, 167

Scott, Robert W. (Bob), 157, 272–73

Scott, William, 266

Seattle, Wash., 316, *317*

segregation. *See* caste system; class; "de facto" segregation; racial segregation; residential segregation

segregation academies. *See* private schools

Self, William, 135–36

Separate Schools, 95–96

Shands, Norman, 70

Sibley Commission, 79–86, 89–92

Sibley, John, 80–81, 83, 90

Silent Americans Speak Out (Greenville), 255

Silent Majority; in Charlotte, *140*, 141–42, 147–50, *152*, 153–54, 157–58, 220; class divisions within, 10, 14, 18, *187*, 198, 227, 250, 302–3, 319; and "color-blind" ideology, 1–2, *149*, 198, 217, 227, 325; and political realignment, 6, 226, 231–32; and Richard Nixon, 5, 158, 241, 260, 267, 302, 313–14; and southern/northern convergence, 3, 17, 249, 300; suburban mobilization of, 1–2, 8, 19, 118, 121–22, 159, 173, 176, 221, 225–26, 255, 301–2, 305, 311, 319, 323, 328–29; and updating of trope, 320, 322. *See also* antibusing movement;

Concerned Parents Association; grassroots politics; homeowner politics; Middle Americans; populism; residential segregation

"silent moderates." *See* moderates (white)

Smith, Lillian, 69, 102

Smith, Muggsy, 65, 78

Sobeloff, Simon, 161

socioeconomic privilege. *See* class

Solid South: dissolution of, 15, 27, 39–40, 46, 228–31, 321–22; and failure of Southern Strategy, 274–75; and Republican strategies, 227, 231, 239–41, 249–50, 312–13, 319–20; and segregationist campaigns for white unity, 6, 28, 45, 64, 68, 92, 228

South: busing battles in, 18–19, 107–9, 121–23, 134–74, 184–212, 219–21, 242–48, 255–58, 276–80, 285–300, 324–29; and fading of regional distinctiveness, 4–6, 15–17, 301–18; geographic subregions of, 16; massive resistance/school desegregation in, 13–14, 17–18, 23–43, 45–46, 54–107, 131–33; metropolitan/Sunbelt development in, 9–14, 47–53, 109–18, 123–31, 175–84, 212–19, 280–85, 327–28; political transformation of, 1–8, 15, 225–42, 249–54, 258–75, 319–22. *See also* Black Belt; Deep South; New South; Outer South; Sunbelt; Upper South; *specific states and cities*

South Carolina, 16, *27*, 246; busing controversies in, 255–58, 279; political developments in, 228, *229*, 230, 233, *235*, 237, 254, 258–61, 270. *See also* Greenville

Southern Leadership Project (SLP), 23–26, 31, 35–43. *See also* business leaders; Muse, Benjamin; Southern Regional Council

Southern Manifesto, 29–30, 258

Southern Regional Council (SRC), 319; attacked by segregationists, 84, 96; and Charlotte, 129, 132, 143, 173, 208; criticism of Nixon administration by, 243; criticism of northern liberals by, 308, 311; criticism of token desegregation by, 75, 103, 105; philosophy of, 23, 25–27, 42–43, 63; struggle to defeat massive resistance by, 23, 31, 35–39; support for busing by, 108, 298; support for open-schools movement by, 41, 45, 62, 67, 70–71. *See also* liberalism; Southern Leadership Project

Southern Strategy, 229; and Barry Goldwater, 230, 241; and debate about political re-alignment, 3–7, 226–28, 303; failure in 1970 elections of, 251–75, 319; and Kevin Phillips, 251, 262, *263*, 271, 273; and Richard Nixon/Nixon administration, 17–18, 137, 233, 240–41, 244, 246, 249–51, 267, 301, 312–13

SouthPark Mall (Charlotte), *127*, 153, 155, 211, 214, 327

Spangler, C. D. (Dick), Jr., 191–92, 204

Spong, William B., 262, 266

sprawl. *See* antisprawl movement; South, metropolitan/Sunbelt development in; suburbs; *specific cities*

St. Louis, Mo., 110

States' Rights Democratic Party. *See* Dixiecrats

Stennis, John, 248

Stevenson, Sarah, 200, 210, 219

Stewart, Potter, 315

suburban annexation: in Atlanta, 52–53, 111–12, *277*; in Charlotte, 124, 128, 180, 183–84, *215*, 276; in Memphis, 297–98; in metropolitan South, 13–14, 276–77; in Richmond, 280–85

suburbs: exempted from integration reme-dies, 18, 107–9, 289–94, 298–300, 304–17; grassroots politics in, 3–9, 13–14, 25–26, 30, 137–41, 150–55, 165–67, 301–4, 323; included in metropolitan busing plans, 123, 167–72, 193–97, 203–7, 277–79, 295–97; and political transformation of South, 6, 40–41, 227–40, 258–75, 319–22; residential segregation in, 1–2, 9–12, *15*, 28, 42, 47, 50–52, 126–28, 142–43, 212–13, 215; Silent Majority in, 1–2, 17–19, 121–22, 141–42, 148, 157–59, 163, 173, 176, 198, 217, 220–21, 225–26, 328–29; subsidized by government, 1–2, 8–10, 281. *See also* African Americans, living in sub-urbs; antibusing movement; class; "color-blind" ideology; homeowner politics; "island suburbs"; neighborhood schools; suburban annexation; *specific cities*

Sugrue, Thomas J., 7, 9

Suit, Hal, 270

Summer, Albioun, 248

Sunbelt: and fading of southern distinctive-ness, 3, 15; metropolitan patterns in, 10–14; and political trends in South and West, 6–11, 231–2, 237, 240, 319–21. *See also* Sunbelt South; *specific states and cities*

Sunbelt South: contrasted with Black Belt, 6–7, 15, 28, 45–46, *249*; contrasted with Deep South, 6–7, 28, 47–48, 95, 97, 131, 233, 249–50, 263–64. *See also* South, metropolitan/Sunbelt development in; South, political transformation of; Sunbelt Synthesis; *specific states and cities*

Sunbelt Synthesis: in Atlanta, 46–48, 111, 115; in Charlotte, 126, 128, 327; defined, 11–14, 276; and transformation of nation, 227; and transformation of South, 15, 17, 304

Supreme Court, U.S.: approval of token de-segregation by, 74, 132; and busing, 161–63, 170–72, 226, 286–87, 298, 314; criticized for regional double standard, 247–48; and housing segregation, 307–8; invalidation of "freedom of choice" by, 107, 133, 136, 243; nominations to, 246–47, 313; and political reapportion-ment, 15, 28, 68, 101; and racial quotas, 210; rejection of city-suburban school con-solidation by, 18, 209, 293, 314–16; and school desegregation/massive resistance, 13, 23–25, 29, 32, 58–59, 67, 85; and school funding equalization, 318; and school resegregation, 324, 364n.4; unitary schools/"immediate integration" requirement of, 151, 243, 254; and voting rights, 27. *See also* constitutional law; *specific cases*

Swann, Darius, 132

Swann v. Charlotte-Mecklenburg, 132–37, 160–63, 170–72, 185–86, 195–96, 202–3, 206–8, 210, 226, 280, 291, 293, 298, 309, 315, 325, 328. *See also* McMillan, James B.

Syracuse, N.Y., 144

Talmadge, Eugene (Gene), 54–56

Talmadge, Herman, 54–58, 77, 79

Tampa, Fla., 278

Tate, Allen, 212–13

taxpayer politics: and antiannexation move-ments, 112, 283, 295, and antibusing movement, 140, 153, 220, 296; and Middle Americans, 302–3; and municipal inequal-ity, 179, 183; and "New South Democrats," 267, 269; and property taxes, 318; and

taxpayer politics (*continued*)
Richard Nixon, 5, 137, 236–37, 312; and suburban conservatism, 231, 240; as suburban populist identity, 1, 4, 7–8, 113, 122, 141–42, 198, 304, 320, 322. *See also* grassroots politics; Silent Majority
Tennessee, 16, 27; busing controversy in, 278, 297–99, 312, gradual/token desegregation in, 29–30, 36; political developments in, 229–31, 237, 272
Texas, 16, 27, 225, 299, 309, 318; gradual/token desegregation in, 29–30; political developments in, 229–31, 237
Thurmond, Strom, 225, 228, 229, 231, 233, *234*, 243, 254, 256, 258–61, 271
Time, 69–70, 113–14, 270, *271*, 301
token desegregation/integration. *See* school desegregation
Truman, Harry, 228
Trust Company Bank (Atlanta), 76, 80, 108, 111
Twitty, Frank, 87–88

Unified Concerned Citizens of America (UCCA), 170, 225–26
United States Information Agency, 99
University of Georgia (UGA), 56, 79, 81, 88–91
University of North Carolina at Charlotte (UNC-Charlotte), *127*, 194, 215, 328
upper middle class. *See* middle class (white)
Upper South, 32; defined, 16; massive resistance in, 28, 35; political developments in, 6, 239, 272. *See also* Outer South; *specific states and cities*
urban renewal, 306; in Atlanta, 51, 100, 109, *110*, 111, 117; in Charlotte, 1, *125*, 126, 129, 134–35, 150, 180; in Richmond, 281, *282*, 289; in Sunbelt South, 10–12, 276

Vandiver, Ernest, 59, 67–68, 74, 77, 79–80, 84–85, 87–91, 97, 101, 344n.30
Vietnam War, 225, 232, 236, 272, 312
Virginia, 10, 16, 27, 43; massive resistance in, 29, 31–35, 40, 66, 71, 85, 131; political developments in, 225, 229–31, 234, 237–38, 261–66, 270, 273, 281, 285, 320. *See also* Richmond
Virginia Beach, Va., 281, 283, 320
Virginia Committee for Public Schools (VCPS), 33–35, 41, 72

Virginia Industrialization Group, 33
Voter Education Project, 39
Voting Rights Act of 1965, 15, 41, 261, 284

Wake County, N.C., 296–97
Wallace, George, 90, 246, 273–74; and debate about political realignment, 5–6, 226–27, 303; economic populism of, 28; and gubernatorial election of 1970, 251–54; and presidential election of 1968, 138, 232–35, 237–40; and presidential election of 1972, 192, 310–12; supporters of, 242, 244, 249–50, 255, 258, 260, 262, 265, 267, 269–70, 272–73, 319–20. *See also* Southern Strategy
Waller, William, 270
Warren, Mich., 306, 310
Warth v. Seldin, 308
Washington, Booker T., 108
Washington, D.C., 163, 171, 238, 247, 269, 288, 296, 299, *317*
Washington Post, 31–32, 267, 271
Watkins, Carlton, 144
Watson, Albert, 254, 256, 258–60
Wattenberg, Ben, 240
Watters, Pat, 143, 308
Wayne, John, 301
West: 4, 6–7, 10, 14, 232, 240, 244, 248, 310, 316, 320–21. *See also* Sunbelt; *specific states and cities*
West Charlotte High School, *127*, 166, 168, 187, 192–94, 196, 204–6
West End Concerned Parents and Friends (WECPF), 286
West, John, 254, 259–61, 270
West Paces Ferry (Atlanta), 44–45, *51*, 61–62
West Palm Beach, Fla., *278*
Westchester County, N.Y., 307, 318
white backlash. *See* backlash thesis
White, Byron, 315
"white flight," *300*, 308, *317*; as consequence of inequitable busing plans, 107–9, 163, 188, 192, 260, 279, 288, 290, 293–94, 298–99; as consequence of municipal planning policies, 52, 177, 183, 281, *282*, 289; and fears of antibusing movement, 165, 169, 184, 197, 203–6; mitigated by metropolitan integration remedies, 123, 168, 198, 207–10, 212, 277, *278*, 279, 296–97, 299, 316; as problematic metaphor, 9, 12, 118. See also *specific cities*

white liberals. *See* liberalism
white moderates. *See* moderates (white)
White, R. Cooper, 255, 257, 259–60
white supremacy. *See* caste system
Wilkins, Roy, 307, 310
Wilkinson, J. Harvie III, 364n.4
Williams, John Bell, 247
Williams, Samuel, 105
Wilmington, Del., 316
Wilson, William Julius, 322
Winston-Salem, N.C., 131, 132
Winter, Carrie, 210, 219
Winter, Harrison L., 299
Withrow, Joe, 178
Wofford, Harris, 35
Women's Emergency Committee to Open
  Our Schools (WEC), 24–25, 41, 60, 69

women's groups. *See* League of Women
  Voters; open-schools movement; Women's
  Emergence Committee to Open Our
  Schools
Woodward, C. Vann, 31
Woodruff, Robert W., 48, *49*, 114
World War II, 3, 19, 23, 26, 133, 228, 312
Wright, J. Skelly, 38

Young, Andrew, 115
Young, Mitchell, 225

zoning, 177–79; exclusionary, 13, 50, 52, 135,
  291, 297, 305–8, 317; inclusionary (mixed-
  income), 215, 322, 329, 354n.26. *See also*
  open-housing movement; residential
  segregation

Politics and Society in Twentieth-Century America

Series Editors:
William Chafe, Gary Gerstle, Linda Gordon, and Julian Zelizer

Civil Defense Begins at Home: Militarization Meets Everyday Life in the Fifties by Laura McEnaney

Cold War Civil Rights: Race and the Image of American Democracy by Mary L. Dudziak

Divided We Stand: American Workers and the Struggle for Black Equality by Bruce Nelson

Poverty Knowledge: Social Science, Social Policy, and the Poor in Twentieth-Century U.S. History by Alice O'Connor

Suburban Warriors: The Origins of the New American Right by Lisa McGirr

The Politics of Whiteness: Race, Workers, and Culture in the Modern South by Michelle Brattain

State of the Union: A Century of American Labor by Nelson Lichtenstein

Changing the World: American Progressives in War and Revolution by Alan Dawley

Dead on Arrival: The Politics of Health Care in Twentieth-Century America by Colin Gordon

For All These Rights: Business, Labor, and the Shaping of America's Public-Private Welfare State by Jennifer Klein

The Radical Middle Class: Populist Democracy and the Question of Capitalism in Progressive Era Portland, Oregon by Robert D. Johnston

American Babylon: Race and the Struggle for Postwar Oakland by Robert O. Self

The Other Women's Movement: Workplace Justice and Social Rights in Modern America by Dorothy Sue Cobble

Impossible Subjects: Illegal Aliens and the Making of Modern America by May M. Ngai

More Equal than Others: America from Nixon to the New Century by Godfrey Hodgson

Cities of Knowledge: Cold War Science and the Search for the Next Silicon Valley by Margaret Pugh O'Mara

Labor Rights Are Civil Rights: Mexican American Workers in Twentieth-Century America by Zaragosa Vargas

Pocketbook Politics: Economic Citizenship in Twentieth-Century America by Meg Jacobs

Taken Hostage: The Iran Hostage Crisis and America's First Encounter with Radical Islam by David Farber

Morning in America: How Ronald Reagan Invented the 1980s by Gil Troy

Defending America: Military Culture and the Cold War Court-Martial by Elizabeth Lutes Hillman

Phyllis Schlafly and Grassroots Conservatism: A Woman's Crusade by Donald T. Critchlow

White Flight: Atlanta and the Making of Modern Conservatism by Kevin M. Kruse